The Ashdown Diaries

VOLUME II: 1997–1999

"I DID NOT HAVE COALITION RELATIONS WITH THAT MAN, Mr ASHDOWN."

PADDY ASHDOWN

The Ashdown Diaries

VOLUME II: 1997–1999

To Gillean

Best wishes + good
luck!

Paddy Ashdown

26/9/01

ALLEN LANE
THE PENGUIN PRESS

ALLEN LANE
THE PENGUIN PRESS

Published by the Penguin Group
Penguin Books Ltd, 80 Strand, London WC2R ORL, England
Penguin Putnam Inc., 375 Hudson Street, New York, New York 10014, USA
Penguin Books Australia Ltd, Ringwood, Victoria, Australia
Penguin Books Canada Ltd, 10 Alcorn Avenue, Toronto, Ontario, Canada M4V 3B2
Penguin Books India (P) Ltd, 11 Community Centre, Panchsheel Park, New Delhi – 110 017, India
Penguin Books (NZ) Ltd, Private Bag 102902, NSMC, Auckland, New Zealand
Penguin Books (South Africa) (Pty) Ltd, 24 Sturdee Avenue, Rosebank 2196, South Africa

Penguin Books Ltd, Registered Offices: 80 Strand, London WC2R ORL, England

First published 2001
1

Copyright © Paddy Ashdown, 2001

The moral right of the author has been asserted

Set in 10.25/13.75 pt Linotype Sabon
Typeset by Rowland Phototypesetting Ltd, Bury St Edmunds, Suffolk
Printed and bound in Great Britain by Clays Ltd, St Ives plc
Cover repro and printing by Concise Cover Printers

A CIP catalogue record for this book is available from the British Library

ISBN 0-713-99511-4

To the people of the Yeovil constituency, who have allowed me to do the job that has given a purpose to my professional life.

Contents

List of Illustrations

(Every effort has been made to contact all copyright holders. The publishers will be glad to make good in future editions any errors or omissions brought to their attention.)

List of Plates

(Photographic acknowledgements are given in parentheses)

1. Wednesday, 7 May 1997, Westminster (Press Association/Justin Williams)
2. Sunday, 3 August 1997, Irancy (Jane Ashdown)
3. Saturday, 6 September 1997, London (Camera Press)
4. Wednesday, 17 September 1997, Westminster (Reuters/Ian Waldie)
5. Friday, 21 November 1997, Winchester (*Guardian*/Martin Argles)
6. Sunday, 15 March 1998, Southport (Press Association/Dave Kendall)
7. Tuesday, 26 May 1998, Somerset (Jane Ashdown)
8. Thursday, 11 June 1998, Westminster (Press Association/Andrew Stuart)
9. Tuesday, 23 June 1998, Albania (Roger Lowry)
10. Tuesday, 23 June 1998, Albania (Roger Lowry)
11. Sunday, 2 August 1998, Irancy (Jane Ashdown)
12. Friday, 21 August 1998, Irancy (Alyce Faye Cleese)
13. Tuesday, 25 August 1998, Irancy (Jane Ashdown)
14. Monday, 31 August 1998, Irancy (Jane Ashdown)
15. Saturday, 26 September 1998, Kosovo (Roger Lowry)
16. Sunday, 27 September 1998, Kosovo (Roger Lowry)
17. Sunday, 27 September 1998, Kosovo (Roger Lowry)
18. Sunday, 22 November 1998, Somerset (Stephanie Bailey)
19. Monday, 14 December 1998, Kosovo (Roger Lowry)
20. Monday, 14 December 1998, Kosovo (Roger Lowry)
21. Monday, 14 December 1998, Kosovo (Roger Lowry)
22. Tuesday, 15 December 1998, Kosovo (Roger Lowry)
23. Thursday, 7 January 1999, Alpe D'Huez (Tim Razzall)
24. Wednesday, 20 January 1999, Westminster (Press Association/Peter Jordan)

Preface

'Paddy ... I really do want to seize this opportunity, to demonstrate that we can follow a programme ... which will [form] ... the basis of co-operation in the future ... But I need you to know that I see this as a means of transition to an end position where you come into the show.'

These words, spoken by Tony Blair just after he had accepted the post of Prime Minister from the Queen on the afternoon of 2 May 1997, opened the way to a series of discussions over the next two years whose aim was to change the ground rules of the British political system. Underpinning these attempts was our joint belief that, if we could bring New Labour and the Liberal Democrats into partnership in government, we could heal the schism that had weakened the left in the twentieth century and create a political force, based around broadly liberal values, that would command widespread public support, keep the Tories out of power for ten years and deliver effective government in the century ahead.

The first volume of my diaries covered the nine years from 1988, when I took over as leader of the Lib Dems, to the General Election of 1997, when we doubled our strength in Parliament. This second volume, by contrast, covers just over two years – from the 1997 election to my resignation in August 1999. It is therefore, inevitably, more concentrated. Its central theme, which dominates the early pages almost to the exclusion of all else, is the attempt to create a new kind of relationship between two British political parties, one in government, the other in opposition. This was founded on the co-operation between Tony Blair and myself when in opposition, our shared vision of what could be done and our joint determination to try to make it happen against a background of rising opposition at key levels in both our parties.

In retrospect, I see that this element of the story falls into three distinct phases.

The first phase, covering the period from the General Election until the early months of 1998, concentrates on the sometimes confusing, complex and untidy 'to-ing' and 'fro-ing', as we tested the limits of the new relationship and sought to find structures (such as the Joint Cabinet Committee and the Jenkins Commission on Electoral Reform) to develop it.

The second phase (from spring 1998 to the publication of the Jenkins commission report in the autumn of that year) was dominated by the preparations for what was to become, after much nail-biting negotiation, our third and most developed attempt to cross the crucial threshold of partnership in government. It was planned that this should take place after the publication of the Jenkins report and its acceptance by the Labour government.

This did not, in the end, happen, leading to the third and final phase of these years: the preparations for my resignation as leader of the Lib Dems and the election of my successor, Charles Kennedy. I had informed Tony Blair as early as July 1997 that, whatever happened, I would not fight the next election and would therefore stand down as leader of the Lib Dems, as soon as either we had succeeded in becoming partners in government, or it became clear that this would not happen.

There are, of course, other stories in these pages, too.

By mid 1998 the gathering clouds of war in the Balkans had once again become central to my life, providing the second main theme in the years covered by this book.

Later that year, there was the struggle to get the legislation through Parliament for the first nationwide PR election in Britain (the 1999 Euro elections). And in mid 1999, the formation in Scotland of the first partnership government between the Liberal Democrats and Labour.

At the end of this volume I have written an epilogue, which gives my conclusions on the events chronicled in both books and outlines my hopes for what they might mean for the future.

Paddy Ashdown
Yeovil
May 2001

Acknowledgements

The advice of friends, the help of supporters and the generosity of those kind enough to assist me have been the indispensable ingredients in my career which have saved me from many self-made disasters, not least in the years described in this book. The same is true in the production of the book itself.

Those listed below have, in many different ways, helped me with the publication of these diaries – some by correcting factual errors or adding explanatory footnotes, others by converting the jumble of a diary often recorded in a state of tiredness not conducive to the production of tidy prose, into what I hope is a readable text.

Those who have read extracts and given me their views, comments and factual corrections include Julian Astle, Stephanie Bailey, Menzies Campbell, Neritan Ceka, Kenneth Clarke, Becks Darling, Brian Donnelly, Richard Holme, General Sir Michael Jackson, Roy Jenkins, Archy Kirkwood, David Laws, Roger Lowry, Tom McNally, Michael Moore, Morgan Morris, Steve Radley, Neil Sherlock, David Slinn, Paul Tyler, Sir Richard Wilson, Ian Wright and my wife Jane.

The small army who have transformed verbal gobbledegook and indecipherable handwriting into text – including Sarah Frapple, Pat Gibbs and Holly Kirkwood – have been valiant and indomitable.

Sally Holloway, my fierce and uncompromising editor, has been at once a joy to work with and completely intimidating in her determination to keep me up to her standards. She and my copy-editor, Trevor Horwood, have brought forth relative order from complete chaos.

Ian Patrick has been the ringmaster behind the whole complex operation. He has been responsible for most of the research, for the control of voluminous and often highly sensitive paperwork and has kept me from despair in the face of a task which at times I didn't think could possibly be concluded.

Stuart Proffitt of the Penguin Press has remained the inspiration behind my publishing these diaries, and his wonderful staff have certainly been more patient with me than I suspect they should have been.

I am grateful to Tony Blair and Richard Holme for their kind permission to use documents and letters. My thanks also to Martin Argles, Jane Ashdown, Julian Astle, David Austin, Stephanie Bailey, Steve Bell, Dave Brown, Alyce Faye Cleese, Nick Garland, Peter Jordan, Dave Kendall, Roger Lowry, John Minnion, Chris Priestley, Tim Razzall, David Rose, Martin Rowsengg, Andrew Stuart, Geoff Thompson, Ian Waldie, Justin Williams and others for the photographs and cartoons in these pages, and to so many others who have helped by their encouragement, like my agent Michael Sissons; or by carrying some of the burdens I should have carried while working on this, like Sue Weeks and my wonderful staff in Yeovil; or just by understanding why I was distracted and pretending not to notice, like my wife Jane, my daughter Kate and her family, Sebastien, Matthias and Lois, my son Simon and our dog Luke, who has lost many good walks to these pages.

To all of these I owe a great debt for the production of this book, but to none should be ascribed any of its errors, infelicities or inaccuracies. Those are all my own.

Kosovo and Surrounding Area

Federal Republic of Yugoslavia

Background Note

Volume Two of this diary picks up where Volume One left off. Tony Blair and I have already had the conversation quoted in the preface; the high drama of the election has subsided; Blair is busy assembling his government, having won a landslide victory, and I am returning to my constituency and the life of an opposition MP and party leader.

Within a few days, however, I had started a fresh round of negotiations with Blair. And within a few weeks I had concluded that our vision of the realignment of the left could not survive the inevitable pressures which, under our confrontational system, were bound to take over, if the Liberal Democrats stayed long on the opposition benches.

So, my immediate task was to prevent a quick slide back into the conventional stances of opposition politics, by adopting what I christened 'constructive opposition', i.e. speaking out against the new Labour government where we differed, but working with them where we agreed, especially on the programme of constitutional reform set out in the Cook/Maclennan agreement of spring 1997, when we were both in opposition.

1997

Saturday, 3 May, Somerset

Back to the constituency. Life, at the moment, is sweet. We're going to Irancy for a few days next Thursday. Something to look forward to.

On the train down to Yeovil I was astonished by how many people came up to me wanting to celebrate Thursday's victory over the Tories. There is a new sense of hope in the country; a real feeling of optimism. Spent most of my time on the train beginning to map out the shape of our new team in the House of Commons. I've decided that although we have forty-six MPs we must use them all in some capacity. I want our new people to be active rather than hang around the back benches getting up to mischief.

Then at 8 o'clock off to the constituency celebrations. Jane and I got home after midnight, both feeling a little woozy.

Sunday, 4 May, Somerset

Roy Jenkins left a message last night, which I returned this morning. Apparently, Blair spent an hour on the phone to him yesterday. Was he [Blair] right in detecting a certain cooling of my enthusiasm for the project? Was it because I felt disappointed at not being in government? Roy said no, probably just a sense of anti-climax. Blair told him that he intended to have us in government 'within a matter of months'.

This is bizarre. As I said to Roy, I have consistently told Blair that if we are to come in, it must be on the basis of a proper coalition agreement. He must know by now that for him to form his government (especially with Jack Straw as Home Secretary), set its policy and budget and then invite us to join in the party later is impossible. Can he still not have understood this?

Nevertheless, I passed back via Roy that we were still fully in favour of the project, that it would not be easy for us to do as Blair suggested now that he had formed his government, but that he and I should meet in the near future.

Spent the rest of the morning working on spokesmanships.[1] It's like

1 The Liberal Democrats in Parliament were organized into 'spokesmanship teams', each covering a government department (Health, Education, Home Affairs, etc.).

fitting a jigsaw together, but at least I have more pieces to play with now.

At about 6 o'clock I started to write my article for the *Independent*[1] but I stopped halfway through so that I could think about it overnight.

I also sent the following (unsigned) fax to Blair at Downing Street:

Dear Tony,

Here are some initial thoughts, in no particular order.

1. We need to get the Electoral Reform Commission [prefigured in the Cook/ Maclennan agreement] started, as soon as possible.[2]

2. If we are to go ahead [with establishing a series of Cabinet committees], I think there are four candidates for consideration. Constitutional reform: I would want Bob Maclennan to be on this, rather than me. If there is a Europe one (which I think would be useful for both of us), then I would want Menzies Campbell to take that place. Given that Northern Ireland is an area of normal cross-party co-operation, that seems a natural candidate: Richard Holme has strong credentials in this area, gets on well with Mo[3] and can give her good support. And finally, as you will remember, we previously agreed that welfare reform would be better and easier, the more it can be achieved on a cross-party basis. We are well equipped here with Steve Webb,[4] who won Northavon for us. He was on Dahrendorf and Borrie[5] and will be well known to Frank.[6] And Archy Kirkwood will do Social

---

1 In this article I committed the Party to 'constructive opposition'. The key passage was: 'The single most crucial decision which Labour and the Lib Dems have agreed to implement in this parliament is a referendum on PR. If this is won and implemented before the next election, then the foundations will be laid for an historic period of change ... then the relationship between the Liberal Democrats and Labour will [provide] the foundations upon which a programme for the ... modernization of Britain can safely be built.'

2 Under the Cook/Maclennan agreement a commission would be established under the new government to look into and report on a proportional alternative to the present first past the post (FPTP) system of voting.

3 Mo Mowlam, Secretary of State for Northern Ireland. Member of Parliament (Labour) for Redcar since 1987. Mo later resigned, became a minister in the Cabinet Office and stood down as an MP at the 2001 election.

4 Member of the Social Security Team. Member of Parliament for Northavon since 1997.

5 The Dahrendorf and Borrie Commissions were two separate bodies set up in the last parliament by (respectively) the Liberal Democrats and Labour to look into the welfare system and its impact on wealth generation. They were chaired by Ralf Dahrendorf (Lib Dem) and Gordon Borrie (Labour), both now in the House of Lords.

6 Frank Field, Member of Parliament (Labour) for Birkenhead since 1979. Minister at the Department for Social Security. He later resigned when Harriet Harman was sacked as Secretary of State for Social Security.

Security for us; he is close to Frank and gets on well with him. I would also be more than happy to participate in this area, supporting Archy.

3. We need to create an effective informal structure for co-operation, in order to promote trust and good working relationships between our main spokespeople. I am going to encounter resistance to a continuation of the Lib/Lab line with my new MPs, all of whom will have come fresh from a campaign fighting Labour on the ground. Most of them will feel understandably triumphalist after years of defeat. Hence the article in the *Indy* (attached), to be published on Wednesday, which lays down the line I want us to follow in the new parliament. This will cause unhappiness. So it is important that they see the fruits of this approach early. Although, of course, our senior spokespeople will be used to having cordial relationships with your people and I shall openly encourage them to pursue these. Can you please ensure they get positive responses? Some specific things would be of particular help. Could appropriate ministers ask to see their senior Lib Dem opposite numbers as soon as the dust has settled? Could we have sight/knowledge of the bare bones of the Queen's Speech early (if necessary on Privy Council terms[1])? Could Jim Wallace have access to the White Paper on the Scottish Parliament[2] in time to make suggestions and have them seriously considered? In all these small but, for us, crucial ways the bonds of mutual trust can continue to be cemented.

4. I cannot stress to you too heavily the importance of PR for the 1999 European elections. This would be the first real show of Labour's good intentions, as we see it.

Monday, 5 May, Somerset

Andy Marr from the *Independent* rang mid-morning. He has had a long discussion with Blair, who apparently said he was nervous that the Lib Dems had done so well that we might strike out on our own and abandon the strategy of Lib/Lab co-operation. I assured Andy we would not and pointed him to my article in his own newspaper.

1 Under Privy Council terms a Privy Councillor (at this stage only Alan Beith, Bob Maclennan and I among the Lib Dems) can receive a government briefing, the details of which he or she can refer to only when speaking to another Privy Councillor.
2 Labour had been elected with a manifesto commitment to devolve power in Scotland and Wales to a parliament and an assembly respectively. The White Paper paving the way for legislation on the Scottish Parliament was due in July. Devolution came under the remit of the Cook/Maclennan agreement.

Tuesday, 6 May, London

Up to London. Blair rang just as I arrived at the flat. Our conversation was lengthy and cordial. But he didn't say anything of much substance, except towards the end.

TB: Look, there are all sorts of things we can do together. But there's one thing we don't agree on. I think we need to put our relationship with you on a proper footing. Both public and formal. Which could eventually lead to merger . . .

PA: Please can we get off this merger stuff? It's just not on. Look, if you had made a serious pitch for us to join with you in government after the election I would have considered that and probably said yes. But the moment has now passed. I have my own thoughts about how to go forward, which I can put to you when we meet. Meanwhile, the only mechanism through which we can achieve what you are talking about is PR.

TB: My people are saying to me they can't see the point of having anything to do with you lot, since we have such a huge majority. To which I reply, 'What the Lord giveth, the Lord taketh away.'

I asked him if he had read my article for the *Independent* which had made precisely this point. An electoral system which gave him a victory on 44 per cent of the vote could also take it away at 44 per cent. The only basis on which we could found a partnership that would last over ten years was PR. Structural relationships handed down by party leaders simply wouldn't do. And any mention of merger would be death to the whole project. But if PR were to be introduced, we could go into the next election on a series of heads of agreement, on which we could jointly campaign, which presumed a coalition afterwards. That would then lead to a government in which the two parties could work together. If we did that successfully, who knew what could happen afterwards?

TB: But surely you lot are not now talking about re-establishing equidistance?

PA: There's no question of that under my leadership. Provided, of course, you deliver on what you promised. If you do so, then we have a genuine partnership that should last ten years while the Conservatives sort themselves out. Then the relationship between Labour and the Liberal Democrats would become the primary axis of British politics.

Just as we were finishing, Jane shouted upstairs for the car keys. The police were going to tow away our car, which was double parked outside the flat, unless she moved it immediately. I told him I had to finish the call. 'I know what it's like. I always have to jump when Cherie calls as well.'

A very unsatisfactory conversation. Blair still doesn't seem to understand the central importance of PR to us and why it will change everything.

In the evening I had dinner at Methley Street with Paul Tyler, Archy Kirkwood and Bob Maclennan. We talked primarily of spokesmanships and also of Paul taking over from Archy as Chief Whip.[1] I had warned Archy of this. He took it well, but I thought that when he left he seemed terribly sad. I felt bad about it, too. But I am sure it is right for Archy to move on and for us to have a new face as Chief Whip – and Paul is the obvious person.

Wednesday, 7 May, Westminster

THE FIRST DAY OF THE NEW PARLIAMENT

Off at 6.30 to do the *Today* programme. All about the new government (they are moving very fast!) and the Tories in disarray over their leadership now that Major has resigned.

William Hague is the bookies' favourite as the new leader at the age of 36! So we are likely to have a 44-year-old Prime Minister, a 36-year-old leader of the Conservative Party and a 56-year-old leader of the Liberal Democrats. I feel ancient.

At 11 o'clock the Lib Dem MPs – all forty-six of us – walked into Westminster through the Old Palace Yard Gates. I hadn't quite grasped how many there were of us until I saw everyone together in the flesh. We had our photograph taken in the garden under Big Ben.

At 1 o'clock lunch with Roy Jenkins. He is puzzled by Blair. He thinks he is being driven by events and by the triumphalism of his colleagues.

Into the chamber at 3.00 for the ritual of welcoming the Speaker. We now occupy three benches in the Commons, when we barely used to fill one. We take up almost a quarter of the opposition side of the House. The

---

1 Archy had been our Chief Whip for the 1992 parliament and the indispensable and unshakeable rock upon which I had relied since taking over the leadership. Member of Parliament for Roxburgh and Berwickshire since 1983, Archy is now chair of the House of Commons Social Security Select Committee.

usual palaver to start with. My speech was very short. I started with a half joke, saying that for the first time I could refer to 'these benches'.[1] It got a small laugh.

Dinner at around 7.30 was a jolly affair. Nearly all the new people were there and we took up three tables. I recall in past parliaments having to huddle together on our little oval table in the middle of the Members' Dining Room;[2] now we spread well up into the Tory area. These little things suddenly bring home the scale of our achievement.

Thursday, 8 May, London

Arrived at Downing Street with Nick South[3] at about 8.20am, going in the back door via the Cabinet Office so as not to be seen.[4]

1 In debate, MPs refer to their side of the House of Commons as 'these benches'.
2 In the Members' Dining Room of the House of Commons each party has an area where its MPs usually sit. The Labour tables are grouped on one side and the Tories take the other. The Lib Dems had traditionally occupied a single oval table in the centre.
3 My Press Secretary.
4 This was the first of many meetings with the Prime Minister, organized between his office and mine. We went to some trouble to keep their existence secret. with me always entering No. 10 through the Cabinet Office in Whitehall, rather than via the main entrance on Downing Street itself.

We were ushered straight through to the Prime Minister's study, where we were met by his Chief of Staff, Jonathan Powell. Jonathan said that he hadn't slept for more than four or five hours a night since the beginning of the election campaign. Interestingly, he told me that they had no gauge of the national mood from inside Downing Street, but they had heard that there was great excitement and anticipation. Was it true?

He spoke about the Blair family living next door at No. 11. Apparently, it had been agreed with Gordon Brown that the Blairs should occupy the flat in the Chancellor's official residence. 'A much nicer flat than the one in this place.' They had the use of three storeys and there was a door to the garden. The Blair children were coping with it well. How strange it must be, he said, for them to arrive back on the tube from school and walk through the gates of Downing Street.

In due course Tony came in, took his coat off and sat down. He looked rather crumpled and a little tired. He was carrying two red boxes, which he handed over to Jonathan. He sat on one end of the sofa and I sat on the chair under the window. I had said previously that I wished to have a meeting with Blair alone, so Jonathan and Nick left.

PA: I think it is important not to beat about the bush, particularly since you will probably have less time for these meetings than before. I want you to know that I am absolutely committed to the project we have been discussing for the past four or five years. I see our two parties as natural partners for a great decade of reform in Britain. If you think I have wavered in any way on that as a result of the General Election, then I can assure you I haven't. Apparently you have doubts about whether we will go back to equidistance. That will not happen, at least not while I am leader, provided, of course, the Cook/Maclennan deal is delivered. If it is – and I think you understand that, for us, the centrepiece of this is PR – then we are natural partners for the period of this government. Since we remain on the opposition benches there will inevitably be things you do on which we will oppose you. But our overall position will be one of constructive opposition and partnership where possible.

I know you want merger. But I can't agree to this. I can't rule it out, of course, after I have gone. But even if it happens then it will only do so organically. Meanwhile, I am as worried as you are that the natural pressures of opposition politics will lead us in different directions. But you have five or six months of honeymoon at least. In that time I hope my members will see clear evidence that you are serious about the Cook/Maclennan agreement. As soon as we know that, and become confident about PR, we will not be able to part company from you, because we will have to remain with you in order to deliver it. Then, I believe, it will be possible, even necessary, for us to go into the next election on the basis of heads of agreement established between our two parties (like the kind I drew up last summer)[1] and the presumption of a coalition government afterwards if we win.

But the relationship between the parties can only grow through good will and trust. I hear from Roy Jenkins and others that you would be interested in bringing us into the government at some later date. I must underline again that if we are to come in, there can be no question of us doing so simply to administer a Labour programme. It could only happen on the basis of a separately negotiated coalition agreement. No member of my parliamentary team is falling over backwards to take up a Cabinet seat, and neither am I. We are enthusiastic about working with you, but only on a sustainable basis and in a genuine partnership.

TB: Thank you for telling me where you stand. That's helpful. I think we have been getting the wrong messages about what you wanted. I must now think about what to do next. But I am very clear that, unless we do something special, we will simply settle back into the old antagonistic positions of opposition and government. The first step, it seems to me, is your idea of setting up Cabinet committees. That will send out a very powerful message about the new kind of relationship we want to have.

After a discussion, we agreed to investigate four areas of joint work including the constitution and social security.

He said he would discuss this with his 'senior people' – all of whom are quite amenable to the idea. If we are to do this, he suggested, we should announce it next week.

I then turned to the Electoral Reform Commission:

PA: A chill went down my spine yesterday when you announced that Jack Straw was considering names for the Electoral Reform Commission. Please give me

1 'Partnership for Britain's Future', see Vol. I, Appendices G and H.

an undertaking that he will not put people on this who are hostile to the whole thing.

TB: Yes. You will be fully consulted on names. I won't let Jack scupper this.

PA: What we desperately need from you now is some earnest of good intent on PR, especially PR for Europe in 1999.

TB: That will be very difficult to put into the Queen's Speech, which is already heavily overburdened. We will probably not include Freedom of Information [FoI] in the Queen's Speech either, as we need to get in some important stuff on health, but that does not indicate any waning of our resolve either on FoI or PR for Europe.

PA: Well, if FoI does not appear in the Queen's Speech, then you can expect to hear some strong criticism from our benches. But can I have an undertaking from you at least that it will be in the programme of government for next year?

TB: Yes, that is our intention. But you must understand how crowded our programme is. Look, I want you guys in, I want you to be part of the government. I can't tell you how much fun it is taking decisions. And I think you would all be very good at it.

Finally, he said, he wanted to change the form of PMQs – did I have any suggestions? I suggested looking at the unstarred question procedure in the House of Lords.[1]

TB: Yes, I will look at that. It would be particularly applicable if I wanted to change to one PMQ a week of half an hour. Would I have your support on that?

I said he would, and that I would try to strike a different attitude in PMQs anyway, in line with our policy of constructive opposition. He said that he intended to do the same.

We finished off with a brief chat about our families. Cherie is enjoying being next door, and so are the kids. 'It's a great house for children,' he said, and told me an amusing story about Robin Cook losing his way in the maze of corridors between No. 10 and No. 11. So Blair had asked Euan, in his pyjamas, to guide the new Foreign Secretary through the corridors of Downing Street to the front door.

A good meeting. Straightforward, straight-talking and constructive.

---

1 An unstarred question in the House of Lords introduces a mini debate on the subject of the question, in which peers are only allowed to speak once.

Tuesday, 13 May, Irancy

I have been doing a lot of thinking about my long-term future over the week we have been here. I have more or less decided to stand down as leader of the Party. The question is whether I do this in September, or next year. At the moment I favour this year.

The arguments for standing down are:

1. I will be 60 at the next election, which is too old to hang on for another full term.

2. There are other things I want to do with my life, so the earlier I start doing them the better.

The arguments for standing down this year are:

1. It gives my successor more time to get his or her feet under the table. No elections, either locals or Euros, are scheduled for 1998.

2. My London staff will only have to stay with me until September, so I won't have to recruit new staff just for one year, which would be unfair on them.

3. If I am to do something else, why not give myself an extra year to do it in?

If I do go, the announcement must come as a complete surprise. I will simply say I am retiring at the end of my speech at conference. Nobody will know beforehand except Jane. And to anybody who asks, I will say that I am naturally considering my position but there is no hurry. The greater the element of surprise the less destabilizing the speculation beforehand. After all, I will have done nine years if I go this year and ten years if I go next. You get less for murder!

Having set off at 7.00am, we had one of our best journeys home ever, arriving in London at a little after midday.

It looks as though the Tories will ask for a judicial recount of the Winchester result and we may have to fight a by-election.[1]

---

1 Our candidate Mark Oaten's majority was only two votes. The Tories were petitioning for a judicial recount. A successful petition would void the original result, necessitating a by-election.

In the afternoon I worked on my response to the Queen's Speech tomorrow, and then walked across to St Ermin's Hotel for a gathering of the Parliamentary Party and the Lords contingent. A huge meeting – about sixty people. Alan Beith, among others, suggested we should vote against the Queen's Speech, but I said that was nonsense. We shouldn't be voting against a Queen's Speech which contains so many of our own measures. Eventually they agreed, but it wasn't easy.

Wednesday, 14 May, Westminster

THE STATE OPENING OF PARLIAMENT

I fell in alongside Ken Clarke in the traditional Commons procession to the Lords to hear the Queen's Speech. I wished him luck in the Tory leadership election: 'If your party doesn't elect you, they are mad.'[1]

He replied, 'That's the problem – they probably are.' He thinks it's between him and Hague.

Afterwards down to the Commons for the Speaker's reception. The usual crush getting in there. I saw Mo Mowlam and several other Cabinet ministers for the first time since the election and congratulated them. They all seem very happy. And so does everybody else. I didn't stay long.

Back to my office to do some last minute work on my speech. Then to the chamber at about ten past two.

There was fifteen minutes of swearing in,[2] after which the Queen's Speech debate. Gerald Kaufman[3] proposed. Brilliantly funny; he had the House rolling about. Mullin[4] next. Not as amusing as Kaufman but the House has great respect for his courage and integrity.

Major next. I thought his first ten minutes were excellent. Light, dignified and decent. But then he suddenly went into election campaign overdrive, claiming that the government had inherited a golden Britain from the

1 Following John Major's resignation as leader of the Conservative Party, a leadership contest was held. The initial candidates were Kenneth Clarke, William Hague, John Redwood, Peter Lilley and Michael Howard.
2 After each election MPs are 'sworn in' at the start of the parliament.
3 Member of Parliament (Labour) for Ardwick 1970–83, Manchester Gorton since 1983. Chair of the House of Commons Select Committee on Culture, Media and Sport.
4 Chris Mullin, Member of Parliament (Labour) for Sunderland South since 1987. Chair of the House of Commons Select Committee on Home Affairs 1997–9.

Tories. There wasn't a touch of humility about him, nor did he show any understanding of why he had been so comprehensively defeated. An uncharacteristically misjudged and unintelligent speech for Major; he should have left that kind of stuff behind at the election hustings.

Then Blair. I thought he would rise above it all, but he didn't. He immediately started mixing it with Major, re-running all the election arguments again. It sounded bad.

At our first full post-election Parliamentary Party Meeting afterwards, Jackie Ballard asked a question about strategy towards Labour. I replied that there were two possibilities: if Labour delivered on PR and constitutional reform we were tied to them as partners for the next five years and would have to swallow some unpleasant fare to see through what we wanted; if they did not, then we would revert to conventional opposition politics. We'd have to wait and see. Alan Beith interrupted, saying that under no circumstances would he go along with Labour. A good-tempered if slightly chaotic meeting.

Thursday, 15 May, Westminster

At 1.00 Nick and I went to Downing Street via the back door again, through the Cabinet Office, where I bumped into Robin Butler,[1] who was very complimentary about what he called 'the new lot'.

'They have come in incredibly well prepared. On the Friday morning after the election they already had the draft letter for the independence of the Bank of England written and ready to present to the Governor. The Civil Service worked on it over the weekend and the Governor received it by 10.00am on Monday. They are better prepared than any others I have seen in my time in the Civil Service.'

'And,' he added, putting his worried face close to mine, 'do you know, they don't eat lunch!'

He was especially impressed by Labour's press operation. 'We in the Civil Service can learn a lot from them.'

I told Alastair Campbell this later. He harrumphed and said that wasn't saying very much since the Civil Service press operation was absolutely dreadful. 'Most of the last government's problems were caused by them

---

1 Sir Robin Butler, Head of the Civil Service and Secretary to the Cabinet. He now sits as a cross bencher in the House of Lords.

not having their press story straight among themselves. But having an inefficient press operation in the Civil Service didn't help.'

We were quickly ushered into Blair's study. He was sitting, as always, in shirtsleeves on the sofa. I said I wanted to speak with him, initially, by myself, so Jonathan and Nick left.

I commented to Blair that I had seen him better than in his response to Major's taunts on the Queen's Speech. He should have hardly mentioned the election campaign at all, and concentrated on the future.

He looked at me rather quizzically, then said, 'Yes, I suppose you're right. I thought that afterwards, too. But I was in a quandary. This was, after all, the first time my people had been together and I wanted to give them something to cheer about. But I agree, it wasn't my best day.

'Now, here's where I think we are. I think we both know what needs to be achieved. But I am still not sure that you and I agree about the end destination.'

PA: Look, I think we *do* agree on an end destination. I proposed about two years ago that you and I should try to mend the schism that split apart the progressive forces in British politics in the early years of this century, giving the Tories more chances to govern than they deserved. And I am still committed to that.

But that will only happen if the will exists on both sides. And it won't happen if we try to force it. I know you want to start talking about merger, but that is not an option in the short term, while I'm around. The Lib Dems are, and will remain, an independent and separate force for as long as either of us can reasonably foresee. If you adopt the same policies as us, then of course all sorts of things become possible. But much water will have to flow under the bridge before that happens. Meanwhile, if you want my prediction about the likely course of events if you deliver on PR then it is this: that we will be linked to you indissolubly in a shared project to bring about constitutional reform during this parliament. We may not agree on everything, but once PR is delivered for the next election we will fight that election on four or five joint heads of agreement with the presumption of a coalition in the next government. And if that's successful, then, with a full and successful partnership government behind us, all sorts of things may become possible. Although I still don't believe merger is one of them, I can't exclude it totally.

TB: Yes, that is broadly the way I see it, too. I'm obviously more enthusiastic about merger than you are, but let's at least go ahead on the basis that it is neither written in in the short term nor written out in the long.

PA: Agreed.

TB: You know, we discussed the whole question of Lib/Lab relationships at some length in Cabinet today. I was surprised at how easily my colleagues took it. There is broad agreement that we should continue along current lines. But some of my people, are saying, 'Fine. They have got a lot out of this, but what's in it for us?' That's the question I now want to turn to.

PA: What's in it for you is very simple: two terms. What's in it for us is room to expand and grow and share in government. And what's in it for both of us is keeping the Tories out for ten years. It's a genuine 'win–win' situation, if we get it right.

But you must understand the absolute centrality of the Cook/Maclennan agreement to all this. Our people are under some pressure at the moment, particularly from journalists who point out that there is no PR for Europe or FoI in the Queen's Speech. Our reply is that we didn't expect either of these to be included this year. But Cook/Maclennan has been delivered in good faith so far, and we have no reason to believe it will not continue to be delivered in the future. Our line will become more difficult to sustain, however, without some signs from you that PR and FoI will happen. Last night, at our Parliamentary Party Meeting, I made it clear to my colleagues that if you delivered on Cook/Maclennan, then in the course of the next two or three years we must be prepared to put up with some difficult things. But we must see signs from you soon. The first is PR for Europe in 1999.

TB: Yes, I have got the message very clearly. I can see advantages in PR for Europe in 1999 for us as well.

At this point we agreed that Jonathan Powell, Alastair Campbell and Nick should join us.

Blair started going through my memo of 4 May. The first item was the membership of the Electoral Reform Commission, which we agreed that Jack Straw and Bob Maclennan should sort out bilaterally.

PA: When will the Electoral Reform Commission start?

TB: Very soon.

PA: What does that mean. Before the summer recess?

TB: Oh yes, bound to be. I mean, I haven't spoken to Jack about it yet, but I can see no reason why not.

I said that the setting up of the Commission was very important to us symbolically.

We turned to tactical voting.

PA: Most of my MPs understand very well that they are only here because of tactical voting. But you need to understand the psychology of our people. For them there's no such thing as a safe seat. Each one of them has had to fight for a long time to win. And one of the ways they won was squeezing down the Labour vote in their constituencies. Indeed, it took me eight years and two elections to win my seat and I only eventually did so because I persuaded Labour voters to vote for me. I didn't just come in at the beginning of an election campaign and walk out an MP, you know.[1] That changes the way you view politics.

He grimaced and turned to the next point on my minute, which was the Cabinet committees.

TB: I raised this at Cabinet today. An interesting suggestion came forward from a rather surprising source. Instead of scattering your people in Cabinet committees all over the place, we should have a single Cabinet committee, consisting of me and you and our most senior lieutenants, which could range freely over all subjects. It would, of course, tie you into the government a bit more. On the other hand, it would also give you much more influence over the progress of events generally. It struck me as a useful idea. What do you think?

I replied that I could see some attractions, but we would need to establish the terms of reference very carefully. I doubted it would formalize our relationship. 'In the end we cannot be held together by structures. We can only be held together by shared objectives.'

I suggested we discuss this in more detail in the week after the Whitsun recess.

Nick and I left at about 1.50.

1 The reference is to Tony Blair's own selection process as an MP. He was adopted for the safe seat of Sedgefield only weeks before the 1983 election.

Friday, 16 May, Somerset

I have been thinking about my future again. I desperately want to stand down. But I have now embarked on a project with Blair which could bring Labour and the Lib Dems closer together and change the shape of politics. I cannot leave before this is brought to a conclusion one way or the other.

Jane and I went out for a walk, during which I explained to her that I felt I might have to stay on for an extra year, or even longer, to see the project through. She said she had waited a long time to 'get me back', but ended by saying, 'If that's what you feel you must do, I won't stop you.'

I think this means I must remain as leader until either Blair has agreed to PR, or it has become clear to me he is not going to deliver.

Monday, 19 May, London

At 6.15pm off with Jane by taxi to the Chelsea Flower Show. A lovely evening with a beautiful clear full moon. I selected some catalogues for marsh plants and began to formulate an idea of how to redesign our back garden. We were continually stopped and congratulated by complete strangers on how well we did in the election. I have never had a public reaction like this before.

Then to the dinner organized by the sponsors. Gordon Borrie also there, with whom I discussed relations with Labour. He is very much in favour of co-operation.

Alastair Goodlad,[1] the Tory Chief Whip, came to join us. He tells me that his party is in a complete mess. No anchor, no leadership and no prospects. They are at war with themselves. His tone was intended to be jokey, but you could tell he was deadly serious underneath.

We left at about 10.30, eventually picking up a taxi at the end of Battersea Bridge. At home Jane and I sat outside under the stars and drank a glass

1 Conservative spokesman for International Development. Member of Parliament (Conservative) for Northwich 1974–83 and Eddisbury 1983–99. Had been Blair's pair. Previously a minister in the Conservative government and now the High Commissioner to Australia.

of whisky before tumbling into bed at about midnight. A very disturbed night's sleep. I always have these following an election. It takes me a long time to settle down after such a prolonged period of tension.

Tuesday, 20 May, Westminster

A Jo Group[1] meeting in the morning. We discussed briefly what pressure to bring to bear on Labour for PR for the European elections.

We also discussed Blair's suggestion for a single Cabinet committee. I was in favour but thought it should be confined to constitutional matters. Bob [Maclennan] was against, as was Chris Rennard. Bob thought it would take us in too deep and Chris was worried about differentiation. After a long discussion, to which almost everybody contributed, we decided to go ahead with it as soon as the Electoral Reform Commission had started its work. But we should make it clear that, initially at any rate, such a committee should only deal with the constitution and bilateral relations between Labour ministers and our chief spokesmen, and that it should not extend further, at least until the Cook/Maclennan constitutional reform programme had been completed. Meanwhile, I should spell out to Blair what the bottom line on all this was, including his personal position on PR, the early launch of the Electoral Reform Commission and the absolute necessity of PR for the Euros in 1999.

At 2 o'clock a long session with David Rendel,[2] who is adamantly opposed to closer co-operation with Labour, whatever the conditions.

Afterwards, a meeting with the Scottish and Welsh MPs in an attempt to reach a consensus on the respective Scottish and Welsh Referendum Bills,[3] about which opinions were diametrically opposed – with Jim Wallace refusing to vote for the Scottish Bill because of Labour's pre-election

1 A group I established in September 1994 (see Vol. I, p. 278). It was a key steering group which advised me and planned and controlled all our relations with Labour on the project. It included, at this stage, Richard Holme, Tim Razzall, Archy Kirkwood, Paul Tyler, Tom McNally, Bob Maclennan, Ming Campbell and key members of my staff. Later I added Nick Harvey and Chris Rennard to this group.

2 Member of Parliament for Newbury since 1993.

3 The government had introduced two bills to provide for referendums in Scotland and Wales on devolution.

betrayal on the tax-raising powers of the Scottish Parliament.[1] Other Scottish colleagues argued a more conciliatory line and the Welsh wanted to vote in favour. I thought I had got them to agree to an abstention by the end of the meeting, but then Richard Livsey peeled off, saying he was determined to vote for the Welsh Bill, and the consensus disintegrated. I suggested that Paul Tyler should take the protagonists away and see what he could sort out. He came back later to say he couldn't resolve the matter, I would have to.

Voting that evening was a terrible crush. There are so many new Labour MPs that they fill the entire Division Lobby from one end to the other.

During the vote I took Ming (who is one of those adamantly opposed to the Scotland Devolution Bill) to one side and went through the potential problems if the Welsh and the Scots vote in different ways. I begged him not to vote against a collective decision of the Parliamentary Party. But I made little progress. I will have to play Roy in tomorrow.

I gave Jim a lift home, and on the way he told me that the Scottish MPs have definitely decided to vote against a Referendum Bill. If I was to persuade them otherwise I would have to do so myself at the Scottish MPs' meeting tomorrow morning. My heart sank. Failure to agree a common line on referendums for Scotland and Wales will undermine our whole credibility on constitutional issues.

To bed at midnight, very disturbed. Our first big test and it looks to me as though we are going to fail it. There is no point in continuing serious negotiations with Blair if I cannot even get my own colleagues to agree!

Wednesday, 21 May, Westminster

At 9.45 the Scottish MPs' meeting. It proved very difficult. I went through the arguments as I saw them:

1. There is no point blaming the Welsh; they have arrived at their position through their own means, and that is their right as part of a federal party.

---

1 See Vol. I, pp. 441–2. Contrary to the agreement reached between the Lib Dems and Labour on Scottish devolution, in the Scottish Constitutional Convention, Blair had unilaterally introduced an extra question into the planned referendum on whether the Scottish Parliament should have tax-raising powers or not.

2. A split would do our party incalculable damage.

3. I am involved in delicate negotiations with Blair and if we can't hold together on this issue, he simply won't take us seriously and we will lose everything.

There wasn't a single argument I didn't use; nor any emotional leverage I didn't try. But I was pretty gloomy about the outcome when I left.

Later on, however, Jim told me that it had worked. With the possible exception of Ming, they have agreed to abstain.

Only Ming to convince now. I spoke to Roy later, asking him to talk to Ming, which, bless him, he did. By the time I saw Ming in the afternoon, he too was beginning to move.

At 11 o'clock a meeting with David Montgomery (chief executive of the *Mirror*). I told him that the *Mirror*'s support had really helped us, particularly in places where some of our majorities were very tight (such as Torbay), and I was very grateful. He, like me, believes that Blair doesn't understand the implications of constitutional change; Blair has accepted the need for devolution intellectually, but hasn't internalized what it means for him (less power in his hands). We also agreed to work together to put pressure on Labour, particularly for the European elections.

Down to the chamber for Blair's first PMQs. He seemed nervous. I am not surprised.

I noticed he didn't use notes. Labour MPs fed him purely sycophantic questions: 'Does the Prime Minister still agree with the main items of our manifesto, that we stood on two weeks ago?' That sort of thing.

Major, I thought, was below par on his first question, and completely muffed his second. He is finding it difficult to learn the very different technique of asking questions from the opposition benches. Rather endearing.

The new thirty-minute question time has changed the whole dynamic of PMQs. Today Blair used the time to make a number of statements. But if he gets himself into real difficulty, then thirty minutes of effective opposition questioning will feel pretty tough.

Thursday, 22 May, Westminster

Last night I decided I would write Blair a letter which would act as an agenda for when we meet. I composed most of it overnight lying in bed and dictated it first thing this morning. My PA, Becky Vye, sent it across by hand to Downing Street mid-morning.

Dear Tony,

. . . I have now had a chance to consider what we talked about at our last meeting in more detail. I have asked Nick South and Tom McNally to produce a paper [on a single Cabinet committee] which contains our considered response, which they will discuss with Jonathan, I hope, before we meet. But I want to add to that paper with a short, personal note to you, laying out the situation as I see it.

Briefly, we think the way that you have proposed going forward is a useful one. There are some relatively small, but important, points of detail which Nick and Tom can discuss with Jonathan. We need, I think, to reach a conclusion on this relatively soon.

I am nervous, as I know you are, about the present climate of co-operation ebbing away unless there is something firm on which to anchor it.

This brings me to my main point. No amount of institutional framework will hold us together unless there is a common project which we share and which is in the interests of both parties. As you know, I believe that common project is constitutional reform with, from our point of view, PR at the centre of it. If we have PR we are closely linked to you in this parliament and, even more so, in the next one, too. And you, in return, have the near certainty of the second term which we both think is necessary to modernize Britain. And the country gets a modern electoral system.

We have, in Cook/Maclennan, reached our formal agreements about how to handle this. And if these now go ahead, as we agreed they should, that should form the starting point of our co-operation and an appropriate moment to move to the kind of Cabinet committee that you propose. You will, of course, understand our nervousness about this. There have been quite a few reports in the press, including from 'high-placed Labour sources', that, now that you have such a large majority, all this will go on the backburner. I do not believe this and have been strong in saying so. But, together with nervousness about the lack of obvious public progress on Cook/Maclennan, they are causing me concern. Before we take this step, I will want to discuss with you, when we meet, three items, by way of confirmation:

1. What exactly are the plans for starting the Electoral Reform Commission?

2. As you know, your personal position on this is absolutely central to us. I will want briefly to discuss and, I hope, confirm our past discussions about it.

3. As I have said to you repeatedly, PR for Europe in 1999 provides, for my people,

the first test of good faith . . . I have, up to now, confined myself to telling you how important this is, because I had no wish to press it when you had so many other things on your mind. But things have settled down now. And some indications we have been getting have been deeply unhelpful. I will need to confirm with you that it remains the government's 'intention' to introduce PR for Europe by 1999, and that appropriate steps will be taken in the near future to indicate this intention. The whole project will become unsellable to my party (and to me) if the 1999 Euro elections are not part of it . . . By a painful irony, the Boundary Commission's first hearing on the new Euro seats is next month; in Taunton (next door to me), possible changes could destroy any chance that the Lib Dems have of holding on to my own Euro seat in 1999. I am, personally, going to be in the firing line on this very soon.

Yours

Paddy

Saturday, 24 May, Irancy

WHITSUN RECESS; ON HOLIDAY IN FRANCE

A glorious day. Last night we heard the nightingales singing all round the village and today is cloudless and hot. The orchids are in flower in the woods around Irancy and the vines are in full blossom, promising a good *vendange*,[1] if we have a hot summer.

I have been giving a lot of thought to our relations with Labour, and concluded that we cannot sustain a position of realistic partnership for a full parliamentary term unless we have a much stronger framework. We are bound to drift into full-scale opposition, whatever constitutional or even party-based agreement we may have. This is a dangerous moment. All that I have worked for over the last five years could now be at risk.

Labour have started well. And if the economy recovers, our point of differentiation on investment in education and health will be gone, since they will have huge sums to play with in the latter half of this parliament, by which time the two parties will have drifted further apart. I have come to the tentative view that if we are to do anything it must be big and we must do it now. I am considering suggesting to Blair that if he wants us to enter government he should make a proposal soon. We must act now or risk missing the opportunity altogether.

---

1 The *'vendange'* or grape harvest normally follows 100 days after the vines flower.

I have also decided that I won't myself take a Cabinet post. I can then argue for a coalition without my personal position becoming an issue. And after the Party has decided (either way) I can announce that I intend to stand down as party leader. That way, I think, we can take the decision without internal rancour or division. I can simply say that the Party has to take this decision and it is my recommendation to go into coalition. But it's up to the members to decide.

Monday, 26 May, Irancy

Another glorious day. Cloudless blue skies, with the barometer still high.

During the afternoon I wrote my post-election position paper.[1] The more I think about it the more convinced I am that the idea of a Cabinet committee simply won't hold in the long term. I wrote the paper hoping that it would help me to clarify the future.

It has, and in the most frightening way. I have come to believe there is only one way that we can sustain the work Blair and I have done together over the last four years, and that's through a full-blown partnership in *this* government, if such a thing were still feasible. I will have to tackle this at this year's Eastbourne Conference. Sooner or later we must resolve the tension between our parliamentary position, which favours closer co-operation with Labour, and our local government and northern party position, which is hostile to Labour.

But I am dreading it. I still haven't really got the courage to face the conclusion I have reached.

A barbecue for dinner. Afterwards, Jane and I went up to the Jefferies' house and I had a look through Greg's telescope at the stars: bright and crisp and sparkling in a clear night sky.

Wednesday, 28 May, Irancy

Lay awake most of the night thinking, then decided finally to send a letter to Blair, based on the paper I have just written. Rang Jonathan at 8.30am and faxed it through to Downing Street. I made sure Jonathan was standing over it, as I didn't want anybody else to see it.

1 See Appendix A.

There's no way back now. If Blair accepts my proposition, then we will be in for a major decision-making conference at Eastbourne. It will be very difficult. But I am absolutely determined that we should live in the real world. The reality is that we are now indissolubly tied in with Labour if they deliver PR. We might just as well get the benefits of this from inside government rather than remain supplicants outside.

When I sent the fax off I should have felt better, but I kept on thinking about it for the rest of the day.

Dear Tony,

One of the advantages of not being in government is that you have time to think. I have been doing a lot of this in my courtyard, in the Burgundy sunshine.

I have come to the conclusion that we may be missing the great opportunity for which we have both worked these last four years.

And that you are right to fear that, unless we do something very strong, the inevitable pressures of opposition in the House will, over time, push us back to fighting each other in the way our parties used to, before you and I initiated the recent process of co-operation.

If this happens, all our hopes of 'healing the historic rift' will have gone.

I am not opposed to pursuing co-operation at Cabinet committee level. The establishment of a Cabinet committee would be a breakthrough in its own right and would certainly delay a reversion to outright opposition, maybe long enough to enable the parties to grow together through shared aims and the habit of co-operation.

But we should not fool ourselves that there is any guarantee of this. It now seems to me more likely that the inevitable pressure of events (a disagreement; next year's local elections) . . . would provide too strong a pull in the opposite direction for this kind of ever closer co-operation to survive the full five years ahead of us.

In short, I have come to the conclusion that, while the Cabinet committee idea remains the best option if we can find no other, it is an uncomfortable halfway house which provides little of real substance for either side . . .

If we are serious about our joint project then we will probably have to think bigger and bolder.

You said to me (and I understand also to Roy) soon after you became PM that you wanted us 'on the inside within a few months'. Is this still your view?

If it is, then, though I gave a cautious response when you first raised it in the immediate aftermath of the election, believing that the moment had passed, I have come to think differently now. For reasons I shall explain when we meet, I believe it would be preferable if I did not take a position in any such coalition myself.

However, if we were able to reach agreement on the points I mentioned in my letter to you before the start of the Whitsun recess, then I think it would be right, at our forthcoming meeting, to reconsider all the options before us, including full-blown partnership in the present parliament.

This is a very high risk strategy for us (and a difficult one for you, too). But it represents, I have come to believe, the surest way to capitalize on the present opportunity, which, if lost, is unlikely to come again.

I have other thoughts about the detail of how we may handle this. We can discuss these when we meet – which I hope can be no later than Thursday of next week.
Best wishes
Paddy

Sunday, 1 June, Irancy

Not feeling too bright this morning. The weather is wonderful, though.

I received an e-mail this morning from Graham Watson[1] telling me that, at a recent meeting[2] he had attended, the opinion was unanimous that we should now turn away from Labour. I fear he may be right, but I wrote him a sharp e-mail back saying this was just nonsense. I am dreading the fight ahead.

But this matter cannot be left hanging over us. Even the policy of constructive co-operation will become unstitched if it is constantly sniped at by activists and others who want to return to full-blooded opposition to Labour. The Party needs to understand that what we have on offer is the best chance we have ever had of getting PR. But that this cannot be achieved without taking risks and, above all, without recognizing that if Labour delivers on PR we are attached to them in this parliament.

Jane and I have had a wonderful holiday. I feel much rested and have caught a lot of sun. However, I am very nervous about the months ahead, which will, I think, be bloody and unpleasant.

1 Member of the European Parliament for Somerset since 1994.
2 I had heard about this meeting previously. It was, I was told, originally planned as a meeting of the campaign team for Simon Hughes' leadership bid if I had failed in the 1997 election.

Monday, 2 June, Westminster

Back to work. A chat with Nick about my position paper and the letter to Blair. He is against the whole thing. The other members of the Jo Group, however, are very much in favour, especially Tom. A big throw, but he thinks we should take it. After talking to me, Nick changed his view slightly. He now thinks that if we can get a commitment to PR we should go ahead.

At 4 o'clock I saw Ming and showed him the paper.

'I could go down on this,' I said. 'I do not think you should openly support me. It is more important for you to be available to stand for the leadership if I fail.'

Ming disagreed. 'What nonsense! This is what I came into politics for. If you go down I wouldn't want to lead the Party anyway. I am absolutely with you. We must tackle this now.'

Then at 5.30 Paul Tyler and Jane Bonham-Carter, from the Press Office. Both of them agreed that we should go ahead, though they recognized how difficult it would be.

At 6.15 I saw Bob. To my surprise, he is in favour, too. Thank goodness.

Tuesday, 3 June, Westminster

At 8.15am I saw Richard Holme and showed him the papers and the letter. His response was, 'This is really big. Are you sure you are right? I will back you, of course. But you must realize you may split the Party. Although you can probably carry it, if you put your whole weight behind it.'

At 4.15 to Downing Street to see Blair. Through the back door as usual. Our meeting lasted a little under an hour.

We began with the Tories.

TB: They are in a total panic. They just don't know how to be in opposition . . . Though I am getting very concerned that they are planning a fight to the death against reform in the Lords [part of the Cook/Maclennan agreement]. I am worried they will do a 'Balfour'.

PA: You mean 'Balfour's Poodle'?[1] I really don't think that the Tories at the end

---

1 'Balfour's Poodles' was what David Lloyd George called the House of Lords in 1907 because it had an inbuilt Conservative majority which was continually rolled out by the then Tory leader, the Earl of Balfour, to block the 1906 Liberal government's legislative programme.

of the twentieth century would dare to do that. They would look absolutely dreadful. But if they do, you have an easy answer. You can do a 'Lloyd George' and threaten to swamp the Tory hereditary peers by creating your own.

TB: Yes, that's what it may come to. I think the Tories are now so desperate that they will stop at nothing. I am really worried about it.

In front of him was the letter I had sent to him from Irancy, with certain passages highlighted in green.

PA: I see you have my recent fax there. What do you think?

TB: Well, I still want you in. But I have to come back to a point which I have made to you consistently before. What's in it for us at the moment? If we give you PR, then we create the circumstances through which you can break away.

He then pulled out a paper, prepared for him by one of his staff, containing several complex tables, none of which I had time to analyse.

TB: Look, you can see it very clearly from these. If I give you PR, here's what my people say the last General Election result would have been: we would have had an overall Commons majority of only nine seats, and you would have had a total of 146. Under those circumstances, why shouldn't you break away and return to equidistance? We would be tripling your seats and creating the very conditions under which we could not rely on you should things get difficult.

PA: I don't understand why this whole issue is up for review again. I thought we had already sorted this out. Are you now saying that PR itself is in question? If you are, then we shouldn't go ahead, even with the Cabinet committee, until we have sorted it out. You ask what's in it for you. Well, exactly what's always been in it for you. The absolute certainty of having a second term, and of keeping the Tories out for ten years. I thought you and I had agreed that that's what we wanted to do.

TB: But can I be sure of that? It might provide you with the opportunity to part company with us after the next election, if that was held under PR. In short, I believe that the only answer now is merger. It's the only way I can be certain that you are locked in with us for the long term.

PA: I have said this to you before and I will say it again: I am not prepared to contemplate merger. And even if I were, I could not get it past my party, so I won't even try.

TB: Why?

PA: Because our parties are not the same. I trust you and think you believe broadly the same things as I do. But you are not the same as your party. And, as you have said to me before, you are not permanent. Now, a merger of hearts after a period of working together, that's different. But there is no prospect whatsoever of us imposing a merger on our two parties on the basis of an *ex cathedra* pronouncement from their two leaders. Anyway, the Lib Dems have an important independent role to play, as we have already shown. Nobody else was prepared to oppose disgraceful measures such as the curfews Howard introduced in his Criminal Justice Bill before the election. [He grimaced at this.] And if merger is the price you want us to pay for PR, then it is one price I can't pay and won't pay. If, on the other hand, what you want is some kind of assurance that, if we have PR, we are locked in with you for the next ten years, how can it be otherwise? I would like you to describe to me the circumstances in which, after having worked with you for four years as partners in government, and having become utterly dependent on your votes to hold our seats, we could, at the next election, part company. I accept that it is theoretically possible, but in practice it seems inconceivable.

TB: Yeah. But I can't be *sure* of that. And I can still think of ways in which, if we made ourselves very unpopular, that option would be tempting to you.

PA: Look, if all this is up for grabs again, then we are back to square one. There is nothing we can do. Let me repeat my proposition to you in full. I think that the Cabinet committee process will not hold water for long. It will give us some breathing space, but not much. After which the essential dynamics of opposition will lead us further and further away from you. The moment will be lost. I do not object to Cabinet committees as a first step. But I think we can and should go to a full working relationship. But we must decide quickly. If you and I are prepared to agree on this, then I am prepared to recommend to my party that we should work together. If that is passed by both parties (and I would be taking a very, very great risk with mine), then you are free to engage us with you, in your government. For reasons I will explain to you in a minute, I would not wish to be a member of the government myself. Nevertheless, this provides you with a win–win situation. If we go into partnership, then you get ten years of leading a solidly founded government of reform and modernization. You get a second term, and the probability that in the process of working together we create the opportunity for an even deeper relationship. If I don't carry my party, then I go down. Then many of the good people in my party who want to be in government may well simply join you. But that's a risk I am prepared to take, because the prize of PR, a decade of reform and 'healing the rift' is that great. But you must take a risk as well.

TB: But what happens after the ten years? Then presumably you can break away?

PA: For God's sake! If we can deliver ten years of sensible government for this country, isn't that good enough? After ten years all sorts of things can happen. But it is madness to lose this historic opportunity now because of what might happen in ten years' time.

TB: But do you think we can deliver PR before the next election?

PA: Yes, of course we can. If the Electoral Reform Commission produces in the next six months – and I see no reason why it should not – and if this is then followed by a referendum on PR some time next year, then we will have three full years in which to implement the process.

TB: Look, I must tell you that if I give you guys PR, without getting from you a guarantee of merger, or at least some bottom-line assurance that you won't break away later, my party will think I have lost my marbles.

PA: Well, doubtless my party may think I have lost mine, too. But those are the risks we must take for the prospect of leading a broad-based progressive coalition for ten full years. God knows, isn't that enough? I simply cannot agree to a merger. It would be inviting my party to vote for its own obliteration. And I won't do that.

TB: I'm not suggesting you get swallowed up by us. I'm suggesting a genuine merger, one in which we both change.

PA: As the elephant said to the mouse. You know as well as I do that it would be perceived as an assimilation by you, whatever we did to dress it up. By the way, I am getting very worried about this discussion. Are you saying to me that you are going to renege on the Cook/Maclennan agreement? Are you saying that, having failed to deliver on your agreement to support PR before the election, you are now withdrawing the promise to recommend PR after the election as well? The first of these will be seen as a betrayal, which will damage your reputation widely. And the second will be regarded by me personally as an act of profound bad faith. I accepted your first inability to deliver on an undertaking; it will be impossible for me to accept a second.

He shifted the conversation.

TB: What would happen if we took all the steps towards PR before the election but didn't deliver PR until the election after next?

PA: You would then be asking me to propose to my party that they should accept that, at the next election, their number of seats would be halved.

TB: Are you sure about that? I have some figures here which show that, in all your target seats, you depend on the Labour tactical vote, and it is still big enough to be squeezed. If we worked in partnership, then that tactical vote would come your way and all the seats you now have, you would continue to hold. The figures are clear. Where you are standing in opposition to the Conservatives, the Labour vote will come to you.

He then tore off three pages of the report he was holding and gave them to me.

PA: Look, I'm not very enthusiastic about this. But if these figures genuinely do show that, not only could we hold on to the seats we have, but also gain more, then that may alter my view. I have a suspicion, though, that what you have here [pointing to the paper] is a static position, not a dynamic one. It's just as likely that the floating votes in these seats will go back to the Tories, if they recover – which we must assume they will.

TB: I don't think so. Forty-four per cent is a respectable vote. But it's not huge. I am pretty sure we can hold on to, let's say, between 40 and 42 per cent. That would still keep the Tories very low. And I reckon that the substantial bulk of those lost votes would indeed come to you.

PA: What's behind all this? Have you now come to believe that with a majority of 179 you can win the next election by yourselves?

TB: No, certainly not. As I have been saying to my party, winning the next election is a possibility, not a probability.

PA: Well, if the proposition you are putting to me is that you will hold to your personal commitment to support PR in a referendum; you will deliver PR for Europe in 1999; you will allow, in good faith, the Electoral Reform Commission to go ahead; you will ensure that, whatever system it recommends is implemented by the election after next; and if, as your figures suggest, we can indeed not only hold our current seats, but increase them, then I would want to go away and think about it. But we don't have very much time. If you and I are to act, we must act soon. If we do so in the next couple of weeks, then I can recommend an abstention on your first Budget. Otherwise, we will have to oppose you. Which will make the whole process much more difficult later. But if we make the announcement next week I will then have to spend the next two months stomping up and down the country trying to win my party over. So let's get together early next week and make our final decision one way or the other.

Now, I want you to understand why it would be inappropriate for me to take a position in the government. Incomparably the greatest task that I now have, if we agree to go ahead along these lines, is to persuade my party. Which will be much more difficult to do if I have something at stake in this myself. If I can present this to my party as something that I believe is right for them, but without personal gain for myself, my chances of winning will be so much the greater. And that is more important to me than being a Cabinet minister. Secondly, if I make it clear that I won't take a part in government, then your job is made easier, too. You would not have to remove any senior people to make way for me.

As the meeting wound up, he said, almost as a throwaway, 'Incidentally, I am now pretty certain that we can go ahead on PR for Europe in '99. I'm doing some final consultation on it, but I'm optimistic.'

'I take that as a firm commitment,' I said.

He smiled and nodded.

For the final fifteen minutes of our meeting one of the Downing Street secretaries kept popping her head in to tell him that there was somebody else waiting and he really was very late, etc. I learned later that the 'somebody else' was Trevor Kavanagh, political editor of the *Sun*, who had been shoved into Alastair Campbell's office so that he wouldn't see me leaving.

Afterwards, I walked back down Whitehall with Nick. I told him briefly what had happened. He wasn't surprised that Labour wanted to delay PR beyond the next election, but then he has always thought it unlikely we could pull it off anyway.

Later I saw Bob. He's implacably opposed to any delay in the implementation of PR. He also suggested we should use Robin Cook to lobby Blair. I agreed.

I also spoke to Roy by phone, telling him that now was the moment when I really needed him to wade in and help with Blair. He said he'd do so in the next couple of weeks. I replied that I didn't think that was soon enough, as I will probably be seeing Blair for the crunch meeting next week.

Back home on the 159 bus feeling depressed that Labour are once again shifting their ground. I don't know whether it's just Blair's negotiating technique, but I find it very wearing.

A whisky and to bed.

Wednesday, 4 June, Westminster

Into the office by 8.00 and settled down to write another letter to Blair, following yesterday's meeting. I am becoming less and less keen on the idea of a Cabinet committee, which seems a halfway house that delivers nothing of real value to anybody. So I decided I may as well stake out, in rather tough language, exactly where I stand, what I think can be achieved and why I am feeling so frustrated at the goalposts drifting again.[1]

I wrote my letter out in longhand and gave it to Becky to type up. Bob advised me not to send it. He thinks I am getting too confrontational; I should let things take a longer course. I told him I couldn't afford to do that in view of the imminent vote on the Budget. He suggested toning down a couple of paragraphs.

I also showed the letter to Roy, who didn't object to the tone at all and only suggested a couple of minor amendments.

Sent the letter after PMQs, at about four o'clock:

Dear Tony,
I thought it might be useful if I let you have some early further thoughts on our meeting yesterday . . .

The main purpose of this letter is to set out where we have got to on the central issue of PR for Westminster.

You have known our position from the start of our discussions four years ago. That PR for Westminster is the rock on which we can join with you in building the realignment of British politics so that the next century will know progressive government as the rule and not, as in this century, the exception.

Over this period we have dealt with this issue, on which we started from different points and with different priorities, in a constructive and accommodating manner, culminating in the formal public agreements enshrined in Cook/Maclennan. I do feel very serious misgivings that, just as we are on the threshold of taking the first steps to put into effect what we have agreed on PR for Westminster, you seem to be recoiling because you are apprehensive about the kind of outcomes PR might produce.

You quoted the example of the last election in which PR would have resulted in a majority of nine seats for you and a total of 146 for us.

---

1 It was about this time that I realized that, not having regular access to Blair in the way that opponents of the project in the Cabinet did, I had to put everything on paper to him if I was to stand a chance of holding him to what we agreed face to face.

Surely the possibility of such an outcome cannot have come as a surprise, given that we have been talking about this for three years or so? Indeed, the need for a partnership (which is the clear conclusion which must be drawn from these figures) has been the central reason why we embarked on the process in the first place.

But if, now, such an outcome is unacceptable to you, then what happens next?

Does this mean that the Cook/Maclennan agreement is no longer acceptable to Labour? I cannot believe that you would contemplate this, as it would cause real dismay about Labour's intentions in a far wider circle than just the Liberal Democrats.

Does it mean that you would no longer feel able, as we have previously personally agreed, to recommend the Electoral Reform Commission's outcome in a referendum? If so, then that could not but affect the personal trust we have built up, which is the foundation of the whole project. You privately agreed with me in December of last year that you would be able to recommend a sensible PR solution in a referendum, at that time saying that you would do it before the election.[1] In the context of the Cook/Maclennan talks, I accepted that you did not feel able to do this, and that it would be better for you to do it after the election, when the Electoral Reform Commission produced its recommendation. If you are now saying that you would not even then feel able to recommend it, the key foundation stone of our dialogue seems to have been pulled away.

Finally, you seem to be saying that the only way you would feel able to proceed with PR would be if this process was accompanied by the merger of the two parties. I must, very bluntly, say to you that I could not persuade my party to this and would not try to. I accept your complete sincerity when you said that this would not be an assimilation, but a genuine 'coming together' . . . But that is not the way my party (and, I imagine, the wider public) will see it . . .

I appreciate that this involves some risks for you. But they seem, in practice, to be small ones. I do not believe there is a serious possibility, given the complimentarity of our votes on the ground and the similarities of our policies, that the process of genuine co-operation, once started, can be reversed.

I apologize for the length of this letter and look forward to seeing you again – hopefully next week. I think it is very desirable to resolve this matter, one way or the other, before the Budget.

Yours

Paddy

1 See Vol. I, p. 481.

Sunday, 8 June, Somerset

Pottered about this morning, opening my mail and reading the papers. Also had a word with Jane Bonham-Carter. I knew she was lunching with Roy Jenkins and Peter Mandelson[1] yesterday and I had previously asked her to pump Mandelson on his view of developments. She reported that Mandelson, who was in a rather unconstructive mood, couldn't understand why we are so hung up on PR. But apparently Roy (who has yet to speak to me) thought it was all part of the negotiations and he was playing hardball. They are still after merger, and are trying to hold us at arm's length on PR, even saying that Europe is not in the bag yet. Jane felt disappointed. But I'll see what Roy says.

Tuesday, 10 June, Westminster

At around 10.00, an envelope arrived from Downing Street marked 'To be opened by the addressee only'. A letter from Blair. Clearly a result of the Mandelson meeting. Pretty sharp stuff:

Dear Paddy,

Thank you for your letter of 4 June.

I hope, as you say, we can resolve the question of PR in the European parliamentary elections in 1999, although I cannot commit myself on this yet.

I was surprised by your letter since I thought we had had a good discussion with much agreement. I also must just say I feel you are unfairly taking my thoughts as they developed during our discussions as though they were hard commitments. I have never been able to give a guarantee to a particular position on PR yet, in particular because of the problems I have raised with you in our discussions.

I explained to you why it would be difficult to move to PR at the next election. It would require me to go to my party and ask nearly 100 of our MPs to give up their seats even if we did as well as we have in this election. There is also a serious question as to whether the country would be better off governed by perpetual coalition politics.

---

1 Minister Without Portfolio at the Cabinet Office, with special responsibility for the Millennium Dome. Later appointed Secretary of State for Trade and Industry 1998, Secretary of State for Northern Ireland 1999–2001. Mandelson resigned from both positions.

That said, I think the basic question is: Are our two parties in fact both modern social democrat parties? The answer is, substantially, yes.

My concern is that PR becomes an obstacle if the two parties agree they should come together. I understand why it is difficult for you now. But the 'project' is not PR, it is a new progressive alliance in British politics. PR may be a part of that, but it is politically and intellectually absurd to say that it is the end game. The end game is for two groups of people who agree with each other to escape from the inherently unsatisfactory position of fighting one another politically.

In my view, it would be far better for the Liberal Democrats and Labour if they were able, after the election, to come together on a position of strength.

The basic problem may be that you want coalition politics where your party can switch alliances, while I wish to build a permanent progressive alliance. On the other hand, I am not so unreasonable as to ignore your point that to appear simply to yield up the Liberal Democrats to Labour is impossible for you.

The only way through that I can see is to carry on working together, moving closer together – continuing the work on the Electoral Reform Commission and on PR – while not ruling out the possibility of merger. That has the disadvantage of postponing ultimate decisions but the advantage of allowing an organic development of co-operation.

It would really be a huge failure of history if we gave up now. I am and remain utterly committed to our joint enterprise. But progress has to be on a basis saleable to both sides. At the moment I am being asked to sacrifice a large part of my party and accept permanent coalition politics with no guarantee that our coalition partner remains constant.

Let us carry on this discussion quickly. It is too important to let it drift away. Why don't we meet for dinner soon, possibly with Roy Jenkins, and try, honestly, to thrash this out . . .

Yours

Tony

I wrestled with this for a while, and then drafted the following reply, which I showed to Roy just before lunch. He said that he wasn't as depressed by the Blair letter as I was. He thinks Blair has come a long way. Probably true.

Dear Tony,

I was preparing this letter when I received yours of today's date, for which thanks. I apologize if I took the points we made in developing our discussions as 'hard commitments' – an over-anxiousness to reach conclusions with time pressing, I suspect. Nevertheless, I don't think I can have misunderstood the relative personal positions we have agreed to on the question of PR. These, after all, have been clear and established between us for some time; they were most recently amended and re-affirmed by our private discussions at the time of Cook/Maclennan.

You ask me whether PR is the end game. I agree with you that it is not. What we want is not PR for its own sake, but what PR produces – which, incidentally, is not a new duopoly, but rather a new pluralism (to which we are both publicly committed).

If your aim is to use PR to create a new left/right duopoly with the Lib Dems safely and permanently tucked in with Labour *as it is at present*, then we have indeed been working together all this time on a misunderstanding – and you are discussing the wrong instrument to do this. For PR will have the opposite effect – it is the instrument of pluralism, not hegemony.

I still think we share a common analysis. But this is being put under pressure by events . . .

There is, indeed, little or no difference between the Liberal Democrats and New Labour. Over time, I believe there is every probability that we will come together. But Labour is not, despite even your efforts, New Labour yet (not least in your local authorities and among your MEPs) . . .

PR, therefore, is the means by which [five] things can happen which we both say we want. A genuine pluralist form of politics can be created in Britain; a framework can be constructed in which the Liberal Democrats can establish a durable working relationship with New Labour, to our mutual benefit; the two can, through that co-operation, have time to grow naturally together; . . . we can keep the Tories out for a decade or more, and, in this process, the whole shape of British politics can be altered.

That seems a pretty good deal to me.

For it, I risk the (very real) possibility of splitting my party, on the one hand, and being swallowed up by you, on the other. But either way, you win.

You risk losing 100 MPs. But you could (very probably, will) lose them anyway under the vagaries of the present system – you could, indeed, lose that many even if you get almost the same 44 per cent at the next election as you got at this one! The difference between the two options does not, therefore, lie in the reduced number of Labour seats. It lies in the fact that, without PR, this could result in the Tories getting back. With PR it is certain not to.

You are right, we must not fail now.

I look forward to seeing you on Thursday.

Yours

Paddy

I suspect either Mandelson's influence or that Blair has got himself into a position in which he can't deliver and from which he is trying to retreat as elegantly as possible.

Nevertheless, it is very encouraging that we have fixed a meeting for Thursday night, at his request. As Roy said, 'It's incredible that the Prime Minister will arrange such a meeting at four days' notice.'

At 3 o'clock a meeting of the Jo Group. The rest of them take a different view from me. They feel the grand alliance has never been achievable anyway and that I am putting far too much emphasis on pushing things to a definite conclusion; that we should now take a much longer, more cautious view. But I am certain that if we lose this moment we lose the possibility of PR, too.

It has been a bad day. I thought we were making progress. But Blair's letter has been like a bucket of cold water.

Wednesday, 11 June, Westminster

I saw Richard Holme at 8.45. He thinks Labour are just bargaining. He has arranged to meet up with Roger Liddle[1] to see if there is a way round our current impasse, and I wanted to brief him. I stressed the absolute importance of delivering PR for Europe in 1999 and also that, if required, I was happy to consider what assurances we could give that we would not break away.

I also mentioned to Richard my thoughts on standing down as leader. I pretended I hadn't made up my mind, asking him to rehearse the arguments for me on staying or going. He said I should stay, chiefly because there was a lot more political work still to be done which only I could do. I told him – untruthfully – that I had really decided to stay on, but that I wanted to hear the arguments from him personally.

In the late afternoon Richard called to say that his discussions with Liddle had gone well. I was about to get a letter which would make a proposition that we should go into the next election on a joint manifesto; that candidates would stand down for each other in key seats; that there would be a referendum on PR; and that the requisite legislation would be passed through the next parliament but wouldn't be enacted until after-

1 Former Lib Dem who defected to Labour in 1995 and now works on Blair's staff in Downing Street.

wards. More or less exactly what I expected. Richard wasn't aware whether this was specifically to include a coalition beforehand.

We then discussed the chairmanship of the Electoral Reform Commission. Richard proposed Roy. An excellent suggestion! His appointment would be both reassuring to the party and also make it more difficult for Blair to turn down the Commission's outcome.

In the course of our conversation Richard and I came up with a compromise position. Should we be unable to persuade Labour to have full PR before the next election, we could propose the introduction of PR in two stages. Almost certainly the outcome of the Electoral Reform Commission will be Alternative Vote (AV) with an AMS[1] to top up for proportionality: we could then propose that we implement this in two phases the first (AV) would require no changes to constituency boundaries and so could be in place for the next election; the second (the AMS top-up) could be done in the next parliament. I later put this to Chris Rennard and asked him to do a rough calculation. This showed that, with AV, we would hold on to our present seats and could win a few more. So Labour would still maintain their leverage on us but we would have a halfway house to a full PR system. And, most helpfully of all, there would be no need for candidates of either party to stand down, which is what Labour apparently now wants.

Later, I discussed Richard's suggestion about the chair of the Electoral Reform Commission with Roy by phone. He gave me the impression that he hadn't heard of the proposition before, but it suddenly occurred to me that, in telling me the importance of a chair, he may have been hinting that he would like to do the job. I hadn't, of course, spotted this. At all events, he said that he didn't think his being chair would be acceptable to Blair, but if it was he would 'accept the labour'. Excellent! I spoke to Bob about it. He is also strongly in favour.

Much encouraging feedback from Labour today. But we're not there yet. This whole business has been characterized by minor breakthroughs, major hopes and subsequent reversals.

---

1 Alternative or Additional Member System. The idea is that some MPs are elected in single member constituencies while others are elected as Additional Members. The number of additional members awarded to each party is based on the number each party needs to make its overall total of MPs reflect the votes cast for it. It is usual for voters to cast two votes – one for the constituency member and one for the party.

Thursday, 12 June, Westminster

At 10.30, Emma Nicholson came in to report back on the trawls I have asked her to do for possible Tory Party defectors during the current Conservative leadership contest. She says there is desperate unhappiness amongst the pro-European Tories. But they will probably hang on a bit under Hague to see how things develop. There is now general agreement that Hague will win. Apparently even Clarke is despairing. Emma says that Robert Rhodes-James[1] wants to join us – she believes he is an important bridge to what she calls the 'liberal Conservatives'. I arranged to meet Robert with her next week. I tested out on her whether a closer relationship with Labour would discourage the 'liberal Conservatives'. She thought it wouldn't. I wonder.

It now appears almost certain that we will have to fight a by-election in Winchester. Poor Mark [Oaten].

Off at 7.15pm to see Roy in his office in the Lords. He offered me a glass of champagne and we sat, with the sunlight streaming through the window, planning the meeting with Blair this evening. We agreed we must push for PR for Europe. Nothing else will work if we don't have that.

Then by taxi down to the Cabinet Office at 70 Whitehall.

We had to wait a little before they came to collect us to take us to the Blairs' flat in No. 11. We were met on the first floor by Blair dressed in a pair of jeans and a white shirt. He was looking fit and unstressed. Shortly afterwards we were joined by Mandelson, who was in a suit. We went into the No. 11 drawing-room, with Roy Jenkins commenting that it was a room that he remembered well from his time as Chancellor. It had poor proportions; too square. Some joking about this.

Roy sat in an armchair alongside Blair's, while Mandelson and I sat opposite, looking out towards St James's Park.

We started off with about ten minutes of easy conversation about Blair's trip to France. (He and Chirac had worked out that at the time when Chirac was Prime Minister of France under Giscard d'Estaing, Tony had been a barman in Paris!) Blair said that, when he had gone to see Chirac, he had been joined by the French Foreign Minister, Vidrine. Chirac had said, rather ironically, '*Nous sommes tous socialistes maintenant.*' Throughout the meeting, Vidrine kept saying, '*Je suis d'accord, Monsieur*

---

1 Member of Parliament (Conservative) for Cambridge 1976–92.

le Président.' No doubt intended to show solidarity, but somewhat missing Chirac's point.

Then Peter made a little speech flattering Blair by saying how amazed Whitehall was by his attention to detail on the treaty.[1] Blair brushed this off, referring to 'lawyers' tricks', but went on to say that he was astonished at how little his continental counterparts bothered with details. Apparently he had complained to Chirac about one clause which Chirac agreed was foolish. This caused an immediate flurry amongst Chirac's officials with one leaning forward to whisper, '*Mais, Monsieur le Président, nous l'avons proposé.*' Chirac responded by saying that didn't mean it wasn't stupid.

Blair leaned forward on the sofa. 'Now, where are we on all this?'

There followed a long discussion on his problems with PR. If he agreed, he was inviting about 100 of his colleagues to commit suicide. I replied that Labour would lose 100 seats anyway, whatever the system. Roy chipped in, saying that to die naturally was one thing but to be put up against a wall and shot by your party leader was another.

Roy then made the brief statement that we had agreed upon beforehand, that we were very impressed by the fact that the PM had been able to find so much time to deal with this issue, amongst all the other things he was doing. We took that as evidence of a seriousness about the project which we found very reassuring.

Nevertheless, there were solid matters to be dealt with. We wanted Blair to know that we were absolutely sincere about this; we were not talking about a short-term relationship; we were not talking about setting up something that we could ditch later on; this was about a long-term relationship. (Which Roy later described as 'permanent and ever closer'; I said I would prefer the word 'durable' to 'permanent'.)

I then picked up the conversation, repeating what I had said in my letter, that we needed to know from Labour what specific, concrete, confidence-building measures on our part would reassure them that we viewed this as a durable relationship which would not be ditched when we had won PR.

Blair began by describing why, though PR could be legislated for before the next election, it would not be possible to deliver it until after it. He saw us fighting the next election, therefore, on a joint manifesto, with candidates standing down in key seats.

1 The Treaty for Europe, signed by the Heads of State and government at a meeting later on in June in Amsterdam.

I said that I didn't think a joint manifesto was appropriate, but that a joint outline programme (heads of agreement), along the lines of the one I had already drafted before the last election, would be possible. But this had three crucial drawbacks for us.

Firstly, I wasn't certain that election on the present system would deliver us the seats Labour predicted we would get.

Secondly, it would give the Tories a huge campaigning issue at the next election. Staying too long in the middle of 'no man's land' was always difficult, but doing so during an election was sheer folly. Blair himself had described how the Tory press would campaign against any change in the electoral system.

Finally, as Roy Jenkins and I knew to our cost from our experiences with the SDP, the whole process of getting candidates to stand down in seats for the other party was damaging, dangerous and difficult. We could not do this.

'Those are three very serious objections,' said Blair. Then, turning to Mandelson: 'What's your response to that?'

Mandelson went off into a long monologue on how impossible it would be for Blair to get through his Cabinet any proposed change in the electoral system by the next election.

'Look,' he continued, 'I've never said this to you before. I have always ultimately accepted your judgement that you can get through the things you need. If you and Gordon are together, Robin, Jack and the others follow. But on this occasion, Gordon is not necessarily going to back you and Jack will certainly oppose you. I very much doubt that you can get this through the Cabinet on the basis you suggest.'

I asked Mandelson to explain exactly what he meant. Did he mean that Blair couldn't get the project through the Cabinet, full stop? Or did he mean that he couldn't get the introduction of PR before the election, rather than afterwards, through the Cabinet?

He didn't give a clear answer. He was performing a function that he was to perform later, on several occasions, of diverting the conversation into a rather hazy byway so as not to specifically deal with the point at issue.

At this stage, Cherie came in clutching a magnum of champagne with which, she explained, she had been presented at a school governors' meeting. 'But because it hasn't been cooled, we couldn't drink it on the spot.' She laughed and went off, saying that she would be back in a minute for dinner.

We were duly called and we went into the dining-room.

It is a rather nice room, though with the most appalling red wallpaper. There was a brief conversation between Cherie and Roy as to who had been responsible for it. 'Was it you?' she asked.

'Certainly not!' replied Roy.

'I wonder which chancellor did put up this wallpaper, then?' I said. 'Can we guess?'

'Well, which chancellor do you think would have chosen a wallpaper which looks as though it has come out of an Indian restaurant?' said Peter.

We all agreed on Lamont.

We sat down to a dinner of fish followed by medallions of lamb and a splendid pudding which seemed to consist of ice-cream and some fancy chocolate brownies; claret throughout.

'I think we know where the blockage is now,' I said. 'It's in finding a mechanism that will give you confidence that we will stick with you afterwards, but which will give us confidence that PR will eventually be delivered.'

Roy Jenkins used a mountain analogy: we were like two teams on either side of the Alps. We weren't far away from each other, but the barrier was formidable.

I proposed that we leave the obstacle of PR for Westminster and its timing for the moment and deal with PR for Europe. 'Firstly, I want to make it clear that unless we get PR for Europe, nothing else is possible. That has to be a given in everything else we do. Furthermore, it is not an issue on which you can delay. When you go to the European Inter-Governmental Conference in a few days' time, you will find you are being asked to accede to, or reject, a proportional system across the whole of the EU. How you react will be watched closely both by us and by others.'

'Look,' said Peter, 'I am in favour of PR for Europe. I don't see what the problem is. Unfortunately, there was no formal "sponsor" for this in the early days of government.'

'But what about Robin Cook?' I asked.

'Robin wasn't sponsoring it. He had other things to sponsor in the Queen's Speech.'

I forbore from saying that it was at the top of the list I had sent Blair in the days immediately after the election, long before the Queen's Speech was formulated.

I asked Peter what the problem was, then. Was it lack of government time? Mandelson confirmed that it might be difficult, but he could see no reason why PR for Europe should not be fitted into the legislative programme. Blair agreed, saying that, despite other pressures, 'I think we could do this and I think we should.'

'Then let's take it as given that it will go ahead,' I said. 'But a statement to this effect, possibly in the context of the IGC, is vital.'

I then turned to the Electoral Reform Commission. We discussed for some time who was going to be chair. I gave Peter Mandelson every opportunity to propose Roy's name, since Richard Holme had, I knew, suggested this to Mandelson earlier. But he said nothing. I didn't feel I could propose Roy there and then, since it would put Blair in a difficult positoin if he wanted to say no.

Later in the evening, however, when Mandelson, Cherie and Roy were out of earshot, I said to Blair, 'Look, I didn't raise it with you when he was there, but the obvious person to chair the Electoral Reform Commission is Roy. If such an appointment is acceptable to you, it would be hugely confidence-building for us.'

He seemed to like the idea, and said he'd think about it.

The general discussion came back to the problem of PR for Westminster.

Roy, as we had previously planned, put forward our two-phase compromise: phase one, the introduction of AV before the election; phase two, the addition of an AMS-based top-up after it.

Then I came in, pointing out the advantages. Firstly, it would ensure that we stayed linked with the government. Secondly, it would help us to hold on to our current seats and perhaps win more. Next, it had the advantage of not requiring any of our candidates to stand down. (Indeed, it would be detrimental to all our chances if they did because if either party withdrew in a seat, then the alternative votes which would normally go to the other would instead go to the Tories.) And lastly, we would have taken the first, crucial step towards electoral reform, which, once established, would be difficult to reverse.

Blair seemed attracted by the idea and turned to Mandelson for his views, but he started on a long, rather sceptical exposition on the difficulties of explaining it to the public.

At this stage, we finished dinner and moved next door. Cherie joined us for a few minutes, then left.

The conversation moved on to what we dubbed 'the iceberg', i.e. what was visible immediately and what was hidden, to be revealed later. I said that my concern was to cross the ground from where we were to where we wanted to be as quickly as possible. I saw little advantage in going through the halfway house of a Cabinet committee. It was unsustainable over the long term and gave little of substance to either party. As far as I was concerned, the optimum position was to adopt what Mandelson came to call the 'Big Bang' approach. That is that, if we could agree on PR then, within the next two weeks (and before the Budget), Blair and I should jointly draw back the veil on our relationship of the last couple of years and say that we wanted it to continue. We could then recommend to our party conferences in the autumn that we should enter into a formal partnership, with the Liberal Democrats going into government in November.

Blair said he was planning a Cabinet reshuffle for November anyway, but that he couldn't announce to his present Cabinet that some of them would have to give way to Liberal Democrats four months before the reshuffle took place. That would be just too destabilizing.

'Fine,' I said, 'I recognize your problems. Now recognize mine. I must do something with my party which is the equivalent to your ditching Clause 4. But it will take time. I need at least six weeks to move my party to a position where I could win a conference vote on the proposition.'

Mandelson said that was ridiculous, I didn't need a conference vote. I could just do it. 'That's what Tony would do.'

'Well, that's not what I will do – not least because having the decision ratified by the full party makes it more secure in the long term.'

Roy very helpfully reminded Mandelson that, even when the Germans invaded Belgium in 1940, Attlee had insisted on holding a special party conference before going into coalition with the wartime government, and that this had strengthened his position later. To which Mandelson muttered something about Attlee not being a leader.

It was getting late, so Roy started to say that we really couldn't go much further tonight. We had covered a very great deal of ground and it was time to close off the discussion. Mandelson chipped in with, 'But first I want to sum up where we have got to,' and turned to Blair, asking him for his summary. When Blair had finished he said, 'Well, I don't think that was a very good summary. I will change leaders,' and turned to me. I gave him one which didn't seem to please him either.

Nevertheless, we all agreed that progress had been made and that Peter Mandelson and Richard Holme between them should set up a chronology of events, leading us to a coalition.

Out through the Cabinet Office again, where I bade goodnight to Roy, and caught a taxi back to Methley Street.

I lay awake for a couple of hours, thinking. On balance, it was a helpful meeting, although Mandelson seemed rather tetchy. Nevertheless, we have made considerable progress. It is clear now, though, that we will have to take the longer rather than the shorter route to coalition. This invites considerable dangers for me. I am really dreading taking the proposal to the Party.

Friday, 13 June, Somerset

I decided overnight to write Blair another letter setting out how difficult it would be for me to put forward the proposal for coalition in November rather than September. So up at 6.00 and a 6.45 taxi to Waterloo to catch the train back to Yeovil. Having settled myself on the train I drafted the letter, which I e-mailed back to Becky to type up and send.

Dear Tony,

Thank you very much for last night. It was enjoyable and very useful.

I think we have now found a potential way around all the obstacles in front of us.

But, reflecting on all this overnight, I remain very worried indeed about the timing. I understand why it is very difficult – probably impossible – for you to take the shorter route. I will now ask Richard Holme urgently to meet with Peter Mandelson in order to draw up a programme for the longer route, with the interim stage of a Cabinet committee and then the final step [to coalition] in November.

I want to mark up for you, however, my concern that this is likely to make things very, very much more difficult for me and considerably increases my exposure to the possibility of failure.

I am pretty confident that, although I would have a fight, I could win the package we have agreed on at my conference in September. But it is one thing to win a vote which I can spend the next eight weeks preparing for, which takes place in the immediate afterglow of good will generated by PR for Europe and the start of the Election Commission, against the background of your early successes and without any history of serious disagreements between us. It will be quite another winning at a special conference, called, inevitably, at short notice, at a time when your honeymoon period is bound to have peaked and with, almost certainly, a number of occasions on the record when we will have strongly opposed you.

I remain very firmly of the view that if we are to do this (and I think we must), then the moment to do it is soon. The longer we wait the more it will slip away from us.

We will both be, I am told, on the same aircraft flying back from Hong Kong.[1] I don't know if arrangements will permit any privacy, but would it be a good idea to review progress then?
Yours
Paddy

During the day I managed to catch Richard. I briefed him on last night and told him that it was now up to him to draw up a chronology of events which would suit both Blair's needs and mine. Richard, who has been pretty cool throughout all of this, suddenly became enthusiastic. He was amazed when I told him that we had been offered what seemed to be a firm agreement to deliver PR for Europe and that Blair appears serious about taking a further step towards coalition. Later he spoke to Mandelson, who also now appeared very eager to get ahead. Richard is flying out to Brazil on Sunday but has agreed to draft a first attempt at a storyline and timetable from there to give to Mandelson. He's really got the bit between his teeth now. It's as though he has suddenly realized that what he thought was all a dream will now happen.

I suspect that other members of the Jo Group have, up to now, been tolerating me on this because they never thought it would happen anyway. With Richard on board and firing on all cylinders my job with them should become rather easier.

Sunday, 15 June, Somerset

Richard (in Brazil) has produced an excellent chronology, storyline and series of statements.[2] I made a few amendments, in particular linking prizes (such as PR for Europe for 1999) with the steps we must take (such as setting up Cabinet committees). In Richard's scenario these happen as if by accident. I want them tightly interconnected, so that the prize of European PR for 1999 is followed by the logical step of setting up a Joint Cabinet Committee. But I need to create a tension in the Party about whether or not electoral reform for Westminster will be delivered, so that

1 Hong Kong had been leased to Britain from China in 1898 for ninety-nine years, and so the lease ran out in 1997. A handover ceremony had been organized for 1 July 1997, to be attended by dignitaries from the UK and China. My office had arranged for me to hitch a lift back on the Prime Minister's VC10.
2 See Appendix B.

when we pull it out of the hat the cathartic release will help carry us
through into the November special conference. It is a complex plan and a
rather Machiavellian one. But it may work. I will not show the Holme
paper to anybody except Roy and Bob.

Tuesday, 17 June, London

Picked up by taxi at 7.45 for breakfast at Emma Nicholson's with Robert
Rhodes-James. Emma had laid a table upstairs and left the two of us to
spend an hour alone together. He and others on the 'liberal Conservative'
wing of the party had, he said, three options:

1. To stay on and fight a 'lost cause' within the Tory Party;

2. To 'do an SDP' and start their own party;

3. To join another party, preferably the Lib Dems.

He asked me what I saw as the role of the Liberal Democrats on the
current political scene. I said I believed that British politics was in the
process of reshaping itself into a broadly European mould, with a Christian
Democratic Party, a Social Democratic Party and a powerful Liberal Party,
dedicated to the free market, competition, social justice, constitutional
reform, internationalism and Europe. I was in the process of deciding how
to play our hand in forwarding that restructuring process. We had two
options: we could assist Blair in moving the Labour Party towards a 'New
Labour' position, so perhaps encouraging the Labour left to break away.
Or we could provide a decent home for Conservatives such as himself. I
did not believe that these aims were necessarily incompatible. He agreed.

He said he was a 'man in agony', but wanted to move relatively slowly.
He mentioned his colleagues Peter Temple-Morris and Robert Cranborne[1]
(whom he described as 'very unhappy'), a number of MEPs and unspecified
'others' as being 'in the same boat'.

He likes the Liberal Democrats ('There is almost nothing between us'),
but thinks our problem is that we 'don't stand for anything – though it
was much better in the last election'. He couldn't join Labour, even though
they had approached him. New Labour was perfectly acceptable; but
Labour was not yet New Labour – so if he joined anyone it would be us.

1 Viscount Cranborne, leader of the Tories in the Lords.

He is pragmatically pro-European, not enthusiastic for PR, in favour of reform of the House of Lords, but not of regional government or a written constitution, and is passionate about higher education. He used to be very close to Major and was one of his confidants just before Major threw down the gauntlet in June 1995. The Conservatives, he said, were split from top to bottom.

I asked, 'If we were to get closer to Labour, causing a breakaway of their left wing, would this make it easier or more difficult for you to join us?'

He thought it would make it more difficult.

There is now a really tempting proposition opening up as to whether we should make ourselves the receptacle for dissident Tories or continue with my strategy of seeking coalition with Blair. On balance I think we should continue with the strategy, since that is what delivers the most in the long term. We cannot, as some believe, be the Tories' competitors on the right. Eventually, like Labour in the 1980s, the Tories will come back to the centre ground, for it is only from there that they can win again. But this is not a space which can be occupied by the Lib Dems. We are, to our core, a centre left party.

Rhodes-James and I left it that he would discuss coming over to the Lib Dems with 'the others' and return to me later.

The mess the Tories have got themselves in became worse later in the day, with Clarke only pipping Hague to the post by two votes in the second round of the leadership contest. This means that in the run-off Hague is almost certain to win.

At 3.00 a meeting with Nick Harvey at which I initiated him fully into the Jo Group material and gave him my diary notes of the Downing Street meetings to read. He said that he knew something was going on but didn't realize it was this deep or this detailed. He will support me.

At 8.30 down to dinner. Quite a full table, with Alan Beith, Jackie Ballard, Ed Davey,[1] Paul Burstow[2] and others from the new intake. Jackie, who had clearly been waiting for some time for such an occasion to arise, immediately pitched into me on the subject of strategy. A heated debate began on our relations with Labour. I said that I thought we had a vested interest in the success of the first Blair term. Much hostility to this notion and some deliberate misunderstanding. I was somewhat shocked by the

---

1 Member of Parliament for Kingston and Surbiton since 1997. Member of the Treasury team.
2 Member of Parliament for Sutton and Cheam since 1997. Spokesman for Social Services.

virulence. Having come out of years and years of fighting on the ground, it is difficult, I suppose, for them to see beyond their constituency boundaries. That's natural. The dinner ended good-naturedly enough, but I came away worried about how much work I will have to do to achieve what I want.

Meanwhile, the Tories are fighting each other like rats in a sack. Tonight Redwood seems to have indicated that he will back Clarke, which is bizarre given that they come from opposite wings of the party. Out of bitterness towards Hague, I suspect. But Clarke appears to have accepted Redwood's support, which seems even more bizarre. And Thatcher, looking completely dotty, has come out for Hague. Tomorrow will be interesting.

Wednesday, 18 June, Westminster

Into the chamber at 3.00. Major's last Question Time. Blair paid him a short but sincere tribute. I went on a little longer, saying that he was the only Conservative leader who could keep this rabble (pointing to the Conservatives around me) together.

Richard is back from Brazil and has had his meeting with Mandelson. He rang me at 4.30 to say that it had gone well. Mandelson has accepted our suggestions and will now write a paper which he will put to Blair.

Thursday, 19 June, Westminster

A taxi at 7.15am to Richard's for a full briefing on the Mandelson meeting. According to Mandelson, Blair is again having doubts. Firstly, he is worried about the instability of a coalition. Secondly, he is worried about us – will we stay firm? Thirdly, he is worried about having to get rid of some of his own Cabinet – and whether he can carry them.

Later in the day I rang Andy Marr of the *Independent* and asked him if he had any access to Blair. Slightly to my surprise, he said he didn't. Apparently relations between him and the government are very bad at the moment. The *Independent* was severely taken to task (by Campbell?) for not being supportive enough of Labour during the election. Andy said that he thought they were in danger of becoming control freaks.

In the early evening, I heard the results of the Tory leadership election. Hague has won 90–72. Catastrophic for the Tories.

Monday, 23 June, Westminster

I was miserable company over the weekend. I am in a really black mood about the future. I am convinced that Blair will not now go ahead. And the election of a 36-year-old leader of the official opposition has really put the pressure on me. I must snap out of this. It is not good for anybody. I am grumpy with Jane and somewhat incoherent with my colleagues. Why do I feel so exhausted?

Tuesday, 24 June, London

At 2.45pm a meeting with Richard Holme, Ming Campbell and Emma Nicholson to set up a little team to beat around the Tory bushes to see if any more birds will fly out.

Then down to the chamber for Hague's first outing. He was a little pedestrian, but good enough. He has a habit of keeping his head down, so all that shows up on the television is his bald pate. I also find his voice very annoying; like a bandsaw with a severe dose of catarrh.

Later Jane and I picked up a taxi to go to David Frost's summer party, which Jane regards as a highlight of the year – chiefly because she once got to stand close to Bob Geldof. Peter Kellner[1] and his wife Cathy Ashton[2] also there, who told us much about what was going on in the Blair office. I didn't tell them what was happening on our side. But I thanked Peter for his help during the General Election. Cathy and Peter both believe that Blair has made a splendid start, but they are worried about the fact that the place is run by the control freaks (that phrase again).

Wednesday, 25 June, London

At 5.15pm a meeting with Lembit Opik. I expected trouble from him on the position paper, but he said that he agreed with it.

---

1 Political journalist for the *Evening Standard*.
2 Baroness Ashton of Upholland, Labour peer.

The Team Leaders' meeting at 5.30.[1] Quite a head of steam building up that I am being too soft on Labour, particularly from Jim Wallace.

At 8.00 Jane and I caught a taxi to the Reform Club for dinner with Robert Reich[2] and Shirley Williams. Also there were Shirley's daughter (who looks extraordinarily like I imagine Vera Brittain would have looked at that age), Dick Neustadt[3] and a professor from the LSE who was embarrassingly complimentary about our GE campaigns. Also the Labour MP Tony Wright, whom I like. He has been a great supporter of PR and co-operation between the two parties – though he was pretty sharp about us when he had to be before the last election. Robert Reich's delightful English wife sat next to me; she has a soft face, with deep intelligent eyes. Reich himself is an extraordinary little man, his eyes burning like bright coals in his head: one of America's few really powerful liberals. He said Clinton would fail in the end because he has no internal core of belief – and the same is true of Blair.

It was a splendid dinner, though Tony Wright had to go early to vote. David Marquand [formerly of the SDP, now Labour] was also there; he, too, confessed to being worried that the Blair government was becoming far too control freakish: How could they say they were pluralist and operate like this? I said that the battle for the character of the Blair administration was between Blair's own personality and Mandelson's instincts. Wright said Blair regarded Mandelson as his 'lucky charm'. A good description. Much concern about Blair following the Tory plans for public spending. I said that I didn't think the Blair government could retain the trust of the electorate if it presided over a crisis in the Health Service which was worse than that suffered under the Tories.

Saturday, 28 June, Hong Kong

In the evening, a reception at Government House hosted by Chris Patten. Lowering clouds over the Peak and the weather stiflingly hot and sweaty.

We all turned out on to the lawn of Government House to watch a

---

1 I had divided our forty-six MPs into 'teams' each consisting of two to five MPs, covering each main policy area (education/health/foreign affairs, etc.), and each headed by a 'team leader'. The Team Leaders' meeting functioned as a kind of Shadow Cabinet.

2 Secretary for Labor in Clinton's first US administration.

3 A professor at Harvard University and married to Shirley Williams.

Chinese pipe band. Somehow this strange sight of Chinese in full kilts playing Scottish reels against a backdrop of Hong Kong skyscrapers under a scudding monsoon sky seems to sum up the descent of Empire, from grandeur to farce. It was a memorable but rather melancholy occasion. The fragrance of frangipane flowers mixed with the inevitable smell of drains in the humid Hong Kong night.

Sunday, 29 June, Hong Kong

At 8.oopm to *Britannia*,[1] which is moored in the harbour. Lashing with rain and a dramatic thunderstorm as we arrived. A dizzy guest list: [US Secretary of State] Madeleine Albright, [Russian Foreign Minister] Yevgeny Primakov, a whole British delegation including the Heseltines, the Thatchers and, of course, the Prince of Wales. About thirty of us in all. It was a good dinner. Meursault followed by a very nice claret.

On my left was the wife of the Zimbabwean Foreign Minister. She was a delight. Sensible and a pleasure to talk to. But the real surprise of the evening for me was Princess Alexandra of Denmark, who sat on my right-hand side. Unbelievably slim and very beautiful, with an absolutely flawless complexion. Her father is Chinese and her mother Austrian. I thought she was a brittle porcelain doll until she started to speak, revealing a strong character and a very clear mind. She was brought up in Hong Kong but has learned to speak fluent Danish. (I later met the Danish Foreign Minister, who said that she is dearly loved in Denmark.) I found her intelligent and sharp. Just the kind of princess our own royal family could do with.

Monday, 30 June, Hong Kong

In the afternoon to the Royal Navy base for the handover ceremony itself. Almost as soon as we arrived it started to rain, and continued to pour throughout the ceremony. We all ended up drenched.

At the banquet afterwards Marion Roe[2] told me she was soaked right

1 The Royal Yacht carrying the Prince of Wales had been brought out to Hong Kong for the occasion.
2 Member of Parliament (Conservative) for Broxbourne since 1983.

through to her knickers. She had contemplated taking them off so that they didn't leave a telltale mark, but had in the end decided this wouldn't be diplomatic!

There must have been 4,000 to dinner, which finished at about 10.15. After which, upstairs for the formal handover. This time the Patten girls were in the room. I couldn't make up my mind whether they were delightful or a terrible handful, but eventually concluded the former.

We were then lined up in rows as in a school crocodile and walked up into the convention centre for the final ceremony. Suddenly the whole thing shifted gear from an atmosphere of harmless pomposity to that of a Nuremberg rally. It was horrible to see the Union flag being lowered and the Chinese flag raised in its place. The British military contingent were smart but somehow unmenacing. But the Chinese Air Force men who replaced them were dressed in full sky blue uniforms, carried rifles and did the goose step.

Afterwards we all filed outside, where I quickly met up with Cherie Blair and Alastair Goodlad and we were taken down to join the Prime Minister's cavalcade to Kai Tak airport where, at about 1.30am, we were swiftly loaded on to the prime ministerial RAF VC10.

Tuesday, 1 July, Hong Kong–London

On board the plane were eight or nine journalists, the Blairs, the Prime Minister's staff and Alastair Goodlad.

The journos sat at the back of the aircraft while the rest of us sat in the forward cabin. During the first hour of the flight Blair chatted chiefly with Alastair Goodlad and the rest of us exchanged views about the evening's events.

Around 2.30am Cherie shot Tony a look which was clearly intended to mean that he should see me, then go to bed. She had said to me earlier, as we chatted during the handover ceremony, that 'Tony is very tired' and she hoped I wouldn't keep him up too long. I promised not to.

We obviously couldn't chat in the cabin, in the presence of Goodlad, so Blair got up, said he wanted a word with me in private and we went into the sleeping quarters next door. We pulled across the curtains of Blair's bunk and sat crosslegged, leaning against the bulkheads at either end with a bottle of claret balanced precariously between us. For the next hour or so we flew through a pretty heavy thunderstorm (the remnants of the bad weather which had caused such a heavy downpour earlier), which threw the aircraft around quite a lot.

During our conversation, Cherie, in night attire, came by, poked her head in and told Tony not to spend too much time talking, ending by appealing to me for help to see that he didn't. She then returned to her bunk on the opposite side of the aisle and pulled the curtains. Alastair Campbell also walked past twice, commenting on the second occasion, 'Very cosy.'

Blair said that he understood that Richard Holme and Peter Mandelson had agreed that the announcement on European PR and the Electoral Reform Commission should be made before the start of the summer recess. And, coincidental with this, we announce the Cabinet committee.

I replied that arranging the proper chronology of events was very important. We didn't want to crowd things together. I suggested we should announce only PR for Europe immediately. He said he would take PR for Europe and the Cabinet committee proposal through Cabinet on Thursday. Robin Cook would probably then announce PR for Europe the following week. After which we could move on to the Cabinet committee. We should then, I suggested, allow a little uncertainty to grow over the summer months about whether Labour was going to fulfil its pledge on the Electoral Reform Commission or not. He could then announce the start of the Commission in October, and, following this, the proposal for a formal coalition in government between the two parties. We agreed to leave the details on all this to be fixed between Richard Holme and Peter Mandelson.

I then turned to a more detailed discussion of the Electoral Reform Commission, and asked him whether he had thought about my proposal that Roy Jenkins should chair this. He said he was perfectly happy with Roy Jenkins as chair, but that some of his own people might be a bit surprised.

PA: I understand that you are still uncertain about PR for Westminster?

TB: I don't think I can get a proportional system through my people. Peter [Mandelson] said to me the other day, 'Don't believe you can get everything you set your mind on. This, in my view, is the one on which you could fail.' I think he's right. In addition I'm nervous about the instability caused by PR. Why not introduce AV and then consider what to do next, leaving the second step [to a proportional system] open?

I told him that this was totally unacceptable to us; AV could not be an end position. A requirement of Cook/Maclennan was that a new system should be proportional – and, as he himself had admitted on *Breakfast With Frost*, AV is not.

TB (laughing): Condemned out of my own mouth. Well, let's go ahead on the basis that there is a presumption in favour of the second step, which has to be part of the deal.

PA: It has to be not only part of the deal, but part of the legislative programme, too. Meanwhile, I remain firmly of the view that if we go ahead with coalition in November, I should hold myself back from being a part of it. It is far more important that I win the support of the Party in November than that I should be a Cabinet minister. I want to be able to say that I don't have a personal stake in this.

TB: Look, I can only really see two of your people as genuine Cabinet material. Menzies Campbell is one and you are the other.

I replied that Alan Beith was also clearly Cabinet material: he would make an excellent Chief Secretary to the Treasury [i.e. in the Cabinet]. We then discussed some of the more junior ministerial possibilities among the Lib Dems, including Steve Webb, Don Foster and others.

TB: You have some real talent now in your party. We have been looking at them and we're rather impressed.

PA: Yes, I think they are very good, especially some of the new ones. To be honest, there doesn't seem to be much difference between our bright ones and yours. They all come from similar backgrounds and have similar ideas.

We went on to discuss more general matters, among them the new Tory leadership. Blair does not underestimate Hague's abilities, but thinks he has made some bad decisions early on: his Shadow Cabinet was not chosen with a view to uniting his party. Blair is pretty confident that Hague will move the Tories further and further towards Euro-scepticism and the right.

PA: I don't think you'll like this, but I wonder how much you hear from outside your immediate circle now? So I want to tell you what is being said about you, and what is worrying me, too. The word is that this is a government of control freaks. Now, if I heard that from your political enemies, I wouldn't be worried. But I'm hearing it from your friends, as well. I think there is a puzzling mismatch between your own personality and that of the government. I have always found you in private conversation open-minded, pluralist and inclusive. But your government appears the exact opposite. It doesn't brook dissent, and it doesn't appear to tolerate different opinions. You cannot run a government on the basis that everybody who doesn't agree with you all the time is against you. I can see natural reasons why you are like this in the early days, of course. If I had got back into power after eighteen years, I would want to make sure everything was right in the early days as well. And, given the way the final years of Major's government were broken by division, it's hardly surprising that you want to avoid it. But if this is a long-term trend, then eventually it will damage you. It also seems to me to stand at variance with what you personally believe in. [I didn't mention Peter Mandelson by name, but Blair knew who I was referring to by 'control freak'.]

TB: You are right in saying that we are trying to control things in the early days. I keep on saying to my people that I don't mind dissent, if it is about genuine things. But for my lot to agonize about whether to re-nationalize the top 100 companies in Britain is just pathetic. It's pure tokenism. Genuine dissent and genuine argument about our options are, however, what I hope to encourage.

PA: Well, it doesn't look very much like it from the outside.

We finished talking at about 3.30 and I returned to my seat in the front compartment.

At about 7.15am we stopped off at Novosibirsk airport to refuel. I awoke a little before then and sat on the flight deck with the RAF crew as we came in to land across the Siberian tundra. What a rundown place! One and a quarter million people live here. Tumbledown houses and the worst runway surface I have ever landed on – even worse than Sarajevo.

After the aircraft door was opened, and they had started to refuel, I wandered out. A few minutes later Blair came out on to the aircraft steps, too, blinking in the early morning light. We walked down the steps, and were stopped at the bottom by Russian guards who threatened to arrest us for illegal immigration. After a brief discussion, however, they allowed us to walk on the tarmac, but only within a red circle painted around the aircraft, with the guards positioned around the outside, presumably to see that the British Prime Minister didn't illegally attempt to enter Siberia.

We continued our earlier discussion in this somewhat surreal setting.

PA: I have been thinking over what we discussed last night. I am assuming that we have now taken the formal decision to go ahead.

TB (nodding): Yes.

PA: In which case I will get Richard Holme and Peter Mandelson to start mapping out the details straightaway. Can we both agree on next week for a start?

Blair replied that he thought it should happen no later.

After about twenty minutes the press contingent appeared, bleary-eyed, from the aircraft. John Hibbs[1] came up and said jokingly, 'Ah, the Lib/Lab Novosibirsk pact.' (If only he knew!) We laughed and told him we were making jokes about Russian airport management. We spent an hour or so chatting as the aircraft was refuelled and a small hydraulic leak in the tailfin mended. At about 10.00am we bundled aboard again and headed off for London.

Wednesday, 2 July, Westminster

A Jo Group meeting at 8.30am. I set aside a portion of the meeting for anyone to express any concerns they had about the direction we were taking. Nick South was opposed, but he has been consistently so from the start. Nick Harvey thinks it is the right thing to do, but that we should delay until the spring. He was supported by Paul Tyler.

I responded that, whilst I was prepared to keep an open mind on this, I was of the firm view that if we left it later than November the dynamics of opposition in the House of Commons would close the opportunity for us. I also believe that both the Tories and Labour's left wing will really go for us when, eventually, they spot what we're about. Tom McNally and Richard Holme supported this view, as did Archy. Chris Rennard nervous about timing. A general consensus that it will be nip and tuck as to whether I can get it through the Party.

At one stage Nick South said, 'What happens if you lose?' Archy said we ought to start thinking about an exit strategy for me. I told him that there was only one exit strategy possible – and that was the door. Nevertheless, I was heartened by the fact that, however sceptical they been previously about what I an trying to do, they now appreciate the scale of what might be achieved and seem more willing to support it. But there is still a lot of work to do before we launch the first stage.

Richard agreed to organize a group consisting of Tom McNally, Nick South, Nick Harvey, Jane Bonham-Carter and himself to sort out the initial

---

1 Political journalist for the *Daily Telegraph*. John is now political editor of *The Scotsman*.

announcements. There was some discussion on how I would handle the Parliamentary Party: we must get the tone just right. I will have to call a special Parliamentary Party meeting, followed by a special conference, of course.

Spent the rest of the morning and lunchtime refining my speech in response to the Budget and looking for hints of what it may contain in the lunchtime news. Then down to the chamber for PMQs and Brown's first Budget speech.

During PMQs Hague went on a rather thin story about a Budget leak in the *Financial Times*. Blair put him down contemptuously, to roars of laughter from the Labour benches. But it is early days yet for Hague.

Brown's speech was good and well delivered. The House liked it and the Labour Party loved it. At one point he said he was going to be flexible about the spending limits,[1] something we have been pushing for them to release for a very long time. But this wouldn't happen till next year. I quickly amended my speech to say that Brown had been too hard on business and not hard enough on the consumer.

Then Hague's response, which was wooden and tilting at the wrong windmills.

Brown has produced a good Budget which will, I think, be acclaimed, although it has a number of flaws that won't become evident for a day or so. It will probably result in higher interest rates and almost certainly a stronger pound. And it will hit industry where it ought to have hit consumers. Although it will help health and education next year, it will do nothing this year for these crucial services which have been underfunded for so long. And the real problems will not wait that long.

Tuesday, 8 July, Westminster

I saw a number of new MPs[2] today to discuss the position paper and relations with Labour. First Richard Allan,[3] who is one of the best of the new intake: serious, quiet, but a tough and effective politician. He lives in

1 Gordon Brown had committed the government to sticking by the spending limits inherited from the Tories for the first two years. I have always regarded this as one of the new government's most crucial early mistakes as it meant they couldn't fulfil their promises to improve public services before the next election.
2 Of the forty-six Lib Dem MPs elected in 1997, twenty-six were newly elected.
3 Member of Parliament for Sheffield Hallam since 1997.

the middle of a Labour area where the anti-Labour feeling among Lib Dems must be strongest, but he immediately saw the point of the long-term strategy and accepted it.

Donald Gorrie[1] is a dry old stick, though capable of great humour. Lugubrious but sharp with it, when he wants to be. He broadly accepted my position in a taciturn, noncommittal sort of a way. But I sense trouble here later.

At 4 o'clock in the afternoon, Michael Moore.[2] He is intelligent and impressive in a rather understated way. He understood what I was trying to say in the position paper, but I'm not sure I can count on him for support. But he is one of our most effective young MPs, nevertheless – one of those to whom the Party may look as a future leader.

And then Vince Cable.[3] For the first time I saw Vince's brain working. It is first class. Some say he lacks charisma. But there is no doubting the strength of his intellect. He supported most of the position paper with enthusiasm. He should be a pretty reliable aid when the tough times come.

Wednesday, 9 July, Westminster

In the morning another meeting of the Jo Group, but without Richard. We had met to discuss our plans for tomorrow, when we are all assuming that Blair will announce PR for Europe. But Richard rang later to say that there was some query over this now at Downing Street. Apparently 'a bad news day' or something. Meanwhile, a meeting with Blair has been fixed for me this afternoon, after PMQs.

At 4.25pm I went to see Blair in his office in the House. He was alone and looked haggard after an hour and a quarter at the Dispatch Box.

I said he must be absolutely shattered after the NATO summit in Madrid.[4] He said he was. Drumcree[5] had added a lot to the strain of the weekend, too.

1 Member of Parliament for Edinburgh West since 1997.
2 Member of Parliament for Tweedale, Ettrick and Lauderdale (David Steel's old seat) since 1997.
3 Dr Vince Cable, Member of Parliament for Twickenham since 1997.
4 The NATO Heads of State and Government summit in Madrid had taken place a few days earlier.
5 A stand-off had developed between the Orange Order and the RUC in Drumcree, Northern Ireland, when the Parades Commission had refused to allow the Orangemen to march down the Republican Garvaghy Road.

We then turned to tomorrow's announcements.

TB: Look, do you guys really want to go tomorrow? We don't have all our preparations absolutely in place. If you are desperate to go tomorrow, then we will. But would it really matter very much if we wait a week?

PA: My strong instinct is to go tomorrow. I've been told Downing Street is alive with rumours about PR for the European Parliament. I am really worried this will leak and the effect will be lost. But if you're confident it won't, and you feel you must wait until next week, then so be it. It's your decision. But I'll need to know by 7.30 this evening as there are various buttons I have to press [I was thinking of the Parliamentary Party].

He agreed to go back and sort it out straightaway.
We then considered the timing of the coalition announcement.

TB: Peter is advising me – and I want you to be aware of this – that November may be too early for me to deliver with my people. He says that I can't get away with bringing two or three of your people into the Cabinet in one go. We may have to do it gradually, over a longer term.

PA: We have always agreed that each step has to be a 'stand alone' one, but my judgement, as you know, is that if it isn't done in November, it is much less likely to be done at all. Particularly if you have, as I suspect, a difficult winter with the NHS as a result of your decision to stick to the Tory spending cuts. Incidentally, I am glad the Budget has at least reversed this for next year, but I think you are wrong about the five billion for next year.[1]

TB (with a watery smile): Yes, of course you are right. There is a five-billion gap next year. I am doing my best to cover it over with smoke and mirrors, but the problem is that, far from having left us a superb economic inheritance, the Tories have actually left us a disaster. The economy is not just bad; it is in a potentially dangerous condition. Inflation next year will go over our limit of 2.75 per cent unless we control it. I don't know how we are going to solve the five-billion problem, but we will. Why don't you guys go and talk to Gordon about it and see what he says?

PA: Funnily enough, I suggested to Malcolm Bruce [our Treasury spokesman] on the bench yesterday that he should approach Alastair Darling [Chief Secretary to the Treasury], asking for a meeting with Gordon, so that we could, on a confidential

1 It had come to light in the press that there was a £5 billion shortfall in the Labour government's first Budget.

basis, discover how the government intended to find their way out of this hole. I will try and fix it. Meanwhile, my worry is that the Budget hasn't taken nearly enough out of the consumer sector, and this will make the economy much more difficult to control in the future.

TB: I know it's become fashionable to say we haven't taken enough out of consumption. But taking into account fuel taxes, mortgages and, indirectly, Advance Corporation Tax, around 50 per cent of our tax increases were on the consumer. The reason the Stock Market has gone up is because it understands how hard the Budget will bite the consumer rather than industry.

We again discussed Hague. Blair thought he had done a good job at PMQs today. 'He is very capable. I don't underestimate him. But his strategic judgements are bad.'

Dinner at Methley Street with Jackie Ballard, Steve Webb, Ed Davey and Tom Brake.[1] A lively evening. They have all read the position paper and seem at least to be beginning to see why I am proposing this line. Steve is broadly in favour; Ed quite pro, but sceptical; Tom, who is a quiet man, didn't say much. But Jackie remains implacably opposed.

To bed a little before midnight.

Tuesday, 15 July, Westminster

Richard has called to say there will be more delays on the announcement on PR for Europe. The government now want to announce PR for Europe on Thursday, after the Cabinet meeting, then delay the Cabinet committee announcement until next week. I was initially against but, having thought about it, see little wrong with it. Blair wants to keep the European PR and the Cabinet committee announcements separate, so that it doesn't look like a party deal. They should be seen to be doing what is right, rather than what is expedient for the Lib Dems. I don't mind, since it gives us two bites of the cherry.

I arranged to speak to Blair later in the day.

At about half-past eight he called.

TB: Look, I understand you guys aren't in favour of splitting this.

PA: We weren't. But I have thought about it again and, if you want to split it, fine.

1 Member of Parliament for Carshalton since 1997.

Paddy Ashdown Awakening the Spirit of Proportional Representation

You announce PR for Europe, preferably on Thursday, then delay the Joint Cabinet Committee announcement until next Tuesday. But I don't want it to run on beyond that because any later will make life difficult with my Parliamentary Party, with whom I wish to discuss this at the weekend.

TB: No one is intending to delay this. I know you are getting somewhat frustrated by it. But it's quite complex and we have a lot of other things on our minds. Let's do as you suggest. We will announce PR for Europe after Cabinet on Thursday, then go with the JCC early next week.

PA: Thank you. But I need another agreement from you. This must not be allowed to become an Alastair Campbell operation for the weekend papers. If we say Tuesday, it must be announced on Tuesday. No prior leaking.

TB: That's fine, let's go ahead on that basis. I will get my people to ring you first thing in the morning, just to confirm.

I bet myself that they wouldn't ring as promised.

Wednesday, 16 July, Westminster

A morning meeting with Jim Wallace to talk about the position paper. But as I was talking him through it, he suddenly exploded.

I was completely unprepared for what happened next. He laid out for me in detail what I had been up to and what our plans were. He knew about PR for Europe, followed by the announcement of the Joint Cabinet Committee. He knew about Roy Jenkins being chair of the Electoral Reform Commission. He knew about the plan to hold off the Electoral Reform Commission so that I could build up a head of anxiety to release later. He knew about the coalition. He knew about my talks with Blair. He seemed to know everything. I was knocked backwards.

I said that I wanted to terminate the conversation there. But he refused, accusing me of betrayal. I said I understood why he felt as he did, but that I wanted to give him a considered response. Then I asked him if he had told anybody else. He said that yes, he had. Nicol Stephen.[1]

Next I asked him where he had got his information from. He refused to say.

Eventually, I insisted that we finished the conversation there and I would come back to him later. 'Meanwhile, please don't say anything to anybody.'

By this time he was absolutely furious, and shouted at me, 'What's in it for me? What's in it for Scotland?'

I lost my cool, slammed down my file and leapt to my feet. So he leapt to his feet as well, and we shouted at each other for about two minutes. [My office staff later told me that they heard the commotion next door and thought we had come to blows.] Eventually we calmed down and I asked him again not to mention it to anybody else. His response was, 'But what shall I say to the people I said I would report back to?' I replied, 'Say that you had a chat with me, but it hasn't been concluded. I want time to think about this.' He agreed reluctantly and left the office.

I was shaken rigid.

Jim now has information which could destroy the project on which I have worked for four years, and probably me with it. I bleeped Ming to arrange to see him, Paul and Archy.

Meanwhile I decided that I had no choice but to bring Jim fully inside the circle. I rang him to tell him and he asked whether that meant he had to support me. I said no. Good, he replied, because he was wholly opposed to the setting up of a Cabinet committee, especially since it would discuss

1 Member of Parliament (Liberal Democrat) for Kincardine and Deeside 1991–2. Nicol is now a Member of the Scottish Parliament, and is Deputy Minister for Enterprise and Lifelong Learning.

Scotland. Also, he refused to be on it, since that would cause problems for him in Scotland.

I suddenly realized why he was so angry. I should have brought him in earlier. The original mistake was mine. I decided that the best thing to do was to admit my mistake, so I apologized to him and explained that I had been working with the same group of advisers for four years and that I had built up a strong relationship with Blair. If he blew this apart, he could of course destroy me. But he would also seriously damage the Party. He revealed that he had also had a discussion with Charles Kennedy in Brussels. So I suspect Charles knows everything, too.

At the meeting with Paul, Archy and Ming I broached with Archy whether he had told Jim. He admitted that he had had a long session over whiskies with him on Budget night, trying to get him to agree with the proposition.[1] But Jim had gone off in a foul mood, accusing Archy of being an 'Uncle Tom' *vis-à-vis* Labour. I got briefly grumpy about this, but quickly changed tack to a discussion on how to limit the damage. I asked Archy to find out who in the Party knew and to tell Nicol Stephen to keep quiet.

Later Richard came to see me. He has spoken to Mandelson. Over the last couple of hours the story about PR for Europe has, as I feared, started to leak. Apparently Mandelson discussed it at lunch with Elinor Goodman of Channel 4 yesterday at the very moment that Blair was promising me there would be no leaks! All I can do now is say how much we welcome the idea, etc.

In the course of the PPM in the early evening I decided that if I wanted to avoid another Jim Wallace situation I must also put Alan Beith in the picture. I caught him just after the vote in the chamber, explained what was happening and said that he would be on the Cabinet committee. He put up no opposition.

Thursday, 17 July, Westminster

Simon Hughes at 2.30pm. He went through the position paper in some detail and said he agreed with it.

---

1 Archy has since told me that he could see this 'explosion' coming and was trying to avoid it by informally bringing Jim 'into the circle'.

At 3 o'clock Bob Russell,[1] who seemed very relaxed about my plans. He is a nice man, completely uncomplicated. His interests are confined to his beloved Colchester, where he is greatly respected. He is one of those MPs who fits his constituency like a glove. My opinion of him improves all the time.

Then at 3.30 Malcolm Bruce. He fundamentally disagrees with key elements of the paper, although he has a rather unclear idea of what the alternative would be. Something about gaining votes from both parties and coming through the middle.

Saturday, 19 July, Somerset

Richard called at about 8 o'clock to tell me about his dinner last night at the Garrick with Derry Irvine. Well lubricated, by all accounts. Apparently, Irvine became very loquacious; according to him Blair is a man of amazing vision and toughness who wants to seize the moment. But he's back on the merger kick. At one stage, apparently, Irvine said: 'Look, don't you lot realize what's in it for you? You can be a minister of state, Paddy can be Home Secretary and Ming can be Defence Secretary. We really mean business and I cannot understand why you are not impressed by it. Don't you realize that I am a liberal. We are all liberals now?'

Irvine had also spent much time trying to convince Richard that he (Irvine) was more powerful than Mandelson. At one point he had switched from good cop to bad cop: 'Blair could wipe you out tomorrow if he puts his mind to it, you know.'

'Is that what he wants?' asked Richard.

'Of course not,' said Derry. 'He wants unity.'

Richard told me he would write a full account of the meeting.

Still no details, however, on the Tuesday announcement.

Monday, 21 July, Somerset and London

At 9.30am another call from Richard Holme. He has finally spoken to Mandelson: Blair is, as I suspected, having second thoughts. Apparently Mandelson said that he had left a 'worried and anguished Prime Minister'. He is not at all certain that we should go ahead with the announcement of

1 Member of Parliament for Colchester since 1997.

the Joint Cabinet Committee (JCC) tomorrow. The atmospherics are not right, he says. Richard sounded tired and fed-up. 'They are in a terrible mess. They simply don't know what to do next. Events are hitting them at such speed that they seem punchdrunk. The whole business is becoming rather chaotic. I cannot keep pace with them changing their minds.'

Later, as I was on my way up to London in the early afternoon, Richard rang again, saying it looked as though it was off for tomorrow. But by 5 o'clock, when I got into the office for the Jo Group meeting, he came in to inform us that it was on again. The PM wanted to go ahead, but I must speak to him today.

In the Jo Group meeting we put together a plan for tomorrow, on the understanding that all will remain uncertain until I have spoken to Blair. Meanwhile, we had a number of technical problems to deal with. What official papers would we be allowed to see? How many on the committee? Who are they? When would the first meeting be?

Blair rang at about 6.45pm.

TB: Sorry for the hold-ups, but the Irish have been quite impossible. It is going to be a very long night. As soon as I have finished this call I will grab a bite to eat and then we have about four or five more hours' work to do with them.

He then moved on to talking about tomorrow. We quickly agreed that we should go ahead.

TB: But I want to tell you that I am getting a lot of flak from my people about the attacks your guys are mounting on us. Particularly Don Foster on Dearing.[1]

PA: Look, this is just ridiculous. I heard Don on the *Today* programme this morning. He was reason itself! The real problem here is that both of us are subject to propaganda from those in our own parties who want us to believe the worst of the other side. The sooner we get ourselves into this Joint Cabinet Committee the better. And, incidentally, it only goes to show that if we don't strike while the iron is hot then we will lose the opportunity.

I then raised the practical questions on which we need responses by tomorrow. He didn't have answers to any of them. He was clearly bombed out by the Irish problem. I'm not surprised – and it is, of course, a much higher priority for him at the moment. I felt guilty even raising such small details, so I backed off quickly and said, 'Look, these matters are for other people to sort out, not you,' and wished him good luck tonight.

1 The Dearing Report on student funding in higher education.

I then put word out that we were on for tomorrow. But I am getting very nervous about it. I am particularly concerned about kickback from the Party.

At 8.00 a meeting in my office with Jim Wallace. He was in an extremely difficult mood. I showed him the Blair papers, at which point he relented a bit. But he still remains implacably opposed to the whole venture.

Then I spoke to Bob Maclennan by phone. Somehow or other he has heard that there have been last-minute changes to the make-up of the JCC. I explained that Blair has decided there should be five of us on it rather than four, and that since Mandelson was going to be on it, I wanted Richard Holme there as well. At which point Bob went nuclear, demanding that I should ring Blair and reverse the decision. I explained that there were good rational reasons for going along with this – but he would have none of it. Eventually I simply said we should discuss it tomorrow, and put the phone down. Maybe he thinks he is being pushed aside in favour of Richard.

A disturbed night's sleep.

Tuesday, 22 July, Westminster

THE DAY OF THE ANNOUNCEMENT OF THE JOINT CABINET COMMITTEE

Into the office by 8.00am. Saw Bob first thing. He hasn't changed his opinion since last night, but at least he's calmed down a bit.

I also briefed Richard Livsey, who is delighted that we're going ahead, but nervous that his opposite number, the Welsh Secretary Ron Davies, may be on the committee. I assured him he wouldn't be.

The Team Leaders' meeting at 9.30, where I told them of the announcement of the establishment of the JCC. A very strong, very hostile reaction. Malcolm Bruce went up the wall. Matthew Taylor ditto. Much talk of being bounced. I got support only from established members of the Jo Group. This should have warned me of what was to come at the Parliamentary Party Meeting at 10.00. At the PPM I explained the position to a shocked silence. Nobody had any idea of what was about to be announced. Ed Davey led off by saying he thought the whole enterprise was extremely injudicious and that I had bounced them all. Then we went round the room. Pretty predictable stuff. Bob Russell in favour (bless him, he's brimful of down to earth common sense). Jenny Tonge,[1] to my great

---

1 Member of Parliament for Richmond since 1997.

surprise, strongly opposed. Lembit Opik in favour. But the Scots, led by Robert Smith, wholly against.

Alan Beith, who chaired the meeting, sat pretty solidly by. Bob Maclennan, despite our previous row, did a splendid job supporting me – he is magnificent at times like this. The best intervention came from Mark Oaten, who said that no one could ever have guessed that we would have achieved all this.

In the end, I got it through, but at considerable cost. I couldn't understand why the new MPs, who had all reacted so well to the position paper, should have reacted so badly to its natural conclusion. But it might well be because they were genuinely stunned and had not been given a chance to think it through. A lesson for the future. I left the meeting shakily at 11.20.

After the PPM, feeling shattered, I went back up to my office. Nick came in and said he thought that it hadn't gone too badly. But I was really depressed.

The news of the JCC announcement broke around mid-day, after which a hectic round of interviews, including *World At One* and ITN. The press are running the story quite prominently. ITN more so than the BBC, on which it is running at item 4 in the headlines followed by a cursory report. Friendly press people such as Tony Bevins, Patrick Wintour et al. pleased that we have pulled it off and amazed that it had been kept so secret. Wintour kicking himself for not having spotted it earlier. I briefed Andrew Marr on the telephone, who was delighted. I also spoke to Alan Rusbridger of the *Guardian*, who said he was busy but could I speak to his political editor, Michael White. Probably means they will not be giving it coverage.

At 1.45 a quick pre-press conference meeting with Alan Beith and Bob Maclennan and down to the press conference itself, which went well.

Then along to the Federal Policy Committee. To my huge surprise, they unanimously supported me. Richard Kemp[1] said, 'This is great. It will divide Labour in Liverpool. All the good ones will support us and all the bad ones will be utterly furious. Very well done.' Totally contrary to the Parliamentary Party! I was reassured.

Later, back in the House, Simon Hughes came up to me during one of the divisions and showed me a telephone message from one of his constituents: 'Will you please make sure that you raise the question of my pension on this new committee.' Apparently, one supporter has rung Cowley Street

---

1 Our candidate in Liverpool Wavertree in 1992 and 1997. He sits in the Cabinet of Liverpool City Council.

to say that he will never support us again, since I have joined the Labour government!

Andrew Stunell,[1] Jackie Ballard and various others opposed to the move were at the dinner table when I arrived. Obviously in full flow discussing it, but not in a hostile fashion. At the end of dinner, I said to Andrew that if he could pull together five or six of the people most concerned about the developments, perhaps he could bring them to my office for a glass of whisky after the last vote?

At 10.15 they turned up: Andrew himself, Robert Smith, Michael Moore, Jackie Ballard and Adrian Sanders.[2] We had a pretty strenuous but good-natured discussion. Andrew gave me a lift home just after midnight.

It has been a very tough day. TV news reporting has been good and we are over the first hurdle. Previews of the early morning editions sound good, even from the Tory press.

Wednesday, 23 July, Westminster

I was waiting for a bus at 7.30am when a taxi drew up and the cabby offered me a lift. He refused to take my fare, saying how pleased he was that we were working with Labour.

At 9.30 a meeting with David Rendel. He remains totally opposed. He seems to believe that we can overtake Labour and defeat them even in traditional Labour seats with large majorities. The long march par excellence!

Thursday, 24 July, Oxford

PARLIAMENTARY PARTY AWAYDAY AT WADHAM COLLEGE

After a day's campaigning in Manchester with Nick South I flew back to Heathrow and drove to Oxford, arriving at about half-past five.

The opening session was to take the form of Tim Razzall and I putting on a performance as two friends having an 'after-dinner' chat about the Party's future and my ideas. We hoped to use this as a vehicle to promote

1 Member of Parliament for Hazel Grove since 1997.
2 Member of Parliament for Torbay since 1997.

a calm discussion about recent events and the future. I took Tim to one side beforehand and asked him to start by asking me very directly whether there were circumstances in which I would have recommended a coalition after the election. I would look shocked by this and then, after a long pause, would answer yes. I would go on to say that I would have recommended it to the Parliamentary Party before putting it to the Party as a whole, subject to three criteria:

1. There was a hung parliament or a small Labour majority;

2. Blair had previously agreed to PR (I would hint strongly that he would have done so);

3. We had drawn up a proper coalition agreement.

There was real shock in the room when Tim asked the question.

Afterwards, a number of people told him how brave he had been to put the question, and what a good question it had been.

The rest of the day went much more easily than I had anticipated. The session ended well.

After dinner, a sort of topical tips session, which was very useful. Then down to the serious business of drinking at the bar. I kept going until about 1.00am, but some of the others continued long after – and were showing signs of it the next day!

Friday, 25 July, Oxford

Had something of a fuzzy head this morning. During breakfast, Ming pointed out an article by John Lloyd in *The Times* and said, in a voice loud enough for everyone to hear, that this came about as a result of his briefing. The article finished with the words 'Paddy Ashdown is right. Let's hope his famously grumpy party allows him to go ahead.' To which Jackie Ballard retaliated from the next table: 'He doesn't understand. It's the leader who's grumpy, not the party.' Laughter all round.

In the pre-lunch session Charles Kennedy said he thought the aim of the Party now should be to replace the Tories as Her Majesty's official opposition. This statement was greeted by some cheering and clapping. But it is, of course, nonsense, as Charles surely knows. We can borrow votes and even win defectors from the Tories while they are being so awful. But such people will return home when the Tories come back to the centre ground. There will always be a right-wing party in Britain and it can never be the Liberal Democrats.

We started the afternoon session shortly after 3.00. Pretty tough going. Jackie Ballard, Norman Baker,[1] Andrew Stunell and Paul Burstow all put a lot of pressure on me to ensure that the Joint Cabinet Committee didn't stray off constitutional matters unless the Parliamentary Party had previously agreed for it to do so. I flatly refused to accede to this. Norman Baker wanted me to reveal my list of advisers. I told him to jump in the lake.

Eventually the mood changed and Jenny Tonge, John Burnett[2] and David Heath[3] all said that we were behaving like student politicians (true), and that I should be given space to lead the Party. So, in the end, I achieved what I had set out to do: 'undress in public', so that everyone knew what I had been trying to achieve and I could prepare the way for the next move.

It has been a useful away session. Alan Beith is proving a real prop. Charles Kennedy was the only person to make an overt bid for wider support on the basis of a strategy contrary to my own. My room for manoeuvre has not, as I had feared, diminished, and my colleagues have had a chance to see inside my mind and begin to prepare their own positions for what may come next.

Saturday, 26 July, Somerset

A very heavy constituency surgery, which didn't finish until about 11.45. During it, Alastair Campbell called. Apparently a *Sunday Times* article is about to come out based on a book by one of Mandelson's former aides, Derek Draper. It mentions the word merger and also slips in details about the 12 June dinner between Blair, Mandelson, Roy Jenkins and myself. Campbell said Blair was very embarrassed by the whole thing. I rang Nick South and Roy to alert them. Roy's name is now appearing in print as a possible chair of the Electoral Reform Commission. Labour is as leaky as a sieve. Mandelson in particular.

---

1 Member of Parliament for Lewes since 1997.
2 Member of Parliament for Torridge and North Devon since 1997.
3 Member of Parliament for Somerton and Frome since 1997.

Monday, 28 July, Westminster

Blair and I had agreed to meet at 3.00. I had arrived at the Cabinet Office door to be told that I was to go to the Green Room[1] upstairs to 'keep me out of the way' until the 'present lot' had gone. I found out later that Blair had been giving interviews to the *Sun* and the *Mirror*, both on an apparently exclusive basis. So I spent an enjoyable quarter of an hour in the Green Room, looking at the paintings and drinking the obligatory Downing Street cup of tea. I was particularly taken by two paintings: one a profile of Wellington, with his famous beak of a nose, but thinner and more hawk-like than I had imagined; the other of Nelson looking half left, with ruddy cheeks and watery eyes, looking as though he had just come off a dawn watch in the North Sea in the teeth of stiff nor'easterly. Anji Hunter[2] told me later that they are going to rehang all the paintings at No. 10: 'Derry Irvine is coming to advise us on bringing in a whole new set.'

Jonathan collected me at about 3.15. Blair was, as usual, in his shirt-sleeves. Since it was a sunny day, he suggested we went outside. So we sat out on the terrace in two wicker armchairs.

We talked about holidays – he's taking the family to Geoffrey Robinson's villa in Tuscany, as usual, and then spending a week in the South of France. He said he longed to be away from the pressure of events. But he was worried about the Italian press. Would they leave him alone? Apparently Romano Prodi[3] had told him that he was more popular in Italy than he was in Britain. He had replied that it wasn't in Italy he needed to be popular.

We then turned to the events of last week. Blair told me that he thought it had all gone very well. I said I was particularly pleased that the press had decided we were two parties negotiating on an equal basis, rather than the Lib Dems being in Labour's pocket. If someone had told me two months ago that we could have so changed the culture of politics both within and without our parties and outside in such a short time, I would never have believed them.

He asked me whether I had had any difficulty with my lot. I said yes,

---

1 A waiting-room in No. 10.
2 The Prime Minister's Special Assistant.
3 Prime Minister of Italy 1996–8. Prodi is now President of the European Commission.

chiefly on the grounds of their feeling bounced. But I was sure that if I hadn't done it that way, I would never have got it through at all. The new MPs, in particular, were still in constituency campaigning mode. Meanwhile, the experience had done much to reshape people's perceptions of what was happening, and what was possible. I told him about the Oxford Parliamentary Party Meeting, and how I had revealed that I would have recommended a coalition in May had there been a hung parliament or a small Labour majority, subject to a full coalition agreement.

He told me that he had had some trouble from his lot, too, particularly in the South West. 'Our people there came to see me the other day and said, "You are making it impossible for us. You are giving the Liberal Democrats real credibility." '

PA: We need to know whether we are still planning on November for the next big move. I am not at all sure that, if I take this to the Party Conference, I will win. I feel more confident about the outcome as a result of last week, but it will be no walkover.

TB: I am not at all certain I can deliver this later, either. But I agree that our hand has been strengthened for November. If we don't do it soon, we may not do it at all. Events will just overtake us. So let's continue on the basis that we will go ahead in November. I'm not sure I can manage the reshuffle, though, goodness knows, there are one or two people who need to be reshuffled.

PA: This really is a huge gamble, as we both realize. But it's important that we agree to proceed on the basis that it is a possibility, even if not yet a probability. There's a lot of work to be done. For instance, we will have to draw up some kind of agreement. Richard Holme and I will work on that over the summer holiday. So, can I confirm that, as far as you're concerned, the overall plan still remains in place?

TB: Yes. The next thing to decide is what we do for each other's conferences.

PA: Frank Field is coming to ours. The first time in history a government minister has come to an opposition party's conference, I think. Perhaps we should send a senior spokesman along to yours as well.

TB: That's a good idea. I would welcome it. We need to build up reasons why it is beneficial for both our parties to move closer together. So far this has been done from the top down. We must start to broaden support and provide reasons for support lower down.

PA: Look, before we finish, I must tell you something very, very confidentially that I have not mentioned to anybody else except Jane. I agreed with Jane before the election that I would stand down during this parliament. I will be 60 when it finishes. Too old to be leading a party against a Prime Minister in his forties and a Tory leader in his teens. Apart from anything else, I have done this job for nine years. I would like to continue in some way in the public service. But I am not at all sure I want to stay on as an MP.

I am telling you this because I don't want to deceive you in any way. I will see things through with you to a fixed point one way or the other. And then announce to my party, hopefully, out of a clear blue sky, that I am handing over the leadership. There are other things I want to do with my life, and I owe some years to Jane.

TB (looking slightly shocked): That really is a blow. You have a lot to offer in politics. I hope you stay on longer than that.

PA: I am only telling you what is going through the back of my mind at the moment. But I give you an absolute undertaking that, since this is the most important thing I have ever done in politics, I won't relinquish my position until we either have arrived at a fixed point in our relationship or have clearly failed to do so.

He asked me to keep him informed and said he hoped I'd reconsider.

TB: The problem with politics is that the best politicians are always the ones who could do something else.

PA: I think it's important to believe that politics isn't the only thing you can do. It makes you stronger.

I walked back out through to the Cabinet Office door at around 3.45pm.

Sunday, 3 August, Irancy

MY GRANDSON MATTHIAS'S CHRISTENING[1]

I will be glad when this christening is over. It's entailed quite a lot of organization. I know Jane is feeling the pressure as well. The weather today is bright, but very muggy and close.

Everyone out of the house by a quarter to twelve and we drove over to

1 Matthias was born in April during the election campaign (see Vol. I, pp. 547–9). We had arranged with Kate's French in-laws to have the christening at our home in Irancy.

Pallotte, where we took photographs of Matthias, Jane, Kate and Simon. Then down to the church. We had to wait outside for quite a long time while mass finished. Then we entered through the back door.

The baptism service was lovely; the same *curé* who married Kate and Seb. We put the family christening robe, in which my mother, myself and both the kids were christened [handmade of Irish lace by my great-grandmother in the last century] on to Matthias as soon as he was named and accepted into the Church. I said a few words in French, then Simon read beautifully from a part of the Sermon on the Mount. The tears started in my eyes.

Afterwards, back over the vineyards to Irancy, where we opened up the house for the christening party. There were seventeen of us in all including Sebastien's godfather, a lovely gentleman called Jean-Pierre, with his wife Françoise. We got through the best part of a dozen bottles of white, a dozen red and a dozen of champagne.

Then someone suggested we went down to the village for the Fête d'Irancy, which was being held on the same day.

The games started at around 6.30. There were really only two. One involved throwing water-filled balls at some cans, much to everyone's amusement. The other was called '*tinette*', in which you take a long wooden pole and stand in a barrel on a trailer being hauled around by Stefan Podor[1] on his tractor, until you reach a half barrel strung up on a cord between two poles and kept full of water by a hose. Sticking out of the underside of the half barrel is a tab with a hole through the middle; the idea is to put your lance through the hole. But if you hit the barrel instead, its entire contents empty themselves over you. Of course, the barrel in which you are standing fills up with water as well. I was soon very wet, so I pleaded with an English friend to help make up an '*équipe britannique*'. To gales of French laughter, we inevitably got completely soaked.

A very successful christening. Matthias behaved absolutely perfectly throughout. He didn't even cry when he was being baptized in church.

1 An Irancy vigneron.

Wednesday, 20 August, Irancy

Spent much of today sitting in Kate's garden drafting 'Partnership for Britain's Future' [the draft coalition agreement that I had agreed with Blair to write over the summer holiday].[1]

Thursday, 21 August, Irancy

Another beautiful day. Spent all morning and some of the afternoon working on my conference speech. Jane and I have got ourselves into a routine of a light lunch followed by an hour or so's sleep. I am slowly losing weight.

Hugh Dykes is to drop in and spend tonight with us, on his way back to the UK, to discuss joining the Lib Dems. He arrived at just after six, having driven 350 miles from his house in the Ardèche in extremely hot weather. When he arrived we told him we were dining with French friends this evening and he was invited. So we pushed a cup of tea into his hands, stuffed him under a shower and then we all went off to the Charriats.[2]

About fifteen other people from the village there, including the Jefferies. We all sat round a long table under the stars on the Charriats' terrace. It was a beautiful evening. Jupiter bigger than I have ever seen it before. Later on, the moon rose from behind the ridge above the vines, shining its early light through the apple tree across the road. People kept driving past and waving. A fabulous meal – terrific beef, almost raw. And, of course, copious quantities of René's excellent wine. Hugh, who speaks very good French, enjoyed himself. We rolled home merrily under the stars at around 1.00am.

Friday, 22 August, Irancy

Hugh, nursing something of a hangover, stayed until about 10.30. We agreed that he would go and see Richard, and that he and I would have a chat in the week before the conference, so that he could join us as part of

1 See Appendix C.
2 René and Jacqueline Charriat, Irancy friends who are vignerons.

our pre-conference publicity. He is a nice man, but he is finding it very difficult to adjust to life beyond Westminster [he had lost his seat as Conservative MP for Harrow East in the election]. Jane and I both liked him.

Tuesday, 26 August, Somerset

I have more or less decided that if Blair and I do agree to go ahead with the November operation (which is becoming known as 'The Full Monty' [TFM]) then I will put it to the Party at a special conference at the end of the month. By my current calculations it will be a very close-run thing. Everything depends on what we can negotiate with Blair. But if, for whatever reason, on his side or mine, we decide we cannot go ahead, I will want to step down as soon as possible. The project will, in effect, be over.

But I am concerned that this might be perceived as precipitate, given that we have only just established the JCC. I don't want to do harm to either the party or my successor. So perhaps I should make sure both the JCC and the Electoral Reform Commission are up and running, thereby cementing our relationship with the government into something more permanent, before I resign. That would mean stepping down at the Spring Conference in March next year. This happens to be the tenth anniversary of the formation of the Liberal Democrats, so that would work rather well. A number of staff are leaving me soon, including Nick South, so this will also make my recruitment choices easier. I will stress to everyone I interview the transient and uncertain nature of the job.

A bad night's sleep. I had rather hoped that the good long nights I got on holiday would stay with me for a while, but my body fell back into its working sleep pattern immediately. Up at 6.00am.

Wednesday, 27 August, Somerset

[*The government, in Blair's absence, had had a rocky August, with a public quarrel as to who was 'in charge' – John Prescott or Peter Mandelson.*]

Downing Street called at 9.30 and put me through to Blair at Chequers. He was very chatty.

I asked him whether he had had a good holiday. 'Terrific. I have done a lot of reading and a lot of thinking. And had a good rest as well.'

I said that I had seen him on French television and that my French friends had been impressed by his command of the language, but commented that he spoke with an accent from the Midi. He laughed and said it was either just an English accent or bad pronunciation.

I said that I wanted to touch base with him to see if he had done any further thinking about November. We would have to make up our minds on this pretty soon. I had done a lot of thinking over the holidays, and had concluded that, on balance, it was still worth going for. But, as we both knew, the longer we left it, the more difficult it would become to pull off. Events over the summer recess [the 'who's in charge' row] would not help me get it through my party. Everything now hinged on the wording he was prepared to use on PR and on the condition agreement.

He replied that, as far as he was concerned, events over the summer had made it more rather than less necessary for us to go ahead, 'Although whether this will be possible in November – even whether it is within the range of my power to do at all – I haven't yet gauged. I'll spend two or three days thinking about it when I get back to my desk.'

PA: I think we either have to go in November, or not at all. As events go by, such a pile of rubble mounts up in front of the door we want to open that we will soon arrive at a point where we can't even reach it to try.

TB: I quite agree. 'If it were done when 'tis done, then 'twere well it were done quickly.' I just don't know whether I can do it, however. I will have to reassess this.

PA: Well, we ought to make a decision one way or another in the next few weeks. I will be away in my constituency next week, but up in London some of the week following. Could we meet then? Apart from anything else, if we do decide to go ahead, I will want to prepare the ground in my conference speech.

TB: Yes, I've been thinking about my conference speech, too. I want to confront this absolutely head on at conference and have done with it.

I said this must be seen as a joint project, rather than as a unilateral move from him to which we were forced to respond. But we could talk more about that later.

Finally, I privately warned him that Hugh Dykes would be joining us the week after next. 'I'm particularly keen that Alastair Campbell, who lives next door to Hugh, and who, Hugh says, keeps ringing him and asking him to join Labour, should lay off for a bit.'

He promised to pull Campbell back and said, 'I think we have one as well.'

I gained the impression it was an MP; Temple-Morris?

In the evening I had a useful dinner with Richard. We went through all the Blair stuff: the timings, the document and what is going on in Blair's mind. We also discussed whether Richard wants to go on dealing with Mandelson in the build-up towards November. He said he would rather not; he found Mandelson annoying and, he suspected, probably working to his own agenda. He [Mandelson] desperately wants a position in Cabinet. Richard told me that when he met Mandelson the day after the election, he was almost in tears – biting his bottom lip – because Blair hadn't given him a job in the Cabinet. I suggested to Richard that he might be better off dealing with Irvine, who clearly sees himself as a central player. Richard took away the document I wrote at Kate's house to work on. However, we should not give this to Blair at our next meeting. It would just scare him off.

Thursday, 28 August, Edinburgh

A splendid dinner at Ming's in Edinburgh after a day's campaigning in Scotland on the devolution referendum. After the other guests had left Ming and I shared a final glass of claret and discussed the latest developments on the Blair front. I told him that if I had to fall on my sword on this then I hoped he would put his name forward in the subsequent contest. But, of course, Ming wouldn't be able to succeed me if he was seen to be closely linked with me. Ming dismissed the idea immediately, saying this was the biggest thing that had happened in his political career and he would support me to the hilt. Elspeth [Ming's wife] was enthusiastic about it, too. To bed at about 1.30am.

Sunday, 31 August, Somerset

Woken at 4.30am by the phone. I dashed to it with a sinking heart, thinking something had happened to one of the kids. The voice at the other end said bleakly: 'This is the BBC. Princess Diana has been killed in a car accident. Would you like to comment?'

Spent the rest of the morning until about 9.30 coping with interviews. But what do you say? Impossible. I saw Blair on television being interviewed as he was taking his children to church. Over the top, I thought; cracking voice and all that.

The pictures of the car crash were terrible. Such a bright light, so terribly and suddenly snuffed out.

Thursday, 4 September, London

There is an ugly mood developing in the country. Something unpleasantly akin to an eighteenth-century mob on the streets outside Buckingham Palace, demanding that the flag be flown at half mast and the Queen come down from Balmoral so that the people can see her cry for Diana, just like them. Partially generated, of course, by the editors of the tabloids, who are the very people who created the climate that eventually killed her. Such hypocrisy.

Roy has been trying to get hold of me. I told him of my disquiet at the national mood. He said he felt equally uncomfortable. He had been invited to the funeral, but had decided not to go. 'I don't want to go there and gawk,' he said. 'You, of course, must go. And your predecessor David is very keen to go. So I have given him my ticket.'

David has appeared on the box today. Rather bravely, I think, criticizing the tabloid editors. I felt I should have done the same and was racked with guilt this evening that I didn't stand up and make my feelings known. At times like these the liberal voice is important, even if it means going against the overwhelming popular feeling.

Friday, 5 September, Somerset and London

At last, some sensible comment in the serious press criticizing the public mood that has been developing over the past couple of days. I should have done it!

After a day's roving surgery, into the car and up to London. We got there in remarkably good time. Jane and I unloaded everything into the flat, then I left for Downing Street at half-past five. I parked in the House of Commons car park and walked along Whitehall in a sweater and jeans. Large crowds are beginning to gather for tomorrow's funeral, many of them preparing to spend the night on the pavements.

I arrived at No. 10 via the Cabinet Office entrance, as usual. Shortly afterwards Blair arrived and said he had just one quick minute's work to do, then he would be with me. Jonathan came up and we chatted over tea. I said I thought that Blair had done well in the aftermath of Diana's death. It must have been difficult to get the tone right. I didn't, however, much like his first statement. Too theatrical, and the pauses too long and emotionally laden. Jonathan smiled and said, 'Perhaps, but that is a recommendation of perfection. I suspect most people found in it what they wanted to hear.'

True enough.

Blair returned a couple of minutes later and we took our cups of tea into his office. He sat, as usual, in his shirtsleeves, with his feet up and his arms flung over the back of the sofa. I sat down in the chair to his left.

There followed a fascinating discussion of the events of the past few days. I repeated what I had said to Jonathan, that I thought his first statement was over the top. He gave a watery smile.

TB: I really felt it, you know. That wasn't acting. I was genuinely moved. I knew her and liked her. I thought she was really important for the nation.

PA: Nevertheless, a prime minister becomes a genuine leader of the nation when something big and traumatic happens. Usually it's a war. You will remember Major during the Gulf War – his finest moment, in my view. Up to now, I suspect that the public has seen you as an interesting and attractive figure, but still primarily as the Labour leader and only secondarily as prime minister. But these last few days you seem to have genuinely caught the nation's mood, and to have led them. You have done yourself a power of good. There will be a political bonus in that.

[I learned later from Roy Jenkins that Blair had been told by his advisers to lift himself above politics for the week and try not to descend back into them afterwards.]

I went on to say that I hadn't much liked some of the comments in the press which had attributed everything the royal family did to him (such as the *Guardian*: 'Palace bows the knee to Blair'). I said I was also worried about the sense of mob rule, whipped up by the tabloids, especially in London. I couldn't make up my mind whether the last three months have shown the beginnings of a genuinely new, more liberal, mood in the country, or whether this whole rather ugly Diana mood is a truer indication of the nation's state of mind.

TB: I am pretty sure this is positive, not negative. But it is a real question. What does this mean for the future? What will the mood be two or three days after the funeral?

PA: Too early to tell.

TB: It has been odd really. We [he meant 'I'] have had to lead people. Now we must take them through their grief, and then through the constructive process of what to do next. And we must decide what we can do to carry that mood forward after the funeral itself. Meanwhile, you should know that, while I have been close to Charles, it really was him, not me, as the papers suggest, who persuaded the Queen to make a statement. And the decision to go on a walkabout came from her alone.

Towards the end of the meeting we discussed the service. Blair is reading a lesson at the request of the Spencer family.

He then turned to what will happen next between our parties.

TB: I have been doing a lot of thinking about our project. I have also discussed it with Gordon, who is, incidentally, much more welcoming to the whole thing than he has ever been before. But he keeps saying, 'If you reshuffle the Cabinet, I don't see how you can put in Liberal Democrats when you have so many good Labour people waiting. I am not opposed to the project, but that is a serious problem for you.' If I were to be blunt with you, at this stage, I would say that there are just two obvious people I can remove from the Cabinet, and even then only after they have had a fair run at it. And if I can reshuffle those two in November, I still couldn't parachute in two Lib Dems. One Lib Dem might be possible. But two? That really would be difficult.

I was getting nervous at this point that he was going back to saying he would simply add a Lib Dem or two to the Cabinet.

PA: I wonder if, since we haven't met for so long, our perceptions of what is possible are becoming separated? As I've said before, this cannot be a question of just adding Lib Dems to a Labour Cabinet. It has to be something much deeper than that. We have discussed a partnership in the past, and a partnership is what I am committed to.

TB (interrupting): So you believe that you would have to vote with us?

PA (surprised): Of course! Surely you cannot have been in doubt on that? We will vote with you and act with you – which, incidentally, with such a huge majority and such a tiny opposition, could force us to consider changing the shape of the chamber of the House [from two sides to a hemisphere]. You are not, I hope, suggesting that we should be free to oppose you in the vote while having Lib Dems in the Cabinet? It must be a full partnership or it is simply not worth doing.

TB: I am relieved. I was getting very worried about that possibility.

He has a terrible habit of forgetting what we have previously agreed.

PA: Then let me say it again. This must also be a full partnership if I am to get it through my party. And, while we are on the subject, I will have to ask you to be much more generous than you will feel comfortable with, or your advisers will recommend. There are four things that are important:

One, this must look like two sovereign and independent parties coming together in a partnership. Your advisers will tell you that you should graciously offer us the opportunity to join you. But that would be a disaster for me. If we are to succeed, despite the obvious imbalances in our positions, you and I must appear as equals who respect each other and understand both our own party's independence and that of the other party.

Two, a coalition agreement. I have begun to map one out. This shows that the two parties agree on about 90 per cent of the things that really matter to most ordinary people: health, education, etc. I think many people will be surprised by how much we do agree on. But the key thing is that we are seen to get something from you and you are seen to get something from us. The coalition agreement itself will be very, very important, as it will be the cement that holds the partnership together through the next government and beyond. If this is not to appear a grubby stitch-up for party advantage, such an agreement should be framed as a promise of what we can jointly deliver to the British people.

Three, we will need you to shift your position on PR from the 'presumption of opposition' to the 'presumption of constructive open-mindedness', as we have previously agreed. The wording is very important. And we need to decide very soon exactly what that should be.

Finally, although you won't like this, there must be some exit mechanism. Of course, I don't anticipate such a mechanism being used, but a proper partnership must have a way of being broken, as well as of coming together.

Is there anything in these points with which you fundamentally disagree?

TB: No, nothing. That all seems perfectly logical and right. I was thinking about the people, but you are clearly thinking about the substance. That's fine.

PA: I reckon the coalition agreement is going to present the most problems. It will contain some things which your people will not want to see. Their argument will be, 'Why, with a 170 majority, do we have to give these things up to the Lib Dems?' But it's crucial. The coalition agreement is the boat in which we sail.

TB: But such an agreement is just a natural progression from our current position. And I have no difficulties with the concept, although doubtless we will have disagreements about individual policies.

We then returned to timing.

TB: I've still got problems with November, for the reasons you know about.

PA: Are you saying that you would prefer to go in the spring?

TB: Well, in a perfect world I would prefer November. But in the spring it would be possible to move, let's say, four Cabinet members, which would give us two and you two. Then I will at least have given my people a fair chance to prove their worth. On the other hand, I understand your point. The earlier we do it, the easier it will be.

PA: I think what you are really saying to me is that we had better plan for spring. I had been working to November. I can change to the spring – although it has consequences. Whenever we make this move, from my point of view, it must be seen to have come about through something that has benefit to us. You will recall that, when we initially thought of November, it was to have been made in the shadow of the announcement of the Electoral Reform Commission. We must think of something in the spring that 'opens the door' in the same way. Only one thing comes to mind immediately. The Electoral Reform Commission could produce its conclusions early; given that there won't be much contention about the system we arrive at, I see no reason why it should not announce its findings in the spring. These, along with your more 'constructive' words on PR, could provide exactly the right climate to go to the Full Monty then. Bear in mind, though, that by then we will have fought you all through the winter, especially on health and education . . .

TB: Don't be so sure. I'm not so stupid as to have a health crisis in the winter. Watch this space.

PA: Well, I hope not. As you know, that's been worrying me. And it's why I went to speak to Gordon.[1] I was interested in what he had to say. But I wasn't very

1 On 30 July I had met with Gordon Brown to discuss my fears of a winter crisis in the Health Service with him. The minute I did for the meeting records: 'I explained to the Chancellor at the start of our meeting that we all understood that the government had made more money available for next year. But it had first to deal with the crisis for this year. It would seriously damage trust in Labour and the support and confidence of their voters if the Labour government were, as we predicted, to preside over a crisis in the Health Service which was worse than that in any of the Conservative years. The Chancellor said that all the government's advice, and all the lobbying they had received both before and after coming into office, was to the effect that the real crisis in health would present itself not this year, but next. So that is where they had decided to concentrate resources. He believed the government was subject to a good deal of propagandizing from medical circles who were overstating the severity of the crisis this winter in order to get more funds.'

convinced that he would avoid a crisis in health this winter. And if I am right it will do you a lot of damage.

TB: Yes, but Gordon couldn't show you all his rabbits.

PA: Nevertheless, more time equals more risk . . . One further point: even if we had only a limited number of Cabinet positions, we would also need a spread of Lib Dems in junior government positions. That would be important for us.

He confirmed that this would be the case.

We had a brief discussion about elections. He said that if we were to join them that would cause problems for the next election. How would we overcome those, and what would we do about by-elections?

I replied that by-elections were the real problem. But if we were to go to AV as the interim stage before PR, that would solve the by-election problem in this current parliament and the next election shouldn't be a problem, either. We would not have to go around persuading people to stand down, since AV made it both unnecessary and unwise for any party to withdraw its candidate.

As I was leaving, I said, 'I just want to reinforce what I said earlier. I accept your preference for the spring. But my firm view remains that the risks will increase substantially if we delay.'

He responded, 'I know the risk. Maybe something will happen that will make November possible. But at the moment I can't see it.'

I left at 6.40pm.

Then back home through the crowds. London is in a strange mood. Sombre on the one hand, but somehow looking forward to tomorrow as well. Whitehall a mass of people; and an amazing number of flowers laid everywhere.

Saturday, 6 September, London

With Jane to Diana's funeral.

We walked through the crowds which thronged the pavements through Parliament Square and surged right up to the door of Westminster Abbey. As we walked by people insisted on shaking my hand. The mood was very bleak. One man dissolved into uncontrollable sobbing.

In through the great door of the Abbey, down one of the side aisles, into the choir. Virginia Bottomley and Willie Garnett on our right and, on our left, Ffion Jenkins and William Hague with Robin Cook on the other side. The place was very full and very quiet. In the aisle opposite us were Elton John and George Michael. A few politicians there, but not many. Past prime ministers in the top aisle on the other side of the choir: Thatcher and Denis, she looking imperious and he rather lost; Ted Heath large and thunderous; while Norma and John Major seemed just uncomfortable and out of place. We sat there for the best part of an hour. They played, among other pieces, the largo from Dvorak's *From the New World*, and Pachelbel's 'Canon'. Blair came in with Cherie, bareheaded, walking a few paces behind him. Then most of the royal family. God knows how many of them there were. All the little princesses and princes and dukes of this and earls of that. Far too many hangers-on. Then the Queen, the Duke of Edinburgh and the Spencer family.

A sudden hush and the music changed tone.

I watched the remote television camera just above me. It suddenly swung to the great West Door.

The coffin had arrived.

Then we began to hear the terrible soft, measured tramp of the feet of the guardsmen pallbearers. The sound at first was eerily distant, but became steadily louder and sent a chill through my heart. Then the coffin and the guardsmen entered the choir in a blaze of crimson and gold, moving as though burden and bearers were a single entity; and that steady tramp of foot on stone was now insistent, loud and reverberating in the pit of my stomach. I watched the guardsmen strain as they placed the lead-lined coffin covered by the Royal Standard on to the bier in front of the altar. They adjusted the huge pile of lilies on top, on which lay a single card bearing the word 'Mummy'.

Following the coffin, Charles and the children and Earl Spencer. What a mass of red hair Harry has! And how Wills looks, almost shockingly, like his mother.

Then Verdi's *Requiem*. The hairs on the back of my neck stood up. I looked up at the window on the west side and there, through a clear pane among the stained glass, I could see a piercing blue sky with, suddenly, clouds scudding across it. And all the time those wonderful notes rising higher and higher. The pagan rhythms of Verdi seemed somehow absolutely apt.

Then, after the appropriate anthems, a couple of poems read by Diana's sisters, followed by Blair, who read his lesson [1 Corinthians 13] with too much theatrical emphasis for my taste. Those words are good enough on their own. They are better said plainly – even softly.

Then Elton John. 'Candle in the Wind'. How he did it, I do not know. I've never particularly liked his music, but in this context it was intensely moving.

Then Earl Spencer.

What a speech.

He castigated the press and fired some bitter barbs at the royal family. (Ill-judged, I thought. The real people we should be thinking about at this time are the princes. It will do them no good to have their uncle criticize the family into which they were born and in which they must continue to live.)

Throughout the service, and especially during the Elton John song, I could hear what sounded like the pitter-patter of raindrops on the roof. It was the crowd clapping outside. At the end of Earl Spencer's speech, the pitter-patter turned into a thunderous wave of sound. Suddenly it wasn't just outside. It seemed to have been picked up inside the apse and ran forward towards us, like a ripple, right into the chapel. Everybody was clapping, even Wills and Harry. As though the immense torrent of public emotion had suddenly burst through the protocol of state and broken over Diana's coffin. Shocked, I noticed that Charles wasn't clapping, and nor were the Queen or the Duke of Edinburgh. I was amazed to hear afterwards that the TV cameras had missed this crucial tiny moment, which would have scandalized the crowd outside.

[Later I heard that, at Hyde Park, where the service was being televised on a large screen, the crowd rose at the end of Spencer's speech to a spontaneous standing ovation – thousands of them.]

Then the commendation of the body.

And finally, the guardsmen again, this time coming back into the chapel for their burden almost as strangers. Again their muscles strained as they lifted her on to their shoulders. Then slowly they turned with their heavy load and marched back down the aisle and out of sight, the terrible tramp of feet ebbing away to diminuendo and then silence.

The Queen went out first. Then Earl Spencer, his face ashen from the strain of his speech. Next Charles, looking drained and wounded. The young princes seemed composed, but with sadness drawn on their faces. We followed. There was the usual wait just inside the West Door as the great and the good got into their cars and left. I used the opportunity to find and congratulate Elton John.

Jane and I left, to be swallowed up into the crowd, all flowing towards us from Parliament Square. There were tearstains on many of their faces.

Thursday, 11 September, Wales and London

An interview I gave to the *New Statesman* on the possibility of a coalition with Blair has been published today. My intention was to get the Party thinking about what is on the horizon. I also wanted to gauge where the opposition is coming from. The latter, at least, seems to have worked. Much consternation from the usual quarters, especially Conrad Russell[1] and Lembit Opik among others. Nick South grumpy about the fact that I have, as he sees it, thrown a hand grenade into the conference. I told him I didn't want a cotton-wool conference.

My second intention in all this is to push Blair. If I get a furious reaction from the Party at conference, it will strengthen my hand when we start to negotiate seriously.

After a day's campaigning in Wales, back to London for the Federal Executive (FE) meeting at 6 o'clock. Here, as I had anticipated, there was a long discussion about the *New Statesman* article, and a lot of anger. I answered criticism by saying that the next few years would be bumpy and I couldn't consult them on everything.

Hugh Dykes has formally joined us today. There has been a good deal of publicity, with which he has coped well.

After the FE Bob Maclennan said he wanted to speak to me, so we arranged to meet tomorrow. I am worried. I think he may have decided we shouldn't go ahead.

Tuesday, 16 September, London

Bob came to see me at 11 o'clock. We spent an hour together. As I suspected, he has contracted a thorough dose of cold feet. He thinks we have got off to a bad start. He presumes this is because the government is deliberately ignoring us. I think it is because they have been too busy to think straight. The old conflict between the politics of conspiracy and cock-up.

This, however, was a prelude to the main thing he wanted to speak to me about. I had a sense of what was coming. There are occasions with Bob when you can smell the fuse burning and have to simply sit there and wait for the bomb to go off. He came out firmly and strenuously against TFM

1 Earl Russell, Lib Dem hereditary peer and Professor of Heritage at King's College, London.

in November, saying it ought to be delayed. I said, 'In other words, you have joined the Augustinian tendency. We should do it, but not yet. I just don't believe that's right. If we don't do it now, we won't be able to do it at all.'

Bob complained bitterly that we were having this conversation in the office rather than in a more relaxed situation.

Later in the day, I caught him at the [FPC] meeting and said that perhaps we should get together in the week after the Party Conference – could he come down to see us in Somerset? I told him that I couldn't succeed without his support and that his opposition was a devastating blow.

He became stronger and more bitter: 'I am President of the Party and I carry a lot of votes. I am sorry, but that is the way I feel.'

Bob thinks we need to get the whole PR deal stitched up first, and doesn't agree with me that, if we did this, the Party would simply turn round and say, 'We have everything we need, why go into partnership with Labour?'

A fairly tetchy conversation.

This is seriously bad news. If Bob comes out against, then I have no one left in the Parliamentary Party, apart from Ming. And that will not be enough. I will ask Roy to put pressure on Bob as well when he talks to him. Home at 8.30. I cooked myself a pie from the freezer with the usual accompaniment of peas. To bed about midnight. Disturbed about Bob – and tomorrow is our first Joint Cabinet Committee meeting, too.

Wednesday, 17 September, Westminster

At 1.45 I strolled down Whitehall in the sunshine with Alan, Bob, Richard and Ming to Downing Street for the first JCC meeting. Outside the door of No. 10 we stopped for a quick photo op before entering. The meeting started promptly at 2.00. The Labour members[1] of the committee sat on one side of the Cabinet table and we sat on the other. The press came in for some more shots, then Blair shooed them out, took off his jacket and we got straight down to business.

It was an exceptionally warm and friendly meeting, during which Robin Cook, who sat next to Blair, had one or two sharp digs at Straw. Mandelson, a silent brooding presence, sat opposite Richard, chipping in only twice. Ann Taylor, leaning forward and enthusiastically playing

1 Blair, Cook, Straw, Mandelson and Ann Taylor.

weathervane to whatever Blair said. Extraordinary, given that she had apparently been so hostile to all this previously. But she couldn't have been nicer.

The pebble-glassed Jack Straw was owlish and mischievous, as I thought he would be.

At the start, when Alan Beith said something, Blair quickly chipped in with, 'No doubt that accounts for your acerbic comments on the *Today* programme.' I noted that Alan wrote down the word 'acerbic' twice and circled it. Whatever Alan had said on the *Today* programme, it had obviously gone home. But so what? There has to be a hard man in all this and Alan makes a very good one.

Ann Taylor, however, chimed in with a loud 'Yes!' when Blair made this comment and sat nodding her head vigorously like a parcel-shelf dog.

On our side Richard was good, if at times a little delphic. Though Ming said little, he said it effectively. Bob was slow and measured, as ever. But our star was Alan, who was tremendous: sharp and on the ball. He was very convincing, putting our case across confidently without any kind of sycophancy. I was glad to have him there.

Fascinating watching Blair. He really is growing into his role. Gone is all that diffidence and his constant deferrence to Mandelson. He was relaxed and in control of the whole thing. He has adopted an interesting way of pausing in his sentences while he seems to be making up his mind, which makes you believe that he really is thinking about what he says. Whenever there was a difficulty, Blair simply said, 'We'll have a look at that, but there should be a way round it.' He seems serious about genuinely doing business with us and appears determined to make a success of it.

The meeting lasted for ninety minutes and we covered all the ground we wanted to. We left by the front door, stopping to do some press interviews on the way out.

Thursday, 18 September, Westminster

At 8 o'clock a co-ordinating group meeting. I have been getting reverberations of some kind of ambush which is being prepared for me at conference. I have suddenly got the measure of it. Resolutions being put down to ban any talks with 'other parties' on coalitions. I had a discussion with Liz Barker,[1] Paul Tyler and Nick Harvey on how to ride this off.

At 11.30 a meeting with Shirley Williams. She wanted to see me after sending me a letter voicing her concerns about the direction in which the party was going (i.e. towards Labour). She said she agrees with the broad strategy but thinks it would be better to go later rather than sooner. Yet another Augustinian! I took her through some of the reasons why earlier would be better, without letting her know that anything was definite. But

1 Baroness Liz Barker, chair of the Lib Dem Conference Committee.

I suspect she will have added two and two together. She is keen to help, so I asked her whether at conference she could remind the Party just what a historic moment this was. She said she would.

Friday, 19 September, Westminster

THE DAY AFTER THE WELSH REFERENDUM ON DEVOLUTION

[*The Scottish Referendum had been held on 11 September and produced a clear majority of 74.3 per cent in favour of devolution.*]

Woke at 7.00 expecting to hear that the Welsh referendum had not resulted in a substantial majority in favour, as everyone anticipated. In fact the outcome was even tighter than I had feared: a margin in favour of only 0.6 per cent! So I had quite a lot of press to do. Blair, curiously, has said that the government may have to think more delicately about Wales. But this would seem to be encouraging the Tories to make mischief, so I went flat out, saying that a majority was a majority and we now needed to make the Welsh Parliament a success.

At 8.30 Liz Barker came to see me. She wanted to talk about how to handle the conference. I am very sure now about what needs to be done. Though whether I can persuade the Party to it is a different matter. But at last I am beginning to enjoy my politics again. My life is worst when I am trying to decide which route to take, or when I can't see any opening for us. But now I can see it very clearly. I am committed to going for TFM and am now personally ready to take the consequences if I fail. Having made a decision makes my life much, much easier. It removes all the tension from trying to lead.

Sunday, 21 September, Eastbourne

PARTY CONFERENCE

I had expected a fairly easy Parliamentary Party meeting at 11.30, and it was – to start with. Paul Tyler took us through the programme. Nothing contentious there. Then Phil Willis suddenly opened up, saying that I had once again bounced them on coalition.

This started a furious round of discussion in which a good deal of heat was generated, chiefly from the new MPs. Jim Wallace very pointedly put me on the spot on coalitions. I gave as firm an answer as I could, but not firm enough for most of them. I saw several looks darting between them. At one stage Jim, thinking I hadn't noticed, used his hand to make a kind of tipping movement, indicating that I was sitting on the fence trying to keep my options open. I rounded on him hard.

I left the meeting feeling depressed. It is clear that the majority of MPs will oppose anything I do.

Afterwards I invited Phil and a number of others, including Ed Davey and Paul Burstow, to my room so that I could tell them where I was coming from and what I was trying to achieve.

In an attempt to be helpful, I discovered later, Phil then went and told a journalist that I had explained things and reassured him. The press turned this into 'Paddy Ashdown beats up Phil Willis and brings him into line'. I bumped into Phil at the bar later on and said that I knew he was only trying to be helpful, but he really mustn't do this. He is still a little inexperienced; nevertheless, in my view, one of the rising stars of the Party.

In the afternoon a members' consultative session on strategy in the conference centre at which I was again strongly criticized, with some people openly saying that I was proposing to sacrifice the Party for a Cabinet seat. If it goes on like this I will lose and lose badly.

I begin to think it will be impossible to lead the Party to where I think it has to go. I said as much to Jane in a fit of depression. 'Oh good,' she said, 'then you can resign this week and I can have you back.'

Wednesday, 24 September, Eastbourne

THE DAY OF MY CONFERENCE SPEECH

The PPM at 11 o'clock. One of our activists, David Howarth,[1] wants to introduce a motion tomorrow that will rule out the possibility of coalitions. A long discussion on this. It was finally agreed that we would try to stop the motion going ahead. But, to my horror, almost everybody said that if the Howarth motion does get put down, they would vote for it. I managed to persuade them this would be silly. Far better to keep our options open. Although I agreed to have a full debate on party strategy in the spring.

Jackie Ballard, sitting at the other end of the table, muttered 'rubbish' when I said we should keep our options open. She and Phil Willis, among

---

1 Lib Dem parliamentary candidate. Member of the FPC and leader of the Lib Dems on Cambridge City Council.

others, said that they would vote against any possibility of a coalition at this stage. However, in the end they agreed to keep the options open for the moment, with Mike Hancock[1] being particularly supportive. The motion was avoided and a dangerous moment passed, though it was a very close-run thing and took up far too much time.

Thursday, 25 September, Eastbourne

FINAL DAY OF CONFERENCE

At the end of the conference we had an hour-long Jo Group meeting at which we discussed timing. Everyone thought we had moved the Party forward at conference, but that it was still very, very dicey. I would probably lose in the present circumstances. To my surprise, they all now think that next spring is better than this autumn for TFM. But I find this position illogical. The later we do it, the more difficult it will be.

I don't *think* this is cold feet. Just muddled thinking.

Sunday, 28 September, Siena

THE PONTIGNANO CONFERENCE[2]

Up at 7.30. From the monastery terrace, Siena, perched on top of its hill six or seven miles away in the early morning sunlight, resembled a scene in a medieval painting, the outlines of the duomo, campanile, towers and palaces surrounded by olive groves and cypresses bustling against the clear blue sky. The deep reverberations of the cathedral bells sounded across the valley.

Over lunch I had a long chat with the Tory MEP John Stevens, after which he suggested a walk in the monastery gardens. Here he told me that he and others wanted to launch a centre right breakaway from the Tories. (They didn't want to join us.)

I asked how would they, and in particular Kenneth Clarke, react to an early referendum on monetary union? He said that Clarke would, of course, join the other pro-European Tories on the 'Yes' campaign and afterwards,

1 Member of Parliament (SDP, then Lib Dem) for Portsmouth South since 1984.
2 A conference held annually in the monastery of Pontignano, near Siena, between senior British and Italian politicians and businessmen.

if there was PR, break away from the Tories and lead such a centre right grouping. But he would do so only if there was PR at Westminster, as this would guarantee their survival. I asked Stevens specifically if he was passing on this message directly from Clarke. He said he was.[1]

At 2.15 off for the airport with Ralf Dahrendorf and Paolo Galli, the Italian Ambassador to London.

I had a fascinating discussion with Ralf in the back of the Jaguar, while Galli sat in the front seat trying to pretend he wasn't listening.

I told Ralf more or less everything that was happening. He agreed that we had only one option: to go in with Blair, even if the situation was less than perfect. To do otherwise would be to risk the party being marginalized. Either way, our survival was at stake. Ralf's view, which was very sanguine, was that we should be there to influence Blair, even if we did get swallowed up in the process. He tells me that is what has happened to liberalism elsewhere. The paradox is that the more our liberal ideas, thoughts and policies are applied by everybody else, the weaker European liberal parties have become, except in Britain. Ralf's view is that parties are not permanent structures, anyway: they come, they make their contribution and they go. Perhaps liberalism in Britain, as in the rest of Europe, will simply become a way of thought rather than a political party, he suggested. (I disagreed.) Either way, now is the moment for us to use the strength gained at the last election to reshape British politics and drive forward the process of modernization. He was quite emotional in expressing his support and promised to throw his weight unequivocally behind any steps I make towards TFM.

I may not have the numbers on my side. But I am slowly accumulating many of the voices who are most respected and influential both in the Party and outside.

Monday, 6 October, Edinburgh

A DAY'S CAMPAIGNING IN SCOTLAND

After dinner at a local Italian with Lembit, I returned with Ming and Elspeth to their house, and we sat down over a whisky and talked through the finer details of the situation with Labour, including who would be in

---

1 I have since checked this with Kenneth Clarke, who categorically denies this – a truth which becomes obvious later on.

the Cabinet (Ming and Alan), and the likelihood of getting it through the Party.

We stayed up talking until about 1.00am. Ming is fully on board, but his judgement, like mine, is that if Howarth's resolution banning coalition had got on to the floor of the conference at Eastbourne, the majority of the Parliamentary Party would have voted for it. Ming thinks we need to work on the new people a lot more. I told him I thought that, in the end, it would be quite difficult for the Party to reject a coalition if it was based round policies with which we agreed and if its most senior and talented people – Roy Jenkins, Shirley Williams, Bill Rodgers, Ming Campbell, Alan Beith, Bob Maclennan, Ralf Dahrendorf – all argued for it.

Wednesday, 8 October, Somerset

To the South Somerset District Council to catch up on council matters. As I arrived I received a message that Blair wanted to talk to me.

The call came through at 1.45. This was a relatively long conversation, summing up our post-conference positions and looking ahead to November.

I said I thought Labour had had a successful conference, and had achieved everything they needed. They must feel very pleased about it.

TB: From where I was, you looked pretty much in control of your party. You have obviously got some people who don't agree. But I take it that you now have the endorsement you were seeking for the strategy you are following.

I replied that it had not been as easy as it looked; there were still some deep-seated suspicions, especially among our new MPs. But at least we had solidified our position. My strategy with the party has always been to move them on a few inches at a time. We had done that and given ourselves a little more room for further progress.

PA: How do you see the future now? Do you still want to go ahead, and if so, when?

TB: I still want to go ahead. But I am having some difficulties deciding exactly when I should do the reshuffle. I am now being strongly urged to do it sooner rather than later. So it is still possible for November. But I haven't made up my mind yet. I think we should have dinner and decide what routes are now open to us.

PA: You know my views. Most of my advisers take the opposite view to you and me, and think it would be better in the spring than in November. But I continue to believe the earlier the better.

I also pointed out that a decision one way or the other would be needed pretty soon. Apart from anything else, we had the Winchester by-election coming up on 20 November, and I didn't want TFM to happen before then. It would confuse the electorate and it would be damaging if the first event that occurred after TFM was a defeat by the Tories in a by-election. Secondly, we had a lot of work to do if we were to set this up by November. We therefore needed a clear decision from him as soon as possible.

He promised to make a final decision very shortly. He suggested another dinner with Roy and Peter Mandelson. [I later tried to fix up a date with Roy, but we couldn't co-ordinate our diaries for another three weeks, so it would either have to be myself, Blair and Mandelson, without Roy, or wait until the House returned. My instinct was not to wait.]

At the end of our conversation I raised the question of the leaks which occurred during Labour's conference. [The Sunday Times had published a story, clearly inspired by a Labour leak, on possible outcomes of the Electoral Reform Commission.] I explained that my concern now was that so much was being leaked by them that everything we wanted to keep secret for the longer term was in danger of becoming a subject for public discussion. For instance, I had been horrified to note the speculation in Monday's Independent about the finesse that we had set up with AV as an interim step towards full PR in a second parliament. There were only five people who knew about this, I pointed out: himself, Peter Mandelson, Roy Jenkins, Richard Holme and me. He saw the point immediately.

Sunday, 12 October, Somerset

Watched Hague's end of conference speech on Thursday. Pretty impressive. He is a good orator; probably a better natural orator than either Blair or myself. He has had good crits, and he deserves them. So now I have two competitors on the political scene. One who is eleven years younger than me and is Prime Minister; the other who is twenty years younger than me.

On a walk through the fields on Thursday I said to Jane that I was really looking forward to giving up. Time for somebody younger to take over. The Party would probably choose Charles Kennedy, I thought.

I had it in mind at the same time to give up the Yeovil seat. I had said when I was elected that I would retire at 60. Anyway, party leaders are an embarrassment, hanging round the House after they stand down.[1] In addition I want to do other things with my life, though I'm not yet sure what.

Jane and I discussed this at great length and we concluded that I should stand down at next year's Spring Conference. We could then use the dinner the Yeovil constituency Lib Dems are planning in June (for the anniversary of my ten years as leader and fifteen as MP) as a celebration of a task finished rather than the years notched up. Hopefully they won't mind. I can't, of course, let on at all.

Today's papers make fascinating reading. The Tories are breaking up behind the scenes; Hague is competent, but his party will need to go through a long period of catharsis before it settles down again. And the more I think about it, the surer I am that Winchester will be crucial. If we go flat out for validation of 'constructive opposition' at Winchester and win, then I can pocket that as a success, which will help me persuade Blair to go for TFM pretty well straightaway. Which would make it more difficult for the party to oppose. And after that I can bed the process in, before handing over to my successor. But much depends on Blair delivering, and delivering early. Equally, if we go down at Winchester everything will be lost – including me.

Wednesday, 15 October, Westminster

To the Methodist Central Hall for the first PPM of the new session of parliament. Malcolm Bruce questioned the whole idea of constructive opposition, suggesting that some of us should attack Labour (i.e. himself) while others should continue to be nice to them (i.e. me). I said I couldn't see the sense in this. It would only confuse. We must have a flexible policy and use our intelligence in choosing our tactics, our people and our opportunities according to circumstances so as to get the best for ourselves.

Then Phil Willis had a go at me for a speech I had made in Cardiff on student funding which he said departed from party policy. I asked him

---

1 Jane reminds me that I quoted Gladstone's comment about past prime ministers during this conversation: 'Past prime ministers are like untethered battleships in the harbour' (i.e. they are capable of doing a lot of damage).

where he had got that from and he pulled out a Welsh Labour Party leaflet. I told him he shouldn't base his arguments on Labour leaflets.

Then Steve Webb. He said that when I'd rebuked Richard Livsey for saying that the £300 million Labour had put into the Health Service was peanuts, he hadn't expected to hear me defend Labour. I told him I wasn't defending Labour, I was defending rational argument. One of the Lib Dems' most valuable, and hard-won, qualities is that the public by and large trust us because they believe we tell the truth. But if we use too much overheated language, that trust will be diminished.

Norman Baker said that we couldn't enter into a relationship with Labour without being stuffed in the process. I replied that what angers me most about the Party as a whole is its lack of self-confidence. We seem to believe that whenever we get into negotiations with anyone else, we are bound to lose. I don't expect that from MPs.

Thursday, 16 October, London and France

Off to France today. Wonderful.

On the way to the ferry I heard from Richard Holme about his meeting with Mandelson on Monday. Among other things, they had talked about personalities and Richard had made the point that we needed three Lib Dems in the Cabinet. Mandelson, apparently, thinks I'm dotty for not wanting to be in the Cabinet. He wondered what my reaction might be to Education.

Last night I also had a report back from Sean[1] on the meeting he attended with Jack Straw, Alan Beith and Bob Maclennan. Sean was pretty gloomy. Straw, he said, was being arrogant, close-minded and difficult. And determined to drive the Electoral Reform Commission remit back to including AV as a possible outcome by itself.

We may have to come back to AV; but that is for a later finesse. It would be intolerable, however, given how hard we had fought the issue in the Cook/Maclennan talks, if the Electoral Reform Commission was to be set up on the basis that the outcome could be a non-proportional system.

I instructed both Sean and Richard to tell their opposite numbers (Powell and Mandelson) that if Labour were now reneging on their commitment to the Electoral Reform Commission producing a proportional system,

---

1 Sean O'Grady, my new Press Secretary and head of office.

then that was a deal breaker for us. I hope and believe Straw is operating on his own and without Blair's agreement.

I spoke to Bob later about the meeting with Straw. He said it had been difficult, but not as cataclysmic as Sean had made out.

Saturday, 18 October, Irancy

Woken up by a phone call from Sean saying that Brown had given an interview to *The Times* on the euro, in which he said little new, but Charlie Whelan[1] had briefed that it was actually meant to make clear that Britain could not join the euro in this parliament. This, along with the other messages we are getting that the government intends to ditch its commitment to proportionality for the Electoral Reform Commission, would kill off the whole project. I felt pretty depressed all morning.

At about 12.00 Jane and I put together a picnic and walked up through the vines, on to the ridge above Irancy and towards St Bris. At the top of the ridge we stopped for lunch, looking down across the whole of the Yonne plain. The vines are wonderful colours: the *aligote* still green, the *pinot noir* a deep, deep red, and the *César* autumn gold, the whole combining into a patchwork quilt of greens and golds and crimsons. The countryside seems almost blue from the haze of heat. But autumn is just over the horizon.

Monday, 20 October, Irancy

Did a telephone interview for *The World at One* yesterday. Labour have got themselves into a terrible mess over the single currency. Brown is trying to refine their 'wait-and-see' position in order to stop speculation. I spoke to Alastair Campbell before doing the interview, saying I didn't want to damage our relationship with them, but Brown has made such a mess of it that he may have inadvertently opted out of joining the single currency before the next election. In which case, of course, any strengthening of our relationship with the government would be out of the question. Campbell said that the whole farrago had been about them trying to clarify their position. 'Not very successfully, then,' I retorted.

1 Gordon Brown's Press Secretary.

Campbell, however, assured me that Brown's statement and the spin put on it were not intended to close all options on the single currency before the next election. He asked me whether I would give them room to make a statement on this when Parliament returned after the recess, rather than put the pressure on tomorrow. Also, would I say that when Brown did make his statement to Parliament, I hoped he would leave the options open? I agreed to do this, but not uncritically. My words in the interview were: 'Uncertain government, unconvincing politics and extremely questionable economics.'

Spoke to Richard. He has amended the remit for the Electoral Reform Commission. He has produced a good text, which he will now submit to Labour.

Work dogs me everywhere.

Tuesday, 21 October, Westminster

Popped down to see Roy at about 3.40 to plan what we wanted to achieve out of tonight's meeting: a clear timetable for TFM; and that he should chair the Electoral Reform Commission, whose remit must include the words 'broad proportionality'. I also suggested to Roy that we make it clear to Labour that their foolish handling of the euro question [Brown's recent statement] had given rise to the perception that they were closing the options for joining the single currency this parliament, and that this was totally unacceptable to us.

Roy said it would be interesting to see what kind of mood they are in. He anticipated that Blair would be feeling pretty bruised. They had had a terrible weekend: this business with the euro has been their first really big mistake.

We agreed to arrive at Downing Street separately, at about 7.40. He was driving back from Oxford and would go to the front of No. 10. I would arrive on foot via the Cabinet Office at 70 Whitehall.

In the event I arrived first and was shown into Blair's flat at No. 11 by an ex-corporal with whom I served in the Royal Marines in Borneo in the 1960s. Blair was in the drawing-room, sitting in his shirtsleeves and jeans in the middle of the sofa to the left of the fireplace, with Peter Mandelson opposite him in a shirt and tie. On the table between them was a bottle of Mâcon-Villages. Blair poured me a glass and I plonked myself next to Mandelson. Shortly after, Roy arrived.

I wished Mandelson a happy birthday (he is 44) and he made some joke along the lines of, 'That's the difference between the two leaders. You remember my birthday; he didn't know anything about it!' Blair pretended to wince. When I asked him how he was, he smiled wanly and said that they had had a bloody awful few days over the euro thing.

Ten minutes later Jonathan Powell came in, saying, 'I have fixed for you to speak to the President [Clinton] in about ten minutes, so you will have to be ready for that. But I have given you an excuse to cut him short by saying that you were on your way to a banquet.'

Blair explained that Clinton was about to announce an initiative on the environment ('He is very serious about global warming, you know') and wanted to speak to him. He said they speak about twice a week.

We soon got down to discussing EMU. They really have it in for Charlie Whelan. Mandelson was very dismissive, at one stage saying that he hoped Whelan would go away and boil his head. Also, that Gordon Brown couldn't easily do another U-turn. Having let it be believed that the government were not keen on monetary union in this parliament, he couldn't change his position again without 'losing even more credibility'.

PA: Better to suffer a little damage to the ego and get the right policy than preserve one's ego and have to live with the wrong one.

Jonathan nodded vigorously.

PA: Of course, with a chancellor, it is more than just ego. His credibility is at stake. So I understand where you are coming from. But the position you have got yourselves into is crazy. Particularly since you have a real opportunity here to divide the Tories permanently if you go for a referendum on the euro, perhaps even as early as next year.

I got the impression that Mandelson and Powell have been recommending this course of action as well.

I added that I thought it was also very bad politics to delay the single currency decision until the next election: it would in effect become a euro currency election (or perhaps a euro/PR election), which would play right into the hands of the Tories.

TB: No, if we put the referendum the other side of the election, we won't have a euro election, as everybody will defer that decision until later.

PA: On which subject, I want to pass on some information that you may not have heard.

I told him of my conversation with John Stevens at Pontignano in which he purported to pass a message from Ken Clarke, which had now been further reinforced, I added, by a meeting between Alan Watson[1] and Geoffrey Howe,[2] in which the latter had said much the same kind of thing. Perhaps it would be a good idea for them to get someone alongside Stevens to confirm all this?

Roy Jenkins said to Blair: 'You are in great danger of having this issue of Europe undermine your government, just as it did for so many prime ministers before you, including Mrs Thatcher. But if you seize this moment, then you can shape events and not have events shape you. The latest opinion polls show only 57 per cent against a single currency, with 37 per cent in favour. It is amazing that those figures are so good, given that no one has yet argued the case for a single currency. You are in a far better position than we were when we started the 1974 referendum on entry into the Common Market. Then we won by two to one, even though the polls initially showed 70–30 against.'

'I've looked at this very closely,' said Blair, 'and I do not believe we can win over public opinion yet.'

'Look, I will be very blunt on this,' replied Roy. 'You have to choose between leading in Europe or having Murdoch on your side. You can have one but not both.'

'Well, I'm not so sure about that. Murdoch seems to be shifting his position. I think we now have him at the point at which, at the very least, he is prepared to judge the euro question on economics rather than "patriotism". I think we can get him on side if we move at the right pace.'

There followed a brief discussion about other press barons, including Conrad Black (who will never be in favour) and Lord Rothermere (who, Roy Jenkins said – and Blair agreed – would probably go along with it, when push came to shove).

The discussion returned to what had happened at the weekend. Roy couldn't understand how the meeting between Blair and Gordon Brown on the preceding Thursday had become public knowledge. 'When I used to meet Wilson for a chat in that little room between No. 10 and No. 11,

---

1 An expert and adviser to me on Europe. Alan is now a member of the House of Lords.
2 Leader of the House. Member of Parliament (Conservative) for Bebington 1964–6, Reigate 1970–74, Surrey East 1974–92. Member of the Conservative government, most notably as Deputy Prime Minister, Chancellor of the Exchequer and Foreign Secretary. He is now a member of the House of Lords.

it never became public knowledge. How on earth did this information get out?'

At this both Blair and Mandelson exploded. There never had been such a meeting. The story was entirely concocted by the *Observer*. And Jonathan added, rather ruefully, from the corner, 'In fact, there was not even a discussion beyond a one-and-a-half-minute phone call that day. They agreed to speak again later but never did. I know, because I listened in on it.' Peter Mandelson chipped in that the first he knew about the spin being put on the Brown interview was when he opened the papers later on Friday night. Clearly a significant breakdown of internal communications, with Mandelson's annoyance with Brown clearly showing through. He was again exceedingly rude about Whelan.

I said, 'Well, our view is that, while it's unlikely that Britain will join the single currency in 1999, we should not close off options. It is perfectly possible that we will not actually join the single currency before the next election, if that election is held early in 2001. But to close off the possibility of entry into the euro before the next election now would be folly. None of what we proposed doing together can happen if you take that course.'

At this point, and before Blair could respond, the housekeeper came in to say that President Clinton was on the phone. Blair left and the discussion continued between Roy, Peter, Jonathan and myself. I said that I simply couldn't understand the logic of their position: if the case they were making was that entering the euro or not was dependent on whether it would benefit Britain economically, it was simply dotty to say that the decision would be driven by the electoral timetable. Both Mandelson and Powell seem to favour an early referendum.

After about ten minutes Blair came back in saying, 'Well, that was the shortest phone call I've ever had with the President.'

There followed an amusing discussion about what other world leaders were like on the phone. Roy asked Blair whether the President was very loquacious. Blair replied, 'No, he's not actually. He usually gets through business reasonably well. Like all of us, he can sometimes go on a bit, but he is by no means the worst.'

The conversation then turned to Blair's own dealings with European leaders. He apparently speaks to Jospin in French (his French must be good), but with Kohl he uses a translator, a lady who always accompanies Kohl and is much trusted by him. Whenever Kohl goes on a bit, she gives Blair the shortened English translation and rolls her eyes heavenwards.

TB: Our European partners aren't at all fussed by the position we have taken on the euro, you know. They are quite happy with it, provided we join in the end – which they think we will do. The economics will require it.

I forbore to say that of course they took this view: the longer we didn't join, the more influence the French and Germans would have over it.

PA: It seems to me that a referendum on the euro next year has a number of distinct advantages. Firstly, it will bring down the value of the pound, which you want. Secondly, it will bring down interest rates, which you are probably less keen on since that may overheat the economy, although you can take compensating measures. Thirdly, it will increase immensely Britain's bargaining power in Europe. Fourthly, it will show that when you say you want to lead in Europe you understand, as Roy has said, that you can't lead from the sidelines. And lastly it will split the Tories early, before Hague can get a grip on them.

TB: OK, I've got the message on Europe. I know how strongly you guys feel about this.

At this point we moved to the table.

Dinner was a crab starter, followed by some kind of chops in bread-crumbs. We stuck with the Mâcon-Villages, and a rather nice claret.

During dinner Cherie came in to say that the kids wanted Tony to go and say goodnight to them. Kathryn had come in earlier to say goodnight to her father and, it was obvious, to say hello to Roy Jenkins (whom she had not met before). Cherie was very jolly and cheerful, but retired saying that she would leave us to talk about 'serious things' while she went off to do some 'light-hearted work'.

We then turned to the Electoral Reform Commission.

TB: Let's decide where we want to get to. Are you still happy to approach this in two stages? The first would be AV for the next election; the second, full pro-portionality after that. The Commission could recommend the ultimate destination, but ought in our view to recommend the intervening staging-post of AV as well, using the phrase 'The government may want to do this in two stages'.

I responded that we were perfectly happy to stick with this formula, on which we had already agreed.

There followed a long discussion on a draft remit which Richard Holme had circulated, at the end of which we agreed that we should shorten it and maintain the words 'broadly proportional' but not repeat them. They could spin on to their side that AV would be considered, whilst we could argue, legitimately, that since the result had to be broadly proportional, AV by itself could not be the final outcome, only part of it.

Blair explained that he was under serious pressure on all this from his back benchers.

TB: In a strange way, it is more difficult to control our party in government than out. They are getting very uptight indeed about the fact that you are providing more effective opposition than the Tories, whilst I am giving you almost everything you want. This is difficult for me. That's why I need to be sure I can include AV, at least for consideration, by the Electoral Reform Commission.

PA: It must be tough. I have difficulties with my party, too. But our bottom line is that we made an agreement with Cook/Maclennan which we see as the foundation stone of our co-operation. You have also committed yourselves to the Electoral Reform Commission considering 'a proportional system' in your manifesto. If you renege on that you will be reneging both on the foundation of our partnership and on your own manifesto, which would be very serious. But if you go along the lines we have agreed, then I should think that would be OK. I want a little time to think about the implications of all this, but I can undertake to give you a firm answer by tomorrow.

Then Roy said, looking straight at Blair, 'You have not yet asked me formally to do this. If you want me to do it, you will have to find five or ten minutes to spend with me alone to discuss it. There are some points I want you to consider on AV: I am prepared to consider it, but not as a final solution.'

They agreed to discuss this at a later date.

I warned Blair that I am going to launch a winter campaign tomorrow against the underfunding of education and health. There followed a quite strenuous conversation between myself and Peter Mandelson, at the end of which I said to Blair, 'Look, we have narrowed our opposition down to the issue of funding the public services. We must have room to oppose you where we disagree. I will try to make sure that we don't use overheated or unrealistic language. But until we formally join with you, you cannot remove from us all powers of opposition. Health and education funding will be a difficult line, but it is the only line we have to play at the moment. I am going to have to ask you to be patient about it.'

Blair nodded in agreement and turned the subject to PR for the European Elections. He assured us, backed up by Mandelson, that he was very keen to get the legislation through, not least for their own purposes (a cull of

Labour MEPs?). But there was a considerable problem with overcrowding of the government's legislative programme.

'It's not up to us to decide how you programme your legislation,' I said. 'But if this fails because you allow it to be obstructed by anti-PR elements in Labour, cheered on by the Tories, then the project itself will be in mortal danger.'

At this point we moved back to the sitting-room and started talking about TFM. Blair said again that there were two people he could easily move out of the Cabinet at the moment, but he was really worried about the reaction from the party. All his instincts were to go early. Mandelson agreed. Jonathan let slip that he had been in favour of going for a coalition straight after the election and couldn't understand why Blair and I had let the moment slip. Blair said that he also wished we'd done it then, but now he wasn't sure whether he could carry his party. I said that, whatever we do, we must not do it before the Winchester by-election.

After a long discussion, in which both Roy and I pressed the case for an earlier attempt at TFM, we finally reluctantly agreed to delay it until May. Blair expressed concern about whether it was possible for us to fight each other at the local elections; I responded by saying that we must be able to operate our politics at different levels in different parts of the country.

Blair agreed that, when the Electoral Reform Commission was announced, he would make what we have come to refer to as the 'comfortable words' about his readiness to accept its findings. He might also say there was no reason in principle why the Liberal Democrats should not be in government. His aim would be to try to get his party used to the idea.

I responded by saying that this would immediately stimulate a huge debate in my party, but I wasn't unhappy about it. I would have to face it anyway at the Spring Conference, so his words might give me a context in which to do so. This would also enable me to see the extent of opposition from within, and to soften up opinion for TFM when it came. 'But,' I added, 'I believe firmly that the longer we leave this the more difficult it will get. If we wait until next year, the risks of failure are much higher.'

Blair said that in the end he didn't think he could go earlier than May next year, as he would have to prepare the ground.

We concluded that there might well be a small reshuffle of, let's say, two this autumn, followed by perhaps four next May [two of which would make way for Lib Dems]. We also agreed to announce the Electoral Reform Commission and its remit probably after the Joint Cabinet Committee of 4 November. And Blair may drop some comments about the Lib Dems being in government, but not until after the Winchester by-election on 20 November. At which point we could make the appropriate responses.

We turned to discussing my position, and I again explained my reasons for not wanting to be in the first Cabinet.

To my surprise, Roy, who has been opposed to this up until now, said that he thought that I had made a rather cogent argument, and we tacitly agreed to go ahead on this basis.

After a brief discussion on who should be on the Electoral Reform Commission and on the impending by-elections in Winchester and Beckenham, we broke up at about 11.00.

Wednesday, 22 October, Westminster

Having thought about it overnight, I have sent Blair a summary of last night's meeting, reiterating my view about the risks attached to waiting until May for TFM and enclosing the following draft 'Terms of Reference' for the Electoral Reform Commission:

DRAFT TERMS OF REFERENCE

COMMISSION ON AN ALTERNATIVE ELECTORAL SYSTEM

To recommend an electoral system which combines a broadly proportional correlation between seats won and votes cast [with the maintenance of a link between MPs and geographical constituencies and greater expression of choice for voters],* to be put as an alternative to the existing system for parliamentary elections in a referendum.

* The words in square brackets are deletable.

Friday, 24 October, Somerset

Another perfect day. Bright weather and a deep frost last night.

During the day Sean rang to say that Jonathan had sent a letter from Downing Street in a sealed envelope. Could he open it and fax it to me? I asked him to do so straightaway. In it was a covering note from Jonathan enclosing Labour's 'alternative' terms of reference:

To recommend an alternative to the existing system for elections to the House of Commons to be put before the people in the government's proposed referendum.

No voting system shall be excluded from consideration. In forming its recommendations the Commission may take into account the need for stable government, the maintenance of the link between MPs and constituencies, the proportional relationship between seats and power which may result, and the expression of choice for voters.

I was deeply shocked by this. It completely ignored all that we had agreed at the dinner. They had simply gone away and rewritten the whole thing as though we had never had the discussion.

I immediately rang Powell and said I was bloody angry. The remit as he had drafted it didn't even make sense. What on earth did he mean by the 'proportional relationship between seats and power'? After all, the present system provided proportionality between seats and power. He said that he couldn't recall what it meant, but that he had got the message that it was unacceptable to us. I told him that I thought this had been drafted by Straw. He confirmed that it had.

Clearly a try-on.

I redrafted it as follows:

To recommend the proportional electoral system to be put as an alternative to the existing system for parliamentary elections in a referendum.

No voting system shall be excluded from consideration but in making its recommendations, the Commission shall seek to recommend an electoral system which combines a broadly proportional correlation between seats won and votes cast with the maintenance of a link between MPs and geographical constituencies and greater expression of choice for voters.

Afterwards I rang Bob to tell him what had happened. He exploded: this was the last straw; we should pack the whole thing in now. Alan Beith took a rather more relaxed line and thought my redraft was OK (as did Richard). But I won't put the redraft to Blair at the moment; I'll get Richard to complain bitterly to Mandelson, then leave them to stew in their own juice for a bit. I also faxed everything through to Roy, to whom I'm talking tomorrow.

A huge setback. I thought we were home and dry. I get very fed up when we negotiate something and they do not stick to it.

Saturday, 25 October, Somerset

At 5.30 I rang Roy. He too thinks they have gone back on what we agreed at our dinner on Tuesday. Nor can he work out why. I told him I now knew that Straw had got at it. But he doesn't mind their proposed remit as much as I do. There again, he doesn't have to cope with the party like I do – or with Bob.

Sunday, 26 October, Somerset

The end of the recess. It has been a week longer than normal and, by and large, quite a good one for us. I am still nervous, however, about what happens next. The crucial months lie ahead.

At a little after 8 o'clock in the evening Blair rang from the Commonwealth Heads of Government Conference in Edinburgh. He seemed in good form.

I asked him how it had gone and he said that he'd had a very tiring day. 'I had to chair the whole lot, you know. It's terribly difficult getting all these heads of government with opinions of their own to come to any kind of agreement.'

He turned quickly to the question of monetary union. 'I want you to know, but on purely Privy Councillor terms, what we are going to do tomorrow. I think you will be pleased with it.

'We will formally publish the results of all the Treasury studies which Gordon has been setting up over the last few months. We cannot let the uncertainty continue, so Gordon will make a statement to the House on every issue of principle. He will say that:

1. We will express support in principle for the single currency as a concept and will say it will be good for Europe and potentially good for Britain.

2. We do want to join, provided that we are convinced it is in Britain's interest.

3. The ultimate test is not an electoral one but an economic one.

4. Tests will be on two things: convergence and jobs.

5. As the Treasury study will show, we cannot join in 1999 along with

everyone else. This will be followed by a settling-down period, so joining immediately afterwards is not on, either.

6. The purpose of the statement is to produce certainty.

7. We plan to consider holding a referendum on EMU after the next election, but the possibility of holding one before will not be completely ruled out.

8. It is essential to start the preparation work now, so that we can join if we wish. This means effectively working to create a culture of opinion which will produce a 'Yes' vote in a referendum. We will also put in place the mechanisms to encourage industry and the country to make the physical changes necessary to prepare for EMU.

9. We will announce a standing committee to deal with this, which will consist of Gordon, senior businessmen and the Governor of the Bank of England.

The whole tone of the statement will be very strongly pro-European.

As he went through the points one by one, I expressed my support for those on which we are particularly keen. At the end I said, 'This is good news. Frankly I wish you had gone further and faster, but you have made a very substantial shift away from a negative to a positive approach to the euro.

'We will, of course, say that we very much regret the mishandling that's occurred in the last week. But we will give the substance of the statement a broad welcome.'

Monday, 27 October, Westminster

Another bright day, with clear blue autumn skies. Up at 7.30. Rang Roy to tell him about my phone conversation with Blair last night. He agreed that, while the Chancellor's statement was not everything we said we had wanted on Tuesday, it went a long way towards it. Tuesday's dinner must have had some effect.

Later in the morning I spoke to Richard, who has tightened up my 24 October draft of the Electoral Reform Commission remit. Also put a call out to Bob, who is still in implacable mood. He said we should go back to the original form of words. I let him go on a bit, then said I would delay getting back to Powell with our final words until he had spoken to Cook, but that time was running out.

Brown made his statement on the single currency today. Worryingly, the BBC are reporting it as closing off the options in this parliament. So often in politics it isn't what happens but how it's reported that matters. But it has been broadly welcomed. They have probably got everyone on board, including the CBI and the TUC. A clever piece of balancing.

Wednesday, 29 October, Westminster

Woke to hear that Ken Clarke has been quoted in the *Daily Telegraph* as saying that the Tories are wrong on the euro and calling for a cross-party coalition on Europe. I spoke to Alan Watson and Richard Holme immediately, saying we should pick up on this. A real opportunity for us to show that co-operative politics can be played both ways.

Into the office by 8.00, where I drafted a letter to Clarke. I then phoned him to say that I was writing to him. He is pretending that the *Daily Telegraph* has overspun what he said. I don't believe a word of it. But we had a very amiable conversation and exchanged phone numbers.

Another discussion with Blair, this time a difficult one. I still can't get him to agree on the remit. He is obviously being lobbied heavily by Prescott and Straw. He appears worried that he cannot get this one past the Cabinet. Roy is going to see Blair at 3.30 tomorrow to discuss his role as chair, so I rang him to see whether we could talk before he went. We agreed to meet at 12.30.

It's very annoying the way Blair makes agreements, then breaks them.

To bed at about midnight. A rather disturbed night. How do I deal with Blair tomorrow?

Thursday, 30 October, Westminster

To see Roy at 12.30. I took him through exactly where we were: both the position we were trying to negotiate and the fallbacks that Bob and I had put together. I pointed out that the key phrase, 'proportional alternative' had been lifted from Labour's own 1997 election manifesto.

At the end of our meeting, Roy became quite emotional. 'You and I have worked closely together for the last two or three years. This is a very big event indeed. Potentially an historic one. So I just want you to know that I am delighted at the way we have been able to work hand in glove. I think I can say that I have never enjoyed a closer or more constructive relationship in politics.' A typically generous compliment.

Afterwards, lunch with Andrew Marr. He was fascinating on Blair, whom he is seeing this evening. He asked what he should say to him. I said that Blair really had to grasp the nettle: he could lead a genuinely historic government, but he would have to lead more decisively and, above all, relax a bit. He could do things this autumn which he couldn't do later – the euro and the realignment of the left. He must seize the opportunity, or it would be lost.

I took Andrew almost totally into my confidence on TFM. I didn't tell him the details, of course, but he is clever enough to have worked them out.

'Look,' I said, 'this is highly confidential and off the record. But I have been able to rely on your judgement in the past and you are the only person outside my immediate circle of political colleagues with whom I can be absolutely frank. I want to say something to you which is extremely explosive, but I need your view. You know my plan; what you may not know is that I am only halfway through it. I am now kept awake at night by the prospect that I might be the person who, having led his party to its greatest victory, then destroys it. My own judgement is that this is a risk we must take because I am pretty confident we can make this government into a liberal, or at least a more liberal, one. But, with the Tories in their current turmoil, the real dilemma is whether we have an historic role to play as the liberal critic of the government from the outside, or whether it is better to be a partner with the government so as to help them deliver a more liberal agenda from the inside. It is a very difficult choice to make. What do you think?'

Andrew started off by taking the view that we should be the liberal critic outside the government. But at the end we both agreed that it was doing things that mattered in politics, not opposing them. At this historic moment we could either be spectators or participants. Even if we chose to be spectators there was no certainty that Labour would not adopt our agenda and make us irrelevant. So the right thing to do was go with them and take the risks.

I asked if the *Independent* would support us if we did take this step. He smiled wryly and said, 'If we are still in existence then.' The paper is obviously living from hand to mouth at present.

At about 2.45 Blair rang. We spoke for twenty minutes or so. A tough session in which we got nowhere. He told me that it was impossible for him to put to his people the text we had submitted. I told him I was very upset indeed that, having negotiated this between us personally at dinner last Tuesday, I should then have the text we had agreed on completely redrafted by Jack Straw! He responded by saying that since I had Roy Jenkins as chair, what was I worried about? I could accept any remit. I replied that, even with Roy Jenkins on board, the remit was everything. I would prefer another chair to a weaker remit. The word 'proportionality' had to appear in the operative part of the text.

He kept saying that he couldn't carry his Cabinet on this, apparently completely impervious to the fact that, in that case, he shouldn't have agreed to the thing in the first place, or stuck it in his manifesto.

We concluded by saying that we would both think about it and talk again, perhaps tomorrow.

Later I received a memo from Bob Maclennan saying that he had spoken to Robin Cook. As we thought, Jack Straw and John Prescott are putting a lot of pressure on Blair. Cook said he would work on the agreement over the weekend and possibly speak to Blair; but he added that, at this stage, it would be better not to reach an agreement at all than to reach the wrong agreement. Bob shares his judgement, as do I.

In the evening I caught the train down to Blandford, where I was due to present an 'Investors in People Certificate' to North Dorset District Council. From my hotel room I rang Roy to find out how the Blair meeting had gone. 'Satisfactory was the best I could call it,' he said. Blair had told him 'man to man' that he would accept his recommendation. They had talked a little about the membership of the commission, but the central issue had been its remit. Roy, from what I could tell, had stuck to the line tenaciously. But it had been tough going and I could sense some frustration in Roy's voice. A long way yet to go, I fear.

Friday, 31 October, Somerset

Another very disturbed night. I kept worrying about where I was going with Blair. I decided on another letter to him expressing my dismay in straightforward terms. Almost make or break. It all depends on how he responds.

Dear Tony,

I understand we are due to speak around mid-day. I shall be at my home in Somerset. I sense we are reaching a crucial point. I am very worried that we may not reach agreement and that the consequences of this to the project could be very great. It might be useful, therefore, to let you know how I see things before we speak.

Please excuse the straightforward language. But one of the best aspects of our relationship is that we are able to speak pretty bluntly to each other.

This is how I see things:

1. You and I signed up, in public, to an agreement which we saw at the time and described to the public as the foundation stone of a programme of reform for Britain and the beginnings of a new relationship of co-operation, built on mutual trust, between our two parties. As I have always made clear to you, the issue of electoral reform was, for us, crucial both to the reform programme and to the relationship. The terms of the Cook/Maclennan agreement were very toughly negotiated between Robin and Bob and subsequently agreed, in public, between you and me. Whatever private agreement you and I have reached, bulwarked by Roy Jenkins's possible chairmanship, you are, as I see it, now asking me to accept a position where the public and my party will read the remit as my acquiescence to your watering down, in a most crucial manner, that agreement. I do not believe this will do either of us any good publicly. And it is not, frankly, something I can carry with my party.

2. The crucial words [in the remit] – a 'proportional alternative' – were carried in your manifesto. I appreciate that you may be under some pressure from senior colleagues, as indeed am I on the compromises I have already made. But they fought the election on this manifesto. What is more, they have used Labour's manifesto commitments to avoid including a Human Rights Commission in the ECHR[1] legislation, as agreed in the Cook/Maclennan report. ('It did not appear in our manifesto, therefore we do not have to apply it' has been their line.) It is very difficult to accept, therefore, as you seem to be suggesting, that even though this was in your manifesto you do not have to enact it. I appreciate that, because of economic pressures, a manifesto may have to be changed. But this is not a matter of cost, it is a matter of principle.

3. Roy and I both believed that we had concluded an agreement with you on the remit when we came to dinner with you last week. I was, frankly, shocked,

1 European Commission on Human Rights.

therefore, to receive two days later a remit which was so distant from what we had agreed as to be almost laughable. I have subsequently been told that this was completely redrafted by Jack Straw! You cannot blame me for wondering what was the purpose of this element of our discussion over dinner, if the agreement I thought we had firmly made was so easily discarded. As I see it, there is now much more at stake here than just the remit of the commission.

4. I now understand that you wish to introduce what is, for me, a completely new element – a second referendum after the election. This has never been mentioned before, nor even considered. It introduces, again at the last minute, a whole new and, from my point of view, unwelcome element into what was a very delicately constructed compromise.

I am also worried that, as we approach the conclusion of this, extra conditions are now being added. The terms of reference of the commission are, I am afraid, a sticking point for us. But there is more at risk here even than the Electoral Reform Commission. We can only work effectively in the difficult times ahead if, when things are settled between us, we don't keep on returning to them.
Yours
Paddy

Blair rang at 1.00. His tone was affable. 'I have read your fax.' I replied that I felt each of us should know exactly how the other felt before we started this session.

We talked for a full half hour but made little or no progress. Blair did, however, reveal that:

1. Robin Cook is 'on your side', but is in a tiny minority in Cabinet.

2. Prescott and Straw are intransigent.

3. When he told Prescott that Roy Jenkins would be chair of the ERC, it was 'a very good thing he was sitting down, because he exploded'.

4. He still can't understand why I won't accept Roy Jenkins as chair in return for a weaker remit.

5. The weakest argument he can use with his Cabinet is that there is a commitment to proportionality in the manifesto, since they all believe he bounced them into that anyway.

I spent the rest of the afternoon talking to Bob and Alan and going over the remit. Sean has found a most useful amendment the Labour Party put down in the House of Lords in 1922. We may be able to use elements of this in our proposed remit. I had several discussions with Pat McFadden[1] and Jonathan Powell. The latter told me that, following our lunchtime chat, Blair was now working on the text himself. Eventually I faxed through a revised version of the remit to Powell based on the 1922 amendment. He will put it to Blair later on:

To examine all appropriate electoral systems and combinations of systems and recommend one in which the composition of the House of Commons shall proportionately reflect the views of the electorate at General Elections, to be put before the people in the government's proposed referendum.

In forming its recommendations, the commission shall take account of the need for stable government: the maintenance of a link between MPs and geographical constituencies and greater choice for the voters.

Sunday, 2 November, Somerset

Another not terribly good night. Worried about what will happen. Through the weekend I have been keeping in touch with Roy, Bob and Alan Beith.

Spoke to Downing Street, but Jonathan said that the PM was at church. Could he ring me at about 12.30? I said no, make it 5.00. Better to leave it longer so I don't look too eager.

I also spoke to Roy. He is worried, as I am, that Blair may renege on other agreements as well. Bob, on the other hand, is surprisingly mellow. He can go with Blair's revised text providing we write out any mention of AV. We are almost there. But it has been very, very tough.

Blair rang me from Chequers just before 5.00, taking me by surprise. He apologized profusely for not having rung earlier but said he had been terribly busy with Hillary Clinton, who is over on what has been called a social visit, but which has in fact included serious discussions about the future of the left and centre left (billed in the press as the 'Third Way').

'I must speak to you about it sometime,' he said. 'A fascinating set of ideas is emerging, if we can all pull them together. Look, I have been thinking about the remit. There is no particular rush. Let's have a Joint

---

1 Private Secretary (Constitutional Reform) to the Prime Minister and Deputy Chief of Staff at No. 10.

Cabinet Committee meeting in, say, two weeks' time to talk about this, then use next Tuesday's JCC to discuss Europe.'

I said I would much prefer to discuss the Electoral Reform Commission on Tuesday, but agreed that it was more important to get it right than do it early. But if we didn't announce it on Tuesday, then it would have to come after Winchester, which meant in three weeks' time, rather than two.

He said that he had decided to come up to London from Chequers early, so perhaps we could meet tomorrow? He also mentioned that he wanted to see Roy again. I am very nervous about this but didn't say so. Given Blair's habit of agreeing things then going back on them later, what does he want to rediscuss with Roy?

We got down to talking about the remit. He said he had two versions they had been working on which he would fax through to me. I asked him to read them out to me first.

One was totally unacceptable because it specifically mentioned AV; the other had elements that were workable. I didn't indicate that we would accept either, but said I would discuss them with my colleagues and come back to him later.

The two proposed remits were:
Either

To recommend the electoral system to be put as an alternative to the existing system for parliamentary elections in a referendum.

No voting system shall be excluded from consideration. In making its recommendation, the commission shall seek to combine a broadly proportional correlation between seats won and votes cast, with the need for stable government, the maintenance of a link between MPs and geographical constituencies and greater expression of choice for voters.

or

To consider all appropriate systems of election, including the alternative vote (AV), and recommend an alternative to the present system for parliamentary elections to be put before the people in the government's referendum.

The commission's recommendation shall observe the requirement for a broadly proportional correlation between seats won and votes cast, as well as the need for stable government and the maintenance of the link between MPs and geographical constituencies.

At the end of our conversation he said things were getting worse in Iraq.
'Not military action, I hope?'

'No,' he replied, 'but it is not going to be easy. Perhaps we could discuss
it tomorrow.'

He sounded really upbeat and self-confident. Quite different from our
previous conversations, when he had sounded reserved and scratchy. He
clearly thinks things are going well for them. Or it could just be the result
of a weekend with Hillary?

Monday, 3 November, Westminster

To Downing Street at 4.00. Blair and I sat in his little office by the side of
the Cabinet Room in our shirtsleeves. He asked if I would mind Jonathan
and Pat McFadden coming in. I agreed.

We went backwards and forwards over the remit for more than an hour.
He started by rehearsing again all the arguments about the outcome, then
spent about twenty minutes expressing severe reservations about moving
away from a majoritarian system at all. He said that he didn't want a
system that would produce weak government through coalitions. I replied
that, if that was his view, we may as well not go ahead at all.

McFadden chipped in: 'You are going to have to choose, Prime Minister.
You can either have a majoritarian system or a proportional one. But you
can't have both.'

Blair said he was seeing Roy Jenkins again. 'It's important to get things
straight. Roy said he will do the job if I am prepared to agree with his
outcome. That's fine. But I want to get a clearer idea of what that outcome
is likely to be first.'

He seems suddenly to have become very nervous about the whole thing.

Later, McFadden told me that Jack Straw has been creating hell this
afternoon. 'He was cloistered with Tony for an hour, biting chunks out of
him.'

There was also a discussion on the consensus in the Cabinet: all three
agree that Cook is in a minority of one; also that Blair doesn't believe he
can carry his earlier undertaking through Cabinet.

Finally, we got back to the words on the paper.

Jonathan suggested the inclusion of a sentence that said: 'The commission would be free to recommend such systems as it saw fit, but it would
have to observe the requirement for proportionality.'

I said these were two flatly contradictory statements in the same sentence! We should at least split them up. They agreed to do this and fax it through to me.

We finished at 5 o'clock, with Blair saying that he would discuss the remit with his colleagues, particularly Jack Straw, in the near future.

They faxed their new proposed remit through later. It is still slightly defective, so later in the evening I faxed back an amended version as follows:

The commission shall be free to consider and recommend any appropriate system or combination of systems in recommending an alternative to the present system for parliamentary elections to be put before the people in the government's referendum.

The commission's recommendation shall observe the requirement for broad proportionality, the need for stable government, an extension of voter choice and the maintenance of the link between MPs and geographical constituencies.[1]

Everything we have negotiated over the years appears to be up for grabs – again!

Apart from his Cabinet colleagues, I have been told that Prodi has also been at Blair. As has Kohl. All arguing against a proportional system because it produces 'weakness'. I hope this is just last-minute jitters, but I spent a long time thinking about it overnight and have decided to put in a démarche to him, either by letter or in a meeting. He must understand that if he really wants to go for a majoritarian system he cannot also have a proportional one. If he does, he will be breaking the Cook/Maclennan agreement. And if that is the case, then there can be no future relationship between us.

Tuesday, 4 November, Westminster

Rang Powell to express my fears about last night. He agreed that a meeting would be a good idea and suggested Thursday. I asked whether Roy could be there, too.

Afterwards, down to see Roy, who was, as always, extremely supportive and agreed to come. The good news I gleaned from the Powell phone call, though, is that Blair has agreed to the revised text I faxed through yesterday

---

1 This was eventually accepted as the final remit for the Jenkins Commission.

and has instructed Powell to get Straw's agreement to it. This is the first time since the whole negotiation over the remit started that Blair has actually said he agreed to any form of words. But will he get Straw on board?

At 1 o'clock to Downing Street for the Joint Cabinet Committee meeting. The mood was, as ever, good.

At the end Blair said, 'Well, I have to leave you guys, since I have Jane Fonda waiting to see me.' We all laughed and said we couldn't compete with her.

When we emerged from the Cabinet Room, there she was sitting outside. Sixty years old she may be, but she didn't look it, in a long skirt, cut to the thigh and showing an expanse of shapely leg. Richard Holme went straight up to her and said, 'Hello, Jane, I wonder if you remember me? You came to our house in La Jolla for an anti-Vietnam war party back in the 1960s and Vanessa swam in our swimming pool with our children!'

We ribbed Richard unmercifully about this outrageous piece of namedropping all the way down Whitehall.

At 5 o'clock a Jo Group meeting. Not a very full attendance; I note that Tom does not attend much these days. A very sharp disagreement over whether delaying TFM is workable or not. Only I, with less than energetic support from Ming, took the view that it is not. But we did decide to start outlining exactly what we wanted in a coalition agreement, so that when Blair says in December that he has nothing against having Lib Dems in his Cabinet we will be ready with our response.

Thursday, 6 November, Westminster

Some serious jostling is starting for the leadership of the Party, stimulated, I think, by rumours in the press gallery that I may go after the European elections in 1999. Charles Kennedy has got himself on to all the internal party committees. I have also deliberately given Nick Harvey a central role in the operation of the Party so as to build up some competition for Charles. Not that I prefer one over the other – just that I don't want this to be a walkover. Succession planning means having a range of talent to choose from.

Roy and I were dropped off outside the Cabinet Office a few minutes before 4.45pm and we were asked to wait inside Blair's study. While we were sitting there, Gordon Brown came out with Charlie Whelan and chatted with Roy, suggesting they got together in the near future.

Our meeting with Blair lasted about an hour. Also in the room were Pat McFadden, Jonathan and the civil servant looking after constitutional reform matters.

'OK, then,' said Blair, 'where are we?'

He shot a glance at Jonathan, who said that the words of the remit were in front of him. Powell said he had spoken to Straw about them. He had reluctantly agreed, with one minor amendment. However, we quickly agreed that Straw's amendment should not be included and the text should stay as I had faxed it through on 3 November.

Blair then moved to the subject of referendums. He said that, in his opinion, it would be difficult to have a single referendum to cover both changes (first stop AV, second stop PR). He was also worried that AV would be regarded as gerrymandering in favour of the Lib Dems and against the Tories. What arguments could be used to counter this?

I pointed out that AV would have disadvantageously distorted the Tory vote in only one election since 1979 – the last one. In all the others AV would actually have increased the Tory share of seats.

Helpfully, McFadden and Powell both came in reminding Blair that the Tories use AV to elect their leaders. Furthermore, it is used elsewhere, not least in Australia.

I reiterated my view that we should let the commission decide on not only the precise system to be used, but also on the best way of getting public consent for it (e.g. one referendum or two). I was opposed to a second referendum, chiefly because it would give powerful ammunition to the Tories ('If you vote "Yes" in this referendum you'll get . . . yes, that's right . . . another referendum!'). But in the end, I explained, it was not a matter of dogma for me; more a matter of how best to enact the recommendations of the commission in the way that has the greatest chance of winning public support.

Then Roy Jenkins added, to much laughter, 'Look, I don't care how many referendums we have, so long as we win them.' Then, 'I have seen Paddy's diary notes of your previous meeting. I think you may well have been perceiving my position in rather more stark terms than I had intended. I have never said that if I were to take on the chairmanship of the commission I would require, as a precondition, that you accept my recommendations. I couldn't conceivably ask that of a prime minister. However, I don't want to take this on unless you have, at least, a strong disposition to accept what I recommend. Ultimately, if you feel you must reject it, you must do so. But I will want to know at the start that you are at least minded to accept. By the same token, I will want to have some discussion with you and Paddy about what we decide before it is finalized. But I will resist any direct interference in the commission's outcome.'

TB: Well, I would be crazy to ask you to do this on any basis other than the one you have just outlined.

PA: I would just like to be clear about how we define 'proportionality' in the remit. I recognize your worries about an unstable electoral system; I have no wish to create such a system. I also recognize that such a system may well benefit my party, since it would, on the face of it, always put us in a coalition government. But that is not what I am seeking to achieve. I want a more proportional system, though not necessarily one which delivers to the last percentage point of proportionality. If a government obtains, say, 45 per cent of the vote then, in my judgement, it should be entitled to majority control of Parliament in its own right. On the other hand, only 40 per cent of the vote in an election should not confer on a party the right to govern by itself. In these circumstances it should have to seek a partner for government. So while it would be wrong for us to tell Roy what kind of system we want him to arrive at, it is legitimate for us to say that we hope the proportional system he recommends will be one in which the lowest threshold that delivers a majority in the House is around 45 per cent of the popular vote.

There followed a discussion as to how many elections there had been since the war which would have delivered a government on 45 per cent of the vote. Quite a few, we concluded.

At the end Blair said, 'Very well, then. I think we now have an agreement on which we can go forward.'

At last!

As we walked back down a foggy Whitehall I said to Roy, 'No one else knows it yet, but an agreement has been reached with the Prime Minister in front of three civil servants which cannot, in my view, be reversed. British politics ought never to be the same as a result of it. From a bipolar majoritarian system of politics, we are now moving towards a pluralist one. I do not feel elated, but I think we have crossed an historic watershed.'

Roy said he felt the same. We aren't there yet, but it has been a decisive moment.

It has taken a long, long time to put this together. But we have got what we want. Just a little work to be done tying up the loose ends.

Sunday, 9 November, London

REMEMBRANCE SUNDAY

Windy, rainy and quite cold. The usual ceremony. Hague, on his début, obviously very nervous. It rained hard during the act of remembrance itself and we all got rather wet.

There is a real worry building up over Iraq again. I spoke to Jock Slater[1] and to the Chief of the Defence Staff yesterday. They confirmed to me what Blair had said to me earlier in the week: that the situation is getting worse and that military action of some sort is becoming increasingly likely.

The clouds of war are beginning to gather. Let's just hope it's only air action.

Thursday, 13 November, London

In the evening to the Grosvenor Hotel for the Indian Independence Golden Anniversary dinner. Chaotically organized, but somehow or other Indian enthusiasm and decency made it all work.

We were all on the top table. Jane sat with Hague on one side and Major on the other. She said afterwards that Major was the better conversationalist. I sat between Ffion Jenkins and Norma Major. I found Ffion rather appealing: intelligent and easy to talk to. Norma, as always, was a delight and surprisingly flirty. Jim Callaghan, sitting on her other side, had us all in stitches with old stories from the House of Commons. I thought Jane's end of the table looked a lot less fun.

A good speech from L.M. Singhvi, the Indian High Commissioner, and an even better one from the Prince of Wales. Thoughtful and well suited to his audience. Blair's was unspectacular. He is beginning to look pretty haggard now. The growing crisis over Iraq is taking its toll.

---

1 Admiral Sir John (Jock) Slater, First Sea Lord and Chief of the Naval Staff.

Saturday, 15 November, Somerset

Overcast, drizzly and far too warm for the time of year.

Up at 8.00 to chat with Roy about the developing Formula One crisis,[1] which the government is mishandling badly. We agreed that I should ring Blair, partly to voice my worries about it damaging us by association and partly to offer some thoughts on how it might be tackled. I also wanted to tell him that some more Tories were joining us and to find out the latest on Iraq. So I put a call through to Jonathan at 8.45, saying that I would like to speak to the PM some time today.

In the event, the call from Downing Street came through at 10.00pm, in the middle of a constituency fundraising do at home. There was a mighty racket going on downstairs, so I took the call upstairs in my study. Blair's first words were, 'What's that row?' I told him it was a constituency event.

'Oh yes, I remember those!'

'You must have had a hell of a day, so I won't keep you long. But I wanted you to know that I am on *Frost* in the morning, so if there is anything I can do to help on Iraq or the Formula One problem, do tell me.'

He said that he'd had a tiring day but things were fine now (during a previous phone call, Jonathan had told me that Blair had been pretty low over the last two or three days, but had recovered today). He went on to say that he had some friends round and they were relaxing.

We had a brief discussion about the Formula One affair. I told him that Mandelson was doing Labour no favours at the moment. 'He looks like a mortician on television. And the line he seems to be pushing – that you have made no mistakes and have done nothing wrong – is simply untenable. I don't think anyone in Britain regards you as a dishonest person; the charge of corruption will not stick. On the other hand, the charge of not coming clean will, unless you clear it up very quickly. This runs entirely counter to what most people think of you. It's absolutely vital, in my view, that you now come clean about the whole thing and admit that it has been mishandled. There is one word in politics which we politicians never say . . .'

He butted in and said, 'Sorry! And I intend to say it. I agree with you.

---

1 The government had introduced a ban on the advertising of cigarettes on all sports except Formula One racing. It emerged that Bernie Ecclestone, the owner of Formula One racing, had previously donated £1 million to the Labour Party.

This is one we are going to take on the chin, as you will see from tomorrow's papers.'

He went on to say that he really was very upset at the charges of corruption the Tories had been making about him and he felt them deeply.

'I am very cross with myself. The truth is I just never spotted the size of this. I was too busy on other things and didn't believe it would blow up like this. I blame myself.'

'What I think you need to present now is two elements: a little humility and a lot of candour. I am glad that you are doing what you are doing tomorrow.'

The conversation continued in this vein for five minutes or so, but Blair showed no sign of bridling at my criticizing him so directly.

Eventually I told him the line I would take on *Frost*: I would say that Labour had handled things badly and that I disagreed with them on the substance of their decision, but to equate this with the Tories' sleaze was simply wrong. Meanwhile, the important thing was to get this cleared up for all our sakes.

He said that would be very helpful.

We moved on to Iraq.

He said that he had spoken to Clinton several times during the day. Clinton is trying to avoid military action but doesn't quite know how to do it. Blair had said to him that it was vital that we drew attention now to why the UN weapons inspectors were there. The world was being exposed to Saddam's viewpoint and had been allowed to forget the reasons for bringing them in in the first place.

TB: I have now seen some of the stuff on this. It really is pretty scary. He is very close to some appalling weapons of mass destruction. I don't understand why the French and others don't understand this. We cannot let him get away with it. The world thinks this is just gamesmanship. But it's deadly serious.

PA: Then it's vital that such information is put into the public domain as soon as possible. This is a moment to do what Kennedy did during the Cuban missile crisis – publish the evidence. Then it was photos; this time it's intelligence information.

TB: I said exactly the same to Clinton. I know he is thinking about how it might be possible to do that.

I went on to say that I thought the right thing to do was to establish a set of clearly delineated steps for Saddam, each with a threshold and each with a clear exit sign, then go through these methodically and resolutely.

PA: But of course that's easy to say. It's difficult to do when you have to keep a coalition on board [i.e. NATO and the Gulf State allies].

TB: That's the problem.

Wednesday, 19 November, Westminster

Down to PMQs. Hague was quite good on a very weak wicket. He seems to have the capacity to unnerve Blair.

I asked a question on health spending. Blair ended a pretty aggressive response with a very barbed comment which got the Tory and Labour benches whooping with delight. Somebody from behind me said, 'Wow! Bring in the marriage guidance counsellors'. Afterwards, Jonathan Powell phoned Sean to apologize. He said that Blair had seen a leaflet we had put out in Beckenham during the by-election campaign which had made him cross. Blair was going to ring and say sorry to me personally. I rang Powell back and told him not to be so silly; no apology, please – that was political life!

Thursday, 20 November, London

THE QUEEN AND PRINCE PHILIP'S GOLDEN WEDDING ANNIVERSARY
AND THE DAY OF THE WINCHESTER BY-ELECTION

I walked over to Westminster Abbey for the service of thanksgiving [to mark the Queen's Golden Wedding]. A dreary grey morning but at least it wasn't raining. I came in through the West Door and walked down the aisle, just as we had done at Princess Diana's funeral, and took my place behind the choir.

The same dreadful crowd of royal hangers-on. I joked with Jane later that they all had strange names: Black Rod, Pink Knickers and goodness knows what else. When the crowned heads of Europe came in, I thought to myself how odd it was that a hundred years ago we would have been having to guard this lot against bearded anarchists throwing bombs at them. Now nobody knows who they are. It is also very noticeable how the Hanoverian nose comes through on all of them.

The service was good. A kind of atonement, counterbalancing the terrible sadness we had felt for Princess Diana only two months ago. Reminding us what the royals really stand for and reminding us also of their reliability and value to the nation.

Later off to the Banqueting House for a formal lunch. This was another masterly occasion. Blair walked with the Queen from Downing Street through the crowds. It must have made some wonderful shots. There already seems to be a genuine affection building up between them. Blair made a very nice speech – personal and simple. He is not so good in the House of Commons but he is superb at this.

The Queen seems to have found a new way of speaking. I wonder if she has had training? Instead of using pompous words and sounding all nasal and tight-mouthed she now speaks with the more rounded vowels of everyday speech. And makes speeches with passages that are personal and simple.

But I couldn't work out who was supporting whom. Was Labour throwing its mantle of popularity around a damaged royalty; or was the Queen giving her support to the New Labour government? It was beautifully judged.

In the evening, the Winchester result. At 11.30 or so I got a call from Chris saying that he thought it would be OK. Earlier he had said that the majority might be 1,300. At about 11.45 he called back. 'It's a landslide.' He was stunned. The majority was likely to be over 10,000. Over the course of the next few hours this translated into a 21,000 majority for Mark!

And a good result in Beckenham as well, where we held our vote. Unhappily, Labour just missed winning and the size of our vote was bigger than the gap between them and the Tories. In Winchester, Labour lost their deposit. There may be recriminations from them on this.

Friday, 21 November, Winchester

To Winchester to celebrate Mark Oaten's victory. A stunning result, which reflects great personal credit on him.

Monday, 24 November, Westminster

[*We were in the throes of agreeing with Labour the wording of each other's responses to the announcement of the Jenkins commission. We wanted Blair to use words which showed he was open-minded on PR and moving closer to it. Our aim was to have the press repeat this along the lines: 'We still don't know where Blair stands on PR. But there is no doubt about the direction in which he is travelling.' Blair's response, with the so-called 'comfortable words', was crucial. Richard sent Mandelson some proposed wording, as follows:]*

'COMFORTABLE WORDS'

I am very pleased that the government has established this Election Commission under the chairmanship of Lord Jenkins of Hillhead. I know that he will command wide public confidence across parties and that he will give distinguished leadership to his colleagues in their important task.

I have so far been unpersuaded of the case for any particular reformed voting system but I recognize that there is well-founded dissatisfaction with the flaws in our present system for parliamentary elections and I believe we should all be open-minded about the possibility of constructive change.

So I shall await the conclusions of the Commission with keen interest, and I should reiterate that it is the government's intention to submit the system they recommend to the British people in a referendum for their decision.

Saturday, 29 November, Somerset

As I suspected, Labour is playing fast and loose on the 'comfortable words'. Sean faxed me through their amendments which fall far short of what we wanted, so I made some further changes. We are in for a tough battle.

Had a chat with Richard on the way to Chard for the constituency surgery this morning. He tells me that Labour are again retreating from their commitments. Always the way with Blair. He goes three paces forward, then pulls two paces back, so we have to push him forward again. I suspect this will dominate our actions over the next forty-eight hours or so.

Sunday, 30 November, Somerset

A chat with Richard at about 5.30 after he'd spoken to Mandelson. He thinks we are getting there. Otherwise, spent the evening relaxing in front of the television.

Monday, 1 December, Westminster

THE DAY OF THE ANNOUNCEMENT OF THE ELECTORAL REFORM
COMMISSION

I have decided that we need to build on the success of the Joint Cabinet
Committee in order to push the party into making a decision one way or
the other on TFM in the spring. Of course, if they go against I will have
to resign. But I am quite relaxed about that now. Before Christmas I shall
try to build up, through interviews, a very clear picture of where I want
the party to go, explicitly not rejecting the possibility of a coalition in this
parliament.

Last night I rang Powell to tell him that I would like to see Blair after
the Joint Cabinet Committee today so that we could press forward our
success, not least by Blair making his statement before Christmas about
the possibility of us joining the Cabinet.

Jonathan had also agreed that it might be useful if Blair and I touched
base briefly on the phone before the JCC. We eventually spoke at 9.00am,
going through the arrangements for the day. Blair said that the announcement of the commission would come out in a written answer after the
Cabinet meeting.

I asked him what he was going to say. He said that he probably wouldn't
say anything himself, but get Alastair Campbell to say it for him. But the
statement's essence would be that

1. He remained unpersuaded himself, but that

2. He recognized that some believed there were flaws and inadequacies in
the present system, and

3. He was open-minded about the result of the commission.

TB: The problem isn't that I am perceived to be open-minded; it is rather that
everybody now thinks it a foregone conclusion that I will come out in favour of
PR. I will have to compensate for that.

He is probably right, of course. But he has allowed us to push him into
that position. As Roy said when I spoke to him, Blair will find it almost
impossible now to turn down the recommendations of the commission.

PA: I am initiating a major debate in my party culminating in the Spring Conference,
which will, I hope, open the door to what might come after that. I hope your

statement about the possibility of us joining the government will present my party with some very clear choices. The Christmas and New Year break would probably be the best time for you to make your statement, since the holiday period would give people a little more time to think about how to respond.

TB: Yeah, that sounds about right. I anticipate making this before the New Year anyway.

To the Joint Cabinet Committee. At the end Blair hung back a bit and thanked me for my support for his decision to invite Gerry Adams to Downing Street.[1]

TB: It was very helpful, particularly since the Tories look as if they are going to play fast and loose. I am now genuinely concerned that they intend to break the cross-party approach between all parties on Northern Ireland.

We also talked about Bosnia. Blair told Ming (who was also there) that he was convinced we would have to stay in Bosnia and that he would try and push the Americans into doing the same.[2]

The news on the Jenkins commission finally broke in the afternoon.

Spent the next couple of hours overseeing our press operation to ensure that we got our message across about the commission. Coverage was excellent, most people conceding that this is a victory for us. Exactly what I wanted. A good day's work.

Tuesday, 2 December, Westminster

At 3.30 to see Gordon Brown in his office at the House. No one else present.

To kick off, I said that it was really important that when we attacked each other, we did so legitimately.[3] I appreciated that they were trying to defend their figures in public, and not admit they were putting less into health and education this year than the Tories had. But they must know

---

1 As part of the Northern Ireland peace talks. The Tories had shouted 'foul', but we had backed the government's decision.

2 There were discussions going on about what would happen after SFOR withdrew from Bosnia in September 1998.

3 Brown had been mounting a series of very personal attacks in the House on Malcolm Bruce in particular and the Lib Dems in general, on the grounds that our figures were wrong and we were being irresponsible. In fact, Malcolm's critique of Brown's economic policies was accurate, justified and subsequently vindicated by events.

privately that this was wrong. He went into a long stream of figures, trying to explain why our accusation was false. I showed him his own parliamentary answers on which our critique was based, which proved our case. He said he would look at it again.

We then went on to discuss tomorrow's meeting between the Lib Dem and Labour Treasury teams (the first under the new JCC arrangements). I said that I hoped it would be an honest exchange of views between officials of both parties, not a wrangle among politicians.

He went into a long explanation about their tax credit position.[1]

GB: Frankly, it's been very tough and I am not sure we have explained it very well. Many Labour members don't understand what we are doing, either. But you must not look at tax credits simply as a single event, but rather judge their impact on how they affect others in the tax/benefit area, such as single mothers. If we can get this through, we can build a lot else around it. I want to use tax credits as the means by which we can create a ladder back into work. So it's part of a much larger picture. For goodness' sake, don't dismiss the idea entirely at this stage. Wait until you see the full picture.

I pointed out to him that tax credits had been our policy at the time of the Liberal/SDP Alliance.

PA: I am determined that my party does *not* go down the 'tax and spend' route. I have issued instructions that we should look at outcomes rather than inputs: How short are hospital waiting lists, not how much money is put into the NHS? How large are school classes? And so on. I recognize what you are trying to do, and if I were in your position I would probably be doing much the same thing: being very tough this year in order to build up a credit that you can spend as the election approaches.

GB: I want to show people we can be tough with money, so that they will trust us to use that money later on. And we will have lots to use. Far more than a penny on income tax [smiling].[2]

---

1 The working family tax credit was introduced by the government to give extra money to people with families who were out of work or on low incomes. Although in essence a benefit, it was to be called a 'tax credit' and paid by employers via the pay packet. The proposal caused controversy because of the administrative burden placed on employers and because of the perception that it was designed to reduce the benefits bill superficially by retitling benefits tax credits.

2 Referring to the famous 'Penny on income tax for education' which had been the centrepiece of the Lib Dems' last two General Election campaigns.

PA: I know that. That's why I am determined we don't move to the left of you. Never mind the damage it may do to the long-term project; it would be deadly for us to be siding with your left-wingers for more public spending when you are already putting so much in. 'Whatever you spend, we'll spend more' is not a policy.

I went on to explain to him how I saw 'the project': the bringing together of the two progressive forces of British politics; the need for action now; the fact that this was an historic opportunity that shouldn't be lost; and that Blair and I had agreed to go ahead after the last election but had been halted by the size of their majority. And that we had set it up again for this November but then Blair had decided to delay it until the spring.

PA: I really want to stress that this is where I believe we can get to. And I believe you want to get there, too. It will be very difficult to convince our parties. But it can be done. Now, tell me bluntly, are you prepared to see us in government with you? Or is that something you would oppose?

GB: No, of course I want you to be in the project with us. It's the only sensible solution. And we need to get there as soon as we can.

PA: Then we must define what it's about. Let me tell you what I think it's about. I think it's about modernization. And there are, primarily, three elements to that: modernization of our constitution; modernization of our education and welfare system; and modernization of our approach to Europe. But it will take ten years to complete.

He nodded.

PA: Then here's the problem for your party. You seem to the public at the moment an intelligent bunch of well-meaning and rather decent people who are doing things which, in themselves, are sensible. But you need to show where it's all going. There is no coherent vision; no end destination and no integrated set of ideas which could act as a creed.

GB: Yes, that's right. The difficulty is lack of intellectual force behind the movement. There is no intellectual coherence about the position and so nothing to fall back on. You have accused us of being a bunch of control freaks. Well, in a way, that's what we have to be, because we don't have an identifiable aim which is ideologically based: because there's no core idea to hold the party together in tough times we have to use discipline instead. We need to define an overarching aim for the project on which we can all agree. That will provide us with a purpose for moving closer together. There are all sorts of intellectuals we could bring together.

Perhaps a series of lectures? Somehow or other, over the next few months, we must embark on this. I will come back to you with some proposals.

A very amicable and productive discussion.

We agreed to meet again soon. His office will organize this and he will give some thought as to how we can, together, begin to assemble the intellectual case for the project and define a destination on which we can all agree.

Wednesday, 3 December, London

More snow today. Several inches, I am told, outside of London. But slushy and bitterly cold in Kennington.

At 10.00, over to the Treasury meeting with David Laws,[1] Malcolm Bruce and Steve Webb. There's a hell of a row brewing over Geoffrey Robinson, who has been discovered to have some offshore funds in Guernsey held in the unlikely name of a Madame Bourgeois. He has, no doubt, been obeying the exact letter of the law. But it looks as though he has also been doing all he can to avoid paying tax, while being minister in charge of tax avoidance. Pretty embarrassing.

When we arrived at the Treasury reception (which looks like a nineteenth-century bank) we were kept waiting and then shuffled upstairs round the circular corridor past the Chancellor's office into an empty room. The building was clearly constructed to impress, with solid oak doors and panelling. But the corridors are terribly run down and reminded me of some distant outpost of the Foreign Office: undecorated and dingy.

It was explained to us in hushed tones that Geoffrey Robinson was supposed to chair the meeting, but that he was with the PM. Helping Blair to prepare for PMQs, I bet. Would I chair?

The meeting started at about 10.15 in a somewhat desultory way with the medium-term spending review. We weren't very impressed. Then, at around 10.30, Robinson came in with Brown's chief adviser, Ed Balls.

Robinson was pleasant, but surprisingly unassertive. He suggested I continue chairing the meeting (extraordinary since he is the Treasury

1 Director of Policy and Research. As a former managing director of Barclays Bank David was ideally suited to be our head economic researcher. He is now the MP for my old seat of Yeovil.

minister). I asked Ed Balls if he would explain their 'Welfare to Work' plans, which he did, impressively.

In order to prevent the debate becoming confrontational I had arranged earlier that we should start with a dialogue between the experts. David Laws did excellently and Steve Webb was brilliant. At one stage Robinson leaned over and whispered to me, 'My goodness, you have people of real quality here.'

Altogether a very satisfactory meeting that went on for an hour. We managed, as I had hoped, to define the differences between us, which are not great. The government side, in particular Ed Balls, was very open and flexible. But God they're young – all in their mid-thirties.

Later I went to see Roy and had a long chat with him.

We discussed, firstly, the timing of TFM. I said that it was really important it went ahead in May or June. The trigger for this would be his Commission report, so we needed it a little earlier than he had intended. He said he would bear that in mind, but thought it unlikely that the report could be finalized that early. He aimed to finish by the summer recess and then publish in early September. I didn't challenge him on this, but said we could talk about it later.

When I next see Blair I will suggest we try to persuade Roy that the Commission must move faster than that. I don't want TFM delayed any further. It's already becoming difficult enough.

Secondly, I wanted to explain to Roy about the Spring Conference. I have become convinced that we must take a clear-cut decision on this. My tactic will be to recommend to the Party that we should maintain the status quo, i.e. constructive opposition while leaving all the doors open. I anticipate that someone will then put down a motion which will attempt to close the options by saying 'no coalition in this parliament'. That will then give me the opportunity to present the counter argument. But I will need all the help I can get – especially Roy's. He promised his support, as always.

Thirdly, I said that I thought it was really important for us to map out an intellectual case for co-operation between the two parties. I told him about my meeting with Brown and he said he would be happy to help there, too.

Later, home for a Methley Street dinner. Colin Brown[1] and his wife

---

1 Journalist for the *Independent*.

Mandy, together with Hugh Pym,[1] and his wife Sue. The conversation revolved mostly around Westminster gossip. But I shared my thoughts with them on relations with Labour – probably too freely. Hugh, Colin and Mandy all think that the Tories have had it. I told them that I rated Hague, and that we shouldn't dismiss him.

Monday, 8 December, Westminster

To a special dinner for the Queen given by the Privy Councillors at the House of Lords. There must have been three or four hundred in the Royal Gallery and a few more in the Robing Room. I sat a few down from the Queen and opposite Hague. She had Blair on her right-hand side. I had Angus Ogilvy on my left, and on my right the Duchess of Grafton. Major was on the other side of Ogilvy.

It was a pleasant dinner, even rather moving. Ann Taylor, as President of the Council and Leader of the House, gave a good speech. The Queen's speech was brief, plain but rather affecting. The setting was splendid, under all the gilt and the paintings of the Royal Gallery.

I had a brief discussion with Major about his forthcoming book. 'I am not going to smear anybody. I will just tell the truth and let everybody reach their own conclusions. But it will be tough.'

My other dinner companion, the Duchess of Grafton (who is apparently greatly feared by the Ladies of the Bedchamber), I found charming company. Very rude about the Tories and delightfully self-deprecating. She told me that she went to a dinner given by the President of Brazil at the Brazilian Embassy last week. All the waiters had pony tails, rings in their ears and looked very swarthy, so she asked her next-door neighbour, 'Do you think any of these people are British?' He turned to one of the waiters, a dusky gentleman with an especially long pony tail and a ring in his nose, and said, 'My colleague the Duchess of Grafton wants to know which catering firm you come from.' The pony-tailed one looked at her, squinted at her nameplate and said, 'Ah, the Duchess of Grafton. I was at Peter-house.[2] We had a Grafton who became Prime Minister. Wasn't a very good one, I'm afraid.'

1 Former ITN reporter who was the Liberal Democrat candidate for North Wiltshire in the 2001 General Election.
2 Peterhouse College, Cambridge. The Duke of Grafton, Prime Minister 1768–70, attended the college.

We finished at about 10 o'clock. As I left I saw Major and Hague sitting on one of the benches having an earnest chat.

During the dinner I watched Blair talking to the Queen. They seem very close. But Blair is now looking much older. The last six months have really taken it out of him.

Tuesday, 9 December, Westminster

At 4.00 a meeting of the Jo Group. Most helpful. I was thinking in my usual way of confronting the Party on keeping coalition options open. But everyone said that if I did that I would lose, especially in the Parliamentary Party. Instead, we decided to draw up a paper, to be drafted by Andrew Garratt,[1] which will be put down as a 'Take note' resolution for the conference, leaving it to the antis to amend it. It will probably give me a less clear cut decision. But, as Alan Leaman said, the best position is where those who want to close options are seen as spoiling the Party.

Wednesday, 10 December, Westminster

Voting in the House went on very late. As I was coming out of one of the lobbies Don Foster took me to one side and said, 'Look, the rumours about your future are now very widespread. They were questioning me at the *Today* programme Christmas party last night. They seem to know that you are being offered the job of European Commissioner.'

'In which case,' I said, 'they are wrong. That's complete nonsense!'

I wanted to speak to Don anyway before the start of the Christmas recess so as to enlist his help in winning the Parliamentary Party strategy debate. We went up to my office and, over a whisky and a cigarette, we discussed the attitude of the Colleagues. I also explained to him what I wanted to do.

'I need your help and advice. I will fax you a copy of the position paper I am going to write over Christmas to see what you think.'

'A number of people will adamantly oppose you, of course,' said Don. 'Phil Willis will fight you tooth and nail. Evan Harris[2] is becoming increas-

1 Head of Party Liaison in my office 1997–9. Fought Bournemouth for the Lib Dems in the 2001 General Election.
2 Dr Evan Harris. Member of Parliament for Oxford West and Abingdon since 1997.

ingly listened to. Steve Webb and Mark Oaten are also crucial voices in the Party. But the real difficulties will lie with Malcolm Bruce and Jim Wallace. Jim told me the other day that he was now certain the JCC had finished its constitutional work and was turning to other things such as education [Don's area] and that you are not telling me about it.'

I assured Don that this was not true. He suggested that I should talk to Jim in his capacity as leader of the Scottish Lib Dems and Richard Livsey for the Welsh. That way I might be able to draw the sting. A good idea.

Thursday, 11 December, Westminster and Somerset

At 12 o'clock a meeting with Jim, Malcolm and Charles, which went far better than I had expected. I said that the JCC had not discussed anything so far other than constitutional matters. 'Although some, I know, say that it does,' I said, looking straight at Jim. I also explained to them where I was coming from, carefully making it clear that this was my personal strategy. I was committed to it and I wasn't going to be budged. I hoped they would get the message early that if they want me to change the strategy they will have to take me on head to head.

At one stage Malcolm said that people were concerned about conspiracies.

I wasn't going to lie, so I said, 'Of course, there are conspiracies. There was a conspiracy to deliver the Electoral Reform Commission. The important thing isn't that there are conspiracies between me and Blair, but that you judge them by their outcomes and that you have safeguards to ensure that I don't go too far. Look, I understand why people are worried. Labour and the Lib Dems are two independent parties. And it must be frightening for members of those parties to be led by two men who have a tendency for wilfulness and who get on well personally. But you must measure the downside against the potential upside. And, so far at least, we have gained much much more than we have lost.'

At the end, Malcolm said, 'Of course we understand what you are doing, but others are more suspicious.'

A useful meeting.

Then into the car at 1.15 for Yeovil. Pleasant weather on the way down but it's getting colder – we need it. In the car I reflected on the week's events. It has been a bad week for the project. The whole tone of the relationship between Blair and myself seems to have changed. A lot of work still to be done to get it back on to an even keel.

Tuesday, 16 December, Westminster

At 3.00 down Whitehall to the Cabinet Office, wrapping my coat around me against a cutting east wind which was full of stinging particles of snow. Kate Garvey[1] met me at the Cabinet Office door and led me through the passages into Downing Street.

She left me sitting outside the Cabinet Room while she went to tell Blair that I had arrived. I could hear gales of laughter from behind the door of the Cabinet Room. Eventually Jonathan came out and said, 'Goodness me, are you still waiting, Paddy? I'll see you go in straightaway.' He went into Blair's little study and shortly afterwards the door opened and out came Alastair Campbell, Kate and Anji Hunter, all still roaring with laughter, above which Blair's voice could be heard: 'For goodness' sake, ask Paddy to come in, we need some light relief.' Apparently they had been discussing carols for the Downing Street concert, though why this had caused so much hilarity no one said.

I took my jacket off and asked, 'How do you feel?'

TB: Bruised. We have done ourselves some damage over the last week [on the withdrawal of benefits from single mothers]. We must learn to get our story across better. However, it's not terminal and we are still on track. Our opinion polls show the public are still with us. They believe hard decisions must be taken. They strongly support the idea of reforming the welfare system and seem to understand that there will be some casualties in this process. But we have done damage, real damage, within the party. There is very little excuse for the bad handling of last week and the fact that we did not explain what we are trying to do in the longer term. Perhaps it would have been better if we had slightly amended the policy. Anyway, that's behind us now.

PA: Well, I feel very unhappy about what has happened. Not least because I don't like my party being used as a peg for your left-wingers to hang their revolt on.[2] But you left us with no option. The really crucial question is: What are you going to do now? Will you, for instance, turn to disability benefit?

1 The Prime Minister's Diary Secretary.
2 The Lib Dems had combined with Labour back benchers to vote against the government on their controversial plans to cut lone parents' benefits.

TB: No, not in the same way. We will have to think it through rather more carefully. But the bottom line is that the money we are now putting into disability allowance is more than we are putting into education and it is *four* times more than what it was two years ago. No one can convince me that there are four times as many disabled people. I am determined that we remain on track with our reforms, because the dividends, in terms of money and a change of culture, are so great.

The discussion turned to Steve Webb.

TB: Is he as good as he appears?

PA: Yes. He is an IFS[1] man and takes the IFS view. That differs from the Labour Party's view. However, the fascinating thing is that at our first joint Treasury meeting last week, he and Ed Balls couldn't find much to disagree about. He is, in my view, a key player in my party. One of the brightest of the new intake and, in the long term, a potential leader of the Party.

TB: Good. Then let's bring him on board. I will see if I can arrange for him to be fully briefed. We could use his expertise, anyway, and if that helps us to understand each other's positions more thoroughly, then all the better.

PA: But what has really depressed me over the last week is the damage we have, I believe, done to the project.[2] You and I have always been able to manage a climate of convergence between the two parties, irrespective of localized difficulties. But on this occasion I think we are further apart than ever before. We should try to manage the process better so that we don't permanently damage the project. I am not sure we should formalize this into precise 'terms of engagement'. But let me explain to you the broad rules I have set down for my party in criticizing yours:

1. We should never do so in a way which would help the Tories (i.e. no generalized insults of the 'inept', 'corrupt' or 'sleazy' sort).

2. Attack the policy, never the person. There is no point in insulting and demeaning individuals.

3. We should ensure that wherever we criticize the government we do so on the basis of real facts, not opposition hype.

4. If we agree with the government's long-term aim, but disagree with the detail, then we should say so, putting the area of agreement first.

1 Institute for Fiscal Studies, an economic think tank.
2 In the previous Wednesday's PMQs Blair and I had had an especially testy exchange in the course of which he had said Tinky Winky, from the Teletubbies, would make a better economics spokesman than Malcolm Bruce.

5. Our tone should always be more in sorrow than in anger.

I continued, 'We try to observe these rules. No doubt we are not perfect about it. You might consider using them informally as the broad terms on which to criticize us as well. For instance, I thought your personal attack on Malcolm Bruce last week was unfair, unnecessary and unhelpful. Please remember that he is a senior colleague of mine who is doing a very good job – even if you don't like it – and whom I may struggle to get on board for the project.'

In his typically disarming way Blair said, 'Yes, I am sorry. I shouldn't have done that. It was spontaneous [I know that it wasn't – it was planned by Alastair Campbell]. I will try not to do it in future, but he does terribly provoke me.'

PA: He may well provoke. But he has a cogent line of attack and he is right.

TB: Yes, I know. We have presented you with an open goal, so I can't blame you for taking it. That's what politics is about.

PA: Incidentally, while I am on the subject, I must tell you how I hate it when you indulge in personal insults, even with Hague. It demeans you and does you no favours. Prime Ministers only rarely establish a position above politics. In my view, you did that at the time of Diana's funeral. You would do far better to maintain a position above Hague, deal with him coldly, if you like, but politely. With disdain rather than insult.

TB: You're probably right. But half an hour PMQs is a very, very long time when you are under pressure. I find it extremely difficult to keep to my own agenda sometimes.

PA: Well, I certainly couldn't do it. It's as much as I can do to put together two questions effectively and sometimes, even then, the atmosphere of confrontation gets the better of me. But how do you feel we should now go ahead on the project?

TB: Well, my instinct is to go ahead as we originally planned. Do you still want me to say the words about it being possible for you lot to be in a Cabinet?

PA: Yes. As you know, I intend to initiate a debate on all this at my party's Spring Conference. I have come to the view that the sharper and clearer the decision taken, the more use it will be to me later if we move to TFM. If we fudge the motion, which goes before my conference, then I can definitely win. But the victory would be of less use to me. So, broadly, I am happy if you still want to go ahead and say the words we have agreed.

TB: That's fine. Let's go ahead on that basis. I will talk to Alastair Campbell about this and come back to you with a date for it.

I said that it was very important he gave us as much notice as possible, since our response would have to be very carefully calibrated.

I then turned the conversation to the longer timescale. I explained that I'd had a chat with Roy Jenkins about producing the Electoral Reform Commission report and that he felt it would not be ready until early September. This would be fine for my Autumn Conference; presumably for his as well.

PA: But the problem is that Roy Jenkins's report, and your support for it, is supposed to be the trigger for the next stage of the project. So when do you want to move on to the next stage? When were you thinking of doing a reshuffle?

TB: I originally thought May, but now perhaps the end of July. Of course, we can't definitely decide to go ahead now. I presume you are not suggesting that?

PA: No, I'm not suggesting a firm plan. Nor that we commit ourselves, either to a date or to the substance, until nearer the time. But we do need to have a rough timescale 'pencilled in'; not least because we want to tell Roy Jenkins that we need to have his report brought forward. So do I take it that we are thinking now probably the middle or end of July? If so, will you talk to Roy about this?

TB: Yes, I am seeing him shortly; January, I think. So I will discuss it with him then.

I warned Blair that Roy would be very reluctant to speed up the report.

We finished off by wishing each other a Happy Christmas and agreed to meet in the New Year.

At 5.30, Robin Butler came to my office to discuss the Neill Committee.[1] He retires from his job as Cabinet Secretary on 3 January and was rather demob happy.

We talked, among other things, about the Cabinet.

RB: Actually, I think they are doing rather well. I like them. They have a very clear idea of what they want to do. No government that I can remember got into its stride so quickly and had such a remarkable first three months. But the real danger is that Blair is trying to do far too much. He often pays too little regard to collective

---

1 A committee, previously called the Nolan Committee, set up in 1994 to look into standards in public life (see Vol. I, p. 294).

responsibility. He merely bowls up and says, 'Gordon and I have decided . . .' I keep on telling him that this can't last. It's fine when things are going well. But if times get tough he will need his Cabinet's backing. And if the rest of the Cabinet haven't been involved in the decision, he won't get it.

PA: Yes, I know you told him that – he told me.

RB (smiling): How did he tell you? Was he cross?

PA: No, not at all. He said, 'Robin keeps telling me I can't do this. But I find it intensely boring having to consult with people, when the outcome is just common sense.'

RB: Maybe. But it can't go on like this. He is an exceptional man, and his charm is one of his most impressive weapons. But he cannot get away with it for ever.

We had a chat about what Robin and his wife Gill are going to do in their retirement. He said they were busy packing and unpacking. He is a nice man and I shall miss him. I told him so and thanked him for the help and advice that he had given me, particularly in the early days.

I left Whitehall at 7.15 and walked down the Embankment, huddling into my coat, to Joe Allen's in Covent Garden for a pre-Christmas dinner with the Jefferies and some Irancy friends who are over on their first trip to London [the Podors and the Hosottes]. Jean Podor has only ever previously been out of France when he did his *service militaire* in Algeria in the 1950s. Apparently, he tried a London doubledecker bus this morning (the French call them *impériales*). He climbed up to the top deck, and, beret pulled down over his head and Gauloise screwed into his lower lip as ever, proceeded to do the rounds of the bus shaking all the passengers by the hand in true Gallic fashion and wishing each of them '*Bonjour*'. A pretty startling experience for your average Londoner reading their newspaper on the way to work!

I took them back to the House of Commons for a whisky in the Pugin Room.[1] Jean entered into a voluble conversation with one of the House policemen, who spoke near perfect French – with which he was much impressed. Afterwards, I packed the French off in a taxi and caught one home myself. Got back at about 11.15 and fell into bed, feeling exhausted and ill.

---

1 A drinking room in the Palace of Westminster named after the designer of the interior of the Houses of Parliament, Augustus Pugin.

Tuesday, 16 December, Westminster

At 5.30, Hugo Young for half an hour. We had a fascinating discussion about Blair, in which I told him pretty well all there was to know, but upbraided him for saying that the only person who was planning ahead or thinking about power was Blair. I bet him a bottle of best burgundy that Blair would turn out in the end to be a pluralist. Hugo thinks he is going to be a control freak.

An interesting question, and one on which the whole government of Britain depends.

Thursday, 18 December, Westminster

Saw Richard Holme first thing, who has drafted out our response to Blair's statement about having Lib Dems in the Cabinet.

A Team Leaders' meeting at 9.30 to take them through the main points of my position paper, making it perfectly clear (though not in so many words) that this was my strategy and my future depended on it.

At one point, I said that this year's position paper was more important than most. Simon Hughes ribbed me by saying, 'You say that every year.' And Ming chipped in with, 'He is right, you know. Moses every January.'

Much laughter.

Saturday, 20 December, Somerset

Over the past two or three days Richard and I have continued working on how to respond to Blair's impending statement [which had by now come to be known as the 'uncomfortable words'] if he makes it over the Christmas/New Year period. We have been bashing various drafts backwards and forwards between us, as well as discussing them with Roy.

Richard saw Mandelson today and gave him our draft response. Apparently, Mandelson sucked his teeth at some elements of the outlined agreement but, more worryingly (though totally predictably), he is now saying that Blair is so tied up with the internal problems of his own party that he is having second thoughts about doing anything before Christmas. If he does say anything, it will merely be in response to a question about his relationship with the Lib Dems. And they will want to play that down, not up.

Richard asked me what my attitude was and I told him to tell Mandelson (who was just off on holiday) that it was important we knew, firstly, when Blair would say his words and, secondly, what they were. We had already agreed that we should ride with Blair's instincts on this. If he was enthusiastic, we should let him go ahead. If not, we shouldn't push it.

I am having quite severe doubts about the whole thing myself now, though I haven't shared them with anybody else. The way the government is going at the moment is not encouraging. I need Blair to be strong, popular and successful. That is what makes him self-confident. It also makes the task easier for me. The events of the last two or three weeks have weakened his position considerably.

1998

Tuesday, 6 January, Val Thorens

ON OUR ANNUAL SKIING TRIP TO FRANCE[1]

Woke to lowering cloud, filling the valley with heavy snow. I needed to spend some time working over the holiday, so today was the day. Fixed a meeting with Tim and Archy at 10 o'clock to talk about the position paper I wrote a few days ago,[2] paving the way for TFM. Archy was concerned about what I will do if it all goes against me. I looked at him sharply and said, 'You know perfectly well what I will do. I will go. I won't say as much in public, because I don't want the Party to feel blackmailed. But it will be pretty apparent to everyone.'

He pushed me hard on this. Would I resign straightaway? I told him that I would accept the decision of the Party, then, with good grace, say I was handing over to somebody else in my conference speech.

Would I make that clear in the debate?

'No. I will go round the country explaining my views beforehand. But I won't speak in the debate. The Party will have to make up its own mind. I've had a wonderful ten years. I have done all I want to do with the Party and it has been very kind to me. If, at this stage, it doesn't want to go down the route I propose, then I will hand over quite contentedly to somebody else.'

Archy thought that perhaps we should get a few of us together to decide exactly what happens if I do go down in the debate – the chances of which he considered were about 50/50. 'People already seem to be taking up positions. Jackie is staking out her ground for Southport[3] and Conrad Russell has written an article for *Lib Dem News* in which he clearly raises the flag of opposition.'

I told Archy that I had anticipated this, although it's happening a little earlier than I'd expected.

After lunch we went skiing, despite the heavily falling snow.

---

1 As a family we go skiing annually with friends, usually Archy Kirkwood, Tim Razzall, Tim Clement-Jones, Max Atkinson and their families.
2 See Appendix D.
3 The party's forthcoming Spring Conference was to be held in Southport.

Sunday, 11 January, France and London

Left Sens for Calais at about 5.50am. Kate emerged bleary-eyed to say goodbye. As always, it was a very sad parting.

Frosty, with fog patches all the way to Paris.

We arrived at Methley Street at 10.45. Just under five hours door to door – a record! Jane and Simon then set off for Somerset. I spent the next couple of hours wading through my mail and trying to catch up on the press cuttings.

Bob Maclennan came round to see me at 4.00. He believes my position paper is too provocatively worded. He also showed me two very unhelpful articles in the *Observer* and the *Independent on Sunday*, which more or less say that Blair has it in mind to offer us Cabinet positions (as we had planned before Christmas). Bob is still very wobbly. But he agrees about what we should try to achieve at Southport [i.e. a mandate to keep our options open]. He seems obsessed with the idea that the history of politics has been about splitting parties. Of course we run that risk, but if we don't run it, we can't do anything.

At 6.30 the Team Leaders started to drift in: Paul Burstow, Simon Hughes, Charles Kennedy, Archy Kirkwood, David Rendel, Paul Tyler and Matthew Taylor. I gave them each a glass of wine and presented them with the position paper. No expressions of unhappiness, though one or two took exception to my prediction that, in time, the Tories were bound to bounce back. But they all agreed with the conclusions. I was mightily relieved to have got them all on board. They will all adopt a 'no options closed' position at tomorrow's PPM.

Monday, 12 January, London

The day I have been dreading. Up at 6.00 to gather my papers and do some thinking for the meeting ahead. Then off to the Ismaili Centre on the Cromwell Road for our annual all-day Parliamentary Party Meeting. I was the first there, arriving at 9.00.

Gradually the Colleagues started drifting in. Each was given a copy of the position paper. I could see them all scribbling furiously.

The meeting proper started at 11.30. The debate was very firmly against me before lunchtime. Not a single person spoke in favour of the policy I was proposing. To my anger, David Rendel parted company from last night's agreement and said that he had been 'reflecting overnight' and disagreed with the paper substantially. He was swiftly followed by Simon, who took exactly the same line but more subtly. Finally, Charles came in with broadly the same points. I was absolutely livid, though I tried not to show it. This is completely the reverse of what they had agreed last night. I think they were just following the current flow of opinion, there being an obvious and concerted campaign to close immediately any option which could lead to a coalition with Labour in this parliament.

Over lunch I went round the other Team Leaders, asking them to take up the debate in the afternoon.

The afternoon session went much better. Gradually, the consensus that I wished for emerged. Jackie Ballard made a marginally conciliatory speech and both Mark Oaten and Steve Webb spoke well. Nick Harvey pointed out that if they fought me on coalitions and won, it would create a crisis in the party. But if they fought me and lost, the press would say that I'd won the Party's mandate to go ahead with a coalition. So, if they wanted neither of these things, they should, as suggested, keep the options open. The key intervention of the day. Everyone nodded.

Others followed. Alan was particularly helpful in correcting some misconceptions about the Lib/Lab pact, while Phil Willis made a powerful (if, to me, unhelpful) speech. Paul Burstow and Andrew Stunell were both very constructive, even though I know they are among those most worried about coalition.

Charles very cleverly identified that Blair and I wanted two different things: he wanted domination and I wanted pluralism. I agreed that this was indeed the case, but that I was aware of it. And anyway, the question wasn't what we wanted in the longer term, but what we could win from the immediate situation. Next spoke Jim Wallace, angry and against, and Don Foster, who was straight down the line in support. At the end Bob Maclennan made an emotional appeal, which seemed to have some effect. The most dangerous moment of the whole meeting came, unwittingly I think, from Don. Because he was being so supportive, I wasn't really on my guard. He said, 'Look, the one question none of you have asked Paddy is the one everybody said they were going to ask him. Is he planning a coalition with Tony Blair? So, in the spirit of Prime Minister's Questions, I want to ask him that now.' And he turned to me: 'Are you planning a coalition with Blair? Answer yes or no.'

Taken completely off balance, I said, 'No.'

My heart sank. It is the first time I have not told them the truth. So at the very end of the debate I returned to Don Foster's question. 'I want to clarify my answer to Don's earlier question, which was, in hindsight, wrong. Personally, I see very little chance of a coalition. But I do want you all to know that I am trailing my skirt like mad. I am tempting Blair to make us an offer. If he does, then I shall want to examine it with an open mind; if I think it is to the advantage of the Party, I will put it to you to decide.'

I felt mortified at not having given this answer to Don's original question. When I later discussed it with Archy, Paul and others they said I had no option if the whole thing wasn't to blow up in our faces.

Afterwards, I walked down Kensington Gore, thinking about the meeting. The whole Parliamentary Party, according to Alan Beith's summing-up, agreed that it would be inappropriate to close options at this stage. It will be difficult for them (although not impossible, given past U-turns) to go back on their decision at the forthcoming conference.

So a serious and determined attempt to limit my room for manoeuvre has finally been beaten off. But not without cost.

Later, to dinner at the Pizza in the Park with some of the Colleagues, after which back to Don Foster's flat with Malcolm. We had a discussion about who would be the next leader. Don is more of a candidate than I thought he was. They both confirmed that Simon and Charles are preparing fiercely. Good. They also put me under pressure as to when I will stand down: I let them think I will fight the next election. No other option!

Tuesday, 13 January, London

I have now clarified my analysis of what can be done. It goes like this:

1. There is a liberal progressive majority of people in Britain. There always has been, but in the past we haven't been able to assemble it. That majority, however, is now much stronger following Labour's abandonment of socialism.

2. In this period of flux we can convert people to the liberal progressive view as evidenced by the fact that people as diverse as Bob Maclennan from Labour and Emma Nicholson from the Tories are now with us.

3. Blair is heading in broadly the same direction. Our working with him will make it more likely that his government is a more liberal one.

4. We are, therefore, involved in a sort of reverse takeover process. We have already partially succeeded in this on the whole constitutional issue. And we must now try to extend it further.

5. Our future growth will come in this area and not from the Tories. The Liberal Democrats can, in short, be the focal point at which a new liberal consensus can gather to form the predominant political force for our time.

To bed well after midnight, having watched the tail end of a rather silly Clint Eastwood film. A disturbed night. I have a cold which seems to be getting worse. My heart sinks at having to go through the whole process of reassembling policy for the next General Election and fighting it once more through the Party Conferences, especially with such a strong pull in the party to revert to the policies of the 1970s. I long to give this job up. In the middle of the night I lay awake hoping something would precipitate my immediate resignation. But, as usual, by dawn I felt better. I should not be depressed. The Party is doing well. But I just don't have the energy and I am now lacking the interest to push this thing on. Time for someone else to take over.

Wednesday, 14 January, Westminster

Into the leaders' Co-ordinating Committee meeting. Local election results show us improving from 1 May. So no signs of a fallback. But later on, when we came to discuss the strategy paper, there was a determined attempt to ride me on to safer ground. They want to pretend we are not taking a decision at all at Southport. I allowed them to play for the safe ground for the moment, but I shall hype it up later as soon as I am safely past the Federal Executive – probably by leaking the position paper (although I am still not sure about this). I have two options. I can either play for safety, in which case the result at Southport is less useful to me. Or I can play for higher stakes when it will be more useful for me with the stage that comes next.

We are having problems now with Labour over meetings between senior Lib Dems and their ministerial opposite numbers. Prescott has put a block on them in his department. He is using some injudicious comments made by Nick Harvey as the pretext. I suspect the *Observer* and the *Independent On Sunday* articles containing Blair's statement about the possibility of the Lib Dems joining government has caused ructions within the Cabinet. On the other hand, Blair is now making a strong pitch for the agenda of the next JCC to be widened substantially. He wants to talk about health, Bosnia and Northern Ireland. There is danger to us in widening too far.

Thursday, 15 January, Westminster

At 6 o'clock off to the FE. I only went there for the strategy motion [i.e. closing no options]; in the event, it went swimmingly. An amendment was put forward rejecting coalitions in this parliament. Fortunately, it lacked focus and tried to pile too many things on to the original proposal, including limiting our room for manoeuvre on the Joint Cabinet Committee. An extensive debate followed in which Jackie Ballard and Lembit Opik made two very helpful interventions which swung the meeting. In the event, only two people voted for the amendment. But we are not out of the woods yet. The FE and the Parliamentary Party are now overwhelmingly in favour of not taking an amendment on coalitions to the conference. But inevitably someone will put one forward. And at that stage those who want to vote for it will do so. No doubt including most MPs. So the danger is still there.

Wednesday, 21 January, Westminster

I have received an e-mail from Mike Hoban,[1] who tells me that there has been a lot of plotting behind the scenes by unnamed MPs to bring the issue of coalitions to a head at the Southport Conference, with a view to defeating me and then running a leadership election afterwards. I don't believe it. No signs of it on the surface.

Met Jackie Ballard in the corridor, who said, 'You never speak to me these days.' There's some truth in this. I have been rather avoiding her. I suppose I feel somewhat aggrieved that, having done so much together in the past [she was previously one of my local councillors in Somerset] she is now so bitterly opposing me during one of the most crucial periods of my political life. But I am being unreasonable; she is entitled to her opinions, even if I disagree with them. She is an effective MP and capable of being very loyal and professional.

---

1 Our prospective parliamentary candidate for Bridgwater at the 1997 General Election.

Thursday, 22 January, Westminster

At 3.30 down to see Roy.[1] He is having the Blairs round to dinner on Saturday. I told him to assure Blair that, although we had not parted company on the best of terms recently, I was still fully committed to the project.

I also asked Roy to find out how the Cabinet had taken Blair's statement about the possibility of Lib Dems in the Cabinet, over the New Year. Had this caused ructions?

'The big question in Blair's mind is: How trustworthy are the Lib Dems?' said Roy. 'Are we just fair weather friends?'

'Yes, that's the risk he takes with us,' I agreed. 'But he should understand that I am taking an equivalent risk with him, too. Is he genuinely a pluralist or does he want to swallow us up? There are dangers in this for both of us, and that's what makes it a win–win situation.'

It also emerged that Roy had lunch with Ken Clarke last Friday, followed by dinner with Mandelson. Clarke had been ebullient but clearly thought the Tory Party was going in the wrong direction. Roy didn't press him too much but simply acted as a sounding board. Clarke's general dissatisfaction with Hague came out with, 'All things being equal, I want to remain in the Conservative Party, but I am not sure that they are equal.' Afterwards Clarke had written Roy a note thanking him for lunch and saying, 'I suppose events are now pushing you and me closer and closer together.' Roy thought this very significant.

Mandelson was even more fascinating. He had rung Roy to invite himself over for dinner. He was very gloomy and, apparently, spent most of the dinner sounding off about Brown and his advisers, in particular Charlie Whelan. This is not some minor tiff whipped up by the press, but something far more fundamental. Roy described Mandelson as being like a man rebuffed in love who needed a friend to pour his heart out to. Roy suspects that one of his problems is the Millennium Dome, although they didn't discuss it.

I said I thought the decision to carry on with the Dome was crazy. It will come back to haunt Mandelson and hang like an albatross around the government's neck.

---

1 Roy had recently given up the leadership of the Lib Dems in the House of Lords, to be succeeded by Bill Rodgers in the New Year.

The only other interesting thing Mandelson said was that Blair is becoming increasingly dissatisfied with the quality of some of his ministers. Roy concluded that Blair may thus be in a position to reshuffle earlier than he had originally intended. Roy will probe more about this on Saturday. He promised to keep me informed.

Monday, 26 January, Westminster

At 2 o'clock, down Whitehall to the Cabinet Office and into No. 10 for my meeting with Blair. Bright sunshine, though it is still bitterly cold.

Following his dinner with the Blairs, Roy had rung me to say that the PM wanted to have a general '*tour d'horizon*' with me.

Unusually, when I walked in he was wearing a jacket. It later transpired that he had just seen Yasser Arafat, who must have been shown out the other way. Blair is looking much more haggard than before.

He began by talking about the economy, which, he said, had been occupying much of his time recently. Previously he had been worried about it, but he now felt rather more confident that we were in for a 'soft landing'.

TB: . . . but events in the Far East are still pretty tricky and I am worried about their knock-on consequences for Russia and the Ukraine. That said, things are looking brighter than a few weeks ago.

I said that surely the public finances were improving to such an extent that he was bound to reap a huge dividend to distribute (what we have christened his 'war chest').

He responded that public finances were in better shape than before, but that there wasn't yet a 'war chest'. They would have to hold back on public sector pay and go for a cautious Budget.

After a brief discussion on Northern Ireland (where peace talks had reached a critical juncture) he said, 'Well, how did it go with your Parliamentary Party? Roy says you had a pretty torrid time.'

PA: You know my strategy. It has been to lever the Party forward inch by inch. Every time we move a little they get concerned. Then they settle down and start thinking the previously unthinkable. Then, when they get used to it, it is time to lever them on again. At the Parliamentary Party Meeting many of my colleagues seemed to guess what I was up to and were determined to resist me. But they probably didn't understand the scope of it and presumed this was all about my own personal ambition. However, I came out of the meeting with unanimous support for the status quo, which is defined as 'Ruling nothing in and nothing out'. I'm pretty sure a hostile amendment will be put down at our conference at Southport, though. But we should be able to defeat it, even though I suspect one or two of my parliamentary colleagues will vote for it.

TB: Sounds tough. I'm sorry I didn't get to say the words you wanted on *Frost*. I went in there prepared to say them, but he never asked me the question!

PA: Never mind. Don Macintyre's article in the *Independent* [on the same subject] has been useful enough. It has created a backdrop for a debate within my Parliamentary Party and in the party at large. This sharpens considerably the decision they have to take. My view here, as with so much else, is that the fuzzier the decision, the easier it is to get through, but the less use it is in the long term. Whereas the clearer the decision, the more difficult it is to get through, but the more useful it will be. I think the balance we have struck here is just about right.

TB: What happens when we move forward? Do you still want to do this? How will your members react?

PA: My position has not changed. I think we have been presented with the best opportunity ever for a '*grand rassemblement*' of progressive and liberal forces which could form the dominant governing power in this country. As you know, I am not in favour of mergers. So I'm talking about a pluralist system where both parties maintain their distinct authorities. Although, as I said last September, our task has not been made any easier by the passage of time and the inevitable mistakes of the government. But I remain completely committed to it. Do you?

TB: Yes, I haven't changed. It is, in my view, the biggest thing I have to do. We are in the business of changing a culture in Britain and this event, when it comes, will signal that the new culture is wider than just the Labour Party.

PA: But that may not be the way it is viewed by everyone else, especially our enemies. You talk about this being in the interests of the country. But they will portray it as a grubby political deal, in which I have sacrificed my party for an elderly man's ambition and you have sought to create a single overarching movement in order to swallow up everybody else and crush democratic debate. Our problem will be to make sure that what we do is portrayed as genuinely for the good of the country, rather than just good for our political parties, or us personally.

TB: I agree with that. And we will need to return to it later. But will your people on the ground come with you if you ask them ultimately to support a coalition?

PA: That depends on two crucial things: your own personal position on PR, and the nature of the deal. If the Lib Dems are perceived as just an appendage to Labour, then my members will reject it. But if you are seen to have joined with us in a programme which goes further than you would otherwise have gone and which we can, therefore, represent as some kind of victory for liberal values, then I am pretty confident I can carry it. I am also banking on the fact that, by the time we may want to do this, you will have considerable financial resources at your disposal to invest in health and education. Under these circumstances, I hope my party realizes that you will be reaping a political dividend that we should be sharing in, not standing aside from. But, at the end of the day, the deal must be substantial on policy and bigger than the sum of its parts.

Blair changed the subject:

TB: How do you think we are doing in government? And where do you think we are going wrong?

I was slightly taken aback by this.

PA: When people ask me what are the flaws of this government, I tell them I think there are three. The first is that you personally are doing far too much. You have done brilliantly to get this far, but you must delegate more. You cannot take charge of the welfare agenda and the Budget as well as everything else we have read in the papers.

Secondly, you are far too dominated by the news agenda of the next forty-eight hours.

And lastly, as I have said to you before, people perceive two sides to your own personality which are reflected in the two sides of your government. The question is, will you lot become pluralist democratic reformers, or will you continue as control freaks?

TB: I have described our present position to my colleagues as 'post-euphoria and pre-delivery'. We have a tough six months ahead of us. But I anticipate we will be able to start delivering more of substance by the end of the summer. But let me respond to your criticisms. I think you are wrong in saying I am doing too much. I feel very happy, very fit and very confident. And all this stuff in the papers about me not pursuing Cabinet government is just nonsense. Our Cabinet meetings are just as long as the previous lot's.

And the idea that I'm obsessed with the media is also wrong. Apparently, Major routinely used to spend hours every night poring over the early editions. I never even glance at them. And I don't think I should.

PA: Yes, but the fact that you don't read them doesn't mean that your office staff – Alastair Campbell, in particular – aren't manic about them.

We turned to the euro.

PA: As you know, Roy and I, and many others, think you are making a big mistake by not having a referendum soon. We will press you very hard on this, including at PMQs.

TB: But do you really think we can win it?

PA: Yes, I think we can. Although it's a risk, of course. But a referendum in, say, early 2000 could be won, given who would be on the platform for each side and the fact that only the smaller, nastier people in the Tory Party would oppose it.

For the first time since we've talked about this he did not dismiss the idea of a referendum out of hand.

Then I asked him what exactly he'd had in mind when he had called for a 'patriotic alliance' on Europe the other day. And what concrete proposals he was going to make to achieve what he wants.

TB: Frankly, I haven't a clue. Although I have people working on some propositions for me.

PA: Well, why on earth did you say it, then? Your remarks caused real problems for some of the Euro-friendly Tories such as Geoffrey Howe and Ken Clarke.

TB: Yes, I understand that now, but I didn't then. It was rather insensitive of me. I have sent Clarke a message of apology.

Though tempted, I did not say that this was a classic example of Alastair Campbell running a short-term media-driven agenda without thinking things through.

We also spoke briefly about Clinton's impeachment over the Monica Lewinsky affair. He reckoned that Clinton has a 60/40 chance of surviving. He understood the White House were now going into offensive mode, with Hillary leading the charge. 'She's some tough lady.' But this was causing real problems elsewhere in the world. He was very worried about Iraq: the latest weapons inspectors' report said they were quite convinced there was some very nasty weaponry hidden away in the presidential palaces.

I finally asked him when he would do his reshuffle. He was vague on this, indicating some dissatisfaction with one or two members of his government, but giving me no indications of timing. Very disappointing!

To the office at 3.00, where I had time to deal with the post before George Soros[1] came to see me at 3.30. What a nice man. Soft-spoken. He wanted to know all about the state of British politics, what role we were playing, etc. I asked him his view of the world economy. He described the Pacific Basin economic collapse as 'scary' but felt that it was probably now broadly under control and wouldn't get worse. Although he saw the collapse coming, he, like everyone else, had been taken by surprise at its severity and by the knock-on effect on other Far Eastern economies. He is now very worried about the Russian economy, which is heavily dependent on some of the Far Eastern banks, especially the Korean ones. He described the situation in Russia as on a knife edge, and that in Ukraine as 'very precarious'.

We talked about the euro, which he thinks will start on time and will be reasonably well founded. But once established, there will have to be a massive dollar reserve in place to protect it. He is worried about the long-term consequences, the rigidity of the European economies in particular.

Tuesday, 27 January, Westminster

At 4.30 a very useful meeting with Bill Rodgers. He is more or less on board for TFM but is concerned to do his new job as leader in the Lords properly. We had quite a debate about who should handle the Lords reform.

In the middle of this meeting I got a call from Jonathan Powell. Blair, he said, is incandescent. Apparently, the Lib Dems in the Lords are going to combine with the Tories to try and defeat Labour on the Greater London Authority (Referendum) Bill, which, under the Cook/Maclennan agreement, we are helping them to get through the Commons! The Lib Dem lords are, he said, even holding a joint press conference with the Tories on it. Blair (justifiably) regards this as a breach of faith which could seriously damage our relationship. Strongarm tactics. I played for time by saying (truthfully) that I hadn't a clue what all this was about.

I immediately called in Simon Hughes in his role as our Commons spokesman on London. He has put down some amendments in the Com-

---

1 President of Soros Fund Management and one of the richest people in the world.

mons without thinking how these would play through when the Bill came
to the Lords where the Tories are, of course, much stronger.

I told Simon that I didn't mind what we said about the government on
any other issue, but constitutional reform was off limits. Also, that we
simply could not have a joint press conference in the Commons about
working with the government on constitutional issues one minute, and
then another one with the Tories in the Lords, opposing one aspect of
it, the next. And not only because Labour would feel justifiably let down,
but because it would massively confuse the public. He agreed to pull the
Lords press conference and go away and think about how best to handle
this.

Wednesday, 28 January, Westminster

Wrote to Blair explaining the situation in the Lords, which is not as
straightforward as it first appeared – the Lib Dem lords do have some
grounds for opposing the Bill as it stands.

Just as I was going for dinner I had a call from Powell. He hadn't received
the letter I faxed to him. I told him I'd resend it. He said, 'I gather the
whole thing is in chaos and we are going to be overturned in the Lords
again. It really is very grumpy-making.' I warned him that before reaching
any conclusions he should look at the fax I had sent. Some people were
clearly getting at Blair with the usual refrain of 'Bloody Lib Dems'.

Thursday, 29 January, Westminster

Labour were indeed defeated in the Lords last night. Today I received a
letter from Blair:

... I appreciate the efforts you have made but I do have to tell you that there is
serious dissatisfaction in the Labour Party due to the defeat we suffered in the
Lords on your amendment. The defeat was once again dependent on the votes of
hereditary peers ... Of course I accept that we can reverse defeats when Bills come
back to the Commons, but ministers find it difficult to understand why they are
being asked by my office to participate in bilateral meetings over London when the
Liberal Democrats are working with the Conservatives in the Lords to defeat the
government on this matter. I think we can get over this problem and I will make

efforts to calm things down on our side, but I do fear this has soured attitudes on our side in the short term.

Sunday, 1 February, Somerset

Another beautiful day. Up at 9.00. Nothing much in the papers except some ominous rumblings over Iraq. I am very concerned about the possible consequences of a military attack.

Doing nothing could make matters worse. But military action on the basis that it is the 'least worst option' would be unlikely to gain the support of the Middle Eastern countries who joined the coalition before, would seriously destabilize politics in the region, would strengthen Saddam's position and lead to goodness knows what. I will try to speak to Blair. It is vital that a clear aim is established for any action taken.

Wednesday, 4 February, Westminster

At 9.30 Sir Peter de la Billière, former commander of our troops in the Gulf War, came to see me, at my request. He shares my nervousness about the Iraqi situation. He said there is a wide gap between the views of the sheikhs of the Gulf States and the opinions of the souk, the latter being very pro-Saddam Hussein. I asked him what he would do instead of taking military action and he didn't have an answer. It was useful, however, to make contact with him again.

I have fixed up to speak to Blair about Iraq at midday – on the phone, if need be – before he leaves for the US. I guess I have a bit of a reputation about being rather gung-ho about military action, but I am more fearful about the Iraqi situation now than I have ever been about action in Bosnia or the previous Gulf War.

Blair rang almost exactly on time. Richard Holme, who happened to be with me, sat in throughout the call.

I said that, as he knew, I had always solidly backed the government on military action in the past. And in the end I would back them on this one, too. But I wanted him to know that I was very nervous about taking action.

TB: I am, too.

PA: Then let me explain. I have three concerns. The first is, I don't believe you have made the case yet to the British people or to the wider world as to why it is so necessary to take action, i.e. you have yet to convince us of the real danger that Saddam poses.

Secondly, it is absolutely vital that we declare the aim of our actions. Obviously, there will be secret military aims, and no one is asking you to divulge those; but there also needs to be a public aim – and one that has a reasonable chance of being achieved.

Thirdly, British public opinion and, more importantly, world opinion must be convinced that all realistic diplomatic alternatives have been exhausted, before we can expect full support for military action. And I don't believe that has happened yet. The Americans, it seems, may well be playing Iraq, at least in part, for domestic political reasons. The last time Clinton challenged Saddam there was a perception in America that Saddam won and Clinton lost. I am worried that Clinton's judgement may be affected both by this and by his weak domestic position. There needs to be a series of carefully graduated, publicly known steps, each with a very clear threshold. Saddam should know exactly what advantages accrue to him if he conforms and what penalties he will suffer if he doesn't.

TB: I agree with you. It would be helpful if you ask a question at PMQs today along these lines. It will enable me to deploy the case on the dangers of Iraq which will, I hope, help educate the public. You should know that I have, anyway, decided to send every MP today a document which will give full details of the threat from Iraq. As to the aim, I am being advised that we can take actions which will force Saddam Hussein to accept the UN inspectors. And finally, I quite agree with you that we must ensure that all diplomatic options have been fully pursued before taking further action; and we're doing so. We have, perhaps, two weeks left to do this in. I spoke to Yeltsin and Chirac this morning. They believe that if we were to offer Saddam the possibility of having five extra people on the monitoring team – one from each of the Security Council nations – that might be a way forward.

PA: Good. But I hope we will do this on the understanding that he must then agree to access for the inspectors. If France and Russia can give Saddam a facesaving way out, so much the better. In the meantime, we should keep up the military pressure.

We ended there.

Afterwards, Richard and I discussed possible Tory defectors. We have been working together for some time on a group of Tories who seem wobbly: Lord Plumb, former leader of the Conservatives in the European Parliament; John Stevens (to whom I spoke at Pontignano and who laid the groundwork for all this); another former Tory MEP, James Moor-house; and supposedly also Anthony Teasdale, Geoffrey Howe's former aide, who is, apparently, very bright. Richard has done a brilliant job on them. He thinks they have now more or less decided to jump. They say it's just a question of when. Our ideal time for them to come on board, we agreed, would be the week before our conference. But they apparently want to do it when the Tory Party is having a conference on Europe, a few days later. I said we should bow to their timing. With defectors they come when they come.[1]

Then PMQs, in which Blair gave a full answer to my question about the aims of the operation and the nature of the Iraqi threat. He outlined just what the weapons inspectors had found: 38,000 chemical weapons, some 48,000 litres of live chemical warfare agents, 48 scud missiles, 30 missile warheads, and a vast biological weapon production plant which they then destroyed. Afterwards I went down to Blair's office.

I was ushered in at about 3.40. Jonathan Powell and John Holmes[2] there, Holmes taking notes.

I said I thought the document Blair had given to MPs today was exactly what was needed. But why not publish the weapons inspectors' reports? Surely they weren't secret and they would provide a mine of convincing objective information.

TB: I made just such a suggestion to my advisers yesterday, and they are looking into it now. If we can, we will. But I would like to go further than that. I would like to get that nice man Butler[3] who heads up the teams on to British television.

PA: Yes, but the problem isn't British public opinion, which is probably pretty robust; it's world opinion. You must put this on a wider stage.

Blair responded by saying that he could see the importance of doing this but that he didn't see how to do it. As for the French, 'They will support us if we succeed, but they won't if we don't.'

PA: Frankly, I don't think the aim that you identified at Prime Minister's Question

---

1 Richard tells me that he believes this multiple defection from the Tories at this delicate moment was only averted at the last minute by a personal appeal from Geoffrey Howe to Lord Plumb.

2 Sir John Holmes, Principal Private Secretary (Foreign Affairs) to the Prime Minister 1997–9. Sir John is now the British Ambassador to Lisbon.

3 Richard Butler, the United Nations chief arms inspector in Iraq. Butler's official title was the Executive Chairman of the UN Special Commission (UNSCOM).

Time is a sensible one. You said, if I recall, that you believed military action could be taken which would force Saddam to accept free access for the weapons inspectors. Are your advisers really saying this can be achieved?

TB: No. There is nothing to say that if we bomb him, he will accept the UN's resolutions. I've been told there's a reasonable prospect he may do so, but no more than that. Why are you worried?

PA: I don't think it's a suitable aim. We ought to have an aim which is achievable. Otherwise, when we fail to achieve it we have to go on bombing until eventually world opinion forces us to stop even if the aim is still not achieved; then Saddam will be seen to have won. The options are, it seems to me, based on prevention, punishment or a mixture of the two. For instance, it would be foolish to make the destruction of every last chemical or biological warhead the aim – because we could never be sure of achieving it. But we could aim to reduce his capacity to produce these weapons by attacking the relevant production and installation facilities. At the same time we could take actions whose aims are to diminish significantly the military capacity on which Saddam's regime is founded. In other words, we could make sure that he did not flout international law without paying an unacceptable price for it. We don't want to totally destroy his forces. That would leave a dangerous vacuum in the Middle East into which Syria or Iran might move. So the publicly stated aim could, for instance, be to prevent Saddam from increasing his stocks of weapons of mass destruction by reducing his capacity for further production, while forcing him to pay a price he finds painful in terms of the loss of other military assets. This, at least, would be an achievable aim.

The next thing that needs to be done, then, is to convince international opinion that we have genuinely exhausted all alternative diplomatic routes. For instance, if we could assemble some international support for a properly formulated, 'step-by-step' approach, then, if Saddam does not react positively, we have a better chance of gaining international support for military action.

Richard said, 'The problem is that the Americans are extremely reluctant to do anything which will reward Saddam.'

TB: Yes. But over the next four or five days we can probably persuade Clinton that Saddam should be offered a limited set of rewards for good behaviour as well as the threat of clear punishments for bad.

By this time we were being interrupted every two or three minutes by a harassed-looking secretary who was clearly concerned about Blair's time-table.

As I left I said, 'I have said all I wanted to say. I wish you every success in Washington. There is a lot riding on it.'

At 7.30 I returned to the office, tidied up my stuff, then walked across the park in the cold evening air to the Reform Club for Roy's farewell do. The walk cleared my head and did me a lot of good, as I am feeling pretty jaded. I arrived just as everyone was going in to dinner in the library (a splendid room). I sat next to Jennifer Jenkins, who was very candid about her worries about Blair. She thinks he has the potential to be a great prime minister but he isn't showing it yet. There were eighty or ninety of us there: all the Lords, of course, and from the Commons, Charles Kennedy, Bob Maclennan and Alan Beith. Roy's old Oxford friend Basil Wigoder made a nice speech, followed by David Steel, who told a couple of quite amusing anecdotes. Then me. I decided I couldn't sustain the wit, so I did something rather serious and a touch emotional. Roy, as ever, funny, self-deprecating and ever so slightly dismissive of the whole event. A memorable evening.

Tuesday, 10 February, Westminster

A chat with Ming on the Bench about the Iraq statement Cook made this afternoon.[1] Much less bellicose than Blair's tones last week. A definite sense of drawing back. Elinor Goodman asked me afterwards whether I felt this showed a weakening of the government's position. I said I didn't think so. It was important to get the military option firmly on to the table, after which we could withdraw for a couple of weeks and let diplomacy take its course.

Wednesday, 11 February, Westminster

At 12.15 Shirley and Ming came in for a Foreign Office briefing on Iraq. It is clear that the government are pushing the Americans on the diplomatic front and that the Foreign Office is quite optimistic about getting another UN resolution through. But it will depend on allowing sufficient time to pass for the Russians to get bored with Saddam's intransigence and, therefore, not use their veto. A fine judgement call.

---

1 The Foreign Secretary had reported back to the House of Commons on his tour of the Middle Eastern States, where he had received a lukewarm reception.

Tuesday, 17 February, Westminster

The Commons debate on Iraq was held today, although I wasn't there – I was on a campaign visit to Liverpool. I learned later that there have been strong complaints about our position of supporting the government from Phil Willis, Steve Webb, Jackie Ballard, Norman Baker and Andrew George.[1] Jackie, I think, is under pressure from her constituency. But after a meeting with Ming, who was at his most persuasive, all except Andrew George and Norman Baker voted with the rest of the Parliamentary Party. A generous act, especially from Jackie. I later contacted her and Phil Willis to thank them.

Wednesday, 18 February, Westminster

A long and pretty strenuous conversation with Conrad Russell today, which ended in us 'agreeing to differ'. He is implacably opposed to Blair and tells me he prefers the Tories to Blairite Labour. I told him he was just plain wrong. He put me under a lot of pressure to explain why I liked Blair and every time I explained why I thought he should be given the benefit of the doubt, Conrad went over the minutiae of why, since he said this in such and such a speech (always a small textual point), Blair was in fact worse than any Tory.

Off to see John Prescott at 6.45pm.

I found him sitting in his Commons office (a rather small affair) in a very crumpled blue shirt with his tie at half mast and his collar unbuttoned. He asked his secretary (whom he described as 'Neil Kinnock's ex-secretary, but I have re-trained her') to bring me a cup of tea. His office is comfortable but unkempt. Cardboard boxes everywhere, with a small arrangement of trades union statuettes lining the windowsill. A picture of Cromwell on the wall and a pretty cluttered desk. I gained a strong sense that this was a place where he camped, rather than worked.

I started off by saying that things were obviously going well for him. He had developed a personality in his own right and had confounded any critics who had said he could not run a ministry, let alone one as big as the

---

1 Member of Parliament for St Ives since 1997.

one he is heading.[1] Also, I knew he played an absolutely crucial part in determining Blair's position in relation to a number of key issues, including those closest to my heart. So I wanted to take the opportunity to tell him how I saw things.

Firstly, I believed there was a project in hand which would take ten years to complete – that is, the modernization of Britain. It had five key elements: constitutional modernization (to put the power back in the hands of the citizen); the modernization of our welfare state (to provide more opportunities for our people); the modernization of the relationship between individuals and the state and our natural environment; the modernization of our society into a less classbound structure; and the modernization of our relationship with other countries, especially in Europe. In all five areas, I believed, our two parties now basically agreed with one another and had a common interest in working together.

I said that my fellow Lib Dems and I knew that we had a vested interest in the success of at least the first term of his government.

There was, I concluded, a natural progressive majority in this country to be rallied, if only we could become untribal enough to find ways of rallying it. This was the project to which I was personally very committed. But I acknowledged there were risks to both sides. From Labour's point of view, it meant putting trust in 'the Liberals', who, in some people's view, had no experience of power, represented all things to all people, and would have neither the discipline nor the commitment to stick with the project when the going got tough. Then, from the Lib Dem point of view, the Labour Party was seen as an arrogant and hegemonic beast that would swallow everybody else up if it could.

Blair and I both understood these risks, but were prepared to take them in order to achieve what I believed was a win–win situation for both of us, and for the people we represented.

How did he see it?

In characteristic blunt tones, he said, 'Yes, that's your position. You have put it very fairly and honestly. I recognize your analysis – it's exactly the same as Tony's. But I don't share it. I believe that if you are to achieve what you suggest, then you will break up my party. I am a Labour man to the core and I am not prepared to see that. I believe that if we did what you suggest, we would be creating a weak structure in place of a strong one. We would be giving chances to the Tories they wouldn't otherwise have. Perhaps if

1 Department of the Environment, Transport and the Regions.

in the future we have to do it to keep the Tories out we should. But it's not necessary now. We can keep the Tories out on our own. I have no qualms about the Labour Party being in power time and time again, and in between taking our turn at defeat, too. I am not against working with you in any circumstances. I actually voted for the Lib/Lab pact (a fact of which I keep reminding Denis Healey), but I did that because it was necessary as a way of keeping in power. But I will not see the break-up of my party.

'Nevertheless, I do understand that Tony has a wider vision and, frankly, he has been proved right in the past. He keeps on floating off with these airy-fairy ideas, and some of them work. But I am here to keep his feet anchored firmly to the ground. He can ditch that anchor if he wishes – and he probably will at some stage. But he needs to know how much it's going to cost. Meanwhile, it is my job, privately at the moment, but publicly later if I have to, to tell him the limits of his room for manoeuvre.

'I have already said to him that, although I will support proportional representation for Europe – which, incidentally, I think is nonsense because it will give you and the Tories more seats and us less – I would not be prepared to support PR for the constituencies [Westminster]. Under these circumstances I would oppose him privately and publicly.

'Secondly, as you well know, I don't sit on the Joint Cabinet Committee. I just do not want to be associated with it. If Tony actually ordered me to do so, then I would, but I've told him I am not keen and he is not pressing the point.

'All that said, I like you guys. I understand where you are coming from. I respect many of you and I understand your beliefs. And I also understand that there are many, many things on which we agree. But I am tribalist, pure and simple. I think the tribe we have is the tribe we must hang on to, and I think the business of reforming and becoming a larger and broader tribe carries huge dangers which will only give our enemies opportunities. I want to preserve the Labour Party for my children, not break it up. And I have made that clear to Tony.'

'OK,' I said, 'let's talk to each other as two practical politicians. Where do you think we differ, our two parties?'

Instead of answering the question, Prescott changed tack and said: 'Incidentally, I have told Tony that another no-go point for me would be if he has you lot in Cabinet. If you come into our Cabinet after the next election as a result of its outcome, fine. But I will not tolerate anything before that. I don't believe that Tony can carry our party on it either, and I'm not sure you can carry yours, come to think of it.'

I thought I'd better clarify my own position, so I told him I did not have the slightest personal ambition to become a Cabinet minister.

Prescott interrupted: 'I am sure you haven't and I'm not making this personal – I'm talking about parties and principles, not personalities.'

I then returned to the question of where he and I differed.

He honed in immediately on the issue of trade-union representation: 'I think the linkage with trade unions is absolutely vital. Furthermore, I see myself as belonging to a party which is crucially an extension of the unions. What about you?'

I said he was wrong. I believed in a strong and vibrant trade union movement. Trade unions were absolutely central to the kind of structure we were trying to create. And, incidentally, John Monks[1] had often told me that he found us less hostile to the trade union movement than Blair. Prescott agreed, saying that he had sat in on some of Blair's meetings with the trade unions '. . . and it's perfectly clear he hates them!'

We then got on to talking about how the government was faring. I said that in my view they had three major problems: Blair didn't run a proper Cabinet system (Prescott responded by saying that was absolutely true, but they were putting it right); secondly, they were driven too much by short-term newspaper-led agenda – and I couldn't understand why Alastair Campbell and Peter Mandelson exerted so much power (Prescott replied he couldn't understand it either, but thought that was changing, too); and thirdly, having abandoned socialism, there was no core belief system around which they could gather (Prescott agreed enthusiastically: 'The party is a cold, efficient machine. But it has no heart').

PA: If you get rid of the heart of a party, you might be able to control it for a bit by squeezing its balls, but not for long. We experienced a lot of that in our relations with the SDP, and you are in danger of going the same way. So what we need to do is jointly create a set of ideas which can inspire both our parties. When we have done it, I suspect we will find that those two sets of ideas are not a million miles apart. Then the question is whether we allow a situation to continue in which, by fighting each other, we let the Tories back in.

JP: Yes, you are returning to the same old arguments that Tony uses with me. But I disagree. I think the danger of moving from one structure to another is just too great, and we will lose too much in the process. Look, don't get me wrong, I think Tony is quite remarkable. He has done things I didn't think he could do – and I

---

1 General Secretary of the TUC.

have learned on several occasions that he has been right when I've been wrong. But there have been others when I have been right and he has been wrong.

He can't make too many more mistakes without losing the party, or substantial parts of it. That said, the other thing I like about Tony is that, if he is wrong, he will say so. He has a very generous spirit. And he doesn't mind you speaking absolutely bluntly to him, even when your bluntness goes over the limit. That's the sign of a very big man, and I like dealing with big men.

By now we had been talking for an hour. I said, 'Look, I think one of the problems here is that you simply don't trust us as a party capable of facing up to hard decisions when the going gets tough. I disagree. So why don't we try? I know you were upset about our handling of the London referendum Bill . . .'

JP: No, I wasn't upset – I was just using it for effect, so that whenever Tony proposes to Cabinet we do something else with you, I can respond by saying, 'You mean the lot who voted against us in the Lords the other night?'

I went on to explain that the problem with the Lords and the London Bill arose from the fact that our people (in particular, Simon Hughes) hadn't been involved in the consultation; they didn't know what was going on behind the scenes.

PA: You can't just expect us to support you if we have no sense of ownership over what we are supposed to be supporting you on. If you are serious about this, you will have to do rather better than that.

JP: Look, I don't object to that. I have always believed that we should take in the views of opposition parties anyway, so I am quite happy to take our bilateral consultations more seriously than we did then. Maybe we got that one wrong. Perhaps we should try again.

We both had meetings to go to, so I wound up:

PA: I want you to know that, although I have outlined a plan that I may have and Tony may share, I am not obsessed with it. I want to see how far this proposition can be tested. As practical politicians, why not test your resolve to be pluralists and our capacity to act in a disciplined way by bringing the Lib Dems into consultations earlier, and seeing how it works? I start off from the presumption that it can be done. Perhaps you start off from the presumption that it can't. Very well, then, let's at least agree to try it out and see who's right.

JP: No, I don't think I can agree to all of that. But let's see if we can work more sensibly together. Even though you and I disagree about the advisability, let alone possibility, of arriving at the point you and Tony wish to reach, I don't see why we shouldn't have good relations. You and I have at least established good contact. Very straight-talking. Just how I like it. And I will certainly ensure that when my people talk to yours it is on a more constructive basis.

I really enjoyed meeting Prescott. He is straightforward and has a much, much quicker brain than I'd been led to believe. He also has a very clear role in government and he feels comfortable with it. At one stage, towards the end of our conversation, he said, 'I keep on saying to Tony that if it all goes pear-shaped he has another career to follow. He can go off and be a success in the law courts. But I am near the end of my political career: I have perhaps ten more years of this, that's all. This is the only thing I can do. And, if you will forgive me, I want to leave the Labour Party just as I found it, for my kids and for my successors. It's an emotional thing. That's where I'm coming from.'

He sees himself as the anchor person, tying Blair down to reality; he sees himself as the guardian of the Labour Party as an institution; and he realizes his relationship with Blair provides the government with a resonance with the wider party that it otherwise wouldn't have, and that he is, therefore, indispensable. He obviously loves his job, especially his work on the environment: 'I want to go down as a real environmentalist. That's one of the pages I can have written about me in the history books.'

Monday, 23 February, Westminster

[*Jane and I were due to have dinner with the Blairs on 4 March. On 15 February I had written a letter to Blair outlining where I thought we had got to on TFM and trying to push him on to the next stage. Since then, I had had further thoughts about how we should progress, in particular on the intellectual case for coalition, so I sent him a fax, as follows, to serve as a starting point for our discussions at dinner.*]

. . . if we are to go up a gear in our investigation of the feasibility of the 'final act' and in our preparation for it by bringing others in, we must be clear about what it is we are asking them to do.

Firstly, we will need to tell them where we are trying to get to and why (something we, of course, know well, but which we have never put down on paper).

Secondly, if we are to stimulate the production of an intellectual 'case' for the project, we must be clear between us exactly what its ingredients are.

1. Wednesday, 7 May 1997, Westminster

'At 11 o' clock the Lib Dem MPs – all forty-six of us – walked into Westminster through the Old Palace Yard Gates. I hadn't quite grasped how many there were of us until I saw everyone together in the flesh' From left: Simon Hughes, Jackie Ballard (obscured), Andy Kirkwood, PA, Alan Beith, David Chidgey, Ming Campbell, Paul Keetch, Ronnie Fearn (foreground), Richard Livesey, Paul Burstow.

2. Sunday, 3 August 1997, Irancy

'... we drove over to Pallotte, where we took photographs of Matthias, Jane, Kate and Simon. Then down to the church'

3. Saturday, 6 September 1997, London
'In through the great door of the Abbey, down one of the aisles, into the choir'

4. Wednesday, 17 September 1997, Westminster
'The meeting started promptly at 2.00. The Labour members of the committee sat on one side of the Cabinet table and we sat on the other'

5. Friday, 21 November 1997, Winchester
'To Winchester to celebrate Mark Oaten's victory. A stunning result, which reflects great personal credit on him'

6. Sunday, 15 March 1998, Southport
'... at 12.30 off to the conference centre. Bob introduced me as a vintage wine, using the words "full-bodied". My speech was long, very serious and heavy on policy'

7. Tuesday, 26 May 1998, Somerset

'Spent a quiet afternoon sitting in the garden and finished reading our latest policy papers'

8. Thursday, 11 June 1998, Westminster

'After the JCC Blair and I went outside for a photo op with the Constitutional Declaration'

9. Tuesday, 23 June 1998, Albania

'We sat cross-legged on the cloth laid out on the floor of their bare tent and I listened to their story, with Ceka [centre] translating. Eventually, he stopped, his voice choked into a sob and his eyes filled with tears ...'

10. Tuesday, 23 June 1998, Albania

'I ... put my binoculars up and started looking for the tracks that the refugees had followed'

11. Sunday, 2 August 1998, Irancy

'In the evening Kate left Matthias with us while she and Seb went off to stay with friends – the first night we have been allowed to look after him by ourselves. I had such fun!'

12. Friday, 21 August 1998, Irancy

'In the evening Jane and I took the Cleeses on a customary tour of the Irancy *caves* to sample the wine'

13. Tuesday, 25 August 1998, Irancy

'In the morning I did what I had been putting off for days – started the first draft of my conference speech'

14. Monday, 31 August 1998, Irancy

'A cycle ride with Simon and Jane. We rode up to the top of Pallotte ...'

15. Saturday, 26 September 1998, Kosovo
'My first appointment was with Ibrahim Rugova, at his substantial house in what passes for Pristina's residential quarter'

16. Sunday 27, September 1998, Kosovo
'... we [found] a calf trapped in the stream. I insisted that we should rescue it, took my shoes off and jumped in'

Thirdly, if we are to begin to assemble a political programme upon which the final act is based, we must decide who does this, how and when.

And lastly, we must decide who from each side will comprise the team of 'engineers' to put forward a plan . . .

Wednesday, 4 March, Westminster

Chris Rennard came to see me today to express his concern about the pace at which we are moving towards TFM. His view is that Blair must be made to commit to PR, and to deliver on that, before TFM can happen – which probably won't be until November next year. I told him that was far too late. I couldn't hold the party together that long. Constructive opposition is an inherently unstable state which must eventually tip one way or the other: it was already becoming increasingly difficult to make it meaningful and the Joint Cabinet Committee would, by the end of the year, be little more than a cipher. Furthermore, although the best of all possible worlds would be for PR to be delivered before we went to TFM, the fact was that it wouldn't happen, since Blair was unlikely to get it through this year. In the end, it came down to whether we would take the risk.

After the PPM in the evening Jane and I walked together to Downing Street for dinner with the Blairs.

We arrived shortly after 8.00 and were shown up to the kitchen of their flat at No. 11, where we found Cherie, dressed in a grey tracksuit, busy with the food.

We were soon joined by Blair himself, who went to the fridge and pulled out a bottle of champagne they'd just been given, and we all went off to sit in the drawing-room. A couple of jokes about the fact that they didn't have a set of matching glasses.

During our discussions, all three kids came in separately. Euan, who has now grown very tall, popped in to say hello, talking about his piano. Cherie said they were having difficulty getting him to do his piano practice and I told him that I had given up playing a musical instrument as a boy and regretted it all my life. After Euan left we could hear him playing the piano – rather well, I thought – for the next half hour or so.

Then Kathryn came in. I shook her by the hand and she winced. She had fallen over in the playground and badly hurt her right hand, which was quite swollen. She is a delightful girl.

And then finally Nicky, proudly carrying the fixture list for some seven-aside tournament he is playing in this weekend. He told me that he was playing hooker. Blair said this is where he had played and he made some joke about ears.

Delightfully normal kids.

I started, as usual, by asking Blair whether he was still serious about TFM.

TB: Yes, I am. I am deadly serious about it. It's the biggest thing I want to do. And I am determined to do it.

PA: Well, as you know, I met John Prescott and he made it quite clear that he is wholly opposed. He said there were two things he would oppose you on, even in public: bringing us in and PR for Westminster.

Cherie said, 'But he said exactly the same to Tony. We know all that. The point about John is that he never does anything behind your back.'

TB: Yes, Cherie's right. I know that's John's position. But he has made his opposition to things clear to me in the past which he has then gone along with – Clause 4, for instance.

PA: The point is, do you still genuinely believe you can overcome this and it won't stop you doing what we are committed to do?

TB: Yes I do. I'm absolutely convinced. It won't be easy. But it can be done.

At this stage I decided that I needed to make my own position clear to him again.

PA: Look, this is just between the four of us here, but this project is all that is keeping me in politics. It has become the remaining purpose of my leadership. I have had a tremendous ten years, but I am exhausted. I will be 60 by the time of the next election. In all other circumstances I would want to be handing over to somebody else at this stage. But delivering on TFM is the one remaining thing I really want to do. So you need to know that, if you are not serious about this, then the time has come for me to stand down.

TB: I really hope you won't do that. You are important both to your party and to the project. Without you I don't think this will be possible. I hope you're not saying you won't see this through.

PA: No, the exact opposite! I will see it through. I have made a commitment to you and I will honour it. But you need to know that if at any time this is checked, either because one of us can't do it or our parties stop us, then I will stand down almost immediately. But if we do deliver this, then I will see it through until the whole thing is locked in place and stable. And then I'll stand down. Not least because I want to spend some of my active years with this person [pointing to Jane].

Cherie agreed emphatically.

TB: Thank you for that. You have told me this before, of course, but it's important I understand where you are now. I promise you I won't tell anybody else.

I continued, saying that there were, in that case, some practical things we needed to discuss.

PA: My real worry is that, while we know what we want to do and are committed to it, we haven't yet made the preparations to make it a possibility. There are three things that need to be done. The first is the process of putting together the intellectual case.

TB: Yes. This is important. How about getting some 'thinkers', not politicians, to have a go at it? But we should wait until after the May local council elections to launch this part of the project. Those elections are going to be difficult for us; the parties will fight each other, and your lot will probably do well, while we will do badly. So it's probably better to get that trauma over with first.

I said that I thought we'd certainly do quite well where Labour were governing badly, but that we would also, like them, suffer at the hands of the Tories. Also, I didn't think we should wait until after May. It may be that we would want to add in others after then (he suggested Steve Webb again). But we should get it started before.

PA: I would like to assemble a little group of academics who can start thinking about the politics of the centre left along the lines that we have defined, perhaps under the umbrella of *Political Quarterly*.[1] Secondly, we must decide when we will move to TFM. I am working towards November. Do you agree?

TB: That should be our target date.

PA: Well, in that case we must make sure Roy has produced his Commission report by then. He told me he was going to produce it by the end of October, but I am anxious that the date doesn't slip, otherwise we will run out of time.

Blair said he'd spoken to Roy very recently about this and that he had

---

1 A highly respected left-leaning academic political journal.

confirmed the end of October. In that case, I said, I would probably hold a special Party Conference later that month.

PA: Next we must agree when the PR referendum will be. What's in your mind?

TB: I am assuming it will be at a suitable date next year. Perhaps at the same time as the European elections.

I responded that it had to be next year, but I wasn't sure about tying it in with the Euro elections. Having two votes on the same day, one using PR and the other about PR, may confuse people. In fact, I could see some advantages to its being in November. This would allow it to be seen as a separate issue whilst enabling us to get the legislation into the Queen's Speech.

We moved into the kitchen, where we all sat at the table. Tony brought out a bottle of Chablis Premier Cru Montée de Tonnerre and Cherie produced some rose petal wine, which she said she had seen and wanted to try. She thought it was non-alcoholic. Much joking about the fact that I used to make rose petal wine and it was anything but non-alcoholic. She had a taste and declared it to be rather good, but, I noticed, soon changed to the Chablis. I had a sip. It was revolting.

Our first course was leek terrine and the second cod with asparagus, served up in an old chipped Pyrex dish covered in foil – very homely and normal.

We continued with our previous discussion.

PA: There are other practical steps I think we should now take. Firstly, we must get together a group of two or three people from each side to assemble the programme on which TFM will be based. And secondly, we must have some 'engineers' who can plan how to move us from where we are now to where we need to be for TFM. These can both be under the general supervision of Richard Holme and Peter Mandelson. But is Peter really able to spare the time? Isn't he very busy now?

Blair replied that yes, Mandelson was flat out – he had been in Germany speaking to the SPD and had also been involved in establishing close relationships with the new French socialists – but that he'd have a word with him. 'If he is unable to spend time on this – which I suspect is the case – then I'll find somebody else.'

I said that I didn't want Peter to misunderstand – Richard and he got on very well, and we all understood how busy he was – but we needed somebody there who could keep a close and constant eye on progress. I also suggested that Blair and I should in future meet with our closest teams and that these meetings should be minuted. He agreed.

From here the conversation turned to the new politics. He explained to me that his 'policy wonk' discussions with Clinton on the 'Third Way'[1] had already had international repercussions, the full importance of which wasn't yet fully understood in Britain. The Italians were very interested – Prodi was trying to establish a new party and had been very interested in finding out what was discussed between him and Clinton. And Cardoso[2] in Brazil is apparently doing exactly the same thing.

We also talked about Helmut Kohl, whom Blair found impressive and likeable, with a marked sense of history. Apparently, Blair has been reading recently about the attempts of Joseph Chamberlain in the late 1890s to establish a rapprochement between the British and the Germans and how he had been misunderstood by Bismarck. He had casually mentioned this to Kohl, who knew all about it and discussed it in some detail. Following this, Kohl had apparently referred to it in his speech at the Guildhall, saying that Chamberlain had got it right in his relation with the Germans. Those in the audience who were not as keen students of history as Blair and Kohl had been utterly perplexed, presuming that Kohl was referring to Neville not Joseph!

The conversation then turned to the single currency itself and he asked me what I thought should be done.

PA: My view, as you know, is that you should announce that it will be the target of the British government to enter the single currency in the year 2001 or 2002; and that you will follow policies consistent with that aim. The effect would be to bring down the pound, lower interest rates and smash the Tory Party for a decade.

Cherie asked whether I thought Tony should lead this.

PA: Yes. He can't continue to leave it to the rest of us to make the running, so that when he thinks the time is right, and he is confident of winning, he can install himself at the head of the victory parade.

TB: Frankly, that's not far off the truth.

Blair then went off into an extremely interesting exposition on the single

---

1 See diary entry for 2 November 1997.
2 Fernando Henrique Cardoso, President of Brazil since 1995.

currency, saying that he could now see circumstances in which it could be won. 'But I don't want the whole single currency issue to become entangled with my domestic agenda. I must get that out of the way first. Only then will I take on the issue of Europe. What I have learned about Europe is that, provided you put your ducks in a row, you can actually begin to turn domestic opinion on Europe round in a matter of days.'

Blair said he would really like to know what Kenneth Clarke's intentions were.

I said that I could probably help find out and promised to fix a dinner with Clarke to pump him some more on his opinions.

Jane was a constant participant in the conversation, and at one stage Blair said, 'Goodness me – she is much more left-wing than you are, isn't she?' I told him that she was the true radical in our family. Cherie nodded vigorously.

Turning the conversation back to PR, I asked Blair to confirm that he would support the outcome of the Jenkins Commission.

TB: Of course I will, provided it contains what we think it will.

I also asked him whether he would require Cabinet solidarity and he responded, 'Yes, this will be a Cabinet decision which we will take together.'

I then asked about the promised reshuffle.

TB: Hmmm, I certainly need one. And in terms of our plans, I think it's easier to have *a* reshuffle, as it were, before we have *the* reshuffle. If we have one now, people will get used to the idea. Incidentally, I am thinking of making a speech after the local elections in which I will once again explicitly place on the agenda the probability of having Lib Dems in Cabinet. I don't want this to come as a surprise for my party.

PA: You may not want it to come as a surprise to your party, but I want the decision in my party to be taken alongside the programme that we agree. The two mustn't be separated otherwise the decision will be taken in a vacuum and I'll lose.

By now it was nearly 10 o'clock. Nicky came in to ask if Cherie would watch *The X-Files* with him. She bade us goodnight and left, but we stayed on chatting for another ten or fifteen minutes about Kosovo and the right-wing press.

As he had done so many times before, Blair asked me how I thought the government was doing overall. I said I thought they were doing well on the big things but they were screwing up on the small ones.

TB: Exactly. That's the difficulty. For instance, beef on the bone. It just slipped past me.

PA: That's because you are trying to do too much. You must delegate. Also, Jack Cunningham's handling of the farmers has been unnecessarily aggressive and provocative.

TB: Yes, I woke up one morning to suddenly discover that I had made enemies of all these people. And hunting is, for some reason, a really talismanic issue for them. I have enough enemies to cope with at the moment without wishing to turn people in the countryside against me, too.

By now it was 10.20 and he was looking pretty tired. He said he still had his boxes to deal with. 'I get through them quite quickly, you know.'

I promised to send him a summary of the decisions that we had taken, and we left. A really useful evening during which we appeared to cross some important watersheds. I remain convinced that he is committed to the project. But has he the will to make it happen? And how do we create the mechanisms to deliver it?

Thursday, 5 March, Westminster

Sent the following letter by fax to Blair this morning:

Dear Tony,
Thanks so much for last night. It was very enjoyable. I hope we didn't keep you up too late.

I promised to do you a note summarizing what I think we agreed, so that we can get our people working on it.

As I recall it, we agreed that:

1. November will be our target date for the 'final act'.

2. The production date for the Jenkins report will be the end of October after the Party Conferences, and this will be the trigger for (1) above.

3. The PR referendum will be held next year; you suggested perhaps around the time of the Euro election. I thought it was worth considering separating this from all other elections and suggested that November might be better. But no firm conclusion was reached.

4. It is urgent to start work on the 'intellectual case' based broadly on the

ingredients of your discussions after the May elections, but we agreed that it would be better if we could start things earlier. Richard Holme could perhaps initiate this with Tony Wright[1] through *Political Quarterly*. I will speak to him about this.

5. We will establish a team to begin assembling the programme. I have three from my side to do this: probably my Director of Policy David Laws, my ex-Head of Office Alan Leaman and an MP on whom I have yet to decide.

6. Also a team of 'engineers' to start detailed planning. Again, I have three: Nick Harvey MP, my Director of Campaigns Chris Rennard and our new Head of Press David Walter.

7. These two teams to be under the general direction of Richard Holme and Peter Mandelson (if you think he is not already too overloaded). From my side, I will get Roger Lowry[2] (who is already in close contact with Jonathan and Pat) to service these teams.

8. Our future meetings should be, at least in part, with these two teams so that we can oversee progress.

9. We need a few bits of symbolism to push things forward, perhaps best done after the May local elections, so as to give momentum after the setback we both anticipate here. We should consider a joint presentation of the Constitutional Declaration in this context. This could mark the end of the main 'constitutional' thrust of the relationship between the parties and the beginning of its widening to other areas. I understand that the government is planning to produce an annual report in May. What about including the Constitutional Declaration as an annexe to this? You would also invite two Lib Dems to the next Clinton 'policy wonk' exercise. As soon as you know the agenda for this, I will be able to propose a name to you, apart from myself.

I also agreed to see if I could fix a discreet meeting with Kenneth Clarke, to see what his long-term intentions are.
Yours
Paddy

1 Member of Parliament (Labour) for Great Yarmouth since 1997.
2 Joint Cabinet Committee Liaison Officer 1998–9. Roger was responsible for the administration, on our side, of the JCC process. Although officially part of the Whips' Office, Roger was based in the Leader's Office.

Wednesday, 11 March, Westminster

I have decided to go to Paris for a single currency meeting that Ken Clarke is also attending. A useful opportunity to speak to him, and I may also be able to get down to see Kate.

Thursday, 12 March, Westminster

In by 8.00 for an hour's work before the Team Leaders' meeting. There's a growing confidence that we should be all right for Southport. Bob told me beforehand that one of the most damaging amendments would be withdrawn.

At 12.30 a Jo Group meeting. This again confirmed the general view that Southport looks better than we could have imagined a week ago. Until Archy said, 'Well, what is going to happen if an amendment closing the possibility of coalitions goes through?' There followed a furious discussion in which everyone in the room said I would have to accept it and 'spin it away'. I said that I couldn't. At one stage I remarked, 'Look, you guys do not realize where I am coming from. I have spent the last three months going round the party explaining why we need to keep our options open. If that's overturned, they will make it impossible to continue with the Joint Cabinet Committee and I will have to go.'

We then went on to discuss the minute I had sent Blair, which, we now understood, had somewhat taken No. 10 aback with its severity. Richard observed, 'We just need to realize that he leads his party in a different way to you. He makes these laid-back comments whereas you want everything tied up in a bow. I bet he will say he didn't say that.'

I replied, 'Yes, I suspect that's true. It probably comes from what we were both doing in the 1960s. While he was lead guitarist in a pop group I was leading a troop of Royal Marines in Borneo.' We all laughed.

Later I rang Powell: 'I understand that my minute has caused some consternation at your end. It's my military manner. I'm sorry, but I like things neat and tidy. I sent it to you in order to ensure that we were on the right track.'

Powell laughed and said, 'I understand the military mind. My father was in the army. It did cause us some amusement. But at least you are making us think about these things. Anyway, there is no substantive difference between us and we'll get back to you as soon as we can.'

'Look, my Southport Conference is very finely balanced just at the moment. Please, no hand-grenades from your side.'

He assured me that there wouldn't be.

Friday, 13 March, Southport

EVE OF THE SOUTHPORT CONFERENCE

Chris Rennard drove us to Southport. He told me that two things have happened: the most damaging amendment has been withdrawn, which is excellent, and the second most dangerous amendment has been watered down to a degree we would find acceptable. Chris seems to think this is very good news, but I have a nagging doubt in my brain.

The rest of the day was so busy that I never did get to look at the amendment myself. Chris and I arrived at Southport at 3.15 and Jane, who had driven up from Somerset, arrived shortly afterwards.

We are staying in some very poky rooms at a rather dingy hotel. In fact, I think the word dingy was invented for the place. Southport is, of course, not on the sea at all. The sea probably took one look at what they'd done to the front, decided to leave and hasn't been back for a hundred years. Just next door to the conference centre (newly done up, but still the old Southport Conference Centre) is a very forbidding statue of Queen Victoria as Empress of India at the end of her reign. Stout, Boudicca-like and deeply frightening. Perhaps it was her the sea was too terrified of to return.

After Jane and I had collected our badges, we had a look in the hall. Rather better than I had anticipated; they have done the backdrop very well, concentrating on the past ten years. Then back to our room for a speech meeting. A lot of work still to do on it.

I have been talked into supporting the two amendments without looking at them. Then, at 4.30 in the morning, I suddenly sat bolt upright in bed. I hadn't read the final version of the amendment Chris had reassured me about earlier in the day. I got up and took a look at it. My worst fears were realized. It is intended to tie my hands by insisting on 'genuine consultation' with the party before acting. As usual, people trying to spin things away, rather than confront them.

Liberal
Democrats

MR. ASHDOWN
DENIES LUST
FOR POWER

PRIESTLEY

Saturday, 14 March, Southport

Up at 6.45 to start ringing around members of the Jo Group at 7.10. Bob
Maclennan first. I had obviously woken him up. He said there was nothing
to worry about. All the amendment meant was the maintenance of the
status quo. I disagreed and said that if we did get criticized for not 'genuinely
consulting' I would look to him as president of the party to defend our
position both within the party and with Labour. Also spoke to Chris
Rennard, who took much the same line as Bob. I insisted that both of them
come to a meeting at 8.15 to discuss the matter.

Down to breakfast, looked at the papers (not bad), then up to the
meeting. Alan Leaman, Ming Campbell, Richard Holme, Chris Rennard,
Bob Maclennan and David Walter, together with Miranda,[1] Roger, and
Andrew from my office. I told them of my concerns. One by one they told
me not to worry, though Chris was good enough to agree that the wording
was ambiguous. So, at Richard's suggestion, I agreed to ask Lembit Opik,
who was summing up for the motion, to say specifically that if the party
voted for this, it was voting for the status quo on consultation. I then went
round the room, prefixing my remarks with 'My instincts are to oppose
this tooth and nail. It will result in a fuzzy solution, rather than a clean
one. We must confront this sooner or later, and now is the time to do it.'

1 Miranda Green, my Press Secretary 1997–9. Miranda is now assistant home news editor
on the *Financial Times*.

But everyone including, to my surprise, Alan Leaman, advised, 'Accept and spin it out into a solution.' Against my better judgement, I agreed.

Then to the PPM, at which I explained my attitude to the two amendments this afternoon. There was no discussion and the meeting finished swiftly.

During the morning I took Lembit to one side and asked him to ensure that any reference he made to consultation in his speech was to the maintenance of the status quo. Richard fed him some rather good lines on this. Feeling slightly more reassured, I returned to my office to work on my speech. After which, on to the platform to hear debate. Some good speeches – but Lembit's was not one of them. Paula Yates[1] was the star; Shirley was good; Richard Kemp excellent. Tom McNally, Cyril Smith and Phil Willis all desperate to speak but Liz Barker, who was chairing the session, never called them. Lembit's speech was full of jokes which didn't work and, on the key passage on consultation, he merely said, 'We should be doing it already.' The amendment passed.

At dinner with Jane in the evening I was in the depths of depression. Despite my intentions we have ended up trying to spin our way out of a problem, rather than confront it. Tom McNally, Shirley Williams and others came to see me expressing the same concerns. I had gone into this debate wanting to ensure we put the strategy issue behind us, maintain party unity and make sure that none of my options were closed off. To that extent it has been a successful day, but it doesn't feel like it. To bed, disturbed.

Sunday, 15 March, Southport

Down to breakfast at 7.45 and a review of the papers. The *Sunday Times* has almost deliberately misrepresented what we did yesterday, otherwise our story comes across reasonably well.

A photo op for the press and at 12.30 off to the conference centre. Bob introduced me as a vintage wine, using the words 'full-bodied'. My speech was long, very serious and heavy on policy. Not at all a rallying cry. I wanted to tell the party it was time to get back to policy – and the speech worked rather better than I thought it might. Out at 2.00 for a press briefing

---

1 Our parliamentary candidate in North Dorset in 1997.

in which I indicated that we had achieved all we set out to achieve at this conference.

I am very glad it's behind me. It has been hanging over me for a long time. If the Howarth amendment to say no to coalitions with Labour had been taken to the Eastbourne Conference it would have been passed easily, so I suppose we are making progress. At least no options have been closed off. A wonderful night's sleep, at last.

Thursday, 19 March, The Hague

THE INTERNATIONAL WAR CRIMES TRIBUNAL TRIAL OF THE CROATIAN MILITARY COMMANDER GENERAL TIHOMIR BLASKIC[1]

Up at 4.30 and straight out to Heathrow with Miranda, with me driving. We caught the 7.15 flight to The Hague.

When we arrived at the War Crimes Tribunal we met Mark Harmon, the prosecuting attorney. I also saw Mesic,[2] who is giving evidence in another case.[3]

I spent the next couple of hours looking through my testimony, re-acquainting myself with the map of Bosnia so I got everything right. I anticipated that the defence counsel would want to try and discredit the map and my sense of geography. In my diary notes there is much talk about Tudjman and me drinking a lot. He will doubtless also concentrate on that.

At 1.15 Harmon came back to see me. We sent everyone else out of the office and I went through my evidence with him. He thought, as I did, that Hayman, the defence counsel, would try and discredit me on the grounds of the nature of the dinner, the amount of wine consumed, etc.

At 2.45 down to the court. Very high-tech courtroom. Three judges in red robes and television screens everywhere, and, to my left, the lone figure of General Blaskic, in an ill-fitting suit and looking isolated and bewildered. The prosecution on my right and the defence on my left. Harmon briefly introduced me, then asked me to tell my story, which I did. I got through

---

1 The result of my dinner with Franjo Tudjman on 6 May 1995 (see Vol. I, pp. 315–17 and 337–8).

2 Stipe Mesic, President of Croatia since 2000.

3 It later became apparent through a Croat newspaper that he had also testified in a closed session in the Blaskic case – an extremely brave act.

it in about fifteen minutes. Hayman then subjected me to an hour and a quarter's intense interrogation. As I thought, he concentrated on the amount of wine we had drunk and inaccuracies in the map. Quite testing. He certainly got me on one technical point, but it was an insignificant one. On the whole, though, everybody seemed pleased with the way it went.[1]

Afterwards, some press and television interviews (a beautiful day in both The Hague and London), then off to a nearby hotel to do some down the line interviews to London. I was really delighted to do this. This tribunal needs all the support it can get. Disgracefully, the French have refused to allow their diplomats, soldiers or politicians to testify at it. In the interviews, I put much emphasis on setting an example which would be recognized in Kosovo, where the whole ghastly Bosnian tragedy looks set to be repeated.

Monday, 23 March, Westminster

At 3.30 a fairly amicable meeting with Jim Wallace. We discussed his plans for Scotland. He said that, of course, the Scottish Lib Dems couldn't really do a deal with the Scottish Nationalists after the May local elections, but it was important to keep some room for manoeuvre so that the illusion of this possibility was maintained and options were kept open.

Tuesday, 31 March, London–Paris

Up at 3.15am, a bath and a taxi to Waterloo at 4.10. I sat in the Eurostar lounge doing some work and reading the papers. Then on to the 5.05 to Paris. Spent most of the time catching up on reading and thinking about PMQs tomorrow.

A taxi to Avenue Freidland for the conference on monetary union at the French Chamber of Commerce. A very interesting American spoke on how the euro could match the dollar as a world currency in the future. Étienne Davignon[2] presided over the whole thing, smoking his pipe, looking inscrutable and speaking in three or four languages perfectly.

---

1 Blaskic was eventually found guilty of crimes against humanity and sentenced to forty-five years in prison for the massacre of Muslims in Ahmici, Bosnia.
2 Viscount Étienne Davignon, Ambassador of the King of the Belgians, chairman of the Société Général de Belgique.

In the pre-lunch session Domnique Strauss-Kahn, the French Finance Minister, spoke without notes for about thirty minutes. I was impressed. Then Ken Clarke made a prepared speech. Good, but he didn't mark out at all clearly the position the government should take on the euro.

Afterwards, as arranged through our offices, Ken and I went off to a brasserie for lunch. Ken seemed ill at ease with the menu and ordered two starters. Perhaps he has been a minister for too long![1]

An interesting and engaging lunch, however. This is the first detailed conversation we have ever had. Clarke is very good fun and excoriating on Hague and the people around him (according to Clarke, Hague has many skills, but poor judgement and even worse advisers).

It was a good meeting.

Friday, 3 April, Westminster

Sent the following fax to Blair today:

Dear Tony,
You will recall that we talked of Ken Clarke when we met last and I promised to find out his intentions.

When I had lunch with him during a Paris conference on the single currency recently, he told me:

1. He has no intention of either leaving politics or leaving the Tories, 'at least until I am certain that they cannot be dragged back to sense, which won't be clear, in my view, until after the next election'. I asked him if he would stay in politics and he said, 'Yes. I will always be a politician and I will always be a Tory. They might leave me. But I will never leave them.' I got the impression that he could, if things turned out really badly, set up a different party, say, under PR (which he opposes), but not join a different party.

2. His task at the moment, 'together with Michael [Heseltine]' is to keep good people in the party. He said that there were 'about thirty or forty pro-Europeans in the Parliamentary Party'. But not all of these were prepared to break cover because of the mood elsewhere in the party.

3. Hague is intelligent, but at heart a genuine hardliner on Europe.

---

1 When I related this story to Ken he specifically denied this inference, asserting that the one thing he never lost control of in his time as a minister was his food!

4. Clarke is ready to play a full part in moving opinion on the single currency 'but the government must set a lead first. And they haven't yet. They cannot expect us to do their work for them.'

5. He 'and Michael' will firmly commit themselves to the single currency platform in any referendum, which, he said, would 'split the Tory Party wide open'.

6. The Tories are planning a Union Jack election (again?) on the single currency for the next GE and he can't understand why you are giving them the opportunity to do so. Like me, he believes a referendum 'in principle' before the next election is economically and politically right and gives you the best chance to consolidate your position in Europe.

7. I asked him if there was anything I could do to help. He replied, 'Yes. Tell Blair to hold a referendum on EMU before the next election.'

We agreed to meet from time to time.
Yours
Paddy

Monday, 6 April, London

In the evening off to the Grand Paradiso restaurant for dinner with David Steel. A very enjoyable meal. We got through two bottles of wine, which was probably half a bottle too much for either of us. David mostly wanted to talk about Africa and his ambitions for the Scottish Parliament (he wants to be Speaker) and how Donald Dewar has mishandled things. Dewar is getting some rather bad press; his success in delivering Scottish devolution has given way to backbiting and bitterness in the Scottish Labour Party, a rise in the SNP vote and much clumsiness.

I let David into about 80 per cent of my Blair meeting. He gave me his full support: 'This is what I have been after for so long.' We also discussed who in the Parliamentary Party would agree or disagree.

Tuesday, 7 April, London

After a day's campaigning in the Pennines, back by train to London, arriving at a few minutes to seven. By tube to the House to collect my briefcase and then wandered down to meet Alan Beith for dinner at the La Barca restaurant in The Cut, behind Waterloo. I took him through much of the Blair stuff.

PA: Blair has come on very strong on coalitions. I have told him that I could not possibly accede to coalition unless (1) he personally accepts PR and the Cabinet does too; (2) it would be based on a full coalition agreement on policies; and (3) we would get a nominal three places in the Cabinet and throughout government. Blair is interested in you and I have an agreement with him that you would have one of those.

But I cannot be certain this will come off; in fact, in my judgement, it won't. But I still intend to pursue it after the local elections. Now, I can do this with you or I can do it without you. I would prefer to have you on board and I would prefer you to look after the whole business of assembling the policy agreements between us – in effect, the coalition programme. But it is a very dangerous move and you may prefer to stay clear and keep your powder dry [the inference being for a possible leadership battle should I fail]. I know I can trust you not to leak this information, so the decision is yours.

At the very end of the evening, Alan said, 'There isn't a proposition on the table now but when there is I will give you my answer. Meanwhile, I will go away and think about it.'

By the end of the evening I had reached the conclusion that Alan would probably come on board, but he is, quite reasonably, keeping his options open for as long as possible.

Monday, 20 April, Westminster

There has been a rumbling news story that Sidney Cooke,[1] the paedophile about whom there has been so much national publicity, has been holed up in Yeovil police station. During the afternoon a crowd gathered outside demanding his head or some other appropriate part of his anatomy. I put

---

1 Cooke, a convicted paedophile, had been released from prison. There were a lot of rumours about where he was being held pending his release into the community.

out a statement saying that, despite his crimes, he had rights like everyone else and that they were behaving like a lynch mob.

Meanwhile, Blair is pursuing his saintly progress around the Middle East[1] trying to persuade them all back to the peace table. All this is helpful to the long-term project, as long as he doesn't achieve such a position of ascendancy over the rest of us that we are treated as simply chattels to be adjoined to his expanding bandwagon. I am feeling pretty grumpy and snapping people's heads off, partly for the simple reason that I hate coming back from holiday [after the Easter recess], and partly because I know we are being placed in an increasingly difficult position by Blair's rise on the world stage.

Tuesday, 21 April, Kent and London

A day's campaigning for the local elections in Kent.

All the news, however, has been dominated by popular reaction to Sidney Cooke. Further coverage this morning on the *Today* programme and more on BBC Breakfast TV, which had shots of 250 people demonstrating outside Yeovil police station. I spoke to the police, who said that they were under siege and there was an air of mob rule developing outside the station. At 10.00 I decided that I couldn't let things lie and should make a statement calling on the crowd to disperse and leave it to the police. At mid-day we got a call from Joyce Quinn's[2] office, saying my comments yesterday had been the only helpful ones made on this. And another from the Chief Constable of Avon and Somerset saying much the same thing. I drafted a statement reiterating my concerns. I wanted to use the phrase 'lynch mob' again, but eventually, following the strong advice of both my office and the Chief Constable, I took it out.

Wednesday, 22 April, London

The Sidney Cooke affair gathers pace. I am being heavily attacked now by my own constituents. Apparently my Yeovil office received a call saying

1 The Prime Minister visited Egypt, Saudi Arabia, Jordan and Israel in order to try to kickstart the stalled peace process.
2 Member of Parliament (Labour) for Gateshead East since 1987. Then a Minister of State at the Home Office.

local criminal elements are behind the mob. But there are also some ordinary good people who have been misinformed by the tabloid papers there, too. So I rang two local churchmen, Will Thompson, the Baptist minister, and Mark Ellis, a close friend and Yeovil's Anglican vicar, and asked them to use their influence to calm things down. Will Thompson was, as always, strong, direct and immensely helpful. Mark Ellis said he was very worried but that he didn't know what to do. I said a public word about leaving justice to the law would be helpful.

Also rang Martin Heal, editor of the *Western Gazette*, appealing to him to use the paper to inform people and cool matters down. To my alarm, he started accusing the police of failing to inform the public and of playing 'a cat and mouse game' with us all. He has obviously taken the protesters' side. I spent some time explaining the full situation to him as I saw it, then agreed to submit myself to a phone interview with one of his reporters – an aggressive-sounding young man who would have been more at home on the *Sun* (which is no doubt where he would like to be heading). Heal, however, finished by saying he would try to use the paper to take some of the heat out of the situation. I thanked him.

Later he rang me to say that a statement was due from the Home Office this afternoon, but that it would come out after their deadline. Could I use my influence with the Chief Constable to get an indication of what that statement contained so that he wouldn't be beaten to it by the other newspapers? I said I would try. [The police were most helpful and subsequently rang him back with the information he needed.]

'Incidentally,' I said, 'I've been told confidentially by the police and others that the same local gang who have been responsible for the recent attacks on Yeovil ethnic minorities[1] are behind this.'

'Oh yes,' he said, 'we've been using them for information.'

I was absolutely horrified. 'Surely you can't use them. Those people have terrified our town and are responsible for personal attacks and racism.'

'Yes,' he replied, 'but they have been helpful to us. They have provided us with inside sources and some background information.'

I didn't want to tell him how angry I felt about this at the time, but have decided that I will write to him tomorrow.

At 11 o'clock, sitting in my office and waiting for the vote, I got a call from Paul Tyler. Charles has apparently given an interview to the first edition of one of the BBC's political programmes due to be shown tomorrow night, in

1 See Vol. I, p. 361.

which he attacks constructive opposition, saying that it is unstable, he doesn't agree with it and that I 'tolerate him'. All deeply unhelpful.

Thursday, 23 April, Westminster

In the afternoon the first edition of the *Western Gazette* was faxed through to me. It was outrageous. Far from informing, it has deliberately inflamed. A huge photograph of Cooke on the front and a disgusting editorial saying he should get out of town, nobody cares where he goes providing he goes, etc. The very worst style of journalism.

I hit the roof. Asked Cathy Bakewell [my PA] to call the editor. She tracked him down to an editorial meeting in Bristol. I ripped into him, saying that he had shamed our community and disgraced his profession. Furthermore, the fact that I had rung him asking him to calm the situation down and he had responded by writing in his paper that he had 'relayed the feelings of the people of Yeovil to me' was a straightforward lie. I told him this was the most disgusting piece of journalism I had ever seen.

After I had finished, Cathy, who was standing outside, said, 'God, I'm glad I wasn't on the receiving end of that.' I was almost crying with rage. I wrote him a stinking private letter plus the following for publication:

Sir,

In your edition last week you claimed that you 'relayed to Paddy Ashdown' the feelings of the people of Yeovil on the issue of Sidney Cooke.

This is, as you well know, completely untrue. I rang you to express the hope that the *Western Gazette* would help calm the situation outside Yeovil police station. I said to you that I believed that a local newspaper had a role to inform.

I deeply regret that you chose to report our private conversation in this way, not as me appealing to you to be responsible, but as you informing me about the 'feelings' of the town I have represented for fifteen years. This falls, I fear, far short of the standards of accuracy in journalism which the *Gazette* ought to be upholding.

But the concern I may feel about your misreporting our private conversation is nothing alongside the anger I feel about the disgraceful front page of last week's *Gazette*.

I am shocked that, in a delicate, difficult and explosive situation, in which our community was being watched across the nation, you chose to use the power of the *Gazette*, not to inform, but to inflame.

I have had a long and constructive relationship with your newspaper, which, up to now, I have respected as an important and positive force for good in our community.

I fear, last week, you shamed your profession, your reputation and our town.
Yours faithfully
Paddy Ashdown MP

Friday, 24 April, London and Swansea

A number of interviews, including with the local press, on the Sidney Cooke affair. There were riots last night in Bristol because they think Cooke is there: hooligans breaking shop windows and forty policemen injured. Really disgraceful.

Off to the Welsh Party Conference in Swansea. We arrived early, so I sat down, had a cup of tea and caught up with my post. Then the usual frantic round of press interviews. As I expected, they played Charles's comments back to me at the press conference arranged to launch the event. Charles had said that constructive opposition was causing us to pull our punches, the Party wasn't in favour of it and neither was he. Wasn't he right? Wasn't this a split? How did I respond? I decided to play it very cool and said, 'He is an ambitious young man, Charles.' There was a sharp intake of breath and a suppressed giggle from the journos. Then someone followed up with, 'But surely you are cross about this?' I replied, 'No. He has started too early and he is riding the wrong horse.'

Later in the evening I spoke to David Walter, who finally made contact with Charles. Charles said his comments had been taken out of context. My eye! But what makes me really furious is that they have dominated the Welsh Conference when we intended to use it as an opportunity to set out our policies ahead of this year's local elections. Instead Charles has given the press an opportunity to say the Party is split!

Saturday, 25 April, Yeovil

Surgery not too busy today, so I rattled through it pretty fast.

Then downstairs to the Liberal Club hall to meet the crowd of Sidney Cooke protesters – about 150 in all. They had marched in a well-ordered fashion through the town and filed into the hall. It soon became clear that they were determined not to let me get a word in edgeways. A very tough meeting.

I spent about forty-five minutes being generally abused and shouted at. But I couldn't have expected less. Then, in an obviously stage-managed and pre-planned move, they got up and walked out in front of the TV cameras covering the event. I fear I didn't win any friends.

Then upstairs for a pint of beer with Jane, Simon and Kate [who was over from France], who said I looked shocked and ashen.

Wrote the following letter to Charles, attaching an extract from a newspaper report of his interview and my response.

Dear Charles,

Given that we agreed to put this matter to bed after Southport and are trying to fight local elections, this is VERY unhelpful.

I am told that you say you didn't mean it and have been quoted out of context, but that would require me to believe that you are naïve – which I don't.

Concluding, therefore, that you are not stupid either, I can only presume that this was intentional – in which case we had better speak soon.

I wanted to have a chat anyway about your spokesmanship.

I have asked Cathy to fix a time to see you – soon!

Yours

Paddy

Tuesday, 28 April, Westminster

In the evening, I caught up with a vast bundle of mail. About half the letters are for my position on Sidney Cooke and about half, including some pretty incoherently angry ones, against.

I am seeing Charles tomorrow. We passed each other in the division lobby and exchanged wary smiles. Paul told me that Charles insists this is all a misunderstanding. Difficult to believe.

Wednesday, 29 April, Westminster

At 5.30 Charles came to see me, flushed and with a very firm grimace on his face.

I opened with, 'You are obviously angry, so sit down and say your bit first.'

He said he was extremely cross to discover what I had said about him at the Swansea press conference. He also reminded me that he had been president of the party for many years, during which time we had never had a cross word.

He said that he hadn't believed, until he'd actually heard it, that I had attacked him so openly at Swansea. It hadn't been his intention to do the same to me. Moreover, I had damaged him in the process.

It was a sharp confrontation which lasted about ten minutes. He was perfectly polite, but red in the face with anger. He has, however, a very direct way of looking at you, which I admire. He held my eyes throughout and was perfectly coherent.

I told him I hadn't brought this problem on him, he had brought it on himself. I had read the transcript of what he had said. There were only two conclusions. Either he was naïve – which I knew wasn't the case, since he was an intelligent and subtle politician. Or he was ambitious, in which case his timing was bad, as was his choice of horse to ride.

CK: I don't want your job.

PA: I don't believe that. And if it was true I would think less of you for it. One job of a leader is to have a succession plan. In due course, I will give up . . .

CK (interrupting): I want to reassure you. I do not want your job.

PA: Then I do think less of you. It's not your wanting my job that concerns me. You should be ambitious, with your ability. What I am furious about is that the pursuit of your ambition results in disturbing the messages the party is trying to get across in the run-up to the local elections. In due course, when I decide to give up, there are in my view only three talents capable of doing this job in the present Parliamentary Party, and you are one of them. I have no wish, therefore, to damage you. But if, as a result of what you said, every journalist reports that you and I are at loggerheads, then I am bound to react strongly. You got your fingers burnt and you deserved it. However, if I have hurt you, that was not my long-term intention and I am happy to put it right. Perhaps I haven't been as frank with you in the past as I should have been. I have always counted you as a supporter, which is why your recent comments came as such a surprise. However, you are entitled to know what's going on in my mind. There's a lot more to come in the future.

CK: You know I'm one of the more cautious.

PA: If you are not cautious about what we are doing – indeed, if you are not scared to death about it – then you are a fool.

He laughed.

We parted company on good terms, with him putting his hand out to shake mine, which was both unusual and generous.

Thursday, 30 April, London and Leeds

A bad night's sleep. Out of the house by 7.30 for an hour of regional press interviews in my office. What I refer to as the 'ageing gunslinger round'. Young, frisky reporters coming in to see if they can notch up a party leader scalp on their belt. It requires infinite patience to deal with them because some are not very good, just rude. However, it seemed to go OK.

Then to Leeds for *Question Time*. Jack Straw, Nita Mann[1] and Michael Ancram[2] also on the panel.

I was not good. I took Jack Straw to town on the Mary Bell[3] case, on which I think he has behaved disgracefully.

However, I was really damaged by one person from the audience – a Labour plant, of course – saying I was pious, sanctimonious, and lecturing. I watched myself afterwards and concluded that, even though he was doing this for political effect, the average ordinary voter would conclude that he was right. I have become too strident.

Rang Jane, who also thought I wasn't as good as I should have been. I must (a) have more time to prepare for these things (I just cannot go into them after a strenuous day's campaigning at the end of three weeks of the same) and (b) slow down and appear more rational. I am in danger of looking and sounding a bit of a ranter with a tendency to preach. I will have to go back to square one and relearn some of my communication skills. To bed very depressed by a bad performance.

---

1 Journalist for *Tribune* magazine.

2 Member of Parliament (Conservative) for Berwickshire & East Lothian Feb.–Oct. 1974, Edinburgh South 1979–87, Devizes since 1992. He is currently Chairman of the Conservative Party.

3 A book had been written by the eminent historian Gitta Sereny about Mary Bell, who had killed two other children at the age of 11. There was public outcry when it emerged that Bell had been paid for assisting with the book.

Tuesday, 5 May, Westminster

On my way to Downing Street just before 5.00 for a meeting with Blair, I bumped into Chris Buckland of the *Express*, who apologized to me for cancelling a meeting today. 'I had to go to see the Prime Minister,' he said. Little did he know.

Kate Garvey met me and took me through, explaining that the PM was with a senior Italian politician (Prodi, I later found out), so they had better smuggle me through the back door. In the event they put me in the Private Office, where, with all the business of government going on around me, I sat quietly writing a letter to one of my constituents.

Jonathan Powell came in and commented in a mock shocked tone, 'Goodness, you are getting your feet under the table!'

Then into my meeting. Blair was, as always, sitting in his shirtsleeves on the sofa. I took my jacket off, hung it over the back of a chair and plonked myself down opposite him.

PA: How are you?

TB: Absolutely knackered. But you are looking very suntanned. Been campaigning up and down the country for the local elections?

PA: Partly. But partly doing something you can't do, planting my garden with my wife!

TB: God, that sounds attractive. I have been dealing with one succession of obdurate people after another recently, ending up today with the Middle East peace conference.

We had a very relaxed discussion. He started off by telling me about the shenanigans at the monetary union meeting[1] over the weekend, which Blair had chaired as Britain was in the presidency.

TB: Frankly, we were just outspun. We didn't have our lines prepared. And we hadn't done any of the background work to enable us to explain the story to the public.

1 The heads of government of the Council of European Union met in Brussels to discuss participation in the single currency and the make-up of the board of the Central European Bank. There had been much confusion over the very bad press reports on the future of Wim Duisenberg, a former Dutch Finance Minister, as president of the Central European Bank.

He went on to tell me, in considerable detail, exactly what had happened. He had been told on the day before the meeting of the council (Friday) that the Duisenberg question had been stitched up between the Germans, the French and the Dutch that Duisenberg should stand down. Only later did it become apparent that the Dutch weren't part of the deal and refused to accept it. Duisenberg wouldn't accept it either, and the remaining fifteen members were wholly opposed to it as well. All this produced a crisis about mid-day on Saturday which was simply dumped in Blair's lap. There followed a frantic three or four hours, during which Chirac insisted that if the deal between him and Kohl didn't stick, then they should go for a third candidate (i.e. not Duisenberg), a Finnish lady, who was not only unacceptable to everyone else but who subsequently made it clear that, if offered the post, she would turn it down anyway!

At this stage, Blair realized that the whole summit could fail. Then, at around 4.30, the coalition behind Kohl fell apart. This gave Blair the opportunity he had been waiting for to nobble Chirac. So, just before the plenary session, he said to Chirac in private, 'Look, if you go ahead, I will say publicly that you are taking a position which wrecks the whole project. I am prepared to blame you directly. I am not taking the flak for this.'

Then he wheeled in Kohl, who announced that he now no longer had the support of his own Cabinet and that the Finnish lady didn't want the job.

In the end Chirac backed down. So the best that could be arranged was that Duisenberg would make a statement to the other fifteen saying that he wouldn't have a date imposed on him for standing down early. Nevertheless, as he had already explained publicly, that was his intention. Unhappily, when it came to selling the outcome to the press, the government's spin doctors completely overlooked the previous Duisenberg comment that he didn't want to do the full term, so in the end it all looked like a grubby compromise instead of a deal to accommodate Duisenberg's own wishes.

TB: Now on to the project. How are things going?

PA: Far too slowly. You have shown over the last month that when you focus your attention on something, it happens and you can overcome obstacles that seem insurmountable. Unless you take a clear personal interest in our thing now and give it a real push, there will be far too much ground to cover for any prospect of success by November. We will have to wait now until after the local elections, but it is absolutely essential that you and I put this project back on the tracks as soon as possible. I hope we will be able to send you a draft of the Constitutional Declaration by the end of the week.

He agreed, and said that he would give thought to making a speech, possibly next week, about the importance of the project.

TB: I have just seen Prodi, you know. He is trying to do exactly the same thing. He says he intends to convert the Olive Tree Alliance[1] into a political party. I want you to know that this is the most important thing I have yet to do at this stage of my premiership. It's a big task – and I am not sure I can take all of my party with me – but I am absolutely confident it needs to be done.

Then we turned to Northern Ireland [where they were due to hold a referendum on the Good Friday Agreement]. It has been suggested that Blair, Hague and myself all go there together and share a platform.

I said I thought it was a bad idea which could be counterproductive: Westminster leaders telling the people of Northern Ireland how to vote on devolution was very likely to produce the wrong reaction. Much better if the three of us made separate visits arguing the same case, but not at the same time. Blair's speech would be the only one that would be reported anyway.

We moved on to the local elections. I told him I thought Labour would do better than we had originally envisaged.

TB: Yes, that's my view too, though obviously we are not saying it.

I went on to say that I thought two things were happening. As regards the Tories, it may be that the electors would consider voting for them again, but they were so demoralized on the ground that there was little evidence of any real campaigning strength there. The second was that, although Labour support in their traditional areas was less enthusiastic than last year, his support amongst the middle classes was, as far as I could tell, undiminished and maybe even hardening.

He responded by saying that he was worried about their traditional voters, but that as soon as he put money into public services he could win them back. He was pleased about the middle-class position. (This is a deadly threat to us, however.)

TB: Frankly, we expect to take some losses, but I don't mind if you win seats where our councils need a good kick. People tell me I ought to, but I don't.

---

1 A centre left umbrella organization covering a number of political parties and others in Italy.

I suggested we should co-ordinate a common line on the results, since it was in both our interests to knock down the Tories. I agreed to put Chris Rennard in contact with Margaret McDonagh.[1]

PA: So are you still fixed on a referendum on PR for next year?

To my horror, he said, 'No.' Then he quickly added, seeing my face, 'Not if you want it some other time. When do you want it?'
    I said that I definitely did not want it any later than next year.

PA: It ought not to be during either the May or the June local and Euro elections, since that would be confusing for the public. So the best time would be November. This would give us time to build the campaign up and get away from the inevitable dogfight which will occur between us over the European and local elections.

He said he would talk to his people about it.
    At this stage his staff were coming in almost every two minutes, seeking to hurry him on.

PA: Thanks for giving me so much time. I think this has been very useful. I do hope you get some rest. I assume you are not getting away over the Whitsun break?

He shook his head ruefully. 'Let's have a word after the local elections.'

Wednesday, 6 May, Westminster

Lunch with Roy, at his request. We went through my meeting with Blair yesterday. Apparently Roy is giving him dinner at East Hendred in a fortnight's time. Roy then came on to why he had really wanted to see me.
    He went through a long explanation of why Blair wouldn't give us Single Transferable Vote (STV) and that AV was not acceptable and anyway would be seen as a conspiracy between the two parties against the Tories and therefore unfair. But at 12.30 on Monday he had suddenly had a brainwave (typical of Roy the diarist to record the exact time and date). The system he would recommend should fulfil two criteria: it must be workable and durable; and it must secure Blair's agreement. I added a third, that it had to be the system most likely to gain a 'Yes' vote from the British people.
    STV may not be the most suitable, as it would invite people to change

---

1 General Secretary of the Labour Party.

not only the electoral system but also the one bit of the present system of politics they like, their attachment to their local MP. Any system that we had would have severe downsides when we came to the referendum. STV would break the constituency link; AV would be unacceptable and unfair to the Tories; and AMS would create two different types of MPs.

Roy then told me of some thoughts he had been having about how to get round this problem. He will also be speaking to Blair about them. What were my views?

I said I thought his ideas were very interesting. But we need to be careful about the proliferation of types of election. We are in danger of building too much complexity into our voting systems.

In the evening, a very amusing dinner at Millbank with Don Foster, Paul Tyler, Paul's son Dominick and Ming. Ming at his scurrilous and gossipy best. Most of the jokes were about Charles Kennedy's informal 'launching' of his leadership campaign.

Thursday, 7 May, Westminster

LOCAL ELECTION DAY

Rather a nice day. It has been cold and overcast the last few days, but today there are signs of spring again. Good for voting.

At 10.00am John Alderdice.[1] I told him that I had suggested to Blair that we should go separately to Northern Ireland rather than together. This coincided with his view and he said he would speak to Blair about it. Later we heard that Alastair Campbell had been briefing journalists that the three party leaders would not go to Northern Ireland as the Three Musketeers, but separately. Excellent.

To Cowley Street at 10.00pm for the election results. I stayed there until about 3.30 before going home to bed, dog tired. Not a bad night. We have lost some seven councils, and the ones we have held have smaller majorities. But the compensation was winning Liverpool. We have done well in some areas, but it is really patchy, and impossible to draw any firm conclusions about the national standings of the parties. Turnout was terrible.

---

1 Lord Alderdice. Leader of the Alliance Party, our sister party in Northern Ireland. John is now the Speaker of the Northern Ireland Assembly.

Friday, 8 May, Westminster

Up at 7.00. Spoke to Richard. We finalized the Constitutional Declaration draft yesterday, which he is to hand over to Mandelson today.

Richard also told me that Roger Liddle was already doing a comprehensive policy comparison between the two parties. I agreed to tell Alan Beith next week that the proposition was now underway and he must choose between either joining in or standing aside. Meanwhile, we will get David Laws and Alan Leaman to work on a joint policy document. Richard will make all these points to Mandelson.

Thursday, 14 May, Westminster

I was shocked to read this week's *Western Gazette* on the Sidney Cooke affair, which still rumbles on. There has been a *Panorama* programme about it which was deliberately sensationalist. Also a highly inflammatory BNP leaflet is circulating Yeovil. Apparently, it has also been displayed in the Liberal Club. And now I hear that the primary school in Reckleford whose fête I am to open on Saturday has had parents complain because I am going along. I have done myself a lot more damage over this than I thought.

At 3.30 Nick Harvey came to see me about Alan Beith's role in TFM. Yesterday, after the PPM, I took Alan into my office and said, 'Look, Blair has now made the proposition that I thought he was going to make. He wants us to talk about the possibility of a coalition and I have told him the terms on which I would consider this. I want to pursue this to see where we can get to. I would like you to head up a small policy unit consisting of Alan Leaman and David Laws to mark out the areas where we might be able to reach common positions. Would you do this?' I also explained that Richard would act in a co-ordinating role. Again, Alan said that he would go away and think about it.

Saturday, 16 May, Somerset

Richard has had a response from Mandelson on our Constitutional Declaration. He will send it through to me in due course. He thinks we can cover most of the points. They are particularly nervous about anything which predicts an outcome on PR.

In the afternoon, off to open Reckleford Infant School's May Fair. Some hostility here, including one man who quite deliberately passed with his children to the other side of the road as I approached.

Monday, 18 May, London

On the way up to London I worked on the revised Constitutional Declaration sent through by Mandelson.

Just as I got to the flat Downing Street rang. Blair wanted to speak to me.

'I gather you are going off to Northern Ireland tomorrow,' he said. 'Things are much worse there than we thought and Trimble is apparently worried about Hague going. It would be most helpful if you were to say that those who are arguing "No" in the referendum are doing more damage to the union than those who are arguing "Yes".'

I said I wanted my visit to be fairly low-key, as the Northern Irish people didn't want queues of Westminster politicians going out to tell them how to vote. But I agreed to toughen up my language slightly and to take on Paisley, if he felt that was useful.

At 7 o'clock, to the Chelsea Flower Show with Jane. Not up to last year's, I thought.

We ended up having dinner once again with Gordon Borrie and his wife (in an even more striking hat than last year) and Mark Fisher[1] and his wife. I got into conversation with Mark over dinner about Blair and the project. He agreed with me that Blair is a liberal – apparently they actually call him 'the liberal' in the Cabinet. Clearly a supporter of the project.

---

1 Member of Parliament (Labour) for Stoke on Trent since 1983, Minister for Arts.

Thursday, 21 May, Westminster

Alan Beith came to see me yesterday saying he needed to give me his answer to my question on where he stood on TFM.

As I was coming back from Gatwick on Tuesday Nick Harvey rang to say Alan had asked him to join in saying to me that they weren't prepared to do as I asked and they were wholly opposed to the project.

I didn't want to queer Nick's pitch for any subsequent leadership bid, so I suggested he should say to Alan that I had asked him to do something different from Alan – his task was purely practical and a natural extension of contingency planning in the party, for which he was responsible. This enables Nick not to jeopardize his future chances if everything goes wrong.

After the Team Leaders' meeting Alan and I went into my office, and he immediately said that he had been speaking to Nick and they both disagreed with what I wanted to do. It was very dangerous and the party wouldn't tolerate it.

In the end Alan didn't quite close the door – he left it ajar, just. He wasn't opposed in principle, he explained, but he, Nick and Chris Rennard all agreed, he claimed, that this wasn't the right time.

I explained to him that the later we leave it the harder it'll get. And that, anyway, we aren't dictating timing, Blair is, and we may have to take it or leave it.

I told Alan I would think about what he'd said and respond later, but I left him in little doubt about what my conclusion would be.

Tuesday, 26 May, Somerset

The Northern Irish vote came through on Saturday – a tremendous 71 per cent 'Yes' vote. Did a number of interviews over the weekend on it. Most of the coverage will be for Northern Irish politicians and for Blair.

Spent a quiet afternoon sitting in the garden and finished reading our latest policy papers. The education paper is terrific – Don Foster has done some really good work here and he has been radical as well. The economy paper also good. But the environment paper not so hot; nor the health paper – it retreats too readily into Old Labour positions.

Wednesday, 3 June, Westminster

My adviser Mark Payne came to see me to stress how important it is that I make it absolutely clear I intend to continue as leader. He thinks it is damaging that people are uncertain about this, with the result that the rival campaigns are starting.

I asked him which campaigns. He said he thought that Simon had been running a campaign for some time. Nick Harvey is apparently also running a campaign, and, as I suspected, Charles has been very active.

At PMQs the Tories groaned as usual when I got up, but soon shut up when they heard that I was speaking on Kosovo. I had warned Blair of my question beforehand, suggesting strong, early preventative action. He seems to be talking seriously about taking strong action, including putting the NATO force on the Albanian border for which we have been pressing for some time. Good.

Sunday, 7 June, Somerset

The Kosovo situation worsens. There is a piece in one of the newspapers saying the government should basically follow my advice. Whatever I say, they should do. But Kosovo is a province of Serbia, not a recognized state like Bosnia, and the situation is much more difficult.

Monday, 8 June, En route to London

On the train up to London I heard that we at last have the go-ahead for the Constitutional Declaration.

Tuesday, 9 June, London

Into the office by bus early. Nervous we haven't got things absolutely tied up for the launch of the Constitutional Declaration on Thursday.

To the gym. I did my full round of exercises, during which I decided we needed to map out a clearer position on Kosovo. The government is going at it slightly wrongly. The key thing is to persuade Milosevic, if necessary by force, that he can't achieve a military answer to the Kosovo problem and that he must seek a political one. We could perhaps use air power to remove the heavy weapons which are doing such terrible damage to Albanian villages and causing the flood of refugees which is threatening to destabilize neighbouring states such as Macedonia. I have decided that I must go out to see for myself. But the Serbs will not give me a visa, so I am beginning to replan my visit just to take in Macedonia and Albania.

After the JCC Blair and I went outside for a photo op with the Constitutional Declaration, after which we had a thirty-minute conversation in his office which covered familiar territory (my misgivings over the lack of progress on TFM, whether the Tories would go further to the right, and our capacity to carry our parties), without much new emerging.

Wednesday, 10 June, Westminster

At 2.15 a meeting with Alan Beith. I told him that I have been giving his concerns about Labour's proposition considerable thought over the Whitsun recess. But in the end I decided that we simply couldn't turn the opportunity down. Labour had asked us to explore the possibility of a joint agreement on policy and we had to take that opportunity. He repeated the arguments for not doing so. But I said that I had taken the decision. He then asked how many other people knew about this and I told him Richard, David Laws, Nick and himself.

'When are we going to start?' he asked.

I said probably within the next fortnight.

He will think more about it.

Then off to a special dinner I am throwing for all our Team Leaders at the Royal Commonwealth Society in their new 'floating dining-room'. Don took me to one side before the dinner to say that he was worried I was putting myself right out on a limb on the Lib/Lab stuff and that I needed somebody further out than me to provide 'cover'. He and a few others were prepared to do this. I told him to hold his horses. Good people like him must be protected if I go down. To which Don replied, 'Well, I'll do it anyway, but only if you give me the undertaking you will stay on as leader.'

I gave him an equivocal answer. He was clearly a bit shocked by this and said, 'Look, you will drop us all in the shit if you stand down. I am only doing this because I really want you to lead us into the next election.'

Thursday, 11 June, Westminster

THE DAY OF THE ANNOUNCEMENT OF THE CONSTITUTIONAL
DECLARATION

In at 7.30 by bus to prepare for the announcement of the Constitutional Declaration and the JCC today. During the morning it became evident that a story in the *Guardian* that Brown was making a major statement on public expenditure (more money for education and health) would be the major news item of the day. By lunchtime it was being broadcast as 'a statement as important as the Budget'. Very cross-making, since this would swamp the Constitutional Declaration story.

We called in the press politicos and spent half an hour with them going through it, but they were pretty sceptical and put me under a good deal of pressure. [The story appeared reasonably well in the following day's papers, but we got absolutely nothing from the broadcasters.] The whole day swamped by the Brown declaration.

Later, I rang Jonathan Powell to relay my anger about this. We should, of course, have spotted that there was the Mansion House speech today, but couldn't they have let us know privately beforehand that something large was coming up?

Roger and others think it's a conspiracy. I think not. But it does indicate that Labour regard all this as less important than we do.

To the JCC at 1.30, picking up Ming and Alan along the way. Bob and Richard arrived later. We were kept waiting outside and as we entered Downing Street I saw Mandelson and Derry Irving in a close huddle.

After the JCC Blair and I went outside for a photo op with the Constitutional Declaration.

Later in the afternoon, his office rang mine. The PM had just seen Ibrahim Rugova[1] and he particularly wanted me to see him as well. I agreed to meet Rugova after a dinner he is due to have with Cook this evening 'for a whisky in my office'.

---

1 Leader of the Democratic League of Kosovo; the self-declared and unrecognized president of Kosovo since 1990. Rugova's party had won the greatest share of the votes in the recent elections in Kosovo.

My dinner was at Fleming's Bank, after which I returned to the House and wandered into Central Lobby to wait for Rugova. He arrived a few minutes later with an entourage of three, an interpreter and his Foreign Office guide. I took them up to my office, got some glasses out and we discussed Kosovo for an hour or so. Rugova is a dignified but sallow-faced Albanian, slightly balding and with the tousled hair and open, somewhat perplexed face of a university professor. He understands English but won't speak it.

I asked him what the Serbs were doing. Surely they didn't want to ethnically cleanse the whole of Kosovo? He thought they did. And if they succeeded in running out all the Albanians, they wanted to turn Kosovo into a national park. Unlikely, I felt. But I could understand why he took that view. I said we were very concerned for his safety because of the radicalization of the Serb population against the Albanians. He said that he had always lived dangerously but that he was safe enough.

I then put to him the idea of putting a token UN or Nato force on the Albanian border, strengthening the Macedonian border and using air power along the lines discussed with Blair. Would this work? Yes, he said, it would.

Rugova was very firm about wanting Kosovan independence. I said this was impossible at the moment and the international community wouldn't tolerate it, but that we ought to follow a 'Bosnia solution'; the *de jure* borders could stay but their importance would be diminished. The only circumstances in which we could put troops in would be to police a Dayton-style agreement. And even then Kosovo would have to pass through an interim position of greater autonomy from Serbia before, eventually, perhaps gaining independence.

A very interesting meeting.

Afterwards I gathered my belongings and caught the 159 bus home.

Tuesday, 16 June, London

A lot of planning for my forthcoming visit to the Balkans (Macedonia, Albania and, if the Serbs will let me, Kosovo). Spoke to the Serbian Ambassador today. He wants to come and 'interview me' for my visa. I told him I would submit to no such thing. I would be happy to see him and to be briefed by him if I was going to his country, but if I was not going to his country I couldn't see the point.

Furthermore, I continued, they have had our visa applications [Roger Lowry[1] was also coming with me] for more than two weeks now, so to suddenly say at this stage that I must have a visa which required special clearance was nonsense. I had to make decisions about my programme and I would give him until 11 o'clock on Wednesday before deciding this. If I hadn't heard from him by then, we would go ahead with our planned visit to Macedonia and Albania, but make it clear, publicly, that the Serbs had made it impossible for me to get a visa.

In the afternoon Alan Beith came to see me.

'I have been speaking to Paul and Nick,' he said. 'They tell me I ought to do this, but I will only do it on a number of conditions. First, Alan Leaman should not be involved.'

I informed him that it was already too late for that. Alan Leaman is already engaged and the first meeting took place this morning.

Secondly, he proposed that he should not be too involved with the Cabinet committee, and so on. He has also spoken to Nick and Paul, who have provided him with a 'cover'. If it comes out that he has been involved and that he has been damaged by this, they would be prepared to say they had recommended him to do it.

I later learned from Nick and Paul that Alan had asked them, 'What do you think will happen if I don't do this?' They said I would go ahead anyway and then ask Don to do the policy work.

Considerable problems yet to come, I suspect.

Meanwhile, we've had the first indications of some leaking. Apparently there is a story going round that No. 10 is working on a coalition deal. All the signs point to this coming from Labour. It will reinforce Alan's view, however, that we can't do anything like this without seepage.

Wednesday, 17 June, London

No word from the Serbian Ambassador. But we received official notification today from the Foreign Office that we must be careful going to Macedonia, and, especially, to the 'badlands' of northern Albania. They may issue us with flak jackets when we get there.

---

1 Roger was responsible for the administration of the Joint Cabinet Committee from our end and also accompanied me on my visits to the Balkans.

Thursday, 18 June, Westminster

More stories in the press today about me being Foreign Secretary. Someone from inside Labour is briefing hard to discomfort Cook.

Put together the final plans for my Balkans trip. We are clearly not going to get into Serbia.

The Foreign Office people came to brief me at 3.30. They again warned me off northern Albania – 'very dangerous', they said. I asked them whether or not I could go over the border into Kosovo. They said no, a New Zealand journalist had been killed recently in an ambush whilst accompanying a KLA unit into Kosovo.

Friday, 19 June, London

Up at 7.30 following a rather turbulent night. Thinking about Kosovo. A lot of packing and preparation still to do.

A story in the *FT* today about Downing Street's preparations for a coalition. More leaking from Labour! No. 10 want to dismiss it all. But I think that's hazardous. Better to suggest that the leak was a corruption of the preparations for the Constitutional Declaration.

Sunday, 21 June, Macedonia

THE START OF MY SIX-DAY BALKAN TOUR

The weather glorious but there were scattered cloud as we flew south over the Alps down the Danube over Belgrade and directly over Kosovo to land at Skopje. As we dropped in I saw the long snow-capped line of the Sar Planina mountains. A great 6,000-foot ridge of peaks poking south like a giant finger, separating Kosovo from Macedonia.

We were met at the airport by the British Ambassador, Mark Dickinson, who drove us up to the Kosovan border, about twenty minutes from Skopje. All quiet. It could have been a frontier post on any border in Europe. A car coming through from Kosovo was being quietly searched by the Macedonians. The only thing that suggested a crisis was half hidden on a peak about a quarter of a mile away – a sandbagged fortification with the UN flag flying above it, similar to the British ones in South Armagh. It was manned by Americans, apparently.

Monday, 22 June, Macedonia

A morning's meetings with Macedonian politicians, including the Prime Minister, Branko Crvenkovski. He is only 36, but has been Prime Minister since 1992. He has a way of looking at you very directly and not taking his eyes off you when he speaks. He gave cogent, clear answers to all my questions. He also reinforced the need for a regional solution to the Kosovo crisis which would include Macedonia and Albania. I said when I left that he should meet Blair: 'You two would get on well together.'

It has become increasingly clear to me since getting here that our idea of using force only on the Serbs, without also dealing with the KLA, will have to be revised. The problem is that the wider Balkan war we all fear could be detonated if either the Serbs *or* the KLA triumph in Kosovo. If the Serbs win, the Kosovar Albanians will be driven into Macedonia, thereby destabilizing the country by upsetting the delicate balance between native Macedonians and the increasingly restless Albanian population in the west of the country, close to the Albanian border. On the other hand, a win for the KLA would lead to an independent Kosovo and almost certainly to a push for the 'Greater Albania' for which some Albanian politicians, particularly Sali Berisha,[1] have been working. This, too, would destabilize the whole region, starting with Macedonia. So Macedonia is the fuse which could detonate a wider war risking the possible involvement of Greece and Turkey. But Kosovo is the spark.

The prevailing view is that the KLA are gaining ground on the Serb security forces, but this is only because Milosevic, who has been trying to show restraint to the international community, has so far not used the full force of the Yugoslav army. If he does, then bloody havoc is likely to follow and the KLA will be driven back. The only answer for the international community is to encourage a stalemate, thereby creating the opportunity to broker a peace deal. We may also be able to put pressure on Milosevic to conform by threatening military force if he does not. But that would only help the KLA to win. So, how to control the KLA? The only way

1 Dr Sali Berisha, chairman of the Democratic Party of Albania and Head of State.

appears to be to close off the main route for their arms supplies, through the lawless mountain region surrounding Bajram Curi in northern Albania, which is currently controlled, not by the Albanian government, but by Sali Berisha and the mafia.

It is vital, therefore, that, one way or another, I go up to this region to look for myself.

At around mid-day we left Skopje in a car provided by the Macedonian Liberals and headed off for Lake Ohrid and the Albanian border. A two-hour journey under cloudless skies.

We travelled first west to the Macedonian towns of Tetovo and Gostivar, where the minority Albanian population rioted last year. Mosques and minarets prominent here, with occasional orthodox churches scattered amongst them, indicating mixed communities. The countryside is trim and well-cultivated. Not like in Bosnia, where so much has fallen into disrepair through the ravages of war.

We then swung south for the Albanian border, following the line of the Sar Planina range which towered above us, the last remnants of snow still caught in its ridges and valleys. Everybody says these mountains are uncrossable, but I'm not so sure. Maybe during the winter months. But at this time of year they would appear no block to really desperate refugees.

Finally, as we approached the border, the mountains gave way to a rump of ridges with large stands of trees, alpine meadows and pretty little villages, opening up at the end to the great open bowl which contains Lake Ohrid, a huge inland sea with snow-capped mountains sweeping down to its shores. It was here that Alexander the Great rested his troops after his first and only defeat, as a very young general, at the hands of the Illyrians (today's Albanians).

At the Albanian/Macedonian frontier there were large crowds waiting to cross in both directions.

The Macedonian border guards, who, like so many officials in the Balkans, seem to find it impossible to change their Eastern Bloc officiousness, even though their states have long since abandoned communism, wanted to know exactly where we were going, why we were here, etc., etc. The fact that our car had been provided by the Macedonian government made not the slightest difference. They insisted that we carry our suitcases and walk the three or four hundred yards between the two border posts to the Albanian side. We bade goodbye to our taciturn Macedonian driver and set off across the 'no man's land' in the blazing sun. Roger muttered, 'Very John le Carré.'

To my delight, at the Albanian border post I could see two white Land Rovers and the figures of two ECMM[1] monitors. One of them, an ex-Royal Marine called Jim Cooper, filled our journey with excited talk about how dangerous Albania was. The other was a rather silent Swede named Bjorn. As Jim sought to negotiate our passage with the Albanian border guard, the man behind us in the queue pushed past, quite openly gave him a $20 note and was swiftly waved through. For us, long discussions and filling in of forms ensued, along with complaints that we didn't have diplomatic passports. But as soon as Jim produced a $10 note things moved rather more swiftly.

Then off on the long, dusty journey to Tirana over appalling roads.

The differences between Macedonia and Albania are strikingly obvious. Macedonia has good roads and well-cared-for countryside. Albania, though impressive, with magnificent mountains, deep valleys and clear mountain streams, is unkempt and grindingly poor. In the region we passed through, there was hardly a tree left standing and the terrible scars of erosion marked almost every valley and mountain slope. But most bizarrely of all, the whole countryside, even in the remote mountain areas, is covered with what are called 'Hoxha mushrooms', named after Albania's Maoist ex-dictator Enver Hoxha,[2] who used forced labour to construct them in the mistaken belief that he was about to be attacked by either the Warsaw Pact from the east or NATO from the west (he could never make up his mind which). These concrete constructions, shaped, as the name implies, like the caps of mushrooms, each contain a gun position and a family-sized shelter. According to estimates there are 115,000 of them in all, distributed higgledy-piggledy and without detectable military logic, right across Albania. Scattered amongst them are a few larger shelters capable of taking a tank or artillery piece, in the same basic design. This desperately poor little country must have exhausted millions and millions of man hours constructing these ridiculous, useless, but virtually indestructible edifices.

Eventually we zigzagged down out of the mountains into a broad valley where a vast Chinese steel factory and strip-rolling mill, covering hundreds of acres, lay derelict, empty and rusting – another monument to Maoism and the Great Leap Forward, Albanian style.

1 European Community Monitor Mission. Established by the European Community in 1991, their observers, who wear a distinctive, all-white uniform, monitor political, security, humanitarian, military and economic issues within the Balkan states. They report back to the European Union Council of Ministers.
2 Communist leader of Albania 1954–85.

Then out of the valley again and along one of the most lovely roads I have ever driven, following the crest of a sharp mountain ridge towards Tirana (I later learned that the Albanian custom is to build roads on the tops of mountains rather than in valleys). To our north, the great mountain peaks of central Albania and to the south wave upon wave of ridges broke blue down to the Adriatic glinting in the distance.

After four hours we dropped down out of the bright sunlight and into a thick blanket of smog, beneath which, almost invisible in the gloom, lay Tirana.

Tirana is like Calcutta transplanted to Europe. Sprawling, unplanned, teeming with humanity, stiflingly hot and paralysingly chaotic.

We made straight for the British Embassy, where we met one of the First Secretaries, who had arranged our visit and who had recently been shot by bandits on the Dajte mountain behind the city when she was returning from lunch there. At the Embassy's recommendation we left our valuables (street robbery is rife) and made our way to our hotel.

On our way we met Neritan Ceka,[1] a former Minister of the Interior, who was to accompany us for the next few days. A big brown-faced man, very handsome, with grey hair and a commanding air of confidence.

He gave me my programme, which consisted of a helicopter trip with him to the northern region of Bajram Curi, a couple of hours there and then a flight back. The rest of my time was to be spent meeting ministers and officials.

I took the British Ambassador, Stephen Nash, to one side before dinner and told him that I really didn't want this. I intended to tell Ceka that we were most grateful for his assistance – and especially the helicopter trip – but could he leave us to our own devices in Bajram Curi for just twenty-four hours?

Nash looked worried. Bajram Curi was not a place to stay overnight, he advised. Ceka reinforced this by saying that it was bandit territory and very dangerous. But I was politely insistent. I would put myself under the protection of the ECMM observer team there, I promised.

In the end Ceka conceded, saying he would assign an Albanian 'friend' to protect me and we agreed to meet in the morning.

---

1 Leader of the Macedonian Liberals. Neritan has remained a close friend. Since this date his party (the Democratic Alliance) and the Liberal Democrats have had a close relationship and he has spoken at several Liberal Democrat conferences.

Tuesday, 23 June, Albania

Up at 6.15 and down to breakfast. A skimpy affair of bread, some very hard cheese and a few slices of extremely undelicious tinned ham. The coffee, however, was Turkish and excellent.

Ceka met us as planned and we drove out to the landing site and jumped into his helicopter.

The flight to northern Albania was magnificent. We flew over range after range of majestic mountains and deep ravines filled with lakes. Eventually, we arrived at a broad alpine valley on the shoulder of which lay Bajram Curi, looking like a cross between a town in Tibet and a dusty Wild West film set, complete with gun-toting population.

Our first visit was to the police station, where they have only one car (a battered Yugo, incapable of reaching the next village, let alone managing the rough tracks up to the mountainous border area with Kosovo) and no communications at all, beyond a walkie-talkie which couldn't even reach as far as the outskirts of the town. Yet this is one of the most fragile borders in Europe.

Afterwards, we were taken to see the mayor and local corporation, who went through the problems of Bajram Curi in the usual ex-communist way. Lots of statistics, but few useful facts. I asked about the Kosovan families who had fled here over the mountain. We were told that Kosovan refugee families were currently receiving full Albanian hospitality, but they would have to be moved down the mountain deeper into Albania once the winter came because there were no facilities for them here.

We were taken to meet one family who had fled over the mountains from Kosovo in the last few days. There were seven or eight of them. The children, from five upwards, were wonderful-looking, the eldest boy with a shock of fairish hair, deep brown face and strongly etched features.

We sat cross-legged on the cloth laid out on the floor of their bare tent and I listened to their story, with Ceka translating. Eventually, he stopped, his voice choked into a sob and his eyes filled with tears, as did mine. Another sufferer of my Bosnian affliction? My heart went out to him.

The mother told us that she had six children and that she lived with her husband in a little farming village just over the border in Kosovo. One day the Serbs had come and taken her husband away. They had beaten and tortured him so much that he had lost his memory and his hearing. She only realized that he was not, in fact, dead, but still at the police station when she heard on a rebel radio station that somebody had been left on the road outside the police station whom no one could identify. She went to collect him.

Some days later, the Serbs turned up on a hill outside her small hamlet and started shooting randomly at the village to scare the inhabitants into fleeing. But they wouldn't budge. So the Serbs brought in mortars, artillery and tanks and started bombarding them.

That night the woman led her weak husband and six children out of the house and left the village with her neighbours under cover of darkness. They would have gone straight to Albania through one of the nearby main frontier crossing points at the head of a low valley, rather than take their young children over the high mountains (6,000 feet, at this point). But they knew that the main crossing points would be full of mines and Serb ambushes. So instead they trekked through the woods out of the Kosovo plain, and over the high mountain passes, travelling always at night. After three days they reached the Albanian border and made their way down the mountain on a goat path into the Bajram Curi valley. The Serbs had shelled the mountain passes through which they had to travel. Several people had died along the way – as usual, the old, the very young and the wounded – but her family had all made it.

Would they go back? I asked.

Yes, they longed to go back.

Did they find it difficult here?

Yes. There is real tension with the locals (there is famously no love lost between the Albanians and their Kosovar cousins).

Would they have stayed if the Serbs hadn't brought in the heavy artillery and tanks?

Of course.

On the way back we met another woman whose husband had been part of a small group of men that had led her and some other families over the mountains before going back to join the KLA. Several of her party had been killed by Serb shelling on the high passes. In the confusion and darkness, she had become separated from four of her children and had feared she would never see them again. But her eldest son, aged 10, had led the other children through the forests and down into Albania. She too was waiting to go back.

Afterwards, off to see the police again. Ceka spent some time trying to convince me that they were keeping control of the arms going through the area, had caught several arms couriers and were pursuing others. I didn't believe him but I pretended to. If this had been Britain and my countrymen were being slaughtered over the border, I don't suppose I would have prevented arms from reaching them either.

Then to the hospital. Here there were several wounded men, clearly KLA soldiers. One young man, terribly wounded in the back by shrapnel, was close to death. Another had been shot by a sniper, the bullet shattering his arm. He had made his way over the mountains to Albania for medical attention and in the process had taken a piece of shrapnel in the leg from a Serb shell. When Ceka inspected the swelling on his knee, he immediately insisted that the man take my empty seat in the helicopter back to Tirana. Médécins Sans Frontières were here doing their usual superb job, but they are terribly under-equipped, with no decent operating material.[1]

After the wounded man was loaded on to the helicopter, I thanked Ceka and said goodbye. He seems greatly admired by the people and respected by the policemen – unusual for an Albanian politician.

Then off to the ECMM office in the town with Milaim Cengu,[2] the interpreter and bodyguard whom Neritan Ceka had deputized to look after me. Brief introductions to the ECMM team and then off in their Land Rover up the valley, heading for the mountains and the Albania/Kosovo border. An appalling journey over very rough roads. On the way up we saw goat herds mixed in with groups of people and trucks moving up with us. We were caught behind one heavily laden, tarpaulin-covered truck, bumping and grinding up the valley. As we came up to it the tarpaulin blew to one side, revealing ammunition boxes stacked to overflowing in the back.

After about half an hour we arrived at the village of Tropoje, in the middle of a valley. Sitting out in the sunshine in the village street were groups of men cleaning and oiling rifles and light sub-machine-guns. Dark,

---

1 The British Ambassador, Stephen Nash, took a list of urgently needed medical equipment from one of the French doctors and, on my return to the UK, I pressed the government to send out second-hand NHS equipment, which duly arrived in Bajram Curi by way of the British Embassy.

2 Member of the Democratic Alliance and Secretary of the prefecture of Kukes, the administrative area in which Bajram Curi and Tropoje lie.

swarthy, with magnificent faces. I could see why Aubrey Herbert[1] called them 'kings in rags'. I wanted to get out and speak to them, but the ECMM man told me he was under strict orders not to let me. I asked if he would drop me off at the corner and turn a blind eye for ten minutes or so. But he was adamant. He had been kind enough to take me, so I submitted, saying, 'OK, but do stop calling me sir. I may be a politician, but out in the field you are the bloke in charge.' He looked much relieved. When I asked Milaim, the interpreter, whether these men were KLA he just raised his eyebrow and said, in a tone I was not supposed to believe, 'Oh no, they are just Albanians.'

The reality, however, is very different. According to the ECMM team, Tropoje and the surrounding area, especially the (heavily fortified) farmhouse we passed, where Sali Berisha's family is based, is used as a kind of huge arms supermarket. Weapons are apparently brought up to the area from Tirana by the mafia and international arms traders. Then the KLA on the other side of the mountains send couriers over who place their orders and the weapons are transported back, either on backpacks or by mule trains. Mostly small arms. But we saw one mule train moving across a mountain track carrying what looked like three stripped-down heavy machine-guns.

From Tropoje we continued on up the terrible dirt path to the Kosovan border, marked by little trig points and a track running along a mountain ridge. Marking the Serb side was a line of watchtowers on stilts, set fifty metres back from the frontier.

Then through a tiny alpine hamlet, finally stopping just short of the crest of the hill overlooking Kosovo. We left the Land Rovers just below the

---

1 While staying in the Ambassador's residence in Skopje, I found in his bookcase a biography of one of my predecessors as MP for Yeovil, Aubrey Herbert, which he had lent me to read on the journey. Herbert, a most romantic figure, was John Buchan's model for 'Greenmantle'. A British agent in Constantinople, he is credited with being instrumental in the fall of the Ottomans. He subsequently became the Conservative candidate in the then safe Liberal seat of Yeovil, failing to overturn the Liberal majority in the election of 1910, but succeeding a year later in the famous Yeovil by-election of 1911. The next time Yeovil changed hands politically was when I won it back for the Liberals in 1983. Herbert, a brilliant linguist, went on to fight (as MP for Yeovil) in the Albanian War of Independence of 1913 and was twice offered the Crown of Albania, which he refused – which I think rather a pity, since the title 'MP for Yeovil and King of Albania' has a certain ring to it. He wrote on one visit to the Balkans, 'I didn't realize how glad I am to have done with Yeovil till I got here. It is such a change to come from niggling non-conformists to people who really are ready to sacrifice all they have for their creed.'

ridge and walked the last two hundred metres through an alpine meadow carpeted with Michaelmas and ox-eye daisies, vetch of every colour and the summer remnants of orchids and alpine crocuses. The air was alive with swallowtail butterflies and chaffinches, and heavy with the scent of flowers and the hum of bees. Somewhere in the woods below a cuckoo called stubbornly and we began to hear the distant sounds of a battle: the heavy crump of artillery, the sharper crack of tank fire and intermittent codas of heavy machine-gun fire rattling through the summer afternoon.

Milaim told me that the Albanians believe a cuckoo is unlucky.

When we reached the ridge we were presented with the whole of the southern plain of Kosovo laid out before us like a Brueghel painting. Its richness was startling after the meagre valleys and unforgiving mountains of Albania. At around 2,000 metres we had a commanding view of the whole fertile patchwork quilt, with its lakes and little red-roofed hamlets stretching away in front of us, like Surrey from the Downs.

Interrupting this picturesque scene, on a bald knoll perhaps two kilometres away, lay a Serb mortar position. And to one side, exposed on a hill in a way that would have been fatal had there been hostile aircraft about, was a tank shooting at a more distant village. Closer by, a cluster of armoured personnel carriers gathered on open ground, waiting for somewhere new to attack. And to our left, about a kilometre away, lay another gun position, exposed like a pimple on the skyline.

Milosevic has obviously decided to end the early restraint he showed and is now using the full force of one of the Warsaw Pact's most efficient armies against the underequipped and ill-prepared KLA and the largely defenceless population whom they were formed to 'protect'.

I crawled forward over the border a little to get a better look at the valley below. Milaim whispered urgently behind me, 'Please, Mr Paddy, come back. Mr Ceka said I must keep you safe and there could be Serb snipers in those trees.' I crawled back, put my binoculars up and started looking for the tracks that the refugees had followed.

Suddenly, on the crest of a nearby ridge, I spotted eight or ten Serb soldiers manhandling a small mountain gun. We saw them fire several shells and heard the dull explosions as they landed somewhere up to the north – bombarding the woods through which the refugees pass.

It was now about four in the afternoon, so, looking at the gathering clouds above us, we decided to get off the mountain before it started raining.

We drove back past the Serb border posts, stopping on our way by the near-vertical slope down which the refugee families had clambered. It must have been a terrifying descent at night, especially with small children.

Then into the valley, past herds of goats and peasant villages unchanged for a hundred years and back to Bajram Curi.

We booked into the only hotel in the town, which was grotty, even by Albanian standards.

Just after dinner we heard the heavy rattle of machine-gun fire on the street outside. Apparently, one of the Kosovans had been seen with blood on him. Much discussion as to whether this was an Albanian blood feud, or *Kanun*[1] (these are desperate things carried out in accordance with a very precise code of chivalry) or just a 'Bosnian unload' (Balkan slang for someone firing in the air, either to celebrate a wedding or some such, or simply after too much raki). We settled on the latter. Then to bed.

At about 2.00am I heard some distant booming and looked out of the window to see flashes up on the hill where we had been in the morning. But I slept well enough.

Thursday, 25 June, Tirana

Having spent the whole of yesterday driving back over the mountains from northern Albania, at 11 o'clock we went to see Sali Berisha. He was smartly dressed and tightly guarded. Armani is obviously the Albanians' preferred tailor for politician, bodyguard and crook alike. It makes it difficult to tell them apart.

We were shown into Berisha's room, where he greeted us with a smile which was both too ready and too oily to be remotely convincing. He has a much more east European air than the other Albanians I have met. To look at he is a sort of cross between Radovan Karadzic and David Owen. I wondered to myself whether these people with their long, lustrous, backswept hair and handsome features were always egotists.

I didn't take to him at all.

I started by saying that I had seen his farmhouse when I was up in Bajram. He replied that it wasn't his farmhouse now – it was owned by his cousins.

1 The full name is 'Kanuni I Lek Dukagjinit', named after the fifteenth-century Albanian prince who drew up this precisely choreographed code of revenge (the only European code of behaviour which matches it for formality and preciseness is the medieval 'Code of Courtly Love').

At this stage, Stephen Nash came in and, in the middle of our conversation, slipped me a telegram he had just received from London. This told me that London was saying they were very concerned about Berisha. They had received confidential information that he was the main backer and arms supplier for the KLA and was intent on stirring up trouble among the Albanian minority in Macedonia. Could I be tough on him?

So I started to get a little more aggressive.

I asked him directly, 'Are you supplying arms to the KLA?'

'No.'

'Well, everyone believes you are.' I said this in a tone meant to convey that 'everyone' included me.

'I assure you I am not. But perhaps my cousins are.'

'Well, who do you think is supplying their arms, then?'

'They are probably coming from Montenegro.'

'But I saw a lot going through Bajram Curi and Tropoje. And everyone says your farmhouse there is the centre of the trade. Isn't that right?'

'It's no longer my farmhouse. I gave it to my cousins.'

'Are you prepared to condemn those who sell arms to the KLA?'

'Of course. But if my cousins disagree, how can I stop them? And anyway, the KLA aren't terrorists. They are a liberation army.'

Another in that category of leaders of whom the poor old Balkans seems to have more than its fair share, who are clever, charismatic and can lie straight to your face.

In the later afternoon, off to the airport and back to Heathrow via Rome. Started writing my report for the Prime Minister on the plane. Landed a little after 8.00.

Saturday, 27 June, Somerset

Finished my paper on the Balkans.[1] Rang Powell. Apparently, Blair is seeing Richard Holbrooke, the American Special Ambassador to the Balkans (whom I am seeing on Monday). Would I fax my report through to No. 10 straightaway?

---

1 See Appendix E.

Monday, 29 June, London

At 4.30 a meeting with Richard Holbrooke. He has just come back from an unsuccessful mission to try and find a solution to the Kosovo crisis and is full of gloom about what will happen next. He said that full-scale war in Kosovo had been within twenty-four hours of breaking out when he arrived, but in the end the Serbs had decided they couldn't launch it while he was there. He also believes that the KLA have a much more sophisticated command structure than has been previously thought.[1]

Wednesday, 1 July, Westminster

At the Jo Group meeting today we had a long discussion about the future of the relatinship with Labour. Nick Harvey said that if TFM goes ahead we will need to get agreement for a coalition from the Parliamentary Party and the Federal Executive before taking it to Special Conference. He's absolutely right.

Also, much discussion about the date for the referendum, in which many disparate views came up. I didn't attempt to chair the meeting tightly. I just wanted to hear their views.

The Jo Group has been meeting for five years. It has delivered a huge amount, but I have decided that this should be its last formal meeting. From now on we will go down to a smaller working group, which I have christened the Next Group, to carry through the last stages to TFM. Though I now doubt we will actually get there. My assessment remains at 70/30 against.

Tuesday, 7 July, Westminster

To No. 10 at 10.30am for our planned 'six-hander' (Blair, Powell and Mandelson from their side and Richard Holme, Roger Lowry and me from ours). I set off alone, leaving Roger and Richard to follow. When I arrived,

1 Over the following weeks, the crisis deepened in Kosovo, as, first, the KLA captured territory from Belgrade control, and then, in September, Milosevic launched a counterattack using the Yugoslav army, leading eventually in spring 1999 to the Kosovo war.

Kate Garvey explained that Blair was running late and showed me up to the ante-room to the No. 10 dining-room. (She had originally tried to put me in a different room, but opened the door to discover there was someone else there. While I was waiting, another Downing Street aide turned up with a cameraman, opened the door and, finding me there, shut it again quickly. Kate then had to lead me to Blair's office via the backstairs to avoid the cameraman. Something of a Whitehall farce.)

Blair's office has had some new paintings hung since I was last there (Derry's work?). In due course, Richard Holme and Roger Lowry arrived and we all sat at the little round table by his desk (rather tatty in comparison to the other furniture in Downing Street).

Then Jonathan Powell came in and moved us over to the chairs by the fireplace. The next person to arrive was Mandelson, who shot us a startled look. It turned out that Richard was sitting in the PM's personal chair. So we swiftly moved amid much joking from Richard about not wanting to take over Blair's seat as well as everything else.

Finally, Blair turned up, apologizing for the delay. He took his seat and we got down to business.

TB: Now, let me see, where are we? Yes. Thanks for the agenda and the note. I am nervous, however, about deciding a date. [I had, as usual, been pressing for one.] I'm not really sure that we can do November. There is so much to do between now and then and I have not got my thoughts in order yet.

PA: Let's come back to that in a moment. As I see it, we are *not* here to discuss if you and I agree to go ahead – that depends on whether the government recommends a 'Yes' vote on the referendum on the Jenkins Commission report, and on reaching agreement on the coalition programme (I wanted to get Blair to restate his previous commitments in front of his own staff).

TB: Yes, I agree. We are not discussing the 'if', just the 'when' and the 'how'. You know my view. If Roy Jenkins proposes something sensible – and I believe he will – I will support that, on which basis we should put together a broader coalition agreement. In policy terms there is not very much between us, and what there is, I believe, will be overcome in the CSR [Comprehensive Spending Review]. Once we have got that out of the way we will, in essence, be on all fours. But I don't want to be tied to a time.

PA: I am not sure that I agree with you. I think that November is the optimum time, and there are a number of reasons for this. Firstly, I will have by far the best opportunity of selling this to my party in the aftermath of your statement in favour of the Jenkins proposals. Secondly, I am very nervous indeed about the extent to which I can hold my party beyond November.

In my view, the window that will have been opened in October/November, by Jenkins and by your response to it, will have closed again by the early spring, when hostilities will start again preceding the huge round of elections next year. Next year is more likely to be a year of fighting than a year of agreement. And all the time, we are adding to the 'folklore' of opposition as you inevitably make mistakes and we attack you for them.

Lastly, and crucially, the economic situation is due to deteriorate next year and with that we will see a rise in unemployment, etc. In other words, the window of opportunity is much narrower than you think.

Mandelson then turned to Blair, saying, 'You have a problem here. If you do your Cabinet reshuffle at the end of July, can you really do another one in November? We all thought you were going to do this in May. And, for some of us it was a considerable disappointment that you did not [much laughter, for Mandelson was clearly referring to his own position]. But, to reshuffle in July and do it again in November would be very, very difficult.'

TB: Well, that's true. But the start of the Scottish and Welsh Parliaments means I will have to reshuffle anyway, so why not then?

I said that there was a good deal of sense in that, but again the question was when?

TB: Maybe the early part of the year. But our relationship with you Lib Dems in the Scottish Parliament will be crucial and could wreck the whole affair.

PA: You know our position on this. A relationship with anybody else but Labour in the Scottish Parliament is difficult to contemplate. But it can't be publicly excluded without damaging our campaign in the Scottish elections. Donald Dewar and Jim Wallace should meet up with you and me to discuss it. But such discussions will be made much easier if we have already proved that we can work together at the Westminster level.

Mandelson jumped in.

Peter: Let me give you my view of this. I have had a look at the two parties' policy documents. There are plenty of areas where we have different policy positions. But, equally, there are many where we either have, or could reach, an agreement. There's nothing on the policy side that impedes what we want to do. But I am very concerned about how this will be received by the outside world. My worry is that it will be viewed, not as like-minded people coming together in the national interest, but as a crude attempt by the Government to buy off the opposition and create an even greater hegemony. Secondly, the Jenkins proposals will, as you know, split the Cabinet, probably around 50/50.

TB: Yes, but I think I can bring them round.

Peter: Well, you may be overly optimistic about that. I accept that you can practically walk on water. But this is something very, very big on which you will find a large number of your Cabinet members opposed. But the even bigger issue is how we sell it to the people as something in the national interest, rather than a grubby deal between parties.

Richard Holme said that the prevailing impression is that Labour were governing well and that the difficulty will be to convince people that TFM will make it even better. 'If New Labour is such a success, why do we now need "New Labour plus?" There will also be a public perception that we are ganging up on poor little Hague, which will not go down well. We must be able to answer the question, "What is this coalition for?" It is certainly not about a parliamentary majority, since you have a huge one already.'

I said I thought that Mandelson's point was right. There were two severe criticisms our political enemies could, and would, throw at us: the first was that this was another conspiracy to create a Blair *'über alles'*, and the second was that I was an old man in a hurry prepared to sacrifice my party for a place in the Cabinet. We must meet these criticisms head on and deal with them from a position of strength. In my view, there is only one way to do that. We must portray this as a new start; a second point of national renewal. Something potentially even bigger than 1 May last year; the completion of a project much grander than a mere general election, which is essential to the nation's long-term interest. And we should also say that this would force a reaction from the Conservative Party, too. They would have to move back to the centre ground. And so, in the long term, we would be creating not just a progressive, non-socialist alternative to the Conservatives, but also a Conservative Party which could offer a more credible opposition. The result would be a much healthier body politic all round.

PA: We should confront the argument about there being no opposition by saying that this is part of a new pluralism. We should make a virtue of this being a break from the culture of control-freakery, and the beginning of a new kind of politics in which dissent and debate play a much more important part. [Mandelson looked startled at this.]

TB: Yes, the point we need to push very hard is that we are doing this, not from a weak position because we have to, but from a strong position because we want to. But I have to do a lot more work on my folk before they understand why this is good for us, so I'd better start straightaway.

PA: I understand what you have to do. But it's the exact opposite of what I must do. I am relying on the fact that the programme we put together will both deliver on PR and cover all the points on which we stood at the last election. I will then be able to say to the Party, 'Here is an opportunity to put into practice all the things you asked people to vote for at the last election – how can you turn it down?'

But my chances of success depend on it being a surprise. If they got to know that coalition was in prospect before they knew the details, I would have a rebellion on my hands that I couldn't stop even before we got to first base. You may have to warm your lot up before you reveal your hand, but I must make sure the wares are on display before I ask my people to decide.

Not many in my party have yet realized it, but constructive opposition is an inherently unstable strategy. I am walking a tightrope. Sooner or later we must tip one way or the other. And the longer we leave it the more chance there is that we will tip into outright opposition. That's why we must concentrate our minds on the end of the year for TFM.

Peter (turning to Blair): What do you think your colleagues' reaction will be to PR? Do you see this as your own decision or a Cabinet decision?

TB: It has to be a Cabinet decision. I don't underestimate how difficult it will be to move some of them, but it will not be quite as difficult as you suggest, Peter. I have been to the Tea Room[1] and had a chat with some of the lads down there. They understand that we and the Lib Dems broadly agree, and that the Lib Dems have been attacking us from a perfectly respectable position.

I found it extraordinary that Blair was actually defending us to his own people!

Peter: Well, I can see why you want to have the Cabinet on board. But I don't think you have much chance of doing that before November.

---

1 The Members' Tea Room in the House of Commons. Used chiefly by back benchers and traditionally the place where senior politicians can sound out back bench opinion in the parties.

TB: I see the end of July as the end of a phase in government. We will have tackled spending on public services; we will have completed the EU Presidency; and, Drumcree permitting, peace will be secured in Northern Ireland. Then, over the summer, I intend to look again at the Labour Party itself. The reshuffle is only part of what I want to do. By then we will have a new General Secretary, and much of the reform in central government and in the institutions of the Labour Party will have taken place. We will then need to decide what kind of Labour Party we are and where we are going. And then, I hope, the Party will see the bigger picture and appreciate it. But I am a little worried about some of the things that are coming out of the Jenkins commission.

By this time Kate was poking her head round the door. Blair's next appointment was waiting. I didn't want him to misunderstand Roy's proposals, so I asked for a couple of extra minutes alone after he had shooed the others out.

PA: Well, there is no electoral system that does not have some disadvantage. You may recall that you and I set the effective threshold of proportionality, so that any party that got more than 45 per cent of the vote should be entitled to a majority in the House of Commons. We can design a system to achieve exactly that. So please don't dismiss his proposals out of hand.

TB: Well, if this produces coalition only when one is appropriate, then that has very considerable advantages. I hadn't realized some of the subtleties of Roy's proposals. I will get someone to look at them again.

PA: It is essential that this isn't known by too wide a circle, though. I know Roy believes that getting a system accepted depends a lot on his being able to move other members of the commission first, and some of them still don't know.

I left the Cabinet Office at almost exactly 12 o'clock. A Rover with Miranda in it was waiting outside to drive me to Canary Wharf for an interview with the *Independent*. I was in a good mood, feeling that the meeting had gone well. It will be difficult for Blair to retreat from what he has said in front of the others. Though, of course, we didn't cover all the details we needed to. But we can return to those later.

Wednesday, 8 July, France

After PMQs off to Waterloo to catch the 4.23pm Eurostar to Paris to spend a few recuperative days in France.

Arrived in Paris at 8.20 exactly. At the Gare de Lyon I checked when my train to Sens left, discovered that I had two hours to spare and wandered across the road to a small café, where I had dinner and spent a most pleasurable hour and a half by myself, watching Paris go by and reading Aubrey Herbert. Away from the hustle and bustle of the House of Commons and living like an ordinary person. I can't remember having quietly enjoyed myself so much for a very long time.

Just after 10.00 I made my way back across the square to the station. Paris is in ferment. The World Cup is on. Walking into the Gare de Lyon I looked at the television screen in one of the restaurants. The crowd were transfixed; the score was France 1, Croatia 1. As the train left I rang Kate in Sens who told me that France had gone a goal up. On the train travelling south to Sens we stopped at Melin station, where everyone was going wild. France had won.

Tried to continue reading my book through the maelstrom. What a remarkable man Aubrey Herbert was. He says that one of the reasons he was elected in the then safe Liberal seat of South Somerset (now Yeovil) was because of the sturdy independence of the local people. *Plus ça change.*

Arrived at Sens exactly on time, at three minutes past midnight, to see Kate running down the platform towards me. What sheer pleasure to travel halfway across France and be met by one's daughter under the stars of a French summer night. I hugged her and wept a little at the joy of seeing her, hoping she didn't notice. We piled into her car and drove off to her house at Véron, where we sat out under the clear night sky for an hour or so drinking a whisky before going to bed. A truly wonderful evening. I suppose this is what life could be like after I retire. Slept well for the first time in ages.

Wednesday, 15 July, Westminster

Strange how the long shadow of Prime Minister's Questions begins to fall even the day before. Already by morning I was beginning to turn my mind to what questions we should ask. Listening to the overnight comments on Brown's Comprehensive Spending Review (CSR), I am very conscious that the government has comprehensively shot our foxes on spending on public services. I don't think my colleagues yet understand the extent to which Labour have cut the ground from under our feet. But Brown has gone much further than even I thought he would.

Saturday, 18 July, Somerset

Woken by the phone ringing. Richard. Apparently Mandelson has gone off to Brazil at the very moment we are supposed to be finalizing the timing of TFM. Infuriating!

I'm increasingly of the view that when I see Blair on Thursday (this date has now been fixed; curious, since it's supposed to be reshuffle day) I will say to him either we do it sometime between November and January or we wait until after the next election; in which case, someone else will be doing it, not me.

The problem is that if, as widely predicted, the reshuffle is next week and Mandelson gets a Cabinet post then he will become completely absorbed in that and I don't see how he can carry our project forward.

Richard also gave me some disturbing information about a conversation he had with Andrew Adonis.[1] Apparently, the project is now the second thing occupying Blair's mind, the first being Scotland (he's up there today). They are, apparently, very worried about the situation there because of the rise in support for the SNP.

I asked Richard to contact Jonathan Powell and insist that Mandy ring him from Brazil because 'Paddy's going to discuss the timetable for TFM with the PM on Thursday and he needs Peter's views'.

1 Ex Lib Dem councillor from Oxford, who joined Labour in 1995 and now works as a special adviser in the Policy Unit at No. 10.

Tuesday, 21 July, Westminster

Met Andrew Marr for half an hour. He's freelance now and clearly enjoying what he's doing. He told me he had had a very long session recently with Blair, after which he'd concluded that Blair is basically a liberal. I told him that the project was still theoretically possible, but that I thought it was unlikely ever to be delivered. Blair simply couldn't get it in place in time and the moment would soon pass.

At 4.00 Hugo Young[1] came to see me. He was, as usual, misanthropic on all fronts. He doesn't think Blair will deliver on PR. But it is a habit of Hugo's to be gloomy.

Then at six o'clock Tony Bevins,[2] who's working for the *Daily Express* now. He was in one of his more dotty moods. Interested in everything I said, but told me it wasn't a tabloid story and couldn't I give him one? I suggested that, if that was the case, perhaps he should save up the information I'd given him and use it as background for the conference. I like Tony very much; he can sometimes appear deeply eccentric, but he has a habit of getting to the bottom of things.

I found it difficult to sleep. I don't think Blair is going to move on the timing question. The crucial meeting will be on Thursday.

Wednesday, 22 July, Westminster

My 'official' tenth birthday as leader. A rather nice piece in the *Independent*. A taxi at 7.00am to Millbank for a round of interviews. Radio 5 first – not great. Then to the *Today* studio. They had done a delightful piece earlier in which Robin Oakley had been very kind about me (Kate had rung Jane to say she couldn't believe what nice things they'd said!). So, to compensate for that, Jim Naughtie went for me really hard. He caught me on the back foot.

Had a chat with Roy later, who is seeing Blair this afternoon. We agreed to speak after his meeting.

During the PPM I received my call from Roy. The meeting with Blair had gone quite well, although they were somewhat inhibited by the presence of two civil servants. It became clear, though, that Roy is proposing a very

1 Now political columnist for the *Guardian*. Former *Sunday Times* political editor.
2 Previously political editor of the *Independent*. Sadly, Tony died in March 2001.

EPIC TEN YEAR MICROLIGHT FLIGHT

decentralized AMS-based system with a small list of about one person per party per county. Blair listened to this suggestion and said that he would think about it.

Rang Chris Rennard to ask him to do some work on it. He reported back that if the system was as I understood it from Roy then it wasn't as proportional as we would wish. Roy later confirmed that such a system would have given Labour a majority of about 50 in the 1997 election. We would have got about 80 seats and the Tories about 120. This is excessively disproportionate, I think. Worrying.

Thursday, 23 July, Westminster

Up blessedly late. Jane dropped me off at the office at 8.00. I cleared a lot of work and looked at the papers. A nice piece from Hugo Young and a good editorial in the *Guardian* saying that my ten years had been a success. But a nasty little editorial in the *Daily Telegraph*, which ended up with 'Pants up, pants down Paddy, we applaud you' – sarcastic and unnecessary. Perhaps evidence, though, that the right wing are now getting worried about what Blair and I may do.

Preparing for my meeting with Blair at 1.00, and having looked more into the detail of Roy's proposals, I went down to see Roy to express my concerns about the threshold for majority government. We need a higher threshold, I said. It was unacceptable that a party could command a parliamentary majority as big as 50 on 43 per cent of the vote. Roy claimed that Labour had taken 44 per cent in May 1997 and that it would be difficult for Blair to admit tacitly that the landslide victory which he had proclaimed gave him such a wonderful mandate should now be declared, by inference, 'illegitimate'.

Then off to see Blair with Roger Lowry. We arrived at the Cabinet Office entrance at a minute or so to one to be met by Kate Garvey, who showed us into No. 10 by the back door and then into Blair's outer office. I stood chatting with Jonathan Powell about Northern Ireland for a few minutes.

Blair came out a few minutes later, disappeared for a moment, returned bearing some papers and we went into his office alone.

We sat, as usual, with Blair in the chair closest to the fire and me on the sofa opposite. He was relaxed and in shirtsleeves. After a few pleasantries he opened with, 'The right wing is really having a go at you, isn't it?'

He told me that he had had a meeting recently with the editor of a right-wing newspaper.

TB: The CSR was a defining moment. After that they knew that I was not, after all, a Tory in 'New Labour' clothing. So they are desperate to convince the public that we are now 'old Labour'. Similarly, they are absolutely scared to death about what you and I are up to. PR in the first place and the partnership in the second.

PA: Which merely proves we are right in what we are doing. I wear it as a badge of pride that the *Daily Mail* spends whole pages excoriating me. These people are scared that if we get our act together the Tories won't be re-elected for perhaps ten years. Right-wingers such as inhabit the editorial room of the *Daily Telegraph* will then find that, not only will their party take a long time to get back into government, but, even when it does, they will not be part of its mainstream, because the Tory left will have regained control. This is about not just the next election, or even the one after that; it's about the next generation of politics.

TB: And they are really worried that Hague may see sense and pull the Tory Party back to a centre right position as well. They have a very low respect for him. Which are all good reasons for going ahead. My only difficulty is finding the ways and the means to do so. I just can't see my way forward for this autumn. I recognize that it must be done. But the barriers in front of me now, in the short term, are really formidable.

PA:That is what I have come here to discuss with you. You will have seen my letter [sent after our last meeting] arguing the case for a November–January window. The more I think about this, the more convinced I am that if it is not done then, it will not be done in this parliament. You know my view. We should have gone a year ago. But, this is our second definitive moment. And I must tell you also that if it isn't done in November–January then somebody else will carry this through with you, not me.

TB: But you *are* going to fight the next election now, aren't you?

PA: No, I'm not, as I have already told you. I have no particular ambition to be a Cabinet minister; it's bringing the project to fruition that really matters to me. But either way I am determined not to fight the next election.

TB: Oh, dear. I thought you had changed your mind. I presumed from last night's speech that you had changed your view.[1] But who will take over from you?

PA: I have been carefully bringing on a number of people from whom the choice could be made, most of whom are committed to the cause. But I am clear that, whatever happens between us, if we don't do this I will move on.

TB: Well, you have been very blunt with me, so let me be blunt with you. This is the big thing that I too want to do. But the question is, how? I have huge problems getting my lot to agree to it by November. There are too many people to get on board and I am faced with a real possibility of splitting my party. I would prefer to do this later if I possibly can. But I don't want to make you a commitment that I then find I can't deliver. I would feel terrible about that.

PA: Look, perhaps there is another window, but I can't see it. You will have to take a clear position on PR more or less straight after Jenkins reports. That is the moment to go for it because that is when you can best tie us in. And, as we've said before, next year will be very tough for you.

TB: Yes, it will. I have told my people that. The economists and all our advisers tell us that if everything goes according to plan, the economy will have a 'soft landing'. But, even under those circumstances, unemployment will go up, which will make it much more difficult for you guys if you are in.

PA: But don't you see? It will be even more difficult if we are out. I want us to go

---

1 I had made a well-covered speech the previous evening at a tenth anniversary celebration party in which, in order to quell damaging speculation about my future, I had implied that I would lead the Party at the next election.

through this together, so that we are partners during the rough times, because that is what builds the relationships. And, anyway, if we are out during the rough times then that will only sharpen the culture of opposition. Frankly, I don't know that I can hold my party to constructive opposition through that period. Which is why I think it must be done before next year. Unless you have an alternative plan.

TB: Well, I have been discussing some of this with Andrew Adonis. He tells me that if Roy's proposals go through as they are currently structured, then he couldn't get them in before the next election. In which case, why have the referendum early if you can't apply it until the election after next?

PA: I'm not sure how workable that is. I will think about it. But there are two halves to the issue. The first half is having proportional representation; the second is having a relationship which proves to the British people that partnerships at government level can work. The two go together and we can't have one without the other.

TB: Well, maybe a step-by-step approach can take us progressively towards our goal. Aren't there ways to do that?

PA: If there are, then of course I am prepared to consider them. If your people have ideas about how we could do it later, then we need to hear them as soon as possible. Incidentally, will you be doing the reshuffle next week?

TB: Very confidentially, yes, I will.

PA: Well, I don't see how you can do that next week and something else in November.

TB: But I will have to do another later anyway, when the Scottish Parliament and Welsh Assembly start.

PA: Then can it be in the November–January window and be part of the project? Can you do it that early?

TB: Yes, I think I can. It won't be too difficult.

I then produced the detailed timetable drawn up by Richard Holme, and agreed by Mandelson. I drew his attention to three key dates. I pointed out the two actions that need to be taken during August – one on procedure, the other on policy – if we are to get our ducks in a row in time for November. The third is the key decision to be taken on 15 September as to whether to definitely go ahead or not in November–January.

PA: So we have a lot of thinking and preparation to do.

TB: Oh, God – is it really that early? I will have to think about it over the holidays. I haven't given it enough thought yet.

PA: If we let matters drift on, we will lose the moment by default. We must come to our decisions on policy and procedure over August. No later. I would have liked to discuss this in front of civil servants, but since that hasn't been possible and we are running out of time, I will get Richard to talk it through with Peter next week. Time is slipping by dangerously.

The conversation turned to PR. Blair confirmed that his meeting with Roy Jenkins yesterday had gone well and that he now needed a chance to think about what Roy was proposing. I explained that the main problem I had with Roy's proposals, as I understood them, was one of thresholds. We had agreed at our Downing Street dinner that we would define 'broad proportionality' on the basis that a party which got 45 per cent or more of the vote was entitled to 50 per cent or more of the seats. But the Jenkins Commission proposals fell somewhat short of that. There were two dangers to this: firstly, the lower the threshold, the easier it would be for the Tories to get back in; and secondly, a lower threshold meant less chance of a coalition government – and working in such a government was one of the prizes on offer to my party. My calculation was that, if we joined Labour in coalition next year, our vote would be reduced by around 4 per cent. Which could damage our chances considerably in both the European and, especially, the Scottish elections. I couldn't see much benefit in us agreeing to actions which would diminish our vote and, for example, give the SNP greater chances in Scotland, unless there was a very good reason for this (i.e. partnership).

TB: But I am opposed to a system where we end up with an almost permanent coalition government. If we had had a system based on a threshold of 45 per cent or more, then effectively only one government since the war would have been an outright government. I don't think that is acceptable.

PA: Have you thought about AV as the directly elected element of the Jenkins proposals? This would, on the one hand, increase proportionality but, on the other, give something to your party, since they were in favour of AV?

We then spoke about the reform of the Lords, which is a major obsession of Blair's at the moment. He thinks that it could take up to two full parliamentary sessions to get the legislation through.

TB: These guys have been at it for a very long time. I have suddenly discovered there is a very good reason why the House of Lords has never been reformed. They seem to be able to pass down some genetic aptitude to be stupid on most occasions, but extremely cunning when it comes to their own survival. I will have to revise my idea about inherited ability! The Lords are also very good at sabotaging other legislation in order to protect their own interests. I keep on telling my people, rather as I had to over the Hunting Bill, that this is a matter not of principle but of practice. How can we make things happen without disturbing the whole of the rest of the parliamentary programme? I will have to talk to you about this soon.

He seems to be thinking of coming to a possible compromise with the Tories in order to get the reforms through more easily.

PA: Well, just don't present us with a *fait accompli* on both the House of Lords and Freedom of Information. That would make life doubly difficult for me.

TB: I promise we won't do that on the Lords – it's too big. But there is a real problem with the Freedom of Information Bill with the parliamentary timetable. I don't know how we can fit it in.

PA: I understand the pressures on the timetable. But, as you know, this is a really important issue for us. And you will be letting yourself in for some strong criticism from your friends – including us – if you cannot, for the second year running, find the will to get it through. What really worries me is that the FoI Bill will become so diluted that it becomes worthless. In which case we will have to oppose it. If it is your intention to dilute the Bill in any way, then I hope we can have a decent debate about it first.

TB: I really don't know what you are talking about. As far as I know, the Bill is going ahead exactly as we originally planned.

At this stage Kate put her head round the door, saying he must move on. As we got up and walked towards the door I asked Blair about Kosovo now that bombs were going off in Macedonia as well.

PA: Macedonia remains the detonator of the Balkans. If it's shown that these bombs have been planted by the Albanian population, then we are close to a catastrophe. A foreign affairs crisis nearly always blows up over the summer and I think Kosovo could well be it.

TB: Well, at least I'll be closer to the action then [referring to the fact that he will be on holiday in Italy!]. I keep saying at every Cabinet meeting, 'What's our policy towards Kosovo?' But we haven't come up with one yet. What do we do? Milosevic has shown a considerable degree of restraint with the KLA, with the consequence that the KLA are now doing rather well. The problem is that, if we intervene now, the KLA may do even better. In which case we will have exchanged the dangers of a 'Greater Serbia' for the equal dangers of a 'Greater Albania'.

PA: We should have acted much earlier.

TB: Yes, but there was no support for it before. I was in favour of using air power early on, but neither the United States nor our European allies supported me. And Washington's current view is that they can't act at present because it will increase the strength of the KLA. What do you think?

PA: Well, I still think the points I made in my report are valid. First of all, shore up both Macedonia and Albania, then suggest a solution for Kosovo based on parallel status with Montenegro [as a state within Yugoslavia as opposed to simply being part of Serbia]. It is now vital that the international community has a clearly stated aim against which policy can be drawn up. This is not like Dayton. You cannot wait for the two sides in Kosovo to come to their own agreement.

He suggested I write him a paper on the subject and said we should keep in close contact over the issue, since it could blow up very quickly, with potentially disastrous consequences.

As we parted company Blair said he had a lot to think about on TFM, but that the others were now reasonably OK about it. Jack Straw is on board [I think he meant for PR rather than TFM] and Gordon is in favour of the overall project, even though he's still uncomfortable about how to get there. John Prescott remains a problem, but he can probably be persuaded.

At 3.30 I went down to see Roy to report back on the Blair meeting. I told him that if we didn't hit the November–January window, then in all probability TFM wouldn't happen in this parliament, in which case, as I had told Blair, somebody other than myself would have to see it through.

Sunday, 26 July, Somerset

Spent much of the evening thinking about the situation we are now in. Apparently the Cabinet reshuffle will happen tomorrow. Mandelson will get a ministerial job and so won't carry through the project from the Labour side, which means that the work that still needs to be done this week, won't be. And if, as seems likely, Blair shifts Cunningham from

Agriculture and puts somebody else in, then it's unlikely we'll get Paul Tyler into Agriculture – rural votes are one dowry we bring to this partnership.[1]

Went to bed feeling really depressed that all the work of the last four years will fall short of the ultimate target. I had hoped we could mend the near century-long schism between the two parties on the basis of a liberal agenda. I now fear that this is probably off for another generation.

There are three problems in dealing with Blair: (1) he tends to say what people want to hear; (2) not having officials present, he says things which the officials do not carry through afterwards; and (3) he thinks so much in terms of the big picture that he doesn't apply himself sufficiently, it seems, to the relatively small things needed to achieve it.

I may be misjudging him, but I don't think so. A little more time will tell. My mind is now turning to when and how I should stand down. I would like to do so in my conference speech in September. But that will probably be before Jenkins reports and Blair's hopeful commitment to the commission's findings. But if I leave it to the spring I will be plunging the party into a leadership election at the same time as the local elections.

Damn! I wanted my time as leader of the Lib Dems to finish with my agenda fulfilled. But I am absolutely clear in my mind that I cannot continue any longer. It isn't good for either me or the Party.

Monday, 27 July, Somerset

The summer recess has begun. I overslept.

Many phone calls to London, in particular about the gradually deepening Kosovo crisis. Also trying to get our message through to Blair that we need a decision. I have decided now to use three channels, apart from myself: Roy to Blair himself, Richard to Derry Irvine and Richard to Mandelson, whom he is meeting this Thursday.

---

1 Paul had been an exceptionally well-respected spokesman on agriculture for our party. The Lib Dems represent more agricultural seats than Labour, so, in the case of a coalition, we could have filled the post – a matter I had previously discussed with Blair.

Wednesday, 29 July, Westminster

Another bad night's sleep. I seem to be waking up at 3.00 in the morning unable to get back to sleep. I just cannot get TFM out of my brain. One day I am very depressed and the next I am optimistic. One day I think Blair is not going to do it and the next that he will. The pressure is building up in my mind. I long for some relaxation.

A breakfast meeting with the Next Group. I took them through my meeting with Blair.

I nearly fell off my chair when Alan Beith said, 'Having looked at the situation, if they accept PR but don't do it until the next election, then I suppose we had better go into government. Otherwise we would suffer all the disadvantages without any of the advantages.'

Worryingly or delightfully (I can't tell which), at PMQs Tony Benn asked Blair whether he would have me in his Cabinet, to which Blair gave a very delphic reply. The hare is running!

Then into the PPM, at which Jackie Ballard attempted to tie my hands down on our likely reaction to the Jenkins report and 'whatever else went on after that'. I said that we should take Jenkins and Labour's reaction to it at face value. We should not assume anything else would happen afterwards. It depended on Blair's response. Don took me out afterwards and said he had never heard me be so devious. Everybody knew perfectly well what was going on. Maybe so. But I cannot let them close our options on matters that haven't even been presented to them yet, and this was a pretty determined attempt to head me off at the pass.

Home at 11.00. *Newsnight*, then bed. But again I couldn't sleep. In my mind I wrote and rewrote the paper I promised to Blair on Kosovo,[1] the letter I am going to write to him about TFM and then finally my speech to the Parliamentary Party when I tell them of the TFM offer. Of course I have forgotten them all now, but they made wonderful sense in the half-light of the early morning.

1 See Appendix F.

Thursday, 30 July, Somerset

Jane picked me up at 2.50 from Crewkerne station. Of all the journeys I take in the year this is the best. The first one home for the summer recess. The weather is good, too. Blue skies, fluffy clouds and Somerset looking at its high-summer best. The whole recess ahead of me. I can throw my suits off, get rid of the formal shirts and the black shoes and live like a human being again. And have my evenings back. Sheer pleasure.

Sunday, 2 August, Irancy

Up at 8.30. A lovely day. Summer at last.

Richard Holme rang at about 11.15 to report back on his meeting with Mandelson. Apparently, Mandelson had said that Blair was now 'fastened on the issue'. He also admitted that they had somewhat separated PR from TFM. Richard made the point that they must be taken together.

Mandelson says Blair doesn't make his decisions until all the 'constellations' are in the right position. Richard commented that this was a bit Zen, to which Mandelson laughed and agreed.

It is now clear that if we are to go ahead in November, this will have to be put together very much at the last minute. Also, that we are the only people who are seriously thinking about it.

In the evening Kate left Matthias with us while she and Seb went off to stay with friends – the first night we have been allowed to look after him by ourselves. I had such fun!

Tuesday, 18 August, Irancy

Off to Kate's today. Just before lunch I got a call from Downing Street. Would I turn the fax on? Then another call from the Prime Minister's French office [he takes an office on holiday with him]. In the event, Kate's machine ran out of paper so I had to take the fax on my laptop.

In his fax, Blair reiterated that his aim is to reshape British politics so as to provide more chances for progressive government; that he believed this could be done without electoral reform, but recognized that electoral reform is important to the Lib Dems – and if this could produce a better system for elections he would support it.

He reaffirmed that he is committed to the project and believes our aim should be to create something as strong and stable as the Liberal Party of the nineteenth century.

The Jenkins commission, he continued, will provide the means, but not the end, in this process. Our task will be to convince our parties, and the country, of what we are trying to do.

The two-stage process (AV first and full reform later) we've agreed on provides one means of doing this. But this system will be difficult to sell to the country because it appears to be unfair to the Tories.

So the best remaining option is a system based either on our current first past the post method of election or on the Alternative Vote, with a top-up. Personally he is attracted to this kind of reform as the best alternative to FPTP. But we need to have clear answers to the criticisms it will attract; a two-tier system of MPs (directly and indirectly elected); near-permanent coalitions and (from his party's point of view) the loss of a significant number of current Labour seats, whose occupants are bound to resist the process. Answers to these deficiencies are not yet apparent.

In addition, he added, electoral reform will be very difficult to get through parliament in the face of such a heavy programme of legislation on schools, hospitals and other measures of constitutional change (e.g. Lords reform). Moreover, we can't get the Boundary Commission changes and the legislation through in time to apply to the next election. The best time for the referendum would therefore be at the same time as the next election, he ended.

This is all most disappointing. Going over old territory again. He now seems to be questioning even the whole idea of electoral reform. I sent it through to Richard Holme so that we could discuss it later on in the day and spent most of the afternoon composing my response.

Another glorious day. The barometer is rising again and the clouds have completely disappeared. Richard rang at around 5.00. I read out to him my suggested reply, which, after a brief discussion, we agreed to send through to Blair, subject to our getting Roy's views.

We had dinner in Kate's courtyard under the stars. I was absolutely whacked and went to bed early. Jane and Kate stayed up talking for an hour or so. Still not a very good night's sleep, though.

Wednesday, 19 August, Burgundy

Another beautiful day. Cloudless blue skies. We left Kate's at a little after 9.00, so that Jane could have time to do the shopping for Friday evening's dinner.

As soon as I got back I put a call through to Roy. I finally reached him at about 4.00 in the afternoon. He said that he was in the process of drafting his final report, but could I send him a copy of my fax to Blair? I said I'd do so. He agreed with it, so, in the morning, I faxed it through to Blair's holiday office:

... You have obviously spent a good deal of time thinking about all this – as, I confess, have I.

I think we now, with a little adjustment, can probably reach an acceptable common position on where Jenkins could lead us.

I understand your point about the two-stage approach (with the AV element for the next election and the rest later). This was, as you will remember, the suggestion we thought provided a way through our respective difficulties at our dinner with Roy last summer at No. 10.

Provided it is preceded by a 'Yes' vote in a referendum for 'AV plus', I nevertheless believe this two-stage approach continues to have considerable advantages. The biggest is that, in the event of our not being able to put Roy's propositions as a whole into practice before the GE, but only stage one, we would not have to consider electoral pacts (about which, more later). Our people could stand in all seats – indeed, there would be a positive advantage in them doing so since our second preferences would go to the other party. This would have the natural effect of drawing us together before the election. The second major advantage is by-elections. Without AV for by-elections, each contest before the next GE will have the effect of pulling us apart, as they did in the last parliament.

For these reasons, I hope we will not allow the 'two-stage' approach to be dismissed too easily. I concede, however, that the 'unfair to the Tories' argument still weighs heavily (despite the fact that AV will actually probably be of positive advantage to the Tories in the next GE, since it exaggerates swings).

I do not think we have a different view about avoiding any system which provides for 'near-permanent coalitions'. I have always made it clear to you that I do not favour this either. I hold firmly to the view that near-permanent coalitions can be consistent with good government (witness the economic record of most of our continental neighbours). But I accept that Britain is not ready for this yet and such a perceived outcome would make it much more difficult to win a 'Yes' vote in a referendum.

In addition, I think there are considerable advantages to us all in making the directly elected element of the system AV. This would make it easier for your lot to find the proposal acceptable. (Jack and co. will be able to claim a victory, etc.) It also increases considerably the element of voter choice (and therefore the saleability in a referendum), while making it easier to choose AV for by-elections (see above).

I think we both agree on the basic principles (including the undesirability of a system which produces permanent coalitions). So we have only to settle on numbers. This will require some delicate balances but is, I believe, achievable.

The timing problem is, however, a much more difficult one.

I think there are two options here. To have the referendum very early, or very late. Anything in the middle is likely to run foul of the natural mid-term unpopularity which you will be bound to suffer from. This means either next spring, or at the General Election.

Your fax seems to indicate a strong preference for the latter. I am very doubtful about this, for these reasons:

1. It will leave three years for the 'rats to get at' Roy's proposals. Opinion polls show a clear majority for a sensible form of PR at the moment. It would, in my view, be dangerous for us to leave such a long time for that to be attacked by the enemies of PR (which would include many in your own party).

2. It would mean the end of any prospect of us moving to the next stage of the project in this parliament. I could not take my party into this if PR were not to be resolved as a question until the next election. The 'next step' would therefore have to wait until after the next election – and would then be likely to be, not easier, but more difficult than now. I don't think my party can be held to 'constructive opposition' for the next three/four years. What would hold them? You would have given your consent to PR and your and the Cabinet's commitment to recommend it in a referendum. My party would be bound to pocket this and return to the joys of all-out opposition. Indeed, our own interests (e.g. in by-elections) would be bound to require this. In other words, the 'Adonis' timetable is, in my view, more likely to provide a framework for the two parties to drift apart than come together. And, after the next election, your lot would be likely to be more hostile to us, not less. You and I have been able to do what we have done because we have worked together in opposition for the last three years. After the next election, you will be asking your people to work with us

after we have spent the last four years attacking them and the last few weeks fighting them in a General Election. And vice versa.

3. Then there is the question of how we fight the next election. I don't believe that your lot will necessarily find it easier to swallow the pill of recommending at an election a PR system, which will rob them of their seat at the following election, than they find it now. And I think it will greatly confuse the electorate, arm our enemies and divide your party to have some of your MPs campaigning for the return of your government, while opposing your recommendation for electoral reform. But my chief concern is not what our people do, but what the Tories do. I have said to you before that if you give the Tories the chance to fight the next election with membership of EMU as an unresolved question you will be giving them the one real campaign issue they would love to fight on, which will unite the Tory newspapers against you. If you now add to this a second campaigning issue – the introduction of an electoral system which will deny the Tories the chance of ever having a purely Tory government again, then they and their friends in the newspapers will fight what I have called a 'Götterdämmerung' election which will powerfully unite all those Tory forces which you have been so skilled at keeping divided. Under these circumstances, we might be forced to consider whether we will need to have an electoral pact in key seats. Having been through this before, it is the very last thing either of us would want in the shadow of an election. It is divisive, grubby and uses up huge amounts of good will and public support – as well as being practically undeliverable for the reason given above.

As you know, when it comes to difficult decisions, what appears the toughest option is nearly always the best one. I know the difficulties that you face are formidable – mine (except on a purely personal level) probably less so. And I realize the problems posed by the Tories making mischief in a very crowded parliamentary programme – though these can be overcome if we have the will.

Nevertheless, the key facts as I see them are these:

1. The long-term realignment that we both want can only be secured if we work together in government, formally. It cannot be done from opposite sides of the House.

2. The best time – and in my view, probably the only time – to do this is now, or at least very shortly. The later we leave it, the more difficult it will get. And, if we leave it too late, it will become impossible.

3. There is a clear majority for a sensible proposition for electoral reform. But this, too, is likely to be eroded the longer we leave it.

4. We can, with a little work, agree on what form this should take.

5. We can bring points 1–4 together best (and possibly, only) if we act decisively and early. We risk most, the longer we wait.

What is clear is that there is much to talk through. Should our staff be fixing something when we are both back?

I hope you and the family are having a good hols.

Friday, 21 August, Irancy

Woke to find it overcast and raining. It has been cloudless for two weeks and this is the day the Cleeses come! [John had rung two weeks earlier to say that he and his wife Alyce Faye would like to come and stay for a weekend.] What a disappointment.

At about 6.00 yesterday evening I got a call from Roy. It is almost certain they will go for AV plus. Apparently Jennifer had commented, 'Paddy has put forward a very powerful argument indeed for not waiting.' Jane and Kate spent most of the morning preparing for this evening's dinner (never-ending cooking, it seems). I spent much of it reading and considering Kosovo. I have decided I probably cannot go out there as I had originally planned next week. Unless I can go as a government 'representative', which is doubtful, the Serbs will, as usual, not give me a visa.

Driving out to Laroche-Migennes to pick up the Cleeses, I started thinking about the month ahead. And about my long-term future. I decided that if, as now seems likely, we do not go ahead with TFM this autumn, then the moment has come for me to stand down. The Jenkins proposals are due out on 27 October. I will probably resign the following week, once the dust has settled. I will then have accomplished all I can accomplish. Blair will have decided on a later referendum. It will be time to hand the party over to somebody else so that they have enough time to prepare it for the next General Election. I cannot see that the parties will do other than grow further apart over the next three or four years. But whatever the eventual outcome, getting Blair to agree to PR (if I can) will be my final act as leader of the Liberal Democrats.

In the evening Jane and I took the Cleeses on a customary tour of Irancy *caves* to sample the wine.

Tuesday, 25 August, Irancy

A beautiful day, thank God. And the barometer is rising.

In the morning I did what I had been putting off for days – started the first draft of my conference speech. Agonized for an hour or so before deciding to scrap it and start again. The problem is that I don't really know what to say. At the last Autumn Conference I could tell the party the direction in which I wanted them to go, and at the Spring Conference map out the policies I wanted us to adopt. But this time everything is up in the air. I don't know if TFM will come off and I don't know what the circumstances for Jenkins will be. I have simply run out of things to say and shall end up repeating myself a lot. Not an auspicious start.

Shortly afterwards Don and Tor Foster dropped in to stay the night. We had a splendid lunch in the sun under our vine. Afterwards we went off searching for some wine for Don to buy. Then we wandered round the village and chatted about TFM and the conference.

Afterwards, back at home, we continued our discussion. Don confirmed that Charles Kennedy is now openly preparing for the leadership. Apparently Charles thinks I will get myself so far out in front of the party that eventually I won't be able to sustain it and will have to give up. A pretty accurate judgement. I said that I hoped that either Don or Nick would also stand (although they had better sort it out between them as they would divide the activist element of the vote). Don more or less admitted that he was interested in standing.

I also told Don that I would not allow those in the Parliamentary Party who wanted to cut off my room for manoeuvre before the Jenkins report was published to do so. I hope the message gets passed on. Don left at about 4.50.

Wednesday, 26 August, Irancy

Another wonderful day. In the morning a chat with Richard and a word with Roger. I am insisting on a two-hour meeting with Blair when I get back. An hour with him alone, then an hour with Richard, Peter and note-takers. We have suggested Wednesday. This will be the crucial one.

Monday, 31 August, Irancy

A beautiful day. Not a cloud in the sky. Fresh and cold to start with. The barometer is dropping slightly. A cycle ride with Simon and Jane. We rode up to the top of Pallotte, then a long, slow freewheeling descent into Cravant with the whole of the Yonne valley laid out below us, the wind streaming in our hair and the sunshine warm on our backs.

Home for a quiet afternoon. Starting to pack up; always a sad time. I got a call from Downing Street in the evening to confirm that Blair will see me on Wednesday.

I think Blair has decided to go for PR, but only on a minimal basis, with a referendum at the time of the next election. Lying in bed thinking about it I decided that, in these circumstances, I would announce my resignation at the end of my conference speech, saying my work for the Party was now finished and it was time to hand over to somebody else.

On the bicycle ride I talked this over with Jane, who agrees. But it will all depend on what happens with Blair on Wednesday.

Wednesday, 2 September, Westminster

The House has been recalled for emergency government legislation on terrorism in Northern Ireland.

Blair made his statement and Hague backed it. But the government is trying to introduce extraneous bits of legislation into the Bill which have nothing to do with Northern Ireland. I raised concerns about these. This triggered of a substantial revolt, led by Richard Shepherd,[1] against the government. He made a superb speech. Wonderful rotundity of phrase reminiscent of a speech from the last century. It had the chamber captivated and the revolt spread like wildfire. Picked up first by Benn and others, then some Tories and then, eventually, by Alan Beith. Paul Tyler had unwisely put his name to the government's resolution. Alan didn't agree with this but had said he'd keep quiet. Then, suddenly, he was on his feet making a speech against the government. It wasn't long before a Tory, Alan Clark, said that this was an extraordinary speech, given that he was arguing against what his own Chief Whip had signed up to! At the end Paul got to

---

1 Member of Parliament (Conservative) for Aldridge-Brownhills since 1979.

his feet and said he was terribly sorry, he had changed his mind and could he withdraw his name from the amendment? Howls of derision all round. And rightly so.

This is deeply embarrassing and puts me in a very weak position since we have, once again, laid ourselves open to the familiar Labour charge that the Lib Dems can't be relied on.

To Downing Street at 6.45. I was kept waiting in some out-of-the-way office for about fifteen minutes in the usual pre-meeting game of hide-and-seek before being shown into Blair's office.

PA (referring to the day's events in the chamber): Look, I'm sorry. That really was a fourteen-carat fuck-up. It won't have done you any damage, but it's done us some.

TB: Well, it doesn't exactly help convince my party of the joys of PR and partnership. But these things happen – it's not big on the scale of things.

We started with the economic situation, in particular in the Far East. I said it looked very worrying, but he was still mildly optimistic that we would get through it all right.

TB: We are currently doing some work behind the scenes on reforming some of the IMF's procedures so that it can operate more effectively to stabilize the situation. Our problem is the Americans; we just can't get them to do anything.

He said he was looking forward to seeing Clinton tomorrow. Perhaps they would discuss it further then, but, 'He really is terribly distracted at the moment and pretty depressed. The recent summit with Yeltsin did not go well.'

TB: Actually I am less worried about the Russian economy than I am about Japan. Russia is important symbolically, but it is Japan which could destabilize the whole world economic situation.

We then looked at the decisions before us.

TB: Of course, I have been doing a lot of thinking about this. You must have been a bit surprised to get my fax out of nowhere. I am grateful to you for responding in such detail. I am near to making decisions on all this, but haven't quite arrived at that point yet. I want to do this at a further meeting with you and perhaps Peter and Richard in the next week or so. It is still very much at the front of my mind, though. Over the holidays I have been speaking to a number of my key colleagues, and I am surprised at the extent to which they agree on the project, even if they disagree on the means of getting there. Jack Straw, for instance, says that he is wholly in favour, but wonders if we have to give you PR as a price for it. And Gordon is always supportive when it comes to the crunch. John Prescott remains adamantly against, of course. So, the larger project seems more possible than PR as the means to get there.

Now, we must decide what to do. With respect to PR, I have two major problems. The first is that I simply don't believe the Boundary Commission can do the necessary redrawing of constituency boundaries by the next election.

PA (interrupting): It is possible if you have the will. I think you are telling me it isn't politically possible.

TB: Probably. And Roy Jenkins is opposed to a two-stage approach, largely because he believes we can't make AV by itself look anything other than a conspiracy against the Tories. I think that's right. I think the British people would smell a rat.

And then there's TFM. All these things are interconnected and we must make some decisions, but I need a little more time to think them through. I also appreciate that if we don't go for it now, I must propose a later date.

The conversation turned to his style of government and the accusations of control freakery.

TB: Such accusations are unjustified. Neil [Kinnock] used to really hate those who opposed him. But I don't. I rather like them. I think Tony Benn makes a very good case, and so does Dennis Skinner. And I admire them for making them. Skinner rings me frequently, you know. It's just that, at the end of the day, it's me not them who has to make the decisions. It's true what they say, though. We may now be suffering more from 'spin doctoring' than benefiting from it. And this whole idea that we manipulate everything and ignore the House of Commons is beginning to do us real damage. Though there's nothing in it, you know. Labour helped Thatcher massively during the 1980s by opposing her on everything and adopting policies completely contrary to hers. But this lot don't have any policies on which to attack us. So they are simply attacking us on style, which is very difficult to counter.

I said I thought it was because the Tories didn't really know how to be in opposition. The only time they had been effective in opposition had been in the later years of the Callaghan government, but then largely because Labour gave them so many open goals.

TB: So what do you think the Tories will do?

PA: The mirror image of what you lot did in the early 1980s [i.e. go off to the extreme]. But eventually they must come back to the centre ground, because you can only win elections in Britain from the centre.

TB: Yes, but the difference between the Tories and us is that, even in 1983, there were people in Labour who really wanted to come back to the centre ground if only they had been given the lead. And, try as they might, Labour couldn't get rid of people like Denis Healey. But the Tories now seem desperate to isolate themselves and want to get rid of people like Kenneth Clarke and Stephen Dorrell. They must be mad to kick out a person as gifted as Ken.

We then spoke at some length about working together in Scotland. He seems much less confident about defeating the SNP than he was when we last met.

At about 7.45 Kate put her head in and said that it was time for his next engagement.

Just as I was about to go, Blair said, 'Look, don't your lot realize that working with us will give them the best opportunity not only to keep their seats at the next election but even win some more?'

PA: No, many of them don't. I keep telling them that the real danger to us is not a rise in the Tory vote, but Labour votes in our constituencies returning home. That's what will let the Tories in.

TB: So why can't they see that if we go down, you go down with us? The public more or less sees us as having the same viewpoints. And the same people are voting for us in our different constituencies.

PA: Exactly! There is now a very strong geographical complementarity about our vote distribution. We can't immunize ourselves from you if you do go down, so we may as well be involved and benefit if you stay popular – which I think you will.

As I was leaving, I collared Jonathan Powell about next week's meeting. I explained that Blair and I had agreed it should be a foursome (Blair, Mandelson, Holme and myself) plus note-takers from each side. I also said that the purpose of the meeting would be to reach decisions on (a) the PR system (b) the dates of the referendum and (c) TFM. Powell noted it all down on the back of his hand, and agreed to touch base on dates tomorrow.

Yet again I had hoped that this meeting with Blair would be the 'decision' meeting. And yet again it was mostly just an hour-long gossip, with Blair again walking round and round a decision before taking it. The next meeting, I hope, will at last be the crucial one.

Back to the House just before 8.00 for a meeting, at Paul's request, with the junior whips. They are nervous about what the Jenkins report may throw up; they are also (especially Phil Willis) keen to tie me down on what options we may follow. I asked them to explain to me what they proposed as an alternative strategy but they didn't have one. I pointed out that nobody in the Parliamentary Party should be worried, since, although I would make a recommendation, they would make the decision. They ought to feel very secure about that. Secondly, they should understand that my responsibilities stretched beyond the Parliamentary Party to the Party in the constituencies and Lib Dem voters in general.

I didn't know what would happen after Jenkins reported, but the difficult decision was not on Jenkins itself (which we probably had to support) but on what happened then. In any case, constructive opposition is an inherently unstable position, so, I explained, sooner or later it would have to tip one way of the other. I didn't know what Blair might do in response to Jenkins – he might, for instance, link a closer relationship with us to getting PR through a referendum.

Much consternation at this. Donald Gorrie, in particular, said that would make the Scottish elections next year very difficult. I responded rather angrily, saying that we must grow up; if we had PR, we would all have to operate at a different level of politics. And if we couldn't do that then we shouldn't be asking for PR. It was as illogical for Donald to ask me to run Westminster politics for the benefit of Scotland, as it would be for me to ask him to run the Scottish Parliament for the benefit of Westminster.

'Look, there are two options,' I said. 'Either Blair turns down PR, in which case our relationship with the government is over. Or he says, "If you want PR you will have to come into government with me, and we will deliver what will be, in effect, the entire Liberal Democrat manifesto for 1997, together." What would you say to that?'

'Well, we would have to do it,' they all agreed.

Saturday, 5 September, Somerset

Asked Chris Rennard to prepare a minute for me to send to Blair on the impact of a coalition if we were to fight the next election on FPTP. I faxed it through to Richard and Downing Street. In the evening I rang Jonathan Powell, who was still at the office, apologizing for inundating them with paper. He said they didn't mind as they had 'wet towels wrapped round their heads' on all this at the moment and needed as much information as possible.

Sunday, 6 September, Somerset

Miserable, wet and raining. Spoke to Roy at 9.30. There have been a number of leaks about the commission and there is a real danger it will split unless the leaks stop. Roy was particularly upset about an *FT* leak; we agreed that this almost certainly came from Downing Street. He told me he was seeing Blair at 4.30 on Wednesday and he promised to ring me afterwards.

An excoriating editorial in the *Observer* today, linking our failure to oppose the government with a 'thin' policy document.

I am in the blackest, deepest mood of depression. Too much to cope with; too many big decisions to make. And unable to make any of them because Blair won't make up his mind. Hanging over me, like the sword of Damocles, is my conference speech. Had another go at the first part this evening, but after about page ten discarded it as hopeless. I still don't know what to say. Eventually, having spent a pretty sleepless night thinking about it, I decided to wait until after the meeting with Blair on Wednesday.

I almost wish I could go tomorrow. But Jane tells me I am always like this when I come back from holiday – I lose my enthusiasm and drive. And the weather doesn't help. Close, cloudy, windy, muggy and rainy. The worst thing is that I can't really share my thoughts with others. I don't remember ever feeling so low.

Wednesday, 9 September, Westminster

All agree that today's meeting must be the 'crunch meeting'. So, at my request, Richard Holme and Chris Rennard have carefully prepared our bargaining positions and tactics. Chris has also had some calculations done on the impact for us of fighting the next election whilst having a close relationship with Labour and FPTP; Peter Kellner [the journalist] has, at my request, done some similar calculations for my eyes only (although without, of course, knowing our plans for TFM).

Richard and Chris's list of our priority aims for the meeting is as follows:

1. To obtain Blair's support for Jenkins.

2. To get agreement for an early referendum, possibly including the 'Big Bang' approach.[1]

3. To ensure some change in the voting system in order to provide us with 'insurance' for the next election.

4. To agree a common approach to some of the Jenkins detail:
    i) That we would prefer AV to FPTP as the basic system;
    ii) That we would want no fewer than 150 'top-ups';
    iii) That there should be open lists, not closed ones.[2]

We also discussed whether Blair might make delivery of PR contingent upon our joining the Cabinet and what we might do in such circumstances. Chris and Richard warned me that, without some change to protect our seats before the General Election, they didn't think I could carry either the Parliamentary Party or the party at large. I agreed it would be difficult, but not impossible.

At about 7.50 Richard and I walked down Whitehall to Downing Street. I told him that I had spoken to Roy Jenkins after his meeting with Blair this afternoon, and that he believed that Blair still hadn't made a decision one way or the other. Roy had persuaded Blair not only that a referendum after the next election wasn't on but that it represented a breach of the terms of his agreement and also of Cook/Maclennan. This was extremely useful, since Kellner [who had also met with Blair] was also pushing for a late referendum. Worryingly, Blair's support for Roy's recommendations does not seem secure yet.

We went in by the Cabinet Office entrance as usual, and were shown via the back door into Jonathan Powell's office by one of the secretaries. Jonathan put on his jacket and led us up to Blair's flat, where he offered us a drink. I had a glass of the very nice Sancerre which appears to be the standard Downing Street tipple and we waited. Apparently, Blair was tied up with some London activists at Millbank Tower.

I decided this was a useful opportunity to ask Jonathan about Freedom of Information. 'We are expecting you to publish before the Queen's

1 See entry for 12 June 1997.
2 In a closed list system, voters specify which party they prefer. In an open list system they vote for the individual candidates.

Speech, you know,' I said. I asked him to try and fix a JCC meeting as soon as possible to discuss both FoI and the Lords. We are very disturbed, I continued, that the meeting has been shifted from next Monday to 20 October. That is far too late. Especially if we want to have an influence on either of these important issues.

Powell said he'd do his best but they just couldn't publish an FoI Bill until after the Queen's Speech; David Clarke[1] had left it in too much of a mess. 'There are no substantive changes, but some technical work still needs to be done. I don't think we can publish until January or February. We will take a big hit on this, especially from our friends, who will assume that because Jack Straw is now in charge he will water it down. But I can promise you that isn't the case.'

Richard Holme said that he had received specific undertakings from Derry Irvine that the Bill would be published, hopefully before our conference in September, but at all events no later than the Queen's Speech. 'If it is not in the Queen's Speech people will suspect dirty work.'

'Well,' I said to Powell, 'if that's the case, it is absolutely vital that either Jack Straw or the PM himself (and preferably the latter) makes a speech or statement recommitting the government to the basic principles contained in the White Paper as soon as possible. We must be able to take some comfort from you on this.'

Mandelson arrived at this juncture, shortly followed by Blair, apologizing profusely. He disappeared and returned a few moments later in jeans and an open-neck shirt.

'OK, what have we got to discuss?' he said.

We spent the next three and a half hours depressingly walking round and round the problem without reaching either a conclusion or a decision.

Roy's earlier warning to me that Blair hadn't made up his mind proved entirely correct. It was soon clear that we were here, not to decide, but to join him in yet another long perambulation around the issues.

Richard later described the whole process as 'being condemned to attend endless repeats of *Hamlet*'.

Timing, systems, the reform of the Lords, who in the Cabinet would support TFM, and who would not – the lot.

By about 10.00pm it was more than apparent that the conversation was going nowhere, so I suggested we wind up the meeting so that I could have

1 Member of Parliament (Labour) for South Shields since 1979. Chancellor of the Duchy of Lancaster.

five minutes by myself with Blair ('*mano a mano*', as Jonathan puts it; a favourite expression of his).

The others filed out, and we closed the door.

I loosened my tie, leaned forward and said, 'Thank you for giving me a couple of minutes with you. I want you to know where I am. I have discussed this with Jane. I really do not want to continue with this job if we do not go to TFM. I am exhausted. I want to do something else with my life. But I cannot keep hanging on like this. If you really decide that we can't do this now, then the sooner I hand on to my successor the better. And if I stand down at the height of the successes of constructive opposition, then it's most likely my successor will continue with my strategy which will secure for you our support in the future. If I wait until next year you will become more unpopular and it will be much more difficult for anybody to get elected leader on the platform of continued constructive opposition. Moreover, if I am to say goodbye, I really want to do so at my Party Conference.'

'What, this year's conference?'

I nodded.

'Do you really not want to be a Cabinet minister?' asked Blair. 'You would make an excellent Foreign Secretary, you know.'

'Well, that remains to be seen. But I have lots of other things to do. And if this project is only a way of getting me into the Cabinet, no more, then I am not interested. I would love to be Prime Minister, but unfortunately that job is taken. [Blair smiled.] As I've told you before, the reshaping of politics is far more important to me than a Cabinet position.

'Thank you for telling me this. But I wish you would wait a bit. It doesn't come as a huge surprise, though I didn't think you would go quite so early. I realize I owe you a decision. I will give you one in the near future. Let's meet again soon, and you can decide what to do after that.'

'Next week?'

'Yes, next week.'

I went outside and picked up Richard. We walked back down Whitehall, discussing the meeting. Richard questioned me closely on what I had talked to Blair about in private. Eventually I told him that I had just wanted to increase the pressure on Blair by telling him that if he didn't act soon, he would probably be doing it without me – but that this was just a bargaining tactic.

A taxi home, a whisky and to bed. Waiting for Blair is like waiting for Godot.

Lay awake much of the night thinking about the meeting. Eventually concluded that there were ways of keeping the options open on TFM, but only if Blair is prepared to come along to our Parliamentary Party and explain to them exactly what it is he wants to do. If they hear him commit himself to the convergence of the two parties and I also come clean about my commitment to that, then I can move to a special conference of the Party to decide on the continuation of constructive opposition in the light of the Jenkins proposals. In this way we might just be able to anchor the present position and bring the whole debate to a head so as to enable either me or my successor to continue in the future. And Blair would have to be prepared to tolerate our continuing opposition while acknowledging our contribution when the government does things we have proposed.

It's a pretty desperate throw, but it may be enough to hold the thing together.

Friday, 11 September, Westminster

The Cabinet 'awayday' yesterday obviously involved talk of PR – there was a piece about it in the *Independent* today.

Rang Richard to pass that information on to him. Richard has, very helpfully, mapped out the four basic options available to us.[1] A typically constructive piece of work. He also managed to have a word with Mandelson.

Apparently, Mandy has pressed Blair for a decision today and Blair was at that very moment sitting down to write a paper on his position. Richard faxed through to them his 'four scenarios' piece.

Everything is now in the balance. My own view is that Blair will give lukewarm backing to the Jenkins proposals, which will put the whole decision back to after the next General Election. Depressing. But Richard

1 (1) Lib Dem Golden Scenario, i.e. Blair supports Jenkins, referendum on PR March 1999, legislation on PR December 1999, next General Election held under new system; (2) Blair supports Jenkins, referendum on PR March 1999 but no Bill until House of Lords review i.e. March 2000; AV for next election, top-ups and Boundary Commission after next election; (3) Blair supports Jenkins, no referendum on either PR or House of Lords until after review of 1999 local and Euro elections, i.e. March 2000, Bill on PR November 2000; AV for next election; top-ups and Boundary Commission after next election; (4) Labour Golden Scenario, i.e. Blair supports Jenkins, referendum March 2000, no system changes at next election, Bill after next election.

said to me yesterday that it was quite extraordinary how much we had achieved, given our numbers. We have put the Prime Minister in a position where he is facing an excruciating decision which, though its resolution may not be exactly as we'd have wanted, nevertheless goes a long way towards it. Richard describes it as 'A Sundance Kid Success', i.e. we had no good cards in our hands, but we have played them in such a way as to achieve, even if only in the longer term, something we have wanted for ages.

In the evening a call from Downing Street. Blair wants to fax something through to me. His decision, I hope.

It came through just before 9.00.

ELECTORAL REFORM

1. We want the project – a great progressive alliance for the twenty-first century – to succeed. There are sufficient numbers of people in both our parties who believe in it. Electoral reform would be one way, and certainly for the Lib Dems the most obvious way, of strengthening the co-operation between the parties to achieve that alliance.

2. But there are two problems to be confronted. To get reform through, we have to win our respective parties to the cause; and we have to convince the country in a referendum. Here the obstacles to moving quickly are formidable and mounting.

i. The system likely to be recommended by Lord Jenkins for reform cannot be put in place for the next election. The scale of boundary changes would make it practically, as well as politically, impossible. We will therefore be asking people to vote in a referendum for a system which won't actually be introduced until after the next time they vote-in a government.

ii. We are already making changes in Scotland, Wales, Northern Ireland, London, the European Parliament; and we have reform on the House of Lords to consider. There will be a powerful argument made: that with all this change, we want time to see how it beds down and works, especially in Scotland where an AMS system is being used; and that any change to the House of Commons should not be looked at in isolation from changes to the House of Lords. As yet, however, there is not even the beginning of a process to determine the second stage of House of Lords reform.

3. The effect of this is to make the case for delaying a referendum on electoral reform remarkably strong, were it not for the damaging impact such delay would have on trust between the two parties. The delay could be easily justified to the

public by saying: there is no point in asking you to vote for change now, when it is only at the election after next that it can be in place; and before we get House of Lords reform right and the other systems have a chance to work. In fact, I would go further: this would be a telling argument in any immediate referendum campaign. It would give the opponents of change not merely an argument of principle, but a very British 'common sense' argument of practicality. In a world beset by instability, it would be persuasive. And I agree that it is clear that a referendum would have to be either soon or much later.

4. So, the problem is, then: If there were a delay, what else could repair the inevitable damage to trust in such a delay? In particular, since this would be a Lib Dem problem, how could Lib Dem MPs have some insurance at the next election? And how could we use any delay to build support for radical change?

5. The following, in my view, would offer a way through:
   i. The Jenkins report is published and welcomed. I say that if there is to be change to the House of Commons, this is the best system (subject to the scale of top-up). But, because it is right that the House of Lords is considered along with the House of Commons, because no new system can be introduced until the election after next and to let the other constitutional changes settle down, we will defer the referendum until shortly after the next election, when people can see all the changes in the round and when they will have the results of another General Election (1997 being plainly somewhat exceptional) upon which to base a view.
   ii. Labour and the Lib Dems announce a strengthening of joint co-operation. Such an announcement could come before or after the Jenkins report. It may even be better for it to be trailed before to get a better context of trust for (i). I would even be prepared to say, probably for the first time, it is possible to contemplate Lib Dems in the Cabinet. Such a co-operation would include:
      * JCC broadening out;
      * some specific policy demands by Lib Dems agreed by government, overtly on the basis they are Lib Dem demands.
   iii. Work could begin, privately, on how to support and help those Lib Dem MPs most at risk, plus some real fieldwork on what the dangers and benefits are of tactical voting and Lib/Labbery for them. If we really are talking about as few as 15–20 MPs, we could deal quite specifically with each case and begin working on local Labour parties.

6. What this gives is a real incentive for Lib Dem MPs to be bound in. They have the prospect of change for the election after next, which is the only time it can be

introduced anyway. They can exert real power before it and they can be given at least the best chance of insurance at the next election.

7. It is, of course, not what they want. But, again, talking around to senior Labour people – in Cabinet and party – has confirmed my view that though there is support, even growing support, for the project, they believe the public are constitutionally satiated and could suffer from constitutional indigestion if another big change was put to them now. And it is clear that if it were to be pushed, we would be fighting a referendum with a Labour Party badly divided (possibly with a majority anti) and a press and opposition united. The real danger then would be *losing* the referendum.

I have also thought very carefully about Richard Holme's point about having AV at the next election without a referendum. I wish it were otherwise, but I really believe we could not get away with that. There would be an outcry, and we could end up setting the whole thing back, perhaps terminally.

8. Frustrating though this is, there has been almost a century of division in the progressive camp. To fail, for want of a few years more waiting, would not be sensible. In any event, the waiting can be used to build support, explicitly, both for reform and the project. However difficult this is, it is the only realistic path forward.

Dreadful. He has decided to hold the referendum after the next election. This will crucify me, wreck our relationship, do terrible damage to his government in the eyes of its supporters and ensure that the next few years of Labour's administration will be far less liberal than they would otherwise have been. I faxed Blair's letter through to Richard and Roy. Will speak to them tomorrow.

Went to bed deeply depressed. It ends here. I will have to stand down at conference.

Couldn't sleep – up at 3.00. A cup of tea and a couple of hours on the computer composing my farewell speech to the Party.[1] A little under 1,000 words.

Also began to assemble my response to Blair. This is our last chance. Unless I can dissuade him, the relationship between the two parties will inevitably deteriorate. The project is dead in the water, probably for another generation – or at least until the next time Labour needs us. The opportunity to carry through TFM from a position of strength has gone –

---

1 I finally gave this speech, almost precisely as drafted then, when I said a formal farewell to the Party a year later, in September 1999.

it will now only happen when the electoral arithmetic makes it necessary. Then, and only then, will we get PR. It's all retreated over the distant horizon again.

Saturday, 12 September, Somerset

Dog tired and deeply depressed. Jane is, too. Spoke to Roy Jenkins before I went off to the constituency surgery in Crewkerne this morning. He thinks it is a very bad moment, but not as bad as I do. Bless him, he offered his unequivocal support in whatever I did next.

Sunday, 13 September, Somerset

I faxed my response to Blair through to Downing Street just before mid-day:

Dear Tony,
Thank you for your fax.

I apologize in advance for the length of this reply and for the bluntness of its language. But we have come to the crunch and there is a huge amount to play for.

I feared at the end of our last meeting that you were coming to the view you have outlined, and tried to tell you then that I could not sell this proposition to my party. Obviously we were all a bit tired and I didn't get my message across effectively.

I have given more thought to this over the last two days, after receiving your memo. I fear further reflection has not changed my view.

What will my lot say about this?

They will ask me why I am asking them to reach another agreement with Labour for closer co-operation, when Labour haven't delivered on the agreement we had. To delay the referendum until after the next election is a clear breach of Cook/Maclennan (para. 55: 'Both parties believe that a referendum on the system for elections should be held within the first term of a new parliament'). It is also a breach of your own manifesto. Taken with the delay on implementing FoI, my party will say, 'There you are. We knew we couldn't trust them. They are stringing us along. And you are asking us to be strung along for even longer?' It would have been difficult enough to make a case for closer co-operation on the basis that PR was legislated for before the GE, but not applied until after it. But it was 'do-able' and I was prepared to try to do it. But a proposition for closer co-operation without even this is, I fear, impossible.

What will the Tories say about this?

They will be absolutely delighted. You have seen from the papers how scared they are about you and I getting together and introducing (or at least making irreversible) the introduction of PR. Leaving it till after the next election lets them off the hook in ways which will, I imagine, cause champagne corks to pop in Smith Square. They have time to regroup and everything to play for to kill the opportunity at the next election. And the Tory press will unite to help them do so. As you know, we have had Tories like the MEP John Stevens (representing, he claims, a group of others and speaking, he claims, for Kenneth Clarke) begging us to persuade you to introduce PR before the election so that they can split the Tories. These people will have nowhere to go now and the opportunity to split the Tories will have been lost by the next election.

What will the reformers and modernizers (many of them the youngest and best of your own MPs) say?

They will see this as a defeat – and rightly so. We have got the country's attention on PR now. Kick it into touch for four years and who knows where we will be? Some will say, 'If Labour is able to abandon its manifesto commitment on this now, then what is to stop them doing it again after the next election? Then, Labour will have had two elections to rediscover the joys of FPTP.' There are, after all, some who have changed back to supporting FPTP just on the basis of the last election! I fear you will get a very bad press for this proposal.

Returning to the Lib Dems, I have said I could not carry a closer relationship with you on the basis of this proposal. I don't think I could hold them to constructive opposition, either. Your proposal would be bound to be seen as a grievous blow to me personally. It would be seized on by those who are impatient to prove me wrong about you as a clear sign that they were right all along. Yes, we may need each other again at the General Election. But that is four years away, and after it all will be another country altogether. Meantime, as I explained to you, we have to do well in Scotland and Wales and in the local and in any parliamentary by-elections if we are to keep up rather than fall back. And this depends on opening up the distance with you, not closing it. I would be prepared to pay a price in this area, if we were gaining something solid and irreversible. But another promise, about what will happen the other side of another General Election, is not going to be enough to persuade my colleagues that the prize is worth the pain.

I am afraid that I cannot agree, either, with some of the reasoning in your fax.

You say that the public will not understand why they have to vote now for a system they will not get until the election after next. Leaving aside the question as to whether the boundary changes can be made for the next elections, I am not at all sure this is correct. I think the public will understand perfectly well if it is explained to them that boundary changes take some time. In addition, as Richard Holme and I suggested, there is the question of the Lords. It would be perfectly feasible to say to the British people, 'We want you to vote now to tell us if you would like a fairer voting system. When we know your decision, we will put in motion the wheels to enact it. But it will take time. And we will want to use that time to look at how your decision will affect the reform of the House of Lords and to see how the other changes we have already made work out in practice. In this way, your decision on this crucial issue will help us in making the other changes we want and in ensuring that the new voting system you want is the best we can provide.' Your argument is that we have to complete the other reforms before reforming the voting system. I would have thought the other way round was more logical.

As you know, I also do not believe the arguments against a two-stage approach are as strong as you and Roy Jenkins think. But if they are, then I still think that we could find ways to leave this choice to the electorate in the referendum, by way of a simple two-question approach (e.g. 'Do you want Jenkins?' and 'Would you like the first stage by the next election?'). This would at least have the merit of forcing the Tories to say why they don't think they will do well at the next election – because, of course, if they did well, AV would actually help them.

I am sorry if all this sounds very negative. I have confined this fax to a response to the points made in yours. I still think we can retrieve the situation and have discussed some ideas with Richard Holme as to how this might be done. I have asked him to contact Andrew Adonis or Roger Liddle, in Peter's absence, to pass on our ideas.

A final point.

I know your commitment to this and I have greatly admired the way you have kept the vision at the front of your mind and driven it forward, even with the pressures of government.

We both believe that the big event waiting to happen in British politics is the reshaping of the centre (liberal) left. Once done, this would form the dominant governing force of our times and make the Tories come back to centre ground, enabling British politics better to reflect the true views of the British people.

You and I set our hands, four years ago, to making this happen. And I remain convinced that we still have it in our hands to do it.

It needs two things. A context to enable the change and an issue around which it can happen. PR is the first. Europe is the second. Your judgement is that you cannot, in this parliament, carry Labour for the former, or the country for the latter. You must be the best judge of your party and I respect that. As you know, I think you are wrong on the country and Europe.

But what is clear is that by postponing the decision on *both* until beyond the next election, we are missing the best chance we have of achieving our objective. After the next election, the Tories are likely to be stronger, we weaker and you, though still in government, will not have the level of support, personal and for your government, that you have now. We will have fought each other for four years and through a General Election. If there is a hung parliament (unlikely, in my view), then we will, of course, have to work together. But it will be from a position of weakness, not strength. The good will we can count on between our parties now will by then almost certainly have evaporated.

My own view is that there will be much less chance of us working together then than there is today. The next real chance, therefore, will be after PR. Not at the next election, but at the one after that.

In the tenth year of your premiership!

Yours

Paddy

At about 6.55 the phone rang. It was Downing Street. Would I speak to the PM? Blair came on almost immediately.

TB: Look, I have just read your fax. I have also been back and reread mine. It was a bit hard. I don't want this thing to come to a crisis and I certainly do not want to lose what we have created. Interestingly enough, I spoke to Gordon and he, too, is not at all sure we should delay the referendum until after the election. In your fax you say that we ought to get together to try and resolve this. I am frantically busy at the moment trying to put together a deal with the G7 to stabilize world currency markets. It is proving very, very difficult. So could we try to solve this by getting our people together?

PA: I am sorry my minute was a bit tough, but I really had to signal that this was a crisis for me.

TB: You are absolutely right. We should be able to speak that bluntly to each other. I looked at my minute just a few minutes ago and said 'ouch'.

PA: OK, I will put Richard in touch with Roger Liddle, since Peter won't be back until Tuesday. I have had some constructive thoughts about how we may find our way out of this, but I won't burden you with them now. Thanks for your call.

I wanted to use the opportunity to press Blair on Kosovo [where Milosevic was continuing to build up forces], so I said, 'I am really worried about Kosovo. We still haven't taken any action.'

TB: Yes, I have some news for you on that. It's been God's own job getting the Germans on board. They refused to act without a UN resolution. But, like you, I believe we can act under Article 1 of the UN Charter[1] and the Americans, at last, feel the same, in view of the gravity of the humanitarian situation. So we are now in a position to say to Milosevic that either he stops what he is doing or there will be air strikes – and we will say that very soon.

PA: I am thinking of going out there again. If what UNHCR tells me is true – that there are some 40–50,000 people living in the forest – then a humanitarian catastrophe of terrifying proportions is about to unfold. And I know what will happen to those poor people. Some will starve and freeze to death and others will up sticks and go over the borders into Macedonia and Albania – then the conflict will widen still further. But perhaps UNHCR are over-dramatizing the situation. What are your people saying?

TB: No. They say it is awful as well. And that it cannot be allowed to get further out of hand.

PA: Well, let's keep in touch on this.

TB: Yes, I'll get some information on our plans sent over to you tomorrow. Meanwhile, let's see if we can get this other matter sorted out. I know you have your conference speech to write very soon, so I hope to see you, perhaps towards the end of next week.

After we rang off I immediately phoned Richard and told him what had been said. He had already spoken to Roger, playing up the emotional thing: 'Why the hell are you lot hanging Paddy out to dry?' etc. I relayed to him my conversation with Blair and asked that he and Roger should get together straightaway.

'But Mandy isn't back until Tuesday,' said Richard, 'and you know what he's like. He just hangs around and does nothing until Blair decides.'

---

1 Which, in effect, says that states can act in order to prevent a humanitarian disaster without a Security Council resolution, where this is necessary: 'To maintain international peace and security, and to that end: to take effective collective measures for the prevention and removal of threats to the peace, and for the suppression of acts of aggression or other breaches of the peace, and to bring about by peaceful means, and in conformity with the principles of justice and international law, adjustment or settlement of international disputes or situations which might lead to a breach of the peace.'

'Stuff Mandy,' I said. 'If he's out of the country, then this is a superb opportunity for us to do an end run round him. If you fix up a deal with Roger then Mandy will come back and find that we have negotiated our way out of this.'

Richard agreed to call Roger back, which he duly did. He then rang me to say that he would meet Liddle and Adonis for lunch tomorrow. Apparently Liddle was both exhilarated and scared to death at being suddenly transported from the outer darkness to the centre of the game.

'Great,' I said. 'If Liddle is flattered, we can certainly use that to our advantage.'

Also Liddle, who is an awful old gossip, let an interesting fact slip in his conversation with Richard. Mandy has been trying to persuade Blair that he can't win a referendum on PR. So that's what's behind all this!

I won't get involved at this stage. Better if I stay at one remove by leaving it to Richard.

We have got Blair moving again and Brown seems to be supporting us, at least on the terms of the referendum, which is good news indeed. I thought we had lost it all this morning. Still not looking great, but at least it's progress.

Monday, 14 September, London

Richard tells me that at his lunch with Roger Liddle and Andrew Adonis today he used a good deal of emotional blackmail. The technique he had used was to be very angry about the position they had put me in, then lay down a firm set of minimum conditions, then dangle a tempting way out. This latter is based on what I have been thinking through over the weekend. Downing Street are now suggesting I see Blair at Chequers on Thursday 'to find a way through this impasse'.

Wednesday, 16 September, Westminster

Mandelson called today on his way to the TUC conference. Richard's message had obviously got through.

I'm going to see Blair at Chequers tomorrow.

'Now, old chap,' said Peter, 'how are you feeling about tomorrow?'

'To be honest, pretty let down,' I replied. 'But not suicidal. If this means

I have to go, I will go. If it also means the end of the project, then that is a pity. I can see a way out, but only with the PM's agreement.'

'You know Tony. He walks round and round a problem. But he talks with you in a more honest and more relaxed fashion than he does with almost anybody else [the inference being the exception was Gordon Brown]. The purpose of his fax was more to have dialogue with you than to announce a decision. But he still needs to walk round this one a bit more. Don't get too depressed. You just have to give him more time. I do hope you won't throw in the towel.'

Thursday, 17 September, London and Chequers

Richard came round at 7.30am to discuss my meeting with Blair later today. Then Chris Rennard at 7.50.

We decided we could move forward on the basis of three agreements from Blair: firstly, wholesale agreement to Jenkins, unamended and with the 'list numbers' [i.e. top-up lists] intact; secondly, his agreement to having a referendum on PR this parliament; and thirdly, if possible, to reinforce this with legislation, either enacted or in place by the next election. We have accepted that, although it is technically possible to put through the Boundary Commission changes it is, in fact, politically improbable, since any 'broadly proportional' system would result in getting rid of 100 or so Labour MPs, who would do their best to delay the work of the Commission until after the election. As I put it, 'Turkeys are unlikely to help with the preparation of Christmas dinner.'

If I could get Blair's agreement on all three of these matters, then we proposed a two-stage approach. The first of these, to take place in November, was to lock the party into a policy of constructive opposition throughout this parliament which could be widened specifically to cover the area of Europe. (I suggested that as part of this Blair should speak directly to our Parliamentary Party and that I should do the same with the Cabinet; it was essential that Blair and I both outlined our vision clearly, so that key people from both sides could hear from our own mouths what we were trying to do. We have kept this hidden for too long. One of the reasons why it is so difficult to get people behind the project is because they can only vaguely see what it is about.) We would then propose a second stage if and when a referendum is launched (in the last year of the current parliament). After we had fought for and obtained a 'Yes' vote and the legislation had been agreed, then we could propose a joint programme on the basis of 'heads of agreement' on which we could both go into the next election, with the presumption of a coalition beyond it.

If we can get Blair's agreement to the three conditions we can construct the context for a continuing deepening relationship whilst providing for a contingent approach at each stage, so that every action, once completed, triggers the next action.

Becks drove me to Chequers, arriving there at 12.30. She parked the Rover in the forecourt and we wandered into the largely empty house. Someone went off to inform Blair that 'his guests had arrived' and he turned up almost immediately, dressed in jeans and a rather crumpled, lumberjack-type shirt, looking fit and relaxed. Becks was whisked away and Blair and I went into his study. He explained to me on the way that he was at Chequers to work on his conference speech.

The Prime Minister's study at Chequers is a splendid little room overlooking the garden. It is beautifully decorated, with light wood panelling and some lovely paintings. I remarked that 'it wasn't a bad weekend pad' and he laughed. 'The kids love it, of course. I will spend the day here. Then I am off to town tomorrow and we're all back here on Saturday. But we have to pay for it, you know, when we use it privately.'

We sat down on two sofas opposite each other, and a cup of coffee was brought in for me in a nice little Chequers china cup. Blair drank from a large mug with the name of some pop group emblazoned across it. 'I see you get the best china,' he joked.

Our preliminary chat was, as always, about politics in general.

We talked first about Clinton, the Monica Lewinsky affair and what effect this would have on the US government.

PA: Having passed through a form of this terrifying ordeal and survived myself I found it actually quite liberating. It's perfectly possible that, having endured the worst that can be thrown at him, Clinton will emerge self-confident, emboldened and ready to tackle other difficult issues as well.

I asked Blair about Yugoslavia and he told me that he would be making a speech to the UN next week about what needs to be done. His view is very clear. Although he wants a UN resolution, he thinks we can still go ahead without one; he has persuaded the Americans that we can act against Milosevic alone, on the basis of Article 1 and Article 52, Chapter 8, of the

UN Charter.[1] I asked whether the threshold of military action was sufficient to show Milosevic we meant business but not outrage world opinion.

TB: Yes, we have now worked out a credible first level of action if Milosevic doesn't accede. The problem is that if he doesn't accede beyond that, then the next step up the escalation ladder must be a big one. We will probably have to suppress their air defences within about 400 miles. And that's a very large area.

The conversation turned to the economy. He told me Gordon Brown reckons it will probably grow towards the end of next year.

TB: If we really can turn the economy round that is very good news. The problem is that the press are now focusing on every single job loss, without realizing that other jobs are being created. Unemployment is going down, but we are still being crucified for it. I've spoken to the new CBI chief. His view is that, paradoxically, an economic downturn will make people less in favour of the euro. I think that's probably correct, though it shouldn't be.

PA: The point about the euro is that it will increasingly get into the nation's 'bloodstream'. As from next January, companies will denominate in it, mortgages will be taken out in it. But do you think Hague's decision to hold a referendum in his party on Europe makes you more or less likely to go early?'

He thought for a few moments.

TB: It could be argued either way. It may be clever electorally for me to keep the euro as an unresolved issue for the Tory Party, so that they are split on it during the election. But, on balance, I think a euro referendum, say, a year before the election, will so damage the Tories that they will never recover in time for the election.

Now, where are we on the project?

There followed a long period of verbal agonizing. How it was so difficult. How he was worried that they would lose a PR referendum: 'I know the

---

1 This reads as follows:

i. Nothing in the present Charter precludes the existence of regional arrangements or agencies for dealing with such matters relating to the maintenance of international peace and security as are appropriate for regional action, provided that such arrangements or agencies and their activities are consistent with the Purposes and Principles of the United Nations.

ii. The Members of the United Nations entering into such arrangements or constituting such agencies shall make every effort to achieve pacific settlement of local disputes through such regional arrangements or by such regional agencies before referring them to the Security Council.

polls are currently in favour, but I suspect that the general constitutional upheaval will be played by the Tories very effectively.' He also repeated the view that he couldn't carry his Cabinet on the substance.

TB: Then there is the question of timing. I know it is deadly for you lot after the election.

PA: No, it's not deadly. It's impossible. I just can't carry my party on this. You will kill me if you go after the election. Peter Mandelson has said to you, hasn't he, that you can't win a referendum?

TB: Yes, he has. And although Gordon thinks we must have the referendum before the next election, he too believes that we can't do it soon. It's just not winnable. And anyway, I couldn't carry either Jack Straw or John Prescott.

The conversation lurched back to the Balkans. I told Blair that I was hoping to go to Kosovo next week, but that I was worried the Serbs wouldn't give me a visa.

TB: Leave that to me. I will make sure they understand that this time you are going not just as Paddy Ashdown, leader of the Lib Dems, but on my behalf as well. It will have to be done unofficially, though.

I thanked him for his help, but wondered whether it would have much effect. Then we came back to my main reason for being there.

PA: Look, let me put my cards on the table. I think I can find a way to push the project forward. But it has to be on the basis that (a) you will agree to Jenkins, (b) you will have a referendum before the next election, and (c) if there is any possibility to legislate for it, you will do so. Are you still prepared to say you are in favour of Jenkins?

TB (after a long and ominous pause): Yes, I'm still broadly in favour of it. But not without reservations. [I grimaced.] That would make it difficult for you, would it?

PA: No, impossible. Our understanding from the start has been that you will back Jenkins. If you do less than that then I really cannot go forward. My people will naturally conclude that you are just stringing us along, and the cynics among them will tell me that they were right all along in saying that in the end you would let us down.

This was obviously a crucial moment in the conversation, so I decided to give him the details of our proposition, including asking him to talk to our Parliamentary Party and for me to reciprocate with the Cabinet.

TB (interrupting): Yes, I'm happy to do that if you think it would help you. And [smiling] I am looking forward to you coming to talk to the Cabinet. I'm longing to see them walk into the room and find you sitting at the Cabinet table. I shall have to be careful which seat I put you in! [We both laughed.]

PA: If we can do this, then I can see a way through the impasse. I will put it to my Parliamentary Party that, on the basis of your agreement to Jenkins, we have a vested interest in the survival and success of your government. And it will be clear that we don't want the Tories back. On that basis, I will ask them to agree formally that constructive opposition will remain in place for this parliament and that we will widen it, initially, towards Europe. This would enable me to lock constructive opposition in place so that it couldn't be eroded in the difficult days and years ahead. I would then say to my party that, contingent upon your holding a referendum and us jointly winning a 'Yes' vote, we could then move together into the next phase, paving the way to fighting the next election on a joint 'heads of agreement' programme. But until this is in place, we would have to continue to fight you; we would have to continue to oppose you; we would have to continue to win seats off you; and we would have to continue to be rude to each other at Prime Minister's Questions. And when it comes to the next election we would still both put up candidates in every seat. We could then say that, although we are fighting on a broad 'heads of agreement' programme, there would remain differences between the parties. And, for our part, we would invite people to vote Lib Dem much as we would under PR, so as to get more Liberal Democrats into the next parliament so that we could influence the next government in favour of those things we believe in, such as the environment. The beauty of this scenario is that it provides a context for progressive movement and it makes each step contingent upon the actions of the other party. But the bottom line is that you must recommend PR.

TB: My problem is, if I recommend PR, then those in my Cabinet who are opposed will come out and say they are. The Cabinet will be split. I can't see a way round that.

PA: I think we can find a form of words acceptable to me that will enable you to fall short of outright acceptance of Jenkins. For instance, something along the lines of, 'I have long accepted that there are flaws in our present electoral system. And if it is possible to reform the way we vote as part of the modernization of Britain, then I would be in favour of that. Having seen Lord Jenkins' proposals I think they are the best on offer. On this basis, it is my intention to hold a referendum in this parliament, and when such a referendum is held I would be minded to recommend 'Yes'.

At this stage we went into lunch in what he described as the 'family dining-room'. A very pleasant light meal: some mulligatawny soup, a fish concoction served with what the chef described as a 'primavera' sauce, and a sorbet with a large bowl of fruit to follow. During lunch we spent another fifteen minutes going round and round my proposition. We also discussed Scotland, briefly. I said one of the advantages of the timetable I was suggesting was that if I were to propose to the party now that we should have closer relations with Labour most of my Scottish MPs would oppose me tooth and nail. But after next year's Scottish parliamentary elections the Lib Dems will almost certainly be in coalition with Labour in Edinburgh. It would then be very difficult for them to oppose me doing the same thing at Westminster. Secondly, my proposal would provide a means to get us through the interim years, which are going to be difficult.

PA: As my party comes up to the next election it will at last realize more and more how its survival is linked with that of Labour. And those MPs (especially many of the new ones who oppose me now) who want to keep their seats will do almost anything to keep the Labour vote down.

TB: I hope they will come to that realization without the kind of structure you are talking about.'

PA:Yes, I suppose they will. *Force majeure* will drive them there. But in what mood? There is a substantial difference between our party, having fought yours, coming grumpily to this understanding that constructive opposition helps keep the Labour vote down, and doing that in a spirit of good will after a period of co-operation. The first will lead to a sulky enmity, the second to a position where we can genuinely build the kind of coalition we both want after the next election.

We also talked about the date of the referendum.

PA: Look, why don't you commit to a referendum now, or at least say that is your intention? If later in this parliament the conditions are not right, then I don't mind postponing it. It is not, afterwards, in my interests to hold it at a time when we would lose it.

After about twenty minutes of talking through the advantages and disadvantages of what I proposed, Blair suddenly said, 'Yes, that is the way forward. It will be difficult for me. But we should go ahead on that basis.'

He made the same kind of comment to me when we broke the deadlock on the Cook/Maclennan talks, and again on the European elections. A substantive decision at last.

PA: Well, I think we have reached an agreement. I am delighted. I can now see a way forward.

But can we talk about my own position again? You know I don't want to fight the next election. But I am dedicated to the project, so I just want to get it into a firm position before I stand down. I can tell you privately that when you sent me that fax on Saturday I couldn't sleep all night and got up at 3 o'clock in the morning to compose my farewell speech to my party.

TB: Ouch, I didn't mean it to be that bad. But we can make life easier for you, you know. We can pay you a ministerial salary and give you a car and a driver and more money for your office.

PA: Thanks, but no thanks. Can you imagine what our enemies would say? 'Paddy's being paid off for being Blair's poodle.' It would kill us. Meanwhile, I can only give you the promise that I will stick with this until it is properly established.

We had a brief discussion on Blair's idea that the Lib Dems could be given credit for coming up with ideas which were subsequently adopted by the government. I was sceptical about this, saying that it didn't seem realistic to expect government ministers to defend policies at the Dispatch Box for which we got the credit. But he thought it could be done.

I said that I would much prefer the government to allow us to experiment with our ideas in Lib Dem-controlled areas: a Lib Dem council piloting PR in local government or, perhaps, introducing neighbourhood school trusts on a pilot basis. We agreed to pursue this.

Then, having sorted through the chronology again, we agreed to get our people together to put some flesh on the new position, after our conferences but before Jenkins is published.

Finally, though, I warned Blair that I could easily go down at our conference.

PA: All this could fall flat on its face if the Party decides to go in a different direction. There are some purists for PR in my party who may reject Jenkins on the grounds that it is not STV – and they have the power to call a special conference.

TB (astounded): What?

PA: Yes, in my party, any 200 members can get together to call a special conference.

TB: Good God! If we had that I would have special conferences every day!

PA: We are slightly more democratic than you.

TB (laughing): Well, we'll have to do something about your constitution, then.

PA (sharply, but also laughing): You and I can alter the constitution of the country, but leave the constitution of my party to itself if you don't mind.

We then went up to the Long Gallery and sat in that huge empty room on two sofas either side of the fireplace.

TB: You know, when I outline the vision I will have real problems with some in my party. People like Gwyneth Dunwoody and co., who keep saying, 'We have this huge majority, why are you giving it to the Liberal Democrats?'

I responded that I had equivalent dinosaurs in my party to cope with. But better to deal with this now than in the context of the next election.

I turned the conversation to our conference.

PA: I want to warn you now that I am going to say some pretty tough things about you at our conference. I intend to say something which I think will get on the *Nine O'Clock News*. My aim is to make people feel they are party to one of our conversations. And although they won't realize it, much of this passage of my speech is drawn from just such a conversation we had a few weeks ago in which I told you my concerns about you and your government. I will leave you with a piece of the text that I have written. You aren't going to like it. It is very straight talking. I don't want to change it, but if you really find it intolerable please let me know and I'll think again.

The draft text I left with him was as follows:

So, let me say something very directly to the Prime Minister.

We have disagreed, sometimes strongly, about properly funded health and education. And on other things, too.

But your government has done some very good things.

Peace in Ireland, devolution for Scotland and Wales, a Bill of Rights for Britain, an Independent Central Bank – these are considerable achievements.

You have honoured, when many said you didn't need to, the commitments you made on constitutional change before the election. And I respect you for that.

But I have one great question about you.

Are you a pluralist?

Or are you a control freak?

Your language tells me you're the first. But so many of your government's actions tell me you're the second.

Your government could become, potentially, a historic one. But only if it lets go a little, if it tolerates dissent a little, if it welcomes diversity a little and if it interferes a little less.

You miss the mood of the age if you believe this is the new era of control. You have said you do not want this to be a Britain in which only the red rose of Labour is allowed to grow. Fine – then let it be a nation in which a thousand flowers are encouraged to bloom.

So, Blair the pluralist or Blair the control freak? Your decision on fair votes will tell us which.[1]

After about twenty minutes, we wandered out into Blair's secretary's office and waited for Becks.

We left at about 2.30pm, with Blair waving us goodbye from the front steps. Thinking about our conversation on the way back I concluded that we had broken the log jam. But we must lock everything else in place as soon as possible. I would get Richard to tell Mandelson that we had reached an agreement, but to stress that both on the question of the wording of his acceptance of Jenkins and on the issues of lists and timings I had no further room for manoeuvre.

Afterwards down to tell Roy that I thought we had achieved a breakthrough. [Roy rang me two days later to say that he had spoken to Blair, who agreed that it was a breakthrough, too.] Felt mightily relieved.

Rang Richard Holme as well, who was astounded. But I did suggest he rang Mandelson immediately to confirm the agreement and check that Blair echoed my view that we had achieved a breakthrough. Richard phoned back later to say that Mandy had trotted off to see Blair and then rang back to say that, yes, he reached the same conclusions as me. Excellent! From this the two parties can really begin to reshape British politics and the country can start on the road towards a fairer voting system. Although there is, of course – especially with Blair – many a slip between cup and lip.

Saturday, 19 September, Brighton

THE NIGHT BEFORE THE PARTY CONFERENCE

Having arrived with Jane in Brighton in the evening I wandered, as usual, into the hotel bar. A lot of nervousness in the air. And some deep suspicion

---

1 I subsequently delivered this passage, unamended by Blair, in my speech on 24 September at Brighton. It was, as I thought, the headline story for that event. Indeed, the phrase 'control freak' as applied to the Blair government began with this speech, and is, I think, the only phrase I have contributed to the modern political lexicon.

about what I am up to. Oh well, can't say I blame them. I would feel the same in their position.

Monday, 21 September, Brighton

In a lunchtime debate on Lib/Labbery, sponsored by the *Guardian*, Charles Kennedy stuck to the line perfectly. He had, apparently, been very elegant – arguing all four points of the compass without anyone noticing. Simon Hughes, however, issued a press release talking about no coalition until after PR was actually in place. He knows perfectly well we had agreed to stay off this. Later I just about succeeded in diverting press interest from coalitions on to policy. But I was livid with Simon.

Charles's and Simon's performances were later described as a 'beauty contest' – with Simon winning the tiara by appealing to the audience with the usual easy left-wing tunes.

In the evening, in a live television interview, I was presented with yet another of Simon's unhelpful statements. Now he's said it would be OK to hold the referendum after the next election! So undermining not only our strategy at conference but also my negotiating position with Blair. I was swift and brutal, saying live that Simon must be overtired as he obviously has not paid attention to the fact that both the Cook/Maclennan agreement and Labour's manifesto required a referendum in this parliament. My attack was immediately picked up by the press.

Roger Lowry reported that one of Simon's staff said to him later, 'In the old days when a colleague got out of line, David Steel used to say, "I am sure you quoted my colleague out of context." Why can't Paddy say the same?' To which Roger responded, 'Paddy is not like that. Do something stupid in public and you can expect to get a public kick up the backside.'

Thursday, 24 September, Brighton

Despite my previous fears, my conference speech passed off OK. Fifty-six minutes. I was very nervous to start with and fumbled some of the lines. But the jokes worked and, as anticipated, the 'Are you Tony Blair the control freak?' bit was picked out on all the news programmes. Not my greatest speech ever. As difficult as any I have made, given that it is basically a holding speech at a very fluid moment.

Still no answer from the Serbs on my visa for Kosovo [my plan was to leave for the Balkans straight after my conference speech]. Throughout the day they kept on saying that the answer from Belgrade would come in the next ten minutes; then the next fifteen minutes; then the next twenty minutes. By 2 o'clock I decided that they were stringing us along and I would go back to Yeovil. So Jane and I packed up our stuff and loaded it all into the car. We were on our way by about 2.30.

Friday, 25 September, Somerset

A pleasant autumn day. Low mists make it rather humid, but otherwise lovely weather.

Roger is trying to get some answers out of the Foreign Office as to whether the Serbs will give us visas. I anticipated they won't.

About mid-morning, however, it looked as if I might get one. Blair has given me a letter to give to Milosevic, and that has influenced their decision, so I am told. At 1.30 I heard that I would definitely get a visa. In one way my heart sank; I am shattered after conference. But it will be good to go back to Kosovo and take a proper look.

So I quickly bundled everything into a couple of suitcases (fortunately, Jane had prepared for a possible trip to Kosovo anyway before we went to conference) and half an hour after receiving the call I was in the car and heading for the Yugoslav Embassy in London.

Very heavy traffic on the road, so I didn't get to the Embassy until about 5.30. The place was locked, but I was eventually let in to be told that Paic, the hard-eyed (almost certainly intelligence officer) deputy head of the mission, couldn't see me until 6.30. I kicked up a fuss and eventually he was produced.

Looking very shifty, Paic told me that I could only go if I saw Milosevic first. That, he said, was courtesy. But Milosevic couldn't see me until the end of my planned tour. An obvious ploy to create maximum problems for me. I blew my top and said I wasn't doing anything of the sort, but that I was perfectly happy to tell the world at large that the Serbs had stopped me at the last moment. He claimed that Belgrade hadn't officially told him I could go. I sat tight for an hour and a half, in constant contact with the Foreign Office. Eventually, they got in touch with Brian Donnelly, the British Ambassador to Belgrade, who left an evening reception in order to go and see Milosevic's chief fixer himself.

The Serbian Ambassador was also produced to sit with me. A pathetic drink-sodden man who chainsmoked awful Yugoslav cigarettes throughout. His fingernails and moustache all coated with nicotine. He cast a sad figure. Paic, hatchet-faced but with the capacity to charm when necessary, is obviously the force in the Embassy.

I left at 8 o'clock and went back to the flat to prepare, while Roger [who had arrived by this time] sat it out with my passport at the embassy. The Foreign Office said that they would, if necessary, send someone over to sit there all night until the telegram came through. Eventually, after we had shown them that we would not give up, the Serbs relented and Roger rang to say that I had got my visa and he would meet me with it at the airport tomorrow.

Saturday, 26 September, London and the Balkans

Up at 5.00, a bath, then into the car to Heathrow. Dark and raining slightly. I met Roger at 6.30 and we caught the 7.25 BA flight to Dusseldorf, where we changed for Skopje. The aeroplane, ancient and very tatty, was full of people from the Balkans. I slept a bit and read a couple of chapters from *Captain Corelli's Mandolin*. Now that the conference is over I have time to read again.

We arrived at Skopje at just past 2.00, to be picked up by a member of the British Embassy, who took us into town for a coffee in the old Turkish quarter. Then off to the Kosovo border. Here, just on the Macedonian side, we met Brian Donnelly, a neat little man with a well-trimmed beard, piercing eyes and a careful, rather hesitant way of speaking. I took to him immediately.

With him was David Slinn, the First Secretary at the Belgrade embassy dealing with Kosovo matters.

We crossed the border and drove for an hour or so out of the Macedonian mountains and down on to the plain of Kosovo, passing through the little town of Kacanik, where the Albanians raised the flag of freedom against the Turks in the last century. Then on to Pristina, an awful slab-sided town specially built as the Kosovar capital by the communists in the 1950s.

Here we were installed in the Park Hotel, which, until recently, had been a Serb brothel. My bedroom showed it, too. The bathroom window was precisely positioned halfway up the wall with no curtain, so that all Pristina could see my private parts. And the bedspread and sheets were a lurid pink nylon sprinkled with appalling cheap perfume.

My first appointment was with Ibrahim Rugova, at his substantial house in what passes for Pristina's residential quarter. Wildly overdecorated with heavy wood carvings and an excess of brocade.

I talked with Rugova for an hour. He said that the Hill proposals[1] formed a basis for discussion, but that elements of them (e.g. a Belgrade police force) were unacceptable to him. I asked him directly whether he controlled the KLA. He said he did, although there were 'small Marxist-Leninist elements' outside his control. If he gave the word, a ceasefire would be observed. I told him in language which was probably more blunt than diplomatic that if he really wanted to lead his people, he couldn't do so from his living-room in Pristina. He had shown immense moral courage so far. But why had he not gone out to visit the refugees or see for himself the

---

1 A set of peace proposals made by Christopher Hill, former US Secretary of State. The proposals provided an interim accord for three years during which period institutions would be created for democratic self-determination in Kosovo through elections overseen by the OSCE. Kosovo would have a certain degree of self-government, including control of its own police and internal security, but Yugoslavia would be responsible for Kosovo's foreign policy, external defence, monetary policy, single market, customs and federal taxation. At the end of the three years the future status of Kosovo would be reviewed.

towns and villages that had been so abused by the Serbs? He smiled that delphic smile of his and said that it just wasn't possible.

What the Kosovars need is a Churchill. What they have is someone trying to be Mahatma Gandhi. His eyes are watery and his presence unprepossessing. No doubt he has immense spiritual force, and he is much respected for what he has already done, but, I concluded, Rugova is not someone to lead his people in war. I left feeling depressed.

Afterwards, off to dinner with, among others, Blerim Shalja, a much-respected local journalist, who told me that, contrary to his claims, Rugova probably controlled no more than 20 per cent of the KLA.

I was ravenously hungry and the food was excellent. Very tender beef and quite a lot of strong red Orahovac wine. Much joking that beef is not difficult to come by, since the Serbs were so busy shooting most of the Albanians' cows.

To bed very tired, at about midnight, after the obligatory whisky.

Sunday, 27 September, Kosovo

A beautiful day. Low mist over the Pristina valley, soon burnt off by the morning sun.

Breakfast, then off in Brian Donnelly's Range Rover with David Slinn, Brian himself, and John Crosland, the defence attaché, driving. John, a taciturn ex-Falklands veteran, has spent a lot of time here, speaks some Serbo-Croat and appears to know many of the Serb soldiers who regularly man the checkpoints.

Following on behind us was David Loyn, the BBC correspondent, in a lurid yellow armoured Land Rover, with his camera crew and some interpreters.

We headed out of Pristina towards Pec on the road which had been blocked by the KLA until a few weeks ago, when Milosevic's tanks had come in and swept them all away.

About five miles outside Pristina I suddenly smelled the acrid smoke burning houses. Crosland said that it was the villages in the Drenica triangle, two or three miles to the north of us, unseen in the morning mist, where there had been very heavy fighting. Otherwise we saw nothing more alarming than a few Serb soldiers sitting at road blocks smoking in the bored fashion of soldiers the world over.

Along the sides of the road were small villages and settlements, all of which had been deserted and burnt by the Serbs. We stopped at one for a closer look. The place had been systematically looted, then burnt and its population driven out. There was a strong smell of putrefaction from the dead bodies of farm animals lying the fields – mostly cows, shot by the Serbs as they moved through. The few animals which had escaped were, however, having a wonderful time, roaming freely and grazing on the unharvested corn.

We looked into one of the Albanian houses. A tragic broken family home. The stove still there, the kettle black and the roofless rooms full of charred timbers and blackened tiles. In an outbuilding the family's supply of winter corn and the seeds for next year's planting had been tipped out on to the ground and urinated on.

We left, depressed, after half an hour and continued on our journey to Pec, a peaceful little town where we stopped for a coffee and a chat with some Albanians sawing wood for winter.

I wanted to travel down the road from Pec to Djakovica, which I had seen from the mountains above in July. Brian suggested that, on the way, we should call in at the little Serb Orthodox monastery of Decani, situated in the forest at the foot of the mountains, as it would help us to understand why Serb nationalists attach such importance to the area.[1]

The monastery consists of a glorious little thirteenth-century church, set like a jewel on a sward of grass, surrounded by monks' quarters, and all housed within a walled enclosure.

The walls of the church are constructed in sandwiched stone, rather like the Duomo at Siena, only in this case slightly purple marble interspersed with granite. The building has been completely untouched by the war and is in perfect condition. The inside is quite stunning. Perfect original fourteenth-century frescoes, some particularly glorious ones near the altar, and a wonderful candelabra. We were shown round by one of the monks, Father Sava,[2] who spoke impeccable English, after which we all trooped upstairs on to the veranda of the monks' quarters for a cup of coffee and the obligatory glass of their home-made raki – excellent stuff, but a little strong for empty stomachs in the middle of the day.

---

1 The Pec region of Kosovo is regarded as a religious centre for Orthodox Serbs, as important as Canterbury is to English Christians.
2 Father Sava, known as 'the cyber monk' because of his enthusiasm for the internet, was to become an important point of call on all my subsequent visits to Kosovo and a key representative of non-Milosevic Serbs in Kosovo.

Then back on to the road heading south under the mountain ridges and past the little villages I had watched being shelled back in July. I particularly wanted to speak to some refugee Serb families I had heard of who lived in this area, most of them from the Krajina, made homeless by the Tudjman offensives.[1] When we arrived, there were some drunken armed Serbs swaggering about in the most arrogant manner. The refugees didn't appear at all frightened, although they claimed to be under constant attack from the KLA. But in all the fifty or sixty houses I saw here I spotted only two bullet marks. Meanwhile, every other village we have been through has been completely wrecked by tank rounds, with 30 mm canon shellholes in most houses.

The next village on our route was Prilep, where, apparently, a Serb policeman had been killed a month or so ago. The village had been literally razed to the ground in reprisal by heavy artillery and, according to some claims, aircraft rockets. There was little left except mounds of rubble, out of which suddenly appeared an Albanian woman and a young girl. We asked them if they lived here. Not now, they replied, but they had. By this time other ghostly figures, all old, had started to appear out of the ruins. They gathered round us and explained that they tried to visit their former houses during the day to make sure that what was left of their livestock was kept alive. They said they were staying with friends or relations, often in appallingly crowded conditions, about two hours' journey away by horse and cart. The young men, of course, could not return without risking arrest or worse from the Serbs. I asked if they ever stayed the night. Apparently about a week ago some of them had tried to do so. But the next morning they had all been found with their throats cut.

I wanted to know how the old woman would survive the winter. She shrugged her shoulders and said she was luckier than most. The roof was gone from her house, but the ceiling above her kitchen was still intact and she still had her stove for heating. The problem would be food.

Then across country on a dirt track to a place where the Serbs had claimed that the KLA had executed a number of Serb civilians. John took us to a bleak patch of scrub through which ran a small but fast-flowing stream in a concrete-lined culvert – the scene of the massacre, where apparently some eight to ten bodies had been found lying along the banks and in the stream bed.

We picked up some 7.62 short-chamber cartridges of Chinese origin, so

1 See Vol. I, p. 315.

probably from the KLA. The theory was that KLA soldiers had captured some Serb civilians and then, when they had been attacked themselves, panicked and shot them against the concrete walls of the culvert, some falling into the river. Not unreasonably, much had been made of this by Belgrade and the Serb president, Milutinovic, had recently visited to lay a wreath (still there) for the TV cameras.

Though the bodies had long since been removed from the scene, we did find a calf trapped in the steam. I insisted that we should rescue it, took my shoes off and jumped in. The fast-flowing culvert led to a sharp twenty-foot drop into a small lake, so I tied a rope around my waist which the others held on to. John Crosland quickly followed, taking off his trousers and, in just his underpants, jumped in to help. Between us we managed to get a line round the calf's hind legs and the others hauled it up.

There then ensued a mighty battle with the poor beast, now thoroughly frightened, to disentangle the rope from its rear end. Brian Donnelly was deputed to hang on to the animal while the others struggled with the rope. But the calf was having none of it, broke free and careered off, with Her Britannic Majesty's Ambassador to Belgrade hanging like grim death on to its rear end.

Much laughter from us all as it galloped away into the scrub, trailing the rope still behind it.

What stupid people we are! Here in the middle of all this carnage, having conspicuously failed to save the defenceless Kosovar Albanians, we make ourselves feel better by saving a calf.

I pronounced that it was obviously a Serb calf. Asked why, I said because it had got itself into a hole it didn't know how to get out of and then kicked anyone who tried to help it.

Then back out on to the main road again, heading south-west for Djakovica. This is wine-growing country, the centre of which is the pretty little town of Orahovac, which had been briefly held by the KLA a few months ago. As we rose up the escarpment out of the town we stopped briefly at a rubbish tip where, it was said, some Kosovar Albanians had been killed by the Serbs. We saw freshly dug graves, in one of which lay an exposed coffin. A strong smell of putrefaction.

Then back up the hill in the sunlight until we rounded a spur to see the whole of the Prizren valley laid out before us. As I looked down into the valley I could see burning village after burning village. We started to hear the boom and crash of artillery and mortar shells, which could now be plainly seen bombarding the peasant settlements on the opposite side of the valley.

A little further on we rounded a corner to find a big barrel-chested Albanian standing in the middle of the road. He took us to his roadside garage, which had, he said been recently burnt and trashed by the Serbs. Then to his house, also now a burnt-out shell. In the courtyard the dahlias and the chrysanthemums were flowering brilliantly against the flame-scarred walls and the blackened eyeless sockets of empty window spaces. Once again my old Balkan affliction struck and I couldn't stop the tears welling up in my eyes.

The man told us that the Serbs had given the local villagers a deadline of two weeks to 'give up their weapons', or they would be back to raze their village to the ground. The deadline was up tomorrow. But the village had no weapons, he said. So they had raised DM 10,000 amongst themselves and were going out on the black market today to buy some weapons to give to the Serbs tomorrow.

The barrel-chested garage owner[1] said it was probably pointless. They wouldn't be able to buy enough weapons to satisfy the Serbs, so they would burn the village down anyway.

Meanwhile, across the valley, the whole hillside was now a mass of flames as more and more villages were fired. A perfect terror operation. The Serbs had deliberately chosen villages on the sides of the mountain, so inhabitants of the whole valley below could see what would happen to them if they didn't comply.

John and I reckoned that, apart from tanks, the Serbs were using their full range of artillery pieces, up to 120 mm mortars and 155 mm guns. The main battle units of one of the Communist Bloc's most effective armies being used against a defenceless peasant population to drive them from their homes and livelihoods.

Our friend the garage owner told us that the routine was always the same. The Serbs issued a deadline for a village to give up its weapons. If the villagers couldn't come up with enough weapons to satisfy the Serbs (which was generally the case), then they were told to get out, after which the artillery bombardment started, driving out any villagers who were reluctant to go. Then the looters came in, bringing with them huge 40-ton articulated lorries and trailers to ransack the houses of anything valuable – video recorders, satellite dishes, refrigerators (invariably purchased

---

1 Brian Donnelly has since told me that he strongly suspected this man was, in fact, KLA.

after many years of working away from the family, often in Germany). And finally, after the looters, came teams of soldiers to set the villages alight.

Milosevic has announced to the world today that Serb military offensives in Kosovo have stopped. So Brian got out his satellite phone and rang direct through to the Foreign Office in London to say, with some anger in his voice, that Milosevic was lying (again). When the Foreign Office man at the other end asked him if he was sure Brian replied by holding the receiver up in the air so that they could hear for themselves the sound of the bombardment.

We decided we should try to get through to the Serb gun positions, so we dropped down the hill into the regional capital of Suva Reka. But, as we anticipated, we were soon stopped by soldiers at a Serb checkpoint who, at gunpoint, refused to let us go any further.

By now it was raining hard and we were becoming worried about getting back to Pristina before the 6.30 curfew, so we retraced our steps back up the Pagarusha valley.

On the way we saw several hundred refugee families, many with small children, huddling under plastic sheets in the pouring rain on the back of farm trailers. They had set up a pathetic little market on an exposed windswept hillside, where they were bartering their remaining possessions for food and fuel with locals and fellow refugees. The villages in this valley remain under the protection of the KLA – though doubtless the Serb tanks will soon change that.

On the way back to Pristina we saw the fires burning through the gathering darkness from parallel Serb operations in the Drenica region. Suddenly we found ourselves in the middle of a large Serb military convoy – tanks loaded with soldiers all giving the Serb three-fingered salute and shouting abuse at us when they saw the Ambassador's Union flag. John said that the convoy of tanks, heading south-west, probably meant that operations in the Drenica had finished and the full weight of the Serb offensive would now fall on Suva Reka, where we had just been, tomorrow.

We arrived at Pristina just before dark and over a beer in the hotel discussed the day's terrible sights. After which Brian left for Belgrade for a meeting with Milosevic tomorrow.

Later we met up with the BBC man David Loyn, who had got separated from us on the journey back. He had dropped behind our little convoy to film a burning house by the side of the road and had been harassed at one of the Serb checkpoints. They had demanded his videotapes and ground them into the dust at the roadside in front of him. But he had kept some hidden, so hadn't lost everything.

Tomorrow we plan to go out with Morgan Morris, the UNHCR Field Officer here, to see the refugee situation. So we contacted her and fixed to go back to Suva Reka, leaving very early so as to be there when the next stage of the Serb offensive starts.

To bed far too late and very tired. Dreams of burning houses and weeping refugees.

Monday, 28 September, Kosovo

At 7.30 we piled into Morgan Morris's unarmoured vehicle and set off for Suva Reka with David Loyn and the BBC crew following behind.

We went through Malisevo, where we were stopped by a Serb army checkpoint and told not to go further, it being both dangerous and forbidden. But we talked our way past them.

Five hundred metres up the road we found a couple of KLA soldiers, sitting peacefully and unconcerned against a wall, warming themselves in the early morning sunshine. They were well turned out in smart uniforms sporting brand-new KLA badges and shoulder flashes. Neither their faces nor their uniforms said they had been out the previous night attacking Serbs, even though their enemy was a mere 500m away. No sign of patrols either – or even of sentries to warn of an impending attack. Given that we were a mere five or six kilometres at most from the place where the Serb army was shelling villages and driving out their fellow Kosovars, I had expected to see more aggressive KLA activity here, if only to draw the fire from the Suva Reka region.

We said we were going to see what was happening in Suva Reka, but would pass back this way later in the day – could we speak to their commander when we came back? Vaughan Smith [an extraordinary young ex-Guardsman who was acting as cameraman for the BBC team, spoke good Albanian and had the best access to the KLA anywhere in Kosovo] produced a KLA pass and vouched for our intentions. They promised to pass the word on to their commander and, after a little persuading, posed for photos.

By now it was raining hard and the tracks were starting to get muddy. We dropped down the valley, where we were directed by some locals on to a back route which, they said, was free of Serb police.

A couple of kilometres further on we began to see the Suva Reka valley and houses burning on the other side. Different ones from yesterday. The shelling had mostly stopped, but more villages had been fired in a great semi-circle in front of us.

We went back down to see our garage friend to ask him how the Serb weapon collection had gone. He replied that the villagers had managed to buy around seven or eight weapons in all – but he was sure this would not be enough to satisfy the Serbs when they came. Would we like to see the guns?

We were first taken to a school room, where we sat and talked for half an hour or so with a group of village elders. All of them were over seventy, though, noticeably, as we talked a small group of younger men quietly appeared and stood silently around the walls.

They said the routine was always the same. First the Serbs came to demand weapons. The village mustered what money they could to buy weapons on the black market, which were then handed over to the Serbs. In some cases the Serbs then left the village in peace, but in many they burnt it anyway. Then the Serbs sold the weapons back on to the black market so that the next village they threatened had enough weapons to buy. In this way the Serbs both terrorized the villagers and relieved them of their money at the same time.

After a village had been sacked the people were often allowed back, but the Serbs nearly always left a 'calling card' to reinforce the terror; usually one of the villagers was executed or tortured or both. In one village, we were told, the returning villagers had found the body of one of their number who was mentally retarded and hadn't got out before the shelling had started. He had been tortured; his arms and legs had been cut off, his torso was then burnt and the arms and legs subsequently placed carefully around the ashes. Apparently this often happens to those who are too infirm to leave. Disembowelment before burning is common, too.

We asked to see the weapons the villages had obtained and were taken in a small procession through the rain to a neat little Kosovan house, where we left our shoes outside and trooped up to a first-floor room. Here they dragged a box out of a cupboard and opened it to reveal eight or nine weapons and some plastic bags.

The weapons were mostly Chinese replicas of the Russian Kalashnikov and Simonov assault rifles. Three were immediately usable, two would have had to be cleaned before being serviceable and the rest were rusted beyond use. It was also clear that no one present had the first idea how to use them. There was much alarm when I selected one, unwrapped it from its greaseproof covering, pulled back the cocking mechanism and found that there was a round in the chamber and the magazine was full.

I also looked in one of the plastic bags to find some more rounds and in another a dozen or so hand-grenades, all fully armed with the detonators and fuses in place. These, too, were horribly rusty and, to my eye, extremely unstable. I told the villagers to handle them with great care as they were quite likely to go off at any moment – and it was better that they did so after they had been handed over to the Serbs, rather than before. The villagers told me that four Albanians had recently been killed when grenades they had purchased to hand over had done just this.

They were all terrified. The Serbs were due in a couple of hours.

We took some photos, wished the villagers luck and said we would try to come back to see them later.[1]

Then, following, the villagers' directions, we took the back route to the main Suva Reka–Prizren road to avoid the Serb police.

But as soon as we came on to the main road we bumped into a road block manned by the special Ministry of Interior Police [or MUPP, as they came to be known in Kosovo]. They told us we should not be in the area, as it had been sealed off, and instructed us to go straight to the Regional Headquarters in Prizren, where we were to report our presence. On no account were we to leave the main road, as it was 'dangerous due to terrorist activity in the area'.

We duly headed south down the main road in the direction of Prizren until we were out of sight, and then turned swiftly left on to a viciously bumpy dirt track, making for the burning villages which we could plainly see to our east about two kilometres away.

We hadn't gone far before we came across a terrible little convoy of refugees. Weeping, terrified women and children sheltering from the pouring rain under plastic sheets on the backs of farm trailers bumping towards a small village. I went up to one of these trailerloads of misery to find five children, a heavily pregnant woman with tears streaming down her face, two others with babes in arms and a collection of terrified-looking grandmothers. I tried to speak to them, but had to walk away, my voice choking to a halt and my Balkan affliction of uncontrollable tear ducts shaming me again. The babies reminded me so much of Matthias.

---

1 For reasons that will become clear, we were unable to get back to them on this trip. But on my next trip I did return to this village, which was called Studencane. The Serbs came later that day, seemed satisfied with the weapons handed over and left without disturbing them further.

I suddenly felt an overwhelming rage that people who call themselves soldiers could have done this.

The women were desperate for us to lead them down into the valley to safety, explaining that they were half an hour away from the Serb deadline for shelling the village and they were frightened that it could start at any moment. We, however, wanted to get closer to where the shelling was taking place now, so we advised them to continue down the valley, as it was safe at the bottom, and promised to come back later.

But we had progressed no more than 200m up the road towards the sound of the firing before being told by a young man that there was a Serb checkpoint just ahead. We didn't want to let down the terrified villagers we had just left, so we turned round and went back, intending to see them to safety down the valley before continuing towards the action.

By the time we got back, however, the villagers had decided that they would stay where they were – they had had enough of fleeing. We suggested that at least we should take the women and children to the main road to avoid the shelling, if it came. But they refused, saying they were determined to stick together and would take what came.

It may have been the right decision, but I left with a heavy heart.[1]

We turned the vehicles again and resumed our attempt to get closer to the battlefield, taking a different route to avoid the checkpoint we had been warned of.

But we got no more than two kilometres before bumping into yet another Serb road block. We tried everything to persuade them to let us pass, including me indulging in an outrageous exercise in namedropping (Tony Blair has sent me; I'm seeing Milosevic tomorrow, etc.). But the very tough-looking and highly professional young Serb soldier in charge wasn't having any of it and insisted politely but unshakeably firmly that we must leave immediately under military escort. He was a good soldier following his orders and, although I was furious at being thwarted, I quite admired him.

Nevertheless, I was very reluctant to be turned back, so I decided to start getting angry with them. But Morgan, in an audible whisper, hissed, 'Shut up! If we don't do as he says he could put our Albanian interpreters at risk.'

Meanwhile, the other soldiers manning the checkpoint had got hold of

1 Two days later it came to light that, at almost precisely the time we were stopped at this checkpoint, a massacre of Albanian villagers was taking place at Iraniq, about three kilometres in front of us (see entry for 14 December 1998).

one of our two female Albanian interpreters, Bili Gjonbaliag, and had started to threaten her. She was going to be arrested, the foreigners couldn't protect her now, they would turn up at her home, etc. There was a menacing moment when they tried to order Bili out of the UNHCR vehicle and into a nearby Serb one, but Morgan steadfastly refused to let the Serbs have her and eventually she got her way. So, feeling dejected, we allowed ourselves to be led out of the battle area at gunpoint by the Serbs.

Once our escort had left us, we discussed the possibility of finding another route back in. But Morgan, who is not to be resisted when she makes up her mind, said no. She had just received strict instructions over the radio from UNHCR to get out of the battlezone immediately, and under no circumstances go back.

Back at Suva Reka we had a coffee at an Albanian roadside café before climbing the mountain to take a better look at the destruction. Sixteen or eighteen villages alight. Now and again, the bright flutter of flames as yet another house went up and, on two or three occasions, the deep explosions of artillery still being fired (though much less than yesterday).

Then home by our 'secret' track through Pagarusha, to where we had met the KLA soldiers earlier that morning. Here, true to their word, we met the KLA commander, who turned out to be an old friend of Vaughan's. He repeated what everybody else had told me, that Rugova was not to be trusted and had no power over the KLA. Some in the international community define these people as terrorists – and they probably are. But wouldn't I be if my house had been burnt down and my wife and children forced to flee?

It was about 3.30 by now, so Morgan suggested taking us to see a group of refugees she had recently found in the forests. She had discovered them after spotting a lone figure walking furtively up a forest track away from the road. After a little difficulty she persuaded him to take her to the rest of his village, hidden up the valley. There she had found some 1,500–2,000 women, children and elderly people, who had been living in the forest for several months. Morgan had subsequently been quietly supplying them with food, medicine and plastic sheeting.

So we followed the road back to Malisevo, then turned right towards Pristina. In due course, we passed through the village from which the forest refugees had come. Every house destroyed and dead cattle, bloated with putrefaction, lying in the fields. Then Morgan suddenly turned off the road and we bumped along a rough track for a couple of kilometres, up a narrow mountain valley and into the forest.

A further kilometre or so and then we saw them. Sixty or seventy rough lean-tos made of branches and plastic sheets, the air blue with woodsmoke and people flitting like shadows among the trees.

A group of village elders were called for and showed us round. Each lean-to held an extended family, as many as twenty or thirty people, including the elderly and mothers with small children, huddled under the plastic. Again, no young men.

There had been a frost the previous night. Some rain had got in and the people were wet. Some had managed to bring stoves out of their houses and had installed them in shelters. But the insides of the shelters were fuggy with dampness and already there were signs of chest infections among the kids.

The villagers told me they were too frightened to go back down the mountain by day in case the Serbs found them. A Serb patrol had passed near by not long ago and they were worried they had been seen. Each plastic shelter was covered in branches in an attempt at camouflage, but the leaves on these had all died, which only made the shelters stand out even more.

I asked one child, a girl of perhaps nine, what had happened on the night the Serbs had come to her village. She told me that they had fired small arms at the village throughout the day before. Then, after nightfall, when all the international observers had left for their hotels in Pristina, the Serbs had opened up with mortars and artillery. The villagers decided to leave under cover of darkness. The girl's father was off in the mountains fighting for the KLA. Somehow or other in the darkness she had lost contact with her mother, so she had taken her younger brother and sister by the hand and walked with them and some other villagers through the night, under constant fire from the Serbs along the way. They had found their way to this valley, she wasn't entirely certain how, where they had met up with their mother again.

I told the refugees I was going to see Milosevic tomorrow. He would no doubt deny they even existed. So they gave me a bag of wild cherries to give to him and asked me to tell Milosevic that this is what they have been living off for the last few weeks. They had nothing else – except what Morgan had been able to provide.

How would they survive the winter? They couldn't live here when the snow came.

An old man said that they would rather die of cold and starvation than risk going back to the Serbs.

On our way back to Pristina a message came through on Morgan's radio that fourteen bodies had been discovered in a village in the Drenica region.[1] All had been mutilated. One, an old man, had had the top of his head sliced off, his brain taken out, and laid beside the body of his dead wife. His foot had also been cut off and her throat had been slit and the knife left on her chest. The ECMM observers who had been led to the bodies had also found a six-week-old baby still alive, lying in its mother's blood. I felt sick to my stomach.

We reached Pristina at 6.30, grabbed a sandwich and headed off for Belgrade, David Slinn driving. On arrival at the capital, we went straight to Brian Donnelly's splendid ambassadorial residence to find that he had just come back from a meeting with Milosevic, who, true to form, had denied that any of the things we had seen were happening. Brian said that Milosevic could lie more convincingly than anyone he had ever known.

A light supper and to bed about 1.00. I slept wonderfully – free, thank God, from the nightmares of burning houses and desperate refugees that I have been having for the last two nights.

Tuesday, 29 September, Belgrade

Up at 8.00, a shower, then down to breakfast. The *Guardian* has commissioned an article from me and is putting the Drenica massacre we heard about yesterday on its front page tomorrow.

Over to the embassy itself, where I met the US Ambassador to Macedonia, Christopher Hill, who has been trying to negotiate a peace package with the Serbs aimed at putting a stop to the Kosovo bloodshed.

Then, at about 12.40, off in Brian's ambassadorial car to see Milosevic in the Presidential Palace, one of the old royal palaces.

We arrived a little early but were shown straight in to see Milosevic. I was struck immediately by how much younger he looked than I had imagined. I delivered Blair's letter, reinforcing it by saying that it would be an act of gross miscalculation if he believed the international community weren't serious about using military force if the barbarism in Kosovo didn't cease.

---

1 This subsequently turned out to be one of the most notorious of the Kosovo massacres, was widely covered on TV across the world and escalated the crisis to the point where the international community was forced to act. US roving ambassador Richard Holbrooke was sent to Belgrade to attempt to reach a settlement with Milosevic which would end Serb operations in Kosovo.

I asked him what he was trying to achieve.

He said he was suppressing terrorism, which was every state's right.

I said he wasn't suppressing terrorism, he was creating it.

He replied that I knew nothing about terrorism, to which I rather gruffly replied that I had fought in three terrorist campaigns and had lost good friends to terrorists. I had no time for them. But neither did I have any time for countries that acted like terrorists.

He then switched tack, saying that none of the actions the press were talking about had taken place.

In which case, I said, he was being lied to by his officials. At the very moment two days ago when he was telling the world that military operations in Kosovo had ended, Ambassador Donnelly and I had personally watched his forces shelling and burning villages in the Suva Reka region – and I had seen them continuing right up to late yesterday afternoon. Moreover, these were being conducted, I believed, with his government's knowledge, or even under its direction. This was in flagrant disregard of any UN Security Council resolution.

What's more, I continued, they were also war crimes in their own right and contrary to the terms of the Geneva Convention. I handed him an extract from the Convention on which we had previously highlighted the relevant passages and added that, now he had been officially informed of this, he could be deemed personally responsible and could be indicted for war crimes if they continued.[1]

But, perhaps just as important as this, I went on, these actions were entirely counterproductive to what he had just told me he was trying to achieve. I knew what terrorism was like and I accepted you must sometimes take tough action. But the fact that people shot at you or perhaps even committed atrocities themselves did not excuse a state from acting in ways which were clearly illegal and inconsistent with membership of the civilized community of nations.

In Northern Ireland, we had fought terrorism for a quarter of a century without having to resort to using tanks and heavy artillery against villages. And if we had, we would not only have been rightly condemned by the international community but we would also have lost the support of the local population and given the terrorists all the recruits they needed.

Milosevic was most elusive. As soon as I tried to pursue a subject he

---

1 I subsequently gave evidence on this incident to the Hague War Crimes Tribunal as part of the evidence upon which Milosevic was later indicted for war crimes.

wandered away into history or into the usual propaganda quagmire of which the Serbs are so fond.

I asked him about the refugees. He said there were none living rough. I told him that I had seen several hundred hiding in the forest yesterday. I would have given him the bag of cherries they had given me, but I concluded that this would be unhelpful.[1]

I said that there was a humanitarian catastrophe waiting to happen. He conceded that there may be a few refugees in the forests, but no more than 2,000 at most. I said that was an underestimate by a factor of at least twenty – there could be up to 25,000 lives in jeopardy this winter unless something was done.

He said he would look again at this problem. Some hope!

I also asked him about the Hill agreement, to which he said he thought there was a basis for discussion there.

He would have gone on and on, but I had no desire to be lectured to about irrelevant historical 'facts' or hear nonsensical propaganda and I didn't want to miss my plane. So at 2 o'clock I said, 'Mr President, you have been generous with your time and, if I may say so, also in allowing me to come to your country. I shall have some hard words to say about what I have seen. As a people, I like the Serbs. I do not believe that you can condemn a nation. But I must tell you that the international community will act if you do not stop. And you are, in my view, acting illegally under international law and could be personally indictable. What is more, even from your own standpoint, these actions are entirely counterproductive. I beg you to put a stop to these things which besmirch the reputation of your country.'

Milosevic walked me to the front door personally, which Brian later commented was surprising, given the extremely frank nature of our exchange.

Then a fast dash back to the embassy for a hastily called press conference, at which I said that the actions of the Serb forces which we had witnessed represented a flagrant contravention of the Geneva Convention and could make both local commanders and their political leaders personally indictable under international law. When it was over, I whispered to Brian Donnelly, 'You will never get me another visa now.'

---

1 An error of judgement on my part. By this stage of our conversation Milosevic seemed to become more amenable and I wished to keep the conversation firm, but constructive. But it was only the old Milosevic charm.

Then a quick dash to the airport for the early afternoon flight to Vienna and the onward connection to London.

Just before we left for Vienna I heard from Richard that our attempts to have a Tory defector come across to us at the start of the Tory conference are about to bear fruit. I had been planning to go straight home to Somerset, but Richard asked whether I would go back via London for a photo op tomorrow. I said that I'd rather not unless it was absolutely essential – I was exhausted. Richard, bless him, said that I should go home and get some rest.

Nevertheless, a good coup at the start of the Tory conference.

It seemed unreal flying home from so much human misery. Got to Heathrow about half an hour late, where there was an awful muddle over our luggage, but it was eventually found and I set off for home at about 8.30. Back at Vane Cottage by ten. Drove far too fast in order to keep myself awake. Sat in a daze watching Blair's conference speech on the telly, which seemed to go down pretty well. Went to bed at midnight, drained.

Wednesday, 30 September, Somerset

Flat out this morning, what with the accumulated mail and a huge number of interviews about Kosovo. The massacres were announced today, so I was on everything from the *Today* programme onwards. Roger also took his camera tapes to ITN, who used them throughout the day.

I wrote my report on Kosovo for Blair in the evening.[1] At about 8 o'clock, as we were having dinner, Downing Street rang. Blair wanted to speak to me. Ten minutes later he called, asking for my views on Kosovo. He was in the middle of the Labour Party Conference and clearly very rushed and distracted.

I told him what I thought should happen, including *not* plunging into air strikes on an emotional basis having seen pictures of Serbian atrocities. He asked me to send in my full report by midday tomorrow, which I agreed to do.

I asked him how his conference was going. He said OK, but they were having a tough time on PR. I told him it looked pretty good from where I was sitting. I gain the impression he may be wobbling again, especially on

1 See Appendix G.

timing, so I said, 'I think we must stick firmly to what we have [i.e. the Chequers agreement], otherwise it will unravel from both ends.'

I could barely keep my eyes open. Into bed at about 9.15, which is unheard of for me. I've been very grumpy with my staff today, but I'm just completely exhausted. All the nervous tension and sleeplessness of conference, followed immediately by all the emotional tension and sleeplessness of Kosovo. At last, an excellent night's sleep.

Thursday, 1 October, Westminster

Had a chat with Richard this morning. Apparently there's a lot of talk of Tory defectors. Including, rumour has it, the son of David Howell (a former Tory MP who used to represent Guildford). More interestingly James Moorhouse[1] has also approached Richard. We had hoped to pull John Stevens at the same time, but he wants to go independent instead. There must be huge malice between Hague and this lot, because they are planning to jump ship just as Hague is starting his conference speech. Spoke to Moorhouse later in the day, who says he is firm on joining us. He will resign from the Tories next Thursday, but initially he may pretend he's going independent and come to us later.

Sent my report on Kosovo off to Blair shortly after twelve, together with a covering note saying that Richard and Peter should meet up soon to sort out our next step.

In my report I said that air strikes now were not an option, since Milosevic appears to have more or less ended his operation in Kosovo and is now withdrawing his troops to barracks. Military force should be used to achieve a political objective, not to pursue revenge or for the purposes of punishment. The best we can probably do is keep the military option on a hair trigger in case he starts again, or it emerges that he hasn't stopped.

Saturday, 3 October, Somerset

Crisp and sunny. A proper autumn day. Spoke to Roy, who has just returned from Italy. He thought we had had a very good conference.

1 Member of the European Parliament (Conservative, then Lib Dem) for London South 1979–99.

Labour's had been yet another rally – no more, he said. I told him I thought we were still on track as a result of the Chequers meeting, but I couldn't be sure. Roy promised to give Blair a call over the weekend and tell me the outcome.

Sunday, 4 October, Somerset

Up at 8.00. Phoned Richard and sent him my minute of what I want to happen while I am away in Mauritius [where I had been invited to give a speech by the British Ambassador]. Entitled 'What Happens Next?', this minute has been drafted as though it is for Richard, but its real intention is to lay out the short- and long-term positions for Blair in the hopes of stiffening his resolve. I contacted Jonathan Powell, who is staying with friends in the New Forest, and sent it to him to show Blair.

What Happens Next?

1. Now that the conferences are behind us, we need to pick up the detailed planning of the next steps.

2. First the big picture. You know my aim. It is to use this parliament, the current strength of our party and the opportunity presented by Blair, to bring about the reshaping the left in British politics with the same vision as Grimond and Steel. If we can achieve this, then we will together form the dominant governing force in Britain for the next decade, or more, depending on how long it takes the Tories to get their act together.

3. I have always seen the reshaping of the centre left as the first step in a more general reshaping of politics in Britain. If we can achieve a *rassemblement* of the centre liberal/left, then the right will have to reshape themselves, too, by moving back to a centre-right position. This will isolate both the extreme right and the extreme left, who will still be represented in Parliament, but only in relation to their true support in the country, which is small.

4. The ingredients to achieve this reshaping are in place, as never previously. The splits in the Tory Party are becoming increasingly irreconcilable and Blair is leading Labour more and more on to our territory. If we miss the opportunity now, it is unlikely to come again in our time. Already the 'pull' in both our parties back to the old tribalism is getting stronger and stronger.

5. This 'growing together' of our two parties will, therefore, not happen naturally. It has to be led from the top.

6. Making this happen is the task of my leadership, for which the last ten years have been a preparation. Blair says he sees things in the same way – that this is the 'most important task of my premiership'. His analysis is a more historical one, springing from a desire to heal the schism on the centre left which occurred in the second decade of this century. Mine is more about what could be in the next century. But the outcomes we seek are identical.

7. Although this project will have to be led from the top, it cannot be done in ways which impose. The trick for us is to give the lead for co-operation, set the climate for convergence and enable an 'organic' process to take place, without setting any artificial limits on where this may lead.

8. Given that there is a will on both sides to make convergence happen, what we need is a context which will enable it and an event which can act as a catalyst for it. PR provides the context, since it breaks tribalism. And Europe, or more precisely the referendum of the single currency, will provide the event.

9. I have always seen the project taking place in three phases.

10. In Phase I, we alter the climate of tribalism and hostility between the two parties and replace it, at the national level, with one of good will and the presumption of co-operation. This has been broadly achieved through the policy of 'constructive opposition' and our participation in the JCC, though the process is not yet entrenched and irreversible and it needs to be deepened and widened.

11. In Phase II we move to full co-operation, in government.

12. Phase III occurs after a successful period of working together. In this phase the two parties would consider whether their close identity of interest might be best served by institutionalizing their relationship to reflect the fact that they are now a cohesive unit representing a united political force in the country.

13. We have, essentially, been in Phase I since around the time of the Cook/Maclennan agreement.

14. Blair and I missed the opportunity to move immediately to Phase II after the General Election, and again when we decided we couldn't do it last autumn. I worried then that the longer we leave it, the more difficult it will become – and that is what has happened.

15. We thought we might get the opportunity to move to Phase II this autumn, in the context of Jenkins. But it is now clear that, again, the time is still not right.

16. However, Jenkins offers a real opportunity to push the project forward which must not be missed.

17. As you know, Blair and I agreed at the Chequers meeting that when Jenkins reported he [Blair] would say:

  i. That he recognized the deep flaws in our current electoral system and had always believed that, if it was possible sensibly to reform this as part of the modernization of Britain's constitution, then we should do this. The Jenkins proposals now offered the best way of achieving this reform.

  ii. He would therefore be 'minded to support Jenkins in the referendum which Labour were committed to' and would recommend that the Cabinet would do so, too.

  iii. That, 'in accordance with Labour's manifesto commitments and the Cook/ Maclennan agreement', he 'intended to hold a referendum in this parliament', but only after we had had time to assess how the elections in Scotland and Wales and the reforms of the House of Lords had worked out (in effect, meaning in the last year of the parliament).

18. It might be appropriate to combine any such referendum with one on the future reforms of the House of Lords, in order to decide the future shape and nature of 'our parliament' as a whole, [the so-called 'Big Bang' approach].

19. The form of words which Blair and I have arrived at contains sufficient flexibility to enable him to have the time and space to bring his party to the position we want it to arrive at. It also contains a sufficient element of conditionality for us to use as leverage on our party in order to push the co-operative project forward.

20. My aim over the remaining years of this parliament is to move the Party to the threshold of Phase II ('co-operation in government'), so that, at the best case, it

becomes possible to move to Phase II in the last year of this parliament and, at the worst, to move to it straight after the next election.

I am in Mauritius giving a speech over the next few days. Please contact me if there are any developments.

Thursday, 8 October, London

Am due to see James Moorhouse to discuss arrangements for his defection today. There have been many shenanigans. To my surprise, whilst lying in the bath, I heard that John Stevens and Brendan Donnelly[1] have been expelled from the Tory Party before they could resign. It turned out that Stevens had more or less prompted this by making contact with Peter Kellner about some Mori poll on the euro and then spilling the beans to him.

James turned up a little after 9.00. He is an elderly man, but very firm in his views, with kind eyes. A genuine radical when it comes to matters such as Europe and human rights. I was impressed. I also spoke to John Stevens on the phone. He said he was delighted the Tories had thrown him out because that would turn him into a martyr. But he sounded very uncertain. James Moorhouse agreed to stick to the original plan, that he would announce his intention to join us at 3.30, just as Hague was almost at the end of his speech.

However, at 11 o'clock I heard that Stevens had gone on the radio to say that 'someone' was going to defect to the Lib Dems. In the afternoon the news reports said that the Tories had now persuaded Stevens to rejoin them and had withdrawn their threat of expulsion. So his intentions, which had been set in concrete for more than a year, reversed as soon as he came under a little pressure.

Monday, 12 October, Somerset

Blustery and windy today. Rang Downing Street to find out how Holbrooke was progressing in Belgrade.[2]

1 Member of the European Parliament (Conservative) for Sussex, 1994–99.
2 Richard Holbrooke was at the time negotiating with Milosevic for the introduction of a Verification Mission (subsequently, the Kosovo Verification Mission (KVM)), but nothing had been signed.

Jonathan Powell phoned me back in the latter part of the afternoon to say that, although still confidential, it looked as if Holbrooke had got an agreement from Milosevic. I am worried it will be too weak.

The news began to emerge at about 7.30 that bombing was off. Early indications of the Holbrooke deal are not good, however. Some talk of unarmed monitors and the exact status of Kosovo remains unclear.[1]

Received a minute from Roger Lowry today about Richard Holme's meeting with Mandelson on Friday. Mandelson says Blair will 'comment favourably' on the Jenkins Commission findings but he would not be too gung-ho and the idea that the Cabinet would sign up to it as well was a 'leap too far'. A clear – and worrying – dilution of the Chequers agreement.

Saturday, 17 October, Scotland and London

THE SCOTTISH CONFERENCE

Ming picked me up [from the plane from Dublin, where I had been on a speaking tour] at 10.10 and we drove to Stirling together. A wild, blustery day of blue skies and scudding clouds. On the way we chatted about the next step. Ming, like me, believes that we must bring this thing with Blair to a head or we'll lose it.

The Scottish Conference was very encouraging. A great new sense of energy in the Scottish Party again under Jim Wallace's leadership.

Caught the 3.15 plane back to London. For the last three or four days I have been working on the statement[2] that I think Blair and I should make immediately post-Jenkins. Did some more work on the plane polishing it up.

Powell told me that Blair is spending the weekend with a 'wet towel wrapped round his head' again. I need to show him that there is more to this than taking a tough decision on PR, and that I am committed to the long-term strategy. I hope this statement will reinforce Blair's reasons for sticking with the Chequers agreement. But I'm worried; he seems to be wobbling again.

---

1 My office issued a press release that night saying that the Holbrooke peace plan would be unlikely to work. Unarmed monitors would, in due course, be undermined by the armed men (on both sides) on the ground, unless backed by forces (which they weren't) and Kosovo would be back to war within months.
2 Which subsequently became known as the 'Joint Statement'.

Sunday, 18 October, Somerset

At around 10.00 I sent through to Blair, via Powell, my first attempt at the joint statement. Writing it has helped clarify my own mind considerably and I hope it will do the same for Blair. What we have agreed to now is a 'double-barrelled' approach. Jenkins will offer the Lib Dems the opportunity of PR – but the joint statement, by widening the work of the JCC, will provide the context in which PR, through Jenkins, is linked to a widening relationship between the two parties.

Monday, 19 October, Westminster

At 3.00 Mark Oaten came to see me, very worried. He has spoken to John Sopel,[1] who has told him that he has it from a 'very senior source' that Blair will not have a referendum this parliament, but will put it off until the next. I told Mark that, whilst I wasn't absolutely certain, I thought I had a deal with Blair. It might well have been eroded a bit by the [anti-PR] reaction at the Labour Party Conference. But, broadly, I believed it still held.

Privately I am very concerned about this. Blair can be so slippery on these matters.

Mark was preparing to tell me that even if we had to wait until the next parliament for a referendum we shouldn't kick up about it. I said he may well be right but that I couldn't say that now or I would lose my bargaining position.

Later I saw Roy. We spent a good hour together, during which he outlined his commission's proposals to me. He, too, is nervous about Blair shifting his position. He has now shown his proposals to Blair in full. Roy told me that, in fairness to Bob Alexander[2] who insisted that Hague should see them at the same time as me, he couldn't give me the report. 'If you really insist, I will give it to you. But I will do so with a guilty conscience towards Bob.'

I said that I would not dream of putting Roy under that sort of pressure. 'I have complete trust in you. I believe it will be a great report. You have

1 BBC political correspondent.
2 Lord Alexander of Weston. A Conservative member of the House of Lords and a member of the Jenkins commission.

given me a full brief and that is good enough for me. Frankly, I would rather I get the report late, if it means the Tories get it late too and have less time to load their weapons. Although I assume Hague will now know as much about your proposals as I do, since I suspect he will have been briefed by both Blake[1] and Alexander.

The situation in Kosovo looks more and more bleak. Battles going on pretty well constantly now. As I thought, the KLA are breaking the ceasefire. And with unarmed monitors, how on earth can we control them?

Wednesday, 21 October, London

At 10 o'clock in the evening Brian Donnelly rang. He was in Skopje with Robin Cook. I have been asked to go on the *Today* programme tomorrow to discuss what appears to be the complete breakdown of the Holbrooke agreement and had asked Donnelly if he would ring me with the latest information. Bless him, he did.

Apparently, the Cook talks have gone reasonably well, although Donnelly is still concerned about the situation. The Holbrooke agreement hasn't broken down. But then wars like this don't shut down overnight. However, the intensity of Serb and KLA operations is declining. So we can't yet say categorically that the Serbs are not conforming to Holbrooke. At the end, I said to Brian, 'I am on record as saying this thing won't work. What do you think?' To which he replied, 'I'll play the politician on that one, if you don't mind. I won't answer.' Which means that he is broadly pessimistic.[2] I agreed that on the *Today* programme I am doing tomorrow morning I will say that it is too early to comment but it is vital we get monitors out on to the ground as fast as possible.

Thursday, 22 October, Westminster

An absolutely crucial day today. I hope we will finalize the words of the joint statement. I am seeing Blair for half an hour to talk about it before the JCC at 2.30. But I am also concerned that the JCC is becoming

---

1 Lord Blake. Conservative peer and former president of the Electoral Reform Society.
2 Brian has subsequently told me that he was in fact trying to dissuade me from being too pessimistic, and not to write off the KVM at this stage.

more ceremonial than functional, and I want to say something about that.

At 1.15 Paul Tyler and Andrew Stunell came to see me. I took Andrew through the Jenkins proposals in broad outline, though not in detail. He thinks I will have no difficulty in getting the support of either the Parliamentary Party or the Party at large for Jenkins. But maybe not for the step after that. There's much buzzing and conspiring going on, he says. He is wise and very supportive, even though I suspect he doesn't agree with my long-term strategy.

Then at 1.45 Roger Lowry and I strolled down Parliament Street through the gusting wind and rain to Downing Street. Once again I thought to myself that at last we were through the negotiations and this could be an important moment.

But again it was not to be!

I had taken Roger along with me as a note-taker. However, when we got there, Jonathan Powell said he felt that on this occasion it might be better to have a meeting *à deux*, that Blair's mind was not yet fully made up, etc., etc. So Roger was whisked away while I was shown into Blair's office.

I picked up a copy of the *New Statesman* lying on the table and started to read it when I suddenly became aware of the cacophonous noise of pop music coming form the Cabinet Room. So I wandered into the side office, where Jonathan was sitting, and said, 'Good God, he hasn't converted the Cabinet Room into a pop studio, has he?'

'No, we didn't want to tell you because we felt it was rather impolite. But he has been pressured into watching a video of the Millennium Dome. What you are hearing is Peter Gabriel,' laughed Jonathan, his eyeballs rolling to the ceiling. 'We have told him you are here, but he says it would be rude to leave before the video has finished.'

I said fine, providing we had enough time to discuss what we needed to discuss.

At about 2.15 Blair came through the double doors of the Cabinet Room, in his shirtsleeves as usual, holding a piece of paper.

TB: Life is appallingly busy at the moment. I don't seem to have a second for anything. However, this thing we are involved in, look [he always seems to open with this expression when he has something difficult to say], I have been giving it a lot of thought and my people have been working on the words I should use when Jenkins comes out.

I saw John Prescott earlier this morning. The difficulty is that the firmer I am in favour, the firmer he will come out against. And I don't want that to happen. So, what I am thinking of doing is this: saying that I find the Jenkins report 'very persuasive' and that it has 'affected me'. In essence I am shifting from 'No, but . . .' to 'Yes, but . . .'

PA: Why can't we stick to what we agreed at Chequers? It really is impossible when you and I agree something, which I then get confirmed via Richard and Peter, which then changes yet again when you move the goalposts. Chequers took me as far as I can go. The real point is, how will you answer the question, 'How will you vote in a referendum?' If the presumption is that you will vote 'Yes', that is tolerable. 'Yes, but . . .', is not, I fear, a presumption of voting in favour

TB: Look, this is very, very tough for me. I don't honestly think I can go further than I have said. As I had anticipated, you are telling me now that this is something which you can't accept. But don't underestimate what a big shift it will be seen as for me to have moved from 'No, but . . .' to 'Yes, but . . .'

I was trying not to overreact, so I said that I found his response disappointing but I would go away and think about it. Then, hoping for time to move him again:

PA: What about the timing?

TB: Again, I don't want to find myself boxed in. I need a way out, if necessary.

PA: But that was available in the Chequers words 'intend to'. Of course, if when the time comes we conclude that we would lose a referendum, we certainly wouldn't press you to hold one. That's just common sense. Anyway, I don't mind a bit of conditionality. It is the only way that I can exercise leverage on my party to get them to where I want. And if I can't get it through my party, of course you need an exit, I accept that.

I gained the impression that the timing question was less of a problem than the words. When I asked Blair when he would give me his words, he said, 'Over the weekend'.

I then turned the conversation to what happens post-Jenkins.

PA: You know I want to move ahead fairly fast. I have sent you a form of words, the so-called joint statement – our 'undressing in public'. The more I think about it the more convinced I am that I must use the Jenkins moment to push forward the relationship. Constructive opposition must be locked in place and widened if I am to hold the party at all. But a precursor of that is this joint statement. Are you still OK with that?

TB: The statement you sent seems pretty good to me. But I want to take another look at the words in detail.

PA: They can be agreed later. At this stage it is the act of issuing the statement that I want to confirm, rather than the words.

TB: Yeah, I still think it's a good idea. But we should think about it just a little bit more.

Then into the JCC, at which I voiced my worry that it was losing its efficacy.

Walking back to the House after the JCC with Richard and Bob, I told them about my unsatisfactory meeting with Blair beforehand. They both agreed we should send panicky messages back to Labour to put them under pressure before Blair's words on Jenkins are finalized. So I asked Richard, who is an excellent bully when he wants to be, to set off a few maroons, saying we were really upset by the change of stance. A slight exaggeration. My conversation with Blair was certainly not as I would have wished, but it hasn't taken me into the disaster zone – yet! Maybe we can win something back by making them think we do regard this as a crisis.

Richard went away to speak to Mandelson, Adonis and Derry Irvine, coming back later in the day to tell me that Mandy was saying they didn't think the Chequers agreement was an agreement. To which Richard had tartly asked why, when he had checked it out soon after the event, Mandelson had confirmed that it was.

I also rang Roy at East Hendred to report to him. He was in the middle of a conversation with Adonis when I rang, so I got him to pass on the same messages about our extreme sense of frustration verging on anger at the erosion of the position. He agreed to do this.

I thought this was going to be an historic day, but once again it isn't. There again, I suppose the last stages of a negotiation are always the most difficult.

Sunday, 25 October, Somerset

Bright today, though still blustery. Spent the morning clearing my mail.

Spoke to Jonathan Powell at a little after 11.00 am. He says I won't get the words until tonight 'at best', and even then probably late. Blair is working on them, he says, on the way back from a conference in Vienna. I didn't complain. They are under a lot of pressure. All very nerve-racking.

I consulted with Richard and we agreed not to pester Blair. We should make a fuss about the big things, not the small ones. Though the longer this drags on, the more it becomes an issue, not of detail, but of substance. And I am afraid of being bounced.

At around 7.45 Powell rang. Blair had only just got back. He was exhausted. He hadn't had time to look at the words, but could he contact me again tomorrow? I sighed resignedly and said OK.

Why would he want to delay, except to dilute? On the other hand, he is very cautious.

Monday, 26 October, Westminster

BEGINNING OF THE FATEFUL JENKINS WEEK

We have been putting constant pressure on No. 10 to provide the words they promised, with Roger ringing an increasingly embarrassed Jonathan Powell. First he said it was Saturday, then Sunday, then first thing Monday morning. But nothing so far.

I talked the situation through with Roy. He thinks that Blair is under huge pressure from the Cabinet and that a weakening of the Chequers agreement seems inevitable.

Why does he always do this? He makes an agreement when we meet. Then finds himself subject to individual and collective pressures from the Cabinet. And they have access to him on a daily basis, which I can't counteract because I only see him occasionally.

This is the third time I have asked him to deliver on a confirmed deal only for him to back off later. Richard says he never likes to be cut off and always wants to have room for manoeuvre.

Still, I remain reluctant to ring him because he is under so much pressure from the deepening Kosovo crisis.

Much talk today that NATO is again preparing to bomb Milosevic. It's difficult to insist that sorting out future electoral reform is more important than deciding whether to bomb a fellow European country!

At 6.30 Robert Fox[1] came to see me, full of dire warnings about what will happen to the refugees in Kosovo The snow has started to fall there and those still left in the forest are already dying of cold or starvation. But the real killer will be disease, he says, arising from the overcrowded conditions. Robert spoke of 300 people in a single mosque and private

---

1 Freelance journalist and Balkans expert.

houses with up to eighty occupants. Dysentery is already occurring, as well as serious chest ailments.

By the end of the day, still nothing from Blair. What has gone wrong? To bed around midnight, very perturbed.

Tuesday, 27 October, Westminster

At 10.30am a planning meeting at which we reviewed all the procedures for today and Thursday [the day the Jenkins report is to be published]. Still nothing from No. 10. I brought everybody up to date on where we were (or weren't) with Downing Street.

Later in the morning Roger finally extracted a promise from Powell to send a text through at about 11 o'clock.

Rang Roy to voice my concerns, only to learn that he is seeing Blair at 11.20. I was furious. Blair is trying to do an end run round me by squaring off Roy first. I told Roger to start upping the ante by complaining to Powell about broken promises, etc. Also asked Richard to launch a similar assault on Mandelson. Roy promised to call me after he had seen Blair.

At 11.50 Shirley Williams came to discuss a letter she had sent me suggesting an expansion of JCC discussions to include Europe. I was very frank and told her my long-term plans, asking for her support in getting them through the party. She enthusiastically agreed to help.

Then at 12.10 a taxi to lunch at the *Daily Telegraph*. In the middle of lunch I was paged to call Roger. Then another message saying that something big was about to break which had completely dominated the PM's attention and that of his staff for the last two or three hours[1] – hence the delay on the words.

I told Roger to pull back immediately. If only they had told us before we would have stopped pestering them. Had a pretty strenuous but, I think, respectful difference of opinion on almost everything with the *Daily Telegraph* lot.

On the way back, just as we were emerging from Canary Wharf, I got another message on my pager to say that the PM would be ringing me in a few minutes. As we went through the underpass on the way to the City my

---

1 Ron Davies had resigned as Secretary of State for Wales after a 'moment of madness' when he was robbed at knifepoint having agreed to have dinner with a man he had met on Clapham Common.

phone rang. Downing Street. Could I take a call from the PM? I wasn't about to ask the Downing Street exchange lady to tell him not to bother, so, shortly after he came on the line, I said, 'Thank you for calling, but I'm afraid I am in the car of the editor of the *Daily Telegraph*. Can we speak later?'

'Good God, I wish I had known that. Of course, but when?'

'Well, I'm on my way to the *Daily Express*, so it had better be after that! What about me coming round to see you?'

We agreed to get our offices to fix a time.

Whilst at the *Express* I got the message asking me to see Blair at 5.15. Into a taxi and back to the House of Commons. Dashed upstairs to give the Team Leaders my brief on the Jenkins details under strict terms of confidentiality. Much discussion, in which everybody spoke. All supported the proposals, although all had their individual quibbles of one sort or another. Matthew Taylor and Nick Harvey very good on the need to come out and support this wholeheartedly, whatever our private reservations. An important hurdle cleared.

Then, at the rush, off with Roger to Downing Street. We rattled our way up Parliament Street through the wind and the rain and into No. 10 by the back way.

Blair was in his outer office when we arrived, watching the television report case of the Ron Davies affair. We went into his private office.

I asked him first about Ron Davies. He said that people shouldn't be sacked for their private deeds, unless such actions were either totally outrageous or called into doubt their judgement; but 'there is more to this than meets the eye'. He couldn't risk a protracted scandal as the full story came out little by little. He felt he had to act decisively, otherwise the government would get drawn down into the mire, as Major's had so often been. He would be appointing Alun Michael as the new Secretary of State for Wales. 'He is very close to me and someone who will continue the project in Wales. I will see to it.'

I said I was grateful for that, since I thought that the relationship that had been developing between Lembit Opik (who represents Montgomeryshire for us) and Davies was very important, both to Wales and to the project.

We turned to the matter in hand. He talked me through the words he proposed to use; they were entirely neutral, both as to his attitude to Jenkins and on the timing of a referendum. What did I think? I deliberately let my face fall and sank back on the sofa with a resigned sigh.

PA: This is very depressing. It is entirely contrary to what you and I said at Chequers. We made an agreement between us and I trusted you to keep it; then the Cabinet and your advisers get to you and I find the goalposts moved. The Chequers agreement wasn't easy for me. I stretched my limits to the utmost in order to break the log jam. Frankly, on the basis of what you have just told me, I can't continue. And from your point of view, you will be accused of showing a complete lack of leadership. If you are not clear on this, then four things will inevitably happen: your party will continue to fight a civil war on PR, the push for PR will stop, Jenkins will be put on the shelf; and the opportunity will be lost. This is very bad for me, it could be fatal for the project and it is not good for you, either.

TB: I don't agree. People will see the report and my reaction to it as a massive move forward. And the press will understand that I have moved from 'No, unless' to 'Yes, unless'.

PA (interrupting): If that's the case, fine. But I doubt it. I think they will say that you are sitting on the fence and that by not giving the lead on the question of electoral reform you will be leaving the whole thing in a vacuum which will be filled by your antis.

TB: It has all been very difficult for me. There are some big beasts in the Cabinet who are very hostile to this.

PA: Yes, I recognize you have a difficult decision to make. But the easier you make it for yourself now, the more difficult it will be for me later. I will think about this overnight. But I'm very gloomy.

TB: I think you're wrong. But why don't we call in Ali to discuss it with him?

He walked over to the door and asked for Alastair Campbell to come down. While we were waiting I turned to the referendum.

PA: Could you read me out your words on the referendum again? Because they seem neutral as well. You and I agreed there would be a presumption in favour of a referendum being held this parliament. So why can't you use the words you have already used on the *Today* programme?

TB: What were they?

I couldn't remember the exact words, so I quickly phoned Miranda in my office and asked her. She dug out the *Today* programme transcript and said that the words Blair had used were that he was 'committed to a referendum and it was envisaged that it would be held in this parliament'.

I returned to the sofa and repeated the words.

TB: Look, I just can't close my options on this.

PA: We have been through this time and time and time again. I accept that you can't close options. I am not asking you to. Anyway, I need room to manoeuvre, too. All I am saying at this stage is that it is necessary for you to repeat the words you have already used and say that a referendum is envisaged, and that the presumption will be that it will happen in this parliament.

By now Alastair Campbell had entered the room. I asked him what words the Prime Minister was going to use on Jenkins. Alastair repeated the words that Blair had just said, that he was going to be neutral on both Jenkins and the timing of the referendum.

I then asked him what the press report on this was likely to be. He replied that the Prime Minister was warm about Jenkins, open-minded about the report and not concluded about his own position.

PA: Exactly. That is contrary to what we agreed at Chequers and insufficient for me. What I need to say to my party is that the PM is on our side on this at the moment, but he won't always be. So our working with him is vital if he is to stick to that position. But the more we work against him the less likely it is to happen.

TB: Well, my lot are saying that you guys aren't playing the game anyway. You keep on attacking us. Gordon is always complaining about Malcolm Bruce. I tell him that what Malcolm's doing is perfectly legitimate, but it's tough.

PA: It *is* perfectly legitimate. Yes, Malcolm does sometimes display an irrational dislike of Labour, chiefly for reasons concerned with his seat.[1] But the criticisms he has been levelling at Gordon have been totally fair, and so far have been proved largely right. He is doing a very good job. I know Gordon wants him moved from being Treasury spokesman, but I am not prepared to do that. And nor am I prepared to neuter either him or the Party, when it is not within our agreement.

TB: Yes, I can see that. But still it doesn't improve the situation.

I could see that I wasn't going to get much further.

PA: Look, perhaps there is a solution. Perhaps you can use a form of words that

---

1 Malcolm's seat is Gordon where, for historical reasons, the Lib Dems and Labour are in virulent conflict and where Malcolm nearly lost his seat to the Tories in 1992 because of a rise in the Labour vote.

will satisfy your colleagues but use a press spin which will enable the outcome to be as we agreed at Chequers. Let's work on it a little more.

At this stage Jonathan Powell came in. He looked pretty miserable.

TB: I don't think you quite appreciate what a big step I have already taken. And what a dangerous one it will be in the Cabinet. If some heavy hitters in the Labour Party come out against reform and an overt split develops in the Cabinet, that weakens my government, which doesn't help either you or the project.

PA: I appreciate that. Maybe we should have judged all this, not on what's desirable but on what's possible. But I wish we could have thought of that before. There are two ways our project can go. If you say 'No' to Jenkins and 'No' to a referendum, then constructive opposition and the JCC will end next year. If you find words which stick to the Chequers agreement, then we can move to the next stage. But it all depends on your exact words, so *please* let's see them soon. Then at least we can work on them.

TB: OK. I'll get you the words as soon as possible tomorrow.

By this time Jonathan Powell was pressing him to move to his next appointment. But I said that I wanted a couple more words with Blair in private, so he asked Powell and Campbell to leave.

I was going to tell him about my own future, but then decided against it, as that would be putting him under too much emotional pressure and he knew where I stood anyway. So I stumbled out a few words: 'It'll keep till later, it doesn't have to be said now.' But he almost immediately broke into his own rather emotional speech.

TB: Look, Paddy, I don't want to let you down. We have come a long way together. But you must understand that there are limits beyond which I cannot go at the moment. I remain utterly committed to the long-term process, but I can only do what is possible now.

PA: We have never used the words 'let down' to each other and I'm not going to use them now. Both of us are dealing with the art of the possible. Although I am obviously very disappointed, I don't blame you. You are the best judge of what you can and can't get past your lot and you are right in saying that it would be hopeless if this split your Cabinet. But, as you know, it puts me in a very, very difficult spot indeed. However, let's deal with what we have.

TB: You were going to talk to me about your going, weren't you?

PA: Yes, I was, but you know my position, so I won't labour it. I want to help reshape politics; it's the only thing that is keeping me from standing down. But if this becomes impossible – and on the basis of your words that now looks likely – then it will be time for me to move on. I want to give my successor as much time as possible to get the Party ready for the next General Election. There's no reason why you shouldn't continue to work with him or her. In fact, an early election for the Lib Dem leadership makes the maintenance of constructive opposition by my successor more likely. The later I leave the changeover, the more unpopular you are likely to be. So, if you are going to kick Jenkins and the referendum into touch then there is probably nothing more that can be done to move the project forward until after the next election, which I don't want to fight.

TB: I am terribly sorry about all of this. But I can only honestly tell you how far I can go.

PA: Well, all is not lost yet. I will think some more.

But I left feeling pretty depressed.

Then a fast dash down Parliament Street and across Parliament Square to Cowley Street, where I arrived late for the FE meeting. I took them through Jenkins, which they unanimously supported. Then back to the office for a delayed meeting with Don Macintyre, chief political columnist on the *Independent*. I poured us both a stiff whisky and was just telling him what I thought would happen with Jenkins when we were interrupted by Richard Holme. Don very kindly left so that I could spend ten minutes alone with Richard.

Richard feels as frustrated as I do. He said we must put down markers of severe disappointment straightaway. I asked him to ring Mandelson and say I would consider sending Blair a letter tomorrow.

Then Macintyre again. I was feeling very tired by now, so I curtailed the interview by promising him an exclusive on our plans beyond Jenkins.

Then, utterly exhausted, I signed off my mail and took Miranda home before going back to the flat for supper with Jane.

I am feeling very down. So much out of the window. I really didn't think Blair would do this.

But gradually, as I pondered it further, I realized that things weren't quite as bad as I had first thought. We can perhaps convert Blair's relatively neutral position into one which indicates the direction in which he is travelling. Having gone from 'unpersuaded' to 'undecided', he is at least moving in the right direction.

Not a strong position for me to take to the Party, however. It all greatly heightens the risks I must take to keep this thing on the rails.

Read my way through the press and a UNHCR report on the refugee situation in Kosovo and did some more thinking whilst watching television, dumbly.

Got to bed around midnight, but only slept for an hour or so. Spent most of the night thinking and composing a long letter to Blair in my head, which I got up at 5.00am to write out in longhand. Then rang No. 10 and spoke to the duty clerk. Faxed the letter through to her, asking her to make sure Blair saw it with his breakfast.

Dear Tony,

I am grateful for the fact that we were able to have such a long chat yesterday evening, in what must have been, for you, a very testing day. I promised to think over what we discussed and have decided that it would be useful to let you have, as early as possible, the fruit of this.

Firstly, I need to make it clear that I understand your position. What we are doing here is testing the limits of the possible, not the limits of will. I do not doubt for a second your continued commitment to what we have set our hand to, or your desire to make it possible for me to go to the next step. As you say, it would benefit no one to act in a way which resulted in a split Cabinet and a concerted public campaign against Jenkins by some of your most powerful colleagues . . .

It may, therefore, be that this is another of those moments when, instead of moving fast, we must have patience and move more slowly; when, instead of sharpening the curve of convergence between us, we must be content to leave it as it is.

My worry here, as you know, is that, with a difficult year coming up, there is much risk attached to this.

You are the best judge of what is best for you and the government.

But I am clear what my people will say: 'He's keeping you dangling; he wants to neuter opposition and will ultimately renege' – or some such unfair nonsense which is, nevertheless, what even decent people believe who are not in the loop of politics.

I still think there is room to find a way out of this, based on the words you used on the *Today* programme in respect of timing, and, if we can reach it, a formulation on the main question which leaves your Cabinet colleagues quiescent if not enthusiastic, but enables the press take to be 'Blair moves towards Yes,' or some such.

But, final appeal, it is absolutely vital for us to see your words and make some suggestions as soon as possible. I know you have yet to clear these with Jack [Straw] – but it must surely be possible for us at least to start thinking about them before this happens? We have trusted each other with some very controversial documents over the years and I can, as usual, assure you both of security and of the fact that, in seeing the words, I recognize that they are still not finalized from your end.

I will be in, or around, my office all day – but early is best, for obvious reasons. With very best wishes.

Yours

Paddy

Wednesday, 28 October, Westminster

After much pestering, we finally got their words at about 11.30 am, as follows:

I want to thank Lord Jenkins and the other members of the commission for producing what is an excellent report. I welcome it warmly. The report makes a well-argued and powerful case for the system it recommends. It is very much a modification of the existing British Westminster system, rather than any full-blown PR system as practised in other countries. It preserves the constituency link. It addresses some of the weaknesses of the present system, such as the complete absence of Conservative representation in Scotland and Wales, and the comparable Labour under-representation that occurred in large parts of the South during the 1980s. But before deciding whether or not there should be change, I want both to see this report debated fully and properly in the Labour Party in Parliament and in the country. And we must take account of the radical and ambitious programme of constitutional reform we have already put in place, together with further closely associated changes to come, particularly the reform of the House of Lords. We also need to see how the new systems of elections in Scotland, Wales and for the European Parliament settle down. Constitutional reform should be looked at as a whole before a decision is made and any decision must be made in the interests of the country as a whole, not any party or group. As to the timing of the referendum, we have always envisaged holding one this parliament. The report, however, makes it clear that the system recommended could not be introduced until the election after next. The Home Office has confirmed this practical fact. No final decision need or should be taken now.

They are hopeless. 'Persuasive' has gone and they have taken an entirely neutral position on the timing of the referendum. Completely indecisive and muddled. I am amazed.

If Blair uses these words he is opening himself up to accusations of lack of leadership and ceding the ground to the anti-PR forces in Labour.

Contacted Richard, who is now in Vienna. With his help I amended the words and sent them back to No. 10, together with an annotated text to explain what we were doing.

Deathly silence for the rest of the day.

Sent Roy copies of the correspondence. At about 9.45pm I checked with Roger to see whether he had heard anything. He spoke to Downing Street, who said nothing tonight, but 'something first thing tomorrow morning'. I bet it doesn't come through. They are just playing fast and loose with us.

Went to bed at around midnight feeling increasingly angry.

Thursday, 29 October, Westminster

THE DAY OF THE PUBLICATION OF THE JENKINS COMMISSION REPORT[1]

Up at 7.00 and into the Leader's Co-ordinating Group. Overwhelming support for Jenkins.

As I thought, not a squeak from Downing Street. I rang Roger first thing this morning to ask him to pick up a copy of the report from Roy. He arrived in the office with it at around about 9.00. I dealt with the mail, then got down to reading the document. It is very, very good. Funny and full of Roy-isms. The only government report I have read that made me burst out laughing. Beautifully written.

Then down to see Roy himself to talk it through, telling him of my nervousness at not having heard from No. 10.

At about 11.00, No. 10's rejigged words came through. They have paid no substantial attention to us at all. Blair's main position is still entirely neutral, though he uses warm words about Roy. Persuasive is still out and they have still said nothing about the timing of the referendum. I was furious and tried to reach them to tell them so, but Powell wasn't answering his phone.

From here the day went on down hill. The press conference on the report started off well, but very soon the questions on the referendum began winging in. I put a brave face on it, saying that our strategic aim was to prevent the options being closed for a referendum in this parliament, etc.

1 The Jenkins report proposed a system which became known as 'AV plus': 80–85 per cent of MPs would be directly elected by constituencies, using the alternative vote (AV) system and the remainder (some 100–120 top-up MPs) would be elected by a list system based on geographical area to give a broadly proportional overall outcome.

Our people asked me what line to take. I said, 'Grit your teeth; spin and smile.' But inside I was raging. I felt badly let down.

At 1.00 I did a briefing for political editors, including Colin Brown,[1] Michael Brunson, Michael White and Elinor Goodman. A full room. I came down with a cup of tea and steeled myself to be jolly and upbeat. Somebody asked me whether I admire Blair's style of leadership. I said it wasn't mine: 'I was trained as a commando officer. I lead in a different way. But there is no doubt about the success of his.' I cracked some jokes and Miranda said afterwards that my body language managed to suggest confidence and success. They went away, apparently reasonably satisfied.

At 2.30 a meeting with the peers at which Roy presented his report and I spoke briefly about why it was good for us. During the course of it I whispered to Roy that the words had come through and I would like to show them to him straight afterwards. When he saw them he said he was as depressed as I was. I told him that this was probably it as far as I was concerned, and that I wanted to go. He said he could understand my disappointment, but begged me not to quit too early. I said that if I delayed I might end up leaving with my tail between my legs instead of grabbing the initiative with the Parliamentary Party by doing something early. I promised not to take any rash decisions before speaking to him again.

Roy is very dispirited with Blair himself. I said that Blair's failure to give a lead had left a vacuum which Straw and Labour's anti-PR forces would now fill and by evening the whole thing would probably be kicked into touch. He agreed gloomily.

Richard Holme came into the office afterwards. He thinks we have been bounced and dumped at the same time. And we are both furious about it. He's going to speak to Mandelson again.

At around 5.30 my phone rang. Would I speak to the Home Secretary? Jack Straw came on the line and said that he understood I was pretty upset. Why?

I unloaded my fury on him. He tried to be as close to contrite as he could get. Richard's message had clearly got back to Blair, who (we heard later) had instructed Straw to speak to me. Straw told me he would try to pull things back a bit when he went on Channel 4's news programme at 7.00. I watched it and he did nothing of the sort. Just as I had feared, he started

---

1 Political correspondent at the *Independent*.

dragging out all the reasons for delays in acting on the Jenkins report (very complex; much more complicated than we had thought, etc., etc.). Deadly stuff. If this is pulling back, God knows what attacking it would be like!

Then a couple of glasses of champagne with Roy and the Jo team to 'celebrate' the publication of the report. We put a brave face on it. People genuinely seemed happy, but I think we all know it won't be acted upon.

Then off to see Maureen Thomas to discuss the annual Lib Dem ball that she organizes. Just before I got there my mobile phone rang. It was Robin Cook. I stood out on the pavement in the rain talking to him. He was depressed, too.

Roy made a good case for the report on *Newsnight*, but Jack Straw followed with a complete hatchet job. Just as I had feared, the momentum is now firmly against Jenkins.

Went to bed feeling very angry and very depressed. Spent much time contemplating how and when I should resign. Thursday of next week, I think. But I had better let things settle down a bit. These events always seem worse on the night after they happen.

Friday, 30 October, London

Roger Lowry contacted me this afternoon, at about 2 o'clock, asking if I could take a call from Blair, preferably at home, at around 6.15. Although I didn't feel like it, I decided that I would since I couldn't reasonably claim that I was uncontactable by phone.

He rang on the dot. His tone was soft and mollifying and, if anything, slightly apologetic.

TB: I just thought I'd give you a ring to find out how things are.

PA: Frankly, they are bloody. We are all feeling very bruised. The form of words you used was not what we had originally agreed. And our input made no substantial difference to them. They were, if anything, even worse than the ones you and I discussed earlier in the week. The word 'persuasive' had been removed. And I was shocked that you were not even prepared to use the words you had used the day before at Prime Minister's Questions on the timing of the referendum. It would have cost you nothing but would have been of immense help to me. I spent most of last night wondering whether the whole thing was worth the candle.

TB: But the press has been rather good today. The *Guardian*, in particular, has been excellent. You can thank Alastair for that. He worked very hard on them.

PA: Yes, but you know perfectly well what happened. Today's press reflects only the news until their deadlines of late afternoon. And after that, the spin from your side became much more hostile. I don't know if you saw Jack Straw on yesterday's *Newsnight*. He did a complete hatchet job. We are losing the argument on this. And it's deadly for me.

TB: Look, I have been doing a lot of thinking over the last thirty-six hours. And I have also been talking to Andrew Adonis. He will do me a paper, which I will send you on Monday, about how we can incorporate you guys more into the policy-making process.

PA: Yeah, that's all fine. But it can only happen if I can persuade my party to confirm constructive opposition as our policy for this parliament, and more than that, be prepared to widen it. You haven't given me enough to do that. If I took that proposition to my party now, I would lose. I would go down and the project would end there.

Neither of us wants that. Which is why we need more from you. As you know, for me the timing of the referendum is crucial. I am also at the end of my tether.

It's always us who put the propositions to you. Then you and I agree how to go forward. Then, at the last moment, it's discovered you can't. Then we – never you – go off and find a different way to keep the project on track and the whole depressing cycle starts over again. Frankly, I don't know how long we can keep doing this and, anyway, I'm not sure it's worth doing at all if it falls flat on its face again.

TB: So what you are saying is that it's up to us to come up with a proposal now?

PA: Yes. We can't go on being the *demandeurs* in this process.

TB: OK, I'll make sure Andrew Adonis's paper gets to you as quickly as possible.

PA: That would be very helpful. Then we can review this situation. I'm not saying it's over. In fact, I am desperate to find a way round. But at present I can't see one. So I'll do some more thinking and consulting over the weekend. Meanwhile, it's very important you take some steps to recapture the momentum for Jenkins in the media.

I also asked him specifically about the timing of the referendum. Would it be held after the General Election? And if so, could we really get the system into place before the election after that?

TB: Yes, it is a problem. But I want to look at this one more time before deciding what impact it actually has.

We finished with a brief chat about what we were doing at the weekend. His kids were away, but he had to go to 'some bloody dinner with some bloody barristers' – a favour to Cherie.

It was by far the most human conversation I think we have ever had on the phone and Blair's tone was one of self-reproach, if not outright apology. He is a devil to deal with.

Monday, 2 November, London

Supposedly a day off. Becks had arranged for me to spend today relaxing at Methley Street to make up for a pretty fraught weekend. In the event, I spent the first couple of hours dealing with the mail. Then I got down to some DIY.

At 11.30 Richard Holme came round. I sat him down and told him of my intention to go, saying I needed his advice. He was shocked, but said he understands why. But he doesn't believe this thing can be pulled off without me, etc. He was very kind and understanding. But he told me what in my heart of hearts I already know, but haven't admitted: that I cannot immediately abandon the party. As he said, it would be like taking the party across the Channel and landing them on the Normandy beaches, only to tell them I was handing them over to another general. His view was that I would have to stay until at least after next year's elections.

In the afternoon I went for a walk with Jane and the dog. Blowing a gale and splattering with rain, but we had a good long talk about what next – and when.

Then off to see Roy. I spent an hour with him going through my plans. He also asked me not to do anything rash. If we don't move forward at all this parliament, then I should probably go. But if we do manage to progress then I should stay on until we get bedded down in the new position. He also agrees that Blair has shown a depressing lack of leadership, particularly on the issue of the referendum. But he was very supportive and helpful, as usual.

Tuesday, 3 November, Westminster

Have been pressing for a meeting today with Blair. Eventually No. 10 fixed one for 1.30, but only for half an hour.

So, worried about the lack of time, I rang Jonathan Powell beforehand and told him that:

1. As a result of last week, I believed our relationship was in a crisis.

2. Blair's proposition to me that we should widen the ambit of the JCC to deal with policy matters was unworkable.

3. I would like to go ahead as previously outlined, lock in place constructive opposition with a joint statement and only then widen the JCC's ambit. But I could only sensibly do this if Blair and I had already 'undressed in public' about what the project was about.

4. Furthermore, I could do none of this unless he gave me more comfort on the timing of the referendum. It would be sufficient for Blair to say he was happy to see a referendum this parliament, perhaps at PMQs.

Jonathan promised to pass all this on.

Roger and I arrived on time and were asked to wait in the Cabinet Room. Blair then came out and collected me and we sat down, as usual, in shirtsleeves.

We started talking about Iraq, where Saddam Hussein is contemplating connecting up VX gas [a lethal nerve gas] to missiles, counter to all Security Council Resolutions.

But we then moved on to the main topic.

PA: As you know, I have spoken to Jonathan. We were pretty bloody upset about last week. If this were a commercial negotiation I would be saying, 'This is obviously going nowhere. Let's call it a day and try again later if things change.' But it isn't a commercial negotiation and the action has now shifted from your side to mine. And since you have done less, I have to do more. I must now take this issue to my party and see if I can use Jenkins, even in its very weakened state, to wind things on. But I can't do that unless you give us more.

TB: Yes, I know you have spoken to Jonathan about doing this at PMQs. I don't think PMQs is the right occasion for me to be more positive about a PR referendum in this parliament. It can easily go wrong there. William Hague may push me on it, anyway.

PA: OK, fine. Not in PMQs, then. I don't want to choose the place. You choose that. It is the press 'outtake' that matters. And the press 'outtake' that I need is 'The PM is in favour of a referendum before the next election', or 'The PM would welcome a referendum before the next election'. The kind of words I have in mind are something like: 'The most important thing is that the British public are able to take a well-founded decision. This means taking into account the other major constitutional changes we are making, particularly in Scotland, Wales and the House of Lords. However, if we are able to do this in time to hold a referendum before the next election, then I would welcome that.'

While I was talking he was writing.

TB: OK, I'll see if I can arrange something along those lines. But I would have to consult first. What I don't quite understand, though, is why your lot don't think that being associated with us in delivering an occasional policy success would be useful.

PA: Look, you are confusing the psychology of government with the psychology of opposition. My lot don't have the fruits of government. In fact, they much prefer being in opposition. Talking to you about other policy matters reduces our distinctiveness and ties them more to your coat tails, which diminishes their capacity to act as an opposition party.

TB: I have been giving a lot of thought to this over the last couple of days. My lot keep saying, 'What is in it for us? The Lib Dems are essentially driving the constitutional agenda. Now you have allowed them to get away with changing the voting system. Meanwhile, we get nothing in return.' That's a serious problem for me. An overwhelming majority of the Cabinet are against PR.

PA: Our problems are exact opposites of each other. You have paid upfront with constitutional change and PR, and want something in return. We have pocketed the advantages, but must realize that we too have to pay a price. I shall explain to my party that if we return to outright opposition, then the overwhelming view in your Cabinet against PR is bound to assert itself. But parties don't always behave that logically. Under stress they act like burrow animals; they mass together and go back to what they know best.

This is a crunch time. So far as I'm concerned, on the issue of substance we are almost there. I was wrong. The press have taken the view that you would most likely vote for PR in a referendum, as you said they would. So the real question now is, how can we take this forward? But nothing will happen unless we get the comfortable words from you on a referendum in this parliament before the week-end. Then we can issue a joint statement[1] shortly afterwards. Having done that, you can go away and forget about us. I will spend the next two months campaigning to shift my party. Essentially, putting my leadership on the line. Have you seen my draft of the statement I think we should make?

I pulled it out and gave him a copy.

TB: The words look fine. But this is a pretty big event. I will have to talk to my people about the event, if not the words.

PA: Yes, it is a very big event. And a key element is that you and I will have to pretend to treat each other as equals. The words can be amended, but we need to know pretty soon whether you're prepared to go ahead. Who will handle it from your side?

TB: I think Jack Cunningham is the right person. I will have a word with him.

PA: Unfortunately, Richard Holme is away in New York next week, so Jack had better deal directly with me, initially.

The meeting was now drawing to a close and we had a few words on the

---

1 This is the document I had already drafted on 18 October 1998. My intention was to use the joint statement to lock in place constructive opposition for my successor before stepping down.

economy: borrowing this year will be practically nil and we are on track for a soft landing. Blair and I promised to get in touch again very soon.

From 2.30 to 4.30 a full Jo Group meeting. It was very, very tough. Everybody opposed my going ahead along the lines I have been planning. Chris Rennard was particularly adamant and, for the first time ever, I got quite cross with him. Paul and Nick were also concerned that I am moving too far, too quickly.

They all think I should do nothing. But doing nothing means losing. I can only save this for my successor and prevent the whole thing from going into reverse if I act now. Even Richard is now counselling delay. But they don't understand that I have to leave space for a special conference, which must be out of the way by Christmas, otherwise it will get in the way of next year's campaigning.

There is a real danger that I will split the Party, of course, but that has always been there. Anyway, one of the things I can depend on is that if there is a genuine democratic debate, people will accept the outcome, even if they don't agree with it. That's the great strength of the Lib Dems. I hope it is enough to see me through without a split.

But, of course, I still don't know whether we are going ahead or not. If Blair rejects my proposal, then I will resign before Christmas. The trust between him and me will have been broken and somebody else must manage the relationship on a different basis. The only people who strongly supported me on this were Tim Razzall and Archy, who came in late.

Thursday, 5 November, Westminster

At 1.30 I had a long, long chat with Chris Rennard. He had sent me an e-mail explaining his concerns. This is the first time I will be going against his recommendations. We had quite an emotional discussion, but it was very useful. He, of course, like the others, is frightened of splitting the Party. A real fear, but we must be prepared to debate this properly. Nevertheless, I am nervous about Chris's opposition. But the beauty of Chris is that he gives his opinion as a professional; it is sincere, but never personal.

I nipped down to the chamber at about 4 o'clock to hear the speeches on the Jenkins debate. Straw was outrageous, parodying the report and playing to the Tory gallery. Liam Fox[1] was equally awful, but at least he is

---

1 Member of Parliament (Conservative) for Woodspring since 1992. Tory spokesman for constitutional affairs at the time.

a Tory and we managed to rubbish him. Alan Beith was excellent to begin with, but suffered from being constrained by time and having to make a short speech on a very complex subject.

I have been waiting on tenterhooks all day to hear whether Blair will go ahead or not.

During the debate I got a bleep from Roger saying he had an answer from Downing Street. As soon as Alan's speech finished, I nipped out to speak to him. It appears that Blair *does* want to go ahead in principle. But, as usual, the details remain shrouded in uncertainty. Why is it so difficult dealing with these people? I rang Jonathan Powell myself and asked him to explain exactly what the conversation with Roger meant. Apparently, Blair wants to speak to me tomorrow. But does he want to go ahead on the basis I have proposed? (Roger had gained the impression that he would make the statement on referendums for the Sunday papers and then the joint statement afterwards.) Powell said that the statement (the joint statement, I presume) had been 'in and out of his box three or four times'. So I am no further forward, except in knowing that they will apparently make a decision tomorrow – probably.

Friday, 6 November, London

Another blessed day spent working quietly at home. Lovely weather. Crisp and sunny. The papers, however, are awful. They have all picked up on Jack Straw's parodying of Jenkins. I put a call through to Downing Street to make our displeasure clear. Also tried to contact Roy. I think he should now wade in with Blair. Given the spin the papers have put on Jack Straw's speech yesterday (entirely contrary to what Blair promised me would happen), Jenkins is now dead in the water unless there is a strong counterspin from the Prime Minister himself tomorrow.

I finally got through to Roy at about 4.00. He told me that he had watched the beginning of yesterday's debate on TV, including Jack Straw's speech, but then had turned it off in disgust. I drew his attention to one passage in Straw's speech which left the way open for a referendum to be delayed until after a second independent commission had decided on top-ups. This would effectively mean well into the next parliament.

I spent the day trying to contact Roger Liddle. He spent the day refusing to return my calls.

In the evening Jane and I went out to a restaurant with John and Alyce

Faye Cleese. Great fun. But I went to bed angry, disturbed and full of semi-nightmares about our relations with Labour. Tomorrow will be crucial. But then I've thought so many days were crucial which didn't turn out to be. And as soon as I really think we have come to the end, somehow we lurch on.

Saturday, 7 November, London

Rang Blair at 10.00am, as previously agreed.

TB: Now, where are we?

I said that the ball was in his court. But both Roy and I thought Jack Straw's speech had been a disgrace. Blair told me that he had looked over the speech beforehand and taken the worst stuff out, but that he was cross about it, too.

TB: The problem is that, although the speech itself was broadly OK, he couldn't resist playing to the audience.

PA: Yes, but the problem was that the audience was the Tories! Roy, who watched the speech on television, turned off in disgust. His scheme was being mocked.

TB: Yeah, I'm very sorry about that. I will try and speak to Roy later about it.

PA: If we are to go ahead, one thing must be cleared up first. Some briefing must be done by your office to make sure that those who will be arguing in tomorrow's papers that Jenkins has been kicked into the long grass, find out that it hasn't been. And that it is your wish that a referendum be held before the election. We need that from you and we need it urgently if Jenkins is not to wither and die.

TB: Yes, I remember you telling me about that. When should I do it?

PA: Tomorrow.

He said that he would get Alastair on to it straightaway.

PA: It has to be a strong statement, and not one tucked away at the back of some newspaper. Otherwise my lot will refuse to go along with the next move, which is our joint statement – you have seen my draft?

TB: Yeah, I will submit to you, if I may, a redraft sometime over the weekend. My proposition is that we should do it next Thursday. Is that acceptable to you?

PA: No, it isn't. As I have already explained to you, I am on a tight time schedule here.

TB: Well, what is it exactly you want to do and what part do I play in this?

PA: You put the words recovering the Jenkins position in tomorrow's Sunday papers. Then I can argue to my party that Jenkins is still there to be done. Then we sign the joint statement. Then it's up to me. You have nothing further to do.

TB: The joint statement will be a big thing for me, too.

PA: Really?

TB: Yes, my people are going to think it's a pretty strange thing for me to do. You shouldn't underestimate its impact.

PA: I don't. In my view it will be very big – and needs to be. My lot, however, will be furious; they'll say I bounced them. But will your lot really give you trouble?

TB: Some will. I have to get this through Cabinet as well, which doesn't meet on Wednesday. So for my purposes Thursday is better for this. But I suppose that's too late for you, given that your Parliamentary Party Meeting is the day before.

PA: Yes, I must take it to my PPM on Wednesday.

He then suggested we should do it at the 4 o'clock Downing Street lobby briefing on Wednesday afternoon,[1] after PMQs but before my PPM at 6.00.

PA: That leaves me very little time to alert my MPs properly before it breaks on the television news. That will greatly increase the bounce factor with my MPs and therefore add to my difficulties. But it looks like the only option. Just as long as there aren't any leaks beforehand.

TB: I don't see why there should be.

PA: Your lot are leaky as sieves. I can't even have a private conversation with you without it ending up in the press. I don't now if you have seen the *New Statesman* today, but it says you are about to offer me a number of goodies [a car, extra office allowance, etc.] in order to make my life easier. Leaks like this only go to make my life more difficult.

---

1 There are two daily press briefings at Downing Street – one at 1.00am and the other at 4.00pm.

We agreed to go ahead with the announcement on Wednesday, provided Alastair Campbell got the right words in the press.

Over the phone I could hear a bit of a kerfuffle in the background. He put down his phone and came back after a minute or so, saying, 'Sorry, family things. I promised to take Kathryn to her music lesson.'

He rang off, promising to get back to me once he'd managed to speak to Alastair.

After I put the phone down, I thought, 'At last – it's done. We are on track.' The only difficulty will be if there is a slip between what Blair says and what Campbell actually does. Campbell is, if course, hostile to the project in general, so anything could happen.

I immediately rang Roy in Scotland, who was delighted. Then a wild flurry of phone calls to everyone else I thought should know, although I didn't manage to get through to Richard in New York.

I later found out that Alastair Campbell had spoken to Patrick Wintour of the *Observer*. I am extremely nervous that if it comes out tomorrow it will be a mouse of a story.

All afternoon I was expecting calls from David and Miranda saying they were under siege from the *Guardian*. Eventually, having heard nothing, I asked David to contact Wintour, who confirmed that 'Blair had told friends he did not exclude the possibility of a referendum in the next parliament'. Hopeless. Wintour didn't even see it as a story. I was furious. I couldn't make up my mind whether this was deliberate obfuscation on Blair's part, mischief-making by Campbell or just a failure in communication. One of the latter two, I concluded.

At 5.50pm, after a bath, Jane and I left for the Remembrance Day event at the Albert Hall. There was a splendid youth marching band. And the grand finale of the massed bands led by the Royal Marines was electrifying.

Afterwards, dinner with the British Legion. I was paged halfway through dinner. Could I call Downing Street? Apparently, the *News of the World* is carrying a story tomorrow on Nick Brown[1] being homosexual, his having been shopped by one of his lovers. Downing Street thought I was on GMTV tomorrow and wanted to brief me. It's Ming who's on, not me, so I rang him to pass on the message. Once again we have been derailed by an internal Downing Street crisis.

---

1 Member of Parliament (Labour) for Newcastle upon Tyne East since 1983. Labour Chief Whip 1992–8. Minister for Agriculture, Fisheries and Food 1998–2001.

Sunday, 8 November, London

At 6.45am I rang Ming to brief him on Nick Brown before his GMTV interview. Then I settled down to draft a letter to Blair expressing my concern about the failure to get anything into the *Guardian* and enclosing my proposed statement for him to counteract the damage done by Straw's speech. The statement I suggested was as follows:

The Prime Minister warmly welcomed Jenkins and sees it as very much part of the live programme of his government. It has not been, nor will be, killed off.

As for the timing of the referendum, he still hopes it will be held at the earliest moment when it is possible for the British people to make a well-informed decision. If that can sensibly be done, as envisaged in the Labour manifesto, before the next election, so much the better. If that proves impossible for practical reasons, then it should be held at the earliest appropriate moment afterwards.

I completed this by 9.00 and faxed it to the duty clerk of Downing Street.

At 9.30, to Whitehall for the Remembrance Day service. An hour or so's wait with the high commissioners in the Map Room of the Foreign Office before being led out to the parade. The service was, as usual, brief but dignified. Overcast and raining slightly. Somehow suitable.

By the time I got home it was just past 1.00. Rang David, who had heard nothing. By two he had still heard nothing so I rang the duty press officer at Downing Street and exploded, demanding Campbell should contact David immediately. Shortly afterwards he did.

Over lunch I got a call from Richard in New York, who is nervous about the whole event. I read out my Blair letter to him. Richard has tried to contact Mandelson, but failed. Finally, at 3.30, I heard from David that Campbell had briefed Ewen McAskill at the *Guardian*. I asked David to really build the story up, giving him some quotes from us. But when he rang he was told that tomorrow's papers would be full of Nick Brown; McAskill couldn't fit our story in but would give it a good splash on Tuesday. This is a risk. If it misfires, then it's our last shot before Wednesday. But, on balance, I think, it's a risk worth taking.

Settled down to making some preparations for the week ahead, including a timetable for consultation, etc. This is going to be very tight. Not unreasonably, I am going to be accused of bouncing the Party.

Chris Rennard, who had been working in Cowley Street all day, faxed me through a minute on the implications of a referendum in the next parliament, again stressing his opposition to the joint statement.

It was a strange minute, almost bitter in tone. I was very disturbed and rang him. We cleared the air, but he obviously passionately believes that I am taking a wrong step. He seems to think we can simply sit tight and demand that Labour deliver PR to us. This is unrealistic. If the *Guardian* reports, as we hope, on Tuesday that the Prime Minister is in favour of a referendum before the next election, then the question is how to make that happen. Going into outright opposition won't work. He said he'd rewrite the minute.

I also had a word with Paul, who has been in New York, too, and faxed through to him the exchange of letters between Blair and myself and also the letter for MPs which I have drafted. Paul also thinks I'm moving too fast. But to delay is to lose Jenkins.

To bed rather disturbed. This coming week is crucial. Spent much of the night thinking about it.

Monday, 9 November, Westminster

At 2.30 off to a planning meeting, at which Bob did one of his exploding acts. He said he was completely opposed to the whole thing; it was a disaster; I mustn't go ahead, etc. Chris followed. Then Nick. I listened to them and then said quietly that I had considered their views but I still wanted to go ahead. If we wait, Jenkins will be lost. And if, as they all want, we wait until next year, the window will have closed completely. The only time is now – although I recognize the risks are great. A long and tortuous meeting, but finally we got down to some detailed planning.

Later in the afternoon I had a long chat with Archy Kirkwood. He had been as hesitant as hell before. But now, bless him, he is one of the few providing me with real backbone. Then Don Foster, who also backs the move and has agreed to help during this coming week. But such colleagues – Archy, Ming and Don – are very few in number.

At 6.15 Alan Beith, followed by Diana Maddock, who is now President of the Party. I told them both that I was thinking of pressing to widen the JCC remit and, unsurprisingly, both advised against.

Then back to the office for more planning. We got down to working through each of the various documents and talking about timings. I had wanted to tell the Parliamentary Party on Wednesday morning but in the end decided I couldn't do so until 3.30. That will raise the bounce factor horrendously. Oh dear! We didn't finish until around 9 o'clock, at which time I stumbled down to the canteen to have a bite to eat and then home. No votes tonight.

Tuesday, 10 November, Westminster

At 8.30am a planning meeting. Bob again said it was all impossible, we shouldn't do it, etc. Chris Rennard sent messages to the same effect. Nick Harvey also. All said I could never get it past the Party. But I said I still wanted to press ahead.

Then at 3.45 Bob came to see me again. Still advising against. A long, in-depth discussion. Then Andrew Stunell, who is also, of course, vociferously against. Both are strongly opposed to my plan, but are still giving me their best advice on how to handle it – which is most generous.

Then, at 4.30, another planning meeting for two hours, to make sure we had everything tied up. At 6 o'clock Diana again, to discuss widening the work of the JCC. Would I want a special FE? I said that I was pretty certain I would. She was terribly inquisitive as to why. I told her I was almost certainly going to bid for an extension of the JCC. At this she looked very gloomy and said I'd never get away with it.

Today and yesterday there have been faxes flying backwards and forwards almost on the hour between ourselves and Downing Street. Amending and perfecting the text, accompanying statements and timings, etc. All this somewhat delayed because Blair has been tied up in discussions with Clinton on Iraq. (One of the problems with this whole exercise is that it has been far too confined to Blair and me, so if he is tied up with something bigger, nothing happens.)

Eventually, the final text arrived. Almost perfect. A far better statement than the draft I had sent him. Richard in New York is still advising against.

Amazingly, no leaks yet. But I will be amazed if we get to 4 o'clock tomorrow without someone finding out.

Down to dinner, votes throughout the evening and home at 10.00. Tumbled into bed after midnight. I am very nervous. Last night I slept a bit better – I always do after I have taken a substantive decision – but tonight was full of nightmares. I am also getting a stye in my eye. I haven't had one of those since I was a teenager. A sure sign of tiredness and strain.

Wednesday, 11 November, Westminster

THE DAY WE ISSUE THE JOINT STATEMENT

D Day! Up at 4.30. Made myself a cup of tea, then sat at my desk listing things to do and people to see. I also drew up a brief plan of how to tackle the PPM tonight. After which I e-mailed two pages of questions and answers to Andrew for those who had agreed to speak in favour at tonight's PPM. Then rang Kate and Simon to tell them that I may not be the leader of the Party by tonight. Both wished me luck. Kate finished by saying, 'Come on, Dad, you know you can do it. You always have!'

Then I rang Jane. I told her, 'It'll be very tough today. And I cannot be certain I will win at the Parliamentary Party Meeting tonight'.

She replied, 'Do you really have to do it?'

'Yes. I believe I must.'

She wished me luck.

Left the flat at about 7.30 and caught the 159 as usual to the office for an 8.30 planning meeting. Pretty full attendance. People are well aware of the risks, and are very nervous about it. I talked through the PPM with them, then checked through the letters being sent out to MPs. I asked Nick Harvey if he would be prepared to speak to the press between the announcement at 4.00 and the PPM at 6.00, if, as I anticipated, Alan Beith would not. He was obviously reluctant. I immediately recognized that putting pressure on Nick (who has been utterly splendid throughout this) to carry more of a burden than he wants is unreasonable. If I go down, he will be one of the leadership contenders, and I don't want to damage his chances. So I immediately pulled back. I'll get someone else to do it.

The meeting finished at 9.30 am.

The final joint statement read:

JOINT STATEMENT BY THE RT. HON. TONY BLAIR, MP, AND RT. HON. PADDY ASHDOWN, MP.

In recent years the Labour Party and the Liberal Democrats have been willing to co-operate with one another on a number of different issues in the interests of the country. This made sense and has helped to widen support for important measures in the modernization of Britain.

Nowhere has this been more true than over constitutional reform. Before the election, Robin Cook and Robert Maclennan negotiated a crucial agreement bringing together key elements of constitutional reform such as devolution, the incorporation of the ECHR into UK law and reform of the House of Lords. That agreement also paved the way for the Jenkins Commission on electoral systems, whose report was published a fortnight ago. Together we have moved the government of our country decisively and irreversibly closer to the people.

The Cook/Maclennan agreement has been important to the work of the government and has helped Ministers to make tremendous progress since the election.

Our two parties will continue to co-operate on constitutional reform. The modernization of our politics is a vital part of the modernization of Britain. It will create a more democratic and pluralist Britain where the rights of the people are strengthened and where national diversity, which contributes so much to Britain, is properly recognized.

The key vehicle for co-operation over the past year has been the Joint Consultative Committee. It has met six times and has been an important and valuable forum to discuss how reform is to be taken forward.

Following the last meeting of the JCC, we have now agreed that Jack Cunningham and Alan Beith review its work and consider how to develop its effectiveness.

We believe it is now appropriate to widen the work of the JCC. This will be an important step in challenging the destructive tribalism that can afflict British politics even where parties find themselves in agreement. Of course we are two sovereign and independent parties working together where we agree and opposing each other where we do not. Our parties will continue to offer different choices to the British people in the ballot box whenever the appropriate opportunity arises. To do otherwise would weaken British politics and diminish the choices available to the voters.

We are confident this step forward can deepen co-operation and result in widening support for the kind of progressive change which we wish to see and to which we believe the British people are strongly committed.

Our aims are simply stated.

To work together in building a modern Britain. To create a new, more constructive and more rational culture for our national politics. To ensure the ascendancy of progressive politics in Britain, against a Conservative Party which seems determined to travel further and further to the Right. And to continue the re-shaping of British politics for the next century.

TONY BLAIR   PADDY ASHDOWN

After the meeting I asked Alan Beith to come and see me. I gave him the joint statement and accompanying letters. His face blanched when he saw how bold we were being. I asked him whether he was prepared to go on television to make the announcements between 4 o'clock and the PPM. 'No. That would undermine my position as chair of the Parliamentary Party. I will do it afterwards, but not before.'

So I rang Ming in Scotland who, stalwart trooper that he is, agreed to cancel an event up there and do the television stuff.

Then at 10.30 Diana Maddock. I told her what I was going to do and she sat with her head in her hands, saying, 'Oh dear, oh God, this is terrible, what a disaster.' Then I showed her the documents. The sight of a piece of paper with Blair's and my signatures on it seemed to help. She gave me a long lecture on how to handle the Federal Executive, but she went out calmer than she came in.

Then some work on PMQs. I had thought of something about cannabis, because I wanted to show that we could still take a very clear Lib Dem line. But my office advised strongly against this. Downing Street, meanwhile, had suggested that if I wanted to go on Iraq I would get a substantive and important answer, but I decided against this as well. The big thing today is to carry the Parliamentary Party, and a key part of this is to show them that I can continue to oppose Blair. So we agreed I'd go on pensions. I quickly phrased the question I wanted, then got back to the preparations for this evening.

At 11 o'clock Malcolm Bruce rang asking to come and see me. He feels he has been taken out of the loop; that I never discuss anything with him. I agreed to meet him at 1.30.

Jim Wallace came in at my request at 1 o'clock. I showed him the statement and swore him to secrecy. I expected a huge reaction from him on Scotland. But he was pretty calm. He obviously doesn't agree with what I'm doing – he gave me a long lecture on bouncing the Party – but he sees why I'm doing it. An amicable discussion.

Malcolm Bruce at 1.30. I think he was too dumbfounded to react properly. Then at 2 o'clock Richard Livsey. He said that he thought it was a wonderful idea. I was absolutely right to do it and he would back me fully. I value his support but I suspect he has not thought through the real implication for the Party in Wales.

Then down to the Members' Lobby at 2.40, expecting to be approached by the press because the story had leaked. But nothing! I am amazed. One of the most successful *coups de théâtre* in which I have ever participated. As I wandered through the lobby and into the chamber I saw them chatting away and thought to myself, 'Little do you know.'

At PMQs Hague was not good. My question was adequate, but not startling. A Labour back bencher asked whether, since they were firing retired people off into space, the PM would think of suggesting me for the first passenger list.[1]

Out at 3.30. I had arranged to call the MPs to be bleeped to say that there was an important letter[2] waiting for them to read in the Whips' Office. I had asked Roger to hand out the letters, but to stay there so he could listen to the reaction and report back to me later. As predicted, huge outrage about being bounced. And huddles of people plotting away like mad. I am told that Phil Willis and others had already been planning to put down a resolution at conference to end the JCC. So they are doubly furious, because this heads them off at the pass.

Upstairs, in my office, I scribbled a note to Phil asking if we could have a word. He came up and we had an interesting and surprisingly constructive discussion. I like Phil and rate him highly; he is absolutely straightforward. Although he bitterly opposes what I'm doing, I think he recognizes why I am doing it.

Then a series of journalists: Peter Riddell, Hugo Young, Alan Rusbridger,

1 A reference to retired astronaut John Glenn, who had recently participated in a US space mission at the age of 77.
2 See Appendix H.

Peter Kellner and Phil Stephens.[1] All very satisfactory. Rusbridger told me that they would be fully on board, as did Simon Kelner from the *Independent*. If they honour their pledges in tomorrow's papers, that will be very, very useful. During the ninety-minute press briefing. Roger kept popping in to say that the revolt in the Parliamentary Party was growing. I'm sure it is.

We had fixed to release the letter only two hours before the 6 o'clock PPM so that MPs didn't have time to see the news or react to party input before discussing it. This proved the right judgement.

The PPM was very tough and lasted three and a half hours.

I opened by saying that I had pushed them a long way in the past and had asked them to take some dangerous steps. We had worried about these steps (e.g. the abandonment of equidistance) at the time, but I hoped that, on reflection, they agreed that they had paid huge dividends. This, however, was the last step I wanted them to take. We were now at the destination I wished us to be for the rest of this parliament (unless we fought a PR referendum with Labour). But it was really quite a small step. Just confirming constructive opposition, then widening it. Something which had been widely anticipated.

But, of course, the context was big. Which was why I wanted them to know about not only my long-term vision but also about Blair's. I finished by reminding them of the story of Gaitskell, who, when he made his infamous speech saying that Labour should be out of Europe, was cheered to the echo. But, when he finished, his wife had leaned over to him and said, 'But, dear, the wrong people are cheering.' I said that, before they booed, they should watch who else was booing. I anticipated that the Tories would be booing because they are scared to death that we were, at last, getting our act together with Labour ('Remember Baldwin's injunction to his party: "Never let Labour and the Liberals get together, or it will be the death of us."') And the Labour left would be booing for the same reason.

There followed a tidal wave of criticism, led by Richard Allan. All the usual suspects pitched in, although Phil Willis was more moderate than he could have been, largely as a result of our earlier discussion, I suspect. An hour of unrelenting criticism. Then the mood began to change, led by Matthew Taylor, who gave a powerful speech arguing the opposite case. Roy was also there (at my request) and told everybody that the closer they

1 Political editor of the *Financial Times*.

got to power, the more likely were they to be bounced from time to time. There was a vote at 7.00, so I responded to the main points that had been raised before going down to the lobby and coming back for what I hoped would be the second, cathartic phase of the meeting.

It worked a charm. Slowly, slowly the mood changed.

Simon Hughes had left about halfway through the first session, saying he was off to open some constituency functions. But it was later suggested to me that he was seen on the phone ringing supporters round the country. It was a fatal move, because he missed the shift in mood.

Alan Beith chaired the meeting very well, bringing out all the hostiles first. Ming came in splendidly, as did Archy, Nick and Don. By around 8.45 I reckoned that about 50 per cent were in favour.

At this point Simon came back in, thinking the mood was still as before, and made an impassioned speech against. There were a few more interventions, including a pretty deadly one from David Rendel, who suggested an amendment to the JCC clause saying that we should explore the possibilities of widening its remit but no more. I said that would not do. We should vote on a clear resolution, not one which risked being misunderstood by the press. At this stage Simon unwisely insisted on his vote. I was saved. When Alan called the vote, Simon put his hand up, followed by Adrian Sanders, but no one else – not even David.

The rest all voted for the resolution, including Charles.

In the course of the debate Charles had given a very intelligent speech in which he had outlined areas of opposition, but hadn't said which side he'd come down on. A perfect positioning speech, should it all go wrong for me.

So, thanks to Simon's insistence on a vote, I now have the overwhelming backing of the Parliamentary Party, including Charles.

I thanked them, said I was immensely relieved and fully understood that I had tested them all to the limit.

At 9.30, exhausted, I went back to my office. David and Miranda dashed off to deal with the press while Don and Nick and others came in for a whisky. Miranda was all bright-eyed, saying she'd never seen such a dramatic meeting. She thought it had been as close to a triumph as I could have expected. 'Triumph' is an overstatement, but at least the gamble has paid off thus far – though I have paid a heavy price for it.

Got home at about 10.30, having eating nothing all day apart from a sandwich at lunchtime. So I grabbed some peanuts, a piece of bread and some cheese and watched Liz Lynne on *Newsnight* with Tony Benn – both fulminating against this outrage.

Excellent!

I am not home and dry yet, but I have successfully negotiated the first stage.

Thursday, 12 November, London

On the *Today* programme at 7.30, with Blair coming on after 8.00. I tried to sound very mollifying, saying I understood how difficult it was for some people in my party to understand what we were trying to do, because it was rather unusual. But we had to break with tribalism or we could never get anywhere. Little did I know that this would subsequently be taken as an insult to those who disagreed with me.

Afterwards, the Team Leaders' meeting. People quite calm today. But the Party reaction is beginning to come in, and it's furious.

Then a dash to Waterloo for the train down to Somerset. On the way I looked at my e-mails. Anger reverberating from every corner of the Party. Some people very bitter and insulting. Others saying they would now raise a campaign dedicated to removing me as leader. Betrayal was a frequently used word. One person went so far as to say that I was the Party's Neville Chamberlain, who had come back with a piece of paper. This took me aback. I had expected opposition, but neither in such quantity nor of such virulence. Oh dear. I will clearly have to spend much more time trying to win the Party round than I had anticipated. On the other hand, they said all this when I abandoned equidistance.

At least the newspapers are good today. The *Guardian* is splendid, although the *Independent* has a whiff of the internal revolt.

Jane picked me up at Crewkerne at 7.30. She found me, I fear, somewhat depressed.

The FE meeting on Monday will be very tough. I thought I had got over the key hurdle with the PPM, but the FE and party hurdles will be much higher than I had originally expected. And there are signs of people calling for a special conference, as I'd anticipated. Others, with a better idea of how to campaign, are saying that they will run a four-month campaign leading up to the next Party Conference in Edinburgh in March. If they do that I may have to go to a special ballot of the members. (Although I will have a greater chance of winning if the decision is made by all party members, who are normally more supportive of the leader and less hostile than conference delegates.)

Sunday, 15 November, Somerset

Spoke to Robin Cook yesterday, who told me that the allies were going to bomb Iraq last night. But Saddam backed down at the last moment. The B52s were, apparently, actually in the air when they were turned back by the Americans.

The newspapers aren't bad today, although the *Observer* is a little disappointing. Yet more furious e-mails and further discussions about ballots. This looks increasingly likely to be the only way out. But, I wonder, will the others see it coming?

To bed around midnight, having cleared yet more e-mails (2,500 at the last count). Very nervous about tomorrow.

Monday, 16 November, House of Commons

The FE was predictably horrendous.

It went on for four hours and followed the same pattern as the PPM. A huge outpouring of anger, then catharsis.

Jackie Ballard sat with the antis in one corner, co-ordinating their attacks and trying to move a motion that there should be no widening of co-operation. Excellent speeches in favour made by Dennis Robertson Sullivan[1] and Matthew Taylor, with helpful interventions from several others. Jackie first put forward an alternative resolution, then tried to introduce a wrecking amendment. So we took the amendment first and it went down hard. After which their tactic shifted to 'strengthening' the original resolution I had put down: a paragraph was inserted which expressed regret at my bouncing the Party. The vote went 10–9 in my favour. I didn't expect the vote against to be quite so high. Too tight for comfort.

A discussion in my office afterwards over whiskies: Paul Tyler, Nick Harvey, Chris Rennard, Tim Clement-Jones and Lembit Opik. I said that I wanted a ballot of members, as that would give me the democratic legitimacy to see through the next year. (Discussion of this had been deferred to the next FPC meeting.)

Most were opposed to this, saying that it would be potentially divisive.

1 Chair of the Federal Financial and Administration Committee, and Treasurer of the Scottish Party.

I said we should keep the possibility of a ballot on the table, as a threat to the antis if they insisted on calling a special conference. If they withdrew the call, I would withdraw the all-member ballot.

The Federal Policy Committee tomorrow. I think that might be even worse.

Tuesday, 17 November, London

The Federal Policy Committee at 6 o'clock. Probably the worst meeting I have ever attended. David Howarth[1] acting angrily, bitterly and almost beyond reason. Strenuously backed up by Tony Greaves,[2] Gareth Epps[3] and Conrad Russell. There followed a long debate in which I was criticized up hill and down dale. David Howarth then moved a resolution to end constructive opposition. I responded that this was clearly beyond the competence of the committee. The FPC dealt with policy; the FE with strategy. There was a vote and I won handsomely.

There then developed the most terrifying row, which must have been similar in tone to those suffered by Labour in the 1980s from the extreme left. It was embittered and bad-tempered, with people arguing about procedural matters rather than substantive ones.

Finally Conrad, who had been sitting sulphurously all evening, put forward a resolution that the FPC couldn't see anything on the policy front on which we could co-operate with Labour. It was defeated. The opposition called for a recount. As chairman I had abstained previously, but this time I put my hand up. It was defeated again, 9–6. David Howarth immediately rushed off to fire a blow-by-blow report of the meeting to the Press Association to get his spin across. A really bruising debate.

By the end feelings were running so high that I adjourned for ten minutes before getting down to the ostensible business of the meeting, a policy paper on local government. I sat there dumbly, then left to have some dinner. That cheered me up.

Quite an amusing table. I sat next to Jackie, who barely spoke to me. I never mentioned what an awful time I had just had at the FPC as I particularly didn't want her to know how hurt I felt.

1 Party activist.
2 Made Lord Greaves of Pendle in 2000.
3 Party activist.

Then up to my office to clear the work that had piled up.

At 9.30 a call from Downing Street. Would I speak to the Prime Minister? He wanted to talk about the Bill which is currently in the Lords introducing PR for Europe.

TB: The Tories are continuing to oppose. I think we may have to give up the Bill.

PA: That would mean the end of our relationship and probably the end of me as well.

TB: Why? We will have done our best to get it through. But if the Tories frustrate it there isn't much we can do.

PA: But that's not the way my party will see it. If we cannot get this through, what chance Jenkins? It will cause a riot with my lot if you allow the Tories to kill this Bill.

We ended our discussion by agreeing to talk later and with me saying that I would see if I could find a way round it.

Blair indicated that we had a day or so to think about it. What I didn't realize until later was that they had already decided that the debate in the Lords on PR for Europe would end tomorrow. Why will he never tell me the truth when he thinks it might be uncomfortable?

Somewhat dejected, I signed off my last few letters and rang Paul Tyler to tell him the bad news. Paul's view, like mine, is that our party will judge the government not on efforts, but on outcome. If they cannot deliver PR for Europe then the relationship is over. I agree.

I put on my coat, walked out and got the bus home. Arrived back at the flat after 11.30. Went to bed after the midnight news, but couldn't sleep.

Wednesday, 18 November, Westminster

A glorious day. Beautiful clear blue sky and a deep frost. I woke up to hear Jack Straw on the *Today* programme saying that they would not use the Parliament Act[1] to enforce the Euro Election Bill's passage; if it fails today,

---

1 The Parliament Acts of 1911 and 1949 restrict the powers of the House of Lords and assert the supremacy of the Commons. Under the Parliament Act, if a Bill has been passed by the Commons in two successive sessions it can go for Royal Assent, even if it is not passed by the House of Lords. The government, therefore, could invoke the Bill to overcome opposition in the Lords and put the PR for Europe legislation through.

that is the end of it. I am deeply alarmed. Blair did not tell me last night that they had already taken the decision, or that Straw would be pursuing this line today. So I decided to fire off a very quick letter to him written in the strongest terms. I composed it in my head over breakfast and started dictating it into my dictaphone on the 159 bus travelling in.

Walked across to Cowley Street, about quarter of an hour early, for the Leader's Co-ordinating meeting and spent the next ten minutes finishing my letter so that it was ready for Becks when she came in at about 8.15.

We started the meeting at 8.00. A long discussion on whether there should be a members' ballot. The overwhelming view was that there shouldn't be, but I insisted on keeping it on the table. I would withdraw it if the antis withdrew their threat to call a special conference. Not before.

As we finished, Roger came across with the typed-up letter. Faxed it over to Downing Street at about 11.15.

Dear Tony,

When we spoke last night I did not realize that you were intending to say on the news today that the 'ping-pong'[1] with the European Elections Bill was going to end today and that you would, if necessary, drop the Bill.

I hope this is just a tactical 'raising of the stakes'. Otherwise, we have absolutely no time to work in to resolve this matter. Jack Straw has consistently told Alan Beith that he would have to threaten this at this stage but that, if necessary, you would use the Parliament Act as a last resort. I pray that is the case.

On the basis of the assurances that I have been given and those given to Alan, I have told people in my party, who were telling me that you intended to break faith on this, that this was nonsense. I have just had a very bruising experience indeed getting through the joint statement and the widened remit [for the JCC]. This issue has come up on many occasions. I have told the Party not to worry. I was sure that the Bill was intact and that you had given me that assurance. If now you drop this Bill then you will put me in a simply impossible position. My party will conclude (justifiably, in my view) that if you are not prepared to deliver on the promise of PR in the European elections because of hostility in some levels in your party, there could be no prospect that you would deliver on Jenkins. I simply will not be able to hold them to the widened remit, which has cost both me personally and the party a very great deal to get through. *I have no doubt that, if this happens, my personal position will become untenable and the whole JCC exercise could be in*

1 The House of Commons term for batting a piece of legislation backwards and forwards between the Commons and the Lords, when each disagrees and each makes amendments the other can't accept.

jeopardy. I am sorry to put it to you so bluntly. But it is important that I lay out the options very clearly.

This is a moment of choice. And the choice is between our continuing relationship, along the lines we have worked for the last five years, and those in your party who would wish to have a system for the European elections which is less democratic but which makes little difference to the final electoral outturn.

I am more than happy to play this game of 'ping-pong' with you for a few further rounds. But in the end we will have to make the choice.

Yours

Paddy

At about 12.30 Blair rang again: 'I got your note. Jack was wrong. Of course we will use the Parliament Act.'

I heaved a sigh of relief.

PA: Why don't you keep the thing going through the night? The Tories won't be able to produce their numbers at the dead of night.

TB: No, you're wrong. The problem with hereditaries is that they replenish themselves. We have done a very careful calculation and have worked out that the Tory lot are in fact younger than ours. So ours will drop off their perches faster than theirs.

PA: Then why not carry it through to Monday? The Tories are trying to take you to the wire.

TB: No, we must finish tonight. We don't think we can keep our numbers there.

I concluded the conversation believing that we have actually caused Labour to change their minds on using the Parliament Act. (This was later confirmed by Michael Brunson of ITN, whom I bumped into on the street outside the House after the drama was over.)

I was due to go and see Blair this evening to discuss my future but Downing Street could only give me ten minutes at 7.30. It didn't seem sensible to talk about such matters so briefly and on such a day, so I pulled it. Had a chat with Archy about it, however. He thinks I should go now. 'Everybody else will try to persuade you to stay. But I don't think it's in your best interest.' Then we wandered across to the Westminster pub to have a drink with Jim Wallace and the Scottish team, who were celebrating the final passing of the Scottish Devolution Bill today.

During the evening the Commons completed the last stage of the Euro Elections Bill and it went to the Lords. At around 9.30 the Lords voted.

Against again. But this time the majority against dropped, and some of the Tories had already begun to break away. Tristran Garel Jones[1] made a particularly splendid speech. Bernard Weatherill[2] also warned them of the constitutional dangers of resisting the House of Commons on a constitutional issue which had been in Labour's manifesto at the election. A moment of great tension, which I watched on television. Labour's leader in the Lords, Margaret Jay, responded swiftly by saying that they would use the Parliament Act. A great sigh of relief all round. Many of our Euro candidates had thought the government would renege on this. Lord Cranborne, leader of the Tories in the Lords, made a delphic speech implying that the Parliament Act wouldn't be needed, since they wouldn't resist the passage of the Bill. But I'm not so sure. I think Hague is up for a fight to the death. Foolish, but that appears to be what he wants to do. Bill Rodgers agrees with me, as does Paul.

Off home at 11 o'clock by bus. To bed at about twelve. The emotional strain of the last few days is beginning to tell. I am getting frequent headaches and, I think, another cold.

Thursday, 19 November, Westminster

Up at 7.00. I heard the phone ring while I was in the bath. A message had been left on the machine. The PM. I rang back.

TB: I think we should really go hell for leather now that the Tories have agreed not to oppose the Euro Bill.

PA: I'm not convinced. I was depressed to hear Jack humiliating them in the House yesterday. That only makes it more difficult for them to get out of the hole they have dug for themselves. We should certainly go at them hard, but only when they have made a clear commitment not to oppose the Bill, and I don't think they have done that yet.

TB: No, I think they have. I've been told privately that they have decided not to oppose the Bill.

PA: Then please, please, please let's wait until they announce it publicly. Let's not make it any more difficult for them to retreat.

1 Member of Parliament (Conservative) for Watford and Minister of State for Europe in the Major government.
2 Lord Weatherill (known as Jack), formerly Speaker of the House of Commons, now Convener of the Crossbenchers in the House of Lords.

TB: Yes, perhaps you are right. I had better tell Jack to tone down his remarks today.

I then told him that one of the things that really scared the Tories was that their actions might drive us even closer together. 'So why not make some elliptical comment about encouraging tactical voting?'

He seemed to think this was a good idea.

I then got dressed and headed for the bus.

Later in the morning I rang Jonathan Powell. They have been told that Hague is going on the lunchtime news to say that the Tories in the Lords will, as I suspected, still seek to kill the Bill. Jonathan said we should stick very close together on this. I agreed. We should start hitting the big drum very hard on the fact that the Tories were using hereditary peers to overturn the democratic process. We co-ordinated a line for Blair and I to follow on the lunchtime news.

Up then to brief the Team Leaders' meeting. They all agree with our line, but worry that PR for Europe is now looking less and less likely.

Did a very brief piece for *The World at One*. Hague was on as well. Not impressive. I launched into him, saying that what he had just said was 'hogwash' and used the old Liberal cry of 'Peers against the people'. Margaret Jay was there, too, but she was very weak and as good as admitted that Labour had abandoned any ambition of getting the Bill through. What a disaster.

Later on I rang Downing Street to complain bitterly about Margaret's comments. They hadn't heard her.

Off to do some shopping and back to the office by 3.00. Roger told me that the Press Association had picked on Margaret Jay's piece at lunchtime and were saying that the government had abandoned the Bill. Bill Rodgers then rang me to say that Cranborne had said to him as late as midnight that the Tories didn't intend to oppose the Bill. But Cranborne has been completely isolated by Hague, who spent most of last night up at the Lords. I told Bill that we should pass the word round the press gallery and make sure Downing Street knew.

Bill rang again to say that he had just spoken to Margaret Jay, who had said that Blair had told her not to introduce the Bill unless the Tories specifically said they would co-operate. A wash-out.

I immediately rang Jonathan at Downing Street, who assured me that Margaret had got it wrong. The government Whips and peers had apparently said that they weren't keen to take the Bill back because it would interrupt business. But the PM had insisted. Phew! I passed the word on to Bill and Paul.

Friday, 20 November, Somerset

A very annoying piece in the *Daily Telegraph* today. Its political correspondent, George Jones, had lunched with one of my colleagues, who had said that I would probably have to go soon. I suspect Charles and so do Roy and the press office. I have an interview with John Humphrys on Sunday's *On The Record* and this, rather than the story of our recent successes, will now dominate it. I had wanted to go cleanly, neatly and without any sense of being under pressure. But it looks as though I may not be able to. The press love the idea of a plot to oust me. I doubt such a thing exists, although, given the last few days, it's only natural that some of my colleagues should be preparing in case I 'fall under a political bus'. But I wish they'd stop talking to the press about it. It means that every interview I do now is about my future instead of about the Party's progress.

Sunday, 22 November, Somerset

A blessed day with very little to do. Quite bright and cold, with a west wind blowing. It has been beautiful weather these last three or four days.

Then Humphrys at 12 o'clock. It was not a good interview. I was surly, truculent, uptight and I did not express myself well. At the end, he questioned me about the leadership, of course. 'I have a simple message for those eager to try on the crown – don't hold your breath,' I answered.

This, of course, will just feed the story. I felt very cross with myself. I saw the video later and decided it was one of the worst interviews I have ever done. I must learn how to handle Humphrys better.

Then walked over the field to the pub with our neighbours. Three pints, then home. In the evening spoke to Roy, who agrees that non-delivery of PR for Europe would be deadly for us. He said he'd speak to Blair about it soon.

To bed about midnight.

Tuesday, 24 November, Westminster

QUEEN'S SPEECH DAY

Always a chaotic event. Down to the chamber at 11.20. The usual pomp with Black Rod and the three knocks on the chamber door followed by the traditional procession down to the Lords. I walked there with David Trimble and back with Ann Taylor. The Lords was particularly full. When the Queen read out the government's intention to abolish the sitting rights of hereditary peers the normal convention of silence while the Sovereign speaks was broken by loud 'Hear Hears' from the MPs, echoed by a deep growl of approval from the life peers. I caught Tom McNally's eye and winked at him. Around me all the MPs were saying, 'Where's Jamie Lee Curtis?'[1] She attracted a great deal of attention but she didn't look particularly pretty to me. Wearing a somewhat unnecessary little gold tiara.

Then back to the Commons. On the way I quizzed Ann Taylor on what they plan to do next on the European Elections Bill, but she gave nothing away. I gained the strong impression that they haven't made up their minds yet. This was reinforced later by John Harris,[2] whose view of the government is that they are wandering around in a thick fog of indecision on the matter.

Wednesday, 25 November, Westminster

As I did my exercises this morning I also did a lot of thinking. I'm becoming increasingly certain that now is the time to go. The government is at such sixes and sevens with the European Elections Bill that we may well still not get it through. If that happens, I would want to go anyway. But that would mean the Tories would score my resignation as a success for their policy of destroying the Bill. Going beforehand denies that connection. Secondly, if I go before Christmas, then those who want to put themselves forward for the leadership will have the whole Christmas recess to prepare for a sharp start to the leadership campaign in January, so we can get the whole thing over with quickly.

---

1 As the wife of Lord Haden-Guest, the actress Jamie Lee Curtis is entitled to sit in the House of Lords to watch the Queen's Speech.
2 The late Lord Harris of Greenwich, our Chief Whip in the House of Lords.

Anyway, I now feel I have established the Parliamentary Party at Westminster and nationally after the election; I have secured the Party's finances; and its direction for this parliament. So this is the best moment to hand over to a new leader. If I wait until the middle of next year then there's a real chance that a leadership election will be fought on a change of direction. And Simon, who is the only one who wants to break from the JCC, is at present flat on his back, having comprehensively lost in his attempt to stop the joint statement. I doubt he would get even 20 per cent of MPs supporting him.

In the sauna I started to think about the actual timing. We have our visas now to go to Kosovo.[1] We leave on Saturday 12 December. So I should announce my intention to resign at the Parliamentary Party meeting before that, on 9 December.

Had a long chat with Archy later in the afternoon about all this. He broadly agrees. We're having lunch with Richard on Tuesday of next week, when I'll actually take the decision. I will then slowly widen the circle to include Chris, Paul Tyler and Roger Lowry. But probably not until the end of next week.

A lot of planning to be done. Jane, of course, is delighted. Although I emphasized to her that I hadn't taken the final decision. I know Richard will advise strongly against. He will say it will look a bizarre decision from the outside. But if there's a better time to go, I can't see it.

What's so embarrassing is that I'm now getting a lot of mail from a lot of people right across the party telling me that they hope the *Daily Telegraph* report about me going is incorrect.

In the latter part of the afternoon I called a meeting on the European Elections Bill with John Harris, Alan Beith and a few others. According to John Harris, the government won't now bring the Bill back before Christmas. Alan said he thought Straw was sincere in trying to get the Bill through, but didn't know quite how to do it.

We have a very clear view. If the Tories continue to oppose, then the government must bring things to a head as soon as possible, and certainly before Christmas.

---

1 The situation in Kosovo had temporarily stabilized following the ceasefire. I had arranged a further visit with Shirley Williams in December.

Thursday, 26 November, Westminster

While I was speaking to my office in Yeovil, at about 10.45, Jack Straw came through to me on the other line. They will now bring the European Elections Bill back next Wednesday, take it to the Lords on 14 December and drive it through. Good.

Back by car to Vane Cottage, my mind full of whether to stay until January or go now. It seems all the decisions are crowding in on me.

Friday, 27 November, Somerset

I have had a call out for Blair all day. I want to discuss with him how to get the Euro Bill through. Having spoken to Straw, I think the government are now serious about it. Alan shares that view.

At 4.45, after a cup of tea, off to Chard to turn on the Christmas lights from the balcony at the Guildhall. A wonderful occasion: a great sea of bright-eyed faces turned upwards towards us. Much hearty singing, at the end of which a contralto somewhere in the crowd sang 'Away in a Manger' so beautifully that it sent shivers down my spine.

I was bleeped halfway through the ceremony. Could I get away early to speak to the PM? I managed to get away at 6.00 and was home by about 6.25. He called me about a quarter of an hour later.

PA: You know how vital the Euro Elections Bill is for both me and my party. If the Tories continue to oppose, why not threaten them with a Lloyd George and create fifty new peers?[1] I have already put this to Jack, who feels that it would fuel accusations of control freakery. But it won't if, as Roy has already suggested, a substantial number of those are crossbenchers.

TB: Well, I have one or two ideas myself. I think we should discuss them pretty soon.

We agreed to meet either in his office after the vote on Monday or in Downing Street on Tuesday.

---

1 When Lloyd George presented the Parliament Bill of 1911 to the House of Lords the hereditaries refused to support it. Lloyd George threatened to create enough Liberal peers to ensure its passage.

Saturday, 28 November, Somerset

Into Yeovil at 9.30 for constituency surgeries. A survey of Lib Dems on the *Today* programme this morning showed two-thirds in favour of my strategy of closer relations with Labour and the joint statement. That's why we must keep the possibility of an all-member ballot hanging over the antis until they back off on calling a special conference. But thirty or forty in the *Today* survey said they want a leadership election so they can vote against me.

Sunday, 29 November, Somerset

Yesterday I faxed the following note, summarizing my thoughts on resignation, to Roy, Richard and Archy:

HOW AND WHEN TO FINISH

1. Jane and I decided before the last election that I would not fight a third election as leader of the Liberal Democrats, or as MP for Yeovil.

2. The reasons are:

2.1 Being a politician is not the only thing I want to do. There is more that I would like to do before I retire – though I don't yet know what. Write a book, do some TV, get involved in foreign affairs or just make a little money.

2.2 I would like to have some time to spend with Jane and with my family (especially my grandson). The last ten years have been very punishing on them and on the time I can spend with them.

2.3 By the next election I shall be sixty. Leading a third party like the Lib Dems is pretty gruelling. I am already very tired after ten years and, in little ways, my health is beginning to show it. I am not sure I can find the reserves of energy to lead the Lib Dems as I would want to lead them for the next three years. The prospect of five months of campaigning next year makes my heart sink. The same applies, if less so, to doing the job of MP for Yeovil the way I believe it should be done. I had always planned to stand down as Yeovil MP at the election soonest after my sixtieth birthday.

2.4 I am not sure that it will be good for the Party to have a 60-year-old leader against a mid-forties PM and a late-thirties Tory leader at the next General Election. We are a young party.

2.5 My style of leadership was, perhaps, most suitable to bring the Party to where it is. Maybe we need a new style of leader for the next phase.

3. So the question is, having decided to stand down before the next election, when do I do it?

4. I set myself these tasks to complete after the 1997 General Election, in order to leave a stable inheritance for my successor:

4.1 To establish and bed down the policy of constructive opposition.

4.2 To make the next step on co-operation. I hoped this might be coalition. But it is now clear that won't happen before the election. Widening the remit of the JCC to allow broader co-operation on bread-and-butter issues is possible, and is the next best thing.

4.3 To thus set – and have accepted by the Party – a broadly convergent course with the government which would give the best chance for a PR referendum before the GE, a deeper level of campaign co-operation through the GE and a coalition after it; thus establishing a firmly founded partnership over the next decade to complete the modernizing of Britain and the reshaping of British politics which has been the aim of my leadership of the party since the Chard Speech, seven years ago.[1]

4.4 To place the relationship between the Lib Dems and the government on a wider institutional footing, so that it didn't depend solely on the personal relationship between Blair and me.

4.5 To secure the Party's finances, at least as far as campaigning funds are concerned, for the years ahead.

4.6 To make it most likely and most simple for my successor to follow my strategy (above) supported by the strongest possible democratic mandate.

5. All these have now, substantially, been achieved.

6. So the question is, when?

7. Given that it must be in the next year to give my successor enough time to 'bed

---

1 See Vol. I, pp. 590–94.

in', the choice is between the end of this year and the period July to September 1999.

8. Although coalitions between us and Labour in Scotland and Wales is most likely, there is no guarantee of this and some possibility of an SNP success at Labour's expense in Scotland next May. Meanwhile, across the country, the government will probably be at the lowest ebb of its mid-term unpopularity in the second half of next year. Unemployment will be rising and the slow-down deepening . . . Since any leadership election is bound to be fought on whether to continue the present strategy of 'constructive opposition', a clear-cut, favourable outcome for this would, therefore, be less likely in July–September than it is now.

9. A leadership contest fought now would probably be fought by all the serious contenders on the basis of a confirmation of the present strategy (or a close variant of it). . . . The only person likely to try to challenge the current strategy is Simon. But it must be doubtful that he could, in present circumstances, get sufficient MPs to reach the required nominating threshold of 20 per cent of the Parliamentary Party.

10. An election now would give the new leader the opportunity to get to know the Party over the election campaigns of the early months of next year.

11. So, if now, before or after Christmas?

12. If after Christmas it had better be after the outcome of the Euro Elections Bill. This could drag on until the second half of January. And if the Bill fails (and that seems quite possible), going will be seen a result of that loss. And the Tories would be able to claim my scalp for their strategy.

13. Going before Christmas would also mean that my departure is unconnected to the outcome of the Euro Elections Bill. This would, moreover, give the candidates and the Party time to prepare over Christmas for a sharp and clean campaign, starting very early in the New Year.

14. Given that the best day is a Wednesday (Parliamentary Party meeting), 9 December looks best. Next week is too early and the following week I shall be in Kosovo (itself rather a good thing in the aftermath).

Went for a walk at lunchtime to the Cat Head. But, despite the gloriously clear weather, I was in a very low mood.

When we got back I found Richard had faxed back his views. He is opposed to my going now, and thinks next July after the Euro elections is better. Later in the evening I spoke to him. I said the timing rested on the answer to two questions. Would I be stronger in July than I am now? And would my successor have a better chance of holding on to the strategy then?

In my view, the answer to both these questions is no. He will think further on it.

Roy called me at about 7.00 to say that he had 'been persuaded' by my note. He didn't want me to go, but he understood my thinking. We also agreed to talk later in the week. I asked him to try and find out what Charles's intentions were: would he want to preserve my strategy, or seek to dilute it? Roy said he would try; but it would be difficult if he couldn't tell Charles what my intentions were. Roy asked me what I thought of Ming as a possible leader. I said I thought he would be superb, but could he win and would he stand?

We also had a chat about leaders' relations with their parties. Roy said leaders don't have to love their parties, citing Macmillan, Churchill and Blair as examples. I said I thought this wrong. Parties don't have to love their leaders, respecting them is enough. But leaders have to love their parties; otherwise why would they put up with them?

Monday, 30 November, Somerset

Jane drove me to Taunton to catch the 12.37 to Cardiff. As the train rattled across the Somerset Levels on a sharp blustery winter's day a thought came to me. Why don't I announce my resignation, as intended, on 9 December, but say that I will stay on for another six months, until after the elections? This has huge advantages. It will not look as though I have been forced out, it will give the party time to prepare and it will also force all the leadership contenders to work really hard in the Euro and local elections next year, in order to get themselves seen in the Party. It may make me a slightly lame-duck leader for six months. But it would force those of the wrecking tendency to nail their colours to the mast and I would be able to spend a relatively relaxed next few months concentrating on campaigning.

The downside is that I could go out on some losses in the local government elections. But the upside is that I would still be in post for the first ever nationwide PR election (if we get the Euro Bill through) and be able to preside over the establishment of the first coalitions between the Lib Dems and Labour in Scotland and Wales.

By the time the train had got to Bristol, I had listed the advantages and disadvantages. They came out strongly in favour.

Tuesday, 1 December, Westminster

I am feeling like the leftovers today. I dread the months ahead. All those long train journeys stamping up and down unfamiliar streets, meeting and greeting uninterested shoppers on often badly organized programmes. All those miserable cold January and February nights spent waiting on deserted railway platforms for the last train home, which is almost invariably full of drunken revellers in smoke-filled carriages.[1]

Ten years of this is almost too much. And yesterday's campaigning exhausted me – you have to be on your toes all the time.

Arrived at Downing Street at about 8.55, entering through the Whitehall entrance as usual, going straight into Blair's office. Almost immediately Jonathan poked his head round the door to say that he had David Trimble on the line. I offered to leave but Blair motioned me to stay. They had a long conversation about some cross-border economic body – they are obviously used to talking together and seemed to get on pretty well.

Afterwards, he opened in his usual tone: 'Look, now this is where I think we are', and went on to explain that he had been having secret negotiations on Lords reform (as he had hinted to me before) with the leader of the Tories in the Lords, Viscount Cranborne, and that Cranborne and he had done a deal behind William Hague's back as follows:

1. That the crossbenchers, led by Jack Weatherill, would put forward a proposition for a two-stage reform process. In Stage 1 the hereditary peers would be 'decimated' (by which he meant that one in ten hereditaries would remain in the first stage of the House of Lords reform).

2. Then, after an interim period, in Stage 2 all hereditaries would go.

---

1 I must have been getting really fed up here, as I usually love campaigning. Rather a similar sentiment was expressed by Lord Salisbury towards the end of his career, when he described electioneering as: 'The days and weeks of screwed-up smiles and courtesy, the mock geniality, the hearty shake of the filthy hand, the chuckling reply that must be made to the coarse joke, the loathsome compliment that must be paid to the grimy and sluttish daughter, the indispensable flattery of the vilest religious prejudices, the wholesome dilution of hypocritical pledges.'

3. The one in ten who remained in Stage 1 would be chosen by their parties in relation to their current strength in the Lords. As part of the deal Blair would then be allowed to make up between fifty and sixty new Labour peers. But he would probably only create twenty or thirty now and keep the rest in reserve just in case the Tory Lords didn't behave themselves.

4. The independents would put this proposition forward, the government would indicate that they were interested and Cranborne, for his part, would indicate that he was also interested (against Hague's wishes).

PA: Why on earth should the Tory peers connive in this?

TB: Cranborne is so fed up with Hague that he is prepared to put his duties as a 'shop steward' for the hereditary peers above those as leader of the Conservatives in the Lords. And he wants to go down in the history books as the person who came up with the compromise that enabled the modernization of the House of Lords (like his great ancestor Salisbury).

There was also an 'unspoken' part of the deal, however. Which was that if, when the second reading of the European Elections Bill came to the Lords, somebody put forward a 'reasoned amendment' and if this was passed (as was likely with a Tory majority), then, following House of Lords procedures, the Bill as a whole would fall, causing the Parliament Act to come into force. In this way Cranborne would, in effect, be conspiring with the government to facilitate the passage of the Bill through the Lords. He would not, however, allow any Tories to put forward the 'reasoned amendment'; somebody else would have to do this.

TB: Would Conrad Russell do it?

PA: Under no circumstances. It would be ridiculous for someone from our side to apparently act to wreck the Bill in order to save it. The public would never understand that. How about Stoddart[1] from your side?

TB: Certainly not, for the same reasons. But provided the amendment comes from a non-Tory source, Cranborne would be able to say that he has done his best. The whole plan is extremely precarious. Are you prepared to go along with it?

PA: Of course, although I'd like to check out some of the details.

TB: The real point is not just that it helps get the European Elections Bill through

---

1 Lord Stoddart, a Labour peer.

but also that it enables us to reform the House of Lords without disrupting government business.

PA: And it will do William Hague terrible damage, too.

Look, there's a second item I want to raise with you: my political future. As you know, I don't want to fight the next election, and I've always said I want to stand down some time this parliament. Well, I think that moment is soon approaching. I want to go in June next year. So I am now left with a choice: Should I announce now that I am going to go in June, or just go in June? As yet, I haven't made a firm decision. I think the person most likely to succeed me now is Charles Kennedy, who seems to have climbed back on board the whole project thing.

TB: Well, I could work with Charles Kennedy – although I'm worried whether he is a serious politician.

PA: I think he will be. He is different from me. But that could be a good thing. My skills as a leader, such as they are, were suitable for building the Party, but Charles has tremendous House of Commons presence, and will in time achieve stature and respect. Furthermore, I think having three young leaders of the political parties is good for the country.

TB: Well, I will be in touch if I have any thoughts on this, but I recognize that I probably can't stop you.

Finally, we talked about Kosovo.

PA: I am going over in a couple of weeks' time. But my current judgement is that you will have to deploy troops there early in the New Year.

TB: Yes, I agree. And we are beginning to plan for it now. We probably should have done so earlier. But you know the problem: How to control the KLA? We may get caught in the middle.

I responded that the only way to control the KLA was, as I had been saying for six months, via northern Albania. I promised to report back on my return.

Afterwards I called a meeting of Bob Maclennan, Bill Rodgers, Roger Lowry, John Harris and Miranda to tell them about the ambush Downing Street has laid in the Lords. I pointed out that this was based on a proposal first put forward by Bob at a JCC meeting some months ago. But Bob is now very nervous about this and Bill said I should not go along with it.

In the evening to Windsor Castle for the state dinner given in honour of President Hertzog of Germany.

As we were waiting to go into Windsor Great Hall for dinner, Margaret Jay came up to me and we had a quick word about the Cranbourne–Blair trap laid for the Tories in the Lords tomorrow. She was, as ever, pleasant to deal with. She has very nice smiling eyes and there is something rather flirty about her.

This is the first state occasion for which Windsor has been used since the great fire. It is magnificent. I had forgotten just how stupendous the armoury is. The Great Hall was beautifully done out, with 150 people seated at the great table – the longest table in the world, they say. The Queen spoke first, but rather meaninglessly. Then Hertzog in German. I just about managed to follow the main points provided I kept my eye on the English translation. I sat next to some aristo woman whose husband was the Master of the Horse (I kept referring to her as the Mistress of the Horse because she looked so much like one). On my other side, Gaynor, Robin Cook's new wife. She seems very shy. The only thing I could get out of her was how dreadful the press were and how much she enjoyed travelling with Robin.

The dinner finished at 11.30, but Jane and I were among the first to leave. As we were waiting for our car to be found, being frozen by the blasts of cold air coming in from the open door, William Hague turned up. He seemed nervous and withdrawn, although Ffion looked pretty and lively. On the way back in the car I phoned Bill Rodgers, asking him to get in touch with Margaret Jay first thing tomorrow morning to co-ordinate our actions.

Home at around 12.30am. I wonder if the government's ambush will hold tomorrow?

Wednesday, 2 December, Westminster

Yesterday I had told Paul about my intended resignation. He was terribly shocked to start with, but soon came round to seeing my reasons. Today I told Chris Rennard, who was rather emotional. I asked him what he thought. He said, 'I could tell you were up to something. I could see it in your face. It is my job to read candidates, and you are effectively my national candidate. I knew something was bugging you.'

I asked him who would succeed me. He thought that if it was a short election campaign, Charles; but if it was a longer one, then Nick might be able to do it. I told him I was thinking of making the announcement either just before or just after Christmas in order to retire in July. What did he think? He said that, on first consideration, it appeared a good plan but he would go away and think about it.

Afterwards, much toing and froing on Blair's ambush this afternoon. Eventually I managed to get Bill Rodgers on board. But Bob is still very nervous – I reminded him that it was his idea on which the government has built!

Into PMQs feeling slightly ill and completely confused about what question to ask. To my astonishment, Hague, who had learned of the Cranborne–Blair deal just before PMQs, walked straight into Blair's trap by ignoring the issue of the day and going for Blair on the Cranborne deal. A tactical error – perhaps brought on by sheer anger at what Cranborne had done to him. Blair was able to say, of course, that even if Hague disagreed with him, his leader in the Lords didn't, the Tory Party was split, etc.

The whole House roared with laughter, except for the Tories, who sat very glum-faced. Hague should have waited for Weatherill to announce his intentions, then concentrate on the government's U-turn, rather than his party's split. Instead, he has handed a huge propaganda coup to Blair and opened up a massive division between the Tories in the Commons and the Tories in the Lords.

MPs streamed out of the chamber afterwards bubbling with the story. The rest of the evening was punctuated by one tale after another of the Tories' deepening embarrassment: at about 6.00 we learned that Cranborne had been sacked by Hague in a stormy meeting in which all the Tory peers had voted for Cranborne and none for Hague!

By 7.00 the story was that eleven Lord's front benchers had allegedly resigned; by midnight Hague had chosen a new leader, Strathclyde,[1] but he only agreed to do it if Hague promised him that the Cranbourne deal could go ahead! Hague is looking more and more ridiculous.

As is so often the case in politics, everything has been changed by a single event. At 3.10 before Hague got up, he was reckoned to be winning against Blair on points – he had done brilliantly on the Queen's Speech and the government have been getting bad press because the Europeans (especially France and Germany) appear to be ganging up on Britain on tax harmonization. By 3.20 the situation had reversed. A single bad judgement from Hague and his leadership is in crisis.

---

1 Lord Strathclyde, until then Conservative Chief Whip in the House of Lords.

Thursday, December 3, Westminster

Woke up at 6.00 as usual, then fell asleep again until 8.00, which made me late into the office.

Prior to our trip to Kosovo, I saw Paic from the Yugoslav Embassy at 9 o'clock, at his request. He let slip during our conversation that it wasn't him who had given us our visas for Serbia with so little delay; somehow or other Donnelly had slipped it through the system in Belgrade. He was his usual sly self, but we have both learned to respect one another, so the meeting went reasonably well. I never did find out what he really came to see me about.

Saw Richard afterwards and told him I was thinking of announcing my resignation before Christmas. He strongly recommended that I shouldn't, and, listening to him, I realized that perhaps I was rushing it a bit, what with the trip to Kosovo, etc. He suggested a better time would be the week the House returns after the Christmas recess. On reflection I think that if we are going to delay it, the third week of January would be best. It gives me time to prepare. I asked Roger to fix a JCC for the first week in the January session, which he did.

Excellent. Everything is falling into place and my mind is becoming clearer . . .

Wednesday, 9 December, Westminster

Had a breakfast meeting this morning with the little group of people who are advising me on resigning. Paul Tyler somehow didn't get the call, but Archy was there, as were Richard Holme, David Walter, Chris Rennard and Becks Darling. David thinks I am taking the right decision. The others all said they didn't see why I couldn't fight the next election; it would weaken the Party if I went, etc. etc.

I said this was nonsense. The claim that I am the Party's best asset is a claim made of all past leaders. In a third party, the leader is always its biggest asset (positive or negative).

We then got on to timings. Chris Rennard made the crucial point that if I waited until June next year to make the declaration then I would be plagued by questions, since people were already saying that, if I did intend to go before the next election, then after the Euro elections in June was the most likely time. On this basis, Chris agreed that the best thing was to announce in January and go in June. Richard said I should make it absolutely clear that I would fight next year's elections as my last act for the Party, and that my reason for announcing early was to give the Party time to do the handover 'in good order'.

I wanted to take the first step on widening the scope of the JCC before standing down, so, at the PPM that evening, I suggested that, following my recent joint statement with Blair, we should now widen the remit of the JCC so as to start work immediately on reaching a common position with Labour on a European Common Foreign Security Policy (CFSP). The proposal was about to go through when suddenly Jackie said, 'I want to get this clear. Is Paddy asking us to take a decision now?'

'Yes,' I said. 'We should take the decision in principle now, although the actual work wouldn't start until after the successful conclusion of the European Elections Bill.'

We then nearly lost the whole thing when it opened up into a wide discussion, during which Mike Hancock, to my dismay, said we didn't have a policy to negotiate with.

Fortunately, Alan Beith cut short the discussion with: 'Well, looking around the room, I think we have all decided that we should agree to widen on CFSP.'

David Rendel and Simon Hughes both tried to get in an extra comment but Alan shut the discussion down. I could have kissed him!

So I went away with the agreement to widen the brief of the JCC – a key brick I need in place before resigning.

After PMQs, down to see Roy. We had a long discussion about recent talks he has had with both Blair and Charles Kennedy. He told me that he had spent twenty minutes on the phone to Blair, who is worried about me going. Apparently, he said to Roy: 'The longer Paddy and I can work together the more likely the project is to succeed.' What he doesn't appear to realize is that the project will almost certainly die anyway because he didn't take decisions earlier. The best I can do is to leave him the firm foundations on which to build with my successor.

At Roy's meeting with Charles, Charles apparently had said that he wasn't trying to unseat me. He was happy to wait and he didn't anticipate I would go soon. But if I did go, he felt he stood a good chance of succeeding me.

I asked Roy whether he thought Charles would carry on my policy.

'No, not in the way you would have done. I suspect he will tack to the wind a bit. He will shade his policy back towards safer ground in order to pick up the votes of those in the party who are unhappy. That's probably natural, given that he has a leadership campaign to win. He will dilute your strategy a bit, but he will not alter it.'

To bed around 12.00. A disturbed night's sleep again. Thinking about the future.

Thursday, 10 December, Westminster

At 3.15, I took a call from New York from the UN war crimes people about the operations I saw in Suva Reka. They are trying to get into Kosovo and asked me to lobby Milosevic for visas if I saw him on my forthcoming visit.

To bed around midnight, having packed for Kosovo. Roger Lowry is coming with me again, which will be fun. And this time Shirley Williams, a member of our foreign affairs team, will accompany us, too.

Friday, 11 December, Westminster

I had been contacted by some councillors from the north-west and from Somerset, who told me that they had got wind of the appointments to the Regional Development Agencies in these two areas which were to be announced the following week by John Prescott. They were unhappy, since he appeared to have ignored the relative strength of the Lib Dems in these areas in favour of Labour. I agreed to take this up directly with the Government.

Have sent messages via Downing Street asking Jack Cunningham to ring me.[1] He did so at about 5.00pm, telling me he too was upset about all this. Prescott was riding roughshod over his views as well. Prescott had, for instance, without consulting him, put Cumbria into the north-west region. When Cumbria was in the northern region, he explained, it had a status. But in the north-west region it was relatively insignificant. The county had also been swallowed up into a huge Euro constituency of which it felt no

---

1 Cunningham's seat, Copeland, is in Cumbria. He had recently been appointed by Blair as 'Cabinet enforcer' and, after Mandelson's promotion to the Cabinet, the person looking after the Lib/Lab relationship.

part. 'John is impossible to deal with, you know. If we overturn this, then it will have to be done by Tony when he returns from the Venice summit. John doesn't listen to anybody else.'

Sunday, 13 December, Macedonia and Kosovo

Roger, Shirley and I arrived in Skopje yesterday evening. Bitterly cold today.

After breakfast we were picked up by some frightfully pukka military types and driven off to Kumanovo to see the Extraction Force[1], stationed in an old tumble-down Macedonian army barracks which is being done up at huge expense.

We were taken to meet the British soldiers to wish them all a happy Christmas from home. They seemed in remarkably good mood, despite the fact that they had come out at very short notice and would miss Christmas at home. Some had actually been at Waterloo International Station on their way to a skiing holiday when they had been suddenly pulled back and told that they were going out to Macedonia instead.

They ran through their tasks and briefings and tried to make the best of them, but admitted that, at this strength and under-preparation, the idea of going into Kosovo against hostile Yugoslav army forces to rescue endangered KVM personnel is a non-starter. The Extraction Force has an undoubted political purpose: it puts pressure on Milosevic and indicates the seriousness of international intent.

---

1 One of the provisions of the Holbrooke–Milosevic ceasefire agreement was that a team of unarmed (and largely inexperienced) international observers (the Kosovo Verification Mission, or KVM) should be stationed in Kosovo to observe the ceasefire. President Chirac, following the experience of hostage-taking in Bosnia (where French troops in particular had been in the firing line), insisted that this should be backed up by an Extraction Force on the Macedonia–Kosovo border tasked to rescue the KVM or any of its members if they got into difficulty. These troops were eventually restructured into a force designed to enter Kosovo and maintain the peace after the Serb withdrawal, under the terms of the later Rambouillet agreement. At the end of the Kosovo conflict, in spring 1999, it was covertly planned to use these forces as the nucleus of an allied invasion force of 150,000 troops, under British General Mike Jackson which could, if necessary, drive Milosevic from Kosovo by force. In the event, however, to everyone's surprise, Milosevic agreed to withdraw and Mike Jackson was able to lead his troops into Kosovo on 12 June 1999 to supervise an unopposed Serb withdrawal and establish KFOR, the allied occupation force in Kosovo under whose protection to this day an uneasy peace in the province is being slowly and painfully rebuilt.

Then, at 10.30, off to the Macedonia–Kosovo border, where we met with David Slinn. The Serbs took a cursory look at our passports and waved us through. Then down on to the snow-covered plain of Kosovo and into heavy fog which accompanied us all the way to Pristina. The roads were very icy and visibility nil. As usual, the Kosovars driving at ridiculous speed, taking ridiculous risks.

We arrived at the Park Hotel (the ex-brothel again) at 12.30 to be met by Brian Donnelly, looking his usual alert and courteous self. I quickly changed into a suit and then, accompanied by Brian, Shirley and Roger, set off on an extensive round of meetings with key Albanians.

First, Fehmi Agani,[1] leader of the Kosovar Albanian team negotiating with Holbrooke on his attempt to reach an agreement between them and the Serbs.

Brian wanted me to press him to get his team together with representatives of the KLA in Vienna, where, with international help, they could try and appoint a team able to speak for all the Kosovar Albanians and with a single voice (negotiations with the Serbs have so far been dogged by the fact that there is no single body representing the Kosovar Albanians, only a series of factions).

Holbrooke is now on his fourth draft of the peace agreement. The first draft veered to the Serb side, but was unacceptable to the Kosovars. The second was unacceptable to both. The third draft was excellent for the Kosovar Albanians. But because they couldn't get their act together they couldn't arrive at an agreement to it.

I put Brian's proposition to Agani and he agreed it was a good idea. He was much more amenable and much less dedicated to independence than last time.

Then, at 3.00, off to see Adem Demaqi, the self-styled 'Kosovar Mandela', – so called chiefly because he spent some twenty-six years in jail under the Tito regime for pursuing an Albanian nationalist agenda. A little man with sharp and inquisitive eyes and a shock of white hair. But we didn't get on well. I found him very inflexible. He is said to be the mouthpiece for the KLA. I asked him about whether he, too, was prepared to go to Vienna. He said no, he wanted proper elections for a Kosovar parliament which could then put forward a single negotiating team. I began to lose my temper with him a little and said, rather roughly, that there

1 Subsequently reported as having been shot by the Serbs at the height of the Kosovo war – see 17 April 1999.

wasn't time for that. Peace was eroding as we spoke and such procrastination would soon be paid for in innocent people's blood. Leaders, I said, must sometimes have the courage to act without perfect democratic backing. I had never thought that somebody with his background would lack courage!

Brian said afterwards that he was pretty depressed. Demaqi is the voice of the KLA's most powerful region, the Drenica. Perhaps Demaqi was just playing for time while he found out the views of the KLA? Brian still believes it possible the KLA would tell him to go ahead.

Then off to see Rexhep Qosja, president of the United Democratic Movement – a breakaway from Rugova's LDK. I had expected to find another Demaqi. But Qosja was far more subtle and easier to have a constructive conversation with. We had a good, though strenuous, exchange of views. He is still too strong on independence and hasn't accepted yet that, while this can be a long-term aim for Kosovo, it cannot be a short-term one. But he is in favour of the Vienna meeting.

There is much talk now about a man called Hashim Thaqi, a KLA commander still in his thirties who seems to be emerging as the political voice of the KLA.[1] At thirty-two or so!

Altogether a pretty exhausting afternoon's meetings.

Then at 8 o'clock off to the usual restaurant the Pellumbi (which means 'dove' in Albanian), the semi-official watering hole for the international community in Pristina. The dinner was arranged by the Embassy and included a wide range of representatives from the international community here. They explained that the KVM is about to be reinforced by up to 2,000, of which no fewer than 400 (including something like forty colonels!) will be based in Pristina, rather than where they are needed, out in the field. It sounds like a recipe for sclerosis to me.

To bed around midnight listening to the World Service news.

Monday, 14 December, Kosovo

Down for an early breakfast and off at 7.30 to Prizren. We drove through thick fog to Malisevo and across to the Dulje heights [where the Serb

---

1 Thaqi did indeed turn out to be the political leader and chief spokesman for the KLA. He now leads the second party in Kosovo.

artillery which had bombarded us during my last visit had been positioned]
and then down through Suva Reka to Prizren.

During the day the fog gradually lifted until, in the late afternoon, we
could see the snow-covered mountains edging the plain of Kosovo. We
arrived in Prizren at about 10.00 to join Colonel Mike Morwood and his
British team of KVM observers. Morwood is an alert, small-framed man
with great toughness in his physique and a sharp pair of blue enquiring
eyes. I took to him immediately.

He gave us a brief about what was going on. Not long ago, he explained,
they had negotiated a local agreement which had averted a major clash
when the Serbs of Orahovac had marched on Malisevo to demand that the
Albanians gave up some Serb hostages.

I asked him if we could go and have a look at the site of the massacre
which took place at Vraniq, about a mile and a half from where I had been
stopped by the Serbs when I was last here.[1] He agreed and we drove along
the road from Prizren, through Suva Reka and up into the mountains. We
stopped on the snow-covered road in the middle of Vraniq, where we were
met by a group of children who instantly appeared and gathered round
Brian Donnelly.

I had expected to find an entire village wrecked. But the Serbs had only
picked out about 10 per cent of the houses (the wealthiest) for destruction.
The Serbs had not given them any warning. The first the village knew of the
impending attack was when the shells started to fall. The villagers had fled
to nearby woods but had subsequently been encouraged down by the Serbs
with promises of safe passage. As one group, who had fled in vehicles, drove
back to the village through a shallow valley, the Serbs lining its sides had
suddenly opened fire on them, killing a dozen or so. The villagers had then
undergone about forty-eight hours of interrogation and generalized terror.

I was taken by the village headman (a supporter of Rugova) to another
site where they had found two bodies in the ruins of a house burnt down
by Serbs.

The path led steeply up to the house, which was a few metres away from
one of the buildings still left standing in the village. We stood outside, the
whole of the Prizren valley lying below us under the snow, while one of
the witnesses explained how they had found the two bodies which had
been dismembered, mutilated and then burnt in the house. There was
speculation that the bodies (of a man and a woman in their mid-thirties)

1 See 28 September 1998.

had come from the neighbouring village of Bukavac – further up the mountain and a well-known KLA stronghold. The villagers had followed the trail of blood leading to the house and found the place where they believed the people had been shot. What would appeared to have then happened was that their bodies had been carried down, dismembered and put in the house which was then set fire to.

The humanitarian catastrophe which I had predicted in my last report, however, has not occurred. I, like all the international aid agencies, had completely underestimated the extent to which the Albanian clan system moves in to care for their own when in need. The layout of the traditional Albanian house, with its central courtyard surrounded by outbuildings, lends itself to providing extra accommodation for other family members. There is, however, a real problem now with wheat flour (the last year's harvest was lost and existing stores of grain deliberately destroyed by the Serbs, along with most farm animals). There is also much concern about the spread of diphtheria, dysentery and respiratory diseases amongst an unimmunized and overcrowded population.[1]

After lunch we bundled back into our vehicles and went off to Studencane, where I saw our garage proprietor friend from my last visit.

I asked him what had happened when the Serbs had come for the weapons. Had they left satisfied? He said that the hand-over of weapons to the Serbs had gone peacefully and they had, mostly, been left alone after that. He had even reopened his business. But he was now, if anything, in an even more depressed state than the last time we met, he said. He had been delighted when NATO had said they would bomb the Serbs. And when the international community withdrew their embassies from Belgrade to open the way for NATO's attack, he had started to put a new roof on his house. But then Milosevic had got away with it again. The Holbrooke agreement could never hold, he said, with only unarmed monitors. Tension was rising again and the local Albanian population was frequently subject to renewed bullying by the Serbs. He had gone down to get his identity papers recently and had been thrown in jail for a couple of days and severely beaten. I asked him to pass on my best wishes to the villagers whom I had met last time.

Then toward Orahovac. Along the way we passed a couple of cars which

---

1 In the 1980s word spread amongst the Albanian Kosavar community that the Yugoslav immunization programme was being used by the Serbs to damage Albanian male fertility. As a result of this most Albanians refused to be immunized.

had been in an ambush where five KLA, including the local commander had been killed. We saw the shot-up cars, a lot of blood and, in the second car, a large piece of human cranium still lying on the driver's seat. There was some suggestion that an American KVM team had unwittingly led the Serbs to the whereabouts of the KLA commander through bad radio procedure which the Serbs had intercepted. But, on the heights above the road I could clearly see several Serb positions commanding the valley, so they must have had the area under very close surveillance for a long time.

In Orahovac itself we had a look at an old Dervish temple (there are quite a few members of the Dervish sect in this area). Then, in failing light, we drove up from Orahovac to Dragobilje, where I had met the KLA on my last visit. I wandered up the track to Dragobilje village and soon bumped into some KLA guards, who directed me to their commander. We were kept waiting a few moments outside his headquarters, then, having taken our shoes off, we were led in.

The room was unlit and, with night falling fast, it was not long before we were sitting in almost total darkness illuminated only by the soft glow of cigarettes on all sides.

The commander was a man of about 35, with a sallow face but kind eyes. But he wouldn't answer any question I put to him. Who did he accept as his political leader? I am just a soldier. What did he hope for? I am just a soldier. And so on. I was impressed by his discipline, if nothing else.

However, at the end he said quite suddenly, 'You know, there are Albanian villages being surrounded and attacked near the border now by Serb forces, even as we speak. I have just heard it on the radio.'

At this moment Mike Morwood suddenly got a call over his radio, too. I saw him hurry off to his vehicle and settle down for a rather long and, by the look on his face, worrying conversation.

I heard him say, 'Look, are things bad enough for me to come back?' So I went over to him and said that his job must come first; if he needed to go back we must do so. But he said no – or at least, not yet.

At this stage Brian Donnelly came in and whispered to me that I should be careful not to allow the KLA to use this meeting for propaganda purposes in a way which could further destabilize an already delicate situation. So I said my goodbyes to the commander, and we bundled ourselves back into the vehicles and headed for Prizren, while Brian and John Crosland left to return to Belgrade.

When we arrived in Prizren we checked into our hotel and I phoned Jane to tell her I was OK. Then off for a drink in a local bar with some of the

British members of the KVM. These were almost exclusively former soldiers, including one splendid retired ex-Guards officer, probably in his late fifties, whose improbable uniform while out in the field included a trilby hat and a shooting stick. He claimed that this unusual outfit had saved his life on one occasion, when he rounded a corner in the middle of a battle between the KLA and the Serbs, to be confronted by some very trigger-happy Serb soldiers, to whom he raised his hat and wished good day. They had been so surprised that they had neglected to shoot him.

Gradually over the evening it became clear that this had been a very active day in the British sector. The Serbs were indeed attacking villages east of Prizren, as our KLA friend had told us, and the incident of which Mike had been warned turned out to be a large-scale Serb ambush of KLA forces near the border, in which thirty-five had been killed.

By the end of the night we were able to piece together the full story.

The KLA had for some weeks been trying to infiltrate men and arms over the high mountain which separates the Prizren area from Albania. Two weeks ago, eight KLA trying to get into the area had been killed in a Serb ambush.

This time an infiltration group of about forty fully armed men and women in KLA uniforms, travelling at night, had made the fatal mistake of following the same route and had walked into a pre-positioned claymore mine, booby-trapped to a log across a track. Several had been killed instantly and the rest had scattered. Twenty-five or so ran back up the narrow valley they had just come down, into a well-laid Serb ambush and had been swiftly killed. A further four tried to break out of the valley, but were captured and, it appeared likely, executed.

I saw the photographs later. The KLA soldiers (badly trained) were all bunched lying where they had been killed, in pools of frozen blood in the snow. The four who had been captured, including one very beautiful-looking girl in her early twenties, had all been shot in the head, the girl with a single small-calibre bullet which had gone into her left ear and come out through her mouth. One of the men had been shot in the back of the head, the bullet coming out through his throat. Nine millimetre, by the look of it. Six others had, apparently, been taken prisoner.

Soon details of another killing started to come in. Three armed and hooded gunmen had gone into a bar in Pec which was owned and frequented by Serbs, and shot dead six Serb youths, who were barely in their teens. We speculated as to whether this was the beginnings of a dirty war, as in Northern Ireland. Up until now the KLA have not attacked any Serb civilian targets, such as bars, etc. Indeed, one of the things that has astonished me is the way Serb soldiers can wander round Prizren, unarmed and alone, without so much as an insult from the very population whose mothers, fathers, aunts and uncles they have been bombarding, brutalizing and sometimes killing no more than five miles away in the hills. I asked an Albanian why, with a worldwide reputation for ferocity, revenge and courage, his countrymen were so extraordinarily submissive in the face of such brutality. He replied that Kosovar Albanians were different; they had been occupied so many times that they had concluded that this was the way all occupiers behave. Being submissive was their historical survival mechanism.

By the time we got back to the hotel, there was clearly something on. The streets were full of armed police, looking very nervous and wearing, for the first time, flak jackets. A reaction to Pec, I imagine.

I stood at my hotel window and watched them at the crossroads below me, standing smoking and chatting in a bunch in the middle of the street, and speculated that if the KLA was an effective guerrilla force it would be making the lives of the Serb minority here, and especially their police and soldiers, much more difficult.

A fitful sleep. The image of the young girl who had died this morning in the snow on the mountain above us, the look of terror in her eyes, still haunting me.

Tuesday, 15 December, Kosovo

To Shirley's horror, I insisted on leaving at 7.00. Much joshing about this over breakfast, at which I had three large eggs and Shirley refused to have anything.

Bili[1] was late, so in the end we didn't get away until 7.30. But we still made it to Pristina by 8.30, where we picked up Morgan Morris from UNHCR headquarters and headed off to a much threatened little Albanian community, surrounded by Serb positions near the Blacavac mine.

On the way we passed a lot of very aggressive Serbs, who gave Morgan's UNHCR vehicle the Serb three-finger salute and sometimes gestures requiring only one finger, as we passed through their villages. Then off the main road and across a desolate landscape of old mine workings to a line of

1 The same interpreter as we had last time. See 28 September 1998.

Serb bunkers dominating a narrow valley. These had all been installed post-Holbrooke (which was supposed to 'freeze' the two front-lines and specifically forbade the establishment of new military positions).

In the valley beneath the Serb guns lay the little Albanian hamlet of Sipitula, which Morgan has been visiting frequently with aid and reassurance. We slipped past the surly Serb soldiers, who glowered at us from behind their bunker, and dropped down the valley into the village.

The first person we saw was the head man, carrying a Kalashnikov. He said he was delighted to see us because he had heard rumours that the Serbs were about to attack. 'Seselj's men'[1] had been spotted in the Serb special police positions above them. He took me to the edge of the village to show me the Serb bunkers completely surrounding it, telling me that they often fired into the village to keep the people frightened. But it was quiet today.

By now it was a beautiful day with bright sunlight sparkling off the crisp fresh snow, and Sitipula looked like a picture-book alpine village, with its old Albanian farmhouses, cattle wandering about and the fields and gardens crowded with little fruit trees, bare and etched with snow against a blue sky.

Shirley left us, saying that she wanted to meet the women of the village, while the rest of us were invited by the head man to join the men in his house. After removing our shoes, we all sat in a circle on the floor and were served Turkish coffee and the obligatory raki while we listened to their story. They had been under terrifying intimidation for several days. The head man's eyes filled with tears when I stupidly asked him how his family was. He said that last night, fearing imminent attack from the Serbs, some, including his family, had left the village and run the gauntlet of a Serb ambush to get out. He didn't know whether they had made it or not.

The men insisted they were not connected with the KLA but had got their weapons recently from the black market in order to defend the village. We promised to try and get the KVM to put a patrol through here in the next few days, so that the Serbs would understand that the international community was taking an interest in them.

It was time for us to leave – but no one could find Shirley.

---

1 Followers of Vojislav Seselj, the head of the extreme nationalist Serbian Radical Party in Belgrade, whose irregulars (identified by their black uniform and bandannas – of which we had, indeed, seen several in the Serb positions we had just passed) were much feared, because of their reputation for terror and murder in both Kosovo and Bosnia.

After a worried search, she was eventually found sitting on the floor in the gloom of a darkened room with the remaining women and children of the village gathered around her, telling her what life was like for them in the besieged village. She had seen something I had never seen on all my previous visits. In the Balkans, male-dominated society that it is, conversation with visitors was always conducted by the men, while the women were hustled out of the way. But Shirley had managed to cut through all that.

We dragged her away and waved the villagers a cheery goodbye, but with secretly sinking hearts, wondering if this would be the site of the next Serb massacre, which we would only hear of later.[1]

At 8.00 off to dinner with Blerim Shalja. He is an Albanian intellectual and newspaper editor and is by far and away the most subtle and intelligent Albanian I have yet met. Too young to be the president and not prepared to get involved in politics for the moment, worse luck. He is the kind of man who could really lead the Albanian community. And he is also absolutely correct in saying that if the KLA want intervention then they should sign up to any old agreement and let NATO come in as guarantor. We stayed too long and drank too much, which gave me a headache the next morning.

To bed around midnight, having heard that, as planned, the Lords voted down the European Elections Bill tonight, which means the Parliament Act will, finally, be used and we will get PR for the European elections. A huge relief. I can now do what I have to do in January and will be able to say that I have presided over the first ever nationwide PR elections. Excellent news. But not enough to counter the misery of the day.

Wednesday, 16 December, Kosovo

Visits to Ambassador William Walker of the United States, the head of KVM, and his British deputy, General Karol Drewenkiewicz (popularity known as General DZ).

Next to see Zoran Andjelkovic, accompanied by David Slinn. Andjel-

---

1 The village was indeed attacked very soon after the NATO airstrikes began. Many of the men with whom I had drunk raki had been killed trying to defend their homes. It is suspected that others were taken to Serbia, where they were subsequently killed. The room in which Shirley spoke to the women was torched and the old house in which I had met the men of the village reduced to rubble; only the stables and outhouses now remain.

kovic, a granite-faced Serb, is Belgrade's most senior representative in Kosovo. He started to lecture me and the meeting developed into quite a shouting match, which David Slinn said afterwards he could have sold tickets for. The KLA are trying to provoke a Serb over-reaction which will bring about intervention by NATO – and the Serbs seem determined to oblige. But this doesn't make it any easier to put up with propagandizing by people such as Andjelkovic pretending that the Serbs have done nothing wrong.

Then the five-hour journey to Belgrade, where I saw Nikola Sainovic,[1] the Deputy Prime Minister of the Yugoslav government. We spent about an hour with him. The same propaganda as Andjelkovic, but put more subtly. We ended up having a similar row.

Afterwards off to the British Embassy Christmas party with Brian Donnelly. Here the talk was not of Kosovo but of Iraq, where the tension has been rising steadily over the last few days. All the news programmes are discussing the likelihood of bombing again, soon. Having listened to the CNN reports on what Richard Butler of UNSCOM is saying, I think it is pretty well inevitable. Though whether it comes tonight or not, who knows? I suspect they can't leave it later because of Ramadan.

Afterwards, a dinner at the Ambassador's residence with members of local Serb opposition groups, NGO leaders and key members of the international community.

I was very tired, looking forward to my bed and hoping the guests would soon go, when, at around 11.00, Brian came in and said that the bombing of Iraq had started. Brian shooed the guests out and we went into his private office to watch it all on CNN and Sky. After a flurry of phone calls with Miranda, and having asked Ming to call me. I went to bed at about 1.00. But my sleep was broken half a dozen times or so by Miranda telling me the press arrangements for tomorrow and finally, at about 2.00 am, by a call from Ming during which we agreed the line I should follow on the broadcasts in the morning.

Thursday, 17 December, En route to the UK

On the way back to UK I wrote my report for the Prime Minister, which included the following overview of the situation as I perceived it.

1 In charge of Belgrade's Kosovo policy and subsequently indicted as a war criminal.

1. Summary

1.1. *The Good News*

1.1.1. The situation in Kosovo is better than when I visited at the end of September. There is no large-scale fighting and clear evidence of people having moved back into their villages, especially in those areas where international monitors (Verifiers) have been in operation.

1.1.2. The unarmed Verifiers have (so far) had a greater effect than I had first anticipated. The OSCE[1] verification exercise is, however, as yet operative in only one area (Prizren) and has taken far too long to get out on to the ground.

1.1.3. Whilst many of the internally displaced people (IDPs) are living in difficult and, in some cases, intolerable conditions, there is no evidence of the large-scale humanitarian crisis that many (including me) anticipated. We underestimated the extraordinary effectiveness of the extended Albanian family/clan system . . . (but) families are living with relatives or clan members, often in terribly crowded conditions . . . There is, as far as we could tell, no one still living in the forests, or imminently at risk from cold and starvation.

1.2. *The Bad News*

1.2.1. Tension in Kosovo is rising again.

1.2.2. Yugoslav forces (chiefly MUPP or interior police) are redigging positions around key villages. Regular and threatening vehicle and personal checks by Yugoslav security forces are back in evidence. The number of random killings and incidences of hostage taking is rising on both sides. Some families who moved back into their villages after Holbrooke/Milosevic are moving out again because of increased tension in their area.

1.2.3. Experienced monitors say that the Yugoslav armed forces are getting increasingly angry, especially with the international operation. As they see it, we are tipping the balance back in favour of the KLA. This is especially so where the Serbs have been required, under Holbrooke/Milosevic, to evacuate territory they took control of in the September offensives and this has been immediately re-occupied ('back-filled') by the KLA.

1.2.4. The KLA are actively training and restocking with weapons, including some quite sophisticated ones. New uniforms are everywhere in evidence. There is also

---

1 Organization for Security and Co-operation in Europe, an organization of 55 states dealing with conflict prevention, management and post-conflict rehabilitation in Europe.

clear evidence that they are bringing in new recruits and material through armed incursions (not always successful) from Albania.

1.2.5. The widespread view is that Holbrooke/Milosevic, having initially established a dynamic for peace strong enough to replace conflict in the early weeks, is now ebbing away and a dangerous political vacuum is being created. Albanian leaders (including the KLA) now do appear to understand that full-scale independence is not an option . . . But they are fast losing confidence that the peace process will produce an outcome acceptable to them and many appear resigned to a return to conflict to achieve their aims.

1.2.6. . . . Kosovo is sliding back into war. Unless we act swiftly to stabilize the situation on the ground and reinvest the peace process with new momentum . . . conflict will come again in the spring (or even as early as January).

Friday, 18 December, Westminster

Into the office by 8.00. A word with Richard, who, along with Archy, Chris and David Walter, has drawn up a programme and a letter for me for 20 January. Richard, incidentally, was absolutely certain that at a lunch Roy Jenkins had at East Hendred, to which Richard and Ming had both been invited, Roy had taken Ming to one side and spilled the beans to him.

Drove back to Vane Cottage at lunchtime. When I got home I rang Paul to ask him whether he also thought Roy had told Ming. Paul said that he was practically certain yes. So I contacted Ming, who immediately confirmed that Roy had indeed spoken to him in the context of Roy hearing about Ming's appointment to the Privy Council in the New Year. He had apparently told Ming that I had nearly resigned on 9 December, but Ming should 'keep himself ready' because Roy wanted to back him. I was absolutely livid with Roy. He knows that I do not want this. I have also specifically told him that the very people I do not want to know about my probable resignation are those who may go for the leadership, since it would give them an unfair advantage. I rang Archy, who confirmed that Ming had also spoken to him about this. I told Ming in a further conversation that naturally I was reviewing my position, but I had taken no decisions yet. I'm not sure I convinced him, but I tried.

Monday, 21 December, Somerset

[*Every year Jane and I make 'Christmas visits' to all the post offices, retirement homes, hospitals etc. in the constituency.*]

Up at 5.30 and across to Chard to pay my annual Christmas visit to the Royal Mail sorting office there. A deep frost last night, but the roads were dry. The Christmas post less heavy this year, they say, than in previous years.

Listening to the news today, I think the government is losing the propaganda war on Iraq. Blair was foolish enough to say that Saddam Hussein was now virtually 'caged'. This sounds ridiculous, and all the papers have turned against him. The BBC, and especially John Humphrys, have been particularly outrageous. No doubt they feel obliged to put the opposite point of view, since there has been so little opposition in the House. Nevertheless, their coverage sounds like a party political broadcast on behalf of Saddam Hussein.

In the afternoon I managed to get hold of Jonathan Powell to tell him that no doubt he didn't want any advice from us since they'd be getting enough from elsewhere, but I wanted Blair to know that they were making an absolute pig's ear of putting their message across. The line about Saddam being caged sounded macho and silly – apart from anything else, we couldn't keep him in his cage, and the next thing would be some countries pressing for sanctions to be lifted. Why weren't they playing the line that he was breaching international law? 'That would at least give you the opportunity to claim the moral high ground.'

Jonathan said that he wasn't keen on the caged idea either, but his view had been overruled. He's furious with the BBC for not putting a more balanced case.

Jane drove me up to London, arriving about 4.00. Cleared the mail, then into the FE at 6.00. There was a long discussion on whether to have a ballot [on whether to pursue closer relations with Labour]. Eventually the antis withdrew their suggestion of a special conference, after which the FE overwhelmingly decided there should be neither a special conference nor a ballot. Good!

Friday, 25 December, Somerset

Raining and blowing still (the weather this year has been awful!). Seb and Simon were down late and so opened their stockings by themselves. But Matthias, whose stocking was so big we had to put it in a cardboard box, sat on our bed and made gurgling sounds of delight while opening his presents. He, of course, has been ridiculously spoiled.

Jane got a camera from me; she seemed genuinely surprised and delighted with it. I got a sweater and a video of *Alexander The Great*, which I have wanted to see for ages. Then off to do our rounds, leaving the kids at the house.

St James' House care home forthe elderly at about 10.30, then the fire station and the ambulance station (they were out on a call), then Sunningdale care home, and then the night shelter and home by mid-day.

We opened another couple of presents each and then went down to the pub for a couple of pints. Absolutely packed. Then home and Christmas lunch at about 4.00. We would have gone for a walk, which is our normal thing, but it rained hard all afternoon. Instead, I retired to bed absolutely exhausted and slept for two hours!

Saturday, 26 December, Somerset

Woke up to hear the news that there has been more fighting in Kosovo. It started two days ago – apparently 100 Serb tanks have moved into Podujevo.

After my traditional Boxing Day run with John Bailey [my neighbour], we had a very relaxed day. I worked most of the afternoon on my resignation letter. I'm finding it very difficult to finalize this.

Tuesday, 29 December, Somerset

Down the line interview to the *Today* programme at 7.30. Everybody is saying that the Mandelson thing means the end of the project between me and Blair.[1] Prescott had given an interview to the *Independent* which is very explicit in calling for 'a return to substance and away from rhetoric' – clearly an attack on Mandelson and an attempt to grab the agenda while Blair is on holiday in the Seychelles.

Brown is said to be behind this, and there is a substantial move by junior ministers as well as Cabinet members, to use the opportunity to stamp out the Lib/Lab relationship and the whole project.

To my fury, on the lunchtime news (which carried an embarrassingly glowing account of my leadership) Simon Hughes launched an attack on me; so, instead of the news being what the press office had worked so hard on – the success of 1998 and our messages for 1999 – it was all about Simon sending a message to me. I bleeped him but he never responded. The stupidity is that he launched a brilliant story of his own on hospital waiting lists and nurse shortages – and he has killed that as well!

---

1 Peter Mandelson resigned as Secretary of State for Trade and Industry after it emerged that he had borrowed money from his government colleague Geoffrey Robinson to purchase a house and had not declared it in the Register of Members' Interests.

1999

Thursday, 7 January, France

The World Service reported this morning that Labour is down 7 points in one poll and 3 in another. Later in the day I discovered that we have gone up to 19 in the first poll, and 13 in the other. Excellent! Just goes to show that if Labour trip up (as with this Mandelson stuff) the vote doesn't always go to the Tories, but can come to us. As I had hoped.

Simon, Kate and I did the tunnel run on the Sarenne – a black piste. Kate was furious at us for bringing her this way. I think she was affected by the memorials situated just as you emerge from the tunnel on to the slope dedicated to two people killed on this piste in the last few years. Anyway, she skied down in a bit of a bate and we met at the bottom, where she said, 'Dad, you just wait till you're older – I shall kick your zimmer frame away, just to pay you back for taking me down that slope.' Then we went across the face of the mountain under a heavily snow-laden avalanche gully. It was very beautiful. Clear blue skies and a totally empty mountain; tracking under the crest and across virgin snow. We dropped down to the lake, then up on the chairlift to meet the others. An excellent day's skiing . . .

Andrew Garratt, in the office in London, has done an impressive job of putting together material to counteract a move by the Campaign for Liberal Democracy [those opposed to closer links with Labour] to close my options. Blair is now in South Africa and has started the fight back after the Mandelson affair, saying that, contrary to Prescott's briefing over the Christmas period, the relationship with the Liberal Democrats is firmly on course.

I have been thinking a lot about my resignation. I reckon I will tell Blair as soon as I get back [i.e. before the JCC meeting], firstly, that I am going to resign on 20 January, and secondly, that I would like to secure the policy of 'constructive opposition' for my successor. Then it will be up to Blair and the new leader to take it from there, but he should realize that unless he is prepared to make further concessions, the relationship is probably doomed in the long run.

Sunday, 10 January, London

It was snowing when we got back to the UK. Jane dropped me at Ashford, where I caught the train up to London, while she and Simon drove back down to Somerset. The train was massively delayed – there had been a derailment the day before. I arrived back at Methley Street at about 12.00 and settled down to the huge backlog of work waiting for me.

Spoke to Paul briefly about tomorrow's MPs' awayday. I am nervous, but he thinks it will be fine. It is important that my resignation programme is not disturbed by a revolt.

Monday, 11 January, London

Have been thinking overnight. Richard, Paul and Chris think I may have to delay my resignation for a couple of weeks because the coincidence of my departure with that of Peter Mandelson may suggest that this is the end of the project. But I'm not convinced. Having looked at yesterday's papers, I see that the government is already getting back on to its feet. There's going to be a Cabinet meeting at which Blair has said to me he will make it clear that, despite Prescott and the counterbriefings over Christmas, the project remains one of the central thrusts of his government. Then, at the January JCC, we will both show our determination to continue by widening our work to other areas, such as Europe. And finally, we have just made a very strong showing in another opinion poll.

The more I delay, the more likely it is that my decision to stand down will be leaked and I will lose control of events. So, before the start of the MPs' awayday at the Ismali Centre, I took Paul, David and Chris aside and talked them through my latest thoughts. They are all coming round to my view.

The awayday chiefly consisted of presentations to MPs on (a) polling (which looks very good), (b) campaign issues, and (c) tips on how to hold on to their seats. It was good-natured and very constructive. Chris Rennard impressive, as ever.

At the end I gave them all the familiar stuff about reshaping politics, the need to be doing things rather than being things and the fact that Labour was our only partner in this parliament. But the Tories would come back in due course, probably in the next one. Charles, rather curiously, appealed

17. Sunday, 27 September 1998, Kosovo

'... the little Serb Orthodox monastery of Decani [is] set like a jewel on a sward of grass ... The inside is quite stunning ... We were shown round by one of the monks, Father Sava ...'

18. Sunday, 22 November 1998, Somerset

'... walked over the field to the pub with our neighbours ...'

From left: John Bailey, PA, Sally Radley, Jane, Stephanie Bailey, Steve Radley

19. Monday, 14 December 1998, Kosovo
'We stopped on the snow-covered road in the middle of Vraniq, where we were met by a group of children who instantly appeared and gathered round Brian Donnelly'

20. Monday, 14 December 1998, Kosovo
'We stood outside, the whole of the Prizren valley lying below us under the snow ...'

21. Monday, 14 December 1998, Kosovo
'Then off for a drink in a local bar with some of the British members of the KVM. These were almost exclusively former soldiers, including one splendid retired ex-Guards officer, probably in his late fifties, whose improbable uniform while out in the field included a trilby hat and a shooting stick'

22. Tuesday, 15 December 1998, Kosovo
'[We] were invited by the head man to join the men in his house. After removing our shoes, we all sat in a circle on the floor and were served Turkish coffee and the obligatory raki while we listened to their story'

23. Thursday, 7 January 1999, Alpe d'Huez
'Simon, Kate and I did the tunnel run on the Sarenne – a black piste'

24. Wednesday, 20 January 1999, Westminster
'Then into a mad round of interviews and photos with Jane in my office'

25. Thursday, 21 January 1999, Somerset
'... walked up to Norton village hall for the constituency council meeting ... The village hall was bathed in TV lights with a satellite van and a mass of press outside'

26. Monday, 8 February 1999, Amman
'We stood for a moment at the coffin, bowed our heads, then moved on'

27. Sunday, 7 March 1999, Edinburgh
'The delegates gave me a very warm reception. In the event, the speech went well enough, although my voice started to crack a bit towards the end. I wanted to lift the peroration but couldn't because I was feeling too emotional. I left the platform rather misty-eyed'

28. Tuesday, 4 May 1999, Edinburgh
'After the press conference we loaded on to the "battle bus" with David Steel, Jim Wallace ... and others, before heading off for the Irn-Bru factory for a campaign visit'

29. Tuesday, 4 May 1999, Scotland

'The tour of the Irn-Bru factory lasted an hour or so, during which I had to say wonderful things about Irn-Bru'

30. Tuesday, 20 July 1999, Kosovo

'We were taken to a stable where six bodies had been found, five of them now little more than piles of ashes, but on the sixth the debris from the roof had fallen, thereby protecting it from the worst of the flames. The smoke, however, had preserved the flesh'

31. Monday, 9 August 1999, Westminster

Charles has changed. And so has my attitude towards him … before I found myself uncomfortable with him … he was taking over a party I had helped to create … and had led for more than a decade. But now that … crown has been passed …'

to the rank and file by saying that we should dispense with having both a Shadow Cabinet and a separate JCC team, and all be equal. Lembit made a much more sensible intervention, saying that of course we needed a Shadow Cabinet structure.

Tuesday, 12 January, Westminster

I had invited my closest advisers to a breakfast meeting at Methley Street to discuss my resignation: Richard Holme, David Walter, Chris Rennard, Paul Tyler, Archy Kirkwood, and Becks.

They started turning up at around 7.15.

On the question of timing, Chris is still in favour of my delaying a while, but agrees that, if the JCC is really built up, then I could go next week. The general consensus is that, provided nothing else happens and the JCC is a success, then we ought to stick to our original date of 20 January. We then went through the various drafts of my resignation letter, making some minor amendments. Richard doesn't think that I have explained well enough and wants me to say that I am feeling exhausted, but I am reluctant to do this. I must still lead the Party for another six months and I want to do other things as well. We finished at 8.30am.

I am nervous about not telling anybody else in my office but it has to be done on a strictly 'need to know' basis. And I won't be certain that I'm going ahead until after the JCC on Thursday.

A brief word from Ming. He went over to see Robin Cook in the afternoon to negotiate the expansion of the JCC's remit to the CFSP. It was, apparently, a very good meeting. But Cook is at his wits' end as to what to do in Kosovo. The West is acting too late again, I fear.

At 5.15 I walked down Whitehall to Downing Street for my meeting with Blair. As usual, into the Cabinet Office through Cockpit Passage[1] and into Downing Street by the back door. I was ushered into the Cabinet Room and told that the PM would be 'a few minutes'. In fact, I waited in the Cabinet Room for about twenty minutes, which gave me the chance to have a good look at it for the first time. There are twenty-three chairs

---

1 Cockpit Passage connects the Cabinet Office to the back entrance of Downing Street. It follows the line of the old Cockpit Passage of Whitehall from the days when it marked the north-eastern side of Henry VIII's Royal Tennis Court. The old brickwork of the original passage is preserved and exposed along one side of the Cabinet Corridor.

round the Cabinet table. Behind the PM's chair there is a rather good portrait of Robert Walpole, No. 10's first prime ministerial occupant. And on the opposite wall, facing the window that looks out over Horse Guards Parade, an eighteenth-century painting of the view towards St James's Park across what used to be the terrace of No. 10. A rather charming, almost naïve landscape, with only two or three somewhat diminutive figures (perhaps Walpole himself?) in the foreground lounging in suitably languid eighteenth-century fashion on the balustrade of the No. 10 terrace. In the middle a canal runs diagonally across St James's Park towards what is now Buckingham Palace (then unbuilt). A country woman, a young child and others walk near by.

I also looked along the bookshelves on the walls of the Cabinet Room. What a strange collection! Many biographies of previous occupants, some history, some poetry and a few miscellaneous anthologies, including *The Golden Bough* and, bizarrely, Gertrude Jekyll's *On Gardening*. Almost all the books date from before the 1930s and many of them from the nineteenth century. Only two books I saw were of a more modern nature – one called *The Conservative Party* and the other *The Conservative Enemy*. Clearly, once a book is put there it is never removed! I wondered when that bookcase had last been opened and any of the books in it read.

A little before 5.30 Jonathan came through with Blair. By this time I was sitting at the end of the table doing some work on my laptop.

Powell said, 'Oh, here he is again with his mobile office. If only John Prescott could see this.'

Blair laughed and said, 'Yes, he would have a fit! Especially if Paddy was sitting over there in the seat alongside me.'

I retorted that Prescott had had enough shocks to last him a lifetime in the past three weeks. We moved into Blair's office.

He was looking well, his face very sun-tanned, although his hair is beginning to thin slightly.

We talked briefly about the Mandelson affair. Blair said Peter had made a terrible mistake, which had come as a complete surprise to him. 'In fact, some fool told me about it three minutes before I made the Iraq statement. I was stunned. I couldn't believe Peter could make such an error of judgement.' But the whole post-Mandelson 'counter-revolution' story had been entirely whipped up by the press. It was complete nonsense that Prescott, Brown and Straw were part of it. Prescott had apparently given an interview to Colin Brown of the *Independent* which had been picked up by a junior reporter and translated from page seven to the front page. 'The worry is that, having got rid of Peter and Geoffrey Robinson, the press now believe they can get rid of ministers in this administration, as they did under Major.'

By this time we were sitting in our familiar positions near the fireplace. On the coffee table in front of Blair were a range of papers, including the remit on the CFSP Ming had agreed with Robin only hours before.

PA: As you know, I have been doing a lot of thinking over the holidays, and the main purpose of my coming here today is to tell you that I have now made my decision. Its timing can be altered, but the decision can't. You know I have been thinking of standing down since the General Election. I had, naturally, hoped that we could take the big step of joining your government before I went. But since that has become impossible, my next task has been to secure the relationship with you as far as my party is concerned, so that you and my successor can continue after I've gone. With the expansion of the JCC, that has now been done. So, I have decided to announce next Wednesday that I am resigning as leader of the Liberal Democrats after the elections in June. I have no wish to cause extra problems for you, so, if you want, I am prepared to wait, say, a week or two. What do you think?

TB: I really don't want you to go, but you have clearly made up your mind. I can see the logic of you going next Wednesday. But I will let you know in a couple of days whether I would ask you to delay a little. When must you know by?

PA: Well, there's a lot of work to be done; I would really like to know by tomorrow, but Thursday would do.

TB: OK, if you don't hear from me by then, go ahead along the lines you suggest. But I am going to miss you. And so, I think, will politics.

PA: That's nice of you. But nobody is irreplaceable. Meanwhile, there are a number of things I'd like you to do. The first is to ask your press people to make the very most of the JCC on Thursday. Our press team has produced this paper [I handed it to him]. It could be used to boost the story that the relationship is a central element of your premiership.

TB (after looking at it): OK, I'll make sure we do something along those lines. I said something like this on *Frost*. Your words are rather stronger than mine, but I don't see anything wrong with them.

PA: Secondly – and I am sorry to be in the mode of *demandeur* here – I need to be clear about how many people we can bank on having to balance up the Lords after your deal with Cranborne. It was a clever deal, but it has left the proportion of peers we have at Stage 1 of the Lords reform significantly below what was agreed under Cook/Maclennan. I have had a paper prepared. You are going to make up some lords in February, I believe.

TB: Yes.

PA: Well, perhaps you will look at this, so that you are aware of the scale of our requirements.

Next, there is the question of further Lords reform. It was agreed in principle that we should see White Papers on the issues we were co-operating on in the JCC, but there appears to have been something of a block here. Bob has asked to see the Lords White Paper, but has been refused by both Margaret Jay and Derry Irvine. Would you mind unblocking that?

And incidentally, I understand that you may be publishing the Lords reform White Paper on Wednesday. If at all feasible, please don't do so if I am to go that day. If it's impossible to delay it a day or so, then let me know and I will make my announcement on Tuesday. I don't want my resignation story swallowed up by the Lords. But, above all, I don't want something so clearly inimical to what we signed up to in Cook/Maclennan published on the day I go.

TB: Well, what do you think we should do now?

PA: About what?

TB: About keeping the project going.

PA: I won't stop being party leader on Wednesday. I still have five or six months to go. And I intend to carry on running the party with a very tight hand. The potential leadership candidates will be constrained by the self-discipline of the forthcoming elections. So we can keep the momentum going in the remaining months of my leadership. We could perhaps widen the remit again. Steve Webb is very keen to do this on pensions, for instance. But let's get CFSP properly established first.

TB: So, will I get Charles Kennedy?

PA: Yes. In my view it's Charles's to lose. But he could lose it. However, if he does win, I think you will get along with him very well. He's excellent company and very bright. Though he will probably tack a bit during the leadership campaign.

TB (looking startled): He isn't going to oppose continuing co-operation, is he?

PA: I'm sure he won't. Simon Hughes will also run, and will get a good number of grassroots votes. But Ming is the wild card. If he runs he could win – but I'm not at all sure he'll run because of the age thing. It may be that Don Foster or Nick Harvey will run, too. If they both run, they will cancel each other out; on the other hand, if one of them chooses to go (most likely Don, in my view) then if Charles makes a mistake, he could slip through.

TB: Are you going to recommend any of them?

PA: No. I don't think it is right for party leaders to interfere in the democratic choice of their successor. My job over the last two years, as part of the succession planning, has been to offer the Party a range of choices and I think they now have it in Charles, Simon, Nick, Don and, possibly, Ming.

TB: Will you have a hand in what they do afterwards?

PA: No, I don't believe ex-party leaders have a role except to advise and help when asked to do so. David Steel has been a model for me on this. Mark Twain quoted in one of his books a message posted in the wheelhouse of a Mississippi steamboat which read, 'Don't speak to the helmsman; don't spit on the floor.' It is a good motto for ex-leaders and I shall do my best to stick to it.

TB: Going is the most difficult thing to do in politics. Too many people stay for too long. I would rather stop when people said, 'Why is he going?' than when they said, 'Why isn't he going?' Or, even worse, 'When is he going?' I hope I will be able to do it the same way.

PA: I have loved doing this job. But my life has been a series of seas on which I have sailed, as soldier, diplomat, businessman. Politics is unquestionably the greatest ocean on which I have sailed, and I will never sail on another as big. But it isn't the only thing I want to do. There is another sea I want to explore before it is all over.

TB: What?

PA: I really don't know yet. I could write. I wouldn't mind doing some broadcasting. And, as you know, I love foreign affairs. Perhaps I could get involved in some way in somewhere like Bosnia or Kosovo.

We went on to talk about the euro. I told him that when the euro campaign came up I would like to play a part: 'Europe is going to be the great event of politics in the next few years. You know my view. The reshaping of British politics needs both an event and a context. PR provides the context – and I had hoped it would come first. But a referendum on the euro provides the event. On the 'Yes' platform you will see the modernizers in

British politics (in all parties, including the Tories). And on the 'No' platform the reactionaries. It will be much easier to have the PR referendum after we have fought and won a successful referendum on the euro together.

TB: I couldn't agree more. And we may be able to go earlier than I previously thought. The economy is doing much better than anticipated. I can tell you that the unemployment figures out tomorrow will actually show a decline. Manufacturing is still in a hell of a state, of course, which is very worrying. But I am pretty confident that we will pull out of that before the end of the year, in which case the way is open for a euro referendum.

PA: It will be a huge challenge for you, you know. The defining moment of your premiership. But it will be a tremendous challenge for the nation as well.

By this time Kate Garvey was putting her head round the door for the third time. Blair was clearly running late for his next appointment, so I said, 'I must go. My last word to you is please don't tell anyone of my intentions until next Wednesday. I don't mind if you tell Alastair and Jonathan the morning I go, but not before. It would be a disaster if it broke.'

I wished him goodbye and good luck, and reminded him that next Wednesday wasn't the end of the line, there was a little more travelling yet to do.

I left via the back door, through Cockpit Passage again, then out through the Cabinet Office entrance and into the rain and evening bustle of Parliament Street.

A poignant moment. But it has been coming for a long time. On the other hand, this was one of the most comradely chats I have ever had with Blair. A Rubicon has, at last, been crossed, but not the one I had hoped for.

Wednesday, 13 January, Westminster

I feel rather strange today. Both angry and sad. This whole thing is coming to an end. But I am sure I am right in doing what I'm doing and in the way that I am doing it. Up rather late, however. Richard rang about 8.00 and I told him about last night's meeting.

We did quite a lot of work on PMQs. David Laws (as usual – he is very good) came up with a splendid public services question which gathered together statistics on police numbers, nursing shortages and teacher vacancies. There was considerable anticipation that we were in for a great PMQs. Hague had so much to work on (Mandelson, Robinson, teachers, etc.). But, as is so often the case when he has too much material, he didn't know which to choose. His jokes fell flat, and his attack floundered.

Then there was the usual groan as I got up. A rather clumsy reference to the New Year had been made earlier on, so instead of cutting the groans short by starting my question, I let them roll up into a crescendo and, as it died, said, 'And a Happy New Year to you, too!' A good laugh from both sides.

I really went for Blair and was quoted on most of the leading news bulletins. One of my better PMQs.

In the evening to the Royal Commonwealth Club for a press reception. I walked down the Embankment to the Club with George Parker of the *Financial Times*, who gently questioned me about my future. Played a dead bat.

It was a pleasant little do. Fifteen or so there and some rather nice red wine. Chaired by Ian Wright. I gave a little speech, then left just before 8.00.

I walked back with Tom McNally up Northumberland Avenue and into Pall Mall, heading for the Reform Club, where I had arranged to have dinner with Ming. On the way Tom told me that he wanted to come and see me. How could he help on the project? I asked him to come and see me next week. Was he going to be around on Wednesday [the day I had fixed to resign]? I nearly spilt the beans. I feel bad about deceiving all these people at this stage, but I just can't tell them more.

Ming met me at 8.15 for dinner and we went straight to his favourite table. During the course of our meal, he questioned me closely about my intentions. I am afraid I threw him completely off the scent by saying that if I was to go it would be around June. At one stage he asked if there wasn't an option for me to announce and go later? I said that was one option that I would have to consider, but I gave him the strong impression that nothing was going to happen. He later reported back to Paul that I had seen sense and wasn't going to go. I had deceived him, of course, but it had to be done.

I asked Ming if he would like to lead the Party, to which he replied that he hadn't totally excluded the idea.

Afterwards to the House for a vote and then a very crowded bus home. Cleared away all the breakfast things I'd left and tumbled into bed at midnight. Dog tired. I am feeling exhausted these days. Nervous tension, I suppose.

Thursday, 14 January, Westminster

Some silly shenanigans with Downing Street last night. Late in the evening Jonathan Powell told Roger that 'the PM has decided that Bob can't see the Lords reform White Paper until after the JCC'. This is plain stupid. I am wondering whether we should use this as a means of withdrawing from the JCC. But the next JCC meeting has had such hype in the press today that we can't.

Spent most of the morning trying to get through to Jonathan, eventually sending him a very stern fax. After Cabinet, at 11.45, he rang today, 'OK, send Bob in at 3.00.'

A victory, of sorts.

Then off to the JCC meeting with Alan, Richard and Ming. A lot of press interest – we were photographed walking up Whitehall and into Downing Street – and when we arrived we were shown pretty swiftly into the Cabinet Room. Blair was about twenty minutes late, so we sat chatting. Jack Straw gave us a long lecture on how more policemen didn't necessarily mean less crime and Robin Cook talked gloomily about Kosovo.

When the JCC meeting was over I asked Blair for a couple of words. We went into his office. Margaret Jay had previously confirmed that the Lords White Paper was out on Wednesday, so I told him that, if that had to be the case, then I would go on Tuesday. He said he would look into this, then questioned me closely on quitting again. Did I really want to go? Was I certain we could maintain the course with the new leader? All rather emotional.

On the way back, Roger said, 'What's up?' I said I would tell him when we got back to the office. When we did so I sat him down and gave him my resignation letter.[1] He went ashen-faced. 'This is nonsense. Can't we dissuade you?' I told him no and eventually he calmed down a bit. As usual, in his professional way, he said he would help in any way he could. So I sent him down to the conference room to read the full plan for my resignation. God, I hate this.

Then off with Andrew Garratt to the FE. He, too is becoming suspicious that something is afoot. But I can't tell him yet. I will do so on Monday. The FE was a doddle. No complaints about the expansion of the CFSP. I had feared otherwise, but Andrew's paper silenced them all.

1 See Appendix I.

In the early evening Roger reported that Jonathan had rung to say that of course they would shift the White Paper to Thursday.

Monday, 18 January. Somerset

This is my big week. I am as nervous as a kitten. And suddenly really worried about the outcome.

At 7.30 Hilary Leamon[1] arrived at Vane Cottage for our breakfast meeting. I sat her down and said, 'I'm afraid this will come as rather a shock to you. And I am also afraid that I am dumping on your plate more than you might have expected when you took over as constituency chair. I am informing you in this letter that I will stand down as MP for Yeovil at the next election.'

She looked absolutely startled, then the tears started to well up in her eyes. So I moved quickly on. 'I am terribly sorry to give you such a surprise, but there really is no other way of doing this. Here's my letter of resignation. Why don't you sit down and look through it?'

As she did so I could see the colour coming back into her cheeks.

I said that I would not in any way interfere in the selection of my successor, but that I hoped they would give women a real chance in the selection process and also that they would begin the process of selecting my successor as soon as possible. We spent an hour or so discussing the consequences. She said that she would be meeting the officers tomorrow night; could she tell them? I said, of course, if she wanted, but beyond that we must keep it secret until Wednesday.

Jane dropped me off at the Yeovil office at about 10.30, where I told the rest of the staff.

By 12 o'clock we were on the road for London. I worked all the way up, largely on the documents for Wednesday.

We arrived in Westminster at 2.30 and I immediately called in Andrew and told him. He said, rather alarmingly, that he had already guessed, but he did not in any way upbraid me for not telling him earlier. We immediately got down to discussing what he had to do. He went away to prepare for this evening's meeting. [I had called a meeting of all those 'in the know' over a dinner Jane would bring into the office, to finalize the plans for Wednesday.]

---

1 Chair of the Yeovil Constituency Liberal Democrats.

Afterwards, a discussion with Miranda and David on the revised press programme. Then a word to Paul about the colleagues. I feel particularly guilty about Ming.

Meanwhile, Kosovo has blown up again.[1] Talked to Ming and David Heath. I don't think our present line (just using air power) is adequate for the current situation. If we manage to stop Milosevic, so much the better. But I am doubtful that we will. In my view, the only option will eventually be to put troops on the ground in Kosovo and we ought to start the planning for this now. Milosevic will probably try an 'ultimate solution' of driving out all the Albanian Kosovars. In which case the West will not be able simply to stand by and watch the region turn into a bloodbath. After a long discussion, Ming and David agreed with me – Ming reluctantly (he thinks threatening ground troops is a big risk – he's right).

At 8.00 Jane came in and we laid the tables in my conference room for the evening meeting. Andrew ordered in some pizza, and I got together the wine. The table looked rather merry. At 8.30 we all gathered – Paul, Chris, Miranda, David, Roger, Andrew, George, Jane and I – to go through the programme, make minor amendments, finalize my resignation letters, etc.

Home at 10.15, very nervous. As I left, Miranda told me that she and David had been talking. They are very pessimistic. They don't think the line will hold. It will look as if I am abandoning the project etc. 'It is not our enemies that I am afraid of,' she said. 'It's disappointing our friends.'

To bed at around 11.30 but I didn't sleep very well. Nervous about everything.

Tuesday, 19 January, London

A campaigning day spent in Southwark looking at the Jubilee Line extension, among other things.

At 3.30 back to Westminster.

Spoke to Downing Street about the final details – they will put out a statement at their end. Only Jonathan and Alastair know. We heard later that Mandelson complained bitterly that, although he sees Blair about three times a day (!!), he was unhappy he hadn't been informed. To which Blair replied, 'Paddy asked me not to tell anyone else, so I didn't.'

---

1 On 15 January there had been a terrible massacre of Albanians in Racak, which had outraged world opinion.

I am extremely nervous. Another meeting at 7.00pm to finalize the details for tomorrow. The whole office has been working late – we didn't finish until nearly 11.00. Miranda, once again, began to have serious reservations about the whole thing: 'You will have a very hard job explaining all this tomorrow.' Jane came in to pick me up and we dropped Becks back at her flat.

To bed at 12.00, but little sleep.

Wednesday, 20 January, Westminster

Up at 7.00 with Jane dropping me at the office by 8.00. Cleared my e-mails, then a meeting of office staff not already in the know at 9.00. They were all a bit stunned but took it very well, and immediately settled down to their tasks.

I stressed, heavily, the need for confidentiality. And they maintained it scrupulously.

At 9.15, Jim Wallace came in and I told him. He seemed quietly surprised.

At 10.30, Diana Maddock. She had expected the worst. Her first reaction was, 'Goodness, that's a relief. I thought you might be about to announce we were going into coalition. You know, I had half thought it might be this.' She rebuked me for not telling her earlier. I felt rather guilty.

Then Bill Rodgers at 11 o'clock. He came breezing in expecting to discuss the Lords White Paper and launched into a long diatribe against [Lord] Wakeham who is, we hear, going to chair the Royal Commission. 'He is honest. But I do not think he has the qualities to chair a Royal Commission of this importance.'

When he had finished, I said quietly, 'Bill, I have a bit of a shock for you,' – and handed him my resignation letter.

He had obviously not seen it coming and went completely white. 'Oh my God, oh my God. Are you sure I cannot dissuade you?'

I told him that the Party could be perfectly well led by somebody else now. He left, shaking me by the hand and saying, 'You have done a wonderful job.'

Then at 12.30 Alan Beith, who said that he'd half anticipated this would happen. He made it clear to me that he didn't want to stand for leader, but he was interested in the Speakership. A far better meeting than I had feared.

At 2.15 the meeting I was dreading. Ming. I sat him down, gave him the

"WE WERE NEVER REALLY MARRIED ANYWAY."

letter and said, 'Ming, I am afraid I pulled the wool over your eyes when we dined at the Reform Club the other night. I am so sorry.'

Ming said, 'That is dreadful news. Just dreadful. This is a disastrous way of doing it. I had half a sense that this was coming, but that doesn't make it any better.'

I said that I wouldn't, of course, be taking sides in any leadership election but I wouldn't be surprised if the 'Young Turks'[1] supported him for the leadership, so that they stood a better chance later. 'Young cardinals tend to vote for old popes,' I said. Secondly, a longer campaign would almost certainly expose the other candidates' deficiencies, which would be beneficial to him should he decide to run.

He left, my office staff told me later, looking grey.

Then down to PMQs. Hague was dreadful. A clear sign of a party in decline is that, at times like PMQs, they follow their obsessions rather than the issues of the day. He didn't go on Lords and he didn't go on Kosovo. He went on the ceasefire and terrorist beatings in Northern Ireland. Blair handled him superbly. Quiet, gentle and agonized.

When I got up people groaned; when I mentioned Kosovo they groaned even louder; when I mentioned ground troops the groans turned into cat calls. But Blair's answer was substantive and made it clear (despite Cook's

---

1 The bright new MPs of the 1997 intake.

adamant and repeated statement to the contrary) that ground troops were a serious option.

Then back to my office. At exactly the same time as Blair had started PMQs, Jane began ringing our friends in Yeovil to tell them of my decision. When I got back to the office I started making phone calls, too. To Nick Speakman,[1] Nick South, Alan Leaman, Mark Payne[2] and others.

At 4.30 Richard Livsey, who leapt up, shook me by the hand and said, 'It is a wonderful decision and you have done it at just the right time. I really admire you. Typical Ashdown.'

At 5.00 the Team Leaders. By now people had gathered that something was afoot. There was silence when I announced it to them.

Then at 5.15 the Parliamentary Party. Dead silence again. I read my resignation letter out quietly, after which Diana read out her letter of acceptance and we took a few questions. They were all very, very nice.

After everyone had received a copy of the letter Alan continued with the PPM. Paul took the likely leadership contenders to one side, emphasizing the need not to start the leadership campaign immediately. The plan worked like clockwork.

The news was broken publicly in the chamber just as the PPM started. Poor Ed Davey was on his feet speaking when a Tory interrupted to say that his leader had just resigned.[3] Ed, of course, knew nothing about it, so it was a potentially very difficult moment for him. But he responded brilliantly by saying that even if I had resigned I was still a better leader than theirs!

Then into a mad round of interviews and photos with Jane in my office.

I spoke to several of the key political editors. Miranda had suggested earlier in the day that I ought to bring Jane into the briefing, since the main question we had to answer was 'Why?', and Jane was a key part of the answer. She sat at the back taking a number of questions. Somebody asked her what the reactions of friends had been like. She replied that one of them (Lelly Jefferies) had said I wasn't to be let near a cook book! She drew a tremendous amount of the television attention away from me – which was excellent. Jane's characteristically blunt explanations helped them to see the reasons. Some, however, remained hostile, deeply suspicious that they were not, as they saw it, getting the full story. So I again went through

---

1 My agent in all the elections I have fought.
2 All past heads of my office.
3 I have subsequently been informed that the leak came not from Westminster but from my local newspaper, the *Western Gazette*, whom I had informed through one of their staff.

the whys and the wherefores. [My resignation ran as the lead story in most of the following day's papers, the majority of which were extremely kind.]

Afterwards, Richard, David Walter and Miranda, all of whom had been extremely nervous, said that it had gone well.

At 8.30, after all the journos had gone, we opened a bottle of champagne and had a small, sadness-tinged, celebration.

Down for dinner. As it happened, our table was full, so I said, 'Is there any room for me, or have I been thrown out already?' I went over to a Labour table to get a chair and someone said, 'Do come and join us.' To which I responded with a smile accompanied by a rude sign.

Then votes at 10.00 and home with Jane.

Today has gone well, but I am really nervous about tomorrow's papers. The BBC and ITV news have both said some very kind things. As I'd hoped, the generosity of the British press comes through at times like these. So far they have accepted my reasons, but they will start digging as hard as they can tomorrow, hoping to find something else. They find it impossible to take a simple story at face value.

To bed a little after midnight. I didn't sleep well, however, filled with the subsiding tension of the day and worries about tomorrow.

Thursday, 21 January, London

Up at 5.30 and off at 6.15 for an interview with GMTV which started with, 'You didn't resign because you are ill or there is a scandal about to break, did you?' I tried to sound light-hearted.

Then ITV and the *Today* programme with John Humphrys. Jane said he was noticeably less unkind than sometimes.

I missed the Leaders' Co-ordinating Group meeting but arrived for the Team Leaders' meeting at 9.30. Quite a long debate about the leadership election campaign, etc.

At 4.00 off by taxi with Miranda to Waterloo to catch the 4.35 to Yeovil. The press photographed me boarding the train and I did an interview all the way down to Basingstoke. After which I waded through my e-mails.

Jane met me at Crewkerne and drove me through thick fog back to Vane Cottage, where I got changed, then walked up to Norton village hall for the constituency council meeting. They gave me a very generous round of applause and I made a brief speech. The village hall was bathed in TV lights with a satellite van and a mass of press outside. I did some brief interviews going in and then again coming out.

Then down to the pub for a pint and home for dinner at around 9.00. Steph Bailey (our neighbour) had made us a wonderful shepherd's pie, which we tucked into with gusto.

We opened a bottle of excellent 1990 Irancy and were all feeling a little merry when the phone rang at around 11.30.

The *Daily Mail*. Did I have any comments on the Tricia Howard[1] article in tomorrow's *Daily Express*?

At 10.30 the previous evening, apparently the *Express* had knocked on Tricia's door. And as a result, they were publishing a two-page spread which said some pretty hurtful things; while I would become a lord she would be alone paying her bills. I was plunged into a paroxysm of anger and misery. Jane, too. Rang Tricia, who said she was both furious and hurt – an *Express* journalist had concocted something out of the non-interview Tricia had given them last night. Why does it always keep coming up? Hopefully this will be the last time.

To bed at 1.15. But a disturbed night again.

Friday, 22 January, Somerset

The *Mail* has repeated the *Express* story on Tricia, claiming it for their own but in fact lifting it almost verbatim from their rival, pictures and all. Not nice.

We have been hit by an avalanche of mail, ranging from the genuinely sad to the hagiographically kind. About 400 letters already from all sorts of people – some party members, of course; but many more from members of the public and even some from Tory and Labour MPs. Inevitably one or two nasties among them – and a couple of amusing ones, too:

YOU ARE
GOING
HOORAY
BLOODY GOOD
RIDDANCE
PISS OFF TO GERMANY

1 See Vol. I, pp. 132–3 and elsewhere.

Dear Mr Ashdown,

I will be sorry to see you go, but at least it will save me from the constant frustration and ever mounting anger of listening to you talking perfect sense about the Balkans and being ignored by everyone that matters.

Reluctantly I have come to the conclusion that you have been ignored because, although you talk sense about Bosnia and Kosovo, you talk bollocks about nearly everything else, particularly Europe and PR.

Now that you are free not to have to pretend to embrace these dangerous notions, I hope that you will put some guts and gumption into British and European policies in the Balkans.

Presumably the new House of Lords will be the correct place from which you will lead the world?

Yours sincerely, etc.

Dear Paddy,

When you started you were third out of three. You finish third out of three. In the Job-centre in Barrow St Helens, Merseyside, they are looking for bin men and street cleaners.

Yours, etc.

Dear Sir,

Having found out that Paddy Ashdown is retiring, I wish to apply for the position of Liberal Democrat Party leader. Please grant me an interview. Attached is my CV.

I want to start up the World Space Agency (WSA); the World Army (WA); UK's National Union of Unions (NUU); school governors introducing the space industry; the UK space industry's non-periscope submarine fleet which when permanently submerged will carry launch and land mini-submarines; safer and economical improvements to NHS hospital treatment to babies and more District Council jobs.

Thank you.

Yours faithfully, etc.

Saturday, 23 January, Somerset

Charles has won the unofficial leadership campaign media battle so far,[1] by refusing all press interviews and therefore being talked about for his self-restraint. Clever. Making a news item out of the fact that he is not seeking media attention puts him above the fray, while simultaneously

1 The formal leadership campaigns would not begin until after the Euro elections in June.

marking him out as the front runner. I said to Miranda yesterday that we should start a board game on the leadership election, based on snakes and ladders. The next few months are going to provide some wonderful spectator sport.

Sunday, 7 February, Somerset–Amman

Up at 7.00. Cleared my in-tray, then a morning's work on the computer. I had just finished at about 10.15 and was about to do my exercises when the phone rang. Downing Street. It had just been confirmed that King Hussein of Jordan is dead[1]. Could I be at the Royal Suite at Heathrow at 3.00? [In accordance with normal practice, the PM's office asked the leaders of the two national opposition parties to accompany him in his official plane to the funeral.] I swiftly packed and said goodbye to Jane.

A beautifully bright day today, but with a bitterly cold north wind. They are forecasting snow. I listened to Puccini on the way up to Heathrow, getting there comfortably by 2.00. The others started drifting in at about 2.45. Hague arrived first, with Sebastian Coe in tow. We exchanged a few pleasantries, waited for Blair's party to arrive, boarded the PM's VC10 and took off at 3.30.

I settled down to do some work on the way out. But soon after we took off Alastair Campbell sought me out and said that Blair wanted a word, 'although we'd have to be a bit careful with Hague here'. In the event, however, Coe and Hague fell asleep, so I went into the Prime Minister's compartment and we spent half an hour talking at his table before dinner.

He told me that the Cabinet meeting after my resignation had gone well; they were all very strongly in favour of continuing with the project. Despite what the press said, he believed that the project was still very firmly founded. I said I was more doubtful in the long term. Not because of my resignation, but because there wasn't enough substance for us to be getting on with. Since we aren't going to have PR this parliament, the opportunity to move towards a semi-coalition before the next election has effectively vanished.

---

1 In fact, he had been close to death for a number of days, but the family, reportedly, kept the life-support machine on so that they could give sufficient notice for world leaders to alter their diaries in order to attend – otherwise the Muslim tradition of burial between sunrise and sunset on the day following the death would have created chaos. An appropriate time having elapsed, the machine had been turned off that morning.

We talked about the leadership campaign. He thinks Charles has started well. I agree, although he has been looking a little tense recently.

Then Kosovo. He is 'moderately optimistic', and Robin is, apparently, doing a good job. 'Incidentally, I never thanked you for your reports. They have helped shape our position.'

Then Hague and Coe came in and we had a jolly dinner, telling political stories, before returning to our seats shortly before landing at Amman airport.

We were one of the first foreign delegations to arrive, so we didn't have long to wait before the Jordanian welcoming party came out to greet us. Blair went down the steps first, then Hague and myself. We followed each other, shaking hands and walking through the guard of honour to the VIP suite, where Blair did some interviews. Then into the city. The roads were practically deserted and lined with soldiers nearly all the way. This must be a security nightmare.

We arrived at the hotel and were shown to our rooms. My baggage was still downstairs, so I went to fetch it, passing the open door to Blair's suite on the way. He called me in. Alastair Campbell was also there. We sat on the sofa, drank a couple of glasses of white wine and talked chiefly about the Tories and Kosovo.[1]

Campbell was sitting at a desk taking phone call after phone call arranging press interviews. He said to Blair just before I left, 'Right, that's it all fixed up. Not *Breakfast Time*, that's too early. But you are on Sky, the BBC and the *Today* programme in the morning.' Blair groaned.

Having collected my bags, I went up to my room for a stiff whisky and to collect my e-mails. To bed about 1.00. I was dreading not being able to sleep – my nose is terribly blocked up from a fierce cold. But in the event a couple of Nurofen for my back [which I had injured in the gym], the whisky and some decongestant did the trick.

Monday, 8 February, Amman

I woke at 6.00, as dawn was breaking, to hear the muezzin calling from a nearby mosque. Down for breakfast at about 8.30, after which I took a walk through the streets, which were empty but for VIP limousines cruising

---

1 The first round of Rambouillet talks between Albanians and Serbs, under the co-chairmanship of Britain and France, had recently begun.

quietly about and security guards on every corner. A sharp wind blowing. It rained last night, which is rare in Amman. As our driver commented later in the day, 'Even God is weeping.'

Then, at just past 11.00, we were whisked off for what turned out to be one of the most extraordinary days I have experienced.

First of all we were taken to the Royal Palace complex, which, as in most other Arab countries, is surrounded by a substantial military camp. We were shown to Hussein's previous personal palace, where he lived before the current (and bigger) Ragadan Palace had been built. Here we met up with the Prince of Wales, who was already installed in one of the presidential suites set aside for the British delegation. The Ambassador, Christopher Bettiscombe, was there, as were Blair, Campbell, Hague, Coe, the military attaché and the commandant of Sandhurst (where Hussein had trained as an officer).

Over the next two hours the palace completely filled up with the great and the good of the world.

Blair said he was off to do some 'bilaterals'[1] and there was much discussion as to who they should go and see. Eventually people started to come and see him.

First in was the diminutive Shaikh Isa bin Salamn Al-Khalifa, the Amir of Bahrain – a lovely little man with twinkling eyes and a seemingly permanent and highly infectious laugh in his mouth. They sat chatting like old friends as the shaikh kept cracking what he thought were jokes.

Afterwards, in swift order, the Amir of Kuwait, then the Sultan of Oman – a magnificent-looking man with a big hook nose, wearing the most gorgeous black robe trimmed in gold.

The conversation with these two was very stilted, though.

In the middle of the Amir of Kuwait's bilateral, George Bush [Senior] walked in. Hague immediately moved over to talk to him. Bush apologized to Blair for interrupting and there followed a rather comradely chat between the two of them.

Then Blair went off to do yet more bilaterals with, among others, the French, the Germans and the Saudis.

I decided to go off and explore.

Every room was now full. Heads of state bumping into each other in every corridor and round every corner. I nearly tripped over Chirac and

---

1 Face-to-face meetings between heads of governments, with note-takers present.

Schroeder sitting chatting on the stairs. Apparently, only the British and the Americans were given suites. Everyone else just milled around.

The Ambassador told me, 'It is quite possible to walk down a corridor here and do more business in an hour than you would normally in a whole year – this is what the diplomats call a "working funeral".'

On the ground floor amongst the throng I counted Queen Beatrice of the Netherlands, the King of Norway, King Juan Carlos of Spain, and Kofi Annan (with whom I had a long chat). Yasser Arafat came up and shook me by the hand like a long lost friend, his lip quivering so much he didn't seem able to speak. (I am not at all sure he knew who I was.) He looked terribly ill.

Also Netanyahu, Peres and Weizman[1] in a nervous huddle, with all the Arabs around them. Netanyahu looking shifty and Peres looking magnificent as always.

I went back up to the British suite just as Clinton was coming in. He is terribly touchy-feely. But his face looks even more flushed, fleshy and 'lived-in' than I recall from the last time I met him. His hair has now gone completely white. He went up to Blair, shook him by the hand, then patted him on the right shoulder and kept his hand there for at least five minutes. Then he bumped into the Prince of Wales, shook his hand and, putting his left hand on the Prince's right arm, started patting it then stroking it. As he passed me by he also shook me by the hand, but mercifully spared me the stroke treatment. He seemed to remember me from Portsmouth, which was pretty extraordinary.

At last, at about 2.00, we were taken out to walk up the hill in the sunshine, behind a huge cortège of people. As we neared the Ragaden Palace the gates opened and a Jordanian army corporal rushed out and pushed everyone unceremoniously to one side. A huge black Russian Zil limousine with darkened windows appeared and made its stately way in the opposite direction through the throng and down the hill. Yeltsin apparently, who had flown out against his doctor's orders, arrived in the Ragadan Palace to see the coffin, immediately got 'ill' and left.

Then into the palace itself and an even more pressing crush of heads of state and hangers-on. All pushing and shoving their way into the palace grounds and upstairs into the chamber where Hussein's coffin lay on a beautifully decorated plinth. Our British delegation, led by the Prince of

1 Benjamin Netanyahu, then prime minister of Israel; Shimon Peres, former prime minister of Israel; and Ezer Weizman, president of Israel.

Wales, somehow managed to keep together in the crush. We stood for a moment at the coffin, bowed our heads, then moved on. On the way out I saw Netanyahu, Weizman and Peres waiting to go in – clearly being kept behind, guarded by security people who must have been scared out of their wits about their safety in the middle of so much congregated Araby.

Then downstairs into the courtyard outside, to join the gun carriage waiting for its coffin. By now the sun was roasting, but the crush of the great and the good intensified. After about fifteen minutes the coffin came out and was loaded on to a waiting gun carriage, and we all followed it in a long, ragged and disorganized crocodile up the hill again. At the top, the coffin was dismounted and carried the remaining few yards into the royal mosque. All the Muslims split off to follow it while the rest of us stood around outside. I was standing next to Queen Beatrice of the Netherlands as Clinton came past shaking everybody by the hand and working the crowd like a gathering of the faithful in Milwaukee. I turned to her and said, 'That, Your Majesty, is a royal progression.' To which she giggled and replied, 'You are very naughty, Mr Ashdown, to make me laugh on such a solemn occasion as this.'

In due course the coffin came out again and we re-formed like Napoleon's army struggling back from Moscow and followed it up the hill to the cemetery, where there was yet another almighty crush. Someone had to take charge and once again it fell to our Jordanian lance corporal to do it. He stopped the column and shouted, 'Right – all heads of state to the front!' and then started to upbraid the assembled dignitaries as though they were Sandhurst recruits for not moving fast enough. A glorious moment.

We then headed into a series of tents forming a hollow square around a courtyard while, out of sight, the coffin was lowered into the grave. We heard the fusillade of shots over the coffin, followed by a 21-gun salute. Then we were once again instructed by the lance corporal to move on through a small gate leading from the courtyard to the graveside, to pay our respects to the family.

There must have been around 600 people there. I found myself pressed up against Haris Siladjic,[1] who was in great form. We were just talking about my possibly coming back to Sarajevo when I was called forward by another Jordanian army person. So I wished Haris '*Strettno*' [Serbo-Croat for 'Good Luck'] and was immediately engulfed in the wildest pushing

1 See Vol. I, p. 271 and elsewhere. Chairman of the Bosnian Council of Ministers, formerly Prime Minister of Bosnia.

match I have ever encountered. Behind me was the Japanese Crown Prince and his delegation. They obviously decided that if pushing was the game, they were world experts. They shoved as though they were trying to get on to the bullet train in the rush hour. In the event, I was swept along with them. Suddenly, to my right, I heard someone shouting 'Help!' I looked down to see the diminutive figure of Shaikh Isa of Bahrain. His delegation was trying to get him through because, as an Arab, he ought to be among the first to pay his respects to the Jordanian Royal Family. I put my hands against a neighbouring wall and pushed back against the Japanese behind me, forming an arch under which Isa and his delegation could pass. He was followed in swift order by the Amir of Kuwait and the Sultan of Oman, who, together with their sizeable delegations, passed beneath my outstretched arms, while the Japanese pushed and cursed behind us.

Eventually it was my turn to meet King Abdullah and the Royal Family. I shook them by the hands and then went out and waited for Blair and his delegation, who had been left far behind in the crush. By now it was getting late and cold. We waited around for about half an hour before Blair appeared. He had got caught at the back of the queue along with the Prince of Wales and Clinton. The US security people were going mad with worry.

Then back to our suite in the palace again, where a whole new collection of foreign dignitaries awaited us. These turned out to be chiefly deposed European royals, now living, it appeared, mostly in St John's Wood, all of whom wanted a lift home on the Prince of Wales's aircraft.[1]

After a while, Chirac came in, too. I happened to be speaking to Blair alone when he came to join us. I motioned to leave but they insisted I should stay. They got down to talking about the Rambouillet peace talks in Kosovo. Apparently, they were going reasonably well. 'The KLA are outrageous. They took over a wing of the château and spent the whole night drinking and keeping everyone else awake. But that is their affair,' said Chirac, shrugging his shoulders. I was fascinated to hear Blair and him speak half in English and half in French. Chirac said that he could not put troops into Kosovo unless there was a UN Security Council resolution to support this. Soon their advisers started to crowd round, recognizing that something important was going on. I saw their note-takers fidgeting, so gave my seat to one of them and moved away to talk to the Prince of Wales.

1 One of them was Crown Prince Alexander of Yugoslavia, there with his delightful wife, who insisted on pouring tea and fetching sandwiches for everybody. Alexander gave me his card which told me that his e-mail address was hrhcpalex@ ... .com. When I asked him what 'hrhcpalex' stood for, he said 'His Royal Highness Crown Prince Alexander, of course'.

Meanwhile, on the television monitor, we could see King Abdullah still shaking hands. He was at it for the best part of two hours.

Eventually, it was time to go. Blair and the Prince of Wales went in to say goodbye to King Abdullah while we waited outside. Then we shot off to the airport. The politicians boarded the VC10 while the Prince of Wales and his gang of St John's Wood ex-royals loaded on to his HS11. We were delayed on the runway, so didn't take off until about 8.20. I rang the office to warn Jane that I wouldn't be back until after midnight.

A smooth flight back. Dinner was a pretty appalling RAF meal, during which there was a long discussion on Shiite Muslims and the events of the day. Alastair Campbell said Blair had had seventeen bilaterals. 'And two of them were with people he didn't even know!' Blair went on to recount how he had been stopped on the stairs by two Arabs and had become involved in a long discussion with them. When they had finished with him, he saw them heading towards Chirac, who spotted them coming and darted over to Blair, saying, '*Qui est-ce?*' Blair shrugged his shoulders and replied, '*Je ne sais pas de tout!*'

Then there was Gaddafi's younger son, a long, sallow, obsessed-looking young man, with a fundamentalist beard and a very ill-fitting Chinese-style uniform, who had, apparently, followed a group of Western leaders, including Chirac, Schroeder, Blair and Clinton, up the hill to the mosque. The attendant Western ambassadors had formed themselves into a wall behind their bosses to stop Gaddafi Junior getting close enough for some mischievous photographers to take a picture of them all together.

After dinner, Hague made his excuses and left. This left Blair, Campbell and me alone for about forty-five minutes. We started talking about my successor. I told Blair that he should remember that, although he and I had worked hand in hand for a long time, my successor would be a complete stranger to this 'secret garden'. Blair would have to bring him round slowly to the idea. Above all, he would have to show that he and I had a shared vision. It would be likely that my successor would believe that I had exaggerated Blair's commitment to the project.

I asked him about a euro referendum, to which he replied, 'It will be very difficult to change the timing that has already been agreed. Perhaps the next step – for which industry is pressing me – is to say we would like to join it if it can be done.' I said I thought this put him on a one-way escalator to an early referendum, but he disagreed.

We also talked briefly about Hague. I pointed out that Hague had a negative rating in every single category of voter and in every single region in Britain – even in Yorkshire. Alastair started to say that he could see a way to sell Hague, but Blair, surprisingly sharply, shut him up immediately.

Alastair added that he thought Hague was losing his self-confidence. He had watched him throughout the day: he was quite content to hang back instead of getting up close to where the proper photo opportunities had been; he had even deferred to me in the key photo of the day – the picture of the Prince of Wales, Blair, Hague and myself at Hussein's tomb. And there was something in his demeanour on the plane that was also half-apologetic. A perceptive comment.

Finally, I told Blair about my diary. He blanched. He asked how big it was and I showed him by holding my two hands about eighteen inches apart.

Alastair said, 'When do you get time to do it?' Where is it?'

I said it was all in a Yeovil bank safe.

'Be careful, you have had trouble with safes, Ashdown,' he replied[1] – to laughter.

We arrived at Heathrow, where the temperature was down to zero and it was snowing, at midnight.

Saturday, 13 February, Somerset

Sent the following letter to Blair:

Dear Tony,

I thought it might be worthwhile to put on paper the points we discussed in our conversation on the plane on our way back from Amman.

I do not have worries about the Lib Dems continuing with the project under my successor.

Positively, our relationship brings real and tangible benefits – and can continue to do so.

And negatively, not to follow this strategy would mean risking being made irrelevant by what you are doing.

But I do want to stress that you are, nevertheless, going to have to put some effort in with my successor, and this will, I fear, take up some of your personal time. You can, of course, count on me. But ex-leaders are not the best people to give their successors advice.

1 Referring to the theft of documents from my lawyer's safe in January 1992. See Vol. I, p. 133.

In the end, you and I worked together because we established a personal relationship and learned to trust each other. You will need to do the same with my successor.

Key to this will be four things:

First, you will have to spend a little time telling him (and it will be a 'him') of your vision and convincing him of it. Remember that he will only have heard of this from me. It is possible that he will think that this is just my vision – so it will be important for him to hear about it in your words and from your mouth.

Second, you will need to have a clear framework for our future work together. Since the election, you have had lots of other things to think about. When it comes to future projects, it is mostly Richard and I who have thought of these and pushed them forward. This is not a criticism. It is how it should have been. You and I were so much inside each other's minds on all this that it was right that I should have been doing the pushing since the election – since you had more than enough other things to occupy you.

But please don't underestimate the inertia, which could, in consequence, follow when my successor takes over. You and I have been thinking and working on this for four or five years. He will be coming to it new; as a person does who enters, for the first time, a room they have heard a lot about, but never been inside.

Third, is the importance of keeping up momentum. What we have learned is that the project can only be kept going if we have a target in mind, a framework within which to work and individual projects to work on. It will be up to your lot to provide these for a bit. Should someone start working on this now?

My own view, as I told you, is that the long-term target to work for is to go into the next election on the basis of joint heads of agreement between both parties. This will open the way to more formal co-operation in the next government, in a way which, regrettably, eluded us in this. It is also the natural conclusion to aim for after the programme of detailed co-operation projects, which you wrote down on the aircraft as we flew home.

But *please* always remember the difference between us. You are giving from a position of strength, which always makes one feel good. We are receiving from a position of weakness, which nearly always makes one feel suspicious. You stand to become the monarch of the big tent. We risk being swallowed up into little more than a satrapy. And there is no point in talking about the logic of eventual merger. For my people, this is not a question of logic – it's a question of emotion. People do not go into politics, especially in a party where the rewards have not up to now included power, in order to lose their identity, however rational the arguments may be for doing so. If, eventually, merger happens (and you know that you and I have differing views on this, at least in the short term), it will have to be organic and grow from the bottom up, after a period in power of joint responsibility and shared adversity. Push this too early, and the whole project will be terminally damaged.

Fourth, you will have to be quite generous and very patient with my successor – even if this leads you to more flak from your own side about 'giving the Lib Dems too much'.

Set something aside to give him very early on, so that he can show to the party that (a) he, too, can win things from the relationship of benefit to the Lib Dems and (b) you are as serious about working with him on the project as you were with me.

Finally, you asked me about the future.

I have no particular plans. I am quite content to be the MP for Yeovil for the rest of this parliament. I have plenty to involve myself in; I will take a continuing and, I hope, closer interest, especially, in foreign and European affairs and particularly in the Balkans; I have a book I want to write. And I am being approached from some quarters to get involved in broader issues related to conflict resolution.

So I am not in a hurry to take decisions. But, as I am sure you know, if there is any way you feel I can help you, the project, or the wider public service, then you can count on me.

Yours
Paddy

Monday, 22 February, Westminster

At about 4.00pm Downing Street rang. Would I go and see the PM at 5.15 to talk about a statement the government is making tomorrow on the euro? I set off down Whitehall at 5.00, fighting my way through the crowds and a blustery, biting north wind.

Spent a few minutes in the outer office chatting with the office staff. Also had a brief word with the new Foreign Office man at No. 10, John Sawers. He is pretty pessimistic about the Rambouillet progress.[1] The KLA are being thoroughly intransigent.

Blair and I talked chiefly about the euro, but at the end he switched to Kosovo.

---

1 The first round of the Rambouillet talks had broken down on 17 February and were due to reconvene on 15 March.

TB: What do you think should be done?

PA: That depends on how the talks are going.

He was more optimistic about them than John Sawers, but also said that the problem was the KLA.

TB: We can't bomb Milosevic if he accepts the Rambouillet deal but the KLA don't. That is our firm view. But the Americans seem to think otherwise. Which is putting a lot of political pressure on the relationship.

PA: I think it is absolutely crucial that we only use air power in a manner consistent with the diplomatic strategy, and with a political aim in mind. But there is one other circumstance in which you could use air power. You could, in the absence of any agreement, say to Milosevic, 'We don't trust you with heavy weapons. Every time you use them you do so in a display of excessive force which is clearly contrary to international law and is deeply destablizing to the region. We are therefore going to deny you the right to use heavy weapons and give you a deadline to get them out of Kosovo and will then be prepared to use air power against any which fail to comply.' But we should recognize the consequence of such an action. We would, in effect, be using Western planes as a substitute air force for the KLA. Without heavy weapons the Serbs would probably lose in any sustained fighting. But in the end I think that may be the least worst of the options.

Finally, if all else fails, we have two terrifying options to consider: Verifiers out, or troops in. On the face of it. Verifiers out looks easier. But it isn't. It would be a signal to Milosevic to go ahead with what I still believe he plans: a 'final solution', in which he drives out all Albanians from Kosovo. Would the West then stand idly by watching the bloodshed that ensued (and the destabilization of Macedonia)? Our public opinion simply wouldn't allow that to happen. But even if it did, could we contemplate what comes next? A widening Balkan war.

He leaned forward and said, 'Look, there is no question of us putting troops in if it is opposed by the Serbs.'

I replied that I thought it would be very, very difficult, and casualties could be considerable, but it might be preferable to widening the war in the Balkans. We would have to contemplate it in the end.

At this stage Kate was putting her head round the door every two or three minutes, so I took the hint and left.

Monday, 1 March, Westminster

Windy, muggy, warm and wet. I hate this time of year. Jane is feeling lousy as a result of her cold and flu, which just won't go away.

At 5 o'clock I called a meeting with Ming to see if we could map out a new line on Kosovo. I am getting very nervous about what is happening there – a full-scale mobilization of Serb forces.[1] They exceeded the ceasefire limits long ago and are now massing on the Macedonian border in an obvious attempt to face down NATO. We are very close to a major conflict here. Our line is much tougher than before, saying that independence has to be a long-term option. Kosovo cannot now return to the status quo ante and be part of Serbia. We will have to set up an international protectorate there.

Sunday, 7 March, Edinburgh

The Party Conference – and my last conference speech as leader.

A big profile of Charles in the *Observer*, with a very nice picture. Charles has allowed himself, however, to be put in a position where the headline says that he doesn't believe there is any scope for the expansion of the JCC.

Had my usual pre-speech nerves in the morning. Made some last-minute changes. Then, at 12.45, headed off for the conference centre. God, I hate the waiting. They brought me up on to the stage at about 1.15. The delegates gave me a very warm reception. In the event, the speech went well enough, although my voice started to crack a bit towards the end. I wanted to lift the peroration but couldn't because I was feeling too emotional. I left the platform rather misty-eyed.

Monday, 8 March, Westminster

During the afternoon I got a message. Could I go and see Gordon Brown?

So at 4 o'clock I walked over to the Treasury, where I was quickly taken up to the Chancellor's room.

It is a splendid room, about twenty metres long, with oak panels and the Chancellor's desk at the far end. A screen and some high-tech stuff about;

1 The Rambouillet talks were continuing but showed little progress.

otherwise pretty bare. Gordon told me a hilarious story about Healey[1] and Pardoe,[2] when they had met here during the Lib/Lab pact. Apparently, at one stage Pardoe had got so angry that he'd stormed out, slamming the massive oak door behind him, saying that the pact was over. There had then been silence for ten minutes, after which Pardoe had sheepishly put his head round the door, saying please could somebody show him out, as he was lost!

Brown asked me whether I would be prepared to head up a small team looking into Customs and Excise and the whole question of cigarette smuggling, which was costing the Exchequer a billion a year. They needed someone who was independent to take a look at it, who also knew their way around undercover operations, etc. It was a job which desperately needed to be done, he said.

He made a point of saying that it was his idea to ask me, not Blair's. He had £100m that he was prepared to deploy on the task. I said I'd go away and think about it, but only if he agreed to three conditions:

1. That I wouldn't take any money for it. I would do it as an MP.

2. That I would have proper back-up from the Civil Service.

3. That I could have time off in August.

He agreed to all these.

Back at the office I called Roy, and I told him about the Chancellor's offer. He said that he couldn't think of a reason why I shouldn't do it. But I remain unsure. The more I think about it the more I think this will be confusing and damaging to the Party. I have promised the Party my full attention until the new leader takes over.

Tuesday, 9 March, Westminster

BUDGET DAY

At 11.30 Downing Street rang and the PM came on the line to ask me what I thought about Gordon's proposal.

I told him that, having giving it some thought, I didn't think I could do it. By the end of the conversation, however, he had almost convinced me that I should.

Then the doubts set in again.

1 Denis Healey, former Chancellor of the Exchequer.
2 John Pardoe, Member of Parliament (Liberal) for North Cornwall 1966–79.

Wednesday, 10 March, Westminster

Rang Jonathan Powell in the morning to say that, on reflection, I really didn't feel I could do the Customs and Excise anti-smuggling job. Jonathan had suggested I have a word with Gordon himself, so I left a message on his answer phone. Our offices arranged for us to meet after PMQs.

At about 2.15, while I was in the Whips' Office preparing for PMQs, I was asked if I could bring the meeting forward. So I went over, my mind full of PMQs rather than Customs and Excise, and hung around talking to his very nice secretary for about twenty minutes before he arrived. I explained that I really couldn't do the job. He said he fully understood and we left on the best of terms.

Saturday, 20 March, Somerset

At about 4.30, Robin Cook rang. He said he was furious with the Serbs: Milosevic was the person who had asked for two weeks' grace between Rambouillet 1 and Rambouillet 2[1] so that he could 'persuade the Serb people to accept the deal'. In fact, he had gone home, stoked up the entire population and launched new offensives in Kosovo. Cook felt very aggrieved.

I asked him what would happen next.

RC: The Americans and us are gung-ho for going ahead.

PA: But to what aim?

He didn't seem able to say exactly.

PA: Well, I can think of two possible aims. One is to extract such a high price from Milosevic that he has to sign up to Rambouillet. But if that fails, as it probably will, then we should use it as the first step towards establishing an international protectorate.

RC: There's no question of NATO using ground forces. We reckon the Serbs have

---

1 The second round of Rambouillet (Rambouillet 2) had reconvened on 15 March; the Albanians had finally signed, but the Serbs still refused, and the talks broke up. Now, the international peace monitors in KVM were being withdrawn and Western embassies moving out, prior to possible bombing.

40,000 and we have only 12,000 over the Macedonian border, and with no prospect of any more.

PA: In that case, public opinion will force it. If we don't back up air strikes with at least the threat of troops on the ground, the Serbs will try to ethnically cleanse all Albanians from Kosovo. When the public see that on their TV screens they will force you to act, including using ground troops, whatever you say now.

RC: If you are right – and I accept that you might be – then I just hope people are prepared for casualties. Because they will be heavy.

PA: Well, if the Serbs respond to our strikes with further atrocities on the ground, then I don't see how we can just stick to air action.

We finished the conversation with Cook saying that he was sure it wouldn't come to that – at least, he hoped not.

Wednesday, 24 March, Westminster

I was due to go to the gym at 9.30 but decided I couldn't spare the time. The crisis in Kosovo is deepening. I called together Ming, Shirley, William Wallace[1] and a little Kosovo team and we mapped out the line we needed to take. I anticipate air attacks will start tonight.[2] Everybody else thinks during the day, but I doubt it. At least the first wave will strike during the hours of darkness.

During the day there has been some talk of B52s taking off from British air force bases.

Just as I was going into the PPM at 6.00 I was told that Jonathan Powell had rung. The first bombs would be falling in half an hour. Our press team have done a brilliant job, a rerun of how we dealt with the Iraqi crisis in 1991. I insisted that we must be first in the television studio with our line.

A few minutes afterwards, the news broke that the first bombs had fallen on Kosovo. And in Belgrade.

1 Lord Wallace of Saltaire. An expect on foreign affairs and previously a director of the Royal Institute for International Affairs. See Vol. I, pp. 9, 119.
2 The Serb Parliament had rejected Rambouillet the previous night.

Thursday, 25 March, Westminster

At 6.15 Richard came to see me. I took him to the Pugin Room, where we had a glass of champagne. He wanted to tell me about a recent lunch he had had with Peter Mandelson. He said Mandelson was very depressed. Desperate to get back into government. He would like to do so by next autumn. Did Richard think that was that too early? Mandelson had had a word with others, apparently, including Alastair Campbell, who had thought it could be done about then. Meanwhile, he was busying himself with 'good works' to win back public approval.

Labour are, apparently, particularly worried about who would drive the project (who would be 'the navigator', as they put it) now that I was going.

Saturday, 27 March, Somerset

At 2.15 Blair called. I took my mobile phone outside and sat on the courtyard steps in the sunshine. I told him that I thought his broadcast last night on Kosovo[1] had been very good. 'Even Jane's mum, who is one of your severest critics, thought it was excellent!'

We had a brief discussion on the Euro summit in Berlin from which I had just returned, then on to Kosovo.

TB: I am really worried. I want to pick your brains. The operation is going well enough. But we have a long way to go before we get down to the serious business of removing their tanks and heavy artillery from the field. And I am determined that we do not let the next phase [cleansing Kosovo of Serb heavy weapons] start until it is safe to do so. On the other hand, what is happening on the ground in Kosovo now is terrifying.[2] It looks like an attempt at the 'final solution' you have been talking about. But the real difficulty is that, although this new wave of atrocities makes the case for intervention stronger, it has also caused some people to believe that we are actually making the Albanians' position worse. And I am worried about that. What do you think we should do?

---

1 Blair had done a prime ministerial television broadcast on Kosovo the previous night. By convention, the opposition party leaders have a right to reply. Hague's was that night, and mine the following night.
2 Milosevic had started 'Operation Horseshore' – the complete elimination by expulsion and killing of the Albanian population of Kosovo.

PA: Well, the obvious thing is to get some Albanian voices heard. All we have had, especially from the BBC, are the viewpoints of either NATO or the Serbs. It's the Albanians we need to hear.

TB: Yes, I've asked for that. But so far nothing's happened.

PA: Perhaps, I can help. I know some people at the Kosovo Information Centre. I will also concentrate on the plight of the Kosovar Albanians in my [response] broadcast.

TB: That is good. You are believed on this because you have been there. But you still think we need ground troops, don't you?

PA: Yes, I can't see any way round it. And I will say that in my broadcast. You and I are going to part company on this. I just do not understand how you think you can secure peace on the ground without them. But before you decide whether to use them you must look at (a) the condition of the Serb forces after the bombing is over, (b) how cohesive Serbia is under Milosevic, and (c) whether the Albanian Kosovars can give you assistance on the ground. We shouldn't forget that Albanians make up 95 per cent of Kosovo's population and they will be with us, rather than against us. So this is not, as many say, going to be like the American experience in Vietnam. The population will be with us, not against us. I am glad to notice, however, that there is a very distinct difference between your line and Robin's. You were saying that ground troops 'are not in the plan', whereas Robin is saying that ground troops will 'never be used except to support a peace agreement' – which effectively gives Milosevic a veto on us using ground troops.

I can understand why people want to write ground troops off as an option now. But, for goodness' sake, don't close it off as an option for the future. There is one more point that needs making. All the press reports are about pressures on NATO. But none of them focuses on the real cracks that are now appearing on Milosevic's side. The president of Montenegro, Milo Djukanovic, has, very courageously, declared that the war is all Milosevic's fault. He wants to use the opportunity to break Montenegro away. My sources tell me that the same thing is happening in the Sandjak and Vojvodina.[1] This is very significant. Milosevic is now in danger of being left with a rump Serbia. Surely we should be emphasizing more that Milosevic, too, is under great pressure.

---

1 Two regions of Serbia. In the Sandjak Muslims are in the majority and in the Vojvodina Hungarians make up the most significant group in the population.

TB: That's a good idea. Is there anybody listening to this?[1] [Nobody answered.] Oh dear. No one is listening. They don't normally when I am speaking to you. I will try and make a note of your point.

We talked briefly about holidays and then hung up at about 2.40.

Sunday, 28 March, Somerset

The news this evening on Kosovo is worse. They say 100,000 Albanians have been pushed up the Rugova valley by the VJ[2] from Pec into Montenegro. Over those high passes in the snow! Terrible.

Monday, 5 April, Somerset

Watched the news of Kosovo. Full of columns of refugees being driven from Kosovo and thousands more being herded into trains and pushed over into Macedonia. Chilling and terrible. My worst fears coming true in spades.

Tuesday, 6 April, Westminster

A briefing at the Foreign Office at 2.00. The situation is not good. The first phase (clearing the defences) has gone well. But the second phase (beginning to damage the forces in Kosovo), has been seriously delayed by the weather. In the intervening period, of course, the Serbs have cleared people out of their homes, crushed the KLA (now no longer an effective fighting force of any nature, according to the Foreign Office) and camouflaged their tanks, guns and artillery to such an extent that, although the skies are now clear, the NATO aircraft are having a terrible business finding their targets. The Foreign Office briefer let slip that there was serious planning going on for troops on the ground, whatever the government says. And although Rambouillet is largely dead (it would not be possible to reconstruct peace

1 Normally ministerial phone calls are 'listened to' by a civil servant, who takes notes of the substance of the conversation.
2 Vojska Jugoslavia, the Yugoslav army.

on the basis that the Serbs would continue to govern Kosovo), 90 per cent of the agreement could be recycled, he claims.

I said that I think what will happen next is that Milosevic will make a bid for peace, since he has achieved his military aims and will want to put us on the spot.

I returned to my office and at 3 o'clock word came through that Milosevic had called for an Easter peace! I put out a swift statement saying it should be rejected, which got out before either London or Washington had defined their position.

During the morning I had agreed with Jonathan to call the PM at 6.30. In the event, when I got back to the office at 6.00 after a round of press interviews, Downing Street was already on the line.

Blair and I spoke for about twenty-five minutes. This time there was somebody listening.

We started off with the usual pleasantries and I thanked him for my FCO briefing today. All pretty gloomy stuff, I commented.

TB: Yes, but according to the latest reports it has been much better today. We have started destroying their forces on the ground. And the Milosevic peace appeal, of course, we have dismissed out of hand; it is a clear indication that he is weakening.

PA: I don't think you are right. I see that's the line your people are putting across. But I think it's wrong. I believe he has achieved all his military and political aims (driving out the Albanians; destabilizing Macedonia and Greece; consolidating his forces on the ground; and avoiding major casualities). So he can afford to have a ceasefire without diminishing his own positions, whilst also appealing to his Orthodox co-religionists in Greece and Russia. A typically wily Milosevic move. Also, if you say he is being forced to do it, then the public will think we are winning at a faster pace than we really are. And it's dangerous to raise public expectations.

TB: Yes, we must not mislead the public. This operation will take a long time and we should tell them that. Nevertheless, I have real reasons, the details of which I cannot go into, to think Milosevic did this because he is under pressure. We have done severe damage to his infrastructure and one of his main military units in Serbia has been badly hit by B1 bombers. And now we are beginning to take on targets in Kosovo.

PA: I hope so. But not having access to your reports, you will forgive me if I say that I have not seen any evidence yet of that. I want to return to the central question that I have been pressing you on for months. The strategy that says you will not put troops on the ground except with Milosevic's agreement is tantamount to saying that he has a veto on the return of refugees. But, as you yourself have said, the refugees will not return unless there are troops on the ground to protect them. So Milosevic is effectively deciding whether the people whom he has 'ethnically cleansed' return to their homes. We cannot have that. And furthermore, I don't believe you are right in saying that Milosevic will be bombed into accepting NATO's conditions. If Milosevic accepts NATO's conditions, he is finished and he is not going to commit suicide voluntarily.

TB: Yes, I have come round to that view. I have just done a minute to my people saying that we are faced with three outcomes: the first is that the Serbs win, which is intolerable; the second is that Milosevic will give in under the bombing, which is unlikely; and the third is that, having degraded his forces on the ground, we are then able to put our forces in, even against his opposition. And it is the third of these that I want to plan for now.

PA: That must be right. But then why are we not doing more to reinforce the Macedonian border? George Robertson [Secretary of State for Defence] says that it will take eight weeks to get the troops there. So why haven't we started already?

TB: The problem is how we do it and through whom. I have just had a long chat with the Macedonian prime minister and reassured him that we will provide him with all the support we can. As a result, he is lifting his block on refugees crossing the border into his country.

Look, I know you want to press me on this troops thing. But please don't; it's very tricky. I am also really worried about the Russians.

PA: Yes, and I can understand why. But surely Primakov understands that he has a part to play when we get to the end game of all this? Provided he keeps reasonable relations with us as well as, of course, expressing the worries of the Slav nations, then he will be very well placed to play the key role in the peace which must follow. But if he breaks with us, then he is cutting off his nose to spite his face. It will be immensely beneficial to the Russians if they are seen as the brokers of peace in this – especially Primakov, who wants to become president.

TB: Yes, but it's not so much Primakov. The Duma [the Russian Parliament] is pushing him hard and, of course, public opinion there is very, very strongly against.

PA: Then it seems right that we should tolerate patiently anything the Russians do by way of language – indeed, anything they do short of materially assisting the Serbs. That is a line that must not be crossed.

TB: Yes, but I have information that they have already crossed it. And that's what is worrying me.

I didn't press him, but wondered what it could be. A supply of arms? The swapping of intelligence? I hope nothing nuclear.

I changed the subject to Rambouillet.

PA: It is time somebody said it. Rambouillet is a dead duck. Kosovo can never again be governed by the Serbs. The only solution is an international protectorate.

As we were bringing the conversation to a close, he wondered whether he should speak to Hague.

PA: I suppose so. But the Tories have been all over the place. Ming has driven Michael Howard [the Shadow Foreign Secretary] off the box.

TB: Yes, I heard Major on the radio this morning. He was pretty mischievous and extremely unhelpful.

We finished our conversation about 6.30 and I leapt into a taxi to go off to Kettners in Soho for the Federal Policy Committee, where I rammed things through as fast as I could. I had hoped to get the widening of the JCC remit through this FPC, but in the event there were far too many members of the awkward squad there for me to be sure, so I slipped it sideways for the next meeting.

Wednesday, 7 April, Westminster and Edinburgh

Jane drove me into the office at 8 o'clock and I managed to do an hour's work before my first meeting, which was with Blerim Shalja, who is in London to rally support. Cook is due to meet him later today for a press conference.

I was busy working on my computer when Blerim was shown in and I looked up to see him, accompanied to my joy by Bili, our interpreter on my last couple of visits. Recently I have had visions of her lying dead in a ditch somewhere in Kosovo with her throat cut. The Serbs have been rounding up all those who worked for foreigners in Pristina. I couldn't fight back the tears. I leapt up, clasped her to me and said, 'Oh, it is wonderful to see you alive.' She said it was wonderful to be alive as well.

Blerim was his usual calm, decent self. One of the points he made was that we must convince the Kosovar Serbs that there would be a place for them in Kosovo after the battle has finished. He also said that NATO was now having a real effect on the Serb forces in Kosovo. And that we must keep going. He was planning to go to Macedonia to try and calm down the Macedonian Albanians in order to reassure the government there that they had no intention of making use of the war to destabilize the state. He also wanted to say that Kosovo won't create the greater Albania the Macedonians fear.

We had a very detailed discussion about the present situation and about how Bili and Blerim (separately) came out of Kosovo. Bili had been put on one of the trains the Serbs pack with Albanians, three or four days ago. She said that they had suddenly been rounded up overnight (she had been sleeping in different beds to avoid the secret police, who were targeting people who had worked for foreigners). She was then made to stand with several thousand others in the mud for seven hours until a train pulled up. They were forced on board and the train pulled off – but none of them knew where they were going. It was only later in the evening that they discovered they were heading for the Macedonian border. After a couple of hours' travelling they were bundled out of the train and told to walk up the track for the last two miles. They were warned not to move to right or left, because it was mined. When they arrived at the Macedonian border, Bili had identified herself to one of the British soldiers there as a British Embassy employee and was taken across the border away from the terrible crush of refugees whom the Macedonians were keeping on the Kosovo side of the frontier. It was a harrowing tale.

Blerim told me that Fehmi Agani had not been shot,[1] he was in hiding somewhere; ditto Veton Surroi.[2] But he, Blerim, had decided to take his chances and get out so that the voice of Kosovo could be heard outside, particularly in Macedonia. He had tried to slip through with the crush on the border, but had been spotted by the Serb secret police. For three hours he had bargained for his life. He believed they would either let him through or take him round the back and shoot him. Fortunately, he managed to get

---

1 This turned out to be false. Agani had indeed been shot by the Serbs.
2 Editor of the Kosovan Albanian newspaper *Koha Ditore*. He subsequently became a close friend and someone I regularly visit when in the Balkans.

in touch with the US roving ambassador in the region, Christopher Hill, on a mobile phone, and also with the Russians, who eventually brokered his release across the border into Macedonia.

Blerim seemed totally unscarred by it all and as calm and dignified as ever. As they left, I hugged Bili, wishing her the Albanian greeting of 'Keep Safe'.

In the afternoon to Gatwick to catch the 4.15 plane up to Edinburgh. On arrival I was taken straight to Ming's house, where I let myself in as Ming and Elspeth are away until the evening. The election campaign for the Scottish Parliament appears to be going very well. The party has had an excellent launch, is beginning to be taken seriously by the press and is going up in the polls. So Jim is in a good mood. He was rather tired and grumpy when I last saw him.

When Ming and Elspeth came in they filled my glass up with a huge whisky and we sat down and talked until 1 o'clock. Firstly about Kosovo; then about the leadership election. I repeated that I thought Ming could win but that he should not fight unless he felt he could do the job on his own terms (i.e. continue the project).

To bed far too late, my eyes stinging with tiredness and having drunk a little too much whisky. Bad news on Kosovo today: the Serbs have closed the Macedonian border and driven the Kosovar refugees back into Kosovo. I now fear that they are going to use them as human shields against NATO attacks.

Tuesday, 13 April, Westminster

END OF THE EASTER RECESS

The House is back.

In the afternoon the PM's Kosovo statement. Blair stern and sombre, but good. Hague rambled on. They have invented a new term for when they can put ground troops into Kosovo: when the bombing has created a 'permissive environment'. I asked Blair whether that meant when the risk was permissible or when President Milosevic permitted it. This amounts to a clear shift in policy and is very welcome.

A long and useful telephone conversation (at my request) with Blair again in the early morning.

TB: Perhaps it is best if I explain to you a little more fully what is happening. We have spent a long time thinking about this and we have had a lot of experts looking at it. We cannot broadcast our intentions. But I can assure you that all eventualities are planned for. So what you see is not necessarily all there is. For instance, one of the reasons why we said that we wouldn't involve ground troops in Kosovo except as part of a peace agreement was that our intelligence sources informed us that if we said we were prepared to take Kosovo without an agreement, that would not only have stiffened Serb resolve, but also caused the Russians to support Milosevic more strongly – Slav homeland stuff. In the event, that assessment proved wrong. But it was the best assessment we had and it was echoed by that of every other NATO country. The game has been about camouflaging our long-term intentions, maintaining some element of surprise and keeping the Russians on board. But you have my undertaking that when conditions are semi-permissive we will use ground troops, whether Milosevic agrees or not. And by semi-permissive, I mean when the risks to troops on the ground have diminished to acceptable levels.

Next, the question of refugees trapped inside Kosovo.[1] This has caused us severe headaches, which is why I have concentrated on saying that they are Milosevic's responsibility. But I have also had a group of people looking at what we can do to help them. I take your point that it would give us a huge propaganda advantage to do so. And it is also urgent from a humanitarian point of view. But we must act in a way which does not disrupt the conduct of the war, for instance by using our aircraft to drop in supplies to refugees rather than to keep Milosevic under pressure. Then we would be doing exactly what Milosevic wants us to do.

I have another problem. As you probably know, Milosevic's wife, Mira Markovic, runs the Serbian Red Cross. My lot are really worried that if we draw too much attention to the plight of the refugees, Milosevic will propose that the Red Cross move in and look after them. And if that happens we will have to stop the bombing. But we would have no control over what happens on the ground, since Milosevic would be operating through his wife. So, you see, there isn't any easy answer. On top of this, these refugees are gathered in relatively small groups, and we are not able to drop supplies to them from a height low enough to have a reasonable possibility of landing in the right place, without making our aircraft vulnerable to hand-held anti-aircraft missiles. If we did it from a safe height most of the supplies would go to the Serbs.

PA: Yes, that is what happened in Bosnia. The reality of war is that aid sent on to a battlefield will always go initially to the person with the biggest gun and the

---

1 There had been recent reports of many thousands of refugees gathered in the woods and remote areas who were in a pitiable condition owing to lack of food and shelter.

largest military force. But you have to supply aid in sufficient volume for some of it to filter down to the poor people you are trying to assist. In Bosnia nine-tenths of the aid we sent in ended up on the two opposing front lines. But we went on supplying it because, after we had fed two armies, one tenth got through to the people who desperately needed it.

The real reason I'm ringing you is that I know you are going to the Heads of Europe meeting tomorrow. Milosevic seems to have NATO permanently on the back foot. I think we should start taking some initiatives of our own. There are a number I would like to suggest. You know about the Serb incursion that has been made across the border today, of course; I hope we will return that in kind, although I recognize how difficult it is militarily and politically.

Then there are the diplomatic initiatives. In my view, there is a case now for NATO to map out its long-term aims. Only when people like the Macedonians and the Greeks[1] see what we are trying to achieve in the longer term, will they understand why they should support us in the short-term actions we are having to take now. You and I both realize that a wider Balkan settlement will be needed at the end of this, including perhaps a revisiting of Dayton. So why not put together some framework which ensures that Macedonia, Albania, Romania and Bulgaria all see that they have a part to play in a future which is European and within NATO, but one for which they must now make sacrifices? After all, that is exactly what Serbia tried to do yesterday in its bid to become part of the Russian Federation.[2] Surely we can match them?

TB: Well, I hope we will take some initiatives. I think the first of them could be very soon. Our meeting with Kofi Annan tomorrow is very important. We think he is about 90 per cent on board, which will mean that we can pull in the UN on NATO's side and create a common purpose between us. This is most important. Furthermore, meetings between Madeleine Albright and the Russians the other day went far better than expected. In fact, the Russians are not a million miles away from us. There is now a real possibility of bringing them in on a Security Council resolution that is broadly in line with NATO's aims. But we are not there quite yet.

As for the bigger picture, we started mapping some of that out earlier on. But the moment we did that the Russians became extremely neuralgic. And understandably so. We cannot expect to outline a basically European long-term objective in what they still regard as their backyard, without either deeply upsetting them or giving them a part to play in it. The first we don't want to do and the second isn't

---

1 There had been strong opposition to NATO's actions in Kosovo in Greece and Macedonia.
2 Milosevic had suggested that Serbia should join the Russian Federation in an obvious attempt to drag the Russians in on his side.

possible. We must reoccupy Kosovo and move the refugees back in, before we can unveil a longer-term solution. Then there is the question of Milosevic. We cannot let him off the hook this time. In my view, for as long as Milosevic is head of the state we must treat Serbia as a pariah state.

PA: Not only a pariah state but hopefully a rump state, too. And under those circumstances I hope the Serbs will not continue to tolerate a leader who has lost them Croatia, Albania, Kosovo and possibly the Vojvodina, the Sandjak and Montenegro as well.

TB: That would be excellent. As soon as Milosevic goes, Serbia can be part of the wider Balkan solution. But not before.

PA: The bottom line, as I see it, is that we are in effect creating a European overarching power in the Balkans. But we are not prepared to admit it yet. Big powers worry about their borders, and our most vulnerable one has always been the fault line between Europe and the East that runs right through the Balkans. The Balkans are our 'marches', which we must make sure are secure. Secondly it is worth recognizing that historically these warring states in the Balkans have never been at peace with one another except as part of a larger hegemony. First of all the Ottomans; then the Hapsburgs; then the communists. And in the future that larger structure will be the European Community. I see why the Russians would find that difficult to accept. But it is the reality.

TB: Yes, it is. Look, the public really seems to trust you on this. And I think we should be using you more – I have had a word with Alastair about it. We would like you to consider going out there in the near future and then perhaps on your return doing a joint press conference with George Robertson or some of the military?

PA: Well, I had planned on campaigning in the local government elections over the next few weeks. But if you want me to go, I should go soon. I will think about it overnight.

TB: That would be very helpful. Meanwhile, I will ask Alastair to give you a call about some ideas we've had.

Later in the evening I was bleeped by Alastair Campbell. I managed to call him on my way back to the House for a division just before 10.00pm. He asked me if I would be prepared to tramp around the area, get some publicity and then return for the joint press conference with George Robertson, but 'we can't have you criticizing government policy'.

'Well, OK,' I replied. 'I'll go. But I'm not going to be a government spokesman and I am not going to part company with the established Lib Dem position. Although I am sure we can find a way around that.'

Wednesday, 14 April, Westminster

I called Julian[1] and Becks together and asked them to start planning my trip to the Balkans. I need a letter from Blair to help me gain access to the Albanian and Macedonian prime ministers.

We are having God's own job getting into either Tirana or Skopje, since they have closed all their air space.

A terrible story is breaking tonight about NATO having bombed an Albanian refugee convoy. Of course the Serbs are capitalizing on it.

Monday, 19 April, Tirana

[*Accompanied by two members of my staff, Becks Darling and Julian Astle, I eventually managed to get into the Kosovo war zone by flying to Rome and hitching a lift on a small World Food Programme aircraft to Tirana. Here Becks went off to conduct a survey of conditions in the Kosovar refugee camps in Albania, with instructions to meet me in two days' time at the Albania–Macedonia border near Lake Ohrid, while Julian and I, once again with the assistance of the embassy and the wonderful Neritan Ceka, would try to make our way up to the Albania–Kosovo border at Kukes, where tens of thousands of refugees, driven out by the Serbs, had been coming over in the last few days.*]

After a little waiting, Neritan turned up at our hotel, followed by Patrick Wilson from the embassy. Neritan said he had had no luck with a helicopter. But Patrick rang some Italian friends at the airport, who said the weather looked a bit iffy but they would ring us back. In due course they did and told us that they would be flying if the weather improved a little. So, armed with the name of Captain Gambetti, the Italian in charge of helicopters, we drove out to the airport through the terrible traffic of Tirana, feeling pretty pessimistic about our chances.

---

1 Julian Astle, my new Joint Cabinet Committee officer. Like his predecessor, Roger Lowry, Julian assisted me with my Balkan trips.

Tirana airfield has been completely transformed since my last visit. It is now overrun with military aircraft. About seventy helicopters of all nationalities piled on to the runway in a jumble; a constant roar of jet engines as heavy transport aircraft flew in and out; batteries of surface-to-air anti-aircraft missiles around the airfield perimeter and soldiers everywhere. I finally managed to talk our way past an American guard and Neritan charmed his way past the Albanian ones. Then we hung around in the middle of this military mêlée saying the magical name of Captain Gambetti to every passing soldier who looked remotely Italian, until eventually we found someone who gave the appropriate response and went off to fetch him.

Would he fly us to Kukes? we asked.

'Of course,' he said, pointing to a twin-rotored Chinook, adding, 'Just jump in.'

A bunch of Italian journalists were having their photograph taken against the helicopter while the crew refuelled it, smoking and chatting furiously.

The photo session over, Neritan, Julian and I bundled on board, buckled ourselves into our seats amidst parcels and pallets of aid and prepared for take-off. Then the crew shambled on board, still smoking, jumped in, started her up, opened the windows, stuffed a couple of machine-guns out of each side and one out the back and then, warning us that it would be cold on the flight, took off in a flurry of dust and Italian machismo.

The Italians were right: there was a howling wind and it was bitterly cold. But the flight up was tremendous. Over the snow-covered mountains and deep ravines of central Albania and, eventually, into the broad lake-filled valley at the head of which lie Kukes and the Kosovo border. As we approached the border area the machine-guns were cocked with live rounds and the crew started to look serious.

Then we were over the lakes and the town of Kukes. We circled and below me I could see the tented encampment of perhaps 150,000 refugees. They looked desperate, dirty and disorganized.

We landed at what we later discovered was the Italian camp in Kukes, run by the Genoese fire brigade including a huge fireman called Alessandro, with whom we struck up an immediate and respectful friendship.

The border has been closed today. Only eleven refugees crossed it this morning, as opposed to the 40,000 yesterday. Why the Serbs have closed the border, who knows? Milosevic playing his usual game of cat and mouse with the refugees, probably.

There followed a full day of meetings.

Firstly, I made myself known to UNHCR, who were their usual helpful, but hard-pressed selves. Then off for a chat with local mayor, who complained that his town of 20,000 was now carrying a population of 130,000, of whom 20,000 were without even tents and living in a sea of mud on the main square, on trailers and tractors and under polythene sheets.

But when I went to see the refugees, I found them laughing and smiling as they queued in the rain for food. I was immensely moved by their dignity. An experienced international aid worker said that he, too, was amazed by their self-respect and honesty – this was the only refugee camp he had worked in where you could put down a spade one day and go back the next day and find it still there.

Later, in their makeshift shelters under constantly falling rain, they told harrowing story after harrowing story of their escapes and looked to us with desperate hope and trust that we would get them back. But it isn't going to be that easy. There's a real danger we will let them down.

Then off with Neritan to the local KLA barracks. As we went in, I met an old man proudly delivering his son to the KLA. I thought I was going to have a private discussion with the head of the KLA, but was led instead to an inner courtyard in which stood about 500 callow youths in uniform, all thinking war was glorious and standing stiffly to attention. Their uniforms were good but their boots – always a telltale sign – were of variable quality, many privately bought. I don't think they have a clue what lies ahead of them. Many will soon go, inadequately trained, to their deaths in the forests. Those terrible lines about impending war from A. E. Housman's 'A Shropshire Lad' leapt unbidden to my mind.[1]

The KLA commander turned to me and asked me to say a few words to them. Almost immediately a translator appeared at my side, who turned out to be a dental assistant from Huddersfield. As I spoke to them my gorge rose.

I said, 'I am not Mr Blair and I do not represent him. I speak only for myself. Nevertheless, I have come here bearing a letter from Mr Blair for the

---

1 The lines I was thinking of read as follows:

> On the idle hill of summer,
>   Sleepy with the flow of streams,
> Far I hear the steady drummer
>   Drumming like a noise in dreams.
>
> Far and near and low and louder
>   On the roads of earth go by,
> Dear to friends and food for powder,
>   Soldiers marching, all to die.

Albanian president and the Albanian prime minister. Its contents are not secret. It says that we are here to support you for as long it takes to win this war. [Huge roar of applause.] There will be no victory unless we can get you home. Anything else is a defeat. [More applause.] What I have seen happening in Kosovo cannot be part of your future and it must not be part of Europe's future either. [More applause.] I admire your courage and support what you are doing. I wish every single one of you success and a safe return to your homes. We all have the same aim. To right an injustice. And that makes us comrades in arms. So good luck and here's to a free Kosovo! [the toast Albanians make to each other nowadays].' To tumultuous applause, I turned away before they could see the tears in my eyes.

Then off for a private talk with the KLA commander, a thin-faced, unsmiling man with big bags under his eyes. Perhaps in his mid-forties. He was very suspicious of me to start with, but we soon warmed to each other when he discovered that I, too, had been a soldier. They are, he said, desperately short of ammunition. I have come to the conclusion that we will have to take a risk with these people and support them, despite the UN embargo.

Afterwards, to the local army headquarters for a chat with Albanian army officers about their defences. These are so few and out of date as to be laughable. Half a dozen ancient Chinese artillery pieces and that's about it. But I did find out from them that there is a grass airstrip here, built in King Zog's time, so I insisted on going to see it. It could be useful to fly out refugees and fly in troops if we have to invade Kosovo through the Kukes valley.

Neritan, however, wanted to get back to Tirana and left on the last helicopter flight out.

After waving him goodbye I went out to have a look at the airstrip. With a little engineering work we could land heavy-lift Hercules transport planes here.[1] Even without work it would be fine for helicopters to fly out the refugees, if Milosevic tries to swamp us with another flood of them.

Then a round of TV interviews with the refugees clamouring in the background. They may come from a peasant society in which little has changed for a hundred years, but it's amazing how quickly they have got to grips with the latest in twenty-first-century telecommunications.

Back in the town centre I met up with our Albanian host, Destan Spahiu,[2] whom Neritan had charged with the task of looking after us. He is a stocky, strong little man with a huge heart and a bottomless capacity for showing

---

1 This strip was indeed later opened for Hercules aircraft.
2 Chairman of the Kukes Democratic Alliance (the Liberal Party of Albania).

Albanian hospitality. We had far too many beers and some raki with him and then a bite to eat with the journalist in the American Bar (the only café in town), before being taken back to his little flat in Kukes.

There, with his wife, two wide-eyed children, a nephew who spoke broken English and his grandmother, Julian and I sat talking about the war; the pains of the Kosovars; the last time the Serbs had come over the border (in 1932, when there had been a great defeat of the Serb army at the hands of the Albanians in the battle of Kukes); what the valley was like before it was flooded by the government; the fruit trees which filled it before Sali Berisha had them cut down; and the fact that Albanian peasants always suffer, whoever is in power and whatever happens.

Then, my head swimming with raki, I tumbled into bed in the little bedroom they had given over to Julian and myself – no doubt at the expense of their own comfort. I slept fitfully. We have a big day's travelling tomorrow, and must be up early.

Tuesday, 20 April, On the Albania–Kosovo border

At 5.45 I looked out of the window and my heart sank. Yesterday evening was bright and cloudless, with a beautiful red setting sun. Last night the stars shone as they only ever do in the high mountains. But this morning the mountains have played their usual tricks on us. It is dank and raining, the cloud is low and the helicopters probably won't fly. I grabbed a cup of stiff Albanian coffee (refusing the glass of raki on offer) and, with my mouth feeling like the bottom of a parrot's cage, stumbled out into the rain with my Albanian host skipping merrily alongside me, and Julian, nursing a gentle hangover, following meekly behind. My Albanian host insisted on holding an umbrella over my head and exclaiming loudly to every passer-by the Albanian word for 'personality!' (i.e. VIP).

After some TV interviews we spent the rest of the morning playing the well-known Balkan game of hunt-the-helicopter. Eventually we concluded that no helicopters would be flying today.

At which precise moment two Swiss helicopters lumbered over the mountain and out of the mist to land a mile and half away at the Italian camp and then take off again, before we could persuade someone to drive us down to try and catch them. Now we were stuck without a helicopter and without even a lift down to the Italian camp, where we might pick up any future craft which landed.

So, there was nothing for it but to find a journalist with a satellite phone and try to get through to the Tirana embassy. Luck was on our side, for I bumped into my BBC cameraman friend Vaughan Smith, who directed me to a friend from *The Times* who lent us his. (It is extraordinary how often you bump into old friends in the Balkans who bale you out.) A chat with the London office, who said they would try to contact Tirana, but all phone lines were down.

By this time our wonderful Albanian host turned up and offered to give us a lift to the Italian camp. We accepted with gratitude and joined some goats in the back of a friend's extremely ramshackle trailer and bumped off down the hill.

When we got to the Italian camp at the bottom valley I had a tough job persuading our extremely voluble Albanian host (who had a rather worrying habit of grabbing hold of my arm whenever he wanted to make a point and my knee for a particularly important one) that it was OK now to leave us in the tender care of the Italians.

It didn't take long to find our Genoese firemen friend Alessandro, who was dispensing aid to the refugees in the camp in the mud, in the middle of which was the helipad. Alessandro insisted that we should immediately repair to the Italian tent to have some coffee, which we did.

There followed a long wait peppered with promises that the Swiss were on their way, only ten minutes away, just over the mountain ... We thought we would be there all day.

But eventually the sky cleared and, after several more cups of Italian coffee and some cake, we went down to the helipad to wait in the sun. After about an hour a helicopter came in. But it couldn't take us.

Then two of the long-promised Swiss ones returned. Alessandro said that if he could get us on he would, but the first priority were some mine casualties who had just arrived.

But then, who should emerge from one of the helicopters but my old friend Adolf Ogi,[1] whom I had skied against in the annual Anglo-Swiss Parliamentarians' ski race at Davos two years ago. He came over and asked what on earth I was doing here. I explained and he insisted that we should fly back with him, if there was space after the wounded were loaded. The happenstance of hitchhiking round a battlezone again!

While he did some photo ops with the refugees, the wounded were loaded on, after which we were squeezed in and off we set for Tirana.

1 Then Swiss Minister for Defence, Civil Protection and Sport.

The cloud was low and the flight very bumpy. As we entered the Albanian plain from the high mountains we had to descend a steep valley which was closed off above us by rain clouds, but we arrived back at Tirana airport without incident.

Back into the military mêlée again. How could we make contact with the embassy? Where was Neritan, who had promised to pick us up? We hung around, knowing that if we stayed in the same place for long enough and told everybody by mobile phone via London where we were, something would happen. Like standing at a bus stop hoping someone you know will come by – and sooner or later they did. General Reith, the ex-para British commander in Tirana, emerged from a tent where he had been holding a reception for the Swiss prime minister and recognized me. When I told him of our problem he immediately insisted that we jump into his personal helicopter and we duly flew into Tirana and were dropped off in the sanctuary of the embassy.

I phoned London and made another call to track down Neritan. Apparently he had taken our baggage from the day before and was eventually located in the middle of a Tirana traffic jam, heading out to pick us up. After he had brought back the luggage and I had had a quick chat with Patrick Wilson, we jumped into the Ambassador's Range Rover and headed for the Macedonian border. Despite the shenanigans we could still make Skopje by nightfall.

The usual long drive along the very bumpy road up to Lake Ohrid. The Albanian valleys at this time of year are immensely beautiful. A brush of green covers them now, dotted here and there with clumps of wild almond trees in full blossom.

I slept for the first hour or so, but then tried to gather my thoughts after Kukes. I am becoming increasingly depressed about the likely success of this operation. I can't see a plan, I can't see an outcome and I can't see any easy military solution. And I am really worried that the political situation in the countries behind the front line (Macedonia, Greece and Albania) is now beginning to break up.

We arrived at the Macedonian border at Lake Ohrid at around 5.00, expecting to see Becks. No Becks. And we couldn't cross the border because our driver didn't have a passport. My patience broke. Couldn't these bloody embassies at Tirana and Skopje fix anything between them?

But, after half an hour or so of pretty grumpy phone calls, Becks arrived at the Macedonian side of the border blissfully unaware of what had happened. She had been told that we wouldn't be here until 6.30 and so had gone off for a substantial, and by her account highly bibulous, lunch with her two Macedonian drivers. So, reunited, we said goodbye to our Albanian driver, jumped into the Macedonian car and sped off for Skopje.

As we crossed the Sar Planina foothills the whole beauty of the Macedonian plain lay before us under the gathering dusk. The only thing to spoil our enjoyment was the fact that we were being driven at petrifying speed by two half-mad Macedonians with a great deal of drink inside them who made it a matter of macho principle in the presence of a lady to pass almost every car or lorry on a blind bend. Definitely the most dangerous thing I have ever done in the Balkans.

We arrived at the embassy, unsurprisingly perhaps, earlier than expected. A quick wash and then off with Mark Dickinson (the Ambassador), Becks and Julian to meet General Mike Jackson, the British commander of KFOR – the NATO ground force designated for Kosovo, but who are currently waiting in Macedonia to move over the border. We arrived at his headquarters in a disused shoe factory and were almost immediately sat down to a splendid meal in the canteen.

Then upstairs for a briefing. Very professionally done, but it made my hair stand on end with fear. I had sort of thought there must be a plan behind all this, I just didn't know it. But it quickly became evident that two very dangerous things are now happening.

Firstly, local political support for the operation in both Macedonia and Greece is fast disappearing. Milosevic could win this war without firing a shot in Kosovo by destabilizing the two countries through which our supply lines run.

And secondly, the military have no clear instructions as to what would happen if – and we all agreed this was most likely – the bombing didn't work.

Afterwards, off with Mike Jackson and Mark Dickinson to Jackson's office, where we sat until 2.00am drinking whisky and going through the problems. Jackson thinks we are staring defeat in the face. He doesn't have the troops to go in should the bombing fail to make Milosevic capitulate – which he believes most probable. He also believes that his lines of communication and supplies are at risk because of political destabilization, especially in Macedonia and Greece, where NATO troops are being stoned by the local population. He more or less appealed to me to ask Blair to get NATO to make up its mind. His view is that this operation must be over by September before the winter sets in. Which means that the decision to send ground troops into Kosovo must be made in the next month if it is to happen in time. Meanwhile, his operation is still supposed to be founded on the Rambouillet agreement. But everyone knows Rambouillet is a dead duck. These are the ingredients for a military disaster in which a great number of lives could be lost.

I went to bed feeling extremely frightened and determined to tackle Blair.

A most disturbed night.

Wednesday, 21 April, Macedonia

Up at 6.30 with a very fuzzy head. A shower, then at 8 o'clock off to see the British army locations close to the Kosovo border. We had a look at their armoured positions and chatted to the lads. They all said the same thing. Something has to be done and they want to get on with it. The uncertainty and lack of clarity of what they have been asked to do worries them. Me, too.

As I was clambering out of one of their Chieftain tanks, my mobile rang. It was Blair. He asked me how things were going. I told him, not very well. I would have some tough messages for him when I got back. He was clearly nervous I may be critical of the government's position in the MOD briefing I have agreed to appear on later in the morning. I told him I wouldn't do that, but that I couldn't change my private view. Spoke to Ming earlier, who is equally nervous about being inadvertently hooked into supporting the government.

Then, to Becks' delight, off in a helicopter to view British gun positions covering the main Serb entry points to Macedonia and afterwards back into town to a carpark where, in the back of the Ambassador's car, I changed out of my sweater and into a suit for my meeting with the prime minister, Ljubco Georgievski.

Then to the Alexander Palace Hotel, where I did a live input into the MOD briefing in London, talking chiefly about the plight of the refugees. George Robertson, who preceded me, went ludicrously over the top, trying to sound Churchillian but without much success. He said we now knew NATO had Milosevic on the run, because he is trying to widen the conflict to Montenegro and the Krajina. Rubbish!

After the MOD piece it was off to see the president, Kiro Gligorov. Very much an old-style Balkan politician – feline and intractable.

A quick change back into my sweater in the Ambassador's Range Rover, then out to one of refugee camps, accommodating around 80,000 Kosovar refugees in tents recently put up by NATO soldiers (UNHCR have been completely overwhelmed). Walking through the tented lines and hearing, once again, the harrowing tales of these pathetic people ripped from their homes and livelihoods, I bumped into one of the Kosovar Liberals who had helped me during my September and December visits last year. I had heard that he was dead. He took me to his family living miserably in a tent. Could I do anything to help them? I said I'd do what I could and stumbled out of his tent, fighting back the tears.[1]

Then back to the embassy, where Blerim Shalja was waiting for me. I told him he must speak to the Albanian community in Macedonia. Georgievski was taking real risks in supporting NATO and it wouldn't help anybody, least of all the Kosovars, if the Albanian minority in Macedonia did Milosevic's work for him and broke up the Macedonian state. He agreed to do what he could to calm down the Macedonian Albanians.

We also talked about the KLA. I said I thought we should take a risk and back them. Was there a reasonable chance the KLA would turn into a responsible organization, rather than drug-running radicals bent on destructive Albanian nationalism? He thought it was a risk worth taking. I said that the crude reality for the West was that the more we helped the KLA, the fewer of our own soldiers would be killed if it came to an invasion. It would have to be done secretly, of course, etc. He promised to put me in touch with Hashim Thaqi, the newly emerged political leader of the KLA.

Afterwards, I jumped into one of the First Secretaries' car and we were driven out to the airport, where we had fixed for an RAF Hercules to take us out. But it was delayed. Apparently its anti-missile devices had broken down. At 7.30 in the evening we discovered that it wasn't coming at all and we would have to wait until tomorrow. So it was back to the Ambassador's residence for the night, with me apologizing profusely for putting Mark and his wife to such inconvenience.

At about 9.00 the phone rang. It was Mike Jackson. There had been a Macedonian government security committee meeting, after which the NATO commanders had been summoned to be told of its outcome. The Macedonians said that they were completely fed up because they were

---

1 I subsequently wrote a 'To whom it may concern' letter for him to use, which was passed on to him by a Royal Marine officer running the camp. I also did a letter to the German Ambassador asking for special consideration for him and his dependants for an urgent visa to Germany, where he had family. This was granted and his family spent the rest of the Kosovo war in Germany. They have now returned to Kosovo, where I see them whenever I visit.

bottom of the list for joining NATO and NATO was insulting them. They had therefore decided not to let in any further NATO reinforcements through Macedonia and NATO would henceforth have to ask permission if they moved at all within Macedonia. Furthermore, there could be no question of mounting offensive operations into Kosovo from Macedonia. And, finally, if NATO didn't abide by this they would be kicked out altogether. Much consternation all round.

About ten or fifteen minutes later the brigadier who had actually spoken to the Macedonians came round to the Ambassador's house for a crisis meeting, accompanied by whisky and Macedonian brandy. I said I didn't want to interfere, since I wasn't a member of the government, but in my judgement the Macedonians were staking out their bargaining position and playing to the NATO summit and fiftieth anniversary celebrations currently taking place in Washington. They realized that they had an equivalent position to that of the Croats and Tudjman in the Bosnian war – they own the vital rear area upon which the whole operation depends. And they would use that advantage to squeeze the maximum out of us. They were in a strong bargaining position, and we were going to have to pay up. So we should listen politely, agree there was a problem, then raise the price from our side. We should say to them that of course they could have a fast track to NATO, but they would then be expected to behave like a NATO country – which meant providing full support for NATO troops on the ground and agreeing to having their territory used, if necessary, as a base for offensive operations against Serbia.

Went to bed having drunk rather a stiff glass of Macedonian brandy while poor Mark Dickinson went off to write telegrams to London reporting on this latest twist.

Thursday, 22 April, Macedonia and London

Mark brought me a cup of tea at 7.00 but I slept in until 8.00. Then down for a lonely cup of tea and a piece of toast and a morning spent writing thank you letters and beginning my report for Blair.

Finally, at 12.30, off to Skopje airport with Julian and Becks, where we sat in the sun waiting for our VC10 to arrive. It finally did and we were back in Britain around 7.00 in the evening.

At about 11pm Jonathan Powell called from Washington asking how it had gone.

I said, 'Look, my report is not what you want to hear. But I am really worried about the present situation and I want the PM to know why.'

'Well, even if it is not what he wants to hear, I suspect it is what he is already feeling. The NATO meeting the other day did not go well. Could you get it through to him quickly as he is off to see the President shortly?'

I faxed my report[1] through to the duty clerk at Downing Street at 1.30am, for onward transmission by secure fax to the States, before tumbling into bed.

Monday, 26 April, Westminster

Before going down to the chamber to listen to the Prime Minister's statement on Kosovo I was bleeped by Downing Street. Would I go and see Blair in his office in the House straight afterwards?

When I got there Bruce Grocott, his PPS, was with him and Blair was signing some letters. After a few minutes Grocott left and we were alone. Blair was yawning a great deal and said that he was very tired, so I decided I wouldn't keep him long – although we ended up talking for nearly three-quarters of an hour.

TB: Look, as you will no doubt have realized, we are already preparing ground troops for Kosovo, but we can't say so. At the moment we are changing the make-up of our troops in Macedonia, hoping nobody will notice. But one thing I have learned from all this is that NATO does not have the capacity to deal with this kind of operation – NATO was set up for total war. When it's over we are really going to have to change its set-up.

PA: I heard your *Today* interview the other day. I thought you were excellent.

TB: I have been giving a lot of interviews in the US, too, and they also seem to have gone down quite well. If you think that our press is being nice, you should see what the American press is saying! Anyway, we are now seriously beginning to work out how we should use ground troops and where.

PA: One of the problems now, though, is the time factor. We will have to start the ground troops operation by mid-July, if we are to have completed it by

1 The key recommendation was that NATO was losing the war and so should change tack and be prepared to use ground troops. See Appendix J.

mid-September and have enough time to move the refugees back and get their houses repaired by winter.

TB: Preferably. But I think we may be able to leave it as late as August if we have to.

PA: Perhaps. But even then, to get the forces into place for an invasion, you will need six weeks, which takes you back to the middle of May. By which time you will have to have taken a decision one way or the other.

TB: Yes, in the next three weeks.

PA: In the next two, for preference. Look, I don't want to keep you, so can I make a number of limited points to you? My first question is, do you think you are winning?

TB: No, not yet. But I think that we can.

PA: I don't think you are winning, either. Has anyone ever taken you through the theory of the conduct of wars? [He shook his head.] Well, briefly, wars are fought on three battlefields. There is the deep battlefield, the close battlefield and the rear battlefield. Our rear battlefield is Macedonia, Greece and Albania, through which our supplies come. And our deep battlefield is Serbia, through which Milosevic's supplies and reinforcements come. Milosevic's deep battlefield, on the other hand, is Macedonia and Greece, through which our supplies must pass, and his rear battlefield Serbia. The person who wins the deep battlefield war (for us Serbia; for him Macedonia and Greece) will win the close battlefield war (Kosovo). And on any balance of judgements, Milosevic is doing better than us in the deep war. Although our bombs may be doing real damage to his infrastructure, we have not so far seriously destabilized his rear areas. But he is seriously destabilizing ours. Stonings are now regular occurrences in Macedonia, and our supply convoys using the port in Thessaloniki cannot leave except by night, because there is such public hostility to them. This is a very serious situation. If he wins the propaganda war in Macedonia and Greece, he can win in Kosovo without a shot being fired. And he is winning there.

TB: Yes, we have talked about that at NATO. Yet despite public hostility in the 'front line states' the political leadership in Greece, Macedonia, Hungary and Romania is still firmly with us. They are all perfectly clear that they want to be part of NATO, they will give NATO as much support as possible and that NATO has to win. Do you think the biggest problem is Macedonia?

PA: Yes, the politicians there are standing up for NATO as much as they can. But they are not taking the population with them. In order to win round the people we must relieve the refugee problem so that it does not destabilize their ethnic balance, and assist them in overcoming the economic problems they face as a result of sanctions.

TB: Yes, I know that. I am thinking of going out there on Thursday. What do you think?

PA: A very good idea. It would be helpful if you talked to the Macedonian people via their press. Macedonia is becoming the key political battleground in the war.

Now, can I turn to the military situation? I was really quite shocked by the lack of certainty amongst our troops on the ground. They were put there with a mission and posture related to Rambouillet. But Rambouillet has been overtaken by events. They desperately need more clarity as to what their mission is.

Let me make a suggestion, entirely between you and me. I spoke to Mike Jackson, whom I think is very good. He spoke of some scheme about ground forces going to Belgrade, which is currently under consideration in military circles in Brussels. Neither of us thinks this is remotely sensible – indeed, it's quite mad. Apart from anything else, has anyone thought how many troops it would take to occupy a city like Belgrade? Also, we would be invading the heart of the Serb homeland. I don't think the Serbs will fight to the death for Kosovo, but they will for Serbia proper.

Secondly, Jackson, like me, is worried about the lack of clarity of aims at this stage. He doesn't know what we want him to do next. Can I suggest you have a bilateral with him? He is, after all, your commander on the ground with the lives of your citizens' sons and daughters in his hands. You should see him, preferably alone.

The next thing I want to speak to you about, though, is the KLA.

There are, in effect, three KLAs: there is the village self-defence KLA, which is of no consequence to us; there is the political KLA, which we should stay firmly clear of; and then there is the militarily effective KLA, which, I think, numbers somewhere between 5,000 and 8,000. And the more I speak to them, the more I see them as the people who support the Rambouillet principles. Help them now and we will give them a better chance of becoming a constructive force in Kosovo's future. Continue to ignore them and they may turn back to radicalism. Used effectively, even at this late stage, they could be the eyes of NATO aircraft on the ground, helping us to identify targets and, in the next phase (the invasion and making the peace) a force to help us build a decent peace afterwards. I know there will be difficulties with Security Council resolutions – and I am aware that all help must be covert – but I don't think we should be squeamish about this. I have been told that the Americans are beginning to help them. We are missing out here.

TB: Yes, Bill and I discussed that, too. We agreed to do what we can to support them.

PA: I know you are very pushed, so I will make one more point to you. It is about the tone of the MOD public briefings. In my view, when a democratic leader takes his nation to war he needs to do so with a decent and proper sobriety and reticence. You did this very well on the *Today* programme earlier this week. But some of George Robertson's comments have been way over the top. I heard him declaim the other day Milosevic's 'blood-stained regime'. People know perfectly well that it is blood-stained. Less adjectives, more facts and plain speaking would work far better. I also heard him talk about 'the heroic efforts of the British troops putting up tents'. It's beginning to sound a bit like Kim Il Sung!

TB (laughing): No doubt Guthrie has been getting at him. Soldiers have a habit of using this kind of language. But perhaps we should tone it down a bit.

The meeting ended at about 5.15.

Then back to the office to finish my paperwork. Douglas Hurd had asked to see me and came by at about 6.30. He wanted to know my views on Kosovo. We had an interesting discussion and broadly agreed on what needed to be done. At one stage I said that I thought that we would have to reform NATO and persuade our European partners to take defence more seriously, to which he said, 'That is exactly right. And if my party had any sense and wasn't tearing itself apart, that is what it would be saying. But, of course, we are not prepared to say anything about Europe. The very mention of it causes them to start frothing at the mouth.'

Tuesday, 27 April, Westminster

At 9.30 Ragie Murugan, the man from the UN War Crimes Tribunal, came to see me to get a statement on my visit to Kosovo in September 1998 (when we witnessed the bombardment of Suva Reka). I spent most of the day with him and his colleagues. I handed over my diaries to them, from which they typed up a statement. Apparently some truly terrible things have come to light which they are slowly and painstakingly putting together.

They didn't think the information I gave them on the bombings of Suva Reka was particularly crucial – they have a lot more information relating to that incident, including some which identifies specific individuals. But my evidence, they said, was potentially vital to the future prosecution of

Milosevic, as I was the only person who was prepared to let them use my records of a conversation with him, in which he had been told what was going on and that he was personally indictable under the Geneva Convention for this. They said that if Milosevic does come before the tribunal, I may have to give evidence.[1]

Thursday, 29 April, London

[*Following the passage of the devolution legislation for Scotland and Wales, elections had been fixed for 6 May for the Scottish Parliament and Welsh Assembly. I had spent much time campaigning in both countries where, since the elections were by PR, it was unlikely that any party would get a majority and very likely that the Lib Dems would hold the balance.*]

Back in London by 4.30pm and straight into the office for a meeting with Julian, Miranda and David Laws. I have only just realized the dangers which the outcome of the Scottish and Welsh elections may pose to the project. We are almost certain to hold the balance of power in both, so coalition negotiations are very likely in Edinburgh and Cardiff. If coalition talks fail in either, the whole project could be affected. I asked Julian and David to produce a paper for me on how best to approach next weekend. I told them that I didn't want to interfere in either but I do want to know what's happening and to ensure that we do not miss the opportunity to get the Lib Dems into partnership government in both Scotland and Wales if the opportunity comes our way. If, in the end, we decide not to go into coalition, then there must be good reasons for that and the parties must continue to have good relations. With Jim's agreement, I asked David Laws, who is widely respected in the Party, not least in Scotland, to go up there to provide assistance and act as a point of liaison for me in the negotiations.

Tuesday, 4 May, Scotland

CAMPAIGNING FOR THE FIRST SCOTTISH PARLIAMENT

[*I had flown up the night before and spent the night with Ming Campbell and his wife Elspeth in Edinburgh.*]

1 A month later, on 27 May, Milosevic was indicted for war crimes by the Hague Tribunal.

I couldn't sleep beyond 5.30. My brain has not yet adjusted to the earlier dawns of spring.

During the morning a private word with Willie Rennie, chief executive of the Scottish Lib Dems. I told him how important it was, if there was a hung parliament in Scotland, that we got the Lib/Lab partnership off to a good start. Willie thinks we will get seventeen seats out of a total of 129. Chris Rennard thinks fifteen. I'm more inclined to believe Chris.[1]

After the press conference we loaded on to the 'battle bus' with David Steel, Jim Wallace, Elspeth Attwool[2] and others, before heading off for the Irn-Bru factory for a campaign visit. On the way I had a long chat with Jim, talking through what he will do if there is, as seems most likely, a hung parliament. We agreed that he should set up a small advisory committee to help him with negotiations with Labour. One of them should be somebody in whom the party had confidence and another somebody in whom he had confidence. I was really worried about the negotiations stretching on for weeks, which could do terrible damage to the public's perception of PR. I hoped they could get it all signed and sealed within a week. The future of the project and of PR depends on how such a Scottish deal works out.

The real block with Labour is university tuition fees, which I discussed at length with Jim. He had come out very firmly against their policy of levying fees. I suggested there might be two ways out of the corners into which both sides had painted themselves. Since I didn't think Labour would concede on no tuition fees (the ramifications both for their Comprehensive Spending Review and the knock-on effects in England were too great), he could either go for a free vote, which Labour would find very difficult to refuse, or for a hardship fund. But if he wanted to give himself room for manoeuvre to suggest a hardship fund, then he should start shifting the argument on to the impact on students, rather than the views of the Lib Dems. Then he could afford to play quite hard ball with Labour. After all, Labour in a hung parliament would be left with two options: to reach a compromise with us and provide a stable government, or to try a minority administration on their own in which they would lose any subsequent vote on tuition fees in the Scottish Parliament anyway. So they would still have to move one way or the other.

Finally, I said that it really was important that he and Donald Dewar make private contact with each other now so that each knew broadly what

---

1 Willie, however, turned out to be right.
2 Now Member of the European Parliament for Scotland since 1999.

the other was thinking. No one wanted any nasty surprises. Jim agreed that it would be useful to have some deniable contacts at a lower level before polling day so that each side would know what the other might do. And then perhaps on Thursday (polling day) Jim could speak to Donald directly. I also got Jim's agreement to my sending David Laws up to help in the negotiations.

The tour of the Irn-Bru factory lasted an hour or so, during which I had to say wonderful things about Irn-Bru. At one stage, when asked if I drank it often, I said, 'Don't you know, Menzies Campbell's cellar is full of it!'

Michael Moore and I then left Jim's battle bus and drove across country to Innverleithen to campaign in his area. Lovely weather. A beautiful drive up the Tweed valley, sunshine sparkling on the waters, the bright new leaves on the trees and the great shoulders of the green hills running down into the valleys. We stopped for an ice cream at Innverleithen, then on to Galashiels, where I spent an hour going round a technical college that has become part of Heriot-Watt University. I hope I managed to sound enthusiastic.

Then to Edinburgh airport to catch the 5.25 shuttle back to London. Whilst waiting for the plane I got a call from Becks saying that Blair wanted to speak to me. He rang about half an hour before take-off.

PA: Look, I am not in a very good position to talk since I am in the executive lounge at Edinburgh airport.

TB (laughing): But you can listen, at least.

PA (with some irony): But I always listen to you. Incidentally, you seem to have had a very good trip to Macedonia.

TB: Yes, I had some very helpful discussions with the Macedonians. I have managed to reassure them of NATO's intentions, I think, and have got them to open another transit camp. I also had a good reception from the Romanian Parliament. What these guys want to know is that we are going to win and do so quickly. So I was able to reassure them on that. I also had a constructive meeting with Mike Jackson. I think we understand each other's views now. He certainly knows what I have in mind.

But the reason I'm ringing is, if you have any influence over your Scottish people [I don't think he said this with any trace of irony], then I must tell you that we are getting into a difficult position on this issue of tuition fees. It is a real deal breaker for us. Jim Wallace seems to be painting himself into a corner. We need room for manoeuvre.

PA: Well, the important think is that neither side paints itself into a corner. You say this is a deal breaker for you. But it is also a deal breaker for us. We have taken a very clear line on this for a very long time and you shouldn't underestimate its importance to us. Jim has only reiterated our consistent position. I don't see how we can get through without compromise on both sides.

TB: Well, any change on tuition fees would mean Gordon revisiting the Comprehensive Spending Review, and that's not possible.

PA: I don't think that's necessary. After all, it is you who have given the Scottish Parliament the power to make up its own mind on this. The logical consequence of this is that Scotland can adopt something different from the rest of Britain.

TB: Yes, I have no objection to that. But they would have to find the resources from within their own budget. I can't imagined Donald agreeing to that.

PA: Look, this cannot be negotiated by you and I now and I certainly can't talk about it effectively in the middle of a public place. It is really up to Jim and Donald to sort out. But, as it happens, I have already talked to Jim about it today and I think he may be able to move if you compromise too. But you are not in a strong position. If you don't do a deal with us you will be defeated in the Scottish Parliament on the issue, anyway. If you do a deal with us, however, we can offer less painful compromise positions and the stability to govern Scotland in partnership and with a majority. Which is, of course, what we both want.

But we won't be pushovers on this. I don't think Jim and Donald have talked to each other much about coalition. And there is so much groundwork still to be laid. I have suggested that somebody close to Jim (possibly Michael Moore) should, before polling day, approach somebody close to Donald just to talk about possible procedures. It would be useful if you could ensure that we get a positive response from your side to this. The danger is that in the post-election period both sides misunderstand the messages being sent by the other.

TB: Yes, that is a real danger. Then we would get the parliament off with an unhelpful wrangle and the whole project would be damaged.

PA: Which would damage the whole cause of PR.

TB (laughing): And not just the public's view of PR. I'm not sure my guys are going to be immensely enamoured of PR when they see how we have to negotiate with you in this way.

PA: Well, that's the new politics. Why don't we speak again when I am in a better position to do so?

TB: OK, I'll give you a call tomorrow evening.

Thursday, 6 May, Somerset and London

POLLING DAY FOR THE SCOTTISH PARLIAMENT, WELSH ASSEMBLY AND
LOCAL COUNCILS IN ENGLAND

Beautiful weather. My last set of local elections as leader of the party and
I am feeling very nervous about the results. Up at 7.30. Jane went off to
tell at 8.00. So I pottered about, then went up to vote for the cameras.

Afterwards, I jumped into the car for my usual polling day rounds. Then
back home for a cup of tea and to pack my stuff before catching the 4.30
from Crewkerne to Waterloo.

In the evening, around 10.00, I went to Cowley Street for the results. We
did far better than I had feared. We lost some seats and councils to the
Tories (especially in the West Country) but gained seats and councils from
Labour – including our triumph of the night, taking control of Sheffield.
On balance, a good night.[1]

To bed about 2.00, but far too geared up to sleep. Anyway, I had to be
up at 5.45 for a round of TV and radio interviews.

Friday, 7 May, Westminster

After my early morning media blitz with Miranda in attendance, it was
back to Westminster for our traditional post-studio fried breakfast in the
Lords cafeteria. Then over to Cowley Street for the press conference, which
went very well. My line was, 'A night of satisfaction sprinkled with triumph
– there have been gains and losses, which is normal for any genuinely
national party, which we now are. But the losses were less than we had
anticipated and the gains more than we had hoped for.' The line of moving
from a party of protest to a party of power went down particularly well.
It has, of course, been another triumph for Chris Rennard and local
campaigners, who are the real heroes.

Then into a taxi to King's Cross to catch the train to Sheffield to celebrate
our victory there.

Shortly before the train arrived at Doncaster, the Downing Street exchange rang my mobile. Could I speak to the PM? I explained that I was in a

---

1 The Scottish and Welsh results, being PR, took longer to count and the outcomes of those
two elections were not expected until the following day.

crowded second-class carriage going north to Sheffield and so my capacity to speak frankly was limited. Nevertheless, they put Blair on the line.

TB: Why are you going to Sheffield?

PA: Why do you think?

He suddenly realized it was to celebrate our victory over Labour last night and laughed.

TB: Look, this business of tuition fees. We really cannot give in on it, you know. It would cost too much; it would open up floodgates for England; it would leave David Blunkett hanging out to dry. And it would reopen an internal battle we have already fought at great cost.

PA: As I said to the exchange before you came on, my ability to speak now is pretty limited. But this is bizarre. For the last four or five days the Scottish papers have been full of hints from your side that there's a deal to be done on tuition fees. So my guys were convinced they were pushing at an open door. These press reports, uncorrected by you lot, have served to increase the determination of our people to get a concession on this. For you to send us and everyone else signals in public that you are prepared to talk, then close down any possibility in private, is a ludicrous way of going about things.

TB: We have not been sending signals.

PA: I'll send you the cuttings if you wish. The Scottish papers have been full of it. The public expects a deal now on the basis that we can both reach a compromise. The press expects it and we will look stupid if we cave in to you. Anyway, we won't. We are as attached to our policy as you are to yours. There can't be a compromise on the basis of one side saying take it or leave it. Please recognize that we are quite happy, if necessary, for you to go ahead with a minority government if that's what you choose to do.

TB: I don't understand how this came about. Donald told Jim there would be no compromise on this last Tuesday. I can't be responsible for what the press says.

PA: Your administration, more than any other, has the reputation of being responsible for *everything* that the press says! If something appears in the press my guys presume you have briefed it. If the press is wrong, why didn't your lot correct it? But look, there is a lot more here we need to discuss and it cannot be done with me sitting in a crowded train carriage.

TB: I just wanted you to know how strongly we feel about this.

PA: So do we. I'll try and ring you from a land line immediately I get to Sheffield.

I then rang Julian, asking him to gather a selection of the relevant Scottish press cuttings and fax them through to Downing Street.

Once in Sheffield, off to the city hall, where we had champagne, photographs and innumerable interviews. A long day's travelling just for two or three minutes on ITN and the BBC, but it was worth it.

After Sheffield, on to an even more crowded train down to Leicester, where I met Nick Clegg[1] and our campaigners (six gains there last night), before doing something for Leicester local radio. Then into my car which Ian Patrick[2] had driven up from London and off to Somerset, hoping to get back by 7.30.

I found I did not have time to ring Blair from Sheffield as promised, so he rang again at about 4.30, while we were sitting in a traffic jam south of Birmingham. This time we had an extended conversation in which we rehearsed again all our previous arguments on tuition fees.

But before we got on to that I said there was something else I needed to discuss first. Jim met Donald yesterday, apparently at some television studio, and they discussed the situation. Donald had said that he wanted a very generalized agreement on the foundation document for the coalition agreement. I said this would be unacceptable to us. We wanted a very detailed agreement. If we were in a minority in the Cabinet in Scotland we would need something specific, so we didn't get subsequently steamrollered by their majority in government.

TB: I don't know exactly what Donald said, but I agree with you. And so does Gordon. We need a detailed agreement to tie you guys in.

PA: I'm not sure I like your implication there. But, at all events, we both have a vested interest in coming up with a detailed coalition agreement, not a few general headings. You because you think it ties us in. And us because it protects us from being steamrollered. Can I leave it that you will contact Donald to make that clear to him?

He said that he would.

On tuition fees I reminded him that the other day he'd told me that, providing the money could be found in the Scottish budget, he wasn't fussed. Was he now saying that is wrong?

---

1 Member of the European Parliament for the East Midlands. Before being elected, Nick was Leon Brittan's Chief of Staff at the European Commission.
2 An assistant in my office. Ian is now my Political Secretary.

TB: Yes, I was wrong when I said that. You can't have Scotland doing something different from the rest of Britain.

PA: Then you shouldn't have given the Scots devolution, including, specifically, the power to be different on this issue. You put yourself in a ridiculous position if, having produced the legislation to give power to the Scottish Parliament, you then say it is a matter of principle that they can't use it.

TB (laughing): Yes, that is a problem. I am beginning to see the defects in all this devolution stuff.

PA: Well, is this a matter of principle for you or a matter of practicalities? If it is a matter of principle, then we might as well call a halt right now. The principle we hold to is that the Scottish Parliament should be allowed to exercise the powers you bestowed on it. If you say that's impossible, then we do not want to be your partners. If, on the other hand, it is a matter of costings, then I'm sure we can find a practical way through.

TB: Well, I am under immense pressure on this. Both David Blunkett and Gordon are hitting the ceiling on it. So Jim will just have to pitch his tent somewhere else.

PA: Jim is not going to pitch his tent somewhere else. This is where we pitched our tent during the election. And it is where your lot in Scotland encouraged us to pitch it. If you think we will roll over and die, then forget it. We must work out a compromise. You say you believe in pluralism. Well, that is what it comes down to. You seem to think you are dealing with a minority party – us. But in fact *you* are the minority party in the Scottish Parliament on this. The majority opinion in the Scottish Parliament is with us on this, not with you. But let's get Donald and Jim together to try and work it out. Who knows, they may be able to find a solution.

TB: Yes, let's. I understand they are due to speak to one another tonight. We need to get them down to the substantial negotiations fast. But you and I will have to assist as much as possible.

PA: I am not sure that's wise. You and I may need to bang heads together at the end. But if we are seen to be the people doing the negotiating now, and then handing down solutions, that drags us in too early, is likely to lead to hostility among our Scottish colleagues and will undermine the entire principle of having a Scottish Parliament in the first place. My strong advice is to let them try to come to an agreement by themselves and only come in afterwards if we have to.

We agreed that that would be the sensible way forward and that we should talk again later after Donald and Jim had spoken.

I immediately rang Jim to give him the gist of the conversation. He is obviously (and rightly) getting nervous about me doing too much negotiating from Westminster. About an hour later, while still in the car, another call came through from Downing Street. Gordon Brown. In the event the reception was so bad that I asked him to ring me later after I had got home to Vane Cottage. He called at about 8.15pm and we had a long discussion.

GB: Let me start by saying that Jim Wallace has asked me to issue a public spending statement in October. There is no way I will do that in order just to solve the problem of tuition fees.

PA: I do wish you people would listen to what we actually say, not what your spin doctors say we say. Jim never said anything of the sort. What he, in fact, said was that one of the reasons why he couldn't be certain of needing a penny on Scottish income tax, was that he couldn't know what the true economic situation was until he had seen the books. So we needed a spending statement to see what was possible.

GB: OK, but let me make it clear to you. There is no question of providing Scotland with more money from the Treasury coffers.

At which I exploded.

PA: Will you people *never* listen to what we say? We never said we should ask the English taxpayer to pay for a better deal for Scottish students. We are not so naïve. The Lib Dems made that clear during the campaign. And I have confirmed to the PM since that if we are to find this, it will be from within the Scottish budget.

GB: Well, that's a relief. I can go back and tell Donald that. But the problem is still an insuperable one. If we are to reach our manifesto commitment of raising the higher education quotient in Scotland to 750,000 students by the end of the parliament, then we simply won't have the money for this if you abolish tuition fees. The only way we could do it would be by cutting back on nursery education or something like that.

PA: That's nonsense. It will cost about £30 million. In a £16 billion budget that's not very much to find.

GB: More like £50 million.

PA: Not according to your own figures, given in your own parliamentary answers. But, whatever it is, let's get together rationally and talk about it. Is this about principle or is it about money?

GB: Well, the principle is the money.

Which is, I suppose, the only answer a Chancellor can give. I told him that I strongly suspected that they were opposed to this whatever. If we won the argument on the basis of money, they would say it was principle. If we challenged them on the basis of the principle, they would say it was the money. He had the grace to laugh. And then he tried a different tack.

GB: Look, we can't just go back to how students were funded before. Students and their parents must bear the burden of cost for their education.

I exploded again.

PA: We got to that position long before you did. I fought this through my party five years ago. It was bloody difficult. And at the last election we fought on a system of student funding not dissimilar from the one you are now proposing. But much better, since it didn't include fees for tuition. And nor did we shelter like you behind the Dearing Report during the election. So please don't talk to me about taking hard decisions!

GB: Well, what's the problem then, if you accept the system?

PA: The problem is that the particular system you have chosen is a rotten one. And by including tuition fees you break with the principle of free education, which we think is wrong. We take the view that education, like health, should be free at the point of delivery. Now let's get back to the substance rather than try to score points off each other.

GB: Well, the substance is that we still can't do it. It's impossible.

PA: Fine. We have both rehearsed our positions. But, as I said to the PM, we should really let Donald and Jim get together to try and sort it out on the ground.

GB: Yes, I suppose so. But I can't see a way through. Anyway, let's call a halt here. I hope you found our conversation useful.

PA: Yes, I did.

We have had a good result in Scotland, seventeen MSPs and a hung parliament. Surprisingly, however, Labour got really hammered in Wales by the Welsh Nats. So we have a hung parliament there, too.[1] Spoke to Jim

---

1 The results for the Scottish Parliament elections were: Labour 55 seats; SNP 35 seats; Conservatives 18 seats; Lib Dems 17 seats; others 3. The results of the National Assembly for Wales were: Labour 28 seats; Plaid Cymru 17 seats; Conservative 9 seats; Lib Dems 6 seats.

about how he is going to handle things. Fortunately, the plans are reasonably well laid, now.[1]

A late dinner at around 10.00, then to bed, completely exhausted.

Saturday, 8 May, Somerset

Lots of calls today, including several with Jim and Mike German.[2] Jim tells me he had a really tough time with some of the MSPs. Some of them, including Keith Raffan (an ex-Tory), are being bloody stupid. Some of them think they can let the negotiations go on until 2 June. Jim, however, like me, believes that they must be finished early.

Sunday, 9 May, Somerset

At 8.00am I woke to hear a Radio 4 review of the Sunday papers. The *Independent on Sunday* is saying I had a conversation with the PM straight after the Scottish elections in which I told him to keep his nose out and let the Scots decide. Clearly a leak from our side. I was very embarrassed about this, so I put a call in to No. 10 to apologize. Downing Street rang back and Blair came on the line.

PA: Look, I am so sorry about this. It didn't come from me. But I did brief some of my colleagues in Scotland about what we have been talking about, so it must have come from one of them. I apologize.[3]

TB: It's not very helpful. I haven't read the article but I heard about it on the radio. But these things happen. I am much more worried about the substance of it. I understand your guys are now saying they don't want a solution until 2 June. That

---

1 Anticipating a hung parliament and the inevitable questions that would be asked of us, Jim and some of his advisers had prepared a strategy document, made public three months previously, which set out the process by which negotiations would take place and, crucially, reassured the Party about how it would be consulted and involved in final decisions.

2 Leader of the Lib Dems in Wales.

3 Michael Moore has since told us that this was incorrect. Labour and the Scottish press were trying to bounce the Lib Dems into a quick deal which Jim and his team were, quite rightly, resisting.

is a real disaster. If we take that long we are all going to look fools. I think it is beginning to look at bit of a mess in Scotland already.

PA: I don't think it's looking a mess in Scotland at all. We have got a parliament for four years. If it takes a few more days or hours to get this sorted, then so be it. No doubt some of mine are saying stupid things in public, just as some of yours are. But Jim and I both remain of the view that this should be completed by the middle of the week. That is what we are aiming for. So don't let's get distracted by idiots blurting out their own versions of what's happening to some passing member of the media, who then takes it seriously.

We then rehearsed once again the arguments on tuition fees, without agreement.

PA: Well, fine. If we can't reach an agreement then you will have to govern on a minority basis. But that just means the Scottish Parliament will impose no tuition fees on you. What will you do then?

TB: We could always hold another election.

PA (laughing): You could. But just imagine what vote you would get if you held another Scottish election within a few months of this one on the single issue of tuition fees and on the grounds that the Scottish Parliament had sought to exercise powers you gave them and the Scottish people had voted for. You would be destroyed! I'm sorry, but I can't take the threat of another election seriously, I'm afraid.

He went through the cost element again.

TB: Well, there is one concession we could make. We could have a review in two years' time. If it shows that the system is not working, then we will change it.

PA: And you really think my party will accept that? You and I both know that when politicians want to sweep something under the carpet they call for a review. Especially your government! We would be humiliated in Scotland if we accepted that and nothing more.

TB: No, I think it is a perfectly sensible proposition and a big concession to you guys.

PA: Well, let me be the judge of whether my party will accept this. But in case you are in any doubt, I can say now that they will not.

There followed a lot of despairing about us doing the whole project damage, threatening PR, getting the Scottish Parliament off to a bad start, etc. He was just about to ring off rather grumpily when I floated the idea of using individual learning accounts (ILAs).[1]

[Anticipating that this might provide a way out for both sides, I had first put the suggestion to David Laws on Friday, and had asked him to look into it. He had discussed it with Jim, who had agreed this may provide a possible way forward.]

PA: Look, we must find a compromise. I have been laying awake all night thinking about it. I haven't discussed this with anyone else. But why not use Scotland as a pilot for ILAs. That was our policy at the last election. And according to my recollection Labour are also committed to ILAs. In fact, I seem to remember Gordon Brown making a speech about them. Perhaps they offer a way forward?

He immediately pricked up his ears.

TB: That's really quite interesting. I am not saying yes or no at the moment, but I will go away and think about it.

PA: And I am not proposing it at the moment. I am just saying it is an idea for both of us to think about. If I can get my people interested, it might provide a way through. But if it is to have any chance of success it must appear to come from Scotland, and from our side.

Later on I spoke to Jim, who has seen Donald Dewar. Their meeting was cordial but nothing substantive has come out of it. He was seeing Donald again tonight and would talk to him about ILAs then. So just before midday I rang Jonathan to tell him that Jim was interested, he was thinking of putting the idea to Donald tonight. Could he arrange a welcome for the idea? Jonathan agreed to get Blair to prime Donald. They seem quite interested.

David Laws rang me from Scotland after the policy meeting early this evening. Apparently it went quite well. Each side has now produced their own text of the proposed coalition agreement. So the serious negotiations can begin.

---

1 An ILA is a tax-advantaged, personalized account (paying interest) into which money can be paid to finance lifelong learning. Contributions can be paid in at any time by the state, employers, young people and their families. Money can be drawn out by the individual 'owning' the account in order to fund education and training costs throughout the individual's life – including, under the Liberal Democrat plans, undergraduate tuition fees.

Monday, 10 May, Somerset

We are making little progress in the Scottish coalition negotiations between Jim and Donald. So I decided to have a further word with Blair in order to make clear to him: firstly, that this is clearly going to take time, so they should be patient; and secondly, that Jim has to carry the Party with him democratically and they must accept this. No doubt our democratic procedures would annoy them, but my experience was that if we gave the party the chance to express its view democratically, it would then be locked in rather than split, which would make for a better partnership in the long run. My third point was to underline the importance to us of the tuition-fees issue and why we couldn't back down.

My meeting with Blair was fixed for 6.30. Julian and I turned up at Whitehall, to be met by Kate Garvey. I asked her how long we had and she said half an hour, the PM had a reception to attend at 7.00. I groaned and explained that if we couldn't get through this in half an hour, we might have to come back to it later in the evening since there was a tremendous amount at stake.

We waited for about five minutes as Blair showed out some visitors and then got down to business. But it was a discussion that went nowhere.

I decided to start off with Wales, since I knew this was his weaker flank.

'Look, I just don't understand what has happened in Wales. We have a real opportunity to put together a stable coalition government with you in Wales, which will help the project overall and encourage the Scots to do the same. Given the fact that there are no problems of a tuition-fees nature in Wales, I just can't understand why this isn't happening. It appears that Alun Michael doesn't want a coalition. He thinks he has got a deal with Plaid Cymru. But Plaid will lead him straight into a trap. They will support him now as First Minister and then dump him later when it suits them.[1] And the result will be that the whole thing will collapse in a year or so's time. This is a real opportunity to push the project forward by doing a coalition which will give Alun a stable basis for government, isolate Plaid Cymru and help in Scotland and Westminster. But you seem to have allowed this to be turned down. I don't understand. He will have to come to it in the end, you know.'

---

1 Which is what, in due course, happened.

Blair looked a bit flustered and admitted that he couldn't understand it either. He would have a word with Alun Michael later.

On Scotland, we talked further about ILAs.

They have a problem with these, apparently, because Gordon Brown objects strongly to giving tax incentives to people who have had a university education and so have had a great deal of money spent on them already. A legitimate objection. Blair then raised the whole question of an independent review again, to which I agreed to give further thought.

The conversation was rather bad-tempered at times, I fear, but it ended on a good-natured enough note.

Then back to the office to clear my mail.

Later I heard from Jonathan Powell that Alun Michael had been contacted by Blair and that he had agreed to see Mike German in the morning to talk about a coalition, but, in Powell's words, 'He wants to play it long. Not the same timescale as in Scotland.'

Afterwards I found out that Michael, in fact, intended to make his Cabinet appointments tomorrow, so all this talk of coalition with the Lib Dems was nonsense. It was hardly likely he would dismiss a newly appointed Labour minister in a few months' time in order to make way for a Lib Dem. I was furious with Jonathan, and with Blair for squandering the chance to play out the project on another stage.

Down to dinner. A small crowd at the table, including Donald Gorrie, Andrew Stunell, Phil Willis and Jackie Ballard, to whom I expressed some of my despair about Wales and Scotland. A long discussion ensued, with all the others at the table taking the predictable view that we shouldn't be going for a coalition in either.

Back home, after the vote, by 10.30. To bed, but I couldn't get to sleep. I am pretty pessimistic about pulling off coalition in either Scotland or Wales. And if it doesn't happen, that will mark the end of the project for good.

Tuesday, 11 May, London and Farnham

Up at 5.30am, having been awake since 4.00. I hate these times when we are building up to a crisis. I simply cannot sleep. Got dressed, tidied the flat and was in the office by 7.30. Lots of calls to Scotland and Wales, then to Waterloo to catch the train down to Farnham, where I am campaigning on behalf of Emma Nicholson. Emma is looking tired, but pleased with the way the campaign is going. She is certain to get in, of course. We went

off to a primary school, where I was filmed reading *The Very Hungry Caterpillar* to some children, then a number of local interviews, then back to the office.

In the middle of the afternoon I got an urgent phone call from a very worried David Laws. David fears that the text the Lib Dems and Labour are negotiating on PR for local government in Scotland is too weak to be acceptable to the Scottish Liberal Democrats. A full meeting of MSPs would reject it.

I said, 'That's worrying. But how do I deal with this? I am not supposed to know the information you have provided to me. The only way I can think of dealing with it is if you tell Jim that I have been pestering you to send me the text of some of the agreements and you have done so.'

David sent through the text and later on I had a word with Jim to ask how it was going. He said the mood was good, but that they hadn't yet touched on tuition fees. His aim was to try and get everything else through before moving on to the crunch issue, in the hope that the momentum could carry us through. Exactly the right negotiating strategy.

I said I had seen some of the text. David Laws had sent it through to me. I was terribly worried about the wording on PR. I told him that we were pushing at an open door here and he could, I thought, negotiate a tougher text; otherwise he wouldn't get it through the party. Jim seems to be blaming himself for ever having got caught on the tuition-fees hook. I told him it wasn't his fault; Labour were equally to blame for letting the press speculate about compromise on the issue here. The aim should be to give people sufficient space to change their minds with elegance. This couldn't be done in the immediate aftermath of the Scottish election, but if we could somehow push the issue into a corner for a bit we might give both sides time to come to a more considered view. Anyway, in my view, tuition fees was not the issue on which we should fight to the death; PR was. Jim agreed to look at the PR text again and get it toughened up.

First thing in the morning I had spoken to Blair and suggested that, to help break the impasse, I should speak to Donald and he should speak to Jim. He agreed and I spoke to Donald at about 9.00am, catching him in a state of deep Celtic gloom – something to which he is famously prone. I emphasized how committed both Jim and I were to succeeding in the negotiations.

He seemed reassured by this, and we even cracked a joke or two at the end. But Blair's parallel conversation with Jim didn't take place until much later in the day – at about 6.45pm.

I was siting down to dinner with Rosemary Billinge[1] in the Strangers' Dining Room when my phone went off. It was Downing Street. Could I speak to the PM? We ended up having a lengthy conversation with me pacing up and down the corridor leading from the Members' Dining Room to the Library while MPs of all parties passed backwards and forwards. There wasn't much privacy.

Blair was in a despairing mood. He said Jim had made no concessions at all in the phone call he had just had with him.

PA: But surely you wouldn't expect him to. Jim asked me, before your call, how he should handle it. I said that when you ring the very least he should do is listen, but not negotiate. What you have just heard is a party leader seeking to preserve his negotiating position in the face of a telephone call from the Prime Minister. I thought the purpose of your call was to explain your view to Jim personally, not to negotiate. That's between Jim and Donald.

TB: Yes, well, I don't think they are getting anywhere. I am also really worried about Donald. He is getting himself into a dangerous mood of depression and is quite likely to throw the whole thing in.

I said I would speak to Jim to find out exactly what was going on. After dinner I went back to the flat to ring him.

'What on earth did you say to the PM? He thinks the whole thing is over. Did you say you were packing it in? Because that's what he thinks.'

1 A long-time family friend.

Jim said he had done no such thing, but confessed to feeling low. I tried to gee him up, saying that however late we had to stay up, we must get it through tonight and I felt we were pretty close.

He agreed that it was tonight or never and went back into the negotiations.

The next spate of calls came through at about 10.30. David Laws, in despair again. Jim had just come out of a discussion with his negotiating committee, who had sent him off to see Donald Dewar with a package of measures which included an inquiry on tuition fees to be set up by the Scottish Parliament, rather than the Executive [the Scottish government], the outcome of which would be debated and decided later. I had previously suggested to Jim that one way forward was to set up an independent inquiry. Jim had agreed to this, but the negotiating committee had said no and sent him back to Donald Dewar with a purely parliamentary inquiry.

David's chief worry, however, was the mood of the negotiating committee. They were exhausted and beginning to lose touch with reality. If their package was abruptly thrown out by Dewar, they were quite likely to pack up and go off in a huff. David wanted me to get the PM to persuade Dewar not to reject the proposal roughly, but to do so in a way which would keep the negotiations in play.

I immediately contacted Blair, explained the situation and asked him to contact Dewar.

I then rang David back to find out what was happening. Too late! Before Blair could get to Dewar, Dewar had rejected Jim's proposals out of hand and, just as David had predicted, the negotiating team had packed their bags and left.[1] We were now in a desperate situation. I told David to do whatever he could to keep Jim in the building. 'Lock the doors, if necessary.' David responded that this was probably not necessary since Jim and Donald had already agreed to have a quiet meeting over a bottle of whisky afterwards. Thank heavens!

I rang Blair again.

PA: Our negotiating teams have left the building. But Jim and Donald are still there, without their negotiating teams but with a bottle of whisky. Maybe we can still pull it off. If Donald is prepared to make a proposal to Jim which shows some flexibility, I think we may clinch it. My proposal is that you now tell Donald to

1 I have subsequently learned that, before they left, a press release was agreed announcing the final breakdown of talks, to be issued in the morning.

propose to Jim an independent inquiry whose membership and remit would be proposed by the Scottish Executive, but agreed by the Scottish Parliament, who could amend both. In other words, you get your independent inquiry but Jim is able to feel that he has asserted the primacy of Parliament. If you agree, we can act fast and may be able to save this.

TB: Yes, that is a solution I think we can just about accept. I'll get on to Donald.

PA: No, not yet. I don't want Donald making this proposition to Jim until I have already got Jim to agree to it.

So I rang Jim with the proposition, saying, 'Look, in the end you are going to have to put your leadership on the line on this. But I can't believe your lot will reject this deal if it means losing you. And it's the best deal you'll get. Can you give me your agreement that when Donald puts the proposition to you, you will accept it and that you will present it tomorrow morning to your parties as a joint proposition from the two leaders, agreed late tonight, as the best deal you can both get? You will have hell on this tomorrow. But so will he. And it's the only way to break the log jam.'

Jim replied, 'This is high-wire stuff. But I think my position is on the line anyway. I need five minutes to think about it and I also want to talk about it with Nicol Stephen. I'll ring you back.'

I waited for an agonizing five minutes before Jim rang back. He said he could go along with what I suggested, provided there was scope for us to maintain our position of opposition to tuition fees and give evidence on that basis to the commission.

I said, 'Of course. That is inherent. Though I wouldn't go seeking opportunities to vote against it. That would be bad faith. So you think we can go ahead with this?'

'Yes.'

'Fine. I'll ask the PM to get Donald Dewar to put the proposition to you. Do not go back in to see Dewar whatever you do until Blair has had the chance to speak to him.'

I then rang Blair back to say he should go ahead. Which he did.

Dewar then rang me, so that I could take him through the proposals. He agreed that that was a way forward. Then another agonizing wait of forty-five minutes or so. David, who had been looking through the door at the two of them, reported that their mood had changed to conviviality.[1]

---

1 In a later conversation Jim revealed that, since he had been in the next room when Donald rung me, he had actually heard the whole conversation!

Jim came out at 1.00am, saying the basis for agreement was there. The breakthrough had been made. Dewar hadn't put the proposition to him in quite the terms he had originally thought, but it was close enough. I was delighted and wished them all good luck. This has been a triumph for Jim. He has shown great courage and succeeded in negotiating a superb deal for Scotland and the Party. He will get hell from the Party for a bit, but he will get through it. Scotland will benefit, and so will he.[1]

Finally, at about 1.30am, I rang Blair back. There was a short pause before I was put through. Cherie came on the other end of the line. 'Good morning, Paddy.'

'Good God, are you two in bed?' I replied.

'Yes, of course we are.'

'How awful. I'm sorry to bother you.'

She laughed. 'I'd better hand you over to him.'

'I think this is the first time I have ever spoken to a Prime Minister in bed with his wife,' I said.

'Well,' Blair replied, 'at least he's in bed with his own wife.'

We both laughed.

I told him what had happened and that, provided there were no slips twixt cup and lip, the deal had been done.[2]

Tuesday, 18 May, London and Sheffield

Up at 6.30am to take a taxi to Heathrow for my flight north for a day's campaigning in the Euro elections.

In the evening, at dinner before the Euro rally at Sheffield University, my bleeper went off. Kate is pregnant with our second grandchild![3] I remember

---

1 Jim did indeed have a difficult time getting the coalition deal accepted by the Lib Dems in Scotland and an even more difficult time with the Scottish press, who took some time to get used to the 'new politics'. Negotiations continued throughout Wednesday (when David Steel was elected the Parliament's first Presiding Officer (Speaker)) and Thursday (when Donald Dewar was confirmed as First Minister), allowing the Party's consultation procedures to be concluded. The partnership government in Scotland has proved a considerable success, scrapping tuition fees, agreeing to introduce free long-term care for the elderly and implementing a much more liberal Freedom of Information Act in Scotland than in the rest of the UK. Jim Wallace became the Deputy First Minister and was Acting First Minister after the tragic death of Donald Dewar, posts he has held with great distinction and to widespread acclaim.
2 The actual agreement was finally signed at 1.00am on Thursday morning.
3 Lois Theurel. Born 9 January 2000.

so well when I heard she was pregnant with Matthias – I was in the Theatre Restaurant in Cheltenham. And here I am campaigning again and over dinner again when I hear about the existence of my second grandchild.

Thursday, 20 May, Westminster

[*The bombing had continued in Kosovo and, with better weather, this was now beginning to have an effect on Serb troops in the province. Meantime, in Serbia there were starting to be signs of splits in support for Milosevic.*]
  Wrote to the PM today outlining my views on Kosovo:

Dear Tony,
We are now clearly moving towards the end phase of the Kosovo war.
  It seems to me that there are three possible outcomes:

1. Total collapse of Serbia, or at least of the Serb forces in Kosovo;

2. A NATO agreement to use ground troops, even against opposition, when the appropriate moment arrives;

3. A negotiated diplomatic solution.

  For what it is worth, I assess the likelihood of the above as follows: ·

1. Collapse: 10–15 per cent – perhaps slightly more, as a result of recent signs of unrest in the Serb forces and civilian population – though I suspect that what we are seeing here is only a first glimpse of what has been going on for weeks and is still rather small-scale.

2. Ground troops. 25 per cent or perhaps slightly less in view of the growing divisions in NATO.

3. A negotiated solution: the rest.

  Assuming, therefore, that we are now moving towards some kind of negotiated solution I wanted to make a couple of points to you and to outline what I believe a minimum acceptable negotiated solution might be.
  First, we need to understand that it is not us who will define whether it is defeat or victory. It is the refugees. If they go back, then we have won. If they don't, then, whatever we say about the negotiated agreement, we have lost.
  I believe that a minimum negotiated agreement which would meet these conditions would have the following ingredients:

1. A military force stationed in Kosovo. Frankly I don't mind how this is 'cap-badged' or what its ingredients are. But it ought to have three essential qualities. Firstly, it needs to be under clear NATO command and control. Secondly, it needs to have effective teeth and rules of engagement. And thirdly, it ought to be backed by a clear-cut UN Security Council Resolution. It is also vital that the national disposition of troops within the international force in Kosovo does not assist in creating a *de facto* partition of the province (e.g. placing the Russians in the north).

2. Serbs in Kosovo. I do not mind representatives of the Belgrade government being in Kosovo. Someone, after all, must point out where the minefields are and help clear up the mess. The crucial thing, however, is that there is no Serb *authority* in Kosovo and any Belgrade representatives who are there operate under the authority of the established international government of Kosovo. If Belgrade is left with any remaining authority in Kosovo after this is over, then the refugees will not go home.

3. The government of Kosovo. We need to be clear about the government of Kosovo. This should be an international protectorate. And it should be clearly seen that the establishment of such a protectorate in Kosovo is the first step towards wider Balkan agreement, whose second priority after Kosovo should be the stabilization of Montenegro.

4. The status of Milosevic. He remains, whether we like it or not, the legal authority in Yugoslavia. Someone's signature is going to have to be on the bottom of the peace agreement and it seems likely that it will be his. But nothing in the peace agreement or in any other agreement should provide immunity for Milosevic or any member of his regime from the due processes of the international court in The Hague. And we should make it clear that, for as along as Milosevic remains in his present post, Serbia cannot participate in the programmes of reconstruction and rehabilitation which will be an essential part of the new Balkan settlement.
Best wishes
Paddy

After the second vote I grabbed my bag and walked across Westminster Bridge in the slight drizzle to County Hall for Andrew Neill's[1] birthday party. Miranda said I ought to go since there would be lots of press there. I said it should be re-christened 'Glitz and Tits with the Shits'. But it turned

---

1 Editor-in-chief and publisher of the *Scotsman* and *Scotland On Sunday*.

out to be rather fun. Except that some frightful young woman barrister whose décolletage defied gravity kept bouncing up to me and asking what I thought of her boobs! To which I replied, 'As such things go, they aren't bad.' I finally succeeded in getting rid of her and had a long chat with Trevor Phillips[1] and the Labour MP Bob Marshall-Andrews, whom I like. I got a bit tiddly towards the end and wandered home at about 10.30.

Wednesday, 26 May, Westminster

In the morning, with Ming to a briefing on Kosovo at the MOD. I think the war is not going as well as they are saying publicly. They have only just begun seriously to damage the Serb forces in Kosovo on the ground. I asked our briefer whether they believed we were yet two-thirds of the way through reducing Serb forces to the level where we could enter Kosovo. To which they replied, 'Certainly not. We are nowhere near that far ahead.' Just as I suspected. They also said that they are beginning to lose patience with the Russians, who are clearly playing both sides against the middle. They are pretending to us that they were seriously negotiating with Milosevic. But there is strong evidence that they are in fact helping him. It is in their interests, of course, to see that NATO comes out of this as damaged as possible.

Most interesting of all, we were told that serious discussion is now going on about assembling a major ground force. A race against time to get everything in place for August. But the Americans, who are prepared to build two highways and a railway up from the sea, believe that we can leave it even later. They are talking about going in as late as mid-September, which I think is cutting it very fine if we are to avoid the onset of winter. They are talking about 175,000 troops, 50,000 of them from Britain!

---

1 TV presenter, now a member of the Greater London Assembly.

Wednesday, 2 June, London

Ahtasaari, the Finnish president, is supposed to be going out to Belgrade today with Chernomyrdin.[1] I rang Downing Street early in the morning and spoke to John Sawers, who told me that we still hadn't got NATO's and the Russians' two positions squared off, so the trip to Belgrade would be cancelled until they could get rid of the 'square brackets'.[2] But later in the day I heard that they had both left for Belgrade, so the problem had obviously not been as intractable as I had thought.

This is a serious attempt at peace and I suspect the Kosovo crisis could end quite quickly now. But what is the nature of the deal? The press, later in the day, said that it included a defined, separate area in the north for the Russians; that some, but not all, of the Serb troops would withdraw; and that Kosovo would remain part of Serbia and the KLA would be disarmed and disbanded. All of these are completely unacceptable to the Kosovars.

Thursday, 3 June, Somerset

Blair has been all over the TV. He is looking terrific, too. Just that slight touch of tiredness and weariness that a leader should show when he is on the way to winning a war.[3] It will have done Labour an immense amount of good and put Blair's own ratings into the stratosphere. Bad news for the Tories, however. They have been terribly slippery about the whole affair. We ought to have done reasonably well out of it.

Monday, 7 June, London

Into the home straight now – the last few days of campaigning, which promise to be pretty hectic.

Up at 6.00 and off by 6.45 for early-morning interviews, mostly on

---

1 On 31 May, Belgrade said it agreed to the principles of a plan put forward by the G8 to end the conflict. The West agreed to put together a joint delegation with the Russians, headed by Victor Chernomyrdin (for the Russians) and Martti Ahtisaari (for NATO).

2 Diplomatic term for areas of disagreement.

3 The Serbian Parliament agreed last night to support the G8 plan – with Milosevic reportedly voting in favour.

Europe but also on Kosovo. The news today is that the negotiations between NATO and the Serbs have hit a sticky patch. I suspect that this is military detail rather than a serious attempt by the Serbs to block. But it may well be that they are playing for time, hoping that the discussions over the UN Security Council Resolution in New York will give them a bit more room for manoeuvre than the agreement they signed up to last week. Over the last few days there has also been some press speculation about my being asked to be the international community's High Representative in Kosovo. I am to see the UN Secretary General Kofi Annan soon to discuss it.

Then into the Jaguar and off to Paddington and the Heathrow Express to catch a flight to Manchester for a day's campaigning. I have been wanting to talk to the PM for a couple of days, ever since Jonathan Powell rang me to say Blair wanted to speak to me about 'jobs'. In the event, Downing Street rang at the most inappropriate moment (it's becoming a habit), when I was checking in to British Midland. I moved down one of the quieter passageways and out on to the forecourt, so that we could speak reasonably privately.

TB: Look, I'm sorry about all this speculation in the press. We don't know where it's coming from. I think you would be great for the Kosovo job, but it won't be decided for some time yet. Let's get together and talk about it sometime early next week.

I am going out to France next week but I didn't want to put him off.

PA: Frankly that will be too late. Can we have a preliminary discussion now? In my view your may have some difficulty persuading the international community to have a Brit in charge of Kosovo, since there is already a British General there [Mike Jackson]. Too many Brits, I suspect.

TB: Yes, you're right about the 'two Brits' problem.

PA: The real point I wanted to make is this, though: whoever does the job, their task will be made immeasurably more difficult if a civil administration is put in too late. That is what happened in Bosnia. Firstly, it left a vacuum which other forces, chiefly criminal ones, filled and secondly the Bosnian civil administration under Carl Bildt[1] had a much more difficult job because the military had already taken all the key decisions. So in my view you need somebody who can almost drop everything and go in straightaway – this week.

---

1 Formerly Prime Minister of Sweden and High Representative in Bosnia.

TB: Yes, I agree that would be best in a perfect world. But it is not going to happen. We were too busy at Cologne[1] with other things to discuss this properly. So the decisions will not be taken for some time. But if you like, I can find out when it will be taken and get back to you.

[We later heard that the first step will probably be taken at the Summit of G8 nations in about ten days' time, which will make a proposition to put to the UN – the sponsoring authority will almost certainly be the UN, not the European Community, which is bad news.]

PA: Thank you, that would be most helpful. Meanwhile, I think you have really enhanced your world status through this – although, as you know, I wish you had taken the position on ground troops a little earlier.

TB: Well, it's not over yet. The Serbs are being difficult in the Macedonian border talks with Jackson. But this time I don't think they are just inventing difficulties – there are some substantive matters at stake, about which it is legitimate for them to ask questions. And their negotiators are finding it difficult to co-ordinate, because we have completely destroyed their communications systems. So I think we should be patient. I spoke to Ahtisaari this morning, who told me he is confident Milosevic is serious about withdrawing all troops, and that he will eventually do so.

PA: Perhaps. But I bet Milosevic also has his eye on what's happening in New York [i.e. at the UN Security Council]. If he can prise the Russians away from the joint position they agreed with Ahtisaari, he will do so. Playing for time here may let those divisions open up. Typical Milosevic, of course.

TB: Exactly. I will continue to be very nervous about this until it has been properly settled.

Blair sounded tired and resigned, so we ended the call there – I will have the opportunity to speak to him properly next week.

Wednesday, 9 June, Westminster

LAST DAY OF THE EUROPEAN ELECTION CAMPAIGN

At 8.45 over to the pre-Euros press conference. It was a bit scrappy. Emma Nicholson said that the Tories should be compared with the BNP, which was a mistake. I tried to get her out of it, but didn't entirely succeed.

1 A meeting of the European Council in Cologne on 3–4 June.

Left the press conference sharp at 11.00 to be driven out to the Westland helipad at Battersea. With us in the car, and, throughout the day, were two journalists, James Landale from *The Times* and Jo Dillon from the *Mirror*, who were both doing pieces on what it was like to be a leader at the end of his leadership.

First to Felixstowe, where I was shown around the docks. Then back to the helicopter and south across the Thames estuary to Maidstone. In Felixstowe we met Andrew Duff[1] and in Maidstone Emma Nicholson. Then back to London in the helicopter, arriving there just before 1.00.

The weather is glorious. England at its June best. Bright sunshine; all the trees at their greenest and the countryside is, like an Impressionist's palette, splashed with the blood red of poppies, the powder blue of flax and the brilliant yellow of fields of rape. One of the best helicopter rides I have ever taken, and probably my last as leader.

Then back to the House for PMQs. Mostly on Europe. Blair won. My question OK, but God, I am tired. My knees have been shaking with sheer exhaustion all afternoon.

But now it's over! It's over! No more campaigning.

When I got on the train I rang Jane and my first word to her was 'Yippee!!'

The sun was setting as the train entered Crewkerne station. Jane picked me up and we went down to the Lord Nelson for a couple of pints, then home. I ought to feel elated, but I can't quite until it is all truly over.

Thursday, 10 June, Somerset

POLLING DAY FOR THE EURO ELECTIONS AND THE BY-ELECTION AT
LEEDS CENTRAL

A most glorious morning soon clouded over, becoming rather chilly. Jane went off at 8.00 to do the first six hours of telling. She is feeling more relaxed now, as she thinks the Kosovo job won't materialize – she doesn't want me to do it. But I still think we may have to face up to an awful decision.

A frantic morning. Usually, on polling day, I go round the polling stations, which I enjoy, but this time, apart from going to vote for the

---

1 Member of the European Parliament for Eastern England since 1999. Former vice-president of the Party and director of the Federal Trust.

cameras (for the last time as party leader), I didn't even get out of the house; too much work to do.

Turn-out at Norton was 45 per cent, but 27 per cent for Yeovil and 30 per cent for Somerset overall. Very low.

That evening I watched the results of the Leeds by-election and the exit polls for the Euro elections,[1] which look good for us and the Tories and bad for Labour. In Leeds we reduced the Labour majority to 2,000.

The news from Kosovo is that the agreement with Milosevic was signed today and Jackson's force is gathering on the Macedonian border. Tremendous pictures of them massing on the plain, ready to move in. *Newsnight* is full of it.

---

1 These were counted on Sunday. The final results were Labour 29 (−33), Conservatives 36 (+18), Lib Dems 10 (+8).

Thursday, 24 June, London

JANE'S BIRTHDAY

At 6.30 to the Dorchester to see Kofi Annan to discuss the possibility of me taking over in Kosovo.

After a short wait, I was shown up to his suite.

A few pleasantries, chiefly about Geneva in the old days,[1] then we talked at length about Kosovo[2] and the Balkans.

He was pleased about the recent agreement signed with the KLA for their disarmament – but were they a single organization? Would they all implement the agreement? He was especially worried about criminal elements who had flooded into Kosovo after the NATO takeover – and especially about the vacuum in law and order which had been created by our slowness in establishing a proper civil administration, police and judiciary. There was a good deal of murder, house burning, looting, extortion, kidnapping, etc. still going on, some of it no doubt inspired by revenge and politics – but much of it simple lawlessness. Nevertheless, he said that he thought that the UN operation had been set up much more tightly than in Bosnia.

I said that I was a bit worried about the double-headed command structure in Kosovo, with the UN High Representative having to share command with the senior NATO military commander. I was worried that this would lead to confusion, duplication and lack of co-ordination. He agreed that this was less than perfect. He would have wished to see the whole operation under civilian control. But NATO insisted that NATO soldiers should be under NATO command. So, he continued, much would depend on the NATO general and the High Representative getting on well together personally.

I said I was concerned about who spoke for the Kosovars. Was it the LDP (Rugova) or the KLA? And if the KLA, then was Thaqi the person who spoke for them all, or were they, too, split? When I had gone out there in September I found to my surprise that, even in the areas of hottest fighting, where I could have expected KLA support to be highest, most

---

1 We had met there when I was a First Secretary in the United Kingdom Mission to the UN in Geneva.

2 NATO forces had moved into Kosovo on 12 June and secured the province after all Yugoslav forces had withdrawn.

ordinary people still acknowledge Rugova as their leader. Though that may have changed as a result of the war and the way Rugova had behaved.[1]

My second concern was that, as soon as compassion fatigue set in, the generosity of the rest of the world would ebb away. What could the UN do to ensure that promised resources materialized and what would they do if they didn't?

'Lastly,' I said, 'I think we have wasted time dangerously. Whoever you want to do this job, I hope you will make your decision early. De Mello[2] had done an excellent job. But all long-term decisions have been placed on hold until you announce the permanent appointment and the staff to administer the province is assembled. Every moment wasted now will make the job more difficult and, especially, allow the criminal elements to tighten their grip on the province.'

He said he would make his decision next week.

I then asked him what he believed the end position for Kosovo would be – independence? He said he thought that, in the long term, it might have to be independence in some form or other, but that we couldn't rush this without risking the destabilization of the rest of the Balkans. Much would depend on the extent to which the Kosovars created a functioning state which would be tolerant, stable, and had good relations with its neighbours. Now that we had eliminated the risk of a Greater Serbia in the Balkans, we must be careful not to allow the establishment of a Greater Albania (which would happen if an independent Kosovo combined with their Albanian neighbours). If that happened, we would blow up Macedonia. So the best position for the moment would be to encourage a certain opaqueness about the long-term future, while we did what we could to settle the rest of the Balkans down. In brief, to 'rule nothing in and rule nothing out'.

I said I agreed with this, but was doubtful whether we could keep the question of independence under wraps for too long. It was the one thing the Kosovars wanted before all others and failing to be clear about it could make life very difficult for the UN administration there. For as long as

1 Rugova had been taken to Belgrade by the Serbs and had allowed himself to be used by them as a mouthpiece for their propaganda. He subsequently went to Rome, where he had stayed for the duration of the war, only returning to Pristina some time after NATO had reoccupied the province.

2 De Mello, a much-respected senior UN administrator with wide Balkan experience (see Vol. I, p. 269) had been appointed temporary UN Administrator, pending a permanent appointment made by the Secretary General. De Mello went on to become the Special Representative of the Secretary General in East Timor.

there was doubt about the final status, both sides would seek to resolve that doubt by force: the KLA by trying to force independence and the Serbs by pressing for the maintenance of the status quo.

Subsequently, as I was leaving, Annan's assistant reinforced the need to be 'very delicate about the question of Kosovar independence'.

As our meeting was drawing to a close, Annan told me a little story about pigeons and dancing which I didn't fully understand, but the purpose of which appeared to be to illustrate how important it was for 'leaders' to stand aside at a time of their own choosing and on their own terms – as I had done with the Lib Dems.

I immediately rang Jane to say that there was no news about a final decision and put a message on to Miranda's pager which said, using a previously agreed code: 'The Man from Del Monte he say very little – decision next week!'

Then to the House, where I collected Jane and we walked arm in arm down Whitehall to No. 10 for dinner with the Blairs, discussing the Annan meeting. She was upset that we still haven't got a definite decision.

The Blair dinner had originally been fixed for Methley Street, but during the morning Downing Street had given my office a call asking for the venue to be moved to No. 10. (We later discovered this was because Nicky had just returned from a school camp, having had no sleep at all, and they felt that it was better for them to be at home rather than out.)

We arrived at 8.00 at the Cabinet Office entrance and waited for a few moments before being take up to the Blairs' flat.

Tony met us dressed in jeans and a sports shirt, gave Jane a kiss and led her to a corner table where he wished her happy birthday and presented her with a present. At this point Cherie came out of the kitchen, also wished Jane a happy birthday and chided Blair for handing over what was a present from her!

We then went into their little sitting-room overlooking the corner of the garden next door to Horse Guards Parade, where he pulled out a bottle of champagne and we toasted Jane's birthday while she opened her present (a pretty little Royal Doulton dish).

The conversation was easy, slightly jokey and very frank.

Blair asked me how the meeting had gone with Annan. I replied that, as far as I could tell, it had gone well. But Annan wasn't going to make a decision until next week.

Blair said that Clinton apparently wanted me to do this, but 'lower down in the State Department they aren't so happy'.

'Feeling bruised after your stiffening of the President's backbone on Kosovo, I shouldn't wonder,' I said.

Blair said that he thought that the key reason Milosevic collapsed was because he realized the game was up when Clinton finally took the decision that ground troops would be deployed.

I thought that was one reason, but not the only one. If Milosevic had hung on for another six weeks, I think he could have won. NATO had to take the decision to use ground troops within the next month or so or lose the opportunity to complete the operation before winter. And if we had announced that decision, then NATO's cohesion would have been very doubtful, because many of the NATO nations weren't prepared to go along with it. So, in effect, by giving up when he did, Milosevic snatched defeat from the jaws of victory.

The full reasoning underlying Milosevic's decision and its timing would remain, I believed, one of the great Balkan puzzles. One factor was, no doubt, the US decision on ground troops. Another was the Russians making it clear to him that if it came to a ground war he was on his own. Another was because, at last, some of Milosevic's closest business cronies[1] were being denied access to foreign countries. But all this did not, in my view, add up to sufficient reason for his extraordinary decision to capitulate when he did – a decision which, I reminded Blair, had surprised everybody. I thought something else had happened in Belgrade which we didn't yet know about.[2]

Blair disagreed. He believed that when Milosevic heard that the British were serious about using ground troops, he said to his advisers: 'Oh, that's only the British – they've always been crazy.' But when he heard that Blair had persuaded Clinton, they knew the game was up. It was then that they collapsed.

At this stage Cherie, who had gone into the kitchen with Jane earlier, shouted through, 'Oh, my God, the tarts are burnt, this is a disaster.' I said, 'No it's not, it's just like home', and we all laughed.

1 Especially Bogoljut Karic, the head of Mobtel, the Serbian mobile phone company, who was believed to have been a source of much of the money stashed away by the Milosevic family and who had been refused entry to Cyprus on a business trip in the days immediately preceding the Serb capitulation.

2 Mike Jackson has since told me that he was absolutely astounded when the word came through of the Serb capitulation, 'which took everybody by surprise'. In addition to the reasons I enumerated to Blair there have also been rumours to the effect that Milosevic had a mild heart attack in the preceding days and also that his wife Mira told him he must end hostilities immediately.

On our way into the dining-room Blair and I stopped and stood for some minutes by the window over looking St James's Park. I said, 'Look, I am going to be rather tough with you. We have always been able to speak bluntly to each other. You have told me and everybody else that there are two great strands to your premiership. These are what will make it different. The first is the project with us and the second is converting Britain into a nation which is prepared to take its place confidently in Europe. I thing the first is as good as lost and that you have lost the initiative on the second.'

He didn't flinch at all.

'Well, if you are talking about the recent Euro election campaign, I agree. It was a bad campaign for us. No message. I think I was too much distracted by Kosovo and I have some work to do to put that right.'

At this stage Cherie and Jane came back with the dinner. The tarts were indeed slightly burnt at the edges, but very good, nevertheless. Mozzarella cheese on a bed of red onions and lettuce, followed by a second course of some deliciously cooked lamb together with thinly sliced potatoes, asparagus and leeks. And then a fine lemon tart and some rather nice cheeses. A very pleasant claret throughout. Beaumont 1994, I think.

Continuing our conversation, Blair said he was determined to regain the initiative on Europe.

PA: Do you believe we could still hold a referendum on the euro before the next election?

TB: I don't totally exclude the possibility. But it's a pretty distant one.

PA: I think that everything could have changed by the spring or summer of next year. Hague has made a mistake by pinning his whole anti-European policy on the current level of the euro. The euro is low now, but it is bound to go up as the European economies recover. And they are almost certain to grow next year at a faster pace than us. If by this time next year the pound is coming down relative to the euro, we can expect a good deal of pressure from industry to take the decision as early as possible. We will, ultimately, be in a really dangerous position if our currency is left between the most powerful currency in the world (the dollar), which the pound tends to follow, and the second most powerful currency in the world (the euro), into which we trade 70 per cent of our goods. That will be a recipe for permanent currency instability. I think current opposition to the euro in Britain is very widespread, but not very deep. If the economic externals change, public opinion on it could change quite fast.

TB: Yeah, but you lot want to go in straightaway.

PA: We want nothing of the sort. We want a referendum taken in principle at a time when we can win it. And then we want to leave it to the government to make the judgement when to go in, at a later date.

TB: I don't think it can be won yet.

PA: You know, one of the things that really amazes and perplexes me about you is that you don't understand your own power. If, at the right moment, you were prepared to really lead this debate, it could be won. Remember 1974.[1]

TB: But I just don't think it can be won today. I think there is a lot more work to be done and I don't believe there is much possibility of doing it before the next election. Incidentally, our economic people disagree with you about next year. They think that sclerosis in the European economies will still hold them back and the euro will not recover next year. Indeed, until Europe liberalizes its markets and institutions, it will not recover at a pace necessary to bring the euro up substantially. And that is a long way off yet. I think that, while the political reasons for the euro are pretty clearly in favour, the economic reasons are pretty iffy or, at best, balanced.

We had a brief discussion about the Lib Dem leadership campaign and then turned to talking about the future.

PA: I don't think there's going to be a referendum on PR for Westminster before the next election, is there?

TB: Yeah, that is almost certainly correct.

Cherie thought that unsurprising, given what happened in the Euro elections.

PA: No. You have drawn the wrong conclusions from that.

TB: Yes, Paddy is right about this and I have been telling my lot the same. In fact the European elections would probably have been worse for us under the old system of first past the post.

PA: If this had been a General Election and it had been by FPTP, then, with this distribution of votes, the Tories would now be the government – which ought to be an object lesson to all of us about the need for PR.

1 The referendum on Britain joining Europe in 1975, when public opinion started out 70 per cent for a 'No' vote and ended with 70 per cent voting 'Yes'.

TB: Nevertheless, given the mood in the Party and the other things we have to do, I agree there probably isn't room for PR before the next election for Westminster.

PA: In which case my recommendation to my party would be that we should switch from being the dogmatists on PR to being the pragmatists. If we can get PR for local elections before the next General Election, then we should be prepared to leave PR for Westminster for four or five years until the whole electoral system has settled down a bit. If we blindly press for a PR referendum for Westminster before the next election, as some in my party want me to do, then we would lose it. But once we have PR for local government, Scotland, Wales, the London Assembly and Europe, then we would be fighting a referendum for PR for Westminster with the tide behind us rather than against us. That's the strategy I shall be suggesting to the new leader of the Lib Dems, when he is elected. But the important thing, if you want to keep the project going, is for you to offer the new leader some goodies, so that the Lib Dems can see that he can win advantages from this relationship, too. Holding out the prospect of PR local government and some further relaxations on the Freedom of Information Bill would be the kind of package which would maintain the momentum after I have gone. Otherwise, the dynamics of opposition are bound to take over and the thing will die; the JCC will run out of steam, and of subjects to discuss, by the end of this year, or early next. So, if you want this to continue, it really is now up to you to push it forward.

TB: That sounds pretty sensible.

There followed a long discussion about the Northern Irish situation, which drags on and on as usual. Blair said it was all looking rather depressing.
It was now 10.30.

PA: Look, I know you have still got some boxes to do so we are going to leave you now. I suppose this really is the last time we will meet like this. So I just want to say it has been great fun working with you. And I think we have achieved a lot. I am sorry that we didn't get further. Our working relationship has been the best thing I have ever been involved in and I hope we can keep alive what we have begun together.

He returned the compliment and said that no doubt we would continue to work together, though on a different basis.
We wandered outside and his red boxes were waiting in the hall. I asked him how long they would take him.

TB: Oh, about an hour, an hour and half. But I enjoy it. I love taking decisions.

PA: How many big decisions in a box?

TB: Normally five or six really big ones. The problem is that you can be tripped up by the small ones, too.

PA: That's what I shall miss most about being leader – taking decision.

'And being at the centre of things!' added Jane.

Jane and I said farewell to both of them and left arm in arm, this time, for the first time, through the front door of Downing Street.

Friday, 2 July, Paris and London

RETURNING FROM A CONFERENCE ON INTERNATIONAL INTERVENTION IN PARIS

The Eurostar had hardly begun moving when my phone rang. It was Westondorp[1] ringing me from Sarajevo. He suggested again that I put my name forward to take over from him as the UN High Representative in Sarajevo. But the timing is all wrong. I might just be able to leave Yeovil and the new leader of the Party for something as urgent as Kosovo. But not for a routine appointment like Sarajevo. He was very insistent but very understanding when I explained my reasons.[2]

I arrived at Waterloo at about 4.20 and caught a taxi home. Shortly after I'd arrived back I got a worried call from one of Robin Cook's aides. Robin couldn't speak to me himself because he was tied up, but he wanted me to know that they had just heard from a very good source in New York that the Secretary General was about to announce that Bernard Kouchner[3] is to be the UN Special Representative in Kosovo. Jane is delighted. I don't know whether to be pleased because I won't have to face so much upheaval, or upset. Rather a gloomy supper and to bed.

1 Carlos Westendorp, UN High Representative in Bosnia 1997–9. Formerly a Spanish diplomat.
2 On reflection, I think he may already have heard what I only heard an hour or so later – that I was not going to go to Kosovo.
3 French Minister for Health.

Sunday, 4 July, Somerset

The Yeovil Lib Dems selected my successor today – David Laws, by a clear margin. I am very pleased.

Wednesday, 14 July, Westminster

Down to the chamber for PMQs. I rose to the usual groans and I said, 'Don't worry, it is nearly the last one.' There was a huge shout of 'Hear, hear', so I said, 'That is the biggest cheer you have given me in eleven years.' But I didn't make a very good fist of my question.

In the evening, dinner at Methley Street for the bright young rising stars of the Party before I hand over the leadership (Jane and I had christened them the 'Young Turks'): Miranda Green, Nick Clegg, Lembit Opik, Richard Allan, Mark Oaten and Steve Webb. Michael Moore was invited, too, but he couldn't come. On reflection, Ed Davey should have been there as well.

This lot should be the second-tier leadership of the Party and I told them that if they worked together they could have a real influence on the way the party goes. We had long discussions about the leadership campaign. Mark and Lembit are supporting Charles. Richard Allen supports Jackie, but accepts that she isn't going to get it. Steve Webb, who supports Simon, admits that he isn't as close as he has been saying. A fascinating discussion.

Jane told me afterwards that it was evident that they had already been meeting up. To bed woozy and late again.

Sunday, 18 July, The Balkans

Up at 4.45am and off at 5.30 with David Laws, who kindly drove me to Heathrow, since he was going to London anyway. It gave us an excellent chance to chat about his replacing me in Yeovil.

We got to Heathrow at about 7.15 where I met Julian, who is accompanying me on this trip. We boarded the 9.05 plane to Istanbul, where we changed planes for Skopje.

On arrival at Skopje airport we were met by a young RAF squadron leader, who did his best to see me through the Balkan bedlam; then out in the blistering heat to the military airfield, where we were to be picked up by a Canadian Huey for the flight to Pristina.

We strapped ourselves in and took off, following the route Mike Jackson's army had taken on 12 June. Along the Macedonian plain, then up over the mountains and through the pass above the infamous border crossing point where I had been so often. Then down on to the plain of Kosovo and over Kacanik, where I expected to see great devastation. But there wasn't. It appears that, contrary to received wisdom, the Serbs have not significantly damaged the Kacanik valley. What we did see, however, were plenty of bomb craters. At one point a member of the crew spotted a Serb decoy[1] below us so the pilot quickly circled and flew back over it. Pretty crude, but it was clearly effective at deceiving NATO planes, for there were pockmarks of bomb craters all round; viewed from the air the area looked rather like it had a dose of chickenpox. Having inspected the decoy we continued our journey to Pristina.

Suddenly, the aircraft's missile-warning system activated, four flares automatically fired from the sides of the helicopter and the pilot threw us into a steep downward right-hand dive. But it was a false alarm.

Then down to land at Pristina, which again looked relatively unscathed, except for some of the Yugoslav military installations, which had taken a terrible battering.

At the airport we were met by David Slinn, who very kindly offered to put us up in what's known locally as 'the British house'.[2] On the way into town, we passed the old Serb police headquarters – blackened, with its top storey neatly decapitated by a cruise missile. But Pristina was full of people. No signs of refugees on the road. Everyone wandering around in a daze of happiness that it is all over. All seems back to normal. Incredible.

David is now effectively the British Ambassador here, although he is not allowed to call himself that. He has to refer to himself as a 'Senior Foreign Office Official who happens to be in Pristina', which I shortened

1 The Serbs were highly adept in the use of decoys and camouflage. The one we saw on this occasion was made of hardboard to look like a missile site. Later we were to see a bridge with black holes painted in the middle and strips of plastic hanging off the side to make it look, to the NATO pilots flying at 15,000 feet, as if it had already been hit. And alongside another bridge built of plastic sheets. It worked. NATO successfully bombed the plastic bridge and left the real one intact.

2 Kosovo not being a country, there could not be an embassy there, only a British office.

to FOOWHIP. A quick drink, then down to dinner with some DFID[1] people in the Pellumbi restaurant of blessed memory. It has been trashed but not burnt. The DFID people told us about their attempts to restart the power station which feeds Pristina and get water going. Typical DFID; they are doing important work at a low level, making people's life easier.

Later in the evening we met Blerim. He still has the air of a student politician, but he is getting more serious all the time. Overall, he has been encouraged by what's happening but is still very nervous about the true intentions of the KLA. What we have been hearing about their decommissioning of weapons, that it's going without a hitch, sounds too good to be true.

To bed at about midnight, having had a whisky sitting on the balcony overlooking Pristina. It was cheering to see all the lights on. But here and there in the valley below the occasional tongue of flame shot up, as a house belonging to a Serb or a Roma[2] was set alight by vengeful Albanians. Apparently, it is not uncommon for an Albanian to douse his house with water before setting fire to his neighbours. Albanian families have often returned home to find their houses wrecked and have gone round to their Serb or Roma neighbours to discover all their furniture there. So they have looted back what they could, then set fire to the place. And still the sound of sporadic shooting in the city. Very depressing. And very difficult to stop. Which is why we so desperately need proper policing here. The police and civil power has come in too late once more. Bosnia all over again.

Monday, 19 July, Pristina

Up at 5.00 for interviews with the BBC at 6.15. They have a house, on the hill overlooking Pristina. In front of it they have built a little wooden platform so that Pristina provides the backdrop for all the television shots. My many interviews were made all the more difficult, though, by a dog who thought it his duty to bark at anybody who came into the neighbouring property.

Then back to David's for a quick bowl of muesli and up the hill for the KFOR[3] briefing in a large hangar-type building. Afterwards, I spent about

1 Department for International Development of the British Government.
2 The Roma are a gypsy minority who gave considerable help to their Serb masters in the war.
3 Kosovo Force, or KFOR, is the international military force, under Mike Jackson, charged initially with occupying and then securing Kosovo.

twenty minutes talking with Jackson in his office. He wanted to cover all sorts of things – Blair's forthcoming visit, the local situation – but we soon ran out of time, so we agreed to meet again tomorrow evening for a longer chat over a bottle of whisky. His helicopter would also fly me back to Skopje on Wednesday to catch the plane home.

Then off at 10 o'clock for an exhausting day of meetings. First of all, Bernard Kouchner – his first full day here as UN Special Representative. I discovered him in an office bare but for a photograph of Kofi Annan. He is much smaller than I thought he'd be, and very Gallic. He waves his arms around a great deal. But I found him lucid and clear-minded and we got on well. He has a very, very difficult job ahead of him.

Afterwards, off the see Denis MacNamara, the Australian who heads the UNHCR here. He told me, in slightly miffed tones, that UNHCR had made detailed arrangements to assist the refugees returning home from the Albanian camps. But they had woken up one morning to find the camps empty. The Kosovars had gone back by themselves. 'You know, they never even waited for us to tell them to go back. They just upped sticks and went – hundreds and thousands of them.'

He continued, 'There's a real danger that different nations putting in their own NGOs will cause duplication and inefficiency, and will undermine everything we're tying to do.' (I heard later of a Belgian NGO which arrived at Albania's border with Kosovo and had been frightened by the stories of this being mafia territory. So they had asked for an Albanian army escort all the way into Kosovo. The first KFOR learned about it was when they were confronted by an Albanian army unit on the outskirts of Pristina, nearly causing a major international incident.)

Then back to the headquarters to meet Jock Covey, Kouchner's deputy. A quiet and reassuring American, and a perfect foil for Kouchner. Covey will get down to the detail and keep Kouchner earthed. He said at one stage that Kouchner's job was to act as a foreign salesman for Kosovo so he would be doing a lot of travelling while Covey stayed on the ground. I was impressed by him.

Then lunch with Hashim Thaqi in a Pristina restaurant. He came in wearing a well-cut suit with his interpreter, a very pretty Albanian girl (aren't they all?). He has an impressive figure but a rather expressionless face. But everybody worries about what lies behind the rhetoric and urbane behaviour. Some say he has been responsible for quite a lot of killing, others say he hasn't. I thought he looked more politician than soldier. Having to use an interpreter inevitably made our conversation somewhat stilted. I found him less substantial than people like Blerim or Veton Surroi.

In the afternoon I went to see Andjelkovic.[1] The last time we met I thought him arrogant, haughty and full of propaganda. This time, I found a completely deflated man sitting in his sparse, sad office in the fire-damaged block that had been the Serb headquarters but which had been all but demolished by a cruise missile. I decided I wouldn't rub his nose in it, although the temptation to do so was real enough, given the arrogance and rudeness with which he had treated us on our last visit. I suspect he will be withdrawn by Milosevic and then blamed for the whole Kosovo débâcle. [He was in fact withdrawn the next day.]

Afterwards, a quick dash across town to the British forces HQ on the outskirts of Pristina. Here I met Major General Richard Dannatt, who is the national commander of the British in KFOR. I sat in on the evening briefing, talking through the day's events with some of the key officers. The Brits are doing a stunning job here. Every time I go into Pristina I see the Paras walking calmly but authoritatively through the town, whereas the Italians, Americans *et al.* are all holed up in their bases and only ever seen out in tanks, helmets, flak jackets, etc. The Northern Ireland experience showing.

We left at about 10.00 and dashed across town again for the final meeting of the day, with Veton Surroi at the *Koha Ditore*[2] café. It was wonderful to see Vetont again. He was the only Albanian leader to stay in Pristina throughout the Serb occupation. He told me how he had moved from house to house almost nightly to avoid the Serbs, and how much he feared the knock on the door. I am not surprised. Veton is small, round and stocky, with a wonderful open face. Full of humour and scepticism. The kind of face you instinctively trust. I told him he ought to get involved in politics, but he said he never would. I'm not sure I believe this. He is far too ambitious. He has a huge reputation and leaves people like Thaqi in the shade. And he is deeply loved by all his staff. If Kosovo can be led by people like him there won't be a problem. I stayed with him for far too long and drank far too much, finally getting to bed at about 2.00 in the morning.

---

1 Under the Kumanovo agreement between NATO and the Serbs, Belgrade was allowed to maintain a small office in Pristina. Zoran Andjelkovic, poor man, was instructed to head it as the senior Belgrade representative in Kosovo.

2 *Koha Ditore* – a much-respected local newspaper run by Veton.

Tuesday, 20 July, Kosovo

Up at 5.30 again for some more radio and television interviews down at the BBC house. Then back for a snatched breakfast before more meetings until mid-morning, when we set off on a tour of the province with David Slinn. Cross-country to Lipjan, where I visited a detention centre being run by a rather surprised-looking colonel of the Royal Irish called Corky. Most of the detainees are Serbs being held for war crimes of one sort or another. But I did meet one young KLA fighter called Adrian. A very urbane young man. He was an American mercenary who had joined the KLA, but got too fond of the killing. After the ceasefire he had continued to kill Serbs with abandon. He will almost certainly go down for multiple murder.

Afterwards south and across the Dulje heights to Prizren. To my delight, Prizren, known to nineteenth-century travellers as 'the jewel of the Balkans', has hardly been touched. There had apparently been orders to burn the town down, but Serb authority had collapsed so quickly they couldn't be carried out. To my horror, however, the whole tone of the soldiering here has changed. Leopard tanks manned by Germans in full flak jackets but not a single soldier out on foot patrol. The town, however, has completely reverted to its former bustling self. Shops selling brightly coloured wares, vegetable stalls back on the streets and the little shops selling filigree silver (for which Prizren is famous) doing a flourishing trade again. The tanks and armoured personnel carriers were just getting in the way.

Then out on the Djakovica road for a rendezvous with the War Crimes team who are working on some mass graves. This turned out to comprise three Metropolitan policemen, a forensic expert and an anthropologist from Vienna. They showed me the site of one of the massacres. One old woman who had survived told me her story. She had woken up at 4.00am, looked up the road and seen the place suddenly surrounded by Serb troops. So she had got her family out of bed and fled across the fields. But the people at the top of the village had not been so lucky. They had been surrounded and the men dragged out into the street. Then the women. Then the houses were set on fire. The women were told to go, but one or two had stayed behind to witness what happened next. The men (some forty of them) were herded into a number of little cowsheds in the lower part of the village. The Serbs, some of them allegedly locals, then put on white armbands and white gloves, walked into the sheds and opened fire with machine-guns. Then they burned the buildings down.

We were taken to a stable where six bodies had been found, five of them now little more than piles of ashes, but on the sixth the debris from the roof had fallen, thereby protecting it from the worst of the flames. The smoke, however, had preserved the flesh. The smell of putrefaction hung heavily in the air and the flies were thick around the flesh on the remaining parts of the body.

We were later to hear of one man in a similar incident elsewhere, who had found himself under a pile of bodies when the building he had been in was set on fire. He had crawled out with something like 70 per cent burns and managed to get away and survive.

We were then taken down to another cowshed where a similar massacre had occurred. I was able to work out from the shell cases and the bullet holes in the back wall that perhaps twenty men had been pushed into the shed, then shot with machine-guns from the door. Afterwards, the executioner had walked in and, judging from the shell cases, stood over them and dispatched each of them one by one. Then the building had been burned down on top of them. A horrific scene which stayed with us for a long while.

After about an hour we left for Djakovica. This lovely old town, parts of it dating back to the fourteenth and fifteenth centuries, had been deliberately burnt to the ground. An act of barbarity which had happened only two or three days after the bombing started. We visited a mosque, on the door of which was the date 1499. The outside had been burnt, though thankfully some of the inside had escaped damage. We had to tiptoe around the area as it could easily be booby-trapped or mined. Even among all this devastation, though, people were already beginning to put out market stalls.

From Djakovica, down to Pec by way of Junik and Prilep. At Pec I met Tom Walker of *The Times* and we went off for a beer, since we hadn't stopped all day (it was about 4.00 in the afternoon by now). While we were sitting there a shot went off. The British soldiers who were guarding me immediately went on alert, but it was an accidental discharge from some Italian soldiers. They do look ridiculous in their helmets with plumes of black feathers.

Then on to the road again to return to Pristina. Just outside Pec we saw an Italian road block. Two Leopard tanks pointing in opposite directions. Completely useless as a roadblock, and totally unnecessary in an area in which they are under almost no external threat. On the way back we had to bypass two bombed bridges, one of which will need to be completely rebuilt. A little further on I looked down to my left and saw some houses burning. It was a village in which almost all the Albanian houses had already been burnt. The Albanians had apparently come back and, to even up the score, set fire to their Serb neighbours' houses, too. A spiral of violence like the one into which we have been locked for twenty-five years in Northern Ireland.

Having dropped the others off near Pristina, Julian, David and I headed off for our last appointment at the fourteenth-century monastery at Gracanica, to see Bishop Artemje, the senior Kosovo Serb churchman (and a bravely outspoken opponent of Milosevic). We arrived at around 5.30 to find 150 or so Serb families sheltering there. We were immediately shown upstairs to see the Bishop, who was waiting for us in the monastery's long refectory on the first floor. Shafts of sunlight thick with dust particles illuminated the room, falling across the ancient wood table at which we sat. Sitting next to the Bishop when we entered was my old friend Father Sava, whom I had last met at the Decani[1] monastery. At the far end of the table sat Momcilo Krajsnik, the local Serb leader, a big bluff man with grey hair and an over-florid face.

The first thing Artemje did was give me a dossier of Serb churches that had (he claimed, probably correctly) been blown up by the KLA. I was glancing through this when a thought suddenly struck me: I had seen for myself two such destroyed Serb Orthodox churches, one outside Pec and the other outside Prizren. They had both been very efficiently demolished, with all their walls blown out – something that would have required a considerable amount of both expertise and explosive. Looking at this dossier of destroyed Serb churches, I noticed that they had all been dispatched in the same way. I immediately realized that these were not attempts by local amateurs, they were professional jobs. Probably a NATO- or Warsaw Pact-trained gang of demolitionists working for some extremist Albanian organization.

I hoped I would have a constructive meeting with Artemje and started off in fairly conciliatory mood. But he wanted to lecture me about Albanian atrocities against Serbs, and then Krajsnik joined in. I am not very good at being lectured at by Serbs at the best of times. But having spent much of

---

1 See 27 September 1998.

the day looking at their massacres and with the smell of putrid flesh still in my nostrils, I was even less patient than usual.

It developed into a full-scale row in which I blazed at both of them: They were acting outrageously. They had been responsible for terrible massacres. Had they no shame? They were doing their people no good, etc., etc. David Slinn, beside me, shifted from one embarrassed diplomatic buttock to another, while Julian took a long look at his large glass of raki and swallowed the lot in one go. He told me later that he thought I was going to get up and hit the Bishop. Eventually, realizing that all I was doing was making the situation worse and myself very angry, I asked David to take over. He duly chatted on about nothing in particular until the temperature cooled. I then decided to end the meeting, paid my respects and left fuming. The hair on the back of my head was standing up. Not a very diplomatic exercise on my part.

Then immediately back to Pristina, where, in the evening, we went up to see Mike Jackson. The obligatory whisky and down to dinner. It developed into a post-mortem of how the campaign had run. We are still completely bewildered as to why Milosevic caved in when he did. We agreed that the full story has yet to be told.

Afterwards, back up to the General's and a whisky à deux while Julian and David went back down to the British house. It emerged that on D+1 (June 13) Jackson had had a stand-up row with Wes Clark.[1] Clark had wanted him to occupy Pristina airfield so that the Russians couldn't come in, but Jackson, quite properly, had said that he couldn't do this because there were serious operational risks, it would cause a major diplomatic incident ('launch World War Three', is how he put it) and it would mean breaking his word to the Serbs. And anyway, it was a diversion of resources. Eventually, it came down to Jackson saying to Clark: 'Look, if you want someone to do this you had better pick another general.' He had rung Rupert Smith[2] afterwards to make sure Robin Cook and George Robertson would back him. To their credit, they did.

At about 1.30am, much befuddled by Jackson's whisky, I said I had to go. He was nervous about letting me out alone, since I would be going outside the limits of the camp and down to Pristina by myself. I insisted, wandered uncertainly out of the gate, past the sentries and immediately set

1 General Wesley Clark, a US general who was the Supreme Allied Commander in Europe.
2 General Sir Rupert Smith, Deputy Supreme Allied Commander in Europe since 1998. Previously UN commander in Sarajevo (see Volume I, p. 333).

off in the wrong direction, away from Pristina. I soon realized my mistake and retraced my steps to meet one of the sentries, hurrying towards me in a worried fashion to tell me that I had gone the wrong way. I waved at him cheerily and stumbled off down the hill to the British House, muttering something about too much of the general's whisky.

Wednesday, 21 July, Kosovo

Up at 3.45 to wake Julian. Swallowed large quantities of water to counter the hangover. It was still dark. Wearilypicked up my suitcase and went downstairs to meet David Slinn, who had nobly got up to drive us up the hill to the waiting helicopter for Skopje.

As we drove, the sun was just beginning to rise, the pale red glow of dawn starting to impinge on the blackness of the departing night. A light mist hung over the Pristina valley, with the higher buildings of the city poking up through it.

After some difficulty in finding the helicopter landing site, we eventually wished David goodbye, piled on board and flew off into the sunrise. The flight to Macedonia was incredibly beautiful. The half light of dawn stayed with us for the best part of twenty minutes, becoming redder and redder, but with no discernible point for the sun. A lot of mist in the valleys, drifting low and thin over farmhouses and trees. An intensely peaceful summer countryside. Who would have suspected the place was littered with mines, burnt houses and desperate people? As we rose up over the crest of the mountains between Kosovo and Macedonia the sun suddenly burst through the mist and revealed the Macedonian plain spread out ahead of us. The perfect antidote to a hangover.

Having been dropped on the tarmac at the military airfield by our helicopter we were picked up by yet another voluble baby-faced RAF squadron leader, who bundled us into a car and took us to Skopje airport. There was a scrummage at the airport, where we had to go through the usual ex-communist bureaucratic form-filing before being finally allowed into the waiting-room. And then, in due course, on to the plane.

A smooth and easy flight through to Zurich, from where I rang the office to see what they were suggesting for PMQs (my last as leader). Then on to the 11.30 BA flight to Heathrow, where we collected our baggage without too much delay and jumped on to the Tube back to Westminster, with me rehearsing my PMQs on the way. It was only when I got back to the office that I realized I had left my suit behind in David Slinn's house in Pristina. Panic! But Jane had brought another in for me, bless her. So I got changed and rushed down to the chamber.

This being my last PMQ as leader of the Lib Dems, they cheered rather than groaned when I got up. I said, 'Yes, and I will miss you all too.' Blair paid me an over handsome tribute at the end.[1]

Afterwards back to the office to pack up the last of my things. It looks so bare. All my ornaments and pictures gone. We opened a bottle of champagne and drank it with some cake. I thanked all the staff, then went home to catch up on some sleep.

Tuesday, 27 July, Westminster

At 4 o'clock a pre meeting for my last JCC, then over to Downing Street at 5.15 with Paul, Ming and Alan. Bob is away in the United States.

We arrived in the ante-room to the Cabinet Room to find Jack Cunningham and various others there. There was a hat with a field marshal's baton on it, so I guessed that Peter Inge[2] was with the PM. In due course he came out with Cook and my friend Brian Donnelly, the ex-Ambassador to Belgrade (now, he told me, looking for a new posting since we have broken off diplomatic relations with Yugoslavia). Brian said that he was desperate to go back, but there seemed little prospect in the near future. We both agreed that Milosevic would not fall quickly, although his days were probably numbered. It was sad to see Brian looking slightly lost here, since he has contributed so much to all this. But it's good that he is briefing the PM.

Shortly after we had assembled for the JCC, Blair arrived; in his shirt-sleeves and looking tired. Cook also tired, yawning throughout. Only Jack Cunningham and the Cabinet Secretary seemed perky. Afterwards back to Alan's office for a debriefing.

In the evening, after a reception celebrating our new Lib Dem peers in the Liberal Club, I walked to Waterloo Station across Hungerford Bridge.

---

1 'As this is the Right Hon. Gentleman's last Question Time, I pay tribute to the tremendous contribution that he has made to British politics in the past few years, not least on Kosovo and Bosnia, where he was well ahead of the rest of us and right long before the rest of us.'
2 Field Marshal Lord Inge, Constable of the Tower of London. At the time, Chief of the Defence Staff.

A glorious day. A breeze blowing from the east kept it cool, but everybody out in their summer best, the City aflame with the evening sun and the river looking blue for a change. It took me back thirty or so years, to when I remember walking across the river and watching it swirl below me, imagining what it must be like to be at the centre of power in London.

I caught the 7.35 and sat happily as the train rattled down to Yeovil in the evening sunlight, the dark edges of the hills in the distance and the countryside golden and ripe under the late summer sun.

I said goodbye to my office for the last time today. I am not really emotional about these things, but I did experience a sudden pang as I walked out. And I suppose this is the last journey I will make down from Waterloo to my constituency as leader of the party. But I don't feel miserable about it. I feel as though I have done all the things I set out to do and perhaps a little bit more. I am dissatisfied about only one thing. And that is that the great exercise to which Tony Blair and I set our hand has not been completed. It has been hugely advanced, but its final act has not come off and is unlikely, I feel, to do so. Unless, of course, Blair is prepared to throw himself into it, which I doubt. Sad. But nothing distracted from my peace of mind.

Monday, 9 August, Westminster

DAY OF THE ELECTION FOR THE NEW LEADER OF THE LIBERAL
DEMOCRATS

I had anticipated waking up today feeling slightly miserable. But I don't at all. This is, after all, the day for which I have been planning for a very long time. And I feel utterly comfortable that I have taken the right decision in the right way and with the right outcome.

During the course of the day, people kept stopping me and asking me how I felt. 'Fine,' I replied, 'I am very lucky to be able to finish my term as leader of the Lib Dems at a time of my own choosing and in the way that I would wish. I feel very happy about that.'

Into the office my bus. A small pile of mail to deal with, but not too much. At 11 o'clock Simon Hughes came to see me. By this time word was coming through that Charles had pulled ahead on the first count of votes, although on second preferences, Simon caught up a bit. Everybody agrees now, though, that it looks extremely unlikely Simon can do it. We had a long amicable chat and he told me that he and Charles had met several times during the campaign and had discussed things in detail last night. But he also made it clear that, given the size of his vote, he was in a strong position, and in terms of relations with Labour, Charles would have to listen to what he had to say. However, he did say to me, 'You must not worry about our relations with Labour. We have a lot of constitutional work to do with them and you can be sure that if I become leader I will want to continue with that.'

'In which case, what you are saying, in a polite way, is that the JCC will end,' I replied. 'There is not enough work to carry it beyond about the spring of next year. And, more importantly, Blair is now, not unnaturally, beginning to look towards the next General Election. Many in his party have already criticized him for going on too long with constitutional reform. We may be able to bank some commitment from him for after the next election. And we may even be able to move him forward on some aspects of PR. But the idea that he will spend much time in the last two years of this parliament on a constitutional agenda is unrealistic. If the JCC is limited to constitutional matters then it will soon have nothing left to discuss and will run out of steam.'

Simon looked rather crestfallen. But overall he is in good form and has done very well in the leadership campaign, increasing his stature immensely.

Becks and I drove in the rain to the rehearsal for the announcement of the results at the Commonwealth Club. Charles arrived separately. Simon was so late that we had to go ahead without him.

The room was rather small and very hot under the heat of TV lights, so not the best venue for a crowded meeting. I had a brief part in the rehearsal, shaking the hand of the new leader. We tried to pretend we didn't know who it would be, but everybody, I think, knew the score by this time. Including Charles, who had bought himself a new double-breasted suit, was surrounded by minders, and was paid due deference by everybody. It is extraordinary how, even before the event, the power begins to shift. But he looked the part. Neat, nervous, and poised. I was impressed.

Then back to the flat. Jane and Simon had got caught in a traffic jam on Salisbury Plain, as had Kate and Seb.[1] Eventually, the whole family arrived one after the other. We had a very happy lunch together and then left for the House.

At my office I introduced Matthias to members of staff and then into a

---

1 Kate, her husband Seb and my grandson Matthias had come over from France for a few days for the end of my term as leader.

taxi to the Commonwealth Club. We were under strict instructions to arrive there for 2.00 but I had negotiated to arrive a little later because of my family and because I had nothing much to do in the way of preparation anyway.

In the event, we were the first people there! The others drifted in shortly afterwards. By now, of course, everyone knew what the result was, although it had gone to a third ballot.

The surprise result was Malcolm Bruce, who, according to the first scrutiny of votes, would come last. In fact, he finished a good third behind Simon. David looked cheerful. Jackie quiet. Charles, as ever, arrived late. In fact, so late we were beginning to get worried about him.

Eventually, there was a little buzz in the corridor and he walked in, again surrounded by minders. I turned to Jane Bonham-Carter and said, 'Typical Charles, late even for his own big event.' 'Of course he is late,' she replied, 'That was fully intentional. It's his show.' To make a joke of it, I stormed into the room where all the other candidates were waiting and said in mock rage, 'Well, I had better say it now since it is the last time I will be able to: Where the bloody hell is Charles Kennedy?' They all laughed.

When Charles came in Elizabeth Pamplin[1] handed round the piece of paper on which the results were printed.[2] Nobody said a word. I got up, shook Charles by the hand, and the others did so too. He looked exceedingly nervous, which is as it should be.

Then, at 3 o'clock sharp, into the main room. There was a round of applause as we came in. The candidates entered in reverse order, then me. I sat down next to Jane. Diana Maddock then gave the results by going through each individual's distribution of votes. This took some drama out of the situation, but as soon as Diana declared Charles elected, everyone clapped. I stood up and shook Charles by the hand, first of all for the television cameras, then for the snappers [newspaper photographers]. As I suspected, the place was far too low, far too cramped, far too crowded and far too hot. Charles gave his speech. It was good and well delivered but the sweat was literally pouring down his face and very visible, I suspect, on television.

I left immediately afterwards to find Matthias and Seb. Apparently,

1 Chief Executive of the Lib Dems.
2 Charles Kennedy had won, followed by Simon Hughes, Malcolm Bruce, Jackie Ballard and David Rendel.

Matthias had been clapping throughout, then putting his finger to his mouth saying 'Shush', to the delight of all around. One of the television crews wanted an interview with me, but I said, 'No, this is Charles's day.' Then out on to the street, and, taking Matthias by the hand, I walked down Northumberland Avenue away from the crowd, with the rest of the family following.

At 5.00pm a meeting with Charles. We spent about seventy-five minutes together. I warned him that he would almost certainly get a call from Blair. He did, later that night.

He asked me what jobs I would like and I said none until the New Year, I needed some time to sort myself out.

I also gave to him the substantial handover notes[1] I had prepared for the new leader. After he read them through he said, 'Heavens, you got much further than I thought you did.'

Charles has changed. And so has my attitude towards him. Whereas before I found myself uncomfortable with him, chiefly proprietorially, I suspect – he was taking over a party I had helped to create in its present form and had led for more than a decade. But now that the crown has been passed to him I feel very comfortable about it.

Then back to the Commonwealth Club for the post-election party. I went round thanking everyone who had helped me to build up the Parliamentary Party over the last eleven years.

Charles came in and we raised our glasses to him, after which he made a very good short speech.

I left the celebrations quietly and walked back to the House feeling just a tinge of sadness that I am no longer a leader of one of the great British political parties. But this was more than offset by the feeling of having cast off a very heavy burden.

1 See Appendix K for an abridged version.

It has been a day of showers and rain, but the evening light was extraordinarily bright. Some purplish clouds over County Hall; the distant sky is blue with a pile of cumulonimbus, like a confection of cream in the far distance. The air is rainwashed and the Thames blue, buffeted by the evening winds. I felt very contented.

Epilogue

Epilogue

I am, I confess, a driven man – though, if you have you read this far, you may have already spotted that.

And the thing which drove me through my leadership of the Liberal Democrats was getting the Party into power. I have never been at all attracted to the notion that it was sufficient for us to be the unpaid think tank for new ideas in British politics; or the repository for community politics without a purpose. Liberalism is too important for that.

To me, success or failure in politics is to be judged by a single measure – whether you give the people that you serve the benefit of government according to the principles you believe in. It is against that criterion that I would wish my eleven years' leadership of the Lib Dems to be judged. My aim – some would say, my obsession – was to make the Liberal Democrats sufficiently confident in themselves to win power, to get used to handling it and to be hungry for more.

One of the advantages of looking at things retrospectively is that it is easier to identify events and the broader patterns within which they occurred than at the time they happened. When I took over the leadership of the Liberal Democrats in 1988, I said to my friends that I saw our recovery in three distinct phases. The first was survival from a point of near extinction; the second was to build a political force with the strength, policy and positions to matter again in British politics; and the third was to get on to the field and play in what I believed would become a very fluid period of politics.

The real heroes of the first (survival) phase were our Lib Dem campaigners on the ground, who started the long, tough process of rebuilding the Party through local campaigning and winning seats on local councils. The 1992 General Election ended this phase. We did not disappear, as many predicted we would. Though, as Wellington said at the battle of Waterloo, it had been at times a 'damned close-run thing'. When the new party was launched in 1988 it had lost nearly all its public support, its membership was dropping and its finances were dire. I was also new and inexperienced and made many mistakes in my first years. I was embarrassingly bad at set-piece events in the House of Commons, especially Prime Minister's Questions against Margaret Thatcher. I was also unconfident in the extent of my own powers and my ability to do the job. Leading a political party is like entering a secret garden – there are no maps, very few who can show you the way, and, whatever your past experience, it does not cover the full range of the job you now have to do.

My greatest error in those early days (which nearly did for us over the issue of the new party's name) was to be so single-minded in my vision of the 'newness' of the Liberal Democrats that I underestimated the importance of tribalism as what my successor Charles Kennedy has called, the 'glue which holds parties together'. The new party, and I, were saved by three things: my friends; the refusal of ordinary members to accept that they were dead; and Harold Macmillan's famous 'events'.

Five events, in particular, were crucial in this 'survival phase'.

The first was the demise of the Owenite breakaway SDP and, at much the same time, the failure of the Greens to capitalize on their extraordinary success in the Euro elections of June 1989. Wellington would have recognized this period, too. This was 'hard pounding', as the Iron Duke put it in the early stages of Waterloo. We had just had to stand there and battle it out for the centre ground until the other's weaknesses told.

Next, I was persuaded to write a book, *Citizens' Britain*, which laid out the ideas which I believed would form the new politics. It made almost no public impact at the time, or since. But it acted as a signpost for me and the Party, and it mapped out the ground on which I hoped we would stand.

Then came the massacre at Tienanmen Square and the Gulf War. Not for the last time foreign affairs gave us opportunities as a third party which domestic politics more often denied us. Our decision to argue the (extremely unpopular) case for passports for all British Hong Kong citizens in the aftermath of Tienanmen was crucial in our rediscovering our internationalist roots and voice. A few months later, the Gulf War marked the moment when I 'came of age' as a party leader and we started to be listened to once again.

And lastly, there was Eastbourne. The tragic death of the Conservative MP Ian Gow, assassinated by an IRA bomb in July 1990, gave us that chance that by-elections so often give struggling third parties. In fact, my initial judgement was not to fight it. But I was persuaded otherwise by our head of campaigns, Chris Rennard, and my close advisers, Mark Payne and Archy Kirkwood. The rest is history. The *Evening Standard*, referring to an earlier jibe from Mrs Thatcher in which she compared the Lib Dems with the dead parrot in the famous Monty Python sketch, published a front page headline on the day of our victory, with a majority of 4,500, which said simply, 'The Parrot Bites Back'. The Party went on to rediscover the will and ability to win again.

It is easy to forget that the outcome of the 1992 election produced two surprises. John Major, to even his own amazement, I think, found himself back in government.[1] And we Lib Dems, who were expected to decline sharply, held our ground.

In fact, 1992 gave me the result I had hoped for – a fourth successive Labour defeat and the opportunity to begin in earnest the process of realignment which I had, from the very early days of my leadership, seen as the Party's main opportunity. First, however, we needed to find a clear identity, an eye-catching set of policies and a distinctive role. It was at this time that I remember saying in press interviews that 'I would sell my grandmother for some distinctiveness for the Party'. I knew that we could not move to the next phase of the Party's development – participating actively as a player on the field – unless we had confidence in ourselves and knew clearly who we were and what we stood for.

John Smith helped me here. I liked and admired him very much and I think he could have made a good prime minister. But he was not a good leader of the Labour Party in opposition. He failed to drive forward the Kinnock reforms, having narrowly won a victory on One Member One Vote (OMOV). And he allowed his party to slide back towards its old stances and easy accommodation of the trades unions. This suited me admirably, as it enabled me to begin to move the Lib Dems on to the only ground from which I believed the new centre left could convincingly win again.

I had already mapped this ground out in *Citizens' Britain*. The new politics of the left would, I believed, be about matching rights with responsibility. It would be about the steady and responsible management of the

---

1 One of the most intriguing 'what would have happened ifs' of our modern political history is, where would we be now if the pollsters and the pundits had been right and John Major had lost? I suspect that Neil Kinnock's would have been another one-term Labour government (perhaps in partnership with us), the Tories would have got back in 2001, the Lib Dems would have suffered heavily and the Blair revolution, possibly without Blair, would only now just be starting.

economy, the encouragement of enterprise and the creation of a strongly competitive internal economy. It would be about 'entitlement-based' public services which concentrated on the quality of delivery to the citizen, not who and how it was delivered. It would be about equality of opportunity and not socialist engineering to produce equality of outcome. It would be about making the poor richer without asking the rich to become swinge-ingly poorer. It would be about Europe, green issues and internationalism. And it would be about constitutional reform and handing power back to the citizen.

It was not proving easy to get the Lib Dems on to this ground, but I was confident we could get there eventually and would reap huge political dividends when we did. I had even discussed my enthusiasm for all this with a young Labour MP called Tony Blair, whom I had just met at dinner at a friend's house. To my delight, he saw things exactly the same way as I did.

We met again a few weeks later, this time at my house. In the course of the meal, he said he was fed up with opposition politics and wondered whether it was worth continuing. We agreed to keep in touch for the future. A few weeks later, John Smith was dead and Tony Blair was beginning to take his place in history.

Thus began what, as I look back, I see was the most difficult period of my leadership of the Lib Dems. I knew that Blair, with his novel and powerful appeal and the whole weight of the Labour machine behind him, would now move rapidly on to the ground for which I had been heading with the Lib Dems. That he would succeed handsomely. And what was more, there was nothing I could do about it.

I also knew that our position had now crucially shifted. Instead of being ahead of the pack, we now, as the third and potentially irrelevant force in British politics, had to find some means of surviving a landslide of change in which we could very easily have been swallowed up. Though I hope few but my closest friends and Jane saw it, in the months after Blair's election as Labour leader I went through a severe personal crisis of confidence, with all its attendant physical side effects.

It became quickly obvious to me that it would be deadly for us to be bystanders in the revolution which would now sweep the Tories away. We had to be part of this movement for change, not separated from it. In swift order, we abandoned equidistance (though not without a considerable fight in the Party) and I embarked on a close, if clandestine, relationship with Blair and his main lieutenants. Our aim initially was to combine to maximize the Tory defeat. But this later widened to embrace a much grander vision: that of forming an enduring partnership in the following parliament, healing the schism which had split the left in the early years of the twentieth century and, in the process, creating the dominant governing force in Britain for the next decade or more.

I had always assumed that this could only come about through a hung parliament in which we Liberal Democrats held the balance of power. My relationship with Blair, however, offered something entirely different and much more attractive. We could combine forces with Labour in government even if they had a clear majority and the Lib Dems were a relatively small part of the partnership. We could fulfil the dream of my predecessors, from Jo Grimmond to David Steel, of using the Lib Dems as a catalyst in the realignment of the left from a position of strength within a majority government – not one of weakness in a hung parliament. And in the process, we could introduce proportional representation, which would modernize the electoral system and provide the context for a continuing and stable relationship between the two parties. The last months of 1996 were spent laying the ground work for this, culminating in the Cook/Maclennan Agreement of March 1997, which outlined the areas in which the two parties would work together in the next government.

Despite all this, in December 1996, only months after the election, the position of the Lib Dems was precarious. We were dropping in the polls. Our distinctive agenda had been taken from us, and we were being squeezed out of everything by the unstoppable rise and rise of Tony Blair. I was becoming desperate.

Once again 'events', this time in the formidable shape of Emma Nicholson, came to our rescue. The Nicholson defection ranks with the Eastbourne by-election as one of the key moments in the eleven years these diaries cover. It gave us desperately needed profile and a role. The Lib Dems were the Heineken party: we could reach parts of the Tory Party which New Labour, even with Blair, couldn't reach. We were important because we could add to the Tory defeat in a manner disproportionate to our numbers.

And so the scene was set for the 1997 General Election.

Actually, although we never admitted it to each other until election day itself, Blair and I succeeded beyond our wildest dreams. In fact, we succeeded too well. The Labour majority was much too big.

I do not know quite what happened during the 1997 election campaign to the relationship we had so carefully built up beforehand. I had left detailed plans of what the Lib Dems would do and what we expected after polling day with Tony Blair's office before the election started, so that there could be no misunderstandings. I had asked my broker in these matters, Tom McNally, to see Jonathan Powell, Blair's chief-of-staff, a few days before polling day, to reinforce the message that we were ready to participate in a coalition, but that that could not just mean bolting on one or two Lib Dems to a Labour administration – participation had to be based around a proper programme for government.

Nevertheless, somehow both Tony Blair and I seem to have misread the signals the other was sending. Peter Mandelson has since told me that the message the Blair retinue convinced themselves they were receiving from us in the crucial few days before polling day was that we had lost interest. And, on the day of the election itself (when we doubled our seats), Blair's advisers apparently led him to believe that, because we had done so well, we wanted to strike out on our own. Nothing could have been further from the truth – though my diary does record (somewhat to my surprise) that both Roy Jenkins and I were relieved when it became obvious that Blair was not going to propose a coalition during that fateful conversation between us, just before he went to see the Queen, on the morning of 2 May 1997.

Did we inadvertently send the wrong messages? Was Blair 'got at' by some of the 'anti-project' people on the night of 1 May? I am unable to say, but there was certainly a curious change in tone between the telephone call I took from him in the head teacher's office at Richard Huish College in Taunton on the morning of 1 May and our conversation the following morning. I still do not know with whom and in what proportions responsibility for this missed opportunity lies.

There is, however, a lesson and a conclusion to be drawn from these events.

The lesson is that political leaders should never take big decisions on the day after polling day.

One of the most malign instruments of the British constitution is the polling day removal van. It turns up at the back of No 10 Downing Street on the morning after, carts a dejected ex-prime minister away to relative obscurity and moves in an exhausted new one to immediate cares and instantaneous decisions, many of which have consequences which will be felt for the rest of his or her administration.[1]

1 See the entry for 8 May 1997 for an example of just how tired Blair and his staff were at this point – and how, even this early, the pressures of life in Downing Street were beginning to cut them off.

But it is not just exhaustion that makes this a questionable way of handing over power. The fact is that it is almost impossible for any person, let alone one drained by exhaustion and sleeplessness, to break out of the psychology of an election campaign which only ended in the early hours of that very morning, and adopt the very different mental attitude necessary for government in the years ahead. The US approach of having a period of transition between one administration and another has always struck me as being more sensible.

Whatever part such elements played, it is clear that we lost a historic opportunity during these twenty-four hours, which I (and, I believe, Tony Blair) deeply regret.

The story of the next two years is dominated by our attempt to recover the chance lost on that morning.

A friend who has read these pages tells me that they read like a Greek tragedy – an attempt to take on the 'Fates' which eventually foundered on human frailties and ended in failure.

I am not sure that any of it is as grand as that. And I am not sure that the end was, in the cataclysmic sense of a Greek tragedy at least, a failure – although ultimately that must be for the judgement of others. It is true that in our final aim of 'healing the rift', we failed. But much was accomplished on the way. We Lib Dems won things we could only have dreamed of in previous years. Devolution (albeit flawed) for Scotland and Wales; a Freedom of Information Act (ditto); the first nationwide PR elections (ditto); the reform (albeit partial) of the House of Lords. And in the process, the Lib Dems moved from being a party of protest to being a party of power; the second party of government at local level and partners with Labour in the governments of Scotland and Wales.

Perhaps more important, however, we have shown that there is a place for a new, less confrontational culture in British politics. Charles Kennedy's remarkable success at the 2001 General Election shows that 'constructive opposition' need not mean, as pundits, press and many Lib Dems predicted, electoral loss. This message is even more strongly illustrated by the fact that, in Scotland, despite being partners in government, our Westminster parliamentary majorities did not reduce, they increased. There is a lesson here for some in the Lib Dems. I need to be careful about retrospective self-justification. But I think it nevertheless fair to doubt whether so much would have been achieved had we not followed the course we did over these years.

Nevertheless, ultimately, we did fail to deliver the final act of reshaping of politics on the left and, through this, changing the whole British political scene. And I can find no comfort for this, even in the soothing idea that 'In great things, it is enough to have tried'.

I am still too close to events to provide a reliable analysis of the causes of this failure. Some (chiefly in my own party) have suggested that after the 1997 election the Lib Dems should have moved to outright opposition and that sullying ourselves with support for the government has damaged our liberal credentials and blunted the Party's radical edge. This worried me, too.[1] But, even with hindsight, I conclude that, given the opportunities before us in the months following 1 May 1997, it would have been simply derelict of me not to have taken every reasonable risk to enable the Liberal Democrats to participate in government and to achieve our long-held dream of PR.

The charge that I may have pursued my personal dream for too long is more difficult to counter. Some people, on reading these pages, could conclude that I should have known that Blair couldn't (they would claim, wouldn't) deliver and that the writing was on the wall from, perhaps, the spring of 1998. To this I can only respond that to me and those who were closest to me at the time, it did not seem so. These were the heydays of the new Blair government, when he appeared to walk on water and anything seemed possible. The crucial moment when I knew the project was irre-coverable was on the evening of 29 October 1998, when Jack Straw was allowed to rubbish the outcome of the Jenkins commission in the House of Commons and Tony Blair did nothing to counter him. A few days later I concluded that the time had come for me to put into practice the decision Jane and I had taken before the election of 1997, and stand aside for my successor.

Some have asked me (chiefly members of the press, who are obsessed by this kind of thing) if I feel betrayed? The answer is, 'No.' I think Tony Blair risked a very great deal in a genuine attempt to carry 'the project' through. And, in the end, what prevented it from happening were tribal forces which we both believed could be overcome, but which finally proved too strong. He had to confront these in his own Cabinet before I had to in my party. He decided (almost certainly correctly) that overcoming them could wreck his government before I had to consider whether doing the same would wreck my party. It was a matter of chronology, not of betrayal.

Others say that, if Blair was not a charlatan, then Ashdown must have

---

[1] See my conversation with Andrew Marr of 30 October 1997.

been a dupe – that Blair never meant it and was dissembling all along. Again it will ultimately be up to others to decide the truth of this. But in my view it is impossible to read these diaries and not conclude that Tony Blair was as serious and sincere about the project as I was. The time alone he was prepared to spend on it in the crucial first months of his administration seems proof enough.[1]

Yet others say that all this unrealistic dreaming was the result of political naivety on both our parts. That may be closer to the truth.

The fact is that both Tony Blair and I are not 'of' our parties as most political leaders are. We were not born to them in the same way as, for instance, John Smith was born to Labour. We were both, in our different ways, outsiders. We saw things as they might be, rather than as they always had to be, according to the conventional laws of politics.[2] In this sense it may be that we overestimated the pull of what we saw as a rational outcome – and the push of our own powers of persuasion.

I still, however, believe that, even falling short of what we aimed for, a great deal was achieved. The climate of politics has been altered in profound ways. We have begun, albeit slowly, to dismantle the battlements of confrontation that have dominated politics for so long and, in the process, replaced them, through the Joint Cabinet Committee and through our partnership in Scotland and Wales, with the habit and practice of partnership. If these continue to be built on, and if, especially, the cause of elected reform can continue to be pushed forward, perhaps initially now at local government level, then I think that those who look back at these events will see them as of genuine historic importance, opening the way to a different form of politics in this country.

So my view is that, although the chapter may be closed, the book is not. When will the next major chapter be written? I suspect not now. Nor, I think, in this political generation, unless fighting and winning together in a Euro referendum leads, as it did in the early 1970s, to a whole new set of opportunities.

Perhaps it will recur when Labour perceives it faces defeat again. But then my Lib Dem colleagues will be being asked to prop up a failing Labour government, which I suspect they will be most reluctant to do. Or perhaps it will come through a hung parliament after an election. But then we will be back doing it from a position of weakness in order to keep in power a government which the electorate, it will be said, have just rejected. So my

1 See Roy Jenkins' comment of 12 June 1997.
2 See John Prescott's comments of 18 February 1998.

guess is that the big chance will not come again until Labour has lost again.

Meanwhile, the hard (and for us Lib Dems, dangerous) fact is that Tony Blair has fulfilled his vision of realigning the left without us. I hope it is not overly self-congratulatory to say that this 'Labour-only project' which was the outcome of the 2001 election will be less liberal, less European, less green, less fired by social justice, more inclined to arrogance and, ultimately, therefore much more vulnerable to a Tory revival, than would have been the case had we succeeded in widening this government to include the Liberal Democrats.[1]

On 16 December 1997, I bet the journalist Hugo Young a bottle of burgundy that Tony Blair would end up a pluralist. I fear the time has come for me to pay up.

The truth about our prime minister is that he is, like many really big politicians, a puzzling collection of paradoxes. In person, he is one of the most open-minded politicians I have ever spoken with. He listens; he is unfussy and totally without pomposity; he answers argument with argument; he is completely disarming in admitting his mistakes; he gives space for others' opinions and he takes direct criticism completely without rancour.[2] These are all the attributes of a pluralist. And yet Hugo Young was right; Blair's government is one of the most control-freaky of modern times. And if it continues to be so, that will be the death of it.

The jumble of Blair paradoxes does not end there. He has very strong personal beliefs – and yet none of them adds up to a creed. The first question I can see his brain asking when presented with a proposition, is not 'Do I believe this?' but, 'Will it work?' And it shows. More than for any other prime minister in recent times, Tony Blair's obsession has always been for the big picture – even to the extent of completely missing important small events, which have gone on to blow up into full-scale crises.[3] Time and again, the absence of a firm set of interlocking political beliefs has denied him the sheet anchor he has needed to keep his government's head to the wind in time of storm. Indeed, one of the biggest failures over the years covered by my diaries was his and my inability to construct a joined-up, coherent intellectual vision of what we were trying to do. It was not that such a vision *could* not have been constructed – just that we were so concentrated on the mechanics of the relationship that we never got

1 See Appendix C, 'Partnership For Britain's Future', for examples.
2 See John Prescott's comment of 18 February 1998.
3 See, for example, the Formula 1 scandal (15 November 1997) and the beef on the bone débâcle (4 March 1998).

round to producing one. And the lack of this denied us a clear cause around which supporters of the project from both parties could gather; a deficiency which I regard as one of the chief reasons for our ultimate lack of success.[1]

Tony Blair is very honest. And yet he has a habit of too easily saying what he thinks people want to hear, leaving the impression that agreements have been made which haven't been, or that they haven't been when they have, with subsequent suspicion of bad faith and broken promises.

He is immensely personally likeable. Indeed, charm is his greatest weapon, though it's not quite as powerful as he sometimes things. (It is said of St Augustine that, when he went to see the Devil, he concealed a rusty nail to press into his palm in order to resist temptation. I used, metaphorically, to do the same thing every time I visited Downing Street.) And yet, the public as a whole does not seem wholly to trust, or even to like Tony Blair. They remain, indeed, deeply puzzled by him. I have often said to him that people want to see where their politicians' backbones are – what they would stand against a wall and be shot for. Even after four years in No. 10, the public do not yet know this of Tony Blair. He remains to them an unresolved enigma.

He has been endowed with two fabulous majorities, very weak enemies and extraordinary personal powers of persuasion. And yet he all too frequently fails to use these fantastic advantages to achieve what he himself has marked out as the great things for which he wants to be known (the project and Europe), preferring instead to hoard his popularity, like some Silas Marner holed up in Downing Street. Some say this shows lack of courage. And yet, his personal courage and conviction secured the end of Clause 4 in his party and turned the Kosovo war from almost certain defeat into uneasy victory, when he persuaded the US president, against the overwhelming view of his own advisers, that ground troops should be used.

When we first started working together, I was confident that Tony Blair would be a good prime minister and thought there was a fair chance he could be a great one. He has been the first. But he has so far failed to become the second. He maintains that the true Blair will be revealed in this second term. Then the paradoxes will be resolved and the enigma uncovered. We must hope so: for history will deal hard with him if all these talents and advantages are spent on just governing like any other administration, instead of changing things for ever in Britain, which was his aim and which still remains his potential.

1 See my meeting with Gordon Brown of 2 December 1997.

Finally, what of us Lib Dems?

The good news is that we have achieved an extraordinary further success in the 2001 elections. That success is directly attributable to the ability, courage in backing his own judgement, and campaigning skills of Charles Kennedy. This gives us a very strong base from which to work in the current parliament. But our success should not obscure for us the real challenges and hard choices ahead.

Some believe that we can somehow replace the Tories. I have never shared this view. There is a thoroughly respectable Tory position which, properly led, can garner a steady 35 per cent of those on the centre right in this country. We can borrow some of those voters for as long as the Tory party remains so awful. And it is good tactics to capitalize on this for as long as we can. But it is not good strategy to depend on your enemy being stupid for ever. We will not be able to hold perpetually on to the bulk of this 'borrowed' vote, because we are not a centre right party, we are a centre left party.

Others believe that the right thing is for the Lib Dems to fill the space now open on Labour's left; to become the mouthpiece for the 'producer interest' in public services. I do not think this is wise either. Apart from anything else, this would be a strategy for electoral disaster when a political force appears again which can represent the centre right – as eventually it must. After all, in most of the places to which the Lib Dems must look for growth next time, it is the Tories we must beat. And in nearly all the seats we want to keep, it is the Tories who are the challengers.

I do not believe that we should abandon 'constructive opposition', not least because I think the public likes it. But it is probably now both inevitable and right that the balance between partnership and criticism will shift more towards the latter, especially on Europe, environmental matters, the government's tendency to forget the niceties of handling power and its increasingly illiberal stances, especially on home affairs.

Meanwhile, our role as the radicals doing the new thinking out in front, not defending the old attitudes of the left (however tempting the opportunities to do so), should intensify. And there remains a huge radical field for us to occupy: the environment; the creation of a democratic EU; the need to decentralize the delivery of public services through more accountable local structures, co-operatives and the principles of mutuality; the need to define the limits of free public services which are paid for from taxation (especially in the NHS); the reform of international institutions; a more radical approach to joining the Euro, to name but a few.

The next few years will be difficult and the next election as challenging as any we have fought. But I remain confident that the Party will rise to the challenge, just as it has done in the past. As for me, I finish these years deeply grateful for the privilege of leading the party I love, broadly comfortable about the way we played our opportunities, happy to have ended it at the right time and on terms of my own choosing, and looking forward to the new challenges which lie ahead.

Looking back two years after handing over to my successor Charles Kennedy, I realize that although I set out in 1988 a very driven man, I have become today a very contented one.

ASHDOWN MAN
BY GEOFF THOMPSON

Appendices

Appendix A

The Parties

1. *The Tories*

1.1. Appear to be – and probably are – in a terrible mess.

1.2. Although his ability should not be underestimated, it seems very unlikely that the election of William Hague can solve the Tories' problems either quickly, or without further trouble.

1.3. The composition of the Shadow Cabinet, taken with that of the new Conservative MPs, shows a pronounced shift to the right.

1.4. Europe remains the Tories' key fault line.

1.5. Unless the Blair government fails in its first term, then it is unlikely that the Tories can get themselves back together as an electorally appealing force in time to win the next election.

1.6. However, the temporary disablement of the Tories as a Westminster force does not mean that they cannot recover many of the local government seats that we won from them at the height of our popularity and the depths of theirs ('93/'94).

2. *Labour*

2.1. Labour are now in a superb position. Blair has started exceptionally well and there is a real sense of a new mood in the country. 'Can do' politics and belief in government may be coming back.

2.2. The make-up of the new Parliamentary Labour Party is, at first sight, impressive. They are mostly young, Blairite New Labour, bright, pro-European, pro-PR and from broadly the same mould as many of our new MPs.

2.3. Labour have inherited a near 'golden' economic scenario. Provided that Gordon Brown has a prudent Budget, which contains a fair element of fiscal tightening, the economy will continue to grow as near the top of its 'safe' range, government receipts will swell and the serious PSBR problem which we currently face could have all but vanished in the next two years, leaving room for substantial extra investment in public services towards the end of the parliament.

2.4. Labour will probably have a difficult winter with health and education, which we can capitalize on. And maybe more problems of the same sort next year, too. But after that, our position as the 'big spenders' on education and health is likely to be undermined by substantial increases in spending by the government.

2.5. Relations between us and Labour remain good at all levels, and can be maintained for, perhaps six months, through our policy of 'constructive opposition' – but for how much longer beyond that, as the pressures of opposition, local elections and inevitable by-election struggles begin to bite?

2.6. Meanwhile, all the signs are that Labour:

2.6.1. intends, broadly, to honour the Cook/Maclennan agreement with the single exception of PR for Euro '99 – where the signs so far are, at present, unclear.

2.6.2. will continue to raid the Lib Dem policy cupboard and enact policies that we initiated and have been in favour of for years.

3. *The Lib Dems*

3.1. At first sight, our position is strong, with the biggest parliamentary contingent ever, matched by a similar position in local government and in Europe.

3.2. In the longer term, however, things look much less rosy.

3.3. Whereas the Party traditionally does best off a failing Tory government, we do worst off a failing Labour one.

3.4. The *only* way out of this is through PR, which will give us the 'room' to continue to grow. But we are almost wholly dependent on Labour to deliver this.

3.5. Without PR, the Euro elections in '99 will be very difficult.

3.7. We will have less and less ground to stand on and increasing difficulty differentiating ourselves from New Labour.

3.8. We could try to capitalize on Tory disarray by replacing them as the effective party of opposition. But this would mean sacrificing our relationship with Labour and PR. And anyway, it cannot be done from a position where we are acting as a goad to Labour arguing for *more* public spending than them (a position which we will, anyway, have to work hard to persuade people is not to Labour's left).

3.9. The notion (too widely held in the Party) that we can make progress at a parliamentary level against Labour where we are second to them in the northern cities is, in my view, a dangerous illusion.

3.10. There appears at the moment to be a tempting possibility of taking advantage of the Tories' disarray to make ourselves into the 'real opposition', but we cannot compete with the Tories as a party of the right. There will always be a party of the right in Britain, but it will never be the Liberal Democrats.

3.14. Meanwhile, there is a potentially very dangerous split which could rise between the sentiment of much of the Party's activist base (particularly at local level and especially in the north) and the realities of our position at Westminster. The former want nothing more than a return to red-blooded opposition to Labour. But our parliamentary (and, where we hold power, local government) position remains overwhelmingly an anti-Conservative one.

3.15. The election has, in short, starkly revealed what has been creeping up on us for the last three years – that Labour and the Lib Dems are, geographically (and, in the case of New Labour, increasingly on matters of policy, too) complementary. Where we are strong, they are weak; and if they are not weak in these areas, then it's the Tories who benefited by holding on to the seat. And vice versa. The tensions between this hard, but uncomfortable reality and the sentiment of many of our activists could, if not resolved early, tear the party apart over the next five years. The best (the only) time to resolve this is now, while the success of the election strategy is fresh in minds, while relations with Labour remain good and while the prize of PR remains in front of us.

3.16. The only rational strategy for the party to follow is, therefore, a 'split level' one. Maintaining our co-operative partnership with Labour and outright opposition to the Tories at national level (and in many southern councils), while operating a more flexible, anti-Old Labour strategy where this is necessary at local level.

Conclusions

4. That our first and overriding aim in this parliament is to secure PR for Westminster and, if possible, for Europe as well.

5. That we have a vested interest in the success of the first term of the Blair government.

6. That our relationship with Labour and our clear opposition to the Tories at parliamentary level should not change.

7. But this will be very difficult to hold under the pressure of events, unless it is firmly secured, both by a common project (constitutional reform) and by institutional means.

8. We should apply a 'split level' strategy where this is appropriate, at the national and local level.

10. It would be far better not to leave these questions of strategy unresolved. We may have to have a strategy debate to settle this at Eastbourne.

Appendix B

Schedules

1. Summary timetable
2. The story.
3. July statements on announcement of Joint Cabinet Committee.
4. Draft terms of reference of Election Commission.
5. Draft PM's statement on Election Commission.
6. Possible recommendation of Commission.

1. Summary Timetable

1997

July	Establishment of Joint Cabinet Committee
	Announcement of European Elections Bill
September	Lib Dem Party Conference
October	Labour Party Conference
November	Annoucement of Election Commission
	Cabinet reshuffle and agreed programme
	Lib Dem special conference

1998

November	Report of Election Commission

1999

January	Government reaction to Commission Report

| June | Referendum |
| | European elections |

2000

| February | A V Bill |
| July | Joint programme published |

2001

| May | General Election |

2. The Story

Britain is in a new political era. The long Conservative hegemony has been broken, with over two-thirds of the electorate voting for change and the Conservative Party divided and discredited.

Now Labour's ambitions, as a result of the leadership of Blair, go wider and deeper than merely replacing one government with another.

There is an unprecedented opportunity to modernize and open up Britain's institutions, to end traditional class-based politics for good, and to create a new relationship of trust and partnership between citizens and their government.

The new style is inclusive and pluralistic, and the Blair government believes that the Liberal Democrats are natural allies in this great undertaking.

For their part, Liberal Democrats recognize the new situation and the chance for their own long-cherished principles to be put into effect, without any sacrifice of identity or integrity, by working together with the Labour government for the common good.

This new constructive relationship had been prefigured by the friendly dialogue between the two leaders and Cook/Maclennan agreement on constitutional reform before the election.

Paddy Ashdown signalled immediately after the election that he wanted to replace automatic adversarialism with constructive opposition, just as Blair had made it plain that his government would not be confined by narrow Labour loyalties and ideological orthodoxy.

This mutual recognition of a great project of reconciliation and reform to replace the dead hand of conservatism has engendered its own dynamic momentum.

The first stage following discussion between Tony Blair and Paddy Ashdown, is the formation of a Joint Cabinet Committee, a constitutional innovation, although not without precedent, in which leading Liberal Democrats come together with Cabinet members under the chairmanship of the Prime Minister, to plan the programme of constitutional reform; and to discuss other matters of common interest between the parties (3).

Simultaneously, the Government announces its intention to go ahead with legislation for PR for the European elections in 1999, indicating that no announcement will be made on the Westminster PR commission referendum until the autumn.

Thus the Cabinet committee can be seen both as a prize for those Liberal Democrats looking for further fruits of co-operation, and as a price for PR for Europe by those who are more suspicious.

However, both these pieces of new policy are welcomed with pleasure, both by the liberal press and by most New Labour and Liberal Democrat supporters.

The Liberal Democrat Conference in September passes off well, with the results of co-operation already apparent, although not without anxiety being expressed on the prospects for PR for Westminster.

At the Labour Conference, the Prime Minister goes out of his way to commend the new political approach in contrast to the Tories.

The second stage in November is even more dramatic, demonstrating the effects of shared co-operative momentum.

The Election Commission, a product of the Cabinet committee, is announced, chaired by Lord Jenkins, with terms of reference (4) which are designed to appeal to the public and a renewal of the commitment to a subsequent referendum. Its establishment is welcomed by a positive statement from the Prime Minister (5).

Just as fundamentally it is announced simultaneously that, as part of the Prime Minister's reshuffle, Liberal Democrats are to join the government with an agreed programme and a common commitment to long-term co-operation.

This is put by Paddy Ashdown to a special Liberal Democrat Conference and, despite strong minority protests, is approved, both for positive co-operative reasons and to safeguard the ongoing process of constitutional, and particularly electoral, reform.

The popularity of this development with the public and the evidence of the Prime Minister's radical and imaginative approach is enough to carry the Labour Party, despite again strong minority dissent and some problems with those removed from office.

The third stage, proceeding from a period of co-operation in government, is the run-up to the General Election of, say, 2001, following closely on the Millennium celebrations. This stage effectively starts with the publication of the Election Commission Report in the period Nov. 98 – Jan. 99, and the referendum held in 1999. 'Fair Votes for a New Century' – possibly in June on the same day as the European elections.

The Commission recommends a combination of the Alternative Vote in single member constituencies plus 25 per cent Additional Members, on a regional basis, to give reasonable proportionality between parties (6).

The government decides to legislate in two stages, with the immediate introduction of AV in existing constituencies to be followed after the election, when time allows for the necessary boundary changes, by the introduction of regional Additional Members.

However, the package as a whole, embracing the complete system, is put to a referendum with the support of the government and all parties, save the Conservatives and Unionists – although individual members of both parties support reform. The Prime Minister gives his whole-hearted backing to a 'Yes' vote and the referendum is successful.

Early in the year 2000, a Bill for AV is introduced and passed through both Houses. Later in the year 2000, by the time of the Autumn Conferences of both parties, a broad joint programme, 'New Britain for the New Century', is published and agreed as the basis for a Lib/Lab coalition platform at the upcoming General Election. It includes the second stage of electoral reform.

The fourth stage is the success of this broad-based government in renewing its mandate at the election of 2001, and putting its agreed programme into effect.

3. July Statements on Announcement of Joint Cabinet Committee

Ashdown: Time to change and hope. New government with new energy, new style and new agenda *v.* exhausted and divided Conservatives.

Demands a different response from the Lib Dems – who share many of the goals of the New Labour government even when they differ on means from traditional adversarial competition.

Bringing forward legislation for a fair voting system for the European elections in 1999 is a tangible sign of good faith and commitment to rational reform which we welcome very much.

Foundation of the new Cabinet committee, itself another example of an imaginative response to a new era, demonstrates possibility of close co-operation; initially on the programme of constitutional reform but without any restriction from moving on to other areas of common concern between Lib Dems and the government.

Blair: I have made it clear that I want my government to be different. I want a government which is inclusive rather than exclusive in its thinking – and pluralistic rather than restricted in its scope. This Joint Labour Committee reflects this new approach.

Before the election New Labour and the Liberal Democrats agreed a substantial agenda of constitutional reform. This Cabinet committee, which I shall chair myself, will be a forum where those plans can be refined and the necessary measures for their practical implementation worked out. I hope and expect that the committee will move on to discuss other matters of agreed common concern.

I look forward to working closely with Paddy Ashdown and his colleagues as part of a new era of positive cross-party co-operation.

4. Draft Terms of Reference for the Election Commission

To review the voting system for parliamentary elections, and to recommend an alternative proportional system, so that the electorate can be offered a choice between them in a referendum.

In considering alternative systems, the Commission will take into account the extent to which they might:

encourage citizens' participation in elections,

maintain the local links of the British parliamentary system,

extend voter choice,

produce a more varied and representative House of Commons,

confer a more equal value on each vote cast.

The Commission should report to Parliament within one year from its first meeting.

Note: In the process of taking evidence, the Commission can legitimately popularize the issues.

5. Draft Statement from Blair on Appointment of Election Commission

I am delighted that the Election Commission has been established under the chairmanship of Lord Jenkins. I know that he will give distinguished leadership to his colleagues in this important task.

There are well-founded dissatisfactions with the flaws in our 'winner-takes-all' voting system. It will not be used for elections to the Scottish Parliament or Welsh Assembly, nor, in future, for European parliamentary elections.

We must all be open to the possibility that we can improve the voting system for Westminster elections, too, although I have always thought that would be more difficult.

The government would not have established this Commission were we not open to the possibility of sensible reform. However, we shall await their deliberations with interest. I would like to reiterate that it is the government's intention that, if the Commission can recommend a system which they believe to be an improvement, this new system will be presented to the British people in a referendum for their decision.

6. Possible Recommendations of Commission

Alternative vote in, say, 450 seats.

Additional members numbering, say, 150 seats, elected on a regional basis to top parties up to overall proportionality, using, if possible, the AV votes to compute party entitlement.

Government Response

We welcome the scheme as a whole but it is too complex to introduce in one package. We shall therefore legislate to reform the voting system in two steps.

The first step will be to change the voting system in existing constituencies, to allow voters to cast their votes preferentially in such a way that the candidates elected will either have achieved over 50 per cent of the first preferences in their constituencies or, if not, that they are the most generally acceptable.

The second step will be to recognize constituency boundaries to create

450 new single member seats, complemented by 150 additional regional members, elected on a party proportional basis.

Note: This envisages that this might also be the occasion to reduce the overall size of the House to 600, and (query?) to sort out the over-representation of Scotland?

Appendix C

PARTNERSHIP FOR BRITAIN'S FUTURE

First Draft, 24 August 1997, Veron, France

This parliament will form the bridge between this century and the next. Its task, is to begin the long process of changing and modernizing Britain's institutions and renewing the spirit of dynamism in our country.

We commit our two parties to working together in this government, with the aim of ensuring that this becomes one of the great reforming parliaments of this century, laying the foundations for a decade of reform and renewal in Britain.

As two sovereign and independent parties, no doubt we will continue to have our differences. But we are content to put these aside in order to work together on the greater task which must be accomplished if Britain is to succeed in the century ahead.

In doing this, we also hope that we will help establish a new culture of partnership and pluralism which are central to the new politics we wish to see in Britain for the future.

The Programme

1. Cleaning Up Our Politics
1.1. Our politics has become dangerously discredited.
1.2. The funding of our political parties is murky and corrupting.
1.3. The rules governing the conduct of elected representatives, especially Members of Parliament, have proved to be inadequate.
1.4. Patronage has become endemic.
1.5. Far too much power and far too many decisions relating to public

money are taken out of view of the public and outside the circle of public accountability.

1.6. We will work together in government to:

1.6.1. Clean up and make open the whole system of funding of political parties.

1.6.2. Strengthen the rules governing the behaviour of MPs in the conduct of their public duties.

1.6.3. Make the public appointments system subject to a system of check and scrutiny.

1.6.4 Diminish the number of quangos and make those that remain more open and publicly accountable.

1.6.5. Make those who sit on quangos subject to the same rules of declaration and interests as councillors.

2. Modernizing Our Constitution

2.1. Britain's political system has failed us.

2.2. It is our job to do for our time, what our forebears did for theirs – to modernize, update and democratize our system of government.

2.3. We will work together in government to:

2.3.1. Enable voters to make an early decision, through a referendum, on reform of the voting system for the Westminster parliament.

2.3.2. Reform the House of Commons and the House of Lords.

2.3.3. Protect our civil liberties, initially by the early incorporation of the European Code of Human Rights and ultimately through a British Bill of Rights.

2.3.4. Bring in a Freedom of Information Act before the start of the new millennium.

2.3.5. Establish a *senedd* (assembly) in Wales and a parliament with tax varying powers in Scotland.

2.3.6. Renew, strengthen and democratize local government and create the framework for a regional dimension to government which is locally accountable.

3. Reforming Our Welfare System

3.1. Britain's welfare system has failed us.

3.2. It traps people in poverty instead of freeing them. It makes them dependent instead of providing them with opportunities. It penalizes work instead of rewarding it.

3.3. It is wasteful, demeaning and extensively abused.

3.4. It is time to replace Beveridge's great scheme with something new which meets the new conditions of our time and can take Britain into the new century.

3.5. We will work together in government to establish the broadest base possible for a review and reconstruction of Britain's welfare system.

3.6. Our aim in government will be to create a system which:

3.6.1. Provides effective support for those who genuinely cannot support themselves.

3.6.2. Tackles poverty and exclusion in Britain.

3.6.3. Rewards those who can help themselves and do, above those who can help themselves and choose not to.

3.6.4. Emphasizes the redistribution of opportunities, rather than just of wealth.

3.6.5. Encourages self reliance and discourages dependence.

3.6.6. Enlarges the support role of the community and reduces that of the state.

4. Strengthening the Foundations of the Economy

4.1. Creating a new future for Britain depends on building and maintaining a strong and secure economy based on skill, enterprise, and long-term investment.

4.2. But, in these fundamentals, Britain's economy remains relatively weak.

4.3. Our education and skill levels are lower than nearly all our competitors'. As is our level of industrial investment. Uncertainty about our future in Europe and about our determination to resist inflation, means higher interest rates for British businesses than in nearly all our continental competitors. And the level of government debt remains dangerously high.

4.4. We will work together in government to:

4.4.1. Ensure Britain's education and skills are raised to world levels.

4.4.2. Maintain a firm long-term low inflation strategy with identifiable and publicized targets for inflation (at the moment 3 per cent).

4.4.3. Ensure total public borrowing, expressed as a percentage of GDP is reduced (our aim is to bring this below 40 per cent over the next parliament).

4.4.4. Adhere to the 'golden rule' (i.e. that the level of the government's borrowing should never exceed the level of the government's capital investment).

4.4.5. Maintain Britain's adherence to the Maastricht criteria for entry into the European single currency, which, provided that it is firmly established on the Maastricht criteria, we should enter at the earliest opportunity.

4.4.6. Take tough action to strengthen competition in the British economy.

4.4.7. Provide that special assistance and encouragement is given for enterprise and small businesses.

4.4.8. Expand employment opportunities, especially for the young unemployed.

5. Education

5.1. Britain's education system is failing us.

5.2. If we are to make this country successful again, we must make its education system the best in the world.

5.3. This means making education the nation's first priority in the years ahead.

5.4. We will work together in government to:

5.4.1. Raise standards in our schools to world levels, by concentrating on core skills, constantly challenging pupils to higher achievement and continuously presenting them with new opportunities.

5.4.2. Improve the quality of our teaching by establishing a National Teaching Council, charged with rigorously overseeing and policing professional standards.

5.4.3. Make education funding the first call on the nation's financial resources and ensure that investment in education rises in real terms every year for the next decade.

5.4.4. Provide the resources to give every child in the country access to two years' free high-quality nursery provision before the start of the new millennium.

5.4.5. Modernize and restructure Britain's higher and further education system to provide an efficient, flexible credit-based system capable of providing a higher proportion of our young people with cost-effective, high-quality post-16 education and training to meet the needs of the next century.

6. Europe

6.1. Weak leadership, ambivalence and lack of self-confidence have damaged both Britain's standing and Britain's influence in Europe.

6.2. We believe that Britain's best interests can be better secured by a realistic, but constructive and positive attitude to Europe and our partners.

This is in Europe's interest, too. Indeed, on a number of crucial issues, including competition, economic liberalization and external and security affairs, Britain could have an important leadership role to play in the European Union.

6.3. We will work together in government to:

6.3.1. Change the direction which Europe has taken, away from the creation of a 'Politicians' Europe' and towards the creation of a 'People's Europe', which puts the emphasis on the democratization of European institutions, greater openness, and on issues of interest to Europe's citizens rather than Europe's elites.

6.3.2. Ensure that Britain is in an early position to join EMU, provided this is firmly founded on the Maastricht criteria.

6.3.3. Enable Britain to play a leadership role in building a strong European economy capable of succeeding in the global market place through higher skill levels, greater economic liberalization, stronger competition and the creation of a more flexible labour market, based on minimum standards established under the provisions of the Social Chapter.

6.3.4. Promote closer European integration in the field of defence and foreign affairs.

6.3.5. Press for the reform of Europe's institutions, especially the CAP (Common Agricultural Policy) and for the greater efficiency and accountability of Europe's bureaucracy.

7. Health

7.1. After years of underfunding, neglect and even hostility from the Tories, the restoration and modernization of the NHS is one of the chief tasks of this government.

7.2. We will work together in government to:

7.2.1. Provide stable and adequate resources for the Health Service.

7.2.2. Reduce waiting lists to a maximum of six months by the year 2000.

7.2.3. Shift more resources into primary care and health education.

7.2.4. Bring together health and community care.

7.2.5. Strengthen democracy and accountability in the local delivery of health care.

7.2.6. Create a framework for decision-making on the prioritization of the range of health services provided free at the point of delivery and funded by taxation.

8. Environment

8.1. For too long, politicians have paid lip service to the environment, but done little to tackle the fundamental challenge of altering the way we live in order to preserve the quality of our national and global living space for future generations.

8.2. We accept this challenge and believe that Britain will benefit from becoming a world leader in setting new national and international standards for the preservation and improvement of the environment.

8.3. We will work together in government to:

8.3.1. Start a progressive shift of taxation away from work, goods and wealth and on to pollution and the use of finite raw materials.

8.3.2. Launch a national strategy for energy conservation, starting with the homes of the poorest.

8.3.3. Press forward with the creation of an integrated national and European transport strategy, aimed initially at shifting 10 per cent of British freight traffic from road to rail by the end of this parliament.

8.3.4. Cut CO_2 emissions in Britain by 2000.

9. Defence and Foreign Policy

9.1. Nearly fifty years after Dean Acheson's telling comment about 'losing an Empire but failing to find a role', British foreign policy has still failed to adjust to the world in which we find ourselves at the end of this century.

9.2. Yet we believe that there remains a powerful role for Britain to play in Europe and abroad, which will also be to the benefit of our national interest.

9.3. Europe and the maintenance of an Atlantic relationship will remain Britain's primary areas of interest.

9.4. But, as a medium-sized nation in an increasingly turbulent world, Britain also has a direct interest in strengthening the framework of international law and especially in the area of conflict resolution and control. It is in this area that we believe Britain, with its extensive experience in conflict resolution, its highly proficient armed services, its wide experience in international relations, its Commonwealth links and its seat on the Security Council, has a crucial role of leadership to play in reforming and increasing the effectiveness of international organizations.

9.5. We will work together in government to:

9.5.1. Continue and strengthen the government's present policy of placing a special emphasis on human rights in foreign policy.

9.5.2. Promote, nationally and through the Commonwealth, the strengthening of international law and the effectiveness of international intervention to prevent, control and resolve conflict.

9.5.3. Press for the reform and strengthening of the effectiveness of the UN.

9.5.4. Strictly limit arms sales by Britain only to those countries which are, or are progressing towards, democratic institutions and who observe the UN International Code of Human Rights.

9.5.5. Work for the establishment of an international arms control regime based on a worldwide register for all arms sales.

9.5.6. Increase Britain's aid and development budget with the aim of achieving the UN target of 0.7 per cent of GDP by 2010.

9.5.7. Work for the early establishment of a Comprehensive Test Ban Treaty and the strengthening of the Nuclear Non-proliferation Treaty.

9.5.8. Maintain the effectiveness of Britain's armed services and ensure that these closely match the task of defending Britain in NATO and pursuing our national and foreign policy interests in the modern age.

Appendix D

General

1. We are at the start of what is, potentially, one of the great reforming parliaments of our democratic history. Almost all of the constitutional reforms for which Liberal Democrats and our predecessor parties have fought for a century or more are now either being enacted, or within our reach.

2. But the programme of reform and modernization does not stop at our constitution and political system.

3. The project before us is the wholesale modernization of our country, along the lines we have always proposed and in which our ideas, policies and language are now dominant. This applies, in particular, in five key areas:

3.1. The reform of our constitution and political system.

3.2. The renewal of our public services, especially health, education and welfare.

3.3. The re-casting of our relationship, both individually and nationally, with our natural environment.

3.4. The creation of a fairer, less class-based society.

3.5. The modernization of our relationships abroad and especially with Europe.

4. This 'project' will not be completed in this parliament. It will take a decade or more.

5. So our strategy must be a durable one – capable of lasting, if it has to, not just for the next few months, or even until the next election, but, potentially, for this parliament and the next one. Our tactics will certainly have to vary in this period. But the strategy we choose must be capable of remaining constant.

6. Secondly, our strategy must have account of the political realities, whether they are comfortable ones, or not.

7. One of these is that, in most of the key areas listed above, Labour's positions, or at least the language they use, are very similar to ours; while the Tories will oppose nearly all of them. On these issues, therefore, a return to equidistance is simply not possible.

8. Next it is important to remember that we Liberal Democrats are one of the key reasons why Britain now has this opportunity for change. Our commitment to constitutional change has been crucial in making it happen. We have helped create the agenda; we have made sure that the pace of change has been maintained and our votes will be vital in carrying these changes through when the going gets tough.

9. What is more, if the changes now happening take place without us, or with us confined to the role of mere onlookers, then they will be less likely to succeed, less secure and less liberal. And we will be far, far less relevant to British politics in the future.

10. I do not believe that there is, therefore, any role for us as bystanders to the changes we have helped unleash. It would be a betrayal of all that we have stood for for so long, and all that we have achieved so recently, to choose merely to be a 'good opposition' at a time of change, when we could be participants in making change happen.

11. So our strategy should not be about whether to be active participants in change, but about how.

12. Finally, and perhaps most difficult of all, we have to have a role to play which gives us room to continue to grow and which enables us to be independent and distinctive. I believe this, not just because I am a Liberal Democrat, but because I believe that British politics would not be either safe or successful without a strong liberal voice and only the Liberal Democrats can provide this.

13. *So our strategy has to enable us to play a role which is distinctive, liberal and 'adds value' to the process of change, rather than simply being an 'add on' to the Labour government in bringing it about.*

The Positions of the Parties

Labour

14. The Blair government has, even with the stumbles of the immediate pre-Christmas period, started well. Probably better than any other new administration in recent times . . .

17. In the longer term, however, they are doing what all new administrations do: taking all the hard decisions, especially economic ones, early.

18. The result of this and their healthy economic inheritance means that, barring a serious economic upset, they will have potentially huge resources to hand in years three and four of this parliament (we may see some signs of this, even in the next spring Budget). These are likely to far exceed our spending commitments at the last election.

19. The Blair government seems genuinely committed to constitutional reform, even if they still do not see this as central, in the way that we would. They have, mostly, delivered on the commitments in the Maclennan/Cook agreement and show no signs of reneging on this. It remains my view that, although he says he has not made up his mind, Blair could well support electoral reform, on the Jenkins proposals, in a referendum, provided it fits in with his long-term plans. This is for him an issue of practical politics, not principle . . .

23. Fortunately, Blair too thinks long term and realizes that he needs us for three things which are key to his plans:

23.1. A second term.

23.2. A counterbalance to his unreconstructed left, especially on things like Europe, sound economics and (more recently), perhaps, the environment, which Labour will do their best to make one of their issues.

23.3. Public approval. He realizes (though he is bewildered by) the fact that the public somehow trusts us. We have won a reputation for speaking the truth and he wants that on his side.

24. *But there are already key flaws becoming apparent with this government. The chief of these are:*

24.1. They are obsessed with short-term news management and this is beginning to catch up with them.

24.2. There is a worrying tone of moral authoritarianism about much that they do and say.

24.3. Blair runs too much himself.

24.4. The Labour Party is actually two parties. New Labour is in government. And Old Labour is as far out of government as the Tories. There is a real possibility of Labour splitting in this parliament, especially with PR, if we are prepared to play our hand well enough.

The Tories

25. The underlying divisions in the Tory Party have been cruelly exposed by the election and the first few months of opposition.

26. I do not underestimate Hague. He is clever and quick on his feet. But his judgement is bad and his close advisers are worse.

27. His party is as divided, as riven by civil war and as unprepared for opposition as were Labour in the early 1980s. It will take the Tories more than this parliament to re-find themselves as a political force capable of winning general elections.

28. It may well be that 'One Nation', pro-Europe, 'liberal' Tories will be released by the advent of PR. Some, especially amongst the MEPs, may see this as their lifebelt and some may head in our direction. But their detachment will only serve to emphasize the solidity of the right-wing rump.

30. Watch out, in particular, for the Tories to run a high-profile and well-resourced campaign aimed at taking on the mantle of the protectors of rural England, especially on issues like housing development, hunting and Euro-phobia, particularly in an agricultural context.

31. We must not, however, allow the miserable state of the Tory Party to blind us to the resilience of their base vote, or their capacity for recovery. In our key areas we will have to continue actively to compete with them for votes in all the key elections of the next four years.

The Lib Dems

32. We have responded to the post-election situation better than either of the other two parties, especially in terms of our strategy.

33. 'Constructive opposition' has also delivered us some useful dividends, particularly on the constitutional front and will, I believe, continue to do so.

34. The Cabinet committee seems to be working well at this stage, though its workload is likely to diminish as the reform agenda gets progressively completed.

35. There is (as yet) no sign that this strategy has done us any harm with the electorate or with Lib Dem voters who would otherwise vote Tory.

36. Nor has this strategy stopped us attacking the government where we needed to – as the debate on single parents before Christmas showed.

37. *Despite these successes however, we, too, have a number of weaknesses to address:*

   37.1. We are still living off our 1 May manifesto policies. These are fine for the moment. But they are soon going to be made irrelevant as the government enacts more and more of our 1 May election policies and outspends our spending commitments.

37.2. Our vote is still too dependent on the votes of the other two parties. Historically, our success has been a mirror image of Tory success. When they prosper, we struggle; and conversely, when Labour are successful, so are we . . . We have to find new ways to compete with Labour for the ground of progressive politics in Britain, not to compete with the Tories for the territory of the right.

37.3. We still have much work to do to tell people what a Liberal Democrat vote is *for*. Lack of a clear core policy message is always dangerous for a third party – but in the context of PR, when we will not be able to rely on the tactical vote, it could be deadly.

What We Should Do

Strategy

59. The strategy I have followed is simply expressed.

60. It is to hold out the prospect of partnership with Blair, subject to three conditions:

60.1. It is primarily centred on political reform on the basis of the Maclennan/Cook agreement, with paramount importance to the delivery of PR.

60.2. Beyond this, it is confined to other areas on which we agree.

60.3. It does not threaten the core unity of our party.

61. This has proved a successful strategy for a number of reasons:

61.1. It is founded on the reality of our areas of agreement on policy, especially on the constitution.

61.2. It provides a solid base on which to build the reforms which those who voted for us wished to see and which we have always said were for the good of the country.

61.3. It is what we said we would do in the election.

61.4. It increases our bargaining power.

61.5. It gives us maximum freedom of movement in the most fluid and unpredictable period of politics in recent history.

61.6. It is the only strategy around which it has proved possible for the party to unite.

62. *The essence of this strategy is that we decide; and the basis on which we decide is what is good for us and will deliver the things we believe in.*

63. There will be those who wish to see this strategy changed at Southport

in order to limit our room for manoeuvre by curtailing the extent of partnership with Labour before the next election.

64. I will resist this strongly, because it would:

64.1. Diminish at a stroke our bargaining power, with much of the constitutional agenda, including crucially PR and Blair's attitude to it, still to be delivered.

64.2. Limit our room for manoeuvre at a time when the possibility of splits in the other parties makes the future highly unpredictable.

64.3. Create circumstances where doors we close after divisive debate this spring, may have to be re-opened by a further divisive debate just before the next election.

64.4. Send a message to the public that we were more interested in our own purity than in exercising maximum influence when we get the chance.

64.5. Destructively divide the party by abandoning the current consensus to which both 'sides' can subscribe.

64.6. Give a deliberately negative impression of our attitude to the government, rendering future constructive co-operation much more difficult and, in effect, making the abandonment of our policy of 'constructive opposition' inevitable . . .

65. However, I recognize that there will be many who are nervous about how much further we can go in the present direction. I therefore intend to make it clear that our present strategy will be subject to a 'double lock'.

65.1. The first lock is that the decisions that we take about how, where and at what level we may in the future co-operate with Labour will be driven solely by the extent to which we can progress *our* policy agenda, which extends beyond PR, but in which PR is the irreducible minimum. There can never be any question of co-operation where it merely provides a Liberal Democrat 'add-on' to get through an exclusively Labour agenda.

65.2. And the second lock is that any change of either direction or substance in our strategy will only be done with the specific and active agreement of the Party, operating through its constitutional procedures.

65.3. The Southport debate will be a crucial and difficult one. I do not believe that it would be appropriate for the Parliamentary Party to take a binding collective decision on this. Individuals should be free to take and argue their own positions. But I shall, of course, be proposing this strategy, which I hope the Parliamentary Party as a whole will support, both at Southport and in the party consultation sessions beforehand.

Appendix E

The Situation on the Ground

1. *Military Action in Kosovo*

1. I was able to observe the military action in Kosovo from the high ground on the Albanian–Kosovan border, North of Djakovica. Over a period of four hours, we were able to observe extensive shelling and mortaring on Kosovan farmhouses. The Serbs were using, I estimate, heavy 120 mm mortars. There was also extensive use of tanks to shell villages and of machine-gun fire from both light and heavy machine-guns. I was also able to observe a Serb unit using, I believe, medium mortars to, it is thought, bombard what are believed to be refugee gathering points and camps in the forests close to the frontier.

2. At no time did I observe any return fire, though ECMM monitors earlier in the day say they saw heavy machine-gun fire returned from one of the villages under bombardment, which was quickly silenced by Serb tanks.

3. So far as I could tell, the Kosovan villages being attacked were empty of inhabitants and the Serb activity seemed to be aimed at destruction, or possibly, interdiction against perceived attacking points for the KLA.

4. We were able to observe a number of Serb units. These included a possible Company Headquarters, with APCs positioned outside, a fixed position on an exposed hilltop of about platoon strength, with trenches and weapon pits, containing perhaps three heavy mortars, a tank in support near by, occasionally firing at a more distant village, and, in a different position, a medium mortar position perched on the skyline of a mountain ridge. All the positions we saw were exposed, uncamouflaged and would be very vulnerable to air attack.

5. The mountain ridges along which the Albanian–Kosovo border runs provide superb secure observation locations which command the whole southern Kosovo valley.

2. *Arms from Albania*
1. Despite protests to the contrary it is clear that very large supplies of small and medium armaments are passing through northern Albania to the KLA. They appear to be purchased actually in the area close to the border and then backpacked or taken by mule over the more secure high mountain passes into Kosovo at night.

3. *The Albanian Police and Border Security Forces*
1. These are hopelessly under-equipped for the task they have to do. Even if they were serious about imposing the rule of law in the border areas they haven't the equipment to do so . . .

4. *Humanitarian*
1. The flow of refugees into Bajram Curi has all but stopped. Only two or three families are arriving per day. However, over recent months some 15,000 have come in, nearly doubling the population in this small, very poor alpine valley . . .
2. There are, however, tensions. Kosovars are not liked in Albania . . .
3. The hospital is woefully equipped, especially in terms of equipment for operations . . .
4. The refugees who are arriving are usually exhausted. Typically, they will have been subject first to Serb harassment in their home villages. At this stage the men will be taken away and either beaten and tortured or, occasionally, it is said, shot. If this doesn't move the villagers, then their houses are subjected to small-arms and machine-gun fire. Finally, tanks and artillery are brought to bear. The houses are then burnt or destroyed and the animals killed, to prevent the Kosovars coming back. The refugee families then make for the mountain forests, travelling at night over the high passes to avoid mines and ambushes . . . There is a fear that one reason why the flood of refugees has stopped is that, with the passes increasingly blocked by the Serbs, there are several thousands sheltering in the forests on the Kosovo side, too frightened to cross. UNHCR are especially worried about this possibility, but there is, as yet, no reliable proof of the existence of this group of 'hidden' refugees . . .

7. Infrastructure

There is little or no usable railway infrastructure in Albania and the roads are appalling. If anything, worse than Bosnia. Travelling the 140-odd kilometres from Tirana to the northern border takes seven hours. The mountains are formidable and the roads at best bumpy and at worst precarious and collapsing along on the edge of vertiginous drops. The logistic maintenance by road of forces of any size in Northern Albania would be a nightmare in summer and completely impossible without massive engineering resources in winter.

What we should do

1. The Problem

There are two ways to detonate a new, probably wider Balkan war. By failing to stop the expansion of pan-Serb nationalism. And failing to prevent the growth of pan-Albanian nationalism. In shorthand, we have to stop Milosevic, without launching Berisha.

It is a serious misjudgement to believe this is a re-run of Bosnia. There may be lessons we can learn from Bosnia, but the situation is substantially different in a number of key areas, not least the fact that the danger of a wider conflagration is greater, our military options fewer and our diplomatic room for manoeuvre much more constrained.

2. The Aim

To persuade both President Milosevic and the KLA that there is not a military solution to Kosovo, only a political one. And to achieve this without any change in borders.

3. Timing

There is, possibly, a month to six weeks to get a grip on the situation before it is likely to become increasingly unmanageable. This situation could come even earlier, if a Serb assault in the South, in the Kacanik area, creates a flood of refugees into Macedonia.

4. The Means

1. Strengthening the fixed points. There are two fixed points in this otherwise dangerously fluid situation: Macedonia and Albania under its present government. We should strengthen both of these, by supporting their

governments and encouraging their growing identity of view about what should be done . . .

2. A regional solution sponsored and policed by the international community. I don't believe the Dayton approach of 'holding the ring' while the protagonists produce their own solution stands any prospect of success within the timescale necessary. The international community will have to formulate, promote, if necessary insist on and ultimately police its own plan, based on autonomy for Kosovo along the lines already enjoyed by Montenegro . . .

3. Persuading Milosevic. The international community should accept that it is their responsibility to secure President Milosevic's agreement to this. Sanctions can be tightened, if it is thought this will help (which I doubt). One option might be to make it clear to those (including Milosevic's family and friends) who benefit economically from breaking sanctions that we are, as with drug money, prepared to pursue and seize their economic holdings abroad. The international community should insist on a return to bilateral negotiations between Rugova and Milosevic, only this time with its own representatives in the room and alternate meeting places in Belgrade and Pristina. But ultimately, as we have learned from Bosnia, diplomacy with Milosevic works better if backed by the credible use of force . . .

4. Controlling the KLA. The Albanian government appear to be prepared to play an active role in this, particularly when it comes to persuading the KLA and Kosovar politicians that there is no question of full Kosovan independence in the foreseeable future (the Helsinki principles must apply). They should be encouraged and helped to do so.

5. Military deployments. UNPRODEP should be reinforced, if only for symbolic reasons. A NATO deployment, for the same reasons would be useful, but, in my view, not currently essential in Albania. But this should, chiefly for logistical reasons, be in central Albania, not forward on the border.

Appendix F

Dear Tony,

I promised you some thoughts on Kosovo. These are attached. No doubt your own people will have much more up-to-date ideas; I fear these are rather mundane.

I fear, also, that events are well ahead of us all – again.

Yours
Paddy

Kosovo

1. *Regional Problem – Regional Solution*

1.1. Kosovo has certain superficial resemblances to Bosnia. The cause of the crisis is Serbian nationalism, fanned by Milosevic. And the international community has made many of the same early mistakes.

1.2. But Kosovo is not Bosnia. It is both more complex and more dangerous. Bosnia could be 'cordoned off' as a problem within the ex-Federal Republic of Yugoslavia. But Kosovo could ignite a regional conflict beyond the Balkans, involving NATO members.

1.3. The detonator may be Kosovo, but the bomb is Macedonia.

1.4. And there are two fuses: one in Belgrade and the other in Albania.

1.5. The Kosovo problem is, therefore, a regional problem, which needs a regional solution – one which does for the southern Balkan statelets and nations what Dayton did for the northern ones.

2. *The Problem*

2.1. The 'bomb' goes off if we act either insufficiently to prevent the triumph of pan-Serb nationalism, or in such a way as to enable the triumph of pan-Albanian nationalism.

3. *The Aim*

3.1. To persuade both sides that they cannot have a military solution, only a political one.

4. *The Present Situation*

4.1. Milosevic was told by NATO to use restraint or risk the use of force. He did so, and immediately started losing. So he has recommended full-scale military operations in Kosovo. He is now using excessive force to an extent which, a few weeks ago, would have brought instant threats of NATO retaliation. But we are tacitly acquiescing to this, because it is one way to prevent an outright KLA victory, which we also fear. We hope that, in the military stalemate, there will be a better chance for a peace based on a political settlement.

4.2. In effect, we are, tacitly, using Milosevic's tanks to help us curb the ambitions of the KLA.

4.3. This is an excessively dangerous policy. At best it diminishes our leverage, both with Milosevic and with the Albanian Kosovars. At worst it could (and in my view shortly will) be overtaken either by a flood of refugees out of the forests of central and southern Kosovo (the UN are now reporting 200,000, with winter only a few months away) into, especially, Albania. Or major disturbances amongst the Albanian population of Macedonia. Or both. If the first happens, public opinion will force our hand to, probably, overhasty action. If the latter, the destablization of Macedonia will do the same thing.

5. *The Solution*

5.1. *Not Dayton.* In Dayton, the West 'held the ring', while the protagonists agreed a solution. There is neither the time nor the necessary war weariness among the protagonists for this process to succeed in Kosovo. If a solution is to be found, the international community will have to lay down their own plan and then aim policy at obtaining the warring parties' agreement to it. At present we are pursuing policy in a vacuum.

5.2. *Containment.* The first task is to prevent the conflict spreading. This means taking urgent action in both Macedonia and Albania.

5.3. *Preventing infection into Macedonia.* This is the flash-point. The international community must make it clear to all sides that we are, if necessary, prepared to act to prevent external interference, overt or covert, with the integrity of the Macedonian state and/or its borders. Further strengthening UNPREDEP is one way of doing this. Making it clear to the Macedonian government that the international community will take responsibility for any flood of Albanian Kosovar refugees into Macedonia would be another.

5.4. *Preventing contagion from Albania*. In Albania the problem is the reverse. It is to stop the instability of Albania fanning the flames of Kosovo. The lawlessness of northern Albania provides both a power base for those, like Sali Berisha, who aim to destabilize the current (and constructive) Albanian government, as well as a corridor for arms and support for the KLA. The recent Cabinet paper [that you sent me] complained that we have no leverage over the KLA. This is wrong. If the international community were to make it clear that we will back the present Albanian government in re-establishing the rule of law in northern Albania, then we would at once be backing a government which is trying to follow a helpful policy while, at the same time, gaining control of the flow of arms and materiel on which the KLA depend. This is the best way to persuade the KLA to reconnect with their politicians and accept a political solution. In short, if the threat of NATO aircraft is our means to control Milosevic, then the control of northern Albania, and the arms that flow through it, performs the same function for the KLA. This does not require massive deployments of Western troops. Some decent police equipment, backed by extra numbers of Albanian security forces, would make a huge, and probably speedy, difference at minuscule cost compared to a deployment of Western troops. There may be a case for a symbolic international troop deployment in Albania, but these should be kept well away from border areas.

5.5. *The status of Kosovo*. A couple of weeks ago, when the KLA were ascendant, I doubted that we could get the Albanian Kosovars to accept anything less than full independence. Some say their aspirations may have been reduced by Milosevic's tanks. I am not so sure. I don't know of many occasions in the Balkans, and especially not with Albanians, where blood has made people more reasonable. I suspect that we may, in the end, have to accept full independence for Kosovo. But this will be easier, the more stable we are able to make Macedonia and Albania. In the first instance, however, Kosovo should be offered no more than parallel status with Montenegro, with strong safeguards for minorities (in this case Serbs) and a Dayton-style deployment to reassure Kosovars that Milosevic will not again be allowed to undermine this. Full independence can be held out as an ultimate, possible goal, within a broader regional settlement.

5.6. *The use of force.* Once there is a clear plan, we will have a better idea what we may have to use force for. The worry is that the initial threshold for the use of force may be set too high. The higher the threshold, the more difficult it is to cross, politically. I hope the military people are able to come up with a small first step, as a token of our resolve. But I understand how difficult this is. You know my view about a UN resolution. I would much rather have one than not. But the Russians remain a problem. And, anyway, I suspect time may soon shorten our options. I hope the lawyers are already advising what actions we can take now to start building up a case for action under Articles 1 or 52 [of the UN Charter]. The humanitarian threat is deepening by the day and winter is coming.

6. *Conclusion*

6.1. A regional solution, guaranteed by the regional powers and the international community.

6.2. The international community must put down its own plan.

6.3. First strengthen the 'fixed points' (Albania and Macedonia).

6.4. Autonomy, not independence for Kosovo, underpinned by a Dayton-style deployment.

6.5. Threaten force to back the plan, but make the threshold as low as possible and start building the case for action under the UN Charter, but without a full Security Council resolution.

Appendix G

Programme

2. *The Military Situation*

2.1. The current situation

While I was there the Yugoslav army was ending its operation in the Drenica area and shifting it to the Suvo Reka region, south-east of Pristina. President Milosevic told me that the operations had ended. I told him this was not so, as I had seen myself. However, since the main Yugoslav objectives have now been achieved, I anticipate that Yugoslav operations will end very shortly and their main units will return to barracks, so as to give no pretext for NATO action.

8. *What We Should Do*

8.1. Military action. Troops on the ground in this phase would not, I believe, be militarily possible. Though they will be needed to guarantee a ceasefire and oversee the transitional phase that Hill envisages. With the weather closing in and Yugoslav troops returning to barracks having achieved their objectives, it is almost too late to use air power, too. However the air-power option should be maintained on a 'hair trigger' and used if Milosevic does not stop his current operations or returns to the use of excessive force. In due course, this is bound to happen. The KLA have not gone away, are likely to reoccupy the ground they have lost and will certainly return to (more effective) aggressive action.

8.2. Urgent and unfettered access must be provided for accredited UN aid agencies and diplomatic observers to *all* refugee or Internally Displaced Persons (IDP) sites. I was stopped by Serb police, in the company of the UNHCR and a British Embassy diplomatic representative, from accessing a reported 18,000 IDPs in the middle of a battle zone 'for our own safety'. This cannot be allowed to continue. The humanitarian drive should be to get people back to their homes as quickly as possible, after which large-scale resources will be required to make these habitable and to heat them. Since, in most of western Kosovo, the crops have not been harvested and the Serbs have been deliberately targeting grain supplies, it is likely that food will also be a problem through the winter.

8.3. The Hill plan offers the only realistic proposal on the table. It will need some adjustment to take a more intermediate position between the Serbs and the Albanians. But it should be supported. There is not time to 'do a Dayton', where the West held the ring while the protagonists produced their own solution. This time the West must put its own plan on the table, together with appropriate sticks and carrots to encourage acceptance from both sides. This needs to be based around a ceasefire, an interim period, greater autonomy for Kosovo along the lines of a 'third republic' and a strong and enforceable framework to protect minority rights (in this case those of the Serb population in Kosovo). We should not exclude outright independence for Kosovo as a long-term aim, even if we cannot yet foresee circumstances when it would be wise or safe to achieve it.

8.4. But Kosovo is not just a Yugoslav problem. It is a regional one and will need a regional solution. There will be no point in stabilizing Kosovo if, in particular, Albania (but also Macedonia) remain in such a precarious state. Action to support the present Albanian government against the mischief of Berisha is important, especially to enable Tirana to regain effective control of the border area of Tropoje, which is, at once, Berisha's home and the area through which the main route for arms to the KLA passes. Regaining control of this area would diminish the power of Berisha and give us real leverage over the KLA.

8.5. The Hague trials have had a profound effect on senior Serbs. If it is now too late to use military sanctions against the Serbs for their latest actions, then Britain should ask the International Court to investigate the recent Serb operations in Drenica and Suvo Reka and, if appropriate, take action against any guilty parties. I believe that this would have a profound effect, both on local military commanders and on their political directors in Belgrade, and could make them think twice about doing it again.

Appendix H

Dear—

You will recall that I have for some time indicated that the outcome of the Jenkins report and the government's reaction to it might require a change in the relationship between ourselves and the government. I promised that, if I thought this necessary, I would make some proposals to you for consultation and decision, first by the Parliamentary Party and then by the party at large.

I now believe that, in the light of Jenkins, we should revisit our policy of 'constructive opposition'.

First, the subject we all like not to talk about. You can never say never in politics. I have always thought that a coalition in this parliament was unlikely. It is now, in my view, inconceivable this side of the General Election.

We must also consider, at this stage, what steps we can take which will make it more likely that those (at all levels, including, it appears, the Prime Minister) in the Labour Party and the government who support PR and will press for an early referendum, win the argument.

However, the eventual delivery of PR will make coalition government more likely, at some time in the future and in some form, and this will almost certainly be based on a partnership between us and Labour. We will have to show that this new, more partnership-based politics which PR will encourage can provide reliable government which benefits the country – and the more we can show this before a PR referendum, the more we are likely to win that referendum.

Having reviewed these factors, I have concluded that it is now right for us, in the aftermath of Jenkins, to consolidate and widen our policy of 'constructive opposition', expanding the number of areas where we work with the government whilst maintaining clear areas of differentiation and opposition to the government where we disagree with them.

Alan Beith has agreed that we should discuss this at the Parliamentary Party Meeting tonight. At that meeting I shall propose that we should now:

1. Agree that if the Prime Minister and the government hold to the line they have outlined on Jenkins – as prefigured in the Cook/Maclennan agreement – then 'constructive opposition' should be confirmed as the strategy of the party for the remainder of this parliament.

2. Agree, in principle, to widen the scope of the JCC, where we believe that by so doing we can (i) enable Liberal Democrat ideas and policies to be applied in government, (ii) benefit our party, and (iii) contribute to Britain's national interest.

You will recall that the resolution passed at our Southport Conference this year calls for a widening of the JCC remit to be preceded by a process of consultation with the Party at large. This proposal will therefore be discussed at the forthcoming 'special' FE on 16 November.

I am sending this letter now so that you can have time to consider these proposals in advance of tonight's meeting and so that those colleagues who wish to have time to discuss them with me.

Both the Prime Minister and I believe that it is right, before we take this step of extending co-operation between our two parties, that people have a clear understanding of why we are taking it and the benefits we believe it can bring to our country, as well as to our two parties. We also believe people should be aware of our view on the importance and future potential of the long-term relationship between our two parties.

It is for this reason that the Prime Minister and I have agreed that the attached statement should be released later this afternoon.

I have no doubt that, after the release of the attached joint statement to the press, you will, before our meeting tonight, be approached for comment. I cannot stop people commenting and would not wish to try. However, I believe that the best course of action is to refrain from any comment until we have had a full discussion amongst ourselves in the Parliamentary Party, on all the above.

Please ensure that the 4.00pm press embargo on this letter and the attachment is strictly observed. Neither of these documents should be shown or distributed outside the membership of the Parliamentary Party until after that time.

I look forward to seeing you later this evening.

Yours
Paddy

Appendix I

Dear Colleague

I want to tell you of a decision which I took some time ago, but which I am announcing today [20 January 1999].

After what will have been a very happy and productive eleven years as leader, the tasks I set myself to achieve for the party are now nearing completion. I therefore told our Chief Whip, Paul Tyler, before Christmas that it was my intention, early in the New Year, to inform our president, Diana Maddock, that I planned to stand down after the elections of this May and June.

This is not a new decision. Jane and I resolved, before the last election, that I would not fight another, either as leader of the Party or as MP for Yeovil. Indeed, when I was first elected for Yeovil in 1983, I promised myself that I would not do the job beyond my sixtieth birthday and would stand down no later than the first General Election after that date.

I believe that judgement was right.

Exhausting though they can sometimes be, I have been very proud to be the Member of Parliament for my community and leader of our party. But I have a clear idea how both these jobs ought to be done and no wish to do either after the point where I feel I can do them justice.

So, after the General Election of 1997, I decided that I ought to stand down no later than mid-1999, in order to give my successor time before the next election.

But before stepping down, I wanted to complete a number of tasks, to ensure an orderly handover. These were:

1. To consolidate the Party's electoral position after the General Election.

2. To establish the policy of 'constructive opposition', which we adopted after the election, on a firm foundation.

3. To begin the process of widening the areas of co-operation in the context of 'constructive opposition' to other areas, where these are to our advantage.

4. To secure the Party's finances.

5. To see the legislation for the first nationwide PR election (for the European elections) safely passed into law.

6. To set – and have accepted by the Party – a strategy which best ensures that we play our role as participants, not bystanders, in the programme of modernization which I believe necessary for our country; which gives us the best chance of fair votes for Westminster; and which opens the way to the reshaping of British politics, which has been the aim of my leadership since the Chard Speech, more than seven years ago.

Last Thursday, the European Elections Bill received the Royal Assent and, on the same day, we reaffirmed and expanded 'constructive opposition' to include co-operation with the government on a Common European Foreign and Security Policy.

So these tasks have now been, substantially, completed. There are still, however, this year's elections to fight.

The mid-term elections in May and June are the key electoral test in this parliament and I am looking forward to fighting them with you. After which I shall formally stand down and make way for my successor.

I have decided that it is right for me to announce these intentions now, so that the preparations for the election of a new leader can be put in hand in an orderly fashion, rather than being an uncomfortable mixture of haste and surprise, as they so often are. The leadership election will also, as has always been my wish, provide an opportunity for the party to confirm democratically the strategy I have set for the future.

This has not been an easy decision to make. I would not, for anything, have missed the privilege of leading the Liberal Democrats for the past decade or so. It has been, quite simply, the best thing I have done in my life. I am deeply grateful to you all for the trust you have placed in me and for the unfailing help and support you have given me, especially when I made mistakes!

I shall lay all this down with great sadness. But also with some sense of achievement.

For Jane and myself, however, this will be a chance to rediscover parts of our life with our family and friends which have had to be pushed to the margins in these past hectic years.

I shall also look forward to continuing to work for the party under our new leader.

No doubt there will also be new challenges to seek out. I do not know what they will be yet. But, I do know that, love this calling though I do, I have never been so obsessive about politics that I see it as the only thing there is in my life!

As for the Party, we are in the fortunate position of having potential leadership candidates of high ability and enthusiasm to take the Party on to fresh achievements. There will, I know, be many new opportunities which a new leader with fresh energy and new ideas will be best able to grasp.

There will be time for goodbyes in due course. For now we have one task on which we must exclusively concentrate. To campaign and win in May and June.

As you know, I love campaigning and this will be my last as leader of the Party – so I intend to enjoy myself and, with your help, give my successor the best possible start for continuing success in the future.

Yours

Rt Hon Paddy Ashdown MP

Appendix J

EXTRACTS FROM A REPORT ON MY VISIT
TO THE BALKANS, 18–22 APRIL 1999

'My people are frightened, because they think NATO has a plan and they are not being told about it. I am even more frightened, because I know NATO hasn't got a plan.'

Ljubco Georgievski, Prime Minister of Macedonia, 21 April 1999

Summary of conclusions

1. I came to the Balkans concerned about the slow progress of the conduct of this war. I leave frightened that all the ingredients are now in place for us to lose it.

2. It is said that we are winning this war. I have, as yet, seen no evidence for that and a great deal of evidence that Milosevic is *not* losing it. I am unable to say to what extent his forces have been damaged, especially on the ground in Kosovo – though I suspect that this is less, and progressing less quickly, then we would like to believe.

3. What is clear, however, is that, after thirty days of war, we have yet to stop Milosevic taking any action that he wanted to take, or made him take any action that he did not want to take. He has retained the initiative in almost all areas. Describing his 'peace overtures' as signs of weakness are nonsense – they were always planned and widely predicted, not least by us. Similarly, claims that his attempts to widen the conflict show he is under pressure are fanciful. He has not even begun to use the full capacity he has to disrupt our rear areas (he has not yet used terrorism against our bases, for instance) – which is one of the key aims of any successful war commander.

Political

4. Nevertheless, he is being successful at what he has already attempted. Hostility to NATO troops in Macedonia is rising, with regular and increasingly serious stoning of NATO soldiers and vehicles. The Macedonian government, already fragile and getting more so, is demanding a higher price for supporting NATO. And in the key NATO supply port of Thessaloniki in Greece, feelings against NATO troops have caused orders to be recently issued [by NATO] that resupply convoys should travel only at night.

5. I am unable to gauge what damage we are doing to Milosevic's rear areas. But whereas political support in his rear areas appears to be, if anything, hardening, political support in ours is weakening. This process is not helped by NATO's clumsiness in dealing with the relevant governments, especially in Macedonia.

6. None of this is irrecoverable, but unless we can turn the tide and point out, again especially to Macedonia, which is our key rear area, why there is long-term advantage to them in supporting NATO and Europe, there could be severe difficulty in persuading them to continue to provide the support the ground operation needs to remain operationally effective, in the face of the short-term problems, especially political and economic ones, which this is causing them.

7. If Milosevic continues to win the battle for our rear areas, then it is not impossible to envisage a situation where the battle for Kosovo is lost and NATO forced to withdraw, without even a shot being fired.

Military

8. There is uncertainty on the ground amongst our military commanders about what they are being asked to do and what happens next. Their mission and make-up remain based on Rambouillet, even though this has long been left behind us. Morale is high and the sense of determination very evident. But they know that an opposed ground operation, in one form or another, is now increasingly likely. They are not, however, equipped for this, have not been asked to plan for it, even as a contingency, and do not know what their aim is or is likely to be. If the Rambouillet mission and posture has been overtaken by events (which they do know), what should they be preparing for now?

9. Meanwhile, time ticks away and the Serbs continue to defensively strengthen ground, which already strongly favours the defenders.

10. NATO has, at most, a month to make up its mind what it wants to do, if there is to be any prospect of a successful completion of a Kosovo operation before next winter. NATO must also decide where any Kosovo ground operation would be mounted from. Macedonia has the right infrastructure, but the wrong politics. Albania has the right politics but hopeless infrastructure. Both can be overcome, but not without a lot of work that ought to have started already.

11. NATO must also decide what its attitude to the KLA will be. I believe we should take a risk with them as I am now convinced that the moderates are, in the main, in charge, that they have a clear if limited military utility and, crudely, that the more we are able sensibly to use them the more effective our air operations will be and the fewer casualties we will take when the ground action starts. At present there is a dangerous ambivalence about our approach to the KLA, which is confusing commanders, prevents us using the KLA effectively, and is beginning to attract from them charges of betrayal which could turn them back to radicalism.

12. Finally, NATO will have to decide which options it is prepared to allow its commanders to consider. The easiest entry into Kosovo would be through the Presovo valley. But this means going in through Serbia. Are we prepared to do this? What about Romania, Bulgaria, Hungary? And if so, do we want Belgrade? My own view is that we can fight the Serbs in Kosovo, but not in Serbia. I think to most Serbs Kosovo is no longer a homeland – it's a monument. Serbia proper, however, would be an entirely different proposition.

Humanitarian

13. The humanitarian situation also gives great cause for concern.

14. It was only because Milosevic shut the Albanian border last week that the little northern Albanian town of Kukes was not completely overwhelmed. If this had happened, we would have had the terrible spectacle of refugees dying in NATO's hands.

15. UNHCR completely lost control of the situation in Macedonia about a week ago. Their performance here has been, by common consent, lamentable. There is a desperate need for proper co-ordination, especially of the NGOs. Had it not been for NATO's intervention in Macedonia, there would have been catastrophe here, too.

16. There must also be concern about what will happen in the camps in a few months' time, if there is no visible progress in Kosovo. These are not Somalis or Ethiopians. The Macedonian camps, in particular, contain the

intelligentsia of Pristina, among the brightest and best in the southern Balkans – doctors, engineers, professors abound. But they are all being treated the same. Aid agency doctors, plumbers and engineers are doing things for them. They are not being allowed to do things for themselves. This is not a problem at the present. The patience and dignity with which the Kosovars are bearing their pain is almost unbearable to see. They all queue patiently and politely. There is courtesy, helpfulness and politeness for all. And almost no stealing. One aid worker said to me, 'This is the only refugee camp in the world where I can put down my shovel and still find it there a day later.'

17. But what will this be like after two/three/four more months, when hope turns to despair and impatience?

18. Milosevic has always used refugees as instruments of war. And in this battle, too, I see no clear sign yet that we are winning. War normally produces refugees as its by-product. This is the first war in history that is being fought *for* refugees. And we have set ourselves an unforgiving measure for judging its success. If they don't go back, we have lost.

Conclusions

19. Overall, this war is not going well.

20. We are beginning to be hemmed in by time. I am not convinced that we are degrading Milosevic's forces on the ground in Kosovo at anything like the speed that is necessary. His rear areas remain firm, while ours are looking decidedly shaky. There is now an increasing likelihood of having to conduct an opposed entry into Kosovo, but no clear decisions on this are forthcoming and the necessary preparations have not even been started, even on a contingency basis. NATO's military are uncertain about what they are being asked to do and the refugee situation, though better in the short term, has not been stabilized and remains vulnerable both to further floods of refugees, whenever Milosevic chooses to release them, and, in the long term, to despair in the camps as this operation drags on and on without visible results . . .

Appendix K

First of all, many congratulations.

Leading our party is the best thing I have done, or will do, in my life.

I hope at the end of your time you will feel the same way.

The purpose of this note is to act as a window on my very personal thoughts and to act as an agenda for our discussions, which I hope will take place shortly after you are elected.

Accompanying this note are two files.

1. A file containing outstanding matters, chiefly engagements which, as the new leader of the party, you might like to consider.

2. A large file of over 100 pages containing highly confidential extracts from my diary detailing some, but not all, of my meetings/conversations with the Prime Minister and others in the government over the last few months. It would be highly embarrassing to me if these got out – so they are for your eyes only and should, please, be destroyed after you have read them.

What I have tried to give you in these extracts is a flavour of the kind of relationship which he and I had, which I hope will serve as a background for you when you talk to him, and a synopsis of the main areas of contention still outstanding; and some indication of what I think is going through his mind on dealing with the party under your leadership.

I hope these are helpful.

To the main substantive items I would like to discuss with you.

1. Relationships with Tony Blair and with the government

This is the biggest early thing you will have to deal with and forms by far the largest portion of this note.

I think you will get a fairly early approach from him, possibly within a few days of your election. He will probably want to have a generalized discussion first with the purpose of 'getting to know each other's minds'. However, I would not be surprised if he made a concrete proposal to you fairly soon. You must decide how to handle this.

You will see from the attached extracts that I have discussed with him the possibility of PR for local government. I have made it clear that if this is to be achieved then it should be for you to obtain it, not me. But I suspect that if he is going to give on this (he has recently told me he has 'an open mind' on it), he will want something in return. Taking a more relaxed attitude to the timing of the PR referendum could be part of it (in our interest anyway, I think). But I expect he will also seek some widening of the JCC.

At the last meeting of the JCC (27 July) we agreed not to have another until after the conference season. FoI is the big issue.

It might be helpful if I outlined the history of our relationship and what has happened during it.

The whole thing started at a dinner at Anthony Lester's house on 14 July 1993, before John Smith died. We got on well and agreed that we would need good relationships between the parties if there were ever a hung parliament.

Since then we have met very regularly. My diaries and notes from these meetings amount to nearly half a million words!

When Smith died, the relationship took off and we worked very closely together, co-ordinating our campaigns, including attacks on Major at PMQs, to a much greater extent than anyone has ever realized.

In the 1997 General Election we co-ordinated our targeting and attacks on the Tories very closely to maximize the effect of tactical voting.

It has been estimated that because of this we increased the Tory defeat by around fifty seats, of which we were, of course, considerable beneficiaries.

My thinking on this has been very simple:

1. I think it has been and will continue to be to our electoral advantage to co-operate with Labour. We won more seats in the GE as a result of the strategy and stand a better chance of holding on to those seats we have or

even increasing them in the next GE, if we continue with it. The reason for this is plain. In the vast majority of our seats, the Tories are our main challengers. The game last time was to get Labour voters in those seats to vote for us, partly because of fear of the Tories, partly because they thought it was a way of voting for a Labour government. They did so in very large numbers. At the next election the biggest threat to our seats will be that those Labour voters, no longer frightened of the Tories because they aren't going to get back in, will go home to Labour because they like the Labour government and want to express their pride in voting for it. That is what happened in Taunton in May when Jackie Ballard's council lost control (c.f. Yeovil, where we still comfortably beat the Tories). The trick for us, therefore, is to act in a way that persuades Labour voters in our held and Tory target seats that voting for us is not just voting for the continuation of the Labour government which they want, *but better than that because we are stronger on the environment, public services, etc.*

2. I happen to believe that British politics is going through a major reshaping in our direction and the new liberal/centre left grouping will be the dominant governing force of our time. I want us to be in the middle of this, not out of it. Particularly since the ideas at its core are ours. Since Baldwin and before, the Tories have been scared to death that 'these two will get together' (to use Baldwin's phrase). They are right to be frightened.

3. Blair is, anyway, intent on occupying our ground. The position he wants to adopt is that of the SDP in the 1987 election or the Lib Dems in the 1992 one. He has decided that he wants us as partners, because this creates the new centre/left grouping, beyond the tribal ramparts of Labour that he wants to create. He describes this to me as one of the two great things he wishes to achieve in his premiership. Only at our last JCC he reiterated his view that he wanted to continue with this plan with you – in part because he believes it is right, but chiefly because he is convinced that it is beneficial for both parties electorally. But if we choose to reverse the co-operation between the two parties, then he will revert to plan B, that is, to take over our territory and policies and make us irrelevant. He has made it explicitly clear that he will try to do this – an option prefigured by Philip Gould. And he has, in my view, both the strength and the appeal to do so.

In short, I believe that the strategy I have pursued is the only strategy for the party because it is the only one which delivers tangible electoral benefits and avoids the potential danger of having the ground cut from under our feet.

There is a view around that we can benefit in the future because Blair will become more and more unpopular as the election approaches. He will with the Tories, of course. But that doesn't help us. With our core voters and with swing Labour ones, I don't think he will become more unpopular at all – quite the contrary. Not many of our voters share our liberal enthusiasms – as Chris Rennard has shown, they are more interested in schools and hospitals. And here, they have been through the worst. Labour have huge sums of money to throw at both. Indeed, I have seen calculations which indicate that, given a little luck, they could greatly increase spending on health and education and cut taxes as well.

Finally, the abandonment of a strategy of co-operation with the government on our areas of policy, together with the consequent takeover of these areas by Blair, would leave us only one place to go – the high-tax, high-spending left. This is not a place from which we are likely to hold on to, let alone win more, Tory seats and votes. I have never quite understood why those in the party most opposed to close co-operation with Labour are also those who would most like to adopt policies closest to those Labour have abandoned, and who represent seats which they won or want to win from the Tories!

As to where our relationship with Labour is heading, Blair has always made it clear that he sees this as merger. I have always made it clear that merger is off the cards for as far ahead as I can see. Although I cannot say what might happen in fifteen years' time, say, having worked together in Scotland and then maybe in the government at Westminster. But for the moment it is a non-starter.

What I did hope to do, however, was take the party into partnership government with Labour – something which we both referred to as 'crossing the Rubicon'.

It is now generally known that we planned this straight after the election but judged that the Labour majority was too big (a judgement we both now regret – never make big decisions on election day). What is not known is that we planned to 'cross the Rubicon' on two occasions since then, in the autumn of 1997 and again the autumn of 1998, after the publication of the Jenkins report. In the end Blair decided on both occasions (almost certainly correctly) that he couldn't carry the Cabinet. I may not have been able to carry our party either, but I was prepared to try. Nevertheless, the planning was very advanced, even down to the coalition programme we would have introduced.

On almost our first meeting after the election, I told Blair that I wasn't going to fight the next election come what may. I wanted to 'cross the Rubicon' with him but to go no further – I did not want a Cabinet post. But if he decided it couldn't be done this parliament, then I would stand down pretty immediately in order to leave my successor enough time to get established before the next election. Which is what happened when our plans to take this final step after Jenkins fell.

And now for the future.

I have explained why I think my strategy is the only one which makes any sense for us.

Nevertheless, I think the 'project' is, to all intents and purposes, dead in the water.

Unless it expands its remit, the JCC will become redundant. There is not enough constitutional work to keep it going beyond early next year. And anyway, Blair is not, I think, interested in it if we are not prepared to widen to the domestic agenda.

You will see from the attached diary extracts that I have made it clear to Blair that he will have to give the whole process some momentum if it is not to be lost. I think, given what happened over Jenkins, you should leave him to do this. The next move is his. But if he does, you must decide how to react.

Meanwhile, we are languishing in no man's land – which is not a place it is wise to rest long, not least because you tend to get shot at from both sides.

I think you have two options.

One will be easier to carry with the Party. But leads, I believe, to a return to oppositionism and a momentum from our activists which you will find difficult to resist, towards policies and a position which, though dearer to our hearts, will make us less and less electable in the Tory areas we must win.

The other will be bold, difficult and risky, but carries huge dividends.

The first means allowing the JCC to wither on the vine and let the gap between us and Labour widen in the hope of capitalizing on Blair's 'growing unpopularity' by creating 'clear orange (for which I fear we all too often mean left) water'.

The second, more difficult, route is to head towards a position where Labour and ourselves go into the next election on a 'joint heads of agreement' manifesto (including, essentially, commitments to PR) with the intention of facilitating, whether openly or not, a coalition afterwards. Blair is up for this and, if I were to have fought the next election, it is the route I would have followed. It will be *very* difficult for you – perhaps impossible. But it will yield the greatest dividends in return of MPs; genuinely 'break the mould'. And it will also mean that you will do what I had hoped to do – lead the Party into government while changing for ever the shape of British politics.

2. The Conference

I wish you great joy with the leader's speech which used to hang across my summer holidays like a malevolent shadow! But I am sure you will have less trouble with this than me – I hated the speechmaking.

Just for your information, however, I have refused all speaking engagements at Conference (though I have agreed to chair two meetings). I understand that I have a brief farewell speech to make, but I intend to do no more than say good bye as elegantly as I can.

My intention at the Conference is to keep as quiet as I can and leave as much of this to you.

Good Luck!